REVOLUTION IN CUBA

OTHER BOOKS BY HERBERT L. MATTHEWS

Half of Spain Died

A World in Revolution

Cuba

The Cuban Story

The Yoke and the Arrows

Assignment to Austerity
(WITH EDITH MATTHEWS)

The Education of a Correspondent

The Fruits of Fascism

Two Wars and More to Come

Eyewitness to Abyssinia

Revolution in Cuba

AN ESSAY IN UNDERSTANDING

Herbert L. Matthews

CHARLES SCRIBNER'S SONS / *NEW YORK*

Library of Congress Cataloging in Publication Data

Matthews, Herbert Lionel, 1900–
Revolution in Cuba.

Includes index.
1. Cuba—History—1959– 2. Cuba—History—1933–1959. 3. Communism—Cuba. I. Title.
F1788.M353 972.91'064 73–1362
ISBN 0–684–14213–9

Map adapted from *Atlas Nacional de Cuba,* Havana, 1970.

1 3 5 7 9 11 13 15 17 19 H/C 20 18 16 14 12 10 8 6 4 2

PRINTED IN THE UNITED STATES OF AMERICA

FOR

Our Beloved Leslie

ACKNOWLEDGMENTS

I desire to express my thanks to the following publishers and the authors concerned for permission to quote a number of passages from their books:

Grove Press, *Reminiscences of the Cuban Revolutionary War,* by Ernesto Che Guevara; and *Fidel Castro Speaks,* edited by Martin Kenner and James Petras.

Simon & Schuster, *Venceremos: The Speeches and Writings of Ernesto Che Guevara,* edited by John Gerassi.

Doubleday & Co., *Ernesto: A Memoir of Che Guevara,* by Hilda Gadea.

I am indebted, as all historians of the Cuban Revolution must be, to Professor Hugh Thomas of Reading University, England, whose monumental work *Cuba: The Pursuit of Freedom* (published by Harper & Row in the United States) is a mine of historic information.

CONTENTS

" 'This—is now *my* way: where is yours?' Thus I answered those who asked me 'the way.' For *the* way—does not exist!"

Thus spoke Zarathustra.

NIETZSCHE

"Sir," said Samuel Johnson, "to leave things out of a book, merely because people tell you they will not be believed, is meanness."

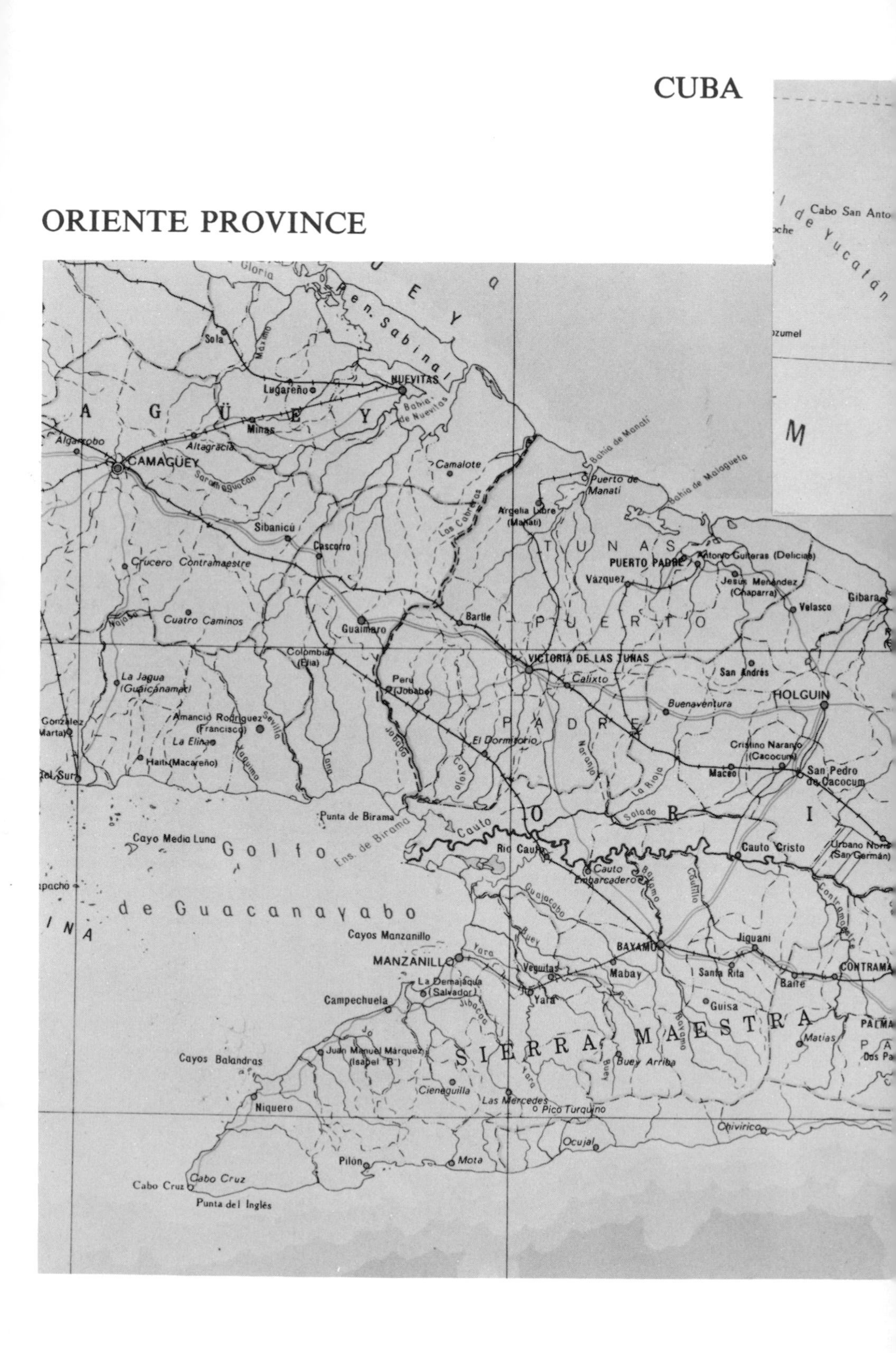

CUBA
ORIENTE PROVINCE
Cabo San Anto
de Yucatán
M
Gloria
Pen. Sabinal
Sola
Máximo
Lugareño
NUEVITAS
Bahía de Nuevitas
A G Ü E Y
Minas
Altagracia
Algarrobo
CAMAGÜEY
Saramaguacán
Camalote
Bahía de Manatí
Puerto de Manatí
Bahía de Malagueta
Argelia Libre (Manatí)
Las Cabreras
Sibanicú
Cascorro
Crucero Contramaestre
T U N A S
PUERTO PADRE
Antonio Guiteras (Delicias)
Vázquez
Jesús Menéndez (Chaparra)
Gibara
Velasco
Cuatro Caminos
Guáimaro
Bartle
P U E R T O
Colombia (Elia)
VICTORIA DE LAS TUNAS
Calixto
San Andrés
La Jagua (Guaicanamar)
Perú (Jobabo)
Buenaventura
HOLGUIN
Amancio Rodríguez (Francisco)
P A D R E
Sevilla
La Elina
Haití (Macareño)
El Dormitorio
Jobabo
Naranjo
Cristino Naranjo (Cacocum)
Maceo
San Pedro de Cacocum
La Rioja
Salado
Punta de Birama
O R I
Ens. de Birama
Cauto
Río Cauto
Cauto Cristo
Urbano Noris (San Germán)
Cayo Media Luna
Golfo
Cauto Embarcadero
Bayamo
Cautillo
Guajacabo
Contramaestre
de Guacanayabo
Buey
Cayos Manzanillo
BAYAMO
Jiguaní
MANZANILLO
Yara
Veguitas
Mabay
Santa Rita
Baire
CONTRAMA
La Demajagua (Salvador)
Jibacoa
Campechuela
Guisa
Bayamo
SIERRA MAESTRA
Matías
PALMA
Dos Pa
Juan Manuel Márquez (Isabel "B")
Cayos Balandras
Buey Arriba
Cienaguilla
Las Mercedes
Pico Turquino
Niquero
Chivirico
Ocujal
Pilón
Mota
Cabo Cruz
Punta del Inglés

CUBA

LA HABANA
Matanzas
Cárdenas
Sagua la Grande
Guanajay
Artemisa
Güines
Jovellanos
Pinar del Río
Güira de Melena
Colón
Camajuaní
Caibarién
Guane
Santa Clara
Placetas
Cienfuegos
Cabaiguán
Morón
Sancti Spíritus
Trinidad
Ciego de Ávila
Florida
Nueva Gerona
Playa Girón
Isla de Pinos
Nuevitas
Camagüey
Holguín
Banes
Victoria de las Tunas
Manzanillo
Bayamo
San Luis
Baracoa
Guantánamo
Palma Soriano
SANTIAGO DE CUBA
Punta del Quemado
Paso de los Vientos
Exuma
Long
Acklins
Mayag
Gra
Cap
Caimán Chico (Gr.Br.)
Caimán Brac (Gr.Br.)
Gran Caimán (Gr.Br.)
Estrecho de Colón
Montego Bay
JAMAICA
Jeremie
PORT AU P
Les Cayes
A n t i l l a s

Cabo Lucrecia
Cañadón
21°
BANES
Antilla
Tasajó
Punta de Mayarí
Bahía de Nipe
Preston
Báguanos (López Peña)
Guaro
Nicaro
Cayo Mambí
Cayo Moa Grande
Moa
Cueto
Mayarí
SAGUA DE TÁNAMO
E N T E
M A Y A R Í - S A G U A - M O A
Arroyo Seco
Mayarí
Mayarí Arriba
Naranjo Agrio
Santa Catalina
S E G U N D O F R E N T E
Toa
Antonio Maceo (Miranda)
Bayate
BARACOA
Caoba
Felicidad de Yateras
Duaba
Realengo
Yumurí
El Salvador (Soledad)
Puriales de Caujerí
(Palma)
Los Reynaldos (Baltony)
Manuel Tames (San Antonio)
SAN LUIS
Jamaica
Gran Tierra
Dos Caminos
Alto Songo
GUANTÁNAMO
Yateras
Río Frío
El Cristo
Imías
Playitas
Punta Caleta
Punta del Quemado
El Caney
Paraguay (Los Caños)
El Cobre
Guantánamo
SANTIAGO DE CUBA
Caimanera
20°
Boquerón
Bahía de Guantánamo

REVOLUTION IN CUBA

Introduction

> But as any historian knows, there can be a wide gap between the history of a country seen from the outside . . . and the history of the same country illumined from inside.
>
> —Fernand Braudel
> (*The Mediterranean*, Vol. II)

A revolution in process is a live phenomenon. It is an experience that a people and a nation traverse. A true interpretation of it has to be found in the joys and sorrows, the sufferings, the accomplishments, the failures, the aspirations, the ambitions, the ideals of the people and of the revolutionary leaders. One cannot encompass it all, as in a photograph, and say, "Here it is!"

One must *feel* the Cuban Revolution in order to understand it. (The Greeks had a word for it: empathy.) So far as it is possible for a foreigner, the Revolution should be looked at through Cuban eyes. A thousand facts will bring no comprehension if they are not interpreted in Cuban terms. The greatest of all the questions to be answered is not "What?" or "How?" but "Why?"

We will sift over the still smoldering ashes of Cuban history, study all the facts, name all the people, praise and blame; but in the end I hope that the reader will understand; that he will see why there is a Cuban Revolution; why it is still so strong at this writing in 1975; why Fidel Castro, its creator, is still the popular *Jefe Supremo*, the Leader. For the most part, I avoid value judgments.

In politics as in religion, the facts can be misleading. What matters most is belief, emotional response, interpretation, desire, hope, faith. The historic causes of the Revolution are what the Cubans of Castro's generation believe them to be. Any other interpretation is quarreling with *Cuban* history. How Cubans ought to think and feel is an academic exercise; how Anglo-Saxon observers feel about the Revolution is largely beside the point.

History is necessarily selective. I have tried to pick out from the historical record those events which contributed to the advent of the Revolution, either in themselves or because of the way Cubans interpreted them. The dynamism of the Revolution has been such that much of what occurred in the first decade—1959–1970—has only historic meaning today. Those dramatic years, in Fidel Castro's breathtaking word, were an "apprenticeship."

No one has written or can claim to write about Fidel Castro and the Cuban Revolution with objectivity, impartiality, balance, lack of bias, or whatever attitude may be considered devoid of emotion. Even the most ignorant would have feelings about Communism, socialism, nationalism, and civil liberties, which must color one's feelings about Cuba.

For sixteen years Americans have been fed a copious but almost universally hostile flow of information on Cuba, although the flow has dwindled to a trickle in recent years. In the early period, when Cuba was open to American correspondents, the news coverage was exceedingly poor. The State Department soon made it virtually impossible for students, professors, or any but accredited members of the mass media to go to Cuba. It built what I called in an editorial in *The New York Times* the "Cuban Wall." In the last seven or eight years it has been very difficult for an American journalist or writer to obtain a Cuban visa. Castro decided that he could not get a fair break from writers; he preferred to let unfolding events do their own talking in good time. He was anyway fed up with all authors and intellectuals after the sensational affair, starting in 1968, of the Cuban poet Heberto Padilla. Many former international literary sympathizers turned on him for imprisoning and muzzling Padilla (see Chapter 18).

I consider myself a special case and have never had any trouble getting into Cuba and talking to all the leaders. The difficulty was not Fidel's desire to admit only writers whom he considered favorable to the Revolution. Among the most important books on the Revolution are five recent ones, all sharply critical and all but one by authors who worked freely in Cuba: K. S. Karol's *Guerrillas in Power* (1970); René Dumont's *Cuba, Est-il socialiste?* (1970); Hugh Thomas' *Cuba, The Pursuit of Freedom* (1971); Lowry Nelson's *Cuba, The Measure of a Revolution* (1972); and Maurice Halperin's *The Rise and Decline of Fidel Castro* (1973). All five were completed under the influence of Castro's failure to achieve his ten-million-ton sugar harvest in 1970 and before a new era in Cuba began.

In 1968 the Associated Press and United Press International

bureaus in Havana were closed down by Fidel and their correspondents expelled. No non-Communist newspaper or magazine has had any regular correspondent in Cuba for years. The only Western news agencies in Havana in 1975 are the Agence France-Presse and Reuters. TASS supplies the Soviet bloc with typical coverage.

Between the restrictions and the censorship, Cuba is singularly isolated from the world. Cubans must rely on the shockingly inadequate, censored, and biased news of their journals and radio, supplemented, for those who have access to receivers and are interested, by the U.S. Information Agency's broadcast propaganda and its chosen, slanted news. On the U.S. mainland the news agencies monitor Cuban speeches and news broadcasts, but they were interested only in publishing brief passages that had the kind of news interest which the American media believed the public expected or wanted.

So long as Fidel Castro and his associates are convinced that the Revolution cannot expect fair coverage in the American and Western European press—and they are wrong about a great many reliable organs—Cuba will remain a closed book to the rest of the world. This suits Castro. He believes that time is on his side and that the longer Cuba is left alone the better the picture will be when the moment comes to open up. Fidel and his colleagues have a profound pride and faith in their accomplishments and in what they are doing. They are not blind to the mistakes they have made or to the great defects and weaknesses of some aspects of the Revolution. But they do not believe that the U.S. press is free or honest. Before the Revolution their own press, with a few honorable exceptions, was venal, corrupt, and directed.

It is as if a fog of war hangs over the island. Those who have followed the Revolution as closely as possible from the outside must make bricks without straw so long as they rely on the meager information that seeps through the surrounding wall of mystery. Only in Cuba is it possible to see clearly. I had read every scrap of information about Cuba that I could lay hands on following my visit in October 1967, but I was not prepared for what I found in August–September 1972.

As the Revolution develops and changes, so must one's ideas about it develop and change. The years between the first time I saw Fidel Castro up in the Sierra Maestra on February 17, 1957, and my latest encounter with him on September 13, 1972, at the Presidential Palace in Havana, have been full of drama, glory, tragedy, error, struggle, and chaotic dynamism. I feel that I have lived with the Cuban Revolution since its birth to its present robust adolescence.

Fidel, his brother Raúl, and virtually all the revolutionary leaders do not look upon me as an outsider. I fully realize both the handicaps and the advantages that this relationship entails. To me, the Cuban Revolution is not object; it is subject.

It stands to reason that the more one knows about Fidel Castro the more forcibly one is impelled to have opinions about him. This imperative is stronger when Castro is an acquaintance or friend. As Dr. Johnson observed, a successful biographer should have eaten his subject's food and drunk his wine—and I would now add, smoked his cigars. Fidel's personality is overwhelming, whether in a tête-à-tête or addressing a mass of half a million people. My attitude toward him has been sympathetic. He has done many things that shocked and sometimes outraged me, many things I consider wrong; and he has made colossal mistakes. I have never hidden my critical opinions from him. But he has also done things that I consider fine and good and right; he is carrying out a revolution which Cuba needed in some form or other; and he has had to deal with enormously complex and difficult problems which no man could have tried to solve without making errors and causing harm to large sectors of Cuban society.

The Cuban Revolution is one of the most striking examples on record of the power of one man to make history. Nearly all writers on Cuba recognize that it is Fidel Castro's revolution. If one misunderstands him, one misunderstands the Revolution.

Fidel Castro lives in a goldfish bowl, on view to all as he goes on his incessant rounds to every corner of the island or makes his long speeches to huge crowds and millions of television listeners. An image has come through over the years that makes Cubans feel as if they know him. In a sense they do; no one can fool an intelligent people like the Cubans over a period of sixteen years.

All the same, Fidel does not wear his heart on his sleeve. In many ways he is an enigma, and he will always remain one because of his withdrawn, jealously guarded temperament. Yet he is accessible. What there is to know about him as a man, living and working, must be grasped now for posterity. We must see him in the framework of the Cuba and the world in which he lived. Only we, who are his contemporaries, who may know him well or slightly, who respond to the same objective world and the same pressures as he does, can provide the precious ingredient of direct knowledge.

The Cuban Revolution is, in one sense, a happy hunting ground for journalists like myself. It is too recent, incomplete, unformed, and bewilderingly dynamic for the historians to tackle confidently with their exhaustive scholarship and laborious "detachment." We newspapermen can give them some material for their histories when the time is ripe for judgment—events seen and heard; personal experience and acquaintance; interpretation based on firsthand knowledge; judgment, understanding, sympathy—elements which cannot be found in or safely extracted from books, official documents, or texts of speeches.

We see the history in the making; we are still living while the policies are made and changed, while the options are open and the future uncertain. No curtain has descended; nothing is over; nothing is dead; the past and present are still only parts of a picture that later generations will have to complete. Cuba, Castro, the Revolution—there they are, alive, vivid, active, exciting, fascinating. Today they belong to us, the journalists.

The history of Cuba since Christopher Columbus discovered it however, can never be out of our thoughts or calculations. One has the sense in Cuba today of living with history, not only the dramatic unfolding history of today's Revolution, but most significantly, the history of the past hundred years since the "Cry of Yara" in 1868 when patriots in Oriente Province rose in arms against Spain.

It would be foolish to deny the value—in fact, the vital importance—of what documentation is available on the Revolution. Unhappily for contemporary historians, a great deal is unavailable, even to the most trusted scholars. Celia Sánchez, Fidel's closest companion, started collecting every scrap of information, every communiqué, statement, speech, broadcast, and statistic that came along day by day since the early weeks in the Sierra Maestra. Later, masses of material were gathered and added about the attack on the Moncada Barracks, the 26th of July Movement, Mexico, the *Granma* expedition, and all phases of the guerrilla war. Then came the flood of official information of the revolutionary government, starting in January 1959, much of it still secret. Few economic and financial statistics have been made available, and they are not always trustworthy.

I began asking about the revolutionary documents a long time ago. Celia Sánchez always assured me that they were being carefully preserved. I begged her in the first years of the Revolution either to put them in safekeeping abroad or to microfilm them and send copies to a friendly country. She told me on one trip that the material had been microfilmed.

But none of it is available to students today. In September 1972 I went hopefully to the Oficinas de Documentos Históricos de la Revolución only to be told that the original material was in the hands, or control, of Fidel Castro and Celia Sánchez and was being kept in a secret locale. At the documents office there is a partial collection of photocopies of documents, but they are available, with official permission, only to students asking for specific items.

The events in Cuba since 1959 can be understood only if one keeps in mind just what a revolution is. The Marxism-Leninism into which the Castro regime gravitated is an attribute of the Cuban Revolution, not its essence. What Fidel Castro dreamed of as a university student, what he fought for when he attacked the Moncada Barracks in Santiago de Cuba in 1953, what he returned to fight for in the Sierra Maestra in 1956, was *a* revolution. Of the varieties of revolution that history has seen since Magna Carta, what Castro had in mind is what we now call a *social* revolution. That in 1961 it took the form of a socialist or Communist, or what Castro calls a Marxist-Leninist, revolution was an accident of history, a forced response to a complicated mass of internal and external events and pressures. The Cuban Revolution has taken a Marxist-Leninist form as a man would don a suit of clothes. It is the man who counts, not the clothes. What matters in Cuba today is the revolution, not the label.

The Concise Oxford Dictionary gives us the bare bones: "*revolution:* complete change, turning upside down, great reversal of conditions, fundamental reconstruction." Yet how much more, how infinitely more, there is in the living event, in the experience that a country and its people go through during the process of a revolution!

It is not only that the dictionary definition misses the tragedy and happiness, the fears, hopes, and hatreds, the passionate devotion, the immense thrill of all the emotions that human beings must feel when their lives are shaken as if by an earthquake. Nor is a revolution only the obvious reversal that takes place in the social and economic positions of the classes—those who lose privileges and wealth and those who gain—for at the heart of the revolution lies the ideal of equality.

A revolution not only transforms the structure of a nation, politically, economically, and socially, but changes the quality of lives, the attitudes of men and women toward each other and toward their society and country. The prototype of the modern social revolution—the French Revolution—not only transformed France but changed the course of world history. We are all heirs of the French Revolution.

The change that a revolution causes is so profound that the exile cannot return to the country from which he fled, for that country no longer exists. It is like a river, in which, as Heraclitus said, one can never bathe twice. Physically, the exile can go back to the geographical locality he left, but the place has altered as surely as if a gigantic hand had wiped out the characteristic features of what was there before. Nor can he restore the *ancien régime*, for true revolutions are irreversible. They have not only destroyed what existed; they have replaced it with new things, new people, new ideas, new desires, new rights and wrongs and vested interests.

On the ruins of the old structure, another house is being built. Cuba in these years has made the most profound of all economic changes possible in our times: from a form of capitalism to a form of socialism. She has turned from the West—the United States—to the East—the Soviet Union and the Communist bloc. She has changed from a nominally parliamentary form of government to a one-man dictatorship, from traditional forms to modernity.

Each day the sun rises over a new Cuba, but new, of course, in being different, not in ceasing to be Cuba. The Revolution came out of Cuban history and is being made by Cubans; this truism must color every consideration of what has been happening on the island. It makes no sense to think of Cuba in North American terms; to measure her with the yardsticks of Western liberal democracy; to expect Latin Cubans to feel and think like Anglo-Saxons and to want what we in the United States want. It seems so trite to say that Fidel Castro is not an Anglo-Saxon; yet it was assumed by Washington and many American writers in the early years of the Revolution that he would or should behave like one.

There has never been mutual understanding between Cubans and Americans. Those Cubans who seemed to understand Americans were simply copying. The Cubans whom Americans understood were the business, banking, landowning, professional elements, who usually spoke English, had likely gone to school in the United States, and had the same social and material values. History is being logical. The exiles in Miami today are turning into exactly that type of Cuban.

We Americans think of the "Rights of Man" in civic terms: equality of opportunity, equality before the law, nondiscrimination, the right to vote, freedom of the press, the sacredness of one's home. In Cuba, as in all of Latin America, individual rights are cherished too, but the emphasis is on personal attributes: personal integrity and dignity, the development and preservation of family life, the domestic concerns of the women, the sexual prowess and physical courage of the men.

How much disillusionment, how much bitterness, how much

frustration could have been avoided in this century if Americans had recognized this fact and had tried to understand Cubans on their own terms!

The reality of a revolutionary world is often the reverse of what we consider real. One goes behind the mirror, as if into a fourth dimension where the logical procedures of investigation as we know them do not apply because they are rejected. So many orthodox American historians satisfied themselves that they had gathered all the facts about Cuba and added them correctly—and so they had, within their own conceptual framework. But Cuba did not fit the frame.

Men who make history are abnormal, and the history they make often seems irrational to outsiders at the time. The Cuban Revolution, in Fidel Castro's constantly used word, should be regarded as a process, with an open mind for the unexpected, the disconcerting, the contingent. Above all, it must never be expected to stand still; a revolution that loses its dynamism is over.

Fidel Castro says (he repeated it to me when I last saw him): "Every year I grow more revolutionary."

The rector of Havana University in 1972, Dr. José M. Millar, said to me: "A revolution is nothing if it is not ideas." Consciously or not, he was expressing a sound Marxist principle: that ideas grow out of the immediate circumstances. Castro's fresh ideas—good and bad—always came out of his immediate problems and circumstances, not out of Marxist literature or any kind of ideology. If Marx stood Hegelianism on its head, there were times when Castro stood Marxism on its head.

Cuba should not be compared to the Soviet Union, the Eastern European bloc, or China. Critics tend to see parallels which do not exist; they apply surface similarities of other Communist governments to the deeper inward lives and feelings of Cubans, who do not necessarily respond to similar policies in the way that Russians, Czechs, or Chinese do.

I repeat, the Castro regime and its Revolution are understandable only in Cuban terms. After all, it is *their* Revolution; they made it; they run it; they live with it. They should have their say, not in the superficial, ephemerally valuable form of C. Wright Mills's famous *Listen Yankee* of 1960, but seriously, in depth, with frank recognition of errors, mismanagement, wrongs, injustices, and other flaws that they generally, but not always, acknowledge. By the same token, they deserve due praise for the many fine things they have done.

A few words on the method and approach. This is not a book by a scholar for scholars. I have deliberately refused to clutter the pages with footnotes that give every page of every reference or quotation. When I quote from a book, I say so, in fairness to the author and as a guide to students who wish to consult a work. The books that I consider important for the general reader are listed in the bibliography.

I believe in the structural interpretation of history in which political events are like the white foam that ripples toward shore while the true drive and force are the ever-moving, changing economic, social, demographic, and cultural tides below. But I am by long training a journalist who for forty-five years on *The New York Times* watched world events unfold in chronological fashion. There are few things harder for a historian than to combine—perhaps "juggle" is a better word—a chronological with a thematic treatment of his subject. In the long process of gathering the material for this book, I found myself working in time and space. Sometimes it made more sense to tell the story as it unfolded; sometimes—for instance, the life and death of Ernesto Che Guevara—it would have seemed foolish to break up a masterpiece like him into a jigsaw puzzle.

"Events are the ephemera of history," as Fernand Braudel writes in his wonderful study of the Mediterranean in the time of Philip II, but he does add: "Every event, to be sure, has some contribution to make, lights up some dark corner or even some wide vista of history." I do not by any means ignore or belittle events; I believe that the important and significant ones are all here. Even if events, as Professor Braudel writes, are "like fireflies" flitting across the stage of history, they illuminate brightly in that brief moment.

CHAPTER 1

The 1970 Watershed

It is the unexpected that happens, as many historians have had occasion to observe and many politicians to discover.

—Algernon Cecil

On July 26, 1970, the "Year of the Ten Millions," a new era began in Cuba. There had been a desperate, year-long effort to achieve a phenomenal harvest of ten million tons of sugar. It had been a colossal mistake which ended in near disaster. The people were confused, worried, tired. The leaders were exhausted and—all but one—discouraged. Enemies and friends outside Cuba gloated or groaned in despair.

In a few hours on the afternoon of July 26, the atmosphere in Cuba was transformed. Fidel Castro, always a remarkable orator, had surpassed himself in the greatest speech of his career. He sensed—or better, he knew—that the Cuban people had not lost faith in him or in what was now *their* revolution. He trusted them; told them the harshest truths in full detail and took the blame on himself and his associates.

Those abroad who read the speech, or devastating passages from it, all but wrote off Castro as a spent, discredited force. Many writers in the United States and Europe said that the Cuban Revolution, if it continued at all, would take many years to recover.

Twice before in his dramatic career Fidel Castro had been written off—the first time on July 26, 1953, when he led a madly reckless attack on the Moncada Barracks in Santiago de Cuba, and the second time when he landed on the coast of Oriente Province from Mexico on December 2, 1956, and all but a handful of his eighty-two men were killed or captured. Yet the Cuban Revolution was to survive those two disasters, and it was to be saved, rejuvenated, and reconstructed as the result of a third great defeat—the 1970 failure of the sugar *zafra*.

Fidel Castro's speeches are made to be heard, not read. Those outside Cuba who read the July 26 speech with its lamentable list of what had happened to this and that branch of the Cuban economy could have had no idea of its effect on his Cuban listeners. And how few foreigners would stop to think, and fewer still be able to judge, the significance of the fact that these Cubans had gone through more than a decade of the Revolution with Castro and his followers. Equally important was the fact that the harvest was produced, not by hungry and ignorant peasants working up to sixteen hours a day for four months and unemployed the rest of the year, but by a combination of experienced cane cutters and volunteers who were politically and culturally aware. They understood what Fidel was telling them in a way that no foreign economist, however well trained or expert, could. Their deductions were not what logic seemed to require. What Castro said was very important; *why* he said it to them and what it meant to them were much more important. Their feelings and their reactions explain why the Cuban Revolution took strength from the lost battle of 1970 and why, in 1975, sixteen years after Castro led his *barbudos* (bearded ones) into Havana, the Revolution is still going strong.

In a way, the stupendous effort to achieve a ten-million-ton sugar crop in 1970 was an extraneous factor. It was a supreme attempt to achieve a high degree of economic independence from the Soviet Union, but meanwhile the Revolution, in all its more important *social* aspects, continued uninterruptedly. The failure of the effort was to make daily life still more difficult for a while, but it was not going to be a vital factor, win or lose. By the middle of May 1970, Castro had had to announce, unhappily, that the goal of ten million tons could not be reached.

"Today," Fidel said in his speech on July 26, "I am going to speak of our problems and our difficulties; not of our successes but of our reverses . . . And we are going, with your permission, to present the essence or what is essential in our difficulties in the most elemental way possible. We desire, above all things, that the masses be informed, that the masses understand, and that the masses prepare to fight their battle. . . .

"In effect, this heroic effort to raise production has turned into deficits in the economy, into a reduced production in other sectors and, in short, into an increase in our difficulties."

Castro presented the facts uninterruptedly and at great length. As always, there was a didactic quality to his talk. Fidel has used his speeches like a teacher lecturing to his pupils, who, in his case, are the Cuban people.

The sugar harvest had fallen short of the ten-million-ton goal by nearly a million and a half tons, as everyone knew. Castro went through a long list of things whose production had slumped heavily because of the distortions in the economy, such as rice, milk, fertilizers, paper, shoes, cloth, bread. It had been necessary to impose "notable" restrictions on the consumption of meat, fowl, vegetables, fruits, lard, beans, beer, and other drinks. Cigars and cigarettes fell so far short of demand that rationing had to be introduced. There were "failures in imports and exports . . . difficulties in railway and truck transportation," and a serious decline in a number of public services. It was, in short, the picture of an economic breakdown.

To these "objective difficulties," as he called them, were to be added even more important "concrete problems"—meaning the question of the personnel involved:

> Let us first begin by pointing out, amidst all these problems, the responsibility of all of us, mine in particular. I have no intention, in any way, to pick out responsibilities that I would claim were not mine as well as those of the entire administration of the Revolution. Unhappily, these self-criticisms cannot easily be accompanied by consequent solutions. It is better that I say to the people: seek someone else! And more —seek other men! It would be better. In reality, for my own part, it would also be hypocritical.
>
> I believe that we, the leaders of this Revolution, have proved too costly in our apprenticeship . . . I include myself in the category of ignoramuses. And we were all, almost without exception—and, of course, one of those exceptions was not I—we were all ignorant. . . .
>
> We are not bringing any magical solutions here to you. We have presented the problems and said: only the people, only with the people, with the mobilization of the conscience of the people, the decision of the people and the will of the people, will these problems be overcome. . . .
>
> Ah! this is not the first time that we said this. We said it when we arrived here the sixth or seventh of January [it was January 8, 1959], and we said that we realized our task was great and that we had much to learn. And we said it in all sincerity, as in all sincerity we say that the apprenticeship of the revolutionaries in the construction of the economy is much more difficult than we had believed; that the problems are much more complex than we believed; and the apprenticeship much longer, very much longer and very much harder. And this is the battle that we now face. . . .
>
> Today we are not fighting against men—unless those men be our-

> selves; we fight against objective factors; we fight against the past; we fight in the presence of that past which is still with us; we fight against limitations of every kind. But this, sincerely, is the greatest challenge that we face in our lives and the greatest challenge that the Revolution has faced.
>
> Our enemies take shelter and base their hopes on our difficulties . . . They are wrong in only one thing: in believing that for the people there is any alternative to the Revolution; in believing that the people, faced with the difficulties of the Revolution, whatever those difficulties are, can choose the road of counterrevolution. Ah! in this you are mistaken, *señores imperialistas!* Yes, in this you are mistaken! In this, no one is ready to grant you a shred of truth! This is where you go wrong. . . .
>
> If we are worth an atom of anything, that atom will be in fulfillment of an idea; that atom will be in fulfillment of a cause; that atom will be for the uniting of a people.
>
> And we are men of flesh and bones, fragile to an incredible degree. We are nothing; yes, we can say it! We are something only in the fulfillment of this or the other task.
>
> And always, always we will be—every time more consciously, every time more intimately, every time more profoundly—at the service of that cause.
>
> Once more, there only remains for me to say to you, our people, in the name of our Party, our Administration, and also in the name of my own feelings at the reaction, the attitude and the confidence of the people—to say to you: many thanks!

The ending, of course, was the traditional *Patria o muerte! Venceremos!* "Fatherland or death! We shall conquer!"

Fidel Castro's speech of July 26, 1970, must be read as far more than a confession of error or a fiercely honest display of the grievous wounds that the Cuban body politic had sustained because of a desperate attempt to achieve the impossible. The address was a call to arms and a pledge that there would be a transformation; that a new leaf would be turned in the history of the Revolution; but that the people—all the people—would have to join in to make a new start and to rebuild what had been damaged. Fidel was able, in this speech, to convey his most deeply felt emotions as a revolutionary. His ideals, his convictions, his passion, his faith in himself and in the Cuban people were all made manifest to those who listened.

A new note had been sounded. Some who were there told me that they saw workers and peasants going away weeping in sympathy for Fidel Castro, who was clearly overwrought. This Cuban response did not and could not show up in any reading of the text in the United States or Europe. Yet the emotions that were conveyed and aroused would have been mere rhetoric if they had not been followed by action. Behind the talk was a furious determination on Castro's part to recover from the economic setback of the sugar harvest, to correct mistakes that were now so obvious, and to move on to new measures.

Nothing was more remarkable about the event than the way the Cuban people responded. Three or four of the revolutionary leaders made the point to me on a visit to Cuba in September 1972 that this proved the unassailable strength of the Revolution. Haydée Santamaría, the heroine of Moncada and the Sierra Maestra, argued that no leader in any socialist country who had made such a colossal mistake could have survived. She was, I would say, overlooking Mao Tse-tung's "Great Leap Forward" of 1958–1962, which was a similar disaster, but the point was well taken. By every logical calculation made abroad, there should have been disillusionment, discouragement, frustration, discontent. There weren't. Castro's popular support was not affected in any way, nor was faith in the Revolution, at least by any outward signs. On the evidence, the people understood, forgave, and set themselves to work hard to repair the damage.

It had been obvious for many years that Castro's enemies could not count on his regime's collapsing because he made mistakes. He made no end of them. The Revolution went on because it had more in favor of it than against it and because it won enough time for the people, including a whole new generation, to understand what was happening and what was being tried. The Revolution evidently carried conviction; it made sense to the Cuban people.

I could see, when I visited Cuba in August–September 1972, that the island had been given a new lease on life in 1970, a virtual transformation since the time, two years before, when Fidel Castro had stood forlornly before his people and confessed failure. The improvement has continued, if anything at a faster pace, in these last few years.

Clearly, the hardheaded men in the Kremlin think so too. They are not charitably inclined. They must have been impressed by Castro's survival and comeback, by the way the Cuban people buckled down to work, and by the new plans and ideas that Fidel started putting into practice. It does not seem possible that the Russians would otherwise have agreed to the extraordinarily generous trade and financial pact which Cuba was given at the end of 1972.

The 1970 speech showed the extent to which Fidel Castro was

relying on government by consensus; government with genuine mass participation as well as support. His revolution is autocratic, but he has based it on popular support and a striving—almost a mania—for national unity.

Most of the men and women who listened to him would have been members of the Committees for the Defense of the Revolution (CDR), the extraordinary mass organization that started in 1960 as a block-by-block network of vigilante groups. It was soon realized that they could perform other functions, mainly of a social nature. They helped organize vaccinations for polio, diphtheria, and measles and saw to it that every family got its injections. They set up campaigns for blood donations for the hospitals. Committees saw to it that streets were kept clean, that parents sent their children to school, that food and other rations were fairly handled.

The CDR grew steadily year after year. At the September 28, 1972, anniversary (the date of its inception is celebrated annually) I was told by Luis Marturelos, then president of the organization, that membership was 4,236,342. Interestingly, 700,471 were new members, and there had been a similar increase the year before—in other words, after the 1970 sugar crisis. By the thirteenth anniversary in 1973, according to the official newspaper *Granma*, the total membership was about 4,750,000. When one considers that the population of Cuba in 1970 was about 8,550,000, of whom 1,500,000 were under sixteen and 150,000 over sixty-five years, this means that almost every able-bodied Cuban adult was watching, helping, praising, or admonishing everybody else. One has an impression of Cuba as a gigantic goldfish bowl. But here, as in other respects, it must be kept in mind that Cubans do not share the Anglo-Saxon mania for privacy; they are a gregarious and friendly people. One has to wonder, though, how many Cubans are uneasy over the fact that the CDR is now completely under the control of the Communist Party of Cuba (PCC). The timid, the opportunist, the oppositionist would all be taking shelter under the CDR umbrella.

Yet all the caveats and reservations cannot diminish the fact that the Committees for the Defense of the Revolution give Fidel Castro a remarkable mass basis for his Revolution. Every one of the members—and the numbers are still growing—*participates* in the Cuban Revolution. Fidel gets a grassroots consensus that is not democracy Western style, but is surely some kind of democracy. It is a kind, of course, that has nothing to do with civil liberties, but we are talking here of the consensus of the people in the processes of government. I believe it was not until the last few years that Castro grasped the fact that the CDR is his greatest revolutionary asset. He is now (since autumn 1974) reinforcing the reliance on a grassroots participation by elections for "organs of People's Power" which are to be made nationwide by 1976.

For more than a century the true ethos of Cuba has resided in the people, not in their mainly selfish, greedy, corrupt leaders. Fidel communes directly with the people in his frequent and usually very long speeches. This would not be possible without the miracle of radio and television. Where Lenin spoke to his hundreds, Fidel speaks to his millions; where Lenin had one of the largest countries in the world to govern, Fidel has one of the smallest. He is always traveling about; there is no Cuban who has not seen Fidel in the flesh, not only haranguing the multitudes, but moving among them on farms and in factories.

Going around Cuba in the summer of 1972 on my tenth visit during the Revolution, I still had the feeling that the greatest strength and the greatest weakness of the Cuban Revolution lay in its dependence on Fidel Castro. Yet for the first time I could see how the Revolution might continue if Castro were assassinated or died of a heart attack. It would have to be carried forward by the Cuban Communist Party, which is not the case now. The party had grown considerably since my previous visit in October 1967. Jesús Montané, the party administrator, told me that there were 140,000 members, but it is still a very selective organization and a vanguard. Almost everywhere I went, when introduced to the man in charge, I was told that he was a member of the Central Committee, or at least a party member. All the comrades of Fidel were then *comandantes* or *capitanes* (majors or captains) and now have ranks up to lieutenant general. The PCC and the FAR (Armed Forces of the Revolution, headed by Raúl Castro) are inextricably intermingled.

I had a long talk with Fidel Castro on September 12, 1972, in his office in the Presidential Palace. He now uses a rocking chair, and so does his guest. He at first rocked violently, but when he got started talking he moved close, as always, so that he could emphasize points by putting his hand on my knee or arm and bringing his face closer. He was in superb health. When I remarked that he had no gray hair, he said, "Oh yes, a few." There were indeed very few—on his chin. He keeps his beard carefully trimmed these days and his hair, as always, rather short.

I had seen him many times since our first dramatic meeting at dawn in a dripping jungle grove of the Sierra Maestra on February 17, 1957. We reminisced—he now entering middle age and I an old man, feeling sure that it was the last time I would see him. It was strange how little he had changed, though those fifteen years were among the most extraordinary that any man of our century has lived through. Obviously, he thrived on work, like an Antaeus drawing strength from the Cuban earth out of which his revolution grew.

We talked of many things about his Revolution which will be appearing in this book. A long history lay behind it; the roots went deep into the past and into the traditions and character of the Cuban people.

CHAPTER 2

Before the Revolution

A corrupt people, having acquired liberty, can maintain it only with the greatest difficulty.
—Niccolò Machiavelli

THE HISTORIC BACKGROUND

There is a charming entry from Christopher Columbus' diary for October 27, 1492, written when he sighted the island: "I never saw anything so beautiful; full of trees, the river all fringed with them; beautiful and green, with flowers and fruits, every one different; many large birds and little ones who sang sweetly . . ."

The passage can be taken as the first words of Cuban history ever written. They were the last that could make Cuba into a paradise on earth, for the story—the longest of any nation in the Western Hemisphere—is in many ways violent and unhappy.

Yet Professor Lowry Nelson, in his classic book *Rural Cuba* (1950), could rightly call the island "one of the most favorable spots for human existence on the earth's surface." Unfortunately, the Spanish conquerors wanted gold and gems, not the fruits of the earth. For two and a half centuries development was slow. The American War of Independence opened the United States as a market for Cuban sugar and other products. After the destructive Haitian revolt of 1791, Cuba was the best U.S. source for sugar and coffee. When Spain finally opened Cuban ports to all foreign trade in 1818, the United States replaced Great Britain as Cuba's primary supplier and biggest market—until 1960.

Cuba, so long in isolation, became a part of the world, but she and Puerto Rico remained Spanish colonies after all the other Latin American possessions had fought for and won their independence early in the nineteenth century. For Cuba, the century meant oppression, social imbalance, slavery until 1886, a Roman Catholic

Church allied to the ruling feudal landowners and military officers, and—at the end—thirty years of cruel, heroic, devastating struggle for independence from Spain.

It was all dominated by the sweet, sickening odor of sugar. Columbus had brought sugar cane to the neighboring island of Hispaniola (now the Dominican Republic and Haiti) on his second voyage in 1493. From there it was taken to Cuba by the Spanish conquerors. In time bananas, coffee, citrus fruits, rice, and beans were introduced. The native Indians, for their part, gave the Old World corn and tobacco.

The evil that sugar brought with it was slavery. The Indians were worked and diseased to death in a half century by the Spanish. Between the beginning of the sixteenth century and 1886, all the Caribbean islands depended almost exclusively on African slaves as a source of plantation labor. The numbers were horrifying; probably a million before the trade ended.

The sugar plantations brought enormous profits to the owners and made Cuba at the turn of the seventeenth century one of the richest—perhaps, per capita, the richest—of countries in the world. But the owners were few, immensely wealthy, and politically powerful. They depended on slavery, which, in turn, depended on a continuation of the Spanish colonial status. At the same time, the planters blocked the formation of a diversified Cuban economy.

This structure was maintained in its basic form for two centuries. After 1886 the cane cutters were no longer slaves, but the struggle for existence kept them tied to the plantations, where their wages were generally not above subsistence level and their work was confined to four or five months a year. After 1898 U.S. investors came to the island, and the Cuban owners ultimately came under American, rather than Spanish, economic domination.

It was true of Cuba, as of all Latin American countries, that racial prejudice was never as strong as in the United States. The Negro slaves had a better legal status than in the American South. In this century, if economically able, they were freely admitted to schools and universities. A number of laws were passed in the 1890s which forbade discrimination in theaters, restaurants, and cafés. There was equality before the written law, but the courts seemed to favor the whites.

The great problems were social discrimination and the subtle ways by which Negroes were unable, because of low incomes and segregation, to qualify by education and training for high posts in business, the professions, and the higher ranks of the armed forces.

They were barred from the more exclusive clubs, the private schools, and in some cases, the newer residential areas. White foreigners were welcomed freely into Cuban upper-class society.

This was the situation up to 1959. Neither government nor business nor society ever made the deliberate effort to *give* Negroes and mulattos the opportunities to be on equal terms with the whites. Fidel Castro has done just that; it is one of the ways in which the Revolution has transformed Cuban society.

It has been easy for historians to trace the roles of slaves, Negroes, and mulattos in the historic background of the Revolution. Not so with the Cuban intellectuals and with the philosophical origins of the Revolution, where, in my opinion, the historians—Cuban, Latin American, and North American—have let their wishes and ideals father their thoughts.

Though a revolution leading to autocracy and Marxism-Leninism would have been completely alien to the thinking of the remarkable group of nineteenth-century Cuban scholars who, incidentally, influenced José Martí, the hero-martyr of the struggle for independence. I can see two ways in which this group, whose roots went back into the eighteenth-century Enlightenment and the French Revolution, provided a degree of background for the Castroites. They insisted on complete independence from Spain, and they believed that it could be brought about only by force, not by legal means. Fidel's generation felt the same way about the United States.

In 1968, looking back a century to the beginning of the Wars of Independence, Fidel Castro and his colleagues saw the embryo of revolution that came to maturity in 1959. It was on October 10, 1868, that an aristocratic sugar-plantation owner in Oriente Province, Carlos Manuel de Céspedes, raised the standard of revolt.

Castro, in a commemorative speech on the anniversary, frankly detailed the quarrels and factionalism that divided Cubans during the Ten Year War of 1868–1878. There was much heroism and self-sacrifice in what was the first stage of the thirty-year struggle for independence from Spain, but there was no possibility of victory. The United States hampered the rebels by selling arms and gunboats to the Spanish.

So the Ten Year War was lost, and so was the Little War *(La Guerra Chiquita)* that followed. It was not until slavery was finally abolished in 1886 that a nationalist movement with mass support, partly Negro, could be created.

The ravages of the Ten Year War had driven thousands of small, independent farmers off their lands and into the cities, where they became a restless proletariat, at the same time that the former slaves, now wage earners, turned into a rural proletariat. The seeds of revolution were being sown, waiting for a climate in which they could sprout.

A great leader, José Martí hovered outside, creating the spirit of revolt that would be released again when he and General Máximo Gómez, the Dominican-born hero of the Ten Year War, landed at Las Playitas in Oriente Province on April 11, 1895.

José Martí was born on January 28, 1853. There were a greatness of character and a love of humanity in this passionate Cuban nationalist that made him one of the noblest figures in the history of the Americas. He was a man of wide culture in many languages, a fine poet, a brilliant prose writer, a great journalist, a warm, tender, and brave man who overcame chronic illnesses, including tuberculosis, with the same willpower and stoicism that Che Guevara was to display against asthma.

He was soon killed—on May 19, 1895. It was as if he knew that he could serve his country best by becoming its martyr—an untarnished symbol of courage, idealism, and patriotism which will forever be Cuba's glory. His work was done. As a political leader in an independent Cuba, he would have been completely hopeless, even if the United States had let him rule. Whatever revolution Martí might then have accomplished would not have been the one that he had promised.

In the event, there was no revolution. The United States saw to that, with the wholehearted support of the Cuban and Spanish landowners. Sugar became a centralized, urbanized industry. Americans bought vast tracts of sugar land at laughable prices.

One of the Spanish soldiers who stayed on in Oriente Province and took a job working on the railway of the new United Fruit Company plantation near Mayarí was a Galician from Lugo named Angel Castro, one of whose children, born in 1926, was Fidel Castro Ruz.

No one contributed more toward instilling a permanent anti-Americanism into the Cuban ethos than José Martí. His last, unfinished letter, written just before he was killed to a Mexican friend, Manuel Mercado, is a never-forgotten classic of Cuban history.

"I am every day now in danger of giving my life for my country and for my duty as I understand it and have the courage to realize it," he wrote, "which is to prevent in good time that, with the independence of Cuba, the United States should extend [its power] over the Antilles and fall with that much more weight on our lands of America. What I have done up to today, and will do, is for this. I lived inside the monster, and I know its entrails; and my sling is the sling of David."

There is a near parallel to this letter in one that Fidel Castro wrote to Celia Sánchez in June 1958 in the Sierra Maestra. A passage from it was reproduced and hung in the Salón de Mayo in Havana during a conference in July 1967. It read: "When I saw rockets firing at Mario's house, I swore to myself that the Americans were going to pay dearly for what they were doing. When this war is over, a much wider and bigger war will begin for me: the war that I am going to launch against them. I am saying to myself that this is my true destiny."

To understand the Cuban Revolution, it must be kept in mind that the threads of United States and Cuban history have been woven together inextricably since the American War of Independence. The Monroe Doctrine, among other things, gave notice that the Caribbean, Cuba included, was in the U.S. sphere of power. This is still the case, as the missile crisis of 1962 proved.

The question of whether the Cuban rebels could have won their independence without American intervention will never be settled and is important only because Cubans are convinced that the United States intervened unnecessarily and for selfish reasons. The probable truth is that the Spanish and Cubans had fought each other to a standstill. Neither side could achieve victory by 1898, although it was obvious that Spanish rule was nearing its end. Sooner or later, Cuba would have won independence without United States help.

The war itself needs no retelling here. Officially, it started on April 21, 1898, and ended 114 days later after only one land battle of importance—San Juan Hill—and a gallant sacrifice by the Spanish of their pathetic naval force outside Santiago de Cuba. The Americans lost about 2,500 men, mostly to disease. The Cubans estimate their losses between 1868 and 1898 at 50,000 men. The island was devastated. The story re-enters the history of the Castro Revolution with the surrender of the Spanish forces in Santiago de Cuba on July 16, 1898. The Cuban guerrillas and their leader, Calixto García, were not allowed to enter the city and take part in the ceremony. The Cubans have never forgiven the United States for that humiliation.

The treaty of peace formally ending the war was signed in Paris —without any Cubans present. It gave the U.S. Congress the right to determine "the civil rights and political status" of the island. The loss of American lives in the conflict was tragic, but otherwise its place in American history was that of a ridiculous war, not "a splendid little war," in Secretary of State John Hay's unfortunate phrase. There were no doubts on either side how it had to end. The Spanish acted as if they simply wanted to make the gesture of fighting for the sake of their national honor and get it over with as quickly as possible.

The humiliations imposed by the American military on the Cuban revolutionaries; the insensitiveness to Cuban feelings; the complacent assumption that it was a "Spanish-American" war in which thirty years of bloody struggle and sacrifice by Cuban patriots counted for nothing—these facts went into Cuban history, and they will never cease to rankle. Fidel Castro and his generation may have been fed on some exaggerations and distortions, but there were also harsh truths and genuine grievances.

Fidel took a measure of revenge in the very first speech he made after President Batista fled. It was on January 2, 1959, in Santiago de Cuba, the city that had been barred to the Cuban *mambises* in 1898. "This time," said Castro, "it is Cuba's good fortune that the Revolution will really take power. It is not going to be as it was in '98 when the Americans came in, took control of the situation, having intervened at the last moment, and then would not even allow Calixto García, who had been fighting for thirty years, to enter Santiago."

Very few Cubans, and fewer North Americans, could have grasped the full significance of that statement when it was made. It was the first of the many chickens that were to come home to roost in the Cuban Revolution.

Cuban nationalists charge the United States with the violation, after the war ended, of Article IV of the Congressional Resolution of April 20, 1898:

"That the United States hereby disclaims any disposition or intention to exercise sovereignty, jurisdiction, or control over said island except for the pacification thereof, and asserts its determination, when that is accomplished, to leave the government and control of the island to its people."

The island was in a dreadful state after thirty years of war. American military occupation between 1898 and the inauguration of the Republic of Cuba in 1902 was efficient and honest but, in later Cuban eyes, lacking in understanding and so manipulated as to give Americans a considerable degree of economic and political control. Moreover, both government and business administration was turned over to Cubans who would cooperate with the United States. For the most part, they turned out to be greedy and corrupt.

When Theodore Roosevelt became President (1901–1909), the Cubans were dealing with someone who looked upon them as what he called "dagoes." He expressed a desire to teach "the cheating, *mañana* lot" a lesson. In 1906, at the time of the first of a series of American interventions, Roosevelt said: "I dread the creation of a revolutionary habit."

The Platt Amendment to the constitution of the new republic (the joint product of Senator Orville H. Platt and Secretary of War Elihu Root) led to the establishment of the still-existing U.S. Naval Base at Guantánamo Bay and contained this crucial and, to Cuban nationalists, highly objectionable Article III:

"That the government of Cuba consents that the United States may exercise the right to intervene for the preservation of Cuban independence, the maintenance of a government adequate for the protection of life, property and individual liberty, and for discharging the obligations with respect to Cuba imposed by the Treaty of Paris on the United States, now to be assumed and undertaken by the Government of Cuba."

President Roosevelt, in a message to Congress on November 10, 1903, was only too realistic about the Platt Amendment.

"It was provided that when the island became a free and independent republic," he wrote, "she should stand in such close relations with us as in certain respects to come within our system of international policy; and it necessarily followed that she must also to a certain degree become included within the lines of our economic policy. Situated as Cuba is, it would not be possible for this country to permit the strategic abuse of the island by any foreign military power."

This, of course, was exactly what President Kennedy was thinking during the missile crisis of 1962.

The way Cuban nationalists felt about the Platt Amendment was well expressed by Fidel Castro in his speech to the United Nations General Assembly on September 26, 1960:

> At the very moment when the people of Cuba, through their Constituent Assembly, were drafting the Constitution of the Republic, a new law was passed by the United States Congress, a law proposed by Senator Platt, of such unhappy memories for the Cubans. That law stated that the Constitution of Cuba must have a rider under which the United States would be granted the right to intervene in Cuba's political affairs and to lease certain parts of Cuba for naval bases or coaling stations. In other words, under a law passed by the legislative body of

a foreign country, Cuba's Constitution had to contain a rider with those provisions, and the drafters of our Constitution were clearly told that if they did not accept the rider the occupation forces would not be withdrawn.

The first President of the Republic, Tomás Estrada Palma (1902–1906), was a man of integrity in money matters but not in political power. His reelection in 1906 was an example of the electoral frauds that were to become commonplace in Cuba. It was a dismal beginning to a consistently dismal electoral history. Fidel Castro could point to the record and say, perhaps rightly, that the Cuban people were fed up with elections by 1959.

Estrada Palma, threatened with civil war, brought on the first U.S. intervention in 1906. For the next three years the island was under the governorship of Judge Charles Magoon of Nebraska, whose tenure has been a source of emotional debate. Cuban historians are almost all critical, and he was unpopular at the time. The President he chose and left behind, José Miguel Gómez (1909–1913), was exceptionally corrupt. During his administration there was a serious Negro rebellion that began on May 20, 1912, with demonstrations and strikes protesting a law forbidding the formation of "movements composed of persons of the same race or color." Gómez's army suppressed the revolt ruthlessly in what he himself conceded was a butchery. According to official figures, three thousand Negroes were killed. The Americans, incidentally, sent naval forces and marines, who were not needed.

The role of Negroes as "Negroes" disappeared from Cuban society until 1959. No Negro was outstanding in that half century and, of course, none even ran for the presidency. They withdrew into their own society, culture, and, in a great many cases, into their Afro-Christian religious practices.

President William Howard Taft (1909–1913) had come along with his "dollar diplomacy." The idea, in his words, was to use "dollars instead of bullets." The phrase inevitably was broadened to describe the United States' Latin American policy as one in which American wealth was used to achieve economic and political hegemony. The popular word now is "imperialism," but the idea is much the same.

When the successor to Gómez, General Mario García Menocal, extended his term as President for a further four years in 1917, there was a brief uprising by the liberals. President Woodrow Wilson supported Menocal and said that the United States would not recognize any Cuban government brought in by revolutionary means. Marines from Guantánamo Base entered Cuba, advancing as far as Camagüey, and stayed until January 1922.

Between 1921 and 1925 the island was virtually ruled by an American commission headed by General Enoch Crowder, who had been brought in because of an economic crisis following the collapse of sugar prices from 23.6 cents a pound to 3.25 cents. When the Crowder Commission left in 1926, Cubans returned to their corruption and disorder—but this time with almost revolutionary force.

General Gerardo Machado, who first took office in 1925 and then extended his term illegally, was not only corrupt; he was brutal, cruel, greedy, and incompetent. The reaction was violent, coming mainly from the student movement.

The fervor, patriotism, and rebelliousness were often expressed in the crudest kind of violence, but out of this ferment came an extreme revisionist interpretation of Cuban history by intellectuals and historians—an interpretation which was profoundly to affect this and the succeeding generation. Fidel Castro was born in 1926. Cuban writers of high distinction had planted the historic roots of revisionism as early as 1910; now they were to flourish mightily.

José Martí was resurrected from his neglected grave. There was no doubt that he would have been bitterly resentful at the events of 1898 and of what happened afterwards. Along with his image came the concept of "the frustrated revolution," the revolution that Martí had wanted to make and, according to the revisionist theory, that Cubans would have made, had it not been for the intervention of the United States.

Therefore, it was argued, the graft, corruption, fraudulent elections, social and economic imbalances, and other evils of Cuban life were the result of American interference and domination, not of the Spanish legacy or the crookedness, greed, and weakness of the Cuban ruling class. Nationalism was channeled like a torrent into anti-Yankeeism. The rationale for Fidel's hostility to the United States was inborn, and then inbred during his student years. The feeling was as natural to him as an Irish-American's antipathy to the British.

Until the late 1920s Cuban textbooks docilely referred to the final episode of their struggle for independence as *La Guerra Hispano-Americana* (the Spanish-American War). The leader of the Cuban revisionists, Emilio Roig de Leuchsenring, and other scholars began using the more accurate description of *La Guerra Hispano-Cubano-Americana.* In 1945 this designation was officially adopted.

The Martí cult flourished during Fidel's childhood and youth among students and politically conscious Cubans. It provided a quasi-religious escape from the ugly reality of Cuban politics and a stick with which to beat the United States. It was not José Martí the writer and political ideologist who inspired Fidel Castro and his followers, but Martí the rebel and martyr who had fought for his ideals. There were giants in those days, Cuban youths thought, looking back to Martí, Maceo, Gómez, de Céspedes, García, Agramonte, and other heroes.

On October 10, 1968, Fidel made the speech to which I referred before, at Manzanillo, Oriente Province, on the hundredth anniversary of the uprising led by Carlos Manuel de Céspedes. Its importance was that it showed how Castro's generation interpreted Cuban history and the role of the United States, and also how Cuban revolutionary ideas are traced to the nineteenth-century patriots:

> Our Revolution, with its style, its essential characteristics, has very deep roots in the history of our Fatherland. This is why we say, and why it is necessary that all revolutionaries understand clearly, that our Revolution began on the tenth of October, 1868. This celebration today is an encounter of the people with its own history; it is like an encounter of the present revolutionary generation with its own roots. . . .
>
> We should know as revolutionaries that when we talk of our duty to defend this land, to defend this Fatherland, to defend this Revolution, we must think that we are not defending the revolution of a generation; we must think that we are defending the labor of a hundred years . . . With the coming of victory in 1959, our country again faced, and on an even higher plane, problems fundamental to the life of our people. For if in 1868 they discussed whether or not to abolish slavery, whether or not man can be the property of man, in our age, in our Revolution, the fundamental question, the essential question, the one that would define the revolutionary character of this epoch and this Revolution, was not the ownership of man by man but the ownership by men of the means of sustenance for Man.

No Cuban alive today can, or will, say: "Let the dead past bury its dead." The past is very much alive in the Cuban heart.

ENTER BATISTA

"Cuban society is disintegrating," the Cuban scholar Fernando Ortiz wrote in 1924, echoing many respected intellectuals of the era. "Cuba is rushing headlong into barbarism."

It was one of those periods when a national atmosphere becomes as tense and ominous as when a barometer drops before a storm. A hurricane was to strike in 1933–1934—and then pass on. The next storm began to brew after Fulgencio Batista's garrison revolt of 1952 and when it broke, it swept the existing Cuban republic away.

The Cuban ruling class could not afford to be independent of the United States, nor could it act as a national bourgeoisie to bring in a revolution. Its money, when not sent to Miami or Switzerland, could go with safety only into Cuban real estate and the tourist industries. Graft, corruption, tax evasion, and usury were the rule among them. Fidel Castro was to call them the "lumpen bourgeoisie."

President Machado had a criminal record, among other things, as a cattle thief. He appropriately began life as a butcher. Aside from being a brute, he was a peculator on a grand scale, a monument of deceit and corruption, and the collaborator for many years with the American business and banking communities and, by accommodation, with the U.S. Government. When in 1927 he arranged for his subservient Congress to extend his term of office for six years without a new election, President Calvin Coolidge indicated that it was all the same to him. This naturally was taken to mean that the United States favored the move. The Platt Amendment was still on the books, although it had been allowed to lapse in practice.

In 1930 came the infamous Hawley-Smoot Tariff Act in the United States, which raised the tariff on Cuban sugar from 1.76 cents a pound to 2 cents, causing untold misery in the already wretched island.

Franklin D. Roosevelt and his "Good Neighbor" policy represented a hopeful change in 1933, but so long as Machado was President and American banking and business interests insisted on maintaining the status quo in Cuba, revolutionary pressures were bound to build up. Strikes, riots, terror, and counterterror brought virtual chaos.

In May 1933, Roosevelt sent his friend Sumner Welles to Havana as ambassador to mediate the crisis. In the crunch the Cuban people, not Washington, drove Machado out on August 12, 1933, with a spontaneous general strike that had begun on the third. Ironically, the Cuban Communists tried to defeat the strike. In the confused five months that followed, Sergeant Fulgencio Batista, a court stenographer, rose to power as kingmaker and dictator of Cuba, a position he was to hold, in and out of office, for a quarter of a century.

Welles had no illusions about Machado and worked to get him

out—but peaceably. The Ambassador could not control events. The departure of the President was followed by exactly the sort of horrifying slaughter that Fidel Castro was successfully to forfend in 1959. On August 12 and 13 hundreds—perhaps a thousand—*Machadistas* were lynched in Havana alone and hundreds of houses were sacked.

As early as August 18, Batista, until then an obscure sergeant, began speaking threateningly. He had taken no part in the overthrow of Machado but saw the opportunities being offered and took advantage of them with a boldness and shrewdness that were innate. A natural gift for oratory helped, and so did a quick mind and a charm of manner.

Fulgencio Batista Zaldívar was born in 1902, the son of a peasant on a sugar plantation in Oriente Province. His parents were of mixed race and he certainly had Negro, white, Indian, and, it was popularly believed, Chinese blood. During his youth he worked at odd manual jobs all over the island. In 1921 he joined the army as a private. There he later learned the profession that was to open the way to power: stenography and typing. In 1932 he became a military tribunal stenographer with the rank of sergeant.

On September 4, 1933, Batista led a group of non-commissioned officers in a bloodless takeover of Camp Columbia in Havana and appointed himself chief of staff and later, colonel.

The island was convulsed by chaos and violence. Batista's force had a showdown on October 2 in Havana with recalcitrant army officers holed up in the Hotel Nacional. It was a bloody affair in which the officers had no chance. Five days later the now strongman Batista held a decisive interview with Sumner Welles in which he made it clear that he was throwing in his lot with the United States and the Cuban establishment. He never was a revolutionary; he was an ambitious, greedy, amoral opportunist, a simple uneducated man who naturally gravitated toward the sources of Cuban wealth and power.

After the uprising a five-man group, called the *Pentarquía*, had been formed by civilians. It included a well-known Havana doctor, Ramón Grau San Martín, who was dean of the faculty of medicine at Havana University and was chosen—not elected—as President on September 10, 1933. The United States withheld the recognition without which Grau's government was doomed. He hung on amid hopeless odds until January 15, 1934. The embittered "Generation of '33" again blamed the Americans for a "frustrated revolution." For Castro's future foreign minister, Raúl Roa, who took part in the uprising as a student, it was "a revolution betrayed." "Machado went, but the *Machadato* remained," he wrote.

At best one can say again that the atmosphere held a revolution in embryo out of which, this time, a truly revolutionary generation emerged. As with the Russian rebellion of 1905, the historic role of 1933 was to be what Trotsky called "a prologue" to the great Revolution. Instead of a revolutionary leader, 1933 had a counterrevolutionary in the strongman Fulgencio Batista. To be sure, there were reasons why Cuba was more ready for revolution in 1959 than in 1933, but the decisive factor was the man: Fidel Castro, who *made* the Revolution. To use Emerson's figure, Batista was the horseman who served the horse; Castro rode it.

The Platt Amendment to the Cuban constitution had become an anachronism. It was no longer needed by the United States, and it was resented by the Cubans, except by those rightists who might have sought U.S. intervention. Roosevelt had it abrogated on May 29, 1934. Nothing, however, could erase the scar it left on the Cuban body politic. It is—and presumably always will be—a source of reproach.

Batista, by now a General, went on playing the role of kingmaker. On September 13, 1938, he made his famous deal with the Cuban Communists, legalizing the party and permitting the publication of its newspapers. In January 1939 the CTC (Confederación de Trabajadores de Cuba—Cuban Workers Confederation) was formed, with the Negro Communist leader Lázaro Peña as secretary general. (He was again secretary general when he died in 1974.) Later, as President in 1940–1944, Batista took two Communists into his cabinet—Carlos Rafael Rodríguez and Blas Roca, both now prominent in Castro's government and Revolution. This term of office coincided with World War II, during which Cuba cooperated with the United States. War was declared on Japan two days after Pearl Harbor and against Germany on December 11, 1941. There were a few Cuban volunteers in the U.S. Army, but no Cubans fought as such. However, the strategic and economic value of a friendly and helpful Cuba was great.

An immensely long—286 articles—constitution was adopted in 1940 to replace the original one of 1901. It promised everything, all the human and civil rights, all kinds of freedom, racial and class equality, compulsory free education for all, social insurance, minimum wages and other workers' benefits. Some of its articles were genuinely revolutionary. One of its few readers was Fidel Castro, who made the mistake at his Moncada trial in 1953 and in the Sierra Maestra of promising to implement its liberal democratic terms.

Batista took credit for holding democratic elections in 1944.

Actually, he miscalculated, fully expecting his (and U.S. Ambassador Spruille Braden's) candidate, Dr. Carlos Saladrigas, to be elected. Instead, Ramón Grau San Martín, now heading the *Auténticos* (Authentic Revolutionary Cuban Party), won, having almost literally promised a Cuban paradise if elected. However, the *Auténticos* did not win a majority in Congress; the Batista coalition kept control.

The unhappy island was now to suffer eight years of misrule, corruption, flagrant peculation, and political gangsterism under the two *Auténtico* presidents, Grau (1944–1948) and Carlos Prío Socarrás (1948–1952). This time it was a bitter disappointment, because Grau was for some strange reason thought to represent honest, progressive, patriotic ideals. He deceived his people shamelessly and, as much as Fulgencio Batista, paved the way for the Castro revolution. If ever there was a *trahison des clercs* in Cuba, it was in the graft-ridden, violent, laissez-faire regimes of Grau and Prío.

Even the restrained, diplomatic U.S. ambassador Philip Bonsal, in the book on his mission, *Cuba, Castro and the United States,* had to write: "I know of no country among those committed to the Western ethic where the diversion of public treasure for private profit reached the proportions that it attained in the Cuban Republic."

A reform movement had begun on May 15, 1947, in the form of a new political party called the Partido del Pueblo Cubano (Cuban People's Party). It claimed to stand for the "orthodox" policies of the once revolutionary *Auténticos,* and hence became known as the Partido Ortodoxo. Fidel Castro joined it. The leader, Eduardo Chibás (known popularly as Eddy), was not only honest himself, but based his whole movement on a quasi-rebellious campaign to abolish corruption in government and business.

Eddy Chibás, as a youth, came out of the revolutionary violence of 1933. His family was wealthy. He had a demagogic and morbid streak which helped to bring about his undoing. There was no good reason to suppose that the *Ortodoxos* could have reformed Cuban society as radically as was necessary. It was a bourgeois party, with ideas of the Machado era, reformist, vague, and disorganized. Chibás talked too big for his possibilities. In a despairing gesture at the end of one of his regular and popular radio commentaries on August 5, 1951, he shot himself. Eddy Chibás would doubtless have brought more honesty into Cuban life, and the best elements in Cuban society had always fought for honesty, but, as Castro was to decide, his movement could never be revolutionary.

General Batista had entered his name, while living luxuriously in self-exile in Florida, as a candidate for senator from Las Villas

Province for the June 1, 1948, elections. He won, and returned in triumph to Cuba on November 19. There he later formed a political party called the Partido de Acción Unitaria (PAU).

The best elements of the "Generation of '33" had failed irretrievably. The idealism, the bravery, the crusade against corruption, the yearning for a Cuba independent of the United States power, the vague but sincere desire for a "revolution"—all these had sunk gradually into a mire of dishonesty, greed, and vicious, unpunished political gangsterism.

Violence had such a long and uninterrupted history in Cuba that some authorities came to believe it was an ineradicable, endemic part of Cuban society. Prerevolutionary Cuban violence was connected with political party factions, Havana University, terrorist private armies, and the trade unions. The university was a hotbed of violence during Fidel's period there, and he was in the midst of it. Assassinations, armed raids (Fidel was never without a pistol), bombs, and dynamite were the ingredients. It was not insurrection; there was no ideology involved; it was a matter of local politics, labor union power, the struggle for student leadership—which was where Castro came in. Communism played no appreciable role.

Another presidential election was scheduled for June 1, 1952. *Bohemia,* the popular weekly, held a public opinion poll in December 1951, which showed the *Ortodoxo* candidate, Roberto Agramonte, professor of sociology at Havana University, in the lead. Carlos Hevia, a respected engineer, for the *Auténticos* was a poor second. Fulgencio Batista, candidate of his own PAU, was a distant third.

Agramonte and Hevia were men of unblemished reputation and transparent honesty. It was a tragedy for Cuba that one of them was not elected and at least given a chance to show what he could do. It seemed almost fated, a part of the "original sin" of Cuban politics, that an honest man could not be allowed to take office peacefully through the electoral system.

General Batista could not win at the polls, but he wanted to become President, and a number of lower-ranking officers in the army, mostly captains and lieutenants, wanted to see him in power. Like Caesar, he let himself be persuaded—or at least he made believe that he was reluctant. Batista's mind was a devious one. His greed for power and wealth was strong and perhaps compulsive.

Early in the morning of March 10, 1952, he and his army followers seized Camp Columbia in Havana, the largest garrison in Cuba. Prío Socarrás, still President, cravenly gave in without a struggle, although there were officers and troops who would have rallied to him. He took refuge in the Mexican Embassy. On March 13 he left for Mexico and then Florida, where he used small amounts of his ill-gotten wealth to arm Cubans trying to overthrow or kill Batista. About $50,000 of his money went to Fidel Castro to buy the yacht *Granma,* in which the revolutionaries sailed to Cuba in 1956.

The Cuban Communists accepted the coup supinely. So did the Workers Confederation after its secretary general, Eusebio Mujal, had been bought off. The peasants were apolitical. Batista shrewdly figured that the big American and Cuban business and landowning interests would support a strong, pro-American government. On March 27, Washington recognized the new government.

The public approval that Batista seemed to have counted upon did not materialize. On the contrary, I was in Cuba a month after the *golpe* and wrote an article from Havana for *The New York Times,* which was published on April 19. In the light of what was to happen, it showed that General Batista's coup was the spark that lighted the fire of a continuing discontent.

"The only safe prediction for the next year or two in Cuba," I wrote, "is that it is going to be a difficult, and perhaps dangerous period. . . . General Fulgencio Batista's coup on March 10 was a simple, old-fashioned and completely successful grab for power by a military leader who knew there was no other way in which he could gain control. It went off so smoothly and has been accepted with such outward calm that the Cuban situation today has a deceptive air of simplicity. It is important to realize that there are complicating factors and that strong forces are and will continue to be at work behind the scenes."

On March 16, 1952, the *Ortodoxo* party convoked a meeting in the Colón Cemetery. At the end of the ceremony a young man jumped on top of the tomb of Eddy Chibás and harangued the crowd. No one knew who he was.

"Eduardo Chibás," he cried, "we have come to tell you that the people will not fail you . . . Eduardo Chibás, we have come to tell you that we will never renounce your ideals . . . Eduardo Chibás, we have come to tell you that we will prove worthy of your sacrifice and we will never halt in the struggle to see the nation free."

It was Fidel Castro, making his public entrance in the drama of the Cuban Revolution in typical oratorical style. Fidel, who received his law degree in 1950, had opened a law office with two friends in Havana under the name of Azpiazú, Castro, and Resende. In this capacity he filed a brief with the Court of Constitutional Guarantees arguing that it should declare General Batista's seizure of power to be unconstitutional. He also entered a charge in the Urgency Court asking that Batista be tried as a criminal.

No attention was paid. The idea and determination to overthrow the Batista regime by a revolution came next.

THE OLD ECONOMY

There was a great deal of controversy in the early years of the Revolution over whether prerevolutionary Cuba was underdeveloped, developed, or at a halfway stage. A persuasive case could be made to prove that Cuba was not underdeveloped, using the figures for per capita income, literacy, automobiles, telephones, television sets, doctors, dentists, average food intake, and the like. Felipe Pazos, one of Cuba's leading economists, called the country "semideveloped." In statistical terms, then, Cuba was comparatively well off at the time the Revolution began.

A great many historians and economists, for reasons incomprehensible to someone like myself, use figures for the per capita income to disparage the Revolution. Professor Hugh Thomas, in his book on Cuba, takes one of the recognized Cuban per capita income figures —$521—and points out that it tells us "no more than the remark that the average Englishman drank in 1964 one-tenth of a bottle of champagne, since 5.5 million bottles were consumed that year." One sign of "prosperity" was not without its irony. There were far more television sets in Cuba than in any other Latin American country. How nice for Fidel Castro, who, in the beginning, almost governed by television.

Most Cubans before the Revolution would not have agreed about how "prosperous" the country was and how gratifying it was that there were so many automobiles, telephones, and TV sets, or that, although they did not know it, their per capita annual income was somewhere between $320 and $520. Professor Lowry Nelson, who in 1950 had called the island "one of the most favorable spots for human existence on the earth's surface," had to write in 1958 that "the importation of food was still a major economic requirement." Food imports in 1958 were $159 million, or 20.5 percent of total imports.

Of the many analyses of the economic situation in Cuba before the Revolution and in its first few years, the most impressive in my opinion was made by the English economist Dudley Seers, then visiting professor at Yale University. He edited a series of papers by a team that went to the island with him, which was published in book form in 1964 under the title *Cuba, The Economic and Social Revolution.*

"Cuba in the 35 years from 1923 to 1958 showed little progress," Seers wrote in his report. "The stagnation was more serious and lasted longer than in any other Latin American economy—excepting perhaps the economies of one or two very small and poor nations such as Bolivia and Haiti. . . .

"The existing state of affairs—in which people were short of food and work but land lay idle and factories not built—could not continue."

Political instability and lack of trust in the law courts led businessmen and investors to seek high profits, to hoard, or to send their money abroad. They induced the government to protect them with high tariffs, and they protected themselves with monopoly practices. The American system of mass production at low prices was not utilized. The tax system, inherited from Spanish colonial times, depended primarily on indirect taxation, which hit the low income brackets and favored the high. Tax evasion was widespread.

One of the few prerevolutionary fields in which there was enlightened social legislation, as even Castro conceded in 1959, was in labor. A forty- to forty-four-hour week, generous paid holidays, prohibitions on work-saving machines in order to protect jobs, maternity leave—these and other favorable measures, which began in 1934, made Cuban trade unions among the most pampered in Latin America. It was almost impossible during Batista's dictatorship to discharge an employee. This is undoubtedly the reason why the industrial workers and nearly all trade union officials supported Batista and were indifferent or hostile to the Castro guerrillas and the civil resistance.

Unemployment was a great and permanent curse, even in the so-called prosperous years. The sugar harvest took only four or five months. During the rest of the year, called the *tiempo muerto,* or dead time, more than 20 percent of the workers were unemployed. Even during the harvest, the figure would be 9 or 10 percent idle.

In 1956 (at the end of which year Fidel Castro landed in Cuba from Mexico) the U.S. Department of Commerce issued a two-hundred-page study called *Investment in Cuba: Basic Information for U.S. Businessmen.* Although the White House, just before the Bay of Pigs invasion in April 1961, was to state in a white paper that conditions in Cuba "constituted an open invitation to revolution," the 1956 study stressed Cuba's potentialities and opportunities for

American businessmen. There was not a word of caution about a political situation which was clearly fraught with hazards. The year 1956 had seen two attempted revolts.

"The only foreign investments of importance are those of the United States," the Commerce Department study stated with apparent satisfaction. "American participation exceeds 90 per cent in the telephone and electric services, about 50 per cent in public service railways, and roughly 40 per cent in raw sugar production. The Cuban branches of the United States banks are entrusted with almost one-fourth of all bank deposits . . . The outlook for additional investments is also good."

Philip Bonsal, U.S. Ambassador at the beginning of the Revolution, listed other American holdings and interests in the book he wrote: an important railroad, the main cement plant, large holdings in the cattle industry, and heavy investments in manufacturing. Americans dominated Cuban imports of automobiles, television sets, household appliances, and other durable consumer goods. Six of the fifteen principal banks were American. Many of the best hotels were American-owned, and the largest interests in the flourishing gambling casinos were held by some of our choicest operators from Las Vegas. "American participation in drug smuggling and peddling and other vices [i.e., prostitution] was suspected," Bonsal carefully notes.

Americans owned the valuable nickel-cobalt mines of Oriente Province. The importing and refining of crude oil and the marketing of petroleum products were in the hands of Standard Oil, Texaco, and the Anglo-Dutch Shell combine, using Venezuelan oil from their own wells. And, of course, there was the American interest in the sugar industry.

"The events of history often lead to the islands," writes Fernand Braudel in the first volume of *The Mediterranean in the Age of Philip II.* "Perhaps it would be more accurate to say that they make use of them. . . .

"How many islands were invaded by foreign crops, whose justification lay solely in their position on Mediterranean or even world markets? Grown for export only, these crops regularly threatened the equilibrium of the island's economy. . . .

"This revolution was carried out entirely in the interest of a Europe which was clamoring for the precious sugar, and not in the interests of the islanders themselves. For the tragedy of sugarcane is that wherever it is grown it prevents the growing of other crops in rotation and restricts the space available for food crops."

Because the sugar plantations needed slave labor, Professor

Braudel continues, it was "the slave trade in Negroes from Guinea and Angola which in the middle of the [sixteenth] century, again because of sugar, reached the shores of the American continent."

The Cuban scholar Fernando Ortiz, who began writing early in the century and lived to see the Castro revolution and accept it, characterized his country in *Cuban Counterpoint* (1947) in terms of "the marriage of tobacco and sugar and the birth of alcohol [i.e., rum], conceived of the Unholy Ghost, the devil, who is the father of tobacco, in the sweet womb of wanton sugar." But what he called the "Cuban Trinity"—tobacco, sugar, and alcohol—no longer predominates. Only sugar has held its place.

"Cane is not cultivated by the plant but in mass," Ortiz pointed out. "The industry was not developed for private or domestic consumption, nor even for that of the locality, but for large-scale production and foreign exploitation."

In the 1950s the industry was unstable and stagnant; yet it was the most important sector of the economy. Eighty percent of Cuban exports was in sugar; nearly three-quarters of the arable land grew sugar; two-thirds of the rail trackage was used for transport of sugar cane and refined sugar; a half a million men—about a quarter of the labor force—worked in the sugar industry.

Cuba was the largest exporter of sugar in the world; the United States was the largest importer. And there was the sugar island right on the American doorstep! Nothing could have been more natural than the heavy American investment in Cuban sugar; the purchase of huge tracts of land, very cheaply, after the 1898 war; and the interlocking of the two economies, which held Cuba in what looked like an unbreakable vise, as many other facets of the economy had also been embraced.

The Cuban sugar quota for the United States was set annually by Congress without consulting the Cuban government. In return for a higher than world market price, Cuba had to grant tariff concessions to American imports. Moreover, as all knowledgeable Cubans realized, the higher price was paid in order to protect domestic American sugar producers, whose costs were higher, and not as a piece of American generosity to Cuba. (Congress was to end the U.S. Sugar Act on December 31, 1974, when world market prices made it useless.)

"The conclusion seems to me unavoidable," Ambassador Bonsal writes, "that the periodical renewals of American sugar legislation and the prospect of such renewals effectively, if not explicitly, limited Cuban sovereignty."

This was a polite, diplomatic way of saying what Che Guevara blurted out in his famous and much ridiculed remark that the American sugar quota was "slavery."

It would, however, be a great distortion to think of the prerevolutionary Cuban economy simply as a sugar monoculture. There was a time, as Fernando Ortiz's book shows, when one thought of the economy in terms of sugar and tobacco. It is nostalgic to read his eloquent tribute to the Havana cigar in these days when Havanas have lost their glory:

"Tobacco is a magic gift of the savage world; sugar is a scientific gift of civilization . . . Tobacco is today the most universal plant, more so than either corn or wheat. Today the world lives and dreams in a haze of blue smoke spirals that evoke the old Cuban gods. In the spread of this habit of smoking, the island of Cuba has played a large part, not only because tobacco and its rites were native to it, but because of the incomparable excellence of its product . . . And that is why as a general thing, in lands remote from the Antilles, the geographical name of Havana is better known than that of Cuba."

As a matter of fact, tobacco exports from Cuba were stagnant for forty years before the Revolution. The reason must have been the high prices everywhere. Now they are still higher, and the quality has deteriorated.

Cuba's most important resources after sugar are minerals. There are considerable deposits of iron, manganese, high-grade chromium, copper, cobalt, and, especially, nickel. A 1958 study said: "Cuba's nickeliferous iron ores in the eastern part of the island are the world's largest potential source of nickel."

For developing countries like Cuba, the problem with minerals in the ground is to find the great sums and technological know-how to exploit them. The United States provided these ingredients, but only for its own investors and market. During World War II the American government developed the nickel in the Mayarí iron mines of Oriente, and by the time the war ended Cuba was producing about 10 percent of the world's supply. In 1947 the mines were closed down because the United States no longer needed the minerals. There was no thought of bolstering Cuba's economy or diversifying her exports. It was only when the Korean War again created a demand for nickel that the U.S. government's mine at Nicaro was reopened. It was still going in 1959.

The mine had been used for American purposes, at American will, for the profit of Americans. Freeport Sulphur had a share in

Nicaro but was primarily interested in the large Moa Bay (fifty miles east of Nicaro) nickel and cobalt deposits. John Hay Whitney, chairman of Freeport, said that the Moa Bay mine represented "the best new source of nickel in the world."

Copper mining started in El Cobre (the Spanish word for copper) in 1530. The mine is in Oriente Province, but there is copper to be found all over the island. The largest mine today is the Matahambre. At one time Cuba produced more than half the world's chemical-grade manganese—for the U.S. Bethlehem Steel Company. The chromium deposits also were once heavily exploited.

The trouble from the Cuban viewpoint was that all these mines were subject to the U.S. economy and U.S. investments. In some cases, as with Moa Bay's nickel and cobalt, Freeport Sulphur exported the unprocessed ore and refined it in the United States.

In all underdeveloped or semideveloped countries in our nationalistic age, the ownership of the products of the soil by foreigners and its exploitation for foreign investors are causes of deep emotional resentment. The United States was curiously blind throughout Latin America for generations and, in Cuba, paid a heavy price. The Soviet Union is not making the same mistake with Cuba.*

*Geographically, a few basic facts on Cuba should be kept in mind. Cuba is larger than all the other Caribbean islands put together—44,218 square miles (110,931 square kilometers). The distance across the Strait of Florida is always referred to as "90 miles"—so much so that the figure is convenient to use. However, the splendid new *Atlas of Cuba* (1972), printed in the Soviet Union and compiled with Russian help, gives the shortest distance between the United States and Cuba as 180 kilometers, which is 112.5 miles. Haiti is 48 miles across the Windward Passage; Mexico 131 miles at Yucatan; Jamaica 87.5 miles.

The length of Cuba from Punta de Quemado in the extreme east to Cabo San Antonio in the west is 781 miles (1,750 kilometers). At its narrowest—just west of the boundary of Havana Province—the distance is 19.4 miles (31 kilometers); at its widest point—Camagüey Province—it is 119 miles (191 kilometers). There are 4,841 miles (5,746 kilometers) of coastline.

The last census before the Revolution was taken in 1953. It gave a total population of 5,829,092. The generally accepted figure when the Revolution began in 1959 is about 6,500,000. The latest census (taken in 1970) gave the population as 8,553,395. The capital of Havana had 1,755,360 inhabitants in 1970. In 1974, Castro said, the population was 9,000,000 "and going for 10,000,000" with an increase of 200,000 a year.

Geographers should note that two important changes were made after 1959 in the provincial boundaries between Camagüey and Las Villas, and between Las Villas and Matanzas. The Zapata Peninsula, with its great swamp, is now part of Matanzas Province. These changes are shown in the new *Atlas*. An alteration was made in the western boundary of Havana Province after the *Atlas* was printed.

FIDEL CASTRO

With Fidel Castro, as with virtually all important historic figures, the years before his prominence are a reconstruction, true and false, imaginative, distorted, colored by favorable or unfavorable bias, and full of gaps. Fidel is a reserved, self-centered, and extremely complex character. He is only superficially an extrovert. He seems to live in a goldfish bowl; in reality, he has an inner self and an inner life that nobody I have met or know of has ever reached or, I think, ever will reach, unless the equally enigmatic Celia Sánchez, his faithful companion, has done so. If she has, she will keep it to herself. Fidel does not give of himself in any intimate way, and he has taken affection only from a few persons in his life. He is a lonely man.

One could draw up a long list of figures famous to history who lived in a constant blaze of publicity, surrounded by apparent intimates, but whose private lives and characters as human beings remained mysteries. They are the enigmas of history, the unsolved puzzles of the chroniclers. Fidel Castro belongs in this class, as did —to pick a perhaps appropriate modern example—Vladimir Ilyich Lenin.

Fidel does not have an affectionate nature; he does not, as I said before, wear his heart on his sleeve; he is one of those people who feel deeply without being able to express their emotions. The July 26, 1970, address was one of the very rare speeches in which he publicly showed a deep, personal emotion. Another was in his elegiac tribute to Che Guevara. There are men who steel themselves against a display of emotion—the stiff upper lip of the English, for instance— but there is also the inherited stoicism of the Spanish.

Yet Fidel has had the rare gift of inspiring the men and women around him with a feeling that can only be called worship. This is why the comrades of the "Generation of '53" have remained a cohesive, blindly loyal group.

He could not have been a sociable young man while he was at Havana University from 1945 to 1950. He shunned dancing and parties—in fact, I am sure that he does not know how to dance. Even now, he dresses formally only when it is absolutely necessary. He hates formality. His brother Raúl once said to me: "Diplomatic protocol and behavior bore and irritate him. Fidel just cannot be bothered." Banquets with toasts are anathema. He is best at public appearances with visiting celebrities, especially when he can make a speech. Gina Lollabrigida found him "unsure of himself; he was afraid of me," although he seemed far from inhibited during her visit in September 1974.

I have had to change my mind about Fidel Castro in some respects as the years passed and as I saw more of him. I have watched him mature from youth into middle age. (He was thirty-one when I first met him and was forty-six in September 1972 when I last saw him.) In my opinion, he has grown in humanity and in his feeling for the people. The idealism, patriotism (or nationalism), the dedication and courage that were always there, but that had a romantic, fanatical, almost frantic quality, are under better control now and more calmly and practically directed. He responds more often and more readily to his innate pragmatism. I think that posterity, including future generations of Cubans, will grant him more respect as a moral being, as well as a revolutionary, than he has been accorded during these hectic years.

Fidel's personal relations with Celia Sánchez will always be a mystery, given the extreme reticence on both sides. Celia is a bit older than Fidel and is not the sexy type who would make any doubts unnecessary. Fidel was, and is apparently, far from being a celibate, but it seems certain that he will not marry a second time after one mutually unhappy experience. Although devoted to his son, Fidelito, he has always insisted on him studying and working quietly on his own. I was assured by several friends that Fidelito, who was at the university in 1972, is entirely loyal to his father and to the Revolution.

There has been no nepotism in the Revolution, at least to date. The prominence of Fidel's brother Raúl is well earned. An older full brother (there are a half-brother and -sister), Ramón, helped Fidel from the Sierra Maestra days, although he was at first somewhat disturbed by his brother's revolutionary activities. He is still working for Fidel in agricultural affairs. Ramón, like their mother, was deeply attached to the family farm, which he ran before the insurrection. The only member of the family who defected was a younger sister, Juana, who could not accept the drift into Communism. She went into exile in 1964 and wrote articles and gave interviews attacking her brother and the Revolution. He was hurt about it, but Juanita proved to be so unreliable and emotional that her attacks did no lasting harm.

Fidel was born on August 13, 1926 (not in 1927 as was sometimes said, even in official publications), on his father's *finca,* Manacas, outside the village of Birán. The nearest town was Mayarí, about twenty miles inland from Nipe Bay on the northern coast of Oriente Province. It was a region partly owned and dominated by the United Fruit Company, which had great properties, mostly in sugar, acquired after the 1898 war. His father, Angel, worked for a time for United Fruit.

Angel, the former Spanish soldier and manual worker from Galicia, was by 1926 a landowner with thousands of acres of mostly sugar-cane land. He was rough, tough, bold, unscrupulous, uneducated. Legality and morality—church or otherwise—bothered him little. One sensed that he was irascible. If he had any political coloring it was rightist, but also anti-Yankee.

Respectability was thrust upon him. His first wife was a schoolteacher. There were two children by the marriage, Pedro Emilio and Lidia. A young woman named Lina Ruz, who was born in Cuba, entered the house as a cook. Angel and Lina would be the parents of five more children—Ramón, Fidel, Juana, Emma, and Raúl—all illegitimate. Lina's family had also come from Galicia in Spain. This made Fidel, like Generalissimo Francisco Franco, a pure *Gallego* by blood. However, nothing should be made of the fact that Fidel was an illegitimate child during the earliest years of his life. In Cuba illegitimate children are never deprived of a normal family life and they have the legal status of legitimate offspring.

When the parents wanted to send several of the boys to the Colegio La Salle, a primary school in Santiago de Cuba run by a religious order, the headmaster insisted on all his pupils being baptized, confirmed, and legitimate. So Angel, his wife having died, married Lina Ruz with the help of the then bishop of Camagüey, Enrique Pérez Serantes, who likewise had been born in Galicia. He was a friend of the family and was later, as bishop of Santiago de Cuba, to play a prominent role in the Moncada Barracks affair.

Fidel's mother, like her husband, had a peasant hardness and that special, covetous attachment to the land that one finds in the farmers of Spain and France. She was angry and dismayed when the 26th of July Movement set about burning sugar cane, including hers, and later, early in the Revolution, expropriating the family property along with all other large holdings. Like nearly all Latin women, she was devoutly religious.

The children were rebellious and must have been hard to handle. Unlike the oldest son, Pedro Emilio, Fidel did not break with his father, although he quarreled with him often and in 1940, when he was thirteen, according to Hugh Thomas, tried to organize a strike of sugar workers against his father. In later life he spoke critically of Angel. At the same time, he let his father support him generously through schools and the university, but I cannot imagine what he did with the money he may have inherited from Angel, who died in 1956 while Fidel was in Mexico. By the time his mother died, in 1963, money meant nothing to Fidel.

After the Colegio La Salle, in Santiago, Fidel went to the Colegio Dolores, a Jesuit primary school in the same city—like his previous school, for children of the well-to-do. In 1941 he started his *bachillerato* in the fashionable Belén preparatory school in Havana, one of the best secondary schools in Cuba. There he excelled in athletics and did well as a student. The note under his photograph in the June 1945 graduating class annual, *Ecos de Belén,* stated: "We do not doubt that he will fill the book of his life with brilliant pages." He was evidently popular, as the reference also said that he won "the admiration and affection of all."

When my wife and I visited the Colegio Belén early in 1959, the charming old Spanish Jesuit director proudly showed us this yearbook. Poor man! His school was to be closed, like every other private school in Cuba, and his favorite pupil was to turn Communist.

In 1945, at the age of eighteen, Fidel entered Havana University and elected to study for the bar. While there he fell in love with a student in the faculty of philosophy, Mirta Díaz Balart, whose brother, Rafael, was a fellow student at the university and whose father was an official in the Batista government. Rafael also was to take a post with the Batista government. The family did not approve of the marriage, while Fidel, for his part, was to find the connection a great embarrassment.

He and Mirta were married on October 12, 1948, in the Roman Catholic church at Banes, Oriente Province, where Mirta was born. Their only child, Fidelito, was born on September 1, 1949. The marriage was clearly unhappy. Fidel must have been a hopeless husband. While he was in the Isle of Pines prison after Moncada, Mirta accepted a salary through her brother from Batista's Ministry of the Interior, causing a scandal. Fidel was bitter. Mirta divorced him while he was still in jail, remarried, divorced again, and, I was told in 1972, had a third husband. Except for a few years at school on Long Island, New York, when Fidel was in the Sierra Maestra, Fidelito had always been in Cuba under his father's care until he went to Moscow in 1974 to take graduate courses in physics.

Fidel's career as a student is tangled in myths, truths, and mysteries. He was exceptionally intelligent, so that when he applied himself he was a brilliant pupil. The system at the university made it possible for students to neglect classes and cram at the very end of the term in order to pass the all-important examinations. This method was ideal for Fidel, who called on his retentive memory.

As an athlete he was always outstanding. His reading was eclectic. He could boast, and be accused of, reading Lenin, but then he also read Hitler's *Mein Kampf.* All that one can glean from Fidel's voracious reading as a youth is that he was not interested in one field of thought, such as Marxism-Leninism, any more than another, despite his opportunistic and demagogic boasts in later years. Because of his excellent memory, surprising literary, philosophical, or historical allusions crop up in his speeches. Raúl Castro once showed me Fidel's university reports for his graduating year, which he had saved. Eight or nine of the professors had written *sobresaliente* (excellent), three gave him *notable,* and only two graded him *aprovechado* (passing).

Fidel is not the most reliable biographer of his own life. Early in the Revolution he was persuaded by the Italian publisher Feltrinelli to attempt an autobiography. Carlos Franqui, a former editor of the newspaper *Revolución,* was entrusted with the task of writing it for him and given the material. He told me in 1963 that he had accumulated the equivalent of eleven volumes.

I asked Castro about it in 1967. He laughed. "I want to *make* history, not write it," he said. This was, perhaps, an unconscious variation on Karl Marx on the role of philosophers: they "have only *interpreted* the world in various ways; the point, however, is to *change* it." In 1972 Fidel again brushed aside the idea in the conversation we had. "I'm too busy living to waste time writing," he said.

But he has never been too busy to talk, starting with his student life. Fidel Castro is a great orator, one of the greatest of our times and, I would think, without a peer in Latin American history. A conversation with him is usually very one-sided because Fidel's flow of ideas and language is close to inexhaustible. He has a remarkable memory, as I said, but perhaps one should add: for what he wants to remember. His hearer is overwhelmed by the talker's enthusiasm, passion, conviction, and complete assurance. One goes away convinced, and then sometimes gets doubts—too late.

His speeches, as I remarked before, are to be listened to, not read. They have no polish, not much form, much repetitiveness, and plenty of declamation. They will never be studied for their literary quality, as Englishmen will always read Churchill or Frenchmen De Gaulle. Fidel uses his speeches as a form of popular education, often going into great detail, with endless data. There is no telling how much is understood, but his efforts seem to be appreciated. The speeches show a respect for the people and for their intelligence and seriousness.

He began to teach himself to be a public orator at Havana University. A feature of Cuban university life all through republican history, and especially from the Machado era onward, was its preoccupation with politics. The romantic, revolutionary fervor of the *Machadato*—what Fidel called "the legend of a heroic epoch"—still permeated the university. It expressed itself in factional quarrels and opposition to the government. The violence had a gangsterlike character.

There were two chief "action groups" while Fidel was there, the MSR (Movimiento Socialista Revolucionaria), whose leader was Mario Salabarría, and the UIR (Unión Insurrecional Revolucionaria). The "revolutionary" names were typical. Fidel joined the UIR after Salabarría's gang almost murdered him in an ambush, writes K. S. Karol in *Guerrillas in Power.* One of the leaders of the MSR was Rolando Masferrer, then Communist, later a strong man for Batista with his own private army of terrorists during the dictatorship; now he is an exile in Florida.

Karol, whose book is venomously anti-Castro, nevertheless asserts that there is no evidence that Fidel indulged in the university gangsterism. This is also my information from some of his fellow students. There is a "black legend" about Castro's supposed hoodlumism and even murders at the university, but no proofs or police convictions. Fidel was never interested in violence for the sake of violence. In fact, in the newspaper articles he was writing for *Alerta* at the time and in his first appearances at the bar he vehemently denounced the prevailing violence.

He and a student named Justo Fuentes had a daily program on the radio station COCO, which apparently led to an MSR ambush in 1949 in which Fuentes was killed. The head of COCO, Guido García Inclán, is still (1975) running the station and ranks as one of Fidel's oldest and most loyal supporters.

The two most sensational episodes in Castro's university career were the abortive Cayo Confites expedition to invade the Dominican Republic in 1947 and the extraordinary outburst of popular fury in Bogotá, Colombia, in 1948, in which Fidel was involved.

The first was a plot to land about a thousand men in the Dominican Republic, then headed by the monstrous General Rafael Leónidas Trujillo. The MSR and UIR went along to help Dominican rebels, one of whose leaders was Juan Bosch. Castro, as a member of the UIR and perhaps looking for adventure, joined the rebels who gathered at Cayo Confites, a little island off the coast of Camagüey. Trujillo, learning of the plot, brought enough pressure on the United

States and the Grau administration to get the expedition broken up. Reliable witnesses say that Fidel swam ashore with his submachine gun lashed to his back.

The *Bogotazo,* as it came to be called, took place during a Pan-American Conference of American States in the Colombian capital. At the same time, a "Conference of Latin-American University Associations" was planned, with General Juan Perón of Argentina providing most of the money on behalf of the Perón Youth League. Perón's interest was to protest against the British possession of the Falkland Islands in the Atlantic, which were claimed by Argentina. There were four in the Cuban delegation. Fidel went to Bogotá with a UIR friend named Rafael del Pino, who was later to betray the *Fidelistas* in Mexico. Early in the Cuban Revolution he joined a sabotaging landing party from Florida and was caught. He is now in a Cuban prison.

On April 9, 1948, the popular Colombian Liberal Party leader, Jorge Eliécer Gaitán, was murdered by a madman in the streets of the capital during a demonstration. The killer was lynched on the spot, and an extraordinary explosion of looting, burning, and murder (perhaps three thousand were killed) went on for three days. The Communists tried to take advantage of the situation but failed. This did not inhibit Secretary of State George G. Marshall and the American delegation from labeling the uprising as Communist.

Fidel and Del Pino were involved in the rioting and seem to have been asked by the police to get out. The Cuban ambassador, Guillermo Belt, a lawyer for American firms in Cuba, took them into the Embassy and arranged for them to be flown back to Havana. He told me in 1960 that he wished to God he hadn't.

The wild stories about Castro and Bogotá have not been bolstered by any proof. A Scotland Yard investigation made afterward found no evidence involving the Cubans except that a few of them —perhaps Fidel and Del Pino—had collected arms in their hotel rooms. The *Bogotazo* has now become a minor incident in the biography of Castro, although innumerable pages were written about it in the early books on the Revolution.

Fidel once spoke of his "vocation for revolution." If there is such a person as a born revolutionary, he is one. Some of Castro's fellow students and his critics and enemies believe that he saw revolution as his road to power and would have made any kind of revolution, right-wing or left-wing, as opportunity presented itself. This makes no sense, if only because a Cuban revolution in the 1950s made by a man born in 1926 could only be anticapitalist and anti-American.

Castro was a rebel against the society of his times, which was rightist and conservative. Moreover, he was later to show a genuine feeling for the poor and an absorbing desire to do something to help the mass of the people, and this could be done only with a radical, leftist revolution.

However, the more one studies his actions and opinions in the prerevolutionary period, the more obvious it is that he had no systematic ideas, no ideology, no political connections. This is one reason why in the Sierra Maestra he was able to make all sorts of democratic, as well as radical, promises with authentic acquiescence and a certain degree of innocence. He was politically immature. In economics, he was a child. If, as he later asserted, he was a Marxist-Leninist in embryo at Havana University, there is no evidence that he, or any reliable witness, can submit to substantiate the claim.

"Fidel never wanted to join any party," his brother Raúl said to me in 1967, "because he didn't want to be restricted or be under any orders or discipline. He never could stand for any kind of formalism. This is a trait of his that he has never abandoned."

Early in the Revolution I suggested that Castro picked up movements and ideas as one would garments, putting them on, taking them off, throwing them away, placing them in the wardrobe—but that in all cases the wearer was the same Fidel Castro. He is not, and cannot be, emotionally dogmatic or orthodox; it is against his nature. It is a vital feature of his character that he must be his own master.

This does not mean that he will not, as he says, be a Marxist-Leninist until the day he dies. It means that Cuban Marxism-Leninism will be what Fidel Castro makes it, not what Marxist ideologues in Moscow or academic scholars consider it should be. Of course, Communism is a determined political and economic system, but so is liberal democracy. Within its limits, Fidel has at all times consciously or unconsciously avoided being caught in a "shirt of Nessus." In a speech in 1968 he said: "Nothing is more anti-Marxist than dogma and thought which are petrified."

His politics had to fit his character, which is that of the "lone wolf," and above all, the leader. The Latin American scene has had a long history of *personalismo.* It is not necessary to be an embodiment of ideal qualities like George Washington or Abraham Lincoln. José Martí was an exceptional figure in Cuban history who died before his image could be tarnished. Latins want their *caudillo* or *jefe* to be different, commanding, strong. His right to rule is his charismatic stature as a hero, and he can achieve that image as much by defying the laws of his country as by climbing a political ladder.

A leader whose supreme virtue is to be like everybody else, only more so (an Eisenhower, for example), would have little attraction in a country like Cuba. Anglo-Saxon historians are wasting their time when they judge Fidel Castro by their own standards of morality and virtue.

Revolution was taking form in Fidel's mind in 1952 when General Batista made his garrison coup. The time had come to do something—but what he did brought on the first of his three shattering defeats. However, as Raúl Castro said to me: "The most important feature of Fidel's character is that he will not accept defeat."

CHAPTER 3

Moncada

Remember that after all, it is more difficult to live than to die.

—Abel Santamaría to his sister Haydée, at Moncada, July 26, 1953

It seemed like madness. Perhaps it was, but history will agree with Celia Sánchez, who said: "The Cuban Revolution was born at Moncada."

The purpose was to attack and take the Moncada Barracks and its arsenal, in the center of Santiago de Cuba. It was the second largest garrison in the country. Control of it would have provided a base from which to dominate the capital of Oriente Province. Castro hoped that it could start an uprising against Batista with volunteers armed from the munitions store in the barracks. A new and better Cuba would then be created.

The attack had to be a surprise, because the Castro band was poorly armed and heavily outnumbered by a garrison of regular troops and Rural Guards. Reinforcements from Holguín in the north would have to be blocked. Therefore a minor attack against the small garrison in Bayamo, west of Santiago, was planned. The date of July 26 in 1953 was chosen because a carnival is held in Santiago de Cuba every year on July 25, 26, and 27. History was with them, for they were raising the standard of revolt in the region where the *mambises* rose in 1868. It was the centennial year of José Martí's birth.

Moncada has been treated by historians either as idealism, self-sacrifice, heroism, and patriotism of the purest sort or as a vainglorious stunt by Fidel Castro at the head of a confused, motley band of sheep being led to the slaughter.

The Cuban Communist Party (the PSP—Partido Socialista Popular) issued a statement on Moncada afterward that is not without its irony in the light of future events.

"We repudiate the putschist methods of the action in Santiago de Cuba and Bayamo," it reads, "which are characteristic of bourgeois political factions and which was a rash attempt to take both military barracks. The heroism shown by the participants in this attack is false and sterile, for it is guided by mistaken bourgeois conceptions."

By coincidence, there was a Communist celebration in Santiago de Cuba at the time, which gave Batista the chance to blame the attack on them, thus increasing their irritation against the Castroites. As it happened, Fidel had no Communists, or at most one, in his group, who would have been the exception to prove the rule. He was bitter about the Communists at the time.

Fidel had prepared a manifesto in advance, but held it to use after his hoped-for success. It was a compilation of all kinds of social and economic reform measures, much like succeeding manifestos and programs up to 1959. There was no coherent ideological line, but the key word "revolution" occurred again and again. It was a word that had been used innumerable times before in previous decades of the Republic, but this time the man who used the word meant it in the strictest sense—a social revolution on the order of the French, Russian, and Chinese Revolutions.

A great deal of new information about Moncada was published during the preparations for the twentieth anniversary of the attack in 1973. All previous accounts of the event have to be rewritten, mainly because of what amounts to the first carefully assembled, official history of the attack, prepared by the history section of the political department of the Revolutionary Armed Forces (FAR). It was first published in *El Oficial,* the magazine of the FAR, and republished in the *Granma* of July 20, 1973.

The account differs in one major and many minor details from previous information, and it adds a number of details not known before. The article contains a certain amount of dutiful Marxist and *Fidelista* propaganda which is easily separated from the straightforward account of what actually happened.

The attackers were not outnumbered by eight or ten to one as all historians, myself included, believed. The official count gives a detailed compilation of the Moncada garrison's force: there were "374 men from Maceo Regiment No. 1 and about 26 men from Squadron 18 of the Rural Guards, making a total of about 402." In addition, there seem to have been some men from the Regimental Intelligence Service and some officers on leave who spent the night in the barracks—perhaps a few dozen, all told. Castro had 131 men with him (29 others took part in the Bayamo attack), so the odds against him were less than three and a half to one. This was more than sufficient, but it made the attack less foolhardy than it seemed.

Another revealing and valuable document is the text published in the weekly edition of the *Granma* of July 8, 1973, of a panel discussion on television on the night of June 26. Ten of the rebel participants in the attack took part, including Haydée Santamaría, Melba Hernández, Jesús Montané, and Ernesto Tizol.

It is now obvious that a much more extensive movement (Fidel refused to give it a name) was formed for the attack than I or other historians of the Revolution had realized. It was also more carefully organized than it had seemed to be. The secrecy maintained until the end was remarkable, considering that hundreds of men were involved over a period of sixteen months.

The movement, Jesús Montané wrote in an article for the magazine *Verde Olivo,* of July 26, 1964, was divided into cells, most of them in and around Havana, especially in Artemisa, but some in Matanzas and Oriente provinces. There was a National Leadership, composed of civilian and military committees. Fidel Castro, as might be supposed, was leader of both committees. They met once a week, training diligently under strict discipline, according to Montané. "The life of the revolutionaries was one of austerity and morality," he claimed. No drinking, and Abel Santamaría, second in command, even lectured the women members, insisting that "your morality should be above all criticism."

Fidel chose the cell leaders and then met the men chosen by them. There were many who were unable to stick it out or who were dismissed as untrustworthy. Everyone who went had been passed as suitable by Castro.

Much came out in 1973 to show the extent to which Fidel was already a leader to whom the others gave unhesitating obedience and who was followed with something approaching blind worship. A good case in point was Juan Almeida, now Deputy Prime Minister and chief administrative official for Oriente Province. He said to me in Santiago in September 1972 that all he knew was that he was joining a movement led by Fidel Castro which was going to make a revolution. All that mattered to him was that Fidel had asked him to take part.

The life story of Juan Almeida borders on the fantastic. He is a mulatto, the eldest of ten children in a family so poor he had to leave school at the third grade. In 1952 he was a mason and happened to visit Havana University with a friend shortly after Batista made his coup.

"That was where I met Fidel," he told Carlos Franqui in an

interview for Franqui's book *El libro de los doce* (better known in its French translation, *Le Livre des Douze*—referring to the Sierra Maestra "Twelve"). "He began to speak about the Revolution, about what the Revolution was. He explained the procedure and how the [Batista] *coup d'état* represented a backward step. He said that they had to unite; that they were the living force and that he was counting on elements who had not been compromised by the past."

Banal words like those from Fidel could not have been enough, nor would they have been necessary with the politically aware *Ortodoxo* youths who formed the majority of his group. Juan (as with nearly all the revolutionary leaders, Cubans invariably refer to him by his first name) had his special reason. He told me about Fidel's treating him with respect and friendliness at that first meeting, putting his hand on Juan's shoulder in a characteristic gesture. No one of Fidel's class, evidently, had done this before.

Fidel won more than a friend for life. Juan not only joined at Moncada but landed from Mexico with the *Granma* and fought with fanatical bravery in the Sierra Maestra, ending as a *comandante,* or major. He was one of the little group I met on my trip to the Sierra to interview Fidel in February 1957, and he figured in my story, for he posed for a now well-known photograph and willingly gave his name when a few others prudently preferred secrecy.

In the Revolution, Almeida rose to high army posts, educating himself as he went along. He had a natural gift for music and learned how to compose songs. He has become one of the most popular songwriters in Cuba. His work as party and government administrator in Oriente Province has been outstanding.

Juan Almeida is a family man now, with a wife and four children. He has authority, distinction, dignity, charm—one of the best products, I would say, of the Cuban Revolution, without which he would have been nobody. His devotion to Fidel approaches adoration.

Juan is worth dwelling upon because he was typical of the men Fidel was choosing in 1952 and 1953 to make the attack on the Moncada Barracks. Both Robert Merle, who interviewed every survivor of the attack for his book *Moncada, premier combat de Fidel Castro* (1965), and Hugh Thomas, who painstakingly pieced together an analysis of the social origins of 154 of the 160 volunteers, conclusively demonstrate, as Almeida put it to me, that "Fidel trusted workers and peasants most, not students, plus a few office workers like Abel [Santamaría] and Jesús [Montané]."

When I asked Fidel in 1972 to tell me about it, he said that he had chosen the volunteers individually, "on basic criteria." He wanted men of the people—*los humildes,* as he called them—not middle class or intellectuals, whom he felt he could not trust as much and who would not have had the necessary revolutionary fervor. There was only a small group of students, four or five of whom opted out at the last moment at the farm in Siboney when Castro told the group what he planned to do.

Of the two women at Moncada, Haydée Santamaría went along because she was living with her brother, Abel, and was in on everything. Fidel was not clear in his mind in 1972 why Melba Hernández, the other woman to go, came along, except that she too was in with the small group and was a member of "The Movement." She was, incidentally, the fiancée of Jesús Montané, whom she later married.

A majority of the men chosen were from the *Ortodoxo* party, Fidel said, "but from the popular level of the party, not the top." Juan Almeida told me that they trained separately, in groups, and did not know one another until they met in Santiago and Siboney. When Juan got word to go to Santiago de Cuba, he thought that it was for more training and to enjoy the carnival. At two o'clock on the morning of July 26, Fidel broke the news to them with what Juan, with an amused gleam in his eye, called "a characteristic speech."

It is interesting that Castro, with his own notorious university record, did not think that his class or his own type as a youth would be serious, suitable, or dedicated enough for his revolutionary adventure at Moncada. Abel Santamaría worked in a sugar refinery. Jesús Montané was an accountant in the Cuban branch of General Motors. Fidel seems to have got in touch with them originally because they wrote and published a magazine, *El Acusador,* which attacked the government. "Montané resigned and handed Fidel all his savings," writes K. S. Karol; "others sold their homes or their small family businesses."

The most famous of the "students" was Fidel's younger brother Raúl, who had just graduated from Havana University. In February 1953 he attended the World Youth Congress in Vienna and then went on to Bucharest and Prague. It was on that trip and on the return voyage with some Communists that he had the idea of joining the Juventud Socialista (really, the Young Communists), which he did in June. On July 24 he left Havana to join his brother without notifying the organization.

"It was wrong," Raúl confessed to Robert Merle, "but I had only belonged to the Party for a month and a half and did not have a very keen [*vif*] feeling of belonging." His early Communism, therefore, was brief and informal. At this time he had little feeling of any kind for politics. He went on the Moncada adventure out of loyalty to his brother. His radical political ideas developed in succeeding years.

Raúl was twenty-two years old in 1953 but looked sixteen, with his small, slim figure and thin, triangular face that remained beardless even when the guerrillas in the Sierra Maestra became *barbudos.* His frail looks were deceptive. He was strong and wiry and stood the hardships of the Sierra better than most. In character, he proved to be tougher than his brother, with a decisive as well as quick mind and a sharp intelligence.

The plotters raised $17,000 or $18,000 to buy arms, selling their shops, donating their savings, pawning whatever they could. The smallness of the total shows that they were, indeed, *los humildes.* "With the money," Fidel said at the first trial of the prisoners on September 21, 1953, in which he acted as a lawyer as well as a defendant, "we bought forty shotguns, thirty-five 22-caliber rifles, twenty-four rifles of other calibers, sixty pistols, three Winchesters from the time of Buffalo Bill and a machine gun that had to be repaired and was almost useless. One of our now dead companions, Renato Guitart, got hold of an M-1 and we got together about 10,000 bullets of different calibers."

The attack was planned in Abel and Haydée's apartment at Twenty-fifth and O Streets in Havana, but there were many meetings in Artemisa, outside the capital on the way to Pinar del Río. The largest group—about thirty—came from there.

The men left Havana for Santiago de Cuba and Bayamo on July 24. In Santiago they scattered into hotels and rooming houses reserved for them by Renato Guitart, the one inhabitant of Santiago in the group. He had also rented a rooming house for the twenty-nine men who were assigned to attack the Carlos Manuel de Céspedes Garrison in Bayamo.

The Bayamo group had three of what the *Fidelistas* called "traitors" who deserted the cause, one of them forcing a complete change of plans. Raúl Martínez Arará, the leader, who was to defect later, had a conference with Castro on the evening of July 25. Fidel was on his way to Santiago, where he arrived at 1 A.M. of the twenty-sixth.

A farmhouse at Siboney, ten miles outside Santiago, had been rented as early as April 1953 by Ernesto Tizol from an unsuspecting owner, José Vázquez. Tizol told him that he wanted to start a chicken farm. The secrecy had been successful, for neither the army nor the police could have had any inkling of what was going to happen. Fidel was counting on a relaxed atmosphere because of the carnival and because it was a Sunday. As it happened, the officers in charge of

Moncada Barracks had increased their guards and security precisely because they feared disturbances by revelers at the carnival.

The full Santiago contingent of 129 men and two women were all gathered at Siboney Farm at 2 A.M., when the weapons were distributed and Fidel told them their objective and the plan of attack.

"You adhered voluntarily to The Movement," Robert Merle has Fidel saying to them. "And today you must take part voluntarily in the attack. If anyone is not in agreement, now is the time to withdraw."

Nine or ten opted out, including some of the few students. The men had trained to make a revolution; they knew the mission would be dangerous and were, in large majority, between twenty and thirty years old and therefore mature enough to know what they were doing.

Moncada Barracks was on the site of the old Spanish colonial Queen Mercedes Fortress. The original building was destroyed by fire in December 1937 and rebuilt the following year. The main garrison building faced on a continuation of the Avenida Moncada, with a parade ground in front. The rear, on the Central Highway (Carretera Central), faced the back of the Hospital Civil Saturnino Lora. There was a Military Hospital at the corner of Moncada and Victoriano Garzón Avenues and behind that, along the Central Highway, was the Palace of Justice, the highest building in Santiago. The street along the south side of the garrison, which cut across the Avenida Moncada at right angles, was then called Trinidad.

The barracks had a wall around it with four entrances, one on each side, each with a sentry post. The key objective was Post No. 3, where the Avenida Moncada led into the parade ground, with the main garrison building on the left. It was this post that had to be taken by surprise if the attack was to succeed.

The plan was for Fidel Castro with ninety men—the bulk of his force—to storm through Post No. 3 and seize the barracks and the rest of the installations, taking the soldiers prisoner and capturing the store of weapons. Abel Santamaría, second in command, with twenty-one men, would occupy the Civil Hospital. With them were the two unarmed girls, Haydée Santamaría and Melba Hernández, who would act as nurses, and Dr. Mario Muñoz, who would take care of any wounded. As the rear windows faced the rear of the barracks, the men could provide covering fire if necessary.

Finally, Raúl Castro with ten men would occupy the Palace of Justice and from its roof have a dominating fire position, with the basic objective of silencing a machine gun that the rebels knew was on the roof of the Officers' Club across the parade ground. As it happened, the roof of the palace did not provide a clear line of fire, so Raúl and his men descended to the top floor and fired from its windows.

There were eighteen cars of varying ages and sizes to take the rebels to the attack.

This was the plan that Fidel Castro outlined to the men early in the morning of July 26, 1953, at Siboney Farm. The official account says that they sang the national anthem and then Fidel made his little speech. Since no one took it down, any version must be approximate, but there are several texts that all agree in general. He invoked the memory of José Martí and the War of Independence and assured them of victory. But if they lost, he added, they would have set an example for other young people to follow.

The cars left Siboney Farm at 4:45 A.M. for the ten-mile drive. The vehicles of Abel Santamaría's group had no trouble reaching the Civil Hospital, which was unguarded. Abel posted his men at the rear windows which commanded the back of the barracks across the Central Highway. The two women and the doctor were welcomed by the nurses and staff.

Raúl Castro and his group disarmed the guards at the Palace of Justice and took their posts at the windows on the fourth floor. As the two groups got into place, they heard firing at Post No. 3, where the main attack was to take place.

Fidel was in the second car. The first, with Renato Guitart and seven others (including Jesús Montané and Ramiro Valdés, who are now cabinet ministers), stopped in front of the sentry post, where the men got out and Guitart shouted to the guards: "Make way! The General is coming." The soldiers fell for the ruse, were disarmed, and the men rushed in.

The rest was tragedy. By an extraordinary chance, a patrol car with two soldiers armed with machine guns came along from Trinidad Street toward Fidel's column. As he explained it at his trial in October, "The clash with the patrol (purely accidental, since the unit would not have been at that point twenty seconds earlier or twenty seconds later) alerted the camp and gave them time to mobilize."

The official account tells what happened in greater detail. The two soldiers, puzzled by the commotion at Post No. 3, stopped and looked back. While they were watching, an army sergeant whose suspicions had been aroused came along on foot. Fidel saw that the whole operation was in danger. As he drove his car toward the patrol, he crashed it into the curb. He and the other occupants jumped out.

"At that exact time," the official story continues, "the occupants of the third car, suddenly realizing that the sergeant was reaching for his gun, were forced to shoot at him. All this happened at once and in a matter of seconds."

The shooting then became general, and any hope of surprise was lost. Only the men of the vanguard had got into the fortress, where they were holding fifty unarmed soldiers prisoner.

The odds were in every way impossible. Officers rallied their men; the machine gun across the parade ground was sweeping the points where rebels showed; soldiers took firing positions. The group who had got in realized that the attack had failed and fought their way out, but Renato Guitart was killed.

Two errors contributed to the failure. The men in the cars behind Fidel's had received orders that when he stopped they were to get out and take the building on their left. This would have been the barracks if Fidel's column had got past Post No. 3, but where he stopped, it was the Military Hospital. They took it, but it meant nothing.

"In the interests of accuracy and even though it may detract from our reputation," Castro confessed in his prison manifesto. "I am going to reveal a fact that was fatal: due to a most unfortunate error, half of our forces—and the better-armed half at that—went astray at the entrance to the city and were not on hand to help us at the decisive moment . . . The reserve group, who had almost all the heavy weapons . . . turned up the wrong street and lost their way in this city, with which they were not familiar.

"I believe that we made a mistake in dividing the command unit we had so carefully trained."

As he also pointed out, ammunition was very short. "Had we had hand grenades, the army would not have been able to resist us for fifteen minutes . . .

"Weaklings may claim that we were wrong, taking into consideration, *juris et de juris*, the abject argument of our victory or failure. Our failure was the result of last minute details, so simple that the very thought of them is enough to drive one insane."

When Fidel saw that the time to withdraw had arrived, he sent Fernando Chenard to carry the order to retreat to Raúl's and Abel's groups. Chenard left on the errand but was killed before he could carry it out.

The official account continues:

> Fidel's idea was to head quickly for the small town of El Caney, near Santiago; capture the little garrison that the Rural Guards had there; and, with the arms they would seize, go into the surrounding

> mountains to begin the guerrilla struggle. A sense of solidarity with the combatants of Bayamo weighed heavily in this idea. Fidel couldn't abandon those men, whose fate he didn't know as yet. However, the comrade who was driving Fidel's car in the withdrawal didn't know the city, and on coming to the point where Vista Alegre crosses Garzón Avenue, instead of going toward El Caney, he took the highway that led to Siboney. They only became aware of this mistake when they were far from the city, which is why they went on to the Siboney Farm.

Raúl Castro's group in the Palace of Justice went on firing until they realized that the main attack had failed. Raúl, in this first test of nerve and intelligence, did the right things. He locked up their four prisoners, and disarmed and drove away an army patrol of five men that suddenly appeared as they walked out. The band then took off the uniforms that covered their civilian clothes and scattered running through the streets.

Here is the finish of Raúl's story in the Batista government's version of the statement that Raúl made in jail after being captured:

> I reached the railway terminal and walked along the tracks to El Cristo. I slept in a canefield, and the next day I continued walking along the tracks to Dos Caminos.
>
> I went into the town, where I purchased bread and drank some water. As I continued walking, I was arrested. They ordered me to halt and asked for my identification. I told them I was from Mercané, that I had come to the Carnival and had run out of money so I had to return home on foot. Since I couldn't provide identification, they took me to the San Luis Garrison. I was there from Tuesday morning to Wednesday afternoon, while they tried to find out what my real name was. Once this had been learned, they sent me to Palma and from there to the Moncada.

There was no happy ending for Abel Santamaría's group in the hospital. Only the two women and one youth were to survive. The bald, official account covers a dramatic story and a famous myth:

> In the course of the battle, some isolated patrols had gone out from the Garrison and tried to recapture the Saturnino Lora Civil Hospital, but they were beaten back. When the struggle against the fortress had died out, the group in the Hospital was still resisting, which is why, when the park was emptied, there was no way for those in the Hospital to withdraw, for the building was surrounded. Then, with the help of the nurses and patients in the Hospital, the combatants took off their uniforms and lay down in beds in the various wards, pretending to be patients.

> After a long time, seeing that no more shots were coming from the Hospital, the repressive forces decided to enter. The photographer Zenén Caravía, a member of the Regiment and a friend of Colonel Río Chaviano, informed on the revolutionaries, who were then arrested.

One old veteran of the 1898 war, I was told by the historian of the provincial government, saved a youth by saying that he was his grandson and had come to visit him.

Abel Santamaría expected to die, and met his fate.

There is a terrible story told about him and his sister, Haydée, which lives on but is legendary. Here is the account in Fidel's words, as he related it two months after the attack in the manifesto he issued from jail, for he believed it at the time:

> Two girls, two heroic comrades named Melba Hernández and Haydée Santamaría, were arrested at the Civil Hospital, where they were giving first aid to the wounded. That evening, at the Army garrison, a sergeant by the name of Eulalio González, nicknamed "The Tiger," approached Haydée. Opening his bloodstained hands, he showed her the eyes of her brother, which his torturers had just pulled out. A little while later, she was told that her sweetheart [Boris Luis Santa Coloma], who was among those taken prisoner, had been killed.

Boris, I was told, had escaped but when he heard that Haydée had been caught in the hospital, he returned to see if he could rescue her.

Melba Hernández wrote an account of their experiences for the newspaper *Granma* of June 11, 1973:

> Abel came in and told us that the firing was coming from only one of the fronts and that meant that the attack had failed. It was about 8 A.M. Abel remained as cool as could be. He called Haydée and me aside and said: "We are lost. You and I know what is going to happen to me and, possibly, to all of us. But what I am most concerned about is that you two don't take any chances. Find a place to hide in the hospital. You must stay alive, no matter what. Somebody must live to tell what happened here." We stood there speechless as he walked away. A few minutes later we saw him in the yard as he was being taken away by the guards, who were beating him with the butts of their guns.

Haydée, in the television panel discussion I mentioned, told her own moving story of what happened in the Saturnino Lora Hospital when they realized that the attack had been repulsed.

> There was a moment, because we feared for Abel's life, we told him that Fidel had said that he [Abel] should stay alive. He replied by saying that Fidel was the one who should live on and that the shooting

> and the fighting there were to give Fidel time to retreat. And the fighting continued. . . .
>
> I also remember that, at a time when I was very downcast and asked him what I had to do after that, he replied, "Don't you realize that Fidel will live, that Fidel really must not die, that Fidel will stay alive and he is now retreating into the hills?"

"Yeyé [Haydée's nickname]," she quotes Abel as saying, "remember that after all, it is more difficult to live than to die. Stay alive because you must."

Haydée told how happy Abel was that morning in Moncada—"the happiest moments of his life"—and no doubt they were. If there was such a thing as the "Spirit of Moncada," it was embodied in Abel Santamaría and his sister.

After the two young women were captured they were taken to the barracks, where they saw prisoners being tortured and murdered. The following night, Haydée learned that her fiancé, Boris, had also been tortured and killed.

What happened at Bayamo—never a clear picture before—is described briefly in the official account:

> The attack on the Carlos Manuel de Céspedes Garrison, site of the Office of the Captain Squadron 13 of the Rural Guards, began at the same time as the attack in Santiago, at 5:15 A.M. The attackers were divided into three groups. The trip from the Gran Casino Rooming House, at the entrance to the city and some two blocks from the Garrison, was made by car.
>
> When a part of the group that Antonio (Ñico) López Fernández commanded had scaled the fence at the rear and found themselves inside the Garrison's grounds, one of the men who hadn't climbed the fence as yet noticed the presence of a soldier in the stables and shot at him without having received any order to do so, thus initiating the shooting. The first shots alerted the Garrison, and a machinegun emplaced on the roof of the building frustrated the attack.
>
> With their surprise factor lost, the revolutionaries had to withdraw after a half hour of fighting. They had inflicted two losses on the enemy. For their part, the attackers had only one wounded.

In short, an ignominious outcome. From what he said later, the leader, Martínez Arará, was not happy with Fidel's plans and did not seem to have had much heart in the adventure.

The official casualty figures for Moncada, now given for the first time, change all previous accounts, including mine. It was believed that only three or four of the rebels were killed in the fighting at Moncada. "The tally at the end of the struggle," the *El Oficial* article states, "was: for the Rebels, eight dead and eight wounded, and for the Government forces, nineteen dead and twenty-two wounded."

In September 1972, on my third visit to the old Moncada Barracks, Dr. Santiago Ramón Guillaume of the Oriente Office of Historical Affairs told me that the Cuban authorities hold the text of a note from President Batista ordering the military commander of the district, General Martín Tamayo, to kill ten rebels for every soldier killed. The official account states that Batista gave the order to Tamayo at an emergency meeting in Havana and that Tamayo, "bearer of the Presidential order that was quickly dubbed '10-for-1,' " flew to Santiago that same afternoon to carry it out.

Of course, General Tamayo could not literally obey, since there were not 190 prisoners to be slaughtered. The reality was horrible enough. Sixty-seven rebels were killed, which means that fifty-nine prisoners were murdered, usually after torture. Thirty-two were spared, mainly because of the public outcry. About sixty of the attackers had escaped.

The Moncada post commander, Colonel Alberto del Río Chaviano, was asleep in his house outside the barracks grounds when the attack started, and he did not show up until the fighting was over, at which time, according to all accounts, he encouraged the brutalities and slaying. So did the second in command, Captain Andrés Pérez Chaumont, whose cruelties earned him the ironical and sinister name *Ojos Bellos* ("Beautiful Eyes"). He seems to have done much of his killing and torturing in a cell in the corner of the main building (which is now shown to visitors), but later he set up a private butchery at El Caney, on the outskirts of Santiago de Cuba. Some innocent civilians were killed in the first forty-eight hours as avenging bands of soldiers scoured streets and houses in Santiago and the surrounding towns and villages.

The news of the atrocities at the barracks spread quickly around Santiago de Cuba. During a visit my wife and I paid to Bishop Pérez Serantes in the Episcopal Palace of Santiago in November 1963, he told us how he intervened to stop the torture and slaughter of the prisoners:

> Santiago was very disturbed. A delegation of magistrates and other leading citizens came to see me and they asked me to go with them to see the commander of the garrison, Colonel del Río Chaviano. "We must do something," they said. I replied that I could not agree more,

> so we all went immediately to see Río Chaviano. He listened; was polite. I said nothing, but afterwards I realized that nothing was going to be done.
>
> So I got into my little auto and drove back to his office. This time I spoke to him, as we Catholics say, dogmatically. "You must stop this killing," I said, "and you must issue a proclamation saying that no more of the youths are to be killed. I will do the same." Río Chaviano was taken aback, but said, "All right, I'll do it." I returned immediately to this office, sat down to my typewriter and put the message down on one small sheet of paper. Just as I finished, an officer came from Río's office and asked to see what I had written. I showed it to him and he said that it was fine, and could he take it to his commander? I said to go ahead. He did so, and the next day my message was printed in all the newspapers. This committed Río Chaviano, although he did not issue a statement himself.

Up at Siboney Farm, Fidel Castro at first had a third of the attackers with him, the official story says.

> There, [it continues] the leader of the Revolution placed the alternatives before them: either to follow him to the mountains or to return to the city and try to escape there. Eighteen decided to follow him to the Gran Piedra range. For a week they reconnoitered an unknown, abrupt terrain, suffering from hunger and thirst. Fidel understood that the physical resistance of many of the comrades had been stretched to the utmost, and he decided that they should go down out of the range and try to make their way through the enemy lines in small groups. He stayed in the mountains with just two men. His plan was to reach the mouth of the Bay of Santiago and cross it in order to continue the struggle in the Sierra Maestra. At dawn on August 1, Fidel and his two companions were captured as they slept, exhausted, in a small, palm-thatched hut on the outskirts of the Mamprivá Farm. Juan Almeida and four other comrades were caught nearby. The patrol that captured them was commanded by Lieutenant Pedro Sarriá Tartabull who, with his resolute attitude, saved the lives of the prisoners, refusing to turn them over to Major Pérez Chaumont and taking them personally to the Santiago de Cuba jail.

There is no doubt that Bishop Pérez Serantes' intervention saved a number of rebel lives, but despite the often-repeated story, it did not save Fidel's. The bishop did not claim to have done so, and Fidel denied the story to me. Lieutenant Sarriá was alone responsible for saving Castro's life, and Fidel has at all times taken pains to make this clear.

The two men saved with Fidel were José Suárez and Oscar Alcalde (the latter now an ambassador).

Robert Merle spoke to the then-retired Lieutenant Sarriá when gathering material for his book. Sarriá, a Negro over six feet tall, was fifty-three years old at the time of Moncada. By extraordinary luck, he was humane, honest, and brave, and based his life on what he called his "ethic," than which nothing could have been rarer in Batista's army. It was accidental that he, instead of another lieutenant who was in bed with influenza, was sent on a patrol to the farm owned by Francisco Sotela Pina, at Siboney. Castro believes that a *chivato*, an informer, had given away that he and some rebels had taken refuge in the Gran Piedra.

Río Chaviano sent Sarriá at 2 A.M., perhaps wanting to get the rebels before Bishop Pérez Serantes, who had also been notified, could do so. While no special instructions had been given to Sarriá, a circular had been issued specifically ordering troops to kill any *revoltoso* found bearing arms—and Fidel was armed. Sarriá, therefore, disobeyed orders. Colonel del Río Chaviano was reported to have been furious, and the lieutenant was punished.

Men of destiny have to have charmed lives or astonishing luck. When I said that once of Fidel to Juan Almeida, he exclaimed, *"No! no! no suerte, testículos!"* ("Not luck, balls!"—or as we would say, guts.)

Juan Almeida was truly, at the last second, saved by the bishop, who by chance happened to be present when Almeida surrendered. "A soldier knocked me down," Almeida told me, "and was going to shoot when Pérez Serantes threw himself in front of the man with his arms outstretched and cried, *'No! no! no tiras'* ['Don't shoot!']. There were eight others in our group and all were saved."

It was impressive how the people of Santiago de Cuba took in and sheltered those who fled from the barracks, as the peasants did in the Gran Piedra mountain region.

I have already told the story of Abel Santamaría's final moments in the Moncada Barracks. The atmosphere in which the Cuban Revolution was born and the devotion, amounting almost to adoration, given to Fidel Castro as early as 1953 by his comrades can perhaps be grasped even better in the words of Abel's sister, Haydée, to Carlos Franqui for his book *Los Doce.* Her account was taped by Franqui in 1961. No one knowing her can doubt its complete sincerity and veracity. Speaking of the height of the combat with wounded and dying around her, she said:

"And in a moment like that one can risk everything to preserve what truly counts, which is the passion that led us to attack Moncada, and which has its name, its face, its strong and welcoming hands, which has its voice and which may be called Abel, Renato, Boris, Mario or another name, but which at a moment like that and for those who come after can be called: Cuba."

Later, a soldier approaches and tells her and Melba Hernández that Abel has died.

"These are the facts that remain in my memory," Haydée continued. "I do not remember anything else clearly, but from that moment on, I thought of nobody but Fidel. Of Fidel who could not die. Of Fidel who had to stay alive to make the Revolution. Of the life of Fidel which was all our lives. So long as Fidel was alive, Abel, Boris, Renato and the others were not dead. They would live in the person of Fidel who would make the Cuban Revolution and would lead the people of Cuba to their destiny.

"The rest was a haze of blood and smoke: the rest belonged to death."

Six months after Castro's triumph in 1959, a government decree ordered the transformation of Moncada Barracks into a school. The hospital was demolished. At the dedication of the "26th of July School City" on January 28, 1960, Fidel made a speech.

"We didn't capture the fortress on the 26th of July [1953] or on January 1 [1959]," he said. "Do you know when we captured the fortress? Today! We captured the fortress today because today we have turned it into a center of learning; today we have won that battle."

The Moncada prisoners were tried and sentenced between September 21 and October 5, 1953, but Fidel was taken out of the trial after two days on false testimony of "nervous illness," although he had given Melba Hernández a letter protesting that he was quite well. She smuggled it into the courtroom in her hair and gave it to the judges, but to no avail.

Fidel was kept in solitary confinement, incommunicado, in Boniato Prison until his trial on October 16 in the nurses' room of the same Saturnino Lora Hospital. A wounded rebel, Abelardo Crespo, was tried at the same time. His attorney was a young lawyer appointed by the court, Baudillo Castellanos, who in 1975 is serving Castro as ambassador to France. Fidel acted as his own lawyer.

Six journalists were allowed to attend but were told that they would not be able to publish the story, as a nationwide censorship was in force. One of them was Marta Rojas Rodríguez, who was then correspondent for *Bohemia.* In 1964 she published her account of the trial in a book called *La generación del centenario en el Moncada,* and while it contains interesting details, she loyally stuck to Castro's heavily doctored version of his defense in *History Will Absolve Me.*

Nothing has been heard from the other five journalists, which means that posterity will never know exactly what Castro said as a lawyer in his own defense. The only books he had in his cell were the works of José Martí and the Civil Code, which were lent to him by Castellanos.

Fidel talked for more than two hours, and two more hours were spent in questioning witnesses. Afterward the judges stayed in their places, discussing his case—and then passed a sentence of fifteen years' imprisonment. Raúl had been given thirteen years, and the others less. The men—there were twenty-seven—were sent to the Isle of Pines prison; the two girls were given light sentences of seven months and were out of the women's prison at Guanajay on February 20, 1954. They immediately began working for "The Movement." Fidel got in touch with them and started smuggling out passages of *History Will Absolve Me.*

What he said he would have done if the Moncada attack had succeeded was a mixture of liberal, democratic, radical, and socialistic measures, plucked by a completely inexperienced young man out of casual reading or memories of *Ortodoxo* programs. Had he been the devotee of Marx and Lenin that he later claimed to have been, he would not have proposed anything so unsystematic. It was not even a socialist program, for private ownership of the means of production was to continue. However, it was truly revolutionary in many ways, and it is surprising how many of his rash proposals were fulfilled.

As with so many pre-1959 pronouncements, a judgment depends on selection. For Castro's critics, the democratic promises led to a betrayal; for his defenders, *History Will Absolve Me* is what Robert Taber in his introduction to an English translation described as "an amazingly accurate blueprint of [Castro's] radical revolutionary program."

It was neither, and the fate of the pamphlet when it first came out was like that of an infinitely more important document, *The Communist Manifesto,* which went as unnoticed in 1848 as Fidel's *History Will Absolve Me* did in 1954. It was not until Castro had the brilliant idea of resurrecting it, first for the fifth anniversary of the Moncada attack in 1958 and then, more effectively, in March 1959, that the document took its place as the most famous of all the prerevolutionary pronouncements. Its importance lies in its effect and the myth created around it, not in its content. There was a romantic, revolutionary fervor in the words and ideas which gave the pamphlet a great spiritual and political value.

"You are well aware," Fidel says in the document, "that resistance to despots is legitimate." He cited Article 40 of the 1940 constitution (which he was later to abrogate): "It is legitimate to use adequate resistance to protect previously granted individual rights."

"The right of rebellion against tyranny, Honorable Magistrates, has been recognized from the most ancient times to the present day by men of all creeds, ideas and doctrines," Castro averred, and he cited a number of authorities from the past, starting with ancient China. It would be interesting to know where Fidel, in prison, got the quotations from John of Salisbury, St. Thomas Aquinas, Martin Luther, François Hotman, John Knox, and others, down to the U.S. Declaration of Independence, from which he also quoted.

Although he read voraciously while in jail, it is hardly likely that the prison library would have contained such books.

The eighteen months that Fidel spent in prison on the Isle of Pines were outwardly uneventful, but they proved to be an important period of gestation for the future revolution. This is clear from a series of letters he wrote to his then friend in Havana Luis Conte Agüero (published in 1959 as *Cartas del presidio*) in Havana, and especially the version of his trial speech, *History Will Absolve Me.* There were also some revealing letters which Robert Merle published at the end of his book on Moncada. Merle does not say to whom they were addressed.

"What a formidable school prison is!" Fidel says in a letter that Merle prints. "Here I have succeeded in forging my vision of the world and finding the direction my life will take. Will it be long or short? I do not know. Fruitful or sterile? But there is one thing that I feel to be taking form within myself: my passionate desire for sacrifice and struggle. I have nothing but scorn for an existence attached to the wretched bagatelles of comfort and self-interest."

"Above everything," he wrote in a letter while he was in solitary confinement, "I see our road and our goal more clearly than ever . . . I have not wasted my time in prison. I have studied, observed, analyzed, made plans, forged a following of men. I know where to find the best of Cuba and how to seek it out. When I began, I was alone; now we are many. The good men will unite and be invincible."

One of the letters to Conte Agüero—Number XI—is important as showing that even then Castro had a fixed idea about the necessity of unity. This became one of the key features of his administration. He compares his ideas to José Martí's efforts to unify all Cubans. "The pages of the history of Cuba that I most admire," Castro wrote, "are not so much the valorous deeds on the fields of battle as that gigantic, heroic and silent struggle to unify Cubans for the conflict."

For a man of Fidel's temperament, imprisonment—especially solitary—must have been torment. In one of the letters to Conte Agüero he wrote, "In many of the terrible moments that I have had to suffer during the past year, I have thought how much better it would be to be dead."

The Moncada prisoners were released on May 15, 1955. The pardon came out of a deal between General Batista, who had arranged to be elected President on November 1, 1954, and the *Auténtico* party, which had agreed to take seventeen seats in the Senate. One of their demands was that the Batista-dominated Congress pass an amnesty freeing all political prisoners.

Little attention was paid to Fidel Castro and his followers at the time they were released. Castro was not well known. It was twenty-two months since the attack on the Moncada Barracks. If General Batista had been afraid of him and his "Movement," he would not have granted the amnesty.

It was on the ferryboat *Pinero,* between the Isle of Pines and the main island, that the decision was made to call their still disorganized group the "26th of July Movement." It did not take an official and separate form until Castro, preparing for the *Granma* expedition in Mexico, wrote and published a letter dated March 19, 1956, breaking with the *Ortodoxo* party. The year before he had referred to his movement as "the revolutionary apparatus of *Chibasismo.*" The new Movement, he now said, "is the revolutionary organization of the humble, by the humble and for the humble."

After his release Castro had started writing articles attacking the Batista regime in the Havana journal *La Calle.* The newspaper was thereupon closed down and Fidel banned from talking on the radio or in public meetings. He was watched by the police, and according to Rodríguez Morejón, one of his biographers, he felt that they were looking for a chance to imprison him again, or even kill him. He had no law practice left.

It was obvious that he was not going to be able to work. Within weeks of his release, he decided to carry out an invasion from Mexico. Raúl Castro and a few followers went ahead to prepare the ground. Fidel left Havana on July 7, 1955, but not before delivering a broadside in the weekly *Bohemia.* "We will return," he wrote, "when we can bring to our people the liberty and the right to live decently without despotism and without hunger . . . Since all doors to a civic struggle are closed to the people, no other solution remains but that of '68 and '95."

He also wrote a letter to a number of prominent political leaders on July 7, 1955, which was reproduced in the collection *La Sierra y el Llano.*

"I am leaving Cuba because all doors are closed in the civic struggle," it began. He was convinced the dictatorship of Batista would last for twenty years, but, "as a follower of Martí, I think that the hour has come to take one's rights, not to ask for them; to seize them, not to beg for them.

"I will reside somewhere in the Caribbean.

"From such voyages, either one does not return, or one returns with the beheaded tyranny at one's feet."

The recipients could have been excused for considering this as rhetoric. Castro had the idea that there was a psychological advantage in calling his punches. Both on a trip to the United States and in Mexico he publicly announced *con toda responsabilidad* that "in the year 1956 we will either be free or martyrs." In that year, Batista was in his strongest phase—secure, powerful, backed by the United States, and enriching himself.

Seventeen months were to pass from the time Castro left Havana until his disastrous and fateful return to Cuba. It was a frustrating, harassed, penurious time. The two great problems were to train his expeditionary force and raise the money for arms and a boat on which to get to Cuba. These had to be done in the face of constant interference by the Mexican police, treachery among the Cubans, and spying by Batista agents. At one time Castro and twenty-two of his comrades spent three weeks in a Mexico City jail for illegally possessing arms.

Men who later became famous had joined the 26th of July Movement. The extraordinary young Protestant teacher who was handling the Cuban end of the invasion, Frank País, had not been at Moncada. At that time he and two other youths who were to become revolutionary leaders—Armando Hart and Faustino Pérez—were members of a once-popular radical organization headed by Professor García Barcena, the National Revolutionary Movement.

País (his full name was Francisco Isaac País García, but he was always known as Frank) had been gathering an impressive revolutionary following on his own in Santiago de Cuba, his hometown. He was an able and gifted leader, very intelligent and very brave. In 1955 he was only twenty-two. After Fidel's release from the Isle of Pines, he joined the 26th of July Movement. Castro recognized his value, and when he left for Mexico, País was made coordinator of the Movement for all of Cuba.

His task was to organize an uprising in Santiago de Cuba that, according to all historians of the Revolution, was to coincide with a landing by Castro and his group from Mexico. This was my understanding. However, in 1972 Fidel told me something I had never heard before and which certainly has not been printed in any of the histories.

"I wanted to make the landing before the uprising in Santiago," he said. "I argued with Frank about that in talking it over beforehand [presumably in Mexico]. I wanted to land; set up a beachhead that would draw the Batista troops away from Santiago and then while the city was clear, Frank and his men could have risen and taken it over and we would have had the army trapped. Frank, however, argued for the simultaneous landing and uprising in Santiago. We were delayed by the weather, and you know what happened."

It is generally accepted that Frank País was against trying the invasion at all that year—1956—and he is believed to have said on his two visits to Mexico that it was too soon to try. He had a streak of realism in his character which was exceptional among the revolutionaries, but it did not inhibit his loyalty to Fidel Castro, for whose Movement he and his seventeen-year-old brother, Josué, were to die.

The man who was to become the most famous of all the revolutionaries—the young Argentine doctor Ernesto Guevara—came on the scene early in the preparations.

"I met Che for the first time a few days after my arrival in Mexico in a house on the Calle El Parám where the Cubans were living," Fidel said in a speech in Santiago, Chile, on November 28, 1971. "For us he was not yet 'Che' but Ernesto Guevara. However, as Argentines have a custom of saying 'che' to everyone, the Cubans began to call him 'Che,' and little by little, everybody knew him by that name, which he later made famous and which has become a symbol." (The name was always written by Guevara with a small "c" when he just wrote "che," but he adopted the word officially as his middle name while in Cuba, and became "Ernesto Che Guevara.")

Professor Thomas gives the address of the meeting as Amparám, No. 49, in Chapultepec, which was the house of a Cuban exile, María Antonia González de Paloma. Che mentions it in his farewell letter to Fidel.

At first, wrote Che Guevara in his *Reminiscences of the Cuban Revolutionary War*, he saw little possibility of victory when he joined Fidel. "I had been linked to him from the outset by a tie of romantic adventurous sympathy, and by the conviction that it would be worth dying on a foreign beach for such a pure ideal."

Another who was to become famous, Camilo Cienfuegos, told José Guerra Alemán, a Cuban newsfilm photographer who was in the Sierra in 1958 and wrote a book about it called *Barro y cenizas,* that he was in California, working in a restaurant, when he read about Castro's threat to invade Cuba. He said that he "had always admired Fidel." So he went to Mexico, arriving as the *Granma* was about to sail. This meant that Camilo, who became one of the greatest of the guerrilla leaders, along with Fidel, Raúl, and Che, had no training in Mexico.

It was not true, Castro told me, that because of the disaster of the *Granma* landing he was forced against his desire or his preparations to go up into the Sierra Maestra. Theodore Draper and a few other historians have made this assertion. "I always had it in mind," Fidel said to me in 1972. "Why, all the men in Mexico were especially trained for guerrilla warfare and our arms were for that type of fighting. Of course, we hoped to take Santiago, make a base there and fight from there if it had been successful."

The guerrilla training in Mexico was under the direction of a Cuban-Spaniard, Colonel Alberto Bayo, then sixty-three, who had first learned the art in Spanish Morocco, fighting against the Moors when Franco was a commander there. Later he fought for the Republicans in the Spanish Civil War. He was a hard taskmaster, according to Faustino Pérez.

After my Sierra Maestra interview appeared in 1957, Colonel Bayo came to see me in New York at the *Times* and, among other things, expressed anxiety over whether the rebels were not being too reckless. He wondered if they were following what he had taught them. Few lived to use their knowledge. Fidel once told me that he himself had not trained with the others in Mexico, and he rather brushed aside the idea that he and his group owed anything much to Colonel Bayo.

Needless to say, Colonel Bayo heartily disapproved of Castro's public boasts that he would invade Cuba before the end of 1956. That was not orthodox. But, as was the case with Moncada, only a few leaders knew the exact destination of the voyage when the men were called down to Tuxpan on the Yucatan Peninsula. One of the ignorant may have been Ernesto Guevara, who at the time was a stranger as well as a foreigner.

In mid-November a large supply of arms destined for the expedition had been seized by the Mexican police in the house of Teresa

Casuso. The Cubans had been betrayed, not for the first time. The Mexican police worked with Batista, except for a brief period when Castro likewise was in a position to bribe them. "Teté" Casuso, who had worked in the Cuban Embassy in Mexico City, was the widow of the Cuban poet Pablo de la Torriente Brau, who was killed in the International Brigade in 1936 during the Spanish Civil War. She was very helpful to the *Fidelistas* in Mexico, and was in the Castro government in 1959, but she defected.

A small reserve of arms had been hidden. Fidel was ordered by the police to leave Mexico City, so the time had come to make his move.

Fidel was raising money wherever he could, and he had no scruples about any of it being tainted. Although he despised ex-President Prío Socarrás and although his revolutionary activities were aimed against everything that Prío stood for, he turned to him for the money to buy a yacht and supplies for his expedition. Prío, for his part, was willing to back anyone who would attack his enemy, General Batista. Fidel sent Teresa Casuso to Prío in Miami to get the money for him. He told me once that the amount was $40,000 and another time $50,000, but whatever it was, it sufficed to buy a piece of junk that was probably worth $10,000 and cost $15,000.

The *Granma* was a twin-engined yacht, much the worse for wear. The badly worn gears meant that speed was impossible; the radio was good only for receiving; the tanks held 1,200 gallons of fuel, which was not nearly enough. Two thousand gallons in cans had to be stored on deck. The yacht was meant to hold a maximum of fourteen men; Fidel put eighty-two aboard.

The empty boat was captured by the Batista forces after it had been abandoned by the *Fidelistas.* Until 1974 it was kept moored on the edge of the Parque Almendares in Havana, which is on the river of that name. The now spic-and-span little yacht resembled one of the pleasure boats on the river. It is incredible, looking at it or clambering awkwardly around it, to think that eighty-two men with their arms and supplies somehow got aboard and survived four days of storm and heavy seas. There is hardly any deck space—a narrow deck along the sides no more than two feet wide, a little more space in the stern, but supplies and arms had to be put there. There is an open deck in the prow about twelve feet long, narrowing to the boat's point. Inside is a small lounge with the engine below it and, up forward, four tiny cabins. The top of the yacht is curved and could not hold anyone in heavy seas. The pilot's cabin is just big enough for the wheel and the simple instrument panel. In February 1974 the yacht was moved permanently into the Museum of the Revolution.

The *Granma* left Tuxpan on the night of November 24, 1956. The weather was so stormy that the Mexican Marine had suspended permission to sail in that region of the Gulf.

It was a truly terrible, sickening journey, on which everything possible went wrong, including the weather, which remained stormy for days. Everyone was seasick; the food was ruined; the bilge pumps failed and the yacht took water, which had to be wearily heaved over the sides in buckets. When calm returned, the men were weak from fatigue and hunger. The storm had blown them off course, making it impossible to keep the rendezvous with Crescencio Pérez, a peasant sent to meet them with arms and supplies, or to make the November 30 timing, on which day Frank País would turn Santiago de Cuba into a city of bombing, shooting, and rioting. País fulfilled his task, controlling the city for a while, but Fidel and the eighty-two men could only hear about it, heartsick, on the *Granma*'s radio.

It would never have occurred to Fidel to turn back to fight another day. The pilot, ex-Naval Lieutenant Robert Roque, who had performed prodigies steering the unwieldy yacht, fell overboard in the darkness when they were close to shore. Fidel ordered a spotlight to be turned on to find Roque, who was saved. This light may have warned the Batista watchers along the coast. It was dawn of December 2, 1956, with no one knowing exactly where they were. They decided to head straight for the land. Soon afterward the *Granma* ran aground in shallow waters about a hundred yards offshore.

The men had to wade ashore in loam and water up to their necks. They could not have hit on a more difficult spot—a soft, slippery bottom, an undergrowth of mangrove roots that formed a dense snarl. "Before our anxious eyes," wrote Faustino Pérez in an article for the book *La Sierra y el Llano,* "we could see only more mud, more water, more mangroves." Rifles, ammunition, food, and almost everything else they carried had to be dropped. It took four hours to get through to dry land, and then they had to keep going to get away from the telltale *Granma.* They were at Playa de los Colorados, ten miles north of Cabo Cruz, the southwestern tip of Oriente Province.

Fidel Castro—all the survivors are agreed—did not lose heart. On the contrary, he started thinking about getting into the Sierra Maestra, whose foothills came down almost to the sea. It should have been the blackest moment of his life.

CHAPTER 4

Sierra Maestra—1957

> We see, therefore, how, from the commencement, the absolute, the mathematical, as it is called, nowhere finds any sure basis in the calculations in the art of war; and that from the outset there is a play of possibilities, probabilities, good and bad luck, which spreads about with all the coarse and fine threads of its web, and makes war, of all branches of human activity, the most like a gambling game.
>
> —Von Clausewitz

Arguments about the relative importance of the *Sierra* and the *Llano*, the mountains and the plain, the guerrillas and the civic resistance, occupy many pages of many histories of the Cuban Revolution. In truth, they needed each other, but this is Fidel Castro's revolution, and he was in the Sierra Maestra. The *Llano* had no leader of its own; the *Resistencia Cívica* was, to a great extent, the work of Castro's 26th of July Movement. The history of the Revolution in 1957–1958 is essentially the story of what happened in the Sierra Maestra, but always remembering the vital role that thousands of brave men and women were playing in every city and town of Cuba.

Fidel's choice of Oriente Province for his revolutionary strike had its roots in Cuban history, but it is also true that all twentieth-century revolutions—in Mexico, Russia, China, Vietnam, Algeria, Cuba—have begun in a peripheral location. It is as if there must be a striking force that comes from the outside.

The discontent and opposition against the Batista regime in 1956 was strong and island-wide, but it was still unorganized and without leadership. There had been an uprising in April of army officers against the regime that had proved a fiasco. Major José R. Fernández, Minister of Education in the present government, then a captain in the regular army, helped organize the uprising. The leader was Colonel Ramón Barquín, Cuba's military attaché in the Washington Embassy. According to Fernández, a number of fellow officers, all lieutenants, captains, and majors, who were revolted by the corruption and brutality of the Batista government, planned the uprising and decided that they needed a leader of higher rank who was well known. Fernández and another officer went to see Barquín and talked him into joining the plot. They were betrayed by one of the officers and the leaders were all put in jail, where Barquín and Fernández were when General Batista fled.

During 1956 there had been many incidents of violence met by much fiercer counterviolence. The vicious circle of terror and counterterror was not a result of the Castro insurrection; it existed before the *Fidelistas* landed. The tensions and bitterness created an atmosphere that made Cuba ripe for revolution.

One evidence was the ease with which Frank País and his 26th of July followers virtually took over Santiago de Cuba on November 30, 1956, the day they thought the rebels on the *Granma* were landing.

Here is the way the exiled General Batista described what happened in his book *Respuesta:*

"On November 30, a seditious outbreak again bloodied the city streets [in Santiago de Cuba]. The teachers' school, the high school, and other buildings near the Moncada Barracks were seized by student groups and Communist elements. They fired from rooftops and destroyed the police headquarters after assassinating the guards. Again civilians and military died in the three days before order was restored."

There were no "Communist elements," and the guards were not "assassinated"; they were killed in a hard fight in which some of the attackers were also killed and wounded. Batista's picture is generally correct; the city was in a turmoil and panic through December 2—but the *Granma* was still out at sea.

Among those helping Frank País were Haydée Santamaría of Moncada fame, the young lawyer Armando Hart (who was to marry Haydée), and Vilma Espín, daughter of the lawyer for the Bacardi rum firm in Santiago. She had been at school in the United States. Returning through Mexico City, she met the Castro group and joined them. Like the others, she played her role in the Sierra, and like Haydée, found a husband—Raúl Castro.

The young person who was to become the most famous and important of the revolutionary women—Celia Sánchez—was out on the coast on November 30, waiting with Crescencio Pérez in vain for the expected landing. They had trucks and supplies for the invaders.

Celia was the daughter of a dentist on the big sugar property of Julio Lobo at Pilón, near Manzanillo in Oriente. She knew the Sierra Maestra from her childhood, when as a Girl Scout she had hiked and climbed in the foothills.

Professor Hugh Thomas, who never met her, characterizes her ungallantly in a footnote referring to events of mid-1957 in the Sierra: "She was an eccentric woman in her thirties, and Lobo had built her on the estate a dovecote where she could 'sleep, write or dream.' She later became Castro's secretary and his most faithful aide."

Actually, at that time she was just twenty-nine, having been born in 1927. I met her in Santiago de Cuba in July 1957. She had slipped through the army lines on one of her trips to the city to buy supplies and talk to the resistance leaders of the 26th of July Movement. I imagine she had also gone for a meeting with Judge Manuel Urrutia, the future President, who was in hiding at a friend's house where I met both of them for the first time. Celia was out of her slovenly khaki uniform of the Sierra. I met a slim, elegant, soft-spoken, big-eyed young woman who had thrived on the mountain hardships and whose revolutionary fervor was singularly impressive.

Lee Lockwood, who got to know her in 1965 when he was gathering material for his book *Castro's Cuba, Cuba's Fidel,* and when she really was in her thirties, describes her in these words: "Black-haired, olive-skinned, petite and sinewy, gracious, soft-spoken and often smiling, she is that combination of sweetness and toughness typical of women from the north of Spain, where her family originated."

No doubt, Celia can be classified as an eccentric; no ordinary or normal woman could have done what she did. In the Sierra she developed the habit of eating only when hungry and sleeping only when tired, regardless of the time. She still follows that practice in Havana, where she is a cabinet minister and Secretary to the Presidency and the Council of Ministers. Courage, brains, idealism, dedication to the Revolution, and a consuming loyalty to Fidel Castro, to whom she is *alter ego,* confidante, housekeeper, and government minister with great responsibilities—this is Celia Sánchez who, in 1957, was a guerrilla fighter with the best of them.

She had belonged to The Movement before it became the 26th of July after Moncada in 1954. Fidel had said that no women were to go on the *Granma* expedition; otherwise she would have gone to

Mexico. Frank País, appreciating her ability and her knowledge of Oriente Province, needed her in Santiago de Cuba. As soon as she learned where Castro and his small band were, she went up to the Sierra to join them. At first she acted as a courier. After the 26th of July Movement's meeting in the mountains in February 1957 (while I was there), Celia, as Che Guevara wrote, "was definitely incorporated into the guerrilla force, never to leave us any more."

An episode of the November 30 uprising in Santiago de Cuba was to have an American angle. Julio Camacho Aguilera (later a *comandante* and chief administrator of Pinar del Río Province) led a group in a foray at the eastern end of the Sierra Maestra facing the U.S. Naval Base at Guantánamo. It was unsuccessful but, he told me in 1972, he stayed there with a nucleus of six men, establishing a liaison with sympathizers at the naval base. Three American boys started smuggling arms out to him after they read my interview in *The New York Times*, and they finally came over to join Castro up in the mountains. They were with a group headed by Jorge Sotús, who had fought in Santiago on November 30. Two of the lads—Victor Buchman and Michael Garney—found the life too hard and left quickly, but the third, Charles Ryan, stayed and saw some action. It was good publicity for the rebels in the American press.

It is time to return to the exhausted, mud-covered, disorganized, and almost disarmed band who had staggered ashore at the Playa de los Colorados on December 2, 1956.

They moved inland. Some of the men got lost, then rejoined the main body. Peasants were neither hostile nor helpful. The invaders had no food and on reaching the cane fields of one of Julio Lobo's plantations, they cut off pieces of the cane to suck for nourishment, making themselves even more thirsty.

Francis McCarthy, head of the United Press International bureau in Havana, reported Fidel Castro's death, even giving details. The army chiefs believed the same stories, and so did President Batista.

On December 5 the rebels reached a place called Alegría de Pío, which was seven or eight miles from where the *Granma* landed and about fifteen miles south of Niquero, their original destination.

"There we were surprised by the troops and the planes of the tyranny," writes Faustino Pérez in the article I have mentioned, "and in that terrible and unequal battle in the midst of the burning cane it was impossible to avoid dispersion and disaster . . . The fate of the small and scattered groups who tried to get away from that unlucky spot was varied. Some were ambushed in the gulleys lined with soldiers; many were captured and immediately killed; other more fortunate ones landed in prison."

"It had been our guide—as we found later—who had betrayed us," Che Guevara wrote in his *Reminiscences.* "We had let him go the night before—an error we were to repeat several times during our long struggle until we learned that civilians whose personal records were unknown to us were not to be trusted while in dangerous areas. It was a serious blunder to release that man."

(It was typical of Che's literary bent that when he was seriously wounded at Alegría de Pío, expecting to die and wondering "what would be the best way," he remembered a story of Jack London's "in which the hero, knowing that he is condemned to freeze to death in the icy reaches of Alaska, leans against a tree and decides to end his life with dignity.")

Juan Almeida seems to have been the man of the hour, brave, cool and, by chance, unwounded. He rallied a group, including Che and Ramiro Valdés, and led them into the shelter of the forest.

"Such was our baptism of fire on December 5, 1956, in the district of Niquero," Guevara concludes. "Such was the beginning of what would become the Rebel Army."

Fidel Castro found himself at first with only two men—Faustino Pérez (like Frank País, a Baptist) and Universo Sánchez, one of the few peasants who was on the *Granma.* Both men attested to Castro's complete confidence which grew by leaps and bounds as straggling groups were brought together to join him.

Fidel was at first guided toward the Sierra Maestra by another peasant, Guillermo García. The "guardian angel" of the group, Guillermo's uncle, Crescencio Pérez, could not have been less in character, though he may not have been as sensational as Professor Thomas describes him: "Cresencio [as is often the case in Cuba, the spelling of names is uncertain] Pérez was a curious figure to find later established as one of the founding fathers of the successful revolution, since he was a bandit more than a radical, a common criminal believed to have committed murder and reputedly father of eighty illegitimate children up and down the Sierra Maestra."

Crescencio, who was then a respectable truck driver on the Lobo plantation, brought wandering groups together in the farmhouse of his brother, Mongo Pérez. Raúl Castro, Juan Almeida, Che Guevara, and their comrades gathered in Mongo's house. Thomas lists fifteen. I believe that the figure was twenty-three. In any case, one has to wonder at another imperishable legend of the Cuban

Revolution: that Fidel Castro finally found himself with twelve out of his original eighty-two men.

It is not known how many were killed at Alegría de Pío or executed later. Twenty-two survived as prisoners. A few escaped.

No doubt, there was a time when Castro and his group numbered only twelve. The figure is useful. Carlos Franqui, in his book *Los Doce,* avoids naming the twelve, but perpetuates the legend. Aside from the obvious relation to the twelve Apostles, there was a story of the first War of Independence which, true or not, provides a striking coincidence.

The day after the *Grito de Yara* (the call to rebellion in 1868), Carlos Manuel de Céspedes, with fewer than forty men, among them some of his slaves, attacked the village of Yara and was repulsed with heavy losses by the Spanish garrison. He turned back, rode for some hours, and then, in a clearing in the woods, counted the men he had left. There were only twelve. Céspedes, the story goes, then said: "It does not matter. Twelve men with me are enough to free Cuba."

"Fidel embraced us," Efigenio Ameijeiras told Franqui in describing the reunion in Mongo Pérez's house on December 17. "He was very happy. He told us that we must not despair, that this was only the beginning, that this first defeat would serve as a lesson for us, that we had to get used to the life of a guerrilla and keep constantly on guard. He also said some of those words he usually says when the occasion presents itself."

"Fidel gave us a fine speech," Universo Sánchez, the peasant who had come over on the *Granma,* added. "He said: 'We have already won the war.' "

Raúl Castro told me in 1967 how, as they were struggling up the foothills with Batista soldiers searching for them, Fidel whispered in his ear: "Now, when we get clear and organize ourselves we can start our campaign."

It was the roughest, wildest part of Cuba, mostly untracked tree- and bush-covered jungle, with the highest mountains in Cuba, including the highest of them all, toward which they climbed—Pico Turquino, about 8,600 feet. The region had the heaviest rainfall in Cuba. There were few peasants, mainly *precaristas* (squatters) and charcoal burners. What fertile land there was generally grew coffee. The peasants were very poor and different from the better-off farmers and sugar workers of the rest of Cuba. At least half were illiterate, and few had more than several years' schooling. There were, in fact, no schools in the Sierra Maestra proper. It was a traditionally lawless and violent zone. The peasants, with bitter reasons to hate the Rural Guard, were suspicious of armed outsiders at first, but were won over. The mountain range is roughly a hundred miles from east to west and no more than twenty-five or thirty miles at its widest. Fidel and his comrades reached the heights near Pico Turquino about Christmas.

President Batista's "Christmas present," in the black humor of the Cubans, was the slaughter of twenty-two men in Oriente Province by Colonel Fermín Cowley in reprisal for some bombings by the 26th of July Movement. He hung several bodies of youths on the trees along the highway outside Holguín at Christmas time. At New Year's there was more terror and counterterror. It went on into January, leading to nationwide censorship on January 16.

These events led me, in New York, to write an editorial for *The Times* of January 31, 1957, headed: "What Is Wrong with Cuba?" It described the tension and expressed puzzlement at "the extent and intensity of the anti-Batista feeling." Yet, at the time I knew virtually nothing about Fidel Castro. In fact, he was supposed to be dead. *Time* magazine, on December 17, 1956, writing of the invasion attempt, could rightly say: "By and large, the Cuban people ignored the whole affair." As I had a few weeks' holiday coming to me, and we liked Cuba as well as being interested, my wife and I decided to go to Havana.

The rebels had already—on January 17—won a small battle.

"Our first victory," Che Guevara wrote in his *Reminiscences*, "was the result of an attack upon a small army garrison at the mouth of La Plata River. The effect of our victory was electrifying. It was like a clarion call, proving that the Rebel Army really existed and was ready to fight. For us, it was the reaffirmation of our chances for total victory. . . .

"This was the first victorious battle of the Rebel armies. It was only in this battle and the one following [Arroyo del Infierno, January 22, 1957] that we had more weapons than men. Peasants were not yet ready to join in the struggle, and communication with the city bases was practically nonexistent."

Two government soldiers were killed at La Plata and five at Arroyo del Infierno without any Rebel losses. Some much-needed arms were captured. Prisoners were taken, the wounded among them being tended and the others released unharmed. This set a precedent which the *Fidelistas* followed for the next two years, in contrast to the way the *Batistianos* treated the Rebels when captured. Aside from being humane, the Rebels' practice paid off in goodwill and propaganda. Che called it "one of the factors in our victory."

"We slip through their hands like soap just when they think they have us trapped," Che wrote his wife, Hilda, on January 28. "Naturally the fight isn't all won, there will be many more battles. But so far, it is going our way, and each time it will do so more."

This was the way Fidel Castro spoke to me three weeks later, and it was what I repeated. But in truth, these were perilous times. The hardships were great; the men were untrained and undisciplined, and some were unfit, physically or morally, to meet the extraordinary demands of their hunted, desperate, dangerous lives.

Writing of the end of January 1957, Che said: "The situation was not a happy one. Our column lacked cohesion. It had neither any ideological awareness nor the *esprit de corps* that could only be attained through hard, bitter struggle. Day after day more comrades would ask to be released and to be assigned to missions in the cities —although this involved even greater dangers—but it was evident that they simply could not stand the rough going."

According to Robert Taber, in his book *M–26,* Batista had committed three thousand men to the liquidation of the guerrillas early in 1957. At Arroyo del Infierno, the rebels had faced the officer who was to be their most able and persistent enemy—Lieutenant (later Colonel) Angel Sánchez Mosquera. The weakness of the guerrilla force lulled President Batista into a false sense of security.

"Except for a few brushes in the first days, for two months there were no signs of any rebels in the surrounding mountain areas," Batista wrote in *Respuesta.* "The General Staff was informed that the group headed by Castro had been dissolved. This information brought an invitation to [Havana] newspapers to send reporters to the zone where Lieutenant Colonel Pedro Barrera Pérez and his troops were stationed. Special planes were put at the disposal of the reporters who, with Army officers, made a broad reconnaissance of the Sierra Maestra. No trace of the rebels was found, and not one shot was fired. This report induced the General Staff, with Presidential approval, to withdraw the troops."

This was a foolish experiment. I saw when I flew over the Sierra Maestra with Juan Almeida in 1972 that one cannot see anyone or anything in the jungle terrain. The government troops did not withdraw from the region; they stayed along the foot of the ranges while Rural Guards kept up their patrols and searches in the Sierra itself.

Batista, as Fidel told Lee Lockwood in 1965, "had his best and only opportunity right at the beginning, when we were very few and inexperienced. Those were our most difficult moments. By the time we had gained a knowledge of the terrain and had increased our force to a little more than a hundred men, there was already no way of destroying us with a professional army."

February and March 1957 were the most dangerous months. The utmost was being asked of the guerrillas. Stout hearts, strong bodies, faith and loyalty were needed to a high degree. These are not easily found qualities. Early in February, Fidel announced that the "crimes" of insubordination, desertion, and defeatism were to be punished by death. "The execution of anti-social individuals who exploited their position of strength in the district in order to commit crimes," wrote Guevara, "was, unfortunately, not infrequent in the Sierra Maestra."

For a long time there was a problem with "bands of marauders" masking as revolutionaries, robbing the peasants under the pretext of revolutionary activities. Some of the "bandits," it seems, were captured and executed by Che Guevara's column. Camilo Cienfuegos was then his captain. Che's account of the outlaws in his book gives a good idea of how tough he could be.

And there were traitors. The most notorious was a peasant, Eutimio Guerra, who, it was learned later, "had been promised a large sum of money and a military rank as a reward for murdering Fidel." His extraordinary journey into Cuban infamy ended the day I made my trip into the Sierra Maestra for the first interview with Fidel Castro, on February 17, 1957.

"One night," Che Guevara wrote in *Reminiscences,* "only a short time before we discovered he was a traitor, Eutimio complained that he had no blanket and asked Fidel to lend him one. It was a cold February night, up in the hills. Fidel replied that if he gave Eutimio his blanket they would both be cold; that it was better to share the blanket, topped by two of Fidel's coats. That night, Eutimio Guerra, armed with a 45-caliber pistol that [Army Major] Casillas had given him to use against Fidel, and two hand grenades that were to be used to cover his getaway once the crime was committed, slept side by side with our leader . . . Throughout the night, a great part of the Revolution depended on the thoughts of courage, fear, scruples, ambition, power, and money, running through the mind of a traitor. Fortunately for us, the sum total of inhibitory factors emerged triumphant, and the night passed without any incident."

As Che wrote, the morale was low by the end of January. They had been machine-gunned from the air, the planes having been directed, they learned later, by Eutimio Guerra.

"In these circumstances," writes Hugh Thomas in the chapter of his book entitled *Herbert Matthews Goes to the Sierra,* "Castro took the critically dangerous but actually fundamental decision, late in January, to send René Rodríguez to Havana to tell his followers in the capital that he would be willing to see a foreign press correspondent, for with the Cuban press under censorship there would be no point in seeing a Cuban."

Faustino Pérez was then in Havana, coordinating the work of the 26th of July Movement. One of the members, Javier Pazos, son of the economist Felipe, spoke to his father about Fidel's idea. Felipe Pazos knew Mrs. Ruby Phillips, *The New York Times* correspondent in Havana, and she, knowing that I was due in Cuba very shortly on vacation, said that she would ask me. Naturally, I jumped at the chance. From early February until Sunday the 24th, when *The Times* published my story, my wife (who accompanied me to Oriente Province to give a air of innocence to our journey) and I lived in a conspiratorial world. Considering how elaborate the arrangements had to be, and how many men and women were involved in the risky business, it was remarkable that secrecy could have been maintained from beginning to end.

My trip coincided with the first Sierra Maestra gathering of the countrywide 26th of July Movement leaders. After an all-night drive to Manzanillo with Faustino Pérez, Javier Pazos, and a Havana society girl, Liliam Mesa, I joined the men and women who had come to Manzanillo from Havana and other places. It seems that Frank País was among them, but I recall only a vague glimpse of some young people standing toward the rear of the garage to whom I was perfunctorily introduced. Celia Sánchez, Haydée Santamaría, and Vilma Espín, all of whom had come from Santiago de Cuba, went up into the Sierra that night and may have been in the garage. The group gathered at a farm near the mountain hamlet of La Montería.

I, meanwhile, with Javier Pazos got through the Batista lines (the whole district was ringed and patrolled) partly by luck, partly by some circuitous driving in a jeep through the narrow roads of the rice paddies. If stopped by the troops, I was to be an American investor interested in the purchase of some rice land. In fact, the boys had pressed some four hundred pesos on me to take to Fidel in my car on the theory that if the money were found on me, it would not seem suspicious. I could see no reason to refuse.

We had a rendezvous at a certain spot in the foothills with a peasant from Fidel's group who was disconcertingly elusive for some hours. According to José Guerra Alemán, the Cuban news photographer whom I have mentioned, he was a *guajiro* from San Antonio de las Vueltas named Rodolfo Peñate.

Peñate, Guerra Alemán wrote in *Barro y cenizas,* had been in the Sierra for fourteen years and "knew its mysteries and bypaths better than anybody . . . Peñate is a fine peasant type and very clever.

He was considered the best courier of the Sierra. He was the one who conducted Matthews over the lower hills of the range for his historic interview with Castro. And he accomplished other missions that demanded caution and safety." (Peñate is now an officer in the Cuban Armed Forces.)

While training under Bayo in Mexico, Ray Brennan writes in his book *Cuba, Castro and Justice,* the men "learned a code system of commands given by soft whistles and bird chirpings by which a commander could lead a group through the jungle without speaking a word."

This low, penetrating whistle and returning whistle accompanied my climb up the mountain in the darkness to what Che Guevara later described as "a thicket of the woods near a stream in a plantation owned by Epifanio Díaz, whose sons had joined the Revolution . . . For the first time we were to be interviewed by a reporter, and a foreign reporter at that. This man was Matthews . . . I was not present at the interview. Fidel told me later that Matthews had asked concrete questions. He had asked no 'loaded' [*capciosa,* "tricky"] questions and seemed to sympathize with the Revolution." (Camilo Cienfuegos, I was told later, was in the group with Che.)

I suppose I acted sympathetically because I was fascinated and impressed, and as my editorials had shown, I was critical of the Batista regime. Fidel had kept me waiting from midnight to dawn, when he joined me with Raúl, Juan Almeida, and some others.

We spoke in whispers at all times, and for good reason. "The area was crawling [*infestado*] with Rural Guards," wrote Che Guevara, who "fired into the wooded localities often, although they actually never entered them."

For purposes of this survey, I believe it will be more useful if I cite what some others have written.

"The significance of the interview," Professor Hugh Thomas wrote in his book *Cuba,* "was considerable. First, Matthews created for North Americans the legend of Castro, the hero of the mountains, 'of extraordinary eloquence, a powerful six-footer, olive-skinned, full-faced, with a shapely beard . . .' For the next three years Fidel Castro was, much to his surprise and even for a time his anger, a North American hero."

(I do not believe the last sentence. Fidel, to my knowledge, was always pleased by hero worship and always made a distinction between Americans and the United States government.)

"Second," Thomas correctly points out, "the interview exaggerated the number under Castro's leadership."

(Fidel would not tell me how many men he had, but said: "We [work] in groups of ten to forty." And in other ways I was given an inflated picture of the number of guerrillas, which I naturally could not check at the time. There were, in fact, only eighteen armed rebels in the group I met, but Fidel was also using some peasants who were not on the spot. There was likewise a small group of guerrillas with Camacho Aguilera on the Guantánamo side. There were, too, all the members of the 26th of July Movement, who, I knew, were somewhere near.

(This inflation of the number of *barbudos* under Fidel's command went on throughout the insurrection. Nearly all the American journalists who went up received an exaggerated idea of the number of guerrillas. There never was any means of checking. Castro naturally wanted to give the impression that his force was greater than it really was.

(I do not believe that I was wrong in adding to my account that in Oriente Province, "thousands of men and women are heart and soul with Fidel Castro and the new deal for which they think he stands." It was a time of great hostility to Batista and to his army and police officers, nowhere more so than in Oriente Province.)

"Matthews's article on his visit to the Sierra was published on 24 February and immediately made of Castro an international figure," Thomas continues.

> Since the censorship was by chance lifted in Cuba the very next day, the news that Castro was alive became known quickly in Cuba also. The imprecise overestimate of the size of Castro's forces helped to attract urban Cubans to his cause. It was supposed that Castro was winning, that Batista's reports could not any more be relied on, and that his side was therefore the right side to be on; Castro's morale was raised. The morale in Batista's Army was further depressed, and afterwards, when the Minister of Defense, Santiago Rey, denied both that Matthews could have penetrated the Army's ring round the Sierra and that Castro was alive, the Government was made ridiculous, since Matthews next published a photograph that he had had taken of himself with Castro.

"Castro deceived Matthews about the size of his forces but not much about his political aims," Thomas goes on to say. However, he asserts that in accepting as Castro's the word "socialism" in a 26th of July underground tabloid, I was being misled, as the article was not written by Fidel and the phrase "social justice" had been changed to "socialism." However, as I stated in my book *The Cuban Story,* Fidel also used the word "socialist" in speaking to me in the Sierra Maestra. It is true, as Thomas writes, "that Matthews himself saw Castro as a social democrat; but it is not of course certain that that was how Castro saw himself." In reality, Fidel had no fixed or precise political ideas of any kind while he was in the Sierra.

General Batista gave his unhappy account of the interview in a passage of his book *Respuesta* headed in italics *"Contradictory Reports and the Matthews Interview":*

> A representative of the United Press, Francis L. McCarthy, reported that Castro was dead and buried. There was no official confirmation of this report, and it was secretly suspected that the rebel leader had taken refuge in the highest mountainous region of the Sierra Maestra.
>
> General Martín Díaz Tamayo, who was still chief of the military territory, and Colonel Barrera Pérez, Chief of Operations, helped to reinforce the belief of the General Staff that the group which had landed on December 2 had given up the struggle.
>
> In this climate of doubt, Herbert L. Matthews, reporter for *The New York Times,* published an interview with Fidel Castro. To prove his statements he produced an unclear photograph of Castro. The military chiefs of the province told the General Staff so emphatically that no such interview had taken place, that the Ministry of Defense publicly denied it had occurred. And even I, influenced by the reports of the General Staff, doubted it. The interview had, in fact, taken place and its publication was of considerable propaganda value to the rebels. Castro was to begin his era as a legendary figure, and end as a monster of terror.

Che Guevara told an interviewer in Havana on January 27, 1959, that "at that time [early 1957], the presence of a foreign journalist, American for preference, was more important for us than a military victory."

It was true enough of that time, but if the argument is extended to the belief, which Hugh Thomas and some early historians expressed, that victory was due mainly to the "skillful use of the foreign press," I do not share it. Nothing but death in the Sierra Maestra could have stopped Fidel Castro. The insurrection would have lasted longer, but Castro had the qualities that would, at that period of Cuban history, have led sooner or later to victory. He also had four outstanding commanders in Che Guevara, Raúl Castro, Camilo Cienfuegos, and Juan Almeida, and there was the urban resistance.

It is a waste of time to say, as so many do, that if I had not written my interview; if Batista had been stronger, wiser, and honest; if the army and the police had not been divided and corrupt and had not acted so brutally; if the middle-class civil resistance had sensed that Castro, as they saw it, would "betray" his promises; if the United States had not imposed an arms embargo; and so many other "ifs," a victory for the guerrillas would have been impossible. Men and things in Cuba were what they were; that is why there was a Castro revolution. Nothing is more futile than quarreling with history.

Of all the nearly impossible things that Fidel Castro and his band had to do in those early months, nothing was more difficult than to survive. Che Guevara was suffering severely from the asthma which was such a terrible burden to him all his life. (The chapter in *Reminiscences* after my visit is entitled "Bitter Days.") A few men joined, and others left. "The physical conditions of the struggle were very hard," Che wrote, "but the spiritual conditions [*condiciones morales*] were even more so, and we lived with the feeling of being continually under siege."

So they were. Batista had sent in a more efficient and intelligent commander, Major Barrera Pérez, who seems to have been better in the field than he was as a staff officer. Rebel reinforcements from Santiago de Cuba, sent by Frank País, could not get through at first. Food was short. Finally, on March 15, the new men—fifty of them—arrived.

Two days before, there had been a sensational attack on the Presidential Palace in Havana whose aim was to kill the General and thus precipitate a revolution.

Batista never understood the strength of the hostile forces that were at work in his country. He knew enough in 1933 and again in 1952 to seize power, realizing that he could get away with it, but he was never rooted in the true traditions of the Cuban people. The two books he wrote after being driven into exile by Castro (*Respuesta*, translated into English as *Cuba Betrayed*, and *Piedras y leyes*) are evidence that he had not understood what was happening or what had happened.

I had long talks with Batista in the Presidential Palace in 1957 and 1958, being received always with courtesy, despite the harm I had done him with the Castro interview and other pieces. He knew that I wrote the critical editorials in *The Times* about Cuba. It was a period when public opinion was clearly against him, but I think that he was sincere in believing the contrary. Or perhaps he thought that support from the establishment and organized labor represented the only popular backing worth considering.

I am sure that he never appreciated the extent to which the peculation, graft, and corruption of his regime—he being one of the worst culprits—had turned a great body of politically conscious middle-class Cubans against him. Faustino Pérez, who became the Castro minister charged with "recuperating stolen properties," claimed to have found about $6.5 million in cash and more than $1 million in shares in Batista's accounts and safe-deposit boxes in Havana. He also owned much Cuban property. It was universally believed that most of his wealth was in Florida real estate and in U.S. and Swiss banks.

On my return to Havana from the Sierra Maestra trip, I had a secret meeting with five university students of the *Directorio Estudiantil*. I did not know it, but the preparations for the attack they were going to lead against the Presidential Palace were almost completed. I had been led to their hideout in the Vedado district by another member of the already flourishing underground. I wrote about them in the third of the three articles on my Cuban trip for *The Times*, this one (February 26, 1957) being based on the threat to "the old corrupt order in Cuba."

"In this struggle," I said, "one other element of prime importance must be added—the Cuban university students with their long traditions of conflict against Spanish oppressors and Cuban dictators."

"The Directorate of the Federation of University Students (FEU) has been on the run from the police for many weeks, thus far successfully. The authorities accuse them of complicity with Fidel Castro, with whom they signed a pact in Mexico City, but they say they are fighting for the same goals."

I told how I managed to see the five students, "including their leader, José Antonio Echevarría, whom the police want most of all and who therefore has considerable fame in Cuba at the moment . . . One boy said: 'My father fought against Machado, my grandfather fought in the War of Independence. I must now fight for the same ideals and the same reasons.' "

"So one sees three elements lining up against President Batista today—the youth of Cuba led by the fighting rebel, Fidel Castro, who are against the President to a man; a civic resistance formed of respected political, business and professional groups; and an honest, patriotic component of the Army, which is ashamed of the actions of the Government's Generals. Together these elements form the hope of Cuba and the threat to General Fulgencio Batista."

The five youths seemed touching to me, who, at fifty-seven, was then an old man to them. They meant business, and in a few weeks three of them were to die. One of the survivors was the badly wounded Fauré Chomón, who lived not only to write the story but to lead a guerrilla band in the Sierra de Escambray and become an ambassador and cabinet minister of the Castro government.

My forebodings received startling confirmation on March 13, 1957, when nearly eighty young men stormed the Presidential Palace. The plan, Fauré Chomón wrote later, was to seize the Palace and kill the President, which, they believed, would result in "the complete decapitation of the regime." To bring in the people, José Antonio Echevarría was to seize Radio Reloj, the main broadcasting station, and call upon the *Habaneros* to concentrate at Havana University, where a headquarters would be installed.

Batista, in *Respuesta,* claims to have known about the plot. There does seem to have been treachery a few days in advance. The General had fortified the top floor of the Palace, which could be reached only by an elevator. It was this which foiled the attackers. However, he did not know on what day or hour the attack was coming, and he was caught partly by surprise.

"The problem," wrote Fauré, who was to lead a group up the palace stairs, "was to corral the dictator." They could not know in what room he would be at the time of the attack. But "the decision was not to back down in any way." Of the drive to the palace he says: "I can affirm that those moments we felt that it was the happiest day of our lives."

They arrived at 3:30 P.M., March 13, 1957. Fauré was wounded entering the Palace. The attack failed because Batista had gone up to the third floor, which could not be reached by the stairs and which was well defended by soldiers. As at Moncada, two other waves of attackers never reached the Palace. They claimed that it had been immediately surrounded by soldiers and police. Fauré Chomón bitterly accused them of cowardice.

Only three of the men who stormed up the palace stairs came out alive. Thirty-five of the attackers and five guards were killed. José Antonio's group succeeded in seizing the radio station and broadcasting an excited message that Batista had been killed. They then blew up the control panel and ran out into the street, where the police came upon Echevarría and shot him dead.

Indirectly, there were many more casualties, for Batista's police and army arrested and killed, in a number of cases after torture, perhaps as many as sixty or seventy suspected students and members of the political opposition. The best-known victim was the lawyer and former *Ortodoxo* senator Pelayo Cuervo, who was found murdered the next morning.

Fidel Castro was not consulted and did not approve. He called it "a useless expenditure of blood," and said that if he had wanted Batista killed it could have been arranged more easily than that. The death of the President at that time would have been premature for Castro, who was fighting desperately to survive in the Sierra. Besides, Echevarría could have become a rival hero and revolutionary leader. Fidel was always worried in the Sierra—and with reason—that the overthrow of Batista would be followed by a military junta.

The issue of *Bohemia* for May 28, 1957, in which Fidel expressed his criticisms, would be embarrassing if resurrected, because starting in 1959, José Antonio and the other victims became martyrs of the Revolution. March 13 is commemorated every year as a glorious landmark of Castro's revolution.

Fauré Chomón exaggerated the effects of the palace attack and its contribution to the success of the Rebels. Batista gloried in an extraordinary wave of sympathy from the whole business and landowning community, the CTC (Cuban Workers Confederation), the American colony, and United States interests. It was the highest point of favor that Batista reached in his career, and there was no one to whisper "Beware of Nemesis!"

Not that I didn't try. I saw him at the palace soon after the attack and argued that there was nationwide opposition to him. He proudly took out of his desk and showed me the photographs of a huge popular demonstration in his favor. The industrial trade unionists did support him, but the appearances were deceptive.

The student *Directorio Revolucionario* was smashed for the time being, but this cleared a way for the 26th of July Movement. A year later Fauré Chomón, who had recovered from his wounds, established his guerrilla nucleus in the Sierra de Trinidad. Terrorism and counterterrorism grew worse.

General Batista had some effective killers. I have mentioned Colonel del Río Chaviano's behavior at Moncada and Colonel Fermín Cowley's 1956 "Christmas present" to Holguín of twenty-two murders with some of the bodies hung on trees to be seen on Christmas morning.

The most notorious civilian killer was the ex-Communist Rolando Masferrer, who had been at Cayo Confites when the young Fidel Castro was also present. "It would be an understatement to say that Masferrer was to Oriente what Capone had been to Chicago," Robert Taber wrote without much hyperbole. Masferrer had a private army of three hundred ruffians, killers, and racketeers. They fattened on the prevailing income sources of gambling, prostitution, and extortion. In addition, Masferrer owned landed property and newspapers. The Cuban revolutionaries blame him for many of the political murders that occured during the seven years of Batista's dictatorship.

(He and Río Chaviano got away to Florida when Batista fled. Cowley was assassinated by the Resistance on November 23, 1957.)

The underground steadily grew stronger. Hugh Thomas accepts this description of it: "The Civic Resistance was supposed to be an independent non-political secret organization composed of middle and upper class people regardless of party; in fact, it was from the start a front organization for the 26th of July Movement in the cities, and a means of getting supplies and money." The first leader in Havana was Raúl Chibás, brother of Eddy, who was soon succeeded by Faustino Pérez.

Cuban law provided no death penalty, which is why one cannot use the word "executions" for the government killings. In the eyes of the resistance, every youth tortured and slain became a martyr, a black mark against the regime, a source of popular bitterness. Neither the resistance nor the guerrillas in the Sierra Maestra used torture. In the first place, there is no evidence that they did, and in the second, it was a deliberate policy on the part of Castro to sustain a popular image of ruthless but straightforward rebellion.

Ex-President Batista gave this version of the terrorism in *Respuesta:*

> As the crimes and cruelties of the terrorists grew, so did the necessary repressive measures. New excesses would take place, followed by another wave of slogan propaganda. Public sensibility would be offended, and corrective action would be the responsibility of the Batista Government (always in his name) and not that of the provocateurs, the bosses who acted as an insatiable Moloch, or the agents who exercised their orders. In this way the unscrupulous groups headed by Fidel Castro, who ordered assassinations and massacres, succeeded in being represented as fighters for the liberty which they themselves assaulted and mutilated. They made it appear that the tyrants were those who opposed the destruction of Cuba by terror and the attainment by the Communists of psychological advantages and strong positions at the door of the giant [the United States] who, democratically, remained confident or asleep.

For Professor Thomas, "Batista was less himself a torturer than a weak man surrounded by cruel ones whom he could not control." This could only have been written by someone who did not know Fulgencio Batista and who was not personally in touch with what was happening in 1956, 1957, and 1958. Batista's career from the *Machadato* on was hardly that of a "weak" man. Besides, by what moral or legal reasoning can one separate the actual torturers from the man who consigns the victims to the torture? I can vouch for the fact that high-level Cuban revolutionaries never considered Batista a weak man.

The universally used figure for killings by the army and the police—twenty thousand—was undoubtedly a gross exaggeration, but there is no doubt that the true figure was very high.

There was relative quiet in the Sierra Maestra from February 9 to the end of May 1957. It was a period used for training recruits, organizing, making contacts with, and winning over the peasant *precaristas* (squatters). The Rebels could now all be called by the name that became famous—*barbudos,* the bearded ones. According to Manuel Fajardo, one of the peasants who joined Fidel after the *Granma* landing, the growing of beards began almost immediately.

"I never shaved," Fajardo told Carlos Franqui for his book *The Twelve.* "Crespo and I were the first. I stopped shaving on December 6 [1956] and from the beginning of May 1957, I stopped cutting my hair. Fidel began to wear a beard about the same time that we did. He was among the first, but he never ceased to have his hair cut."

In mid-March, Castro received the fifty recruits I have mentioned who were sent by Frank País from Santiago. "They came in trucks owned by a rice planter from the area," Che Guevara wrote unkindly in his *Reminiscences,* "who later became so frightened about being implicated in the affair that he took refuge in an embassy, then departed for Costa Rica, and returned to Cuba as a hero, aboard a plane carrying some arms. His name was Hubert Matos."

What Che did not say was that Matos then stayed on and fought well enough to be promoted to *comandante* (major) and to be put in charge of Camagüey Province in 1959.

The cement, the quality that counted above all others, was loyalty. Disloyalty was and still is the unforgivable sin, no matter what services were performed in earlier times. To Castro and all his associates, Major Hubert Matos could never have been loyal; he would always have been a selfish, potentially treacherous opportunist.

On April 23 the Columbia Broadcasting System's correspondent,

Robert Taber, and a photographer, Wendell Hoffman, with their television equipment, arrived for what Guevara called a "famous interview." It was shown throughout the United States in mid-May as "The Story of Cuba's Jungle Fighters," and was invaluable propaganda. Starting in the middle of the year, a steady stream of American correspondents found their way to Castro's headquarters.

In the November 8, 1967, issue of the monthly *Tricontinental,* Efigenio Ameijeiras, referring to May 1957, quotes Fidel as saying: " 'Che, we have to make our presence felt immediately, hit the enemy hard, so hard that they can't keep on telling the people of Cuba that we don't exist in the Sierra, especially now when the tyranny is denying the fact that we had an interview with Matthews.'

" 'I agree with you, Fidel,' said Che, 'but we have to make sure of a successful attack, capturing arms from the enemy and producing many casualties so that it will be hard for them to hide the truth.'

"Thus the idea of attacking El Uvero was born."

Che called El Uvero (May 28, 1957) the battle that was "to have greater psychological impact than any other in the history of the war."

"We had eighty men and the enemy fifty-three," he wrote in his account of the fight, "with thirty-eight—over one-fourth—out of action in less than two and a half hours fighting . . . From that moment on, our morale increased enormously, our determination and hope for victory also increased, and although the months that followed were a hard test, we now had the key to the secret of how to beat the enemy. This battle sealed the fate of every garrison located far from larger concentrations of troops, and every small army post was soon dismantled."

A Rebel standing next to Fidel was killed in the first moments. Juan Almeida, then a captain, had the most important task—to liquidate a post in the center. In a last, desperate rush he took the post, being wounded in the shoulder and left leg. This opened the way to the barracks, as Guillermo García had also taken the post assigned to his group.

The *barbudos* lost six killed, two badly wounded, and seven less seriously hurt. The enemy casualties were fourteen dead, nineteen wounded, fourteen prisoners. Only six of the garrison of fifty-three soldiers escaped.

Che Guevara, with typical modesty, says little of his own crucial and courageous role in the battle. He saw that one of the flanks had no cover. Although still theoretically only the doctor of the force, he asked for a few men, one of them with a machine gun, and attacked with the bravery that helped to make him a legend.

"If, as a guerrilla, he had his Achilles' heel," Castro was to say in his funeral oration years later, "it was this excessively aggressive quality, his absolute contempt for danger . . . He took too many risks and exposed his life in rash actions . . . But that was his temperament: stubborn, combative."

Because of the wounded on both sides who had to be tended, his own severe asthma, and the need for the main column to fight its long way back, Guevara remained behind with a small group of Rebels. When they rejoined the main force, Che was made a *comandante,* the first to achieve that rank after Fidel Castro.

By mid-June 1957, Guevara could write: "It was a pleasure to look at our troop. Close to 200 men, well disciplined, with increased morale, and armed with good weapons, some of them new. The qualitative change . . . was now quite evident in the Sierra. There was a true free territory; safety measures were not so necessary, and there was a little freedom to carry on conversations at night while resting in our hammocks."

However, on July 26 Frank País wrote a letter to Fidel in which he said: "The situation in Santiago is getting more and more tense; the other day we escaped miraculously from an encirclement by the police." The police kept searching, for by then they knew that he was the Movement's leader in Santiago de Cuba. On July 30 the chief of police, Colonel José Salas Cañizares, and one of his men caught Frank and gunned him down. He was twenty-three. As I mentioned, his younger brother, Josué, had been killed similarly during a demonstration in June.

There was an extraordinary manifestation of sorrow in the city. The whole 26th of July Movement went openly to his bier, and hundreds of *Santiagüeros* attended the funeral.

The other big event of 1957, aside from the attack on the Presidential Palace, was an uprising by army and navy officers on September 4 which should have embraced Havana and other cities but inexcusably was left to the conspirators in Cienfuegos on the south coast to fight alone. It had been called off at the last moment by Havana, but Cienfuegos was not notified.

An interesting feature was that the American Embassy had been informed in advance, Ambassador Earl E. T. Smith testified to the Senate Internal Security Subcommittee in 1961. He said that the conspirators had been told by a CIA officer that if successful, any government set up would be recognized by the United States. Ironically, the revolt was crushed with American-supplied bombs, tanks, and guns, which were being used in contravention of the agreement that U.S. arms were for hemispheric defense only. This contributed to the American decision to impose an arms embargo the following April.

The reprisals were monstrous in extent and cruelty. The atrocities—murder, torture, mutilation—were denounced at the World Medical Association meeting in Istanbul, Turkey, in October 1957 by the past president of the Cuban Medical Association, Dr. Augusto Fernández Conde. Taber reports that the January issue of *Medical News* printed a report written by Dr. Louis H. Bauer, secretary general of the World Medical Association, "citing evidence in hand that Government troops in Cienfuegos had buried 200 wounded alive."

This seems too horrifying to believe, but there were persistent reports of prisoners being buried alive. There were no protests in the American press or by the U.S. government for the truly ferocious reprisals. In fact, a few weeks after the uprising USAF Major General Truman Landon made a special flight to Havana to present the medal of the Legion of Merit to Colonel Carlos Tabernilla, who had directed the indiscriminate aerial bombing of Cienfuegos.

Fidel and his followers gradually won the peasantry of the Sierra Maestra over to their side. Che Guevara, in his *Reminiscences,* gives eloquent testimony to the suspiciousness on the part of the peasants that in the early stage of the insurrection led to informing and treachery, but he also tells in a moving passage how the guerrillas in their turn were made to realize the need to help the peasants. Writing of April 1957, he said:

> People in the Sierra grow like wild flowers, unattended. Then they fade away, constantly busy at a thankless task. It was due to our daily contacts with those people and their problems that we became firmly convinced of the need for a definite change in the life of our people. The idea of an agrarian reform became crystal-clear, and communion with the people ceased to be a mere theory and became an integral part of ourselves.
>
> Guerrillas and peasants began to merge into a solid mass. No one can say exactly when, in this long process, the ideas became reality and we became a part of the peasantry. As far as I am concerned, the contact with my patients in the Sierra turned a spontaneous and somewhat lyrical decision into a more serene force, one of an entirely different value. Those poor, suffering, loyal inhabitants of the Sierra cannot even imagine what a great contribution they made to the forging of our revolutionary ideology.

These peasants were not at all like the sugar "proletariat" and the tobacco growers of the rest of Cuba. They were peasants in a more classical sense. Like millions of peasants throughout the underdeveloped world, they had reasons for rebellion, even if they could not express them or conceive of any revolutionary possibility. This was true of the Cuban rural laborers generally, especially on the sugar plantations, but not in the unionized sugar mills (the *centrales*) or among the port workers.

The Rebels were a revelation to the Sierra peasants, paying in cash for what they got; healing the sick when they could; treating the peasants as equals; and operating under Fidel's stern discipline of death for murder, rape, or informing.

Castro was instinctively doing what Mao Tse-tung in his book *On Guerrilla Warfare* and Lin Piao in his famous article "The People's War" had counseled. "Do not steal from the people; be courteous; be honest in transactions; returning what one borrows," Mao advised. One of Lin Piao's points was: "Do not ill-treat captives."

Fidel had not read these works; he was simply being sensible, pragmatic, and humane. He had never been in the Sierra Maestra before, but Guillermo García, one of the first peasants to join him and who became an army commander after 1959, said to Lee Lockwood: "In six months Fidel knew the Sierra better than any *guajiro* who was born there. He never forgot a place to which he had gone."

"We went through very difficult moments," Castro confessed at a press conference in Chile on December 3, 1971. "On several occasions we were on the verge of being exterminated, precisely because of our lack of experience. We gave the enemy a number of opportunities . . . Every struggle entails risks and the possibility of defeat. We, too, went through such risks—and it was quite possible that we might have been defeated."

The fame of the Rebels, adventurism, and romanticism brought many volunteers who then found that they could not bear the hardships and dangers. "Hundreds would join us," Fidel said in a speech on July 12, 1971. "There were times when dozens came every day, and we submitted them to stiff tests. And I remember that, in the more difficult periods, eighty out of every hundred would give up and leave—but the twenty who remained would be really good." Che Guevara had a lapidary phrase for the dangers: "Death is a frequent accident."

What Che in his *Reminiscences* called the battle of El Hombrito at the end of August 1957—really a skirmish—"proved that it was easy, under certain circumstances, to attack enemy columns on the march. We continued this practice until it became an established system, so efficient that the soldiers stopped coming to the Sierra Maestra and even refused to be part of an advance guard."

By July 1957, as Che wrote, Castro had about two hundred armed and trained fighters in what Radio Rebelde later proudly proclaimed as *El Territorio Libre de Cuba* (The Free Territory of Cuba). By early 1958, Fidel's forces pretty well controlled the entire Sierra Maestra, a range as large as the Adirondacks of New York State.

Toward the end of 1957, Castro set up a permanent headquarters at La Plata, on the southern slope of the Sierra Maestra, two days march from Pico Turquino. He was being urged by his followers and the Directorio Nacional of the 26th of July Movement to take fewer personal risks and to delegate more authority. He really had no choice, as he was now directing a complicated guerrilla war and had assumed political leadership of the whole resistance. The wearing effect of his harassing tactics with guerrilla bands, which ranged from one side of Oriente Province to the other and along a hundred miles of coast, has been underestimated by historians of the Revolution. Army commanders who ventured into the Sierra rarely got out with their forces intact.

The peasants all over the range knew where the guerrillas were, especially when Castro set up the La Plata headquarters, where there were soon a hospital, school, kitchens, workshops, a newspaper, and a radio station. He began decreeing "laws."

Batista's problem was no longer one of finding the *barbudos* but of liquidating them. The continuing and considerable efforts that had been made to defeat Castro throughout 1957 proved that the government considered him an important enemy. The Civic Resistance, strong though it was, could have been contained by counterterrorism. The *Fidelistas* were like a cancer on the body politic; either they had to be excised or the disease would spread and prove mortal.

CHAPTER 5

Sierra Maestra—1958

It is the unexpected that happens, as many historians have had occasion to observe and many politicians to discover.

—Algernon Cecil
(A House in Bryanston Square)

The stream of manifestos, platforms, programs, radio talks, and interviews coming out of the Sierra Maestra from Fidel Castro provided more confusion than enlightenment, more soothing talk than serious intentions. There was such a preponderant degree of naïveté, amateurishness, contradictions, and pie in the sky involved that listeners and readers had themselves to blame if they relied upon a liberal-democratic–reformist interpretation of Fidel's "promises." That, or they cynically counted on manipulating the young man.

Washington was to make highly effective propaganda of the "betrayal of the Revolution" by Fidel Castro, and so were hostile historians like Theodore Draper and Philip Bonsal. In truth, no one could make a coherent program out of the Sierra pronouncements. Analyzing the documentation makes a futile and frustrating exercise in scholarship. One can concede that Fidel promised to make a revolution with popular elections and democratic freedoms. At the same time, he promised a genuine radical social revolution.

In reality, of course, he did not know how he was going to make his revolution any more than had Lenin, Mussolini, or Madero in Mexico. Castro was no Hitler, and *History Will Absolve Me* was no *Mein Kampf,* although the Isle of Pines prison document gave a better idea of what was going to happen than much of what was said and written in the Sierra Maestra.

I do not believe that Castro realized any more than the rest of us did that in promising liberal-democratic reforms *and* a radical social revolution he was promising the impossible. His choice was either/or, and there was never any question which way he would go once power was in his hands, because his goal was as fixed as the North Star.

Meanwhile, up in the Sierra Maestra, he was promising all things to all men and seeking support from all sides. He was having great difficulty in uniting the Batista opposition on terms that satisfied his plans and ambitions. The first attempt, made on July 12, 1957, was a manifesto drawn up with the help of Raúl Chibás and Felipe Pazos. It was neither revolutionary nor unrevolutionary; it was liberal, constitutional, and a little radical. But the hoped-for "civic revolutionary front" did not materialize.

On November 1, 1957, by far the largest meeting of exiles and oppositionists was held in Miami, including Felipe Pazos and Lester Rodríguez (who had been at Moncada) for the 26th of July Movement. The seven anti-Batista groups agreed on a "Unity Pact" with a moderate, democratic program. However, Castro had not been notified or consulted.

The text reached him in the Sierra on November 20, a day of three dangerous skirmishes with the army. On December 14 he sent back a long, angry letter, calling the Miami pact "an outrage" and unauthorized. It had been understood at Miami that Felipe Pazos would be Provisional President. Fidel brought forward the name of Manuel Urrutia, the judge who had argued at the trial in May that the eighty-one rebels from the *Granma* landing and the November 30 uprising in Santiago de Cuba had acted constitutionally. Fidel had never met him, but in his own trial defense, published as *History Will Absolve Me*, he had made the same argument—that the Constitution of 1940 justified rebellion against tyranny. As the 26th of July representatives discovered when Urrutia got to Miami as a refugee, their choice was a singularly naïve man. One presumes that Fidel learned as much himself when, in November 1958, Urrutia went up to the Sierra Maestra, but by then it was too late to change.

The differences in the "Mountain" and the "Plain" had come out in the conflict over the Miami pact.

"Our discussions and our internal conflicts were quite sharp," Che Guevara wrote in 1963. He also argued that the opposition groups were a mixture, and that all of them were "infiltrated by Batista agents." While complaining of gangsterism and opportunism, he conceded that the urban underground contained "many brave and honest men, sacrificing their lives to maintain the comfortable existence of such personages as Prío Socarrás."

The Communist PSP, Che continued, "did not understand with sufficient clarity the role of the guerrilla force, nor Fidel's personal role in our revolutionary struggle . . . Later, some of their men, of guerrilla spirit, were to join us, but by then the end of the armed struggle was near."

Fidel once said to me: "You know that I would not take any Communists with me on the *Granma.*" In fact, while there may have been an odd Communist or two in the Sierra Maestra, one can say that for more than a year the guerrilla warfare went on without them. The PSP was critical and even contemptuous of Castro and the *barbudos,* and they sabotaged the attempted general strike in April 9, 1958.

Individual Communists began contacting Fidel in February 1958, but, as Che wrote, the party waited until "the end of the armed struggle was near." Negotiations of a sort began in June or July, perhaps because the 26th of July Movement sought the labor union support that was lacking on April 9 when an abortive general strike was tried. Before that, the Movement would have no dealings with the Communists. Carlos Rafael Rodríguez, Communist party leader who most clearly and quickly realized that the guerrillas were winning, visited Raúl Castro in the Sierra de Cristal and Fidel in the Sierra Maestra in August 1958, but without having been directly invited.

An agreement was finally reached in a meeting of all the oppositionist groups except the Communists, who again were not invited, at Caracas, Venezuela, on July 19–20, 1958. The Frente Cívico Revolucionario Democrático was formed with Dr. José Miró Cardona, president of the Bar Association, as coordinator. Urrutia was named "President of Cuba in Arms," and Castro was acknowledged as the commander in chief of the revolutionary forces. There were the usual constitutional and democratic pledges.

It all looked and sounded good, but there was no substance to it, no true unity of action, and the "Front" never got off the ground. The declaration satisfied Castro, who issued a broad invitation for all concerned to meet in the Sierra. According to Andrés Suárez, in *Cuba, Castroism and Communism,* it was in response to this that Carlos Rafael Rodríguez went up, finding "understanding" in the Sierra de Cristal, where Raúl was commanding, but "suspicion" in the Sierra Maestra, presumably from Fidel Castro.

The Communist PSP in Havana, however, withheld definite approval of unity with the *Fidelistas* and still had not given it by January 1, 1959. The party did not formally offer its support until January 6. Fortunately for the PSP, Rodríguez had gone back to the Sierra Maestra and stayed there until the end.

Castro apparently had taken the position that he was to maintain throughout the Revolution—that the old Cuban Communists were to be a part of the revolutionary administration but never to be allowed to get control of it. When Cuba went Marxist-Leninist, the PSP was pushed into the background.

Batista, for his part, had no desire to suppress the Communists of the Partido Socialista Popular, with whom he got along well, but he had to prove his anti-Communism to Washington, and by labeling the guerrillas as Communists, it followed that he had to be tough with the Communists in Havana.

A curious feature of the situation in 1958 was that the Roman Catholic Church leaders and priests all over the island were showing sympathy toward the *Fidelistas* and opposition to Batista. The Church hierarchy at one time came out for the General's resignation. Both Fidel and Raúl had priests up in the mountains with them, and there was also a Protestant chaplain with Fidel's force for months.

"As for the dissemination of our ideas," Che wrote later, "we started a small newspaper, *El Cubano Libre*, in memory of the heroes of the jungle [1895–1898]." It was printed on a mimeograph machine and apparently was almost unreadable. It was later edited by Carlos Franqui, then beginning his role of unofficial editor in chief of the Revolution, a role that was to end in 1968 in defection and exile.

Che also got the idea of installing a rebel broadcasting station in the Sierra Maestra. It was set up in the safe location of Fidel's military headquarters at La Plata. On February 24, 1958, preceded by the tune of the "Invaders' Hymn," Radio Rebelde officially went on the air. It was soon powerful enough to broadcast overseas, as well as around the island. The content of the programs was mainly about the war. When other fronts were opened up, each had its own local radio receivers and transmitters. Radio Rebelde proved highly effective in circumventing Batista's press censorship. Fidel first polished his oratorical gifts from the "Territory of Free Cuba in the Sierra Maestra."

There had been a lull in the fighting—what Che Guevara called "a period of consolidation"—for a few months at the turn of the year 1957. "We were in a state of armed truce with Batista," as Che put it; "his men did not go up into the Sierra and ours rarely went down."

Early in 1958, Fidel, as always desperately short of arms, sent Pedro Miret to San José, Costa Rica, to appeal for help from President José M. Figueres. The President, one of the outstanding liberal democrats of Latin America, unhesitatingly complied, sending Fidel a planeload of arms at what was a critical time.

The pilot was a Cuban air force officer, José Luis Díaz Lanz, who was to defect in June 1959 over the Communist issue and make a sensational appearance before the U.S. Senate Internal Security Subcommittee. The shipment was in charge of Hubert Matos, about whom Che Guevara wrote. He was to figure in the most sensational of the revolutionary trials. The arms these two brought permitted Fidel to form another column, under Matos, which carried out some successful raids in the plains.

There was never a shortage of men but always a shortage of weapons. The great sums—reportedly more than a million dollars—raised by the Civic Resistance were rarely used to buy arms for the guerrillas. This was a puzzling failure on the part of the Havana underground. The Castro group suspected that because those giving money were mostly of the upper middle class, they did not want to see a real revolution. They were anti-Batista because they wanted to see reforms and were horrified by the counterterrorism. Some, like ex-President Prío Socarrás, had political reasons for wanting to overthrow the regime. Prío earned Castro's undying enmity by controlling caches of arms in the plains and not sending them up to the Sierra.

Skirmishes were numerous, and there was one near-battle at Pino de Agua on February 16, 1958, where, Che asserted, they killed at least eighteen soldiers and captured many arms.

"Fidel was euphoric over the battle," Guevara wrote. "At the same time, he was worried about the fate of our comrades and at various times he took greater risks than he should have. Because of this, days later a group of officers and I sent him a letter asking him in the name of the Revolution not to risk his life needlessly. This rather infantile letter, which was inspired by the most altruistic motives, did not, I believe, warrant even a reading on his part, and needless to say, he did not pay the least attention to it."

Castro's first and, as it turned out, highly successful move to break out of his isolation in the Sierra Maestra came on March 10 when he sent his brother Raúl with a column of about fifty men toward the Sierra de Cristal on the north coast of Oriente Province. Raúl's mission was to disrupt transportation of all kinds and establish a base of operations. His group was called "Column 6" in order to give the idea that there were at least five other columns around—which there weren't.

Raúl, in the diary he kept in order to keep Fidel informed (printed in *La Sierra y el Llano*), told of "the emotional impact that the plain produced, without the protection of the Sierra Maestra with its thick woods, for which reason I decided to drive hard to get away from that difficult predicament, always keeping in mind the tragedy of Alegría de Pío."

They were lucky to encounter no enemies as they cut across roads and railway lines in their jeeps, passing through villages and sugar plantations. The jeeps were abandoned, and the guerrillas walked until exhausted and lame.

"Twenty hours after having left San Lorenzo in the Sierra Maestra," Raúl wrote to his brother on April 20, "ten hours in jeeps and another ten on forced march, and we had succeeded in crossing the province, arriving at Piloto El Medio north of San Luis and opening the Second Front in the northern zone of Oriente. Some of us had not slept for nearly sixty hours."

There were scattered groups of rebels, some of them Communist, already in the Sierra de Cristal, who joined him. With characteristic toughness, Raúl asserted his leadership by executing several marauding bandits.

Raúl, who was then twenty-seven, was for years one of the most underrated figures of the Revolution. He lacked the magnetism of his brother and could not make an impressive appearance in public. Unlike Fidel, he has never been approachable to journalists or strangers. The impression he gave was unattractive, but only to those who did not know him. With friends, he is warm, gay, and animated, with a much keener sense of humor than his brother.

His love affair—and later marriage—with Vilma Espín ("Débora" in her guerrilla days with Raúl in the Sierra de Cristal) was one of the romances of the Revolution.

Within weeks of establishing the Second Front, Raúl had created a truly remarkable organization. After a few unsuccessful skirmishes against outposts, he started showing considerable aptitude for aggressive and clever guerrilla fighting, ridding the region of enemy posts and capturing arms. He had maps made; organized a telephone network, an intelligence corps, public works for transport, an arms factory to make guns and bombs; and established a school, a provisional hospital, and even a *Cuerpo Juridico* through which he imposed a rudimentary code of law and collected taxes. Army columns were ambushed or allowed to waste time going in and out as the Rebels would withdraw into the wooded hills and then return. Raúl had more than a thousand *escopeteras* (musketeers), as he calls them in his diary, mostly recruited from bands roving the area. In addition, he formed five companies of July 26th *barbudos,* scattered over the northern and eastern areas of Oriente Province, directing them from his headquarters on Monte Rus, within a few hours' reach of the town of Guantánamo. Nearly all the column commanders under Raúl became high officers in the Castro government's army and still later, members of the Central Committee of the Communist Party.

Raúl Castro was a tough, strict disciplinarian, with fewer qualms about ordering executions than his brother. He showed his daring when he kidnapped a dozen American and two Canadian engineers from the nearby nickel mines and a busload of U.S. Marines from the Guantánamo Naval Base. He also showed his common sense in seeing that they were treated in a friendly, if firm, way. The escapades provided excellent publicity for the Rebels.

The guerrilla warfare in the Sierra de Cristal deserves, and someday will have, a book of its own, like the many works on the Sierra Maestra, where the main operations of the war took place. However, Fidel, to his great regret, for the moment looked to the Plain.

A manifesto of the 26th of July Movement was read over Radio Rebelde on March 12, 1958, announcing that there would soon be a "revolutionary general strike." The long declaration unfortunately gave the impression that the whole issue of war and resistance hinged upon its success and that the guerrillas were now waging "total war."

No one had harsher words for it than Che Guevara in *Reminiscences:*

> April 9th arrived and our efforts came to naught; the National Committee of the Movement, having blundered utterly concerning the rudiments of mass struggle, had attempted to start the strike by surprise, with no advance notice—with shooting. As could be expected, the workers refused to participate and a certain number of exemplary comrades all over the country died in vain. April 9th was a painful failure which did not for a moment succeed in threatening the regime's stability. Far from it; after this tragic date the Government was able to withdraw its forces [from Havana] and send them little by little to Oriente, to sow destruction as far as the Sierra.

Castro's feelings and ideas about the general strike are anybody's guess. Publicly, he certainly gave the appearance of favoring it and counting heavily upon it. Ray Brennan, correspondent of the Chicago *Sun-Times,* who was in Havana at the time, claims that Fidel was "supremely confident and believed that 80 per cent of the workers would join." The French writer Régis Debray quotes, in his book

Revolution in the Revolution, a letter that Fidel wrote to a certain Nasin on March 23, 1958, two weeks before the attempted strike: "If Batista succeeds in crushing the strike, nothing will have been resolved. We could continue fighting, and in six months his [Batista's] situation will be worse." According to Debray, Fidel went along with the strike in a skeptical mood. "The city is a cemetery of revolutionaries and resources," he said.

The fiasco was tragic for the resistance, as Che wrote, because a hundred or more of them were killed. It was a setback to morale, an encouragement to the government, and a loss of prestige for Fidel Castro. It taught him a valuable lesson.

Guerrilla warfare resembles a boxing match in which there is no knockout for round after round, but one of the fighters is winning on points and a time comes when the K.O. can be delivered. In this case we can use the analogy because we know how the fight ended. In the spring of 1958, it looked like a draw so far as the Sierra Maestra rebels and the government were concerned. The same could be said of the Civic Resistance and the government. Batista could not defeat the guerrillas or crush the civilian underground, but neither could they overthrow his government.

However, the failure of the general strike gave the President hope of liquidating the *barbudos.* He gathered a force that should have been more than ample for the purpose. Fidel Castro drew his own obvious conclusions. The strike fiasco, the earlier failures of the attack on the Presidential Palace and the Cienfuegos uprising, the indecisiveness of the underground struggle—all strengthened his conviction that the battle had to be won in the field, not in Havana.

Batista had not had any combat training, as a soldier, sergeant, colonel, or general. He could decree an offensive, but others had to command in the field. He gathered between 10,000 and 12,000 well-armed troops, supported by American Sherman tanks, armored cars, and mountain artillery, all backed by his navy and air force. The ground troops, to be sure, were poorly trained and physically unfit for mountain fighting. The Rural Guards, who were also thrown into the battle, were tough, hardened veterans, but they were so hated by the peasants that they operated in actively hostile terrain. The government's strategic plan was simple: isolate the Rebel force in the Sierra Maestra, close in, and destroy it. Raúl Castro's front in the Sierra de Cristal could be ignored.

Fidel had plenty of time to prepare. His intelligence was always good, and he knew, day by day, what was being done. To begin, his strategy could only be defensive.

Castro's force in the Sierra Maestra at the time, he said later, was three hundred men under arms. Another four hundred or so were being trained elsewhere, but were without arms. Fidel had pulled in six out of his eight "columns." He, as over-all commander, directed Column One; the others were headed by his veteran *comandantes* —Che Guevara, Juan Almeida, Camilo Cienfuegos, Ramiro Valdés, and Crescencio Pérez. Each column was small in number; the harassing patrols often totaled no more than five or six *barbudos.*

It was no wonder that Batista simply could not see the guerrillas as a *military* threat to his regime. He was calculating, as the United States was to do on a vastly greater scale in Vietnam, that an overwhelming superiority in arms was enough to ensure victory.

The Rebels had some clear advantages: their interior lines in familiar, rugged territory; first-rate intelligence; the fighting spirit of the *barbudos;* and the outstanding leadership of Castro. Fidel at first directed from Pico Turquino; then he went down to command in the field.

They built trenches and tank traps and blew up bridges, while the 26th of July Movement carried out diversionary street bombing and sabotage in Santiago de Cuba, Bayamo, and Guantánamo.

The offensive began on May 24, 1958, with an attack on the Rebel outpost at Las Mercedes. Two Batista forces, one from the north and one from the south, gained ground steadily and penetrated so far that Castro's guerrillas were squeezed into an area no greater than four square miles.

However, the government had only gained ground; they had not defeated or even severely punished the guerrilla force. The soldiers were not trained for the exhausting mountain warfare, always meeting fierce resistance. Two battalions, bravely and efficiently commanded by Lieutenant Colonel Angel Sánchez Mosquera, were dogged and harried by a band led by Juan Almeida. The whole Batista force stopped to regroup and rest—a fatal error.

Sánchez Mosquera's battalions were quartered in the village of Santo Domingo. His name continually crops up in the accounts by Guevara and others of the Sierra Maestra. He was the bravest, toughest, most brutal and tenacious of all Batista's officers. But at this point he found himself surrounded by Castro's riflemen, and his two battalions were cut to pieces in a week-long battle ending on June 20. Only about half his troops got out, bearing their gravely wounded commander, who lived to fight another day.

His unit's shortwave radio equipment was captured, along with a code book. The army kept using the code until July 25, when, by coincidence, another victory gave the Rebels the new code just as a change was made. Fidel claimed later that they intercepted every order and even used the captured transmitter to direct government air strikes on its own positions and to drop food where the Rebels were.

The shortened lines had strengthened the small Rebel force of three hundred, while the enemy had become more extended. The decisive engagement was fought at El Jigüe, near Fidel's headquarters at La Plata, below Turquino, from July 11 to 20 against a battalion commanded by Major José Quevedo. Fidel, who directed the Rebel forces, wrote an account of the battle in *La Sierra y el Llano.* The government troops had been harassed in fourteen skirmishes as they moved in and were short of provisions. Quevedo (incidentally, an acquaintance of Castro's) was trapped, and every effort to break out meant soldiers killed, wounded, or captured. Reinforcements were cut to pieces. On the twentieth, Quevedo and 163 soldiers surrendered. He himself joined Fidel's forces. His soldiers were fed and the wounded tended and turned over to the Cuban and International Red Cross. Their arms were distributed to already trained Rebel volunteers.

By this time Batista's officers were demoralized. Without combat training themselves, they were fighting against veterans of many encounters. Castro's guerrillas struck against advanced or exposed positions, always defeating the soldiers and creating confusion and panic. Late in July, Batista had to order a withdrawal, which became a rout. One battalion after another of the seventeen sent into the Sierra Maestra was decimated or fled. By August 7 it was over, except for stragglers. A great quantity of arms was captured.

The Castro forces lost only twenty-seven killed and about fifty wounded. They had taken 433 prisoners, who were well treated and released, most to the International Red Cross and the rest to the army. It is not known how many soldiers were killed, since the government was not even conceding defeat, but there was a figure of 117 wounded.

The returned prisoners demolished the Batista propaganda of the murders, torture, and ill-treatment of soldiers and peasants by the guerrillas. Psychologically, it had been a brilliant tactic, and also practically, for as Castro broadcast, he did not have enough food, cigarettes, and other supplies for prisoners. The army did not release a single Rebel prisoner and, it was believed, murdered guerrillas after capture.

Cubans learned of the victories from Castro, speaking over Radio Rebelde on the nights of August 18 and 19. Batista gave the

Cuban press a communiqué stating that his soldiers had defeated the guerrillas who fled.

On August 20, Fidel said on Radio Rebelde: "Victories in war depend to a minimum on weapons and to a maximum on morale . . . The sentence of Martí's which could have been merely poetry has become a profound truth for us: 'What matters is not the quantity of weapons available but the number of stars on your forehead.' "

Fidel Castro won the 1958 battle because of his tactical leadership, which, as in the Bay of Pigs invasion, was resourceful and courageous, and because his men fought with skill and spirit from beginning to end.

After Batista's offensive had failed, Castro issued an order of the day saying: "The guerrilla war has ceased to exist; it has become a war of positions and movements." This was true insofar as it meant the spreading of the war from Oriente Province to the rest of the island.

Fidel's strategy was for his and his brother's columns to encircle and capture Santiago de Cuba while another column of 148 men under Che Guevara moved west through Las Villas Province to the Sierra de Escambray and then on to Havana. Che also had the task of imposing Castro's authority on three or four groups of guerrillas fighting on their own in the mountains south of Havana. A fourth column of eighty-two *barbudos* under Camilo Cienfuegos was to move parallel to Che's column and aim ultimately to repeat Antonio Maceo's drive to the westernmost province of Pinar del Río. That proved to be an unnecessary goal.

"The Antonio Maceo and Ciro Redondo [Guevara's] Columns together had little over 200 men and some 182 weapons of various types during the march through Camagüey Province," Raúl Castro was to say in a commemorative speech in 1973, "while the Batista Army had about 2,400 soldiers on operations in the same area equipped with all means of combat."

Early in 1958 a group calling itself the "Second National Front" had been established in the Sierra de Escambray southeast of Havana under the leadership of Eloy Gutiérrez Menoyo, a survivor of the 1957 attack on the Presidential Palace. The band received training in commando tactics from an American war veteran, William Morgan. A smaller but more effective group from the student Directorio Revolucionario, headed by Fauré Chomón, another March 13 survivor, went up into the Sierra de Trinidad. There were a few other bands, one of them composed of barely disguised bandits.

Most historians credit Che Guevara and his Column Four, which made a trek of extraordinary hardship, tenacity, and heroism, with having delivered the decisive military thrust of the war. It had all the ingredients of an epic, but one should not forget what had gone before and the hard-fought campaign by the Castro brothers which was going on almost unnoticed in Oriente Province. Fortunately for posterity, Che told the story of his campaign with classic simplicity in the last chapter of the English version of his *Reminiscences of the Revolutionary War.*

Castro's original idea was that the journey could be made in four days, using trucks and weapons brought in by plane, but the vehicles were destroyed by enemy bombing and the column had to go on foot and horseback. Che's march began on August 21, and Camilo's on August 30, 1958.

> We were heavily loaded with ammunition, [Che wrote] with a forty-rocket bazooka, and everything necessary for a long march and a quick setting up of camp.
>
> Came difficult days in the still-friendly territory of Oriente Province. We had to cross rivers in flood, creeks and brooks converted into rivers; we had to struggle unendingly to keep ammunition, guns and rockets dry; we had to find fresh horses to replace the tired ones; we had increasingly to avoid populated areas as we moved beyond Oriente Province. We marched toilsomely through flooded terrain, attacked by hordes of mosquitoes which made rest stops unbearable. We ate little and badly; we drank water from streams that wound through marshes, or even swamp water itself. We dragged ourselves along, in a pitiable state, during appalling days. A week after we had set out, we crossed the Jobabo, which divides Camagüey from Oriente. We were quite enfeebled and furthermore lacked footwear: many comrades walked barefoot through the mud of southern Camagüey.
>
> During the night of September 9th, on entering La Federal, our advance guard fell into an enemy ambush. Two courageous comrades met their death there. But the worst was that we were spotted by enemy forces who, from that moment on, harassed us without let-up. After a small clash, we reduced their little garrison, at the cost of four of our men taken prisoner. We had to redouble our caution, all the more so now that the enemy's aviation knew our general course. . . .
>
> Came days of grueling trudging across desolate stretches where we came upon nothing but water and mud. We suffered from thirst and hunger and we were scarcely able to move ahead. Our legs were like lead and our weapons weighed us down oppressively. We con-

tinued the march with some better horses, which Camilo left us when he went to fetch the trucks, but we had to abandon them in the vicinity of the Macareño sugar mill. Since the guides who were to meet us had not appeared we simply plunged ahead, feeling our way blindly.

Our advance came upon an enemy post at Cuatro Compañeros and this was the beginning of a grueling battle. Dawn came. We succeeded—not without difficulties—in mustering the majority of the troop in a densely wooded grove, but the enemy flanked us and we had to carry on a long battle in order to permit those who had fallen behind to cross over a railroad track in the direction of the woods. It was then that their planes spotted us. B-26's, C-47's, large reconnaissance C-3's, small planes, all spitting fire within a perimeter of 300 meters or less. After this saturation, they withdrew. We had lost one man to the bombs and we had several wounded, among them Major Silva, who made the rest of the expedition with a fractured shoulder.

There were always peasants who helped them, although others were too terrified and betrayed them. The army continually harassed the column. One day they heard General Francisco Tabernilla Dolz announce that Guevara's column had been annihilated. "The news of our demise provoked delight among our little troop," Che continues.

However, little by little they began to be attacked by pessimism. Thirst, hunger, fatigue, a feeling of impotence in the face of the encircling enemy forces, and especially a terrible foot ailment which made each step a torment, had transformed our group into an army of shadows. Day after day our physical condition deteriorated and our meals —one day yes, another day no, the third day perhaps—were not such as to improve our condition. Our hardest days were those we spent under siege, near the Baraguá sugar mill, in pestilential swamps, without a drop of potable water, harassed by planes, without a single horse to aid the feebler among us to cross that unfriendly slough, our shoes completely rotted by this brackish, muddy water full of vegetation that lacerated our bare feet. When we broke through the encirclement of Baraguá in order to reach the famous road from Júcaro to Morón—a historic spot, the scene of bloody battles between patriots and Spaniards in the War of Independence—we were truly in a disastrous situation. We had no time to recover, because torrential downpours and the general inclemency of the weather, together with enemy attacks, obliged us to resume our march. The troop became more and more exhausted and disheartened. However, at the most critical moment, when insults, entreaties, and tongue lashings were the only way to get

> the weary men to advance, a distant vision sufficed to restore their courage and give new spirit to the group: a blue spot on the horizon toward the west, the blue of the Las Villas cordillera, glimpsed for the first time by our men. From that moment on, privations were more bearable, everything seemed easier. We escaped the second ring of encirclement by swimming the Júcaro, which separates the provinces of Camagüey and Las Villas. We felt as if we had emerged from darkness.
>
> Two days later we were safe in the heart of the Trinidad-Sancti Spíritus mountain range, ready to enter the new stage of the war.

Camilo Cienfuegos kept a field diary which he addressed to Castro from the plains of Santa Clara on October 9, 1958. It is published in *La Sierra y el Llano.*

> To begin with [Cienfuegos wrote] I will tell you that from the time we left the area of the Cauto [River] going westward, we marched without resting a single night, forty days, many of them without guides, using the southern coastline to orientate ourselves and with a compass to direct us. The journey along that coast was disastrous; during two weeks we walked with water and mud up to our knees, every night evading ambushes and troops stationed in the crossings that we had to make.
>
> In the thirty-one days the trip across the Province of Camagüey took, we ate only eleven times [despite] this being the primary cattle region of Cuba.

(On one of the days when they did eat, he writes later, "we consumed a mare, raw and without salt.")

On October 8 they reached a rebel encampment and were received "with a thousand marvels" by the leader, Major Félix Torres. He was a Communist who had joined forces with Che's column when it came along. Other Communist groups also helped Guevara, who disturbed the generally anti-Communist members of the 26th of July Movement by giving Communists commanding posts. They had what he called "the guerrilla spirit."

Most of Camilo's diary contains a detailed account of the arduous, dangerous journey that started at midnight on September 7 at the Jobabo River in Oriente. There was never a stretch without enemy troops, and no place to stop.

On September 16 they encountered a group of nine *compañeros* who joined them, along with two young "musketeers," one seventeen and the other twenty-nine years old. These two, as it turned out, had been attacking and robbing in the name of the 26th of July Movement. "On being unable to deny their guilt, they were tried and condemned to death."

The column often spotted troops ahead of them "in ambush," as Camilo always puts it, and on one occasion knew that they were spotted and watched crossing a river without being attacked. "This is the best proof," he wrote, "that Batista's army does not want to fight and that its discomposed and scanty morale is getting lower every day."

But this proved to be exceptional. It took extreme precautions, daring, shrewdness, and great stamina for Camilo's column to keep going night after night through terrain swarming with regular soldiers who, nearly always, were trying to snare and destroy them.

Camilo tells the story deadpan, in simple and generally unemotional language. He was uneducated, but he had an extraordinary story to tell. The facts needed no adornment.

Both Camilo and Che, incidentally, often found the local 26th of July groups inhospitable and unhelpful.

There was an enchanting day near Ciego de Ávila in a cluster of thirty houses where Camilo's troop took shelter, as the inhabitants, although fearing the brutality of the troops if they had come up, were friendly. A rebel captain, Antonio Sánchez, took over the schoolroom, gave classes, and distributed sweets. "Among these little ones," Camilo, who was young in heart, wrote, "we spent happy hours that for a while made us forget the fatigues and pains of the hours before."

When they went away, the children sang the national anthem and promised that every Friday they would place a floral offering before the statue of José Martí. It was, in fact, terrain made historic by the similar drive of Antonio Maceo's column six decades before. Camilo's column was named for Maceo.

At the end of the journey, he was childishly happy. When they crossed the Jatibonico River into Las Villas Province, he kissed the ground. His pride was simple, natural, and to a high degree, warranted.

"Thus," he wrote, "we achieved one of the greatest triumphs in revolutionary command since, in spite of the many attempts of the Army of the tyranny to try to exterminate us, we crossed the wide sweep of land from Oriente to Las Villas with only three dead."

Fidel was broadcasting about "a flood of rebels" pouring over the whole island. In reality, it was a trickle, but Batista's intelligence was poor and his censorship so strict that the Cuban people were prepared to believe anything, so long as it was not an official handout. The "fog of war" had descended over the island.

Batista had no idea, it seems, that he was being beaten. How could he? His Army was intact. So was his police force. His administration was the legitimately recognized government of Cuba; the Civic Resistance was being controlled, ruthlessly and efficiently. There were only those few hundred rebels, holed up in the eastern end of the island, and some scattered, poorly armed, ragged bands of guerrillas in Las Villas.

But this was where Fidel Castro had shown a touch of genius. Those two small columns led by Guevara and Cienfuegos had the psychological force of two divisions. It was the old story of a David against a Goliath or, one may say, of the mouse frightening the elephant. Weighed in the balance, 2,400 soldiers armed with U.S. matériel had less strength than a handful of men with indomitable spirit and two extraordinary leaders. There was also the fact that the rebels were being supported by a brave and effective urban resistance.

Fidel's problem now was not simply to overthrow the Batista regime. He knew that this was inevitable. Curiously, he did not realize the extent to which he had become a national hero and the only valid symbol of victory. He was right to think that others would try to snatch the fruits of victory from him. The sure way for the *Fidelistas* to win over all the others was to get Guevara, Cienfuegos, and their *barbudos* into Havana while he and Raúl took Santiago de Cuba.

Batista fought on, even holding a farcical presidential election on November 3, 1958, in which his chosen candidate, Andrés Rivero Agüero, naturally "won." Within a matter of days the President saw towns like Placetas, a road junction, and other centers around Sancti Spíritus and northern Las Villas Province fall to guerrilla bands that he hardly knew existed or to the 26th of July rebels in the underground.

Batista was frantically buying arms, tanks, and planes from England and the Continent. It was too late. General Francisco Tabernilla, a Batista man since 1934 and chief of staff after the 1952 coup, evidently realized well before his boss that it was all but over. He and his two sons, "Wince" and "Silito," whom he had made high officers, began plotting their getaway.

Hugh Thomas calls Tabernilla "the evil genius of the Army" and "Batista's *bête noire* and the real author of the Army's defeat." He even considers Tabernilla, not Batista, to have been the strongman of the dictatorship. This was far from the case. Tabernilla was a greedy smuggler and peculator, and he had distributed his own men in command posts around the island. But this is like saying that Haldeman and Erlichman were the strongmen of the White House, not Nixon. Tabernilla and his cronies were the kind of men who suited Batista and his method of governing. The difference was that they were not loyal to him, as the White House clique was to the President.

Tabernilla seems to have gone behind Batista's back to order General Eulogio Cantillo in Santiago de Cuba in mid-December to parley with Castro. They met at the Oriente sugar mill on December 24. Raúl Castro, Raúl Chibás, Celia Sánchez, and Vilma Espín were at this meeting, at which, the revolutionaries say, Cantillo was asked to surrender the Santiago and Bayamo garrisons. He asked for time and then flew to Havana.

As Batista claims to have said to his chiefs of staff: "When an Army loses all its battles and skirmishes, one after the other; when it has been unable to repel an unorganized enemy; when not a day passes without some of its men surrendering—to seek out the chief of such groups [Castro] and ask him what do you want in exchange for a cease-fire is equivalent to surrender." Nevertheless, Batista did agree to a parley.

The end of the war was not the spontaneous collapse of a hopelessly demoralized army that so many historians made it out to be. The victory was won by hard fighting in Las Villas and Oriente provinces, although there were also surrenders of authority and desertions. However, the Rebels were so greatly outgunned and outnumbered that when an army unit had officers and men who stood and fought, which was often the case, the fight could be desperate for the guerrillas.

The battle for Santa Clara, with which the insurrection ended in the west, was a case in point. All emphasis is placed on the ignominious surrender of the formidable armored train sent by Batista without considering the hard fighting and clever tactics that led up to the collapse.

Captain Antonio Núñez Jiménez, who had just joined the rebels and whose unusually pompous title was "chief of topographical services and military liaison" for Guevara's force, tells the story in *La Sierra y el Llano.*

The beginning of the end, he writes, came on December 18 at Fomento, in Las Villas Province, where the municipal authorities accepted revolutionary appointees to run the town. The process was repeated elsewhere as they went along. But these were civilian authorities. The air force had plenty of pilots willing to bomb and machine-gun townspeople, Rebels, and houses indiscriminately and cruelly. By doing so, they aroused a sense of bitterness that led the unforgiving Fidel Castro to take a somewhat illegal vengeance later when some aviators went on trial.

Instead of attacking Santa Clara directly, Che set about capturing all the surrounding localities, isolating the provincial capital. The local garrisons often fought it out. Then he asked Núñez to find him a road into Santa Clara from which he could approach and attack the city undetected. Núñez planned an entry from Las Villas University City, where, before becoming a revolutionary, he had been professor of geography. Guevara set up headquarters there for the assault on December 28. He had broken his left arm in Cabaiguán, near Santa Clara, when he climbed to the roof of a house with a machine gun to fire on a movement of Batista troops and fell off. He had it put in a splint and, with characteristic stoicism, led his soldiers onward.

Batista's last, despairing effort was to send the armored train to Santa Clara, fully outfitted, bearing tanks and 350 soldiers. It might as well have been an elaborate toy.

The city itself had first to be taken piecemeal in a number of attacks on buildings, the main police station, isolated tanks and groups of soldiers. It took desperate and costly fighting, for the Rebels had few men against a numerous, entrenched foe who, in some places, fought well. The civilian population suffered some losses from the aerial attacks on the guerrillas.

Che Guevara had no more than three hundred men—his own column plus recruits from the Directorio Revolucionario and the underground 26th of July Movement. On December 29 the armored train moved into the center of the town. Using tractors, Che's men pulled up the railway tracks in front of and behind the train, derailed it with dynamite charges, and set it afire. The trapped officers and soldiers surrendered, the troops fraternizing with the Rebels. There was some sporadic fighting at four or five points in the city for two days. On December 31, 1958, Santa Clara was added to the *Territorio Libre de Cuba.*

Batista was notified at nine that evening. An hour later he received a telephone call from General Cantillo giving him the equally bad news that Santiago de Cuba could not be held, which meant that all of Oriente Province was lost. It was this combined defeat, not just the loss of Santa Clara, that evidently made the President decide to flee immediately.

The army commander in Santa Clara, Colonel Joaquín Casillas Lumpuy (who had been named to succeed the sinister Moncada Barracks commander, Alberto del Río Chaviano, now a general), was also down in Rebel books as a murderer. He ran away in civilian clothes, but was captured and executed. Command was then turned over by his fellow officers to a valiant but wounded officer, Colonel Hernández.

Che named Núñez and two others as a commission to demand the surrender of the main garrison. They entered the Leoncio Vidal Barracks under a white flag and were warmly greeted by the soldiers.

It was January 1, 1959. As they were talking to Colonel Hernández, an announcement came over the radio of the flight of Batista and the formation of a military junta headed by General Eulogio Cantillo, who had flown to Havana. Núñez got the general on the radiophone and was told that Castro had agreed.

"Knowing that this was impossible, we denied it over the radio," writes Núñez. "We explained to the General by radio and to the officers present by word, that we had direct orders from Major Ernesto Guevara to resume hostilities at 12:15, and this time without concessions, discussions or truce, if the defenders of the Leoncio Vidal Barracks did not surrender before that hour." The officers yielded.

"Thus ended the struggle in Santa Clara," Núñez concludes.

Fidel had not expected Batista to give up so quickly. He would not have been besieging Santiago de Cuba if he had. When I saw him in September 1972, he spoke in an almost aggrieved tone of the fact that all the histories of the Sierra Maestra war give no credit for the campaign that he, Raúl, and others in Oriente Province fought in November and December 1958. The Oriente campaign, Castro said, was *"tremenda."* Four or five times as many Rebel troops were fighting there, but hardly anything had been printed about it. I pointed out that there was very little material on it, whereas Las Villas had a galaxy of Rebel literary stars. He did not begrudge Che and Camilo their fame and credit, but he seemed to feel that he had been slighted. Perhaps there was a touch of envy.

The most important single event of the Oriente campaign was the battle of Guisa, eight miles from Bayamo, which was fought from November 20 to 30, 1958. A brief account of the battle appears in *La Sierra y el Llano.* (On its fifteenth anniversary the *Granma* called Guisa "the most important action waged by the Rebel Army in the revolutionary war.")

Castro, leading Column One, named for José Martí, with 230 men, left the *Comandancia General* in La Plata, reaching the neighborhood of Guisa on November 20, 1958. They blew up the old bridge of Monte Oscuro with dynamite, cutting off the government tanks in Bayamo. At night the Rebels attacked the Batista forces, blowing up a tank and a truck with twenty soldiers in it. By six o'clock in the morning, the reinforcements sent from Bayamo were repulsed "after several hours of intense fighting." That day the enemy bombed and machine-gunned the Rebels and then managed to get in reinforcements of Sherman tanks, mortars, machine guns, bazookas, and a large supply of ammunition. Fidel sat tight.

"We can wait patiently," he commented. "The idea is to make them nervous."

Hostilities were not renewed until dawn of November 25. The enemy sent out a column of two tanks followed by fourteen trucks of soldiers. A mine blew up the leading tank.

"By midday the exchange of fire was getting more and more intense. Thus began one of the fiercest battles of the whole Sierra Maestra campaign."

The enemy finally abandoned their trucks. The Rebels then cut off the retreat of the soldiers and their vehicles, pinning them down without food or drink all through November 26. Early the next day two battalions of enemy reinforcements, accompanied by tanks, entered the combat. Planes bombed. The fighting went on all day.

"That day," says the account, "the Rebel Army covered itself with glory. Before nightfall the tanks and infantry began a general retreat. The road, with its fourteen destroyed trucks, tens of dead bodies and and thousands of helmets blocking the path, gave an exact idea of the importance of the battle. Much booty was captured, including a T–18 tank in perfect condition."

On November 29 a group of rebels, some of them driving a captured tank, entered Guisa and attacked the barracks. The tank was immobilized by enemy bazookas, but the next day, November 30, the tenth day of the battle, "having defeated four battalions sent from Bayamo, the Rebel victory was consummated . . . At 4 in the afternoon, the whole garrison of Guisa took flight, leaving behind a great quantity of arms and ammunition. At 9 in the evening, the first advance group of Rebels entered the town. The Army had suffered more than 200 casualties in dead, wounded and prisoners. The Rebels lost only eight men."

Like the summer offensive in the Sierra Maestra and the experiences of the Rebels in the center of the island, Guisa was proof that the government army would often fight as well as it could up to the end.

Raúl Castro's Second Front from the Sierra de Cristal, Juan Almeida's Third Front west of Guantánamo, Hubert Matos' column, and Castro's Column One now had Santiago de Cuba surrounded and cut off. The garrisons in Bayamo, Holguín, and Guantánamo still gave no signs of yielding. Groups of Batista troops made forays in which the peasants, not the Rebels, were the chief victims. One such column was led by the infamous Captain Jesús Sosa Blanco, who later gained not only fame but sympathy from the American public, which did not know of his many atrocities but who saw him die bravely on their television screens when he was executed. Those soldiers and officers who fought on did so from desperation or discipline, not loyalty to Batista.

Fidel was warning again and again on Radio Rebelde that the people should not take justice into their own hands, as his revolutionary tribunals would see to it that justice was done.

The garrison at Palma Soriano surrendered on December 28, and the last government stronghold, Maffo, on December 30. Fidel made preparations to advance on Santiago de Cuba to set up a provisional government there. The news of Batista's flight reached him on the morning of January 1, 1959. That afternoon Colonel Rego Rubido, acting military chief of Oriente Province, capitulated to Fidel Castro in El Escandel, near Santiago. The same night Castro's force entered the city, and before dawn of January 2 his car, flying the 26th of July black-and-red pennant, drove into Moncada Barracks. For Fidel Castro, the war ended where, in the eyes of history, it had begun on July 26, 1953.

For the Americans of the State Department, the Pentagon, and the Embassy in Havana, it had been a dramatic and bewildering time —and also a very upsetting one. The United States did not want to see Fidel Castro and his *barbudos*—whom many, long before the fears eventualized, considered to be Communist—take over in Cuba.

The U.S. ambassador in 1957, Arthur Gardner, told Professor Hugh Thomas that he had suggested to Batista "that the FBI or CIA should send up a man to the Sierra to kill Castro; Batista answered: 'No, no, we couldn't do that: we're Cubans.' " Considering how many Cubans were killed by Batista's orders or consent, the reply (if the story is true) has to be classified as national pride. If Fidel was to be assassinated, it would be by Cubans, and, in fact, attempts were made.

Both Gardner and his successor, Earl E. T. Smith (1957–1959)—

the protégé of John Hay Whitney, one of the largest stockholders in Freeport Sulphur, which owned the Cuban nickel mines—"were devoted to American business interests in Cuba," as Professor Robert F. Smith wrote in *What Happened in Cuba.*

According to the next ambassador, Philip Bonsal, in the book he wrote, "Ambassador Smith soon developed a visceral conviction that Castro was a tool of the Communists."

The Resistance had a precious spy in the Cuban Embassy in Washington, an army sergeant named Angel Saavedra, who regularly furnished inside information to the Civic Resistance representative in Washington, Ernesto Betancourt. Among other things, he supplied a list of the arms delivered to Batista—which, in fact, were not extensive, as an arms embargo had gone into effect on March 18, 1958. Batista had more than enough arms, but the embargo was a blow to morale and his prestige. Smith was bitter, but as Bonsal wrote, "The absence of the embargo would not have saved Batista."

Bonsal puts the situation toward the end of 1958 in the U.S. Embassy well. He rejects Earl Smith's "belief that the officials of the [State] Department favored Castro and were working for his success."

"The truth, as I see it," Ambassador Bonsal writes, "is that these officials as well as the more knowledgeable members of the Embassy staff in Havana shared an antipathy for Batista's regime; so far as Castro was concerned they had no feeling other than a belief that the movement he headed was destined to take over and that the legal opposition that so engrossed the Ambassador's attention had no comparable significance."

After returning to Havana on December 12 from a trip to Washington, Smith, as he wrote in his book *The Fourth Floor,* reluctantly told Cuban Foreign Minister Gonzalo Güell: "It is my unpleasant duty to inform the President of the Republic that the U.S. will no longer support the present Government of Cuba and that my Government believes that the President is losing effective control."

However, Smith told the Senate Internal Security Subcommittee in 1961 of a conference with Batista on December 17.

"I did not tell Batista he ought to get out," he said. "I would not put it so bluntly as that. I spent two hours and 25 minutes trying to tactfully explain that the Department believed he had lost effective control. To avoid further bloodshed, did he not think it might be in the best interests of all concerned if he retired? This had to be done without giving the impression that I was intervening." Smith was evidently so hesitant and diffident that Batista paid no attention.

According to Ambassador Bonsal, Batista "had already disposed abroad most of the extensive spoils of his years in power; he fled the country he and his friends had plundered in the early morning of New Year's Day, 1959." Bonsal also writes of "the repudiation of a corrupt and bloodstained regime by the people of Cuba," and "the sordid and bloody morass into which the regime of Batista had sunk." This severe judgment on Fulgencio Batista is impressive, coming as it does from so carefully diplomatic and reticent an authority as Philip Bonsal.

Smith was still trying to carry out Washington's desire to find a replacement for Batista who would not be Castro. Professor Thomas was told by Admiral Arleigh Burke, Chief of the Naval Staff, of a New Year's Eve meeting in the Pentagon at which Burke, "with some support" from Allen Dulles, head of the CIA, and Under Secretary of State Robert Murphy, argued that "Castro was not the man for Cuba and something should be done to stop him from taking power." They talked until 2 A.M. without finding a solution, which was not strange. Short of a very costly—in every way—invasion by marines with air and sea cover, nothing could have been done. The meeting showed how little Washington understood of what was happening in Cuba. Poor intelligence in and from Cuba was to continue to mislead the United States throughout the Revolution.

The eyes of the Western Hemisphere were on Cuba in the closing months of 1958. There were times when there was no censorship and periods when, on the surface, life in Havana was normal. Thousands of American tourists thought so to the very end. No one will ever forget the remark of Senator Allen J. Ellender, Democrat of Louisiana, in Havana on December 12, 1958: "Is there a revolution here? I hadn't noticed any trouble."

Batista's decision to leave on the night of December 31–January 1 must have been sudden, as he left behind a small fortune in cash, jewels, stocks, and bonds, and left his palatial country home, Kuquine, untouched, as my wife and I discovered a few days later. However, his chief possessions were in the United States and Switzerland.

He took some relatives and friends in the few planes he used, leaving thousands of other *Batistianos* to their fate. His plane left Camp Columbia at 3 A.M. for Ciudad Trujillo in the Dominican Republic. Others went a little later. Rolando Masferrer, one of the most wanted men, was warned in time and sailed from Santiago de Cuba by yacht. Other Batista leaders escaped during the morning in planes and boats or by seeking refuge in foreign embassies. Some of the most notorious characters thus escaped revolutionary justice.

"Not only politicians fled," Hugh Thomas wryly notes, "but also such men as Meyer Lansky, the gambler." Most of the first refugees had funds in the United States, and some, as Thomas remarks, "carried satchels of stolen money." Many got away because of their social connections or wealth. They were "non-torturable," to use Graham Greene's term in his 1958 *Our Man in Havana.*

Before fleeing, Batista had named supreme court judge Carlos Manuel Piedra as Provisional President. On the morning of January 1, Piedra tried to act as if the appointment meant something.

Fidel had heard the news of Batista's flight as he was having morning coffee. At first unbelieving, then suspicious and angry at General Cantillo for, as he saw it, breaking his word, he announced on Radio Rebelde that he did not recognize the Military Junta being formed, and he called for a general strike.

At 1 P.M. a diplomatic commission headed by Ambassador Smith saw Cantillo in the Presidential Palace in Havana, but refused to deal with Piedra. They were still trying to keep Castro out of power. I met Smith and his confrères coming out of the back entrance to the Palace. He gave me a weak smile and muttered something about "seeking a solution." An hour later Cantillo, realizing the hopelessness of his position, gave up. He must have known that Colonel Ramón Barquín, still in the Isle of Pines prison for his part in the 1956 army revolt, was being called in to take over.

Barquín's brief and puzzling role was partially cleared up by Hugh Thomas, who got the story from Justo Carrillo, banker and liberal anti-Batista politician. Carrillo told Thomas that he and his *Montecristi* group had sought CIA help in getting Barquín out earlier. The CIA was interested, but held back until December 30, when they gave the head of the prison $100,000 to release Barquín. The Colonel was thus able to get to Havana on January 1, before any of the Rebel leaders, and he held a sort of command for a day or two at Camp Columbia, which was turned over to him by Cantillo.

However, the 26th of July underground, now out in the streets and keeping order in Havana, was not taking orders from Barquín. The Colonel tried in vain to contact Fidel. Instead, Armando Hart notified him and his officers on January 2 that Castro's orders were that Camp Columbia was to be turned over to Camilo Cienfuegos and Cabañas Fortress to Che Guevara. Barquín yielded gracefully and greeted Camilo and his *barbudos* warmly. Months later he went quietly into exile.

On New Year's Day, Castro broadcast an urgent appeal to all

Cubans not to take the law into their own hands, as had been the case when Machado left Havana in 1934, and in Caracas, Venezuela, just a year before when the dictator, Marcos Pérez Jiménez, fled. Thanks to the men of the 26th of July Movement, there was hardly any violence in Havana and other cities, and no lynchings. It was Fidel's promise to try *Batistiano* "criminals" in military courts that more than anything prevented a blood bath, although it meant many executions later.

My wife and I were in Havana on January 1 and succeeding days. It was especially remarkable on New Year's Day to see the young men of the 26th take over in the streets with firmness and discipline.

The labor unions, which had never helped and, in fact, sometimes sabotaged the Castro insurrection, came out on January 2 in an effective general strike. Eusebio Mujal, secretary general of the Cuban Workers Confederation, was one of the unsavory characters who took refuge in an embassy. He was believed to be a millionaire.

As a precaution, Fidel at first declared Santiago de Cuba the provisional capital and proclaimed Manuel Urrutia, who was with him, as Provisional President. Urrutia flew on ahead to reestablish Havana as the capital and to form a cabinet, which Castro later told me that he himself had not chosen.

Fidel made a slow, triumphal procession across the island amid delirious enthusiasm, making speeches and appointments and cannily allowing the excitement in Havana to rise to fever pitch. The reception in the capital on the evening of January 8 was joyful to the point of hysteria. It was a popular release of volcanic proportions, a release from years of terror, repression, and corruption, from a species of tyranny.

So much hope, so much happiness! Cubans lived in a dream world, utterly unreal, but wonderful while it lasted. The hopes were differing, and so were the dreams. They did not know—nor could Fidel Castro—that it was not only a release from much that had gone before, but also from the Cuban Republic of six decades, from life as they had known it, from United States domination. It may well have dawned on Fidel Castro that night of January 8, 1959, that Cuba was his to do what he pleased with.

In his pronouncement over Radio Rebelde from Santiago de Cuba on January 1, he had said: *"Revolución, si; golpe militar, no!"* ("Revolution, yes; military coup, no!")

The importance of this *grito*, this call, was not realized in those hours of national euphoria, but they were fateful words. When the Rebel leader said "revolution," he meant exactly that. It took months of conflict and heartbreak before Cubans and Americans grasped the fact. On January 1, 1959, Fidel Castro began to carry out the revolution for which he had been fighting since the attack on the Moncada Barracks in Santiago de Cuba in 1953. He is still carrying it out sixteen years later.

Castro told Lockwood that at the end of the guerrilla war he had about 3,000 men. "We fought our decisive battles with 300 men," he said. The May-August 1958 offensive, he claimed, started with Batista's 10,000-man army against his 300 *barbudos.* "It is true that we had many more ready to join us, but they had no weapons . . . We captured 500 men and some weapons . . . That allowed us, now with 800 armed men, to spread out throughout the country . . . At the end of the war, we had 15,000 soldiers of Batista surrounded in Oriente Province alone. We had some 2,500 men there, plus 500 in Las Villas, a total of about 3,000 men."

After January 1 *barbudos* sprang up everywhere like mushrooms. No one will ever know how many were genuine fighters in the Resistance. Professor Andrés Suárez, in *Cuba, Castroism and Communism,* who became undersecretary in the treasury ministry, said rightly that "it was only during 1958—and in Havana only in December 1958 at that—that opposition began to take on massive proportions."

The close-to-unanimous popular support that Fidel Castro had when he entered Havana in triumph was not because he had promised to hold elections and make democratic reforms; it was the result of a profound public upheaval into which Cuban history, traditions, character, hopes, and emotions all mingled with a revulsion against the Batista regime to sweep Fidel Castro to heights never attained by any Cuban leader. The phenomenon of Batista's fall and Castro's triumph was an enormously complicated process which both pro- and anti-*Fidelista* historians greatly oversimplified at the time.

Batista might have said of Fidel Castro what Porfirio Díaz said of Francisco Madero as the Mexican president went into exile and the 1910 revolution began: "Madero has unleashed a tiger; let us see if he can control him."

CHAPTER 6

The Social Revolution

None goes so far as he who knows not whither he is going.

—Oliver Cromwell

The Cuban Revolution began when the insurrection ended on January 1, 1959. It was not just a *coup d'état,* or a change of government, or an era of drastic reform; it was a transformation of Cuban life and an end to the sixty-year domination of Cuba by the United States. For nearly all Americans, the history of Cuba began on that day. They had been fed on the pap in American history books about the misnamed Spanish-American War. They believed that the United States had been altruistic toward, as well as beneficial for, the Cuban Republic. They saw Communism before it came and, perhaps, helped to bring it to Cuba sooner than it might otherwise have come; and they had been educated to believe that democracy American-style was the best of all systems for every nation.

A lot of trouble and heartache were therefore built into the situation, much of it lying below the surface of the great wave of relief and happiness at the ending of the Batista era. Revolutions must surely be the most unpredictable of all political and social events. They release great forces which, to begin with, are destructive. They demand a process of creation which is painful, complicated, and hazardous.

Criticizing the difficulties and flounderings of the Cuban revolutionaries, Americans tended to forget what a near thing it was for the former English colonies to get started and consolidate their independence. The federal system of our "Articles of Confederation" came close to breaking down, and under Thomas Jefferson, of all people. Like our State Department officials in the early 1960s, officials in London's Westminster must have been gloating over what seemed like a coming disaster. Alexander Hamilton was pessimistic. Resolving the maddening complications of the Revolutionary War was proving a desperate business. Attempts to solve the enormous financial problems were not succeeding. The hostile economic policies of George III's government were proving only too effective. We know, of course, that the fragile, infant government was to survive triumphantly, but contemporaries in the 1780s and 1790s were by no means sure. Without a James Madison, who can say what might have happened?

The comparison cannot be pushed without getting absurd, but it is a fact of political life that the birth of a nation—and a new Cuba was being born—is as painful in its way as a natural birth.

But early in 1959 there was no revolution and little understanding that there was going to be one. Fidel Castro had to make it—he, alone, against a new host of enemies and would-be friends, with only his small, loyal clique of *Moncadistas* and Sierra Maestra *barbudos.* There was naturally no articulate popular demand for a revolution, since no people can know what a revolution is until they experience it. However, the national mood was for a change, a wiping out of the ugly past, a cleansing purge, a new Cuba. Generations of Cuban intellectuals and politicians had resented the United States hegemony but were powerless or lacking in the audacity to do anything about their sentiments. To paraphrase Mark Twain, everybody talked about revolution in Cuba but nobody had done anything about it—until Fidel Castro came along.

He did not know what kind of revolution, or how he was going to make it. He knew little of Marxism, despite what he said later, and he not only felt critical of the Cuban Communists at the time, but was far more radical, nationalistic, and daring than any Cuban or Russian Communist. In fact, Fidel Castro had no ideology whatever in 1959.

There was no question in anybody's mind after a few weeks had passed that Castro was in effect the *Lider Máximo,* the *Jefe Supremo.* He faced what is called in football an open field. The old political parties, the old politicians, the high military officers, the businessmen, bankers, and landowners—all were scattered, divided, powerless, and nearly all, justly or unjustly, discredited in the eyes of the victors. No one man, no party, no movement could stop Castro and his followers, now intoxicated with power. Surprisingly, considering the Cuban republic's history, no element was more helpless than the United States and the American business community.

It was going to be a dictatorship, a one-man show. It was Fidel Castro's revolution, a triumph of personality and an outgrowth of

Latin American *caudillismo.* He exercised power because he was a hero, not because he had a constitutional mandate, although he did acquire one in time. Che Guevara once referred to Fidel Castro as "that telluric force." He hit Cuba like an earthquake, and the response of the people was to him. The Cuban masses were going to follow him, wherever he led them. The government, to them, was Fidel Castro; it was a personal relationship, man to man, as if each individual communed with Fidel Castro and he with them. His political genius lay in carrying the Cuban people along with him, year after year, even though the going was hard. Cubans are not, like the Russians, apathetic or docile or submissive. To get them to accept a revolution, Fidel—long before he triumphed—realized that he required a maximum degree of national unity.

In the circumstances obtaining at the beginning of the Revolution, this was a palpable impossibility. The revolution which Castro was determined to make naturally provoked violent differences. The issue of Communism merely crystallized what was bound to be conflicts of class, race, economics, relations with the United States, and deeply ingrained Cuban habits of thought, prejudices, beliefs, customs, traditions.

Yet there was evidence from the beginning that a large majority of the Cuban people had risen to the occasion. There was a remarkable degree of willing acceptance of what was happening and a quick popular understanding that a transformation of the whole Cuban structure was under way. I, among others, was struck by this fact early in the Revolution and wrote about it. This popular consensus, not the oppression of a police state, is what has kept the Cuban Revolution going for sixteen years. It could not be otherwise, for the Cuban people, with their Spanish heritage, are individualists, quick to violence and characteristically brave. Their instinct is to be against the government—any government. Had they as a people been hostile to the Castro revolution, they would have rebelled against Fidel, as they did against Gerardo Machado and Fulgencio Batista.

Cubans borrowed from Spain the idea of labeling their periods by generations. The "Generation of '53" (Moncada), Fidel claimed, "has nothing to learn from the society in which it grew up." The new men distrusted existing institutions and interests; were suspicious of advice from their elders; had a disdain for orthodoxy and an indifference to individual suffering or injustice so long as it was for what they considered the good of Cuba and the Revolution.

In a dispatch I wrote for *The Times* from Havana on July 4, 1959, I said that the young men around Fidel were all "yes" men. I realized later that I was doing them an injustice, for they were not sycophants or weaklings; they saw eye to eye with Fidel. If not a generation, this was at least a group of men and women who had been brought together by common ideals; who were compatible; who had fought and worked and lived through the great hazards and hardships of Moncada, the *Granma,* and the Sierra; and who were now going to follow Fidel Castro into new and agonizing trials. All the same, as Che Guevara was to say in 1964, "there were internal struggles which at times became very violent." With a few exceptions, these men and women are with him in 1975, leaders of his revolution, members of his government, his Communist Party, and his armed forces. I can think of no historical comparison, unless it be Napoleon's marshals.

As officials, they were beginning at the bottom—inexperienced, ignorant of politics and economics, but full of faith and confidence. They were going to make appalling mistakes, but in the process they were going to construct one of the most complete social revolutions of all time.

Fidel Castro was to be as eloquent as anyone in saying how difficult it was to make a revolution, but this was in later years. In January 1959, I was with him one afternoon strolling in the garden of a villa he had taken over temporarily in the fishing port of Cojímar, the scene of Hemingway's *The Old Man and the Sea.* I made the trite remark that the task he was assuming was going to be infinitely more difficult than anything he had faced in the Sierra Maestra. He nodded thoughtfully at that, but when I added that the power he now held in his hands could do great harm, as well as great good, for Cuba, he stopped in his tracks with a startled look on his face, turned toward me and put his hands on my shoulders.

"But how could I do harm?" he asked in astonishment. "We have the most wonderful plans for Cuba!"

They were not plans; they were dreams, hopes, visions, so earnestly and sincerely felt that they seemed certain of realization to those young revolutionaries. The faith in their visions inspired them, and through them the Cuban people.

It was, in its way, a religious faith which came pouring over the radio waves and through the television screens in the words and presence of Fidel Castro. I coined a phrase at the time: government by television. The Revolution came in on a flood of talk, as Fidel exhorted, explained, reasoned with, and aroused Cuba's millions day after day, night after night, four, five, six hours at a time. The world was amused; Cubans listened enthralled. The art of rhetoric is highly regarded in Cuba, and in Fidel Castro they had one of the great natural orators of our times.

One must listen to him; hear the hoarse, impassioned voice; feel the magnetism of his extraordinary personality. He is a spellbinder. His speeches are, as he put it, a conversation. Like an actor, he senses the feelings of his audience and responds to them. For Che Guevara, in his little book *Man and Socialism in Cuba,* there was "a dialectical unity between Fidel and the mass . . . In the big public meetings one can observe something like the dialogue of two tuning forks whose vibrations summon forth new vibrations in each other." In the early weeks of the Revolution, when the enthusiasm and fervor of his audiences were phenomenal, Fidel's speeches were impassioned and interminable. As the years passed, he cut down from five or six hours to one, two, or three.

"In the early days of the Revolution," he said in a speech on March 13, 1968, "public opinion in the capital, which has always had the characteristic—and I say this in all frankness—of being somewhat inconsistent, required our appearing on television with a certain frequency in order to explain every kind of problem, major or insignificant . . . The struggle of this Revolution has always been to explain problems to the masses."

The speech from which this passage was taken was one of the most remarkable he has made. It contained an incredible mass of economic statistics which would have been indigestible and beyond grasp had they been read in one's home. In detail, the talk must have been incomprehensible, and yet it is more than probable that his audience appreciated the fact that Fidel was treating them with seriousness and sincerity, trying to make them realize the problems which the Revolution faced and why, for instance, the milk ration had to be cut. They undoubtedly heard him with respect and grasped his main arguments about the whys and wherefores of Cuban shortages. It must have been a four- or five-hour speech, and he started by saying: "I want to begin by telling you that this evening's speech is going to be boring." It was indeed. The text runs for sixty-five pages in a book containing a number of his speeches, *Fidel Castro Speaks.*

It was Fidel's extraordinary good fortune to inherit three television and five radio stations in Havana linked to every Cuban city. The press—eighteen newspapers in Havana alone—was another matter. There is a sad fact that journalists in democratic countries hate or refuse to face: that while a democracy cannot function without a free press, a dictatorship or an authoritarian regime cannot function with a free press.

The Cuban Revolution, as Castro soon realized, was being endangered by freedom of the press. One can argue that there should not have been such a revolution or that it was a bad revolution, but for Castro there was no escaping the dilemma: either revolution or civic freedoms. No autocratic revolutionary leader could have both, and there was no question what his choice was going to be. The struggle was not over the abstract merits of free or controlled mass media; it was a practical matter of the making of a revolution. The fact that there was no censorship during all of 1959 indicated that Castro would have liked to keep a more or less free press if he thought he could safely do so.

Critics of Castro's policies, including the Inter-American Press Association, blandly overlooked the extent to which the Cuban press was controlled from the Machado era to 1959. Government after government maintained a high degree of direction through bribery and subsidies. The revelations in January 1959 of the Batista government's bribes to many prominent Cuban journalists, taken from government archives, were no surprise. Of the nearly sixty newspapers around the island, only six earned their way with subscriptions and advertising. Batista had been paying $217,300 a month to newspapers and $22,000 monthly to individual journalists.

The government had also helped by exempting newspapers from corporate taxes and duties on imported newsprint. It paid a far higher price than business firms for advertisements, which were granted or withheld according to the way a newspaper behaved. The government also paid handsomely for official announcements. Some publishers received government favors on public works contracts.

In fairness, one should add that newspapers and magazines often bit the hand that fed them and were frequently critical of, and damaging to, the Batista regime. Moreover, Cuban journalists had to be graduates of a four-year course in journalism, and their professional standards were high. The weekly magazine *Bohemia,* edited by Miguel Angel Quevedo, a liberal, honest, courageous publisher, had been hostile to Batista and a great help to the revolutionary opposition.

It should not be surprising that Fidel Castro never did and never could understand the workings of a free press such as we have in the United States. He is not alone in this inability; in my career I have found that not only Latin Americans, but Italians, Spaniards, and, quite often, Frenchmen are as cynical and disbelieving. Castro, for instance, could not believe that critical editorials in *The New York Times,* which he knew were written by me, truly expressed my feelings. He was sure that I was writing under orders.

When a hostile historian like former ambassador Philip Bonsal writes, "He [Castro] affected to be convinced that the American press was slavishly at the service of 'imperialist interests,'" he is showing a misunderstanding of Castro. He was not *affecting* to be convinced; he *was* convinced.

The abolition of all kinds of subsidies to the mass media was immediately decreed by the Castro government—except for one, the official organ *Revolución,* which had been published in the Sierra Maestra under Carlos Franqui's editorship. He moved it to the plant of the expropriated Havana *Alerta.* A number of newspapers had to close because they could not exist without government help. The famous old conservative journal *Diario de la Marina,* owned by the Rivera family, courageously began digging its own grave by its independent, anti-Communist, and critical line.

Castro's earliest measures were more reformist than revolutionary. Nothing was more extraordinary—in fact, for most Cubans it was unbelievable—than the immediate elimination of corruption in government and industry. There had never been an honest government in Cuba. It was taken for granted that politicians took office to feather their own and their family's nests; that army officers, police officials, customs agents depended on graft; that businesses had to use bribery or go bankrupt. One must add hastily that there were, of course, many politicians, officers, and officials of the highest integrity—but they were exceptions in the Cuban Republic.

Professor Hugh Thomas subtitles his monumental work on Cuba "The Pursuit of Freedom." I do not believe that the Cuban people, as distinct from the intellectuals and an enlightened minority in the middle upper-class, ever cared enough for civic freedoms to fight for them. They did fight against corruption and for honesty in government for generations. The *Machadato* of 1933–1934 was just such a fight; the *raison d'être* of the *Ortodoxo* party under Eddy Chibás was a struggle for honesty.

In a speech on January 13, 1959, Fidel said that "for the first time there are worthy men at the head of the country who neither sell themselves nor falter nor are intimidated by any threat." No more *entreguismo,* he said—no handing over, no sell-out.

One of the major reasons for the popular support behind the Castro regime has surely been an appreciation of the fact that Fidel Castro and his associates are men who have not enriched themselves or their relatives; who have sent no money to Florida or Switzerland;

who have lived modestly and worked themselves to the limits of human endurance. The charges that they are now, in the 1970s, a "privileged caste" is laughable when compared to what happened before the Revolution. This is a subject to which I will return later.

Stealing from the government became a capital offense. Gambling, the lottery, and the numbers game—the great sources of prerevolutionary graft and corruption—were immediately abolished. Cockfighting, a favorite pastime of the *campesinos,* was suppressed.

In the United States the Watergate affair and all its ramifications, revealing the Nixon Administration as the most corrupt in American history, has started a democratic revulsion against dishonesty in high official circles. At municipal levels there has been no change. In Cuba, nothing short of a revolution could have brought a change from top to bottom.

Prostitution (there were said to be more than fifty thousand prostitutes in Havana alone) was vigorously attacked and with remarkable success. "Before the Revolution," Joe Nicholson, Jr., wrote in an article for the April 1973 *Harper's,* "Havana was one of the world's great centers of vice, a paradise for visiting foreigners but hell for the thousands of women forced by poverty to become prostitutes. I was initially skeptical about Cuba's claim that prostitution has been wiped out. But after six weeks, in which I met only one bedraggled and aging veteran of the Batista era, I was convinced."

The same, incidentally, can be said of beggars. During three weeks in Cuba, just before Nicholson was there, I did not see a single beggar in Havana, nor was I approached by one in other Cuban cities.

Why should Americans have thought it complimentary to Cubans that Havana should be a mecca for gambling, prostitution, blue movies, frozen daiquiris, and luxurious living? For responsible Cuban citizens it was a source of shame and humiliation.

There was a puritanism about the new order which still has not disappeared. It was partly a reaction to previous license, but also a reflection of Fidel Castro's ideas. Not that he is straitlaced, having been divorced and being by no means celibate, but he considered the permissiveness sweeping over the United States and elsewhere to be a sign of decadence.

"Much of the quasi-religious fervor attached to the revolution was spontaneous and not simply an invention of Government propaganda," MacGaffey and Barnett wrote in their book *Cuba.* "From an early date the resemblance of Castro and his bearded followers to

Christ and the Apostles caught the popular imagination. Cheap colored prints of Fidel appeared beside those of the saints in humble homes; statuettes were hawked in the streets. Fidel was regarded as a patron, guardian and guarantor of salvation in a sense that had both religious and secular overtones."

The army was swept away, but police were necessary and those not linked to the tortures and corruption of the past were kept on. Discipline and public order were desperately needed as, day after day, the full extent of the terrorism under Batista came out. It was a moment of horror—but only in Cuba; it was not felt in the United States. Bodies were unearthed; torture chambers uncovered; witness after witness told of fathers, husbands, sons—and wives and daughters, too—tortured and murdered by the Batista authorities. The culprits were known. Batista's terror had been calculatedly open. There were insistent, inescapable demands for revenge. It was extraordinary that the new government was able to keep control and prevent mob vengeance.

In the angry letter written in December 1957 to the exiles who had made the unacceptable "Unity Pact" in Miami, Fidel had said: "The nation must know that justice will be done and that crime will be punished wherever it appears." On February 11, 1958, he signed a "law" in the Sierra Maestra providing for the punishment of *Batistiano* "criminals." Up to the last day of the insurrection Castro had been broadcasting appeals to the Cuban people not to take justice into their own hands. He promised that justice would be administered by the revolutionary government. In January 1959 the Cuban people obeyed—but they would have expected Fidel Castro to fulfill his pledge.

I have mentioned the public vengeance after the flight of Machado in 1933 and of Pérez Jiménez of Venezuela in 1958. It was this type of blood bath that Castro set out to avoid—successfully in the first days thanks to the discipline and firmness of the 26th of July underground in Havana and other cities, and later thanks to the revolutionary justice that was meted out in the trials and executions of the *Batistianos.*

Cries of outrage went up all over the United States when a report got out that Raúl Castro, who had been left in charge of Santiago de Cuba by his brother, had more than seventy prisoners killed and, in Ambassador Bonsal's words, "bulldozed underground without any semblance whatever of a trial." Ray Brennan, in *Castro, Cuba and Justice,* writes: "Practically all the goodwill went smash when Raúl Castro had seventy-four convicted war criminals lined up near Santiago de Cuba, shot, and buried in a ditch dug by a bulldozer. People all over the world were shocked, horrified. Charges were made that the revolutionary government was putting Cuba through a barbaric bloodbath, that political prisoners were being killed after drumhead trials." In 1971 Professor Thomas wrote of the Santiago incident as "still shrouded in some mystery."

So far as I know, no historian of the Revolution was able to get at the truth of this incident—and that included me until around midnight of September 14, 1972, when I was sitting in the Presidential Palace talking with Raúl Castro, his wife Vilma Espín, and Jesús Montané, cabinet minister and coordinator of the Communist Party. It was all so intimate and friendly that I finally got up the nerve to ask Raúl what had really happened on that mysterious and unforgettable night. "I hope I am not being indiscreet," I had said out of politeness before I asked. As I should have expected, Raúl answered instantly, frankly, and with complete assurance in the rightness and justice of his action.

"Yes, I had them executed—about seventy," he said passionately.

> They were sadists, murderers, thieves. We did give them trials, but after the first four had been tried by a due, rather slow process, word came through that difficulties were occurring in the Havana negotiations. So I speeded up the trials; everyone quickly, and we went on without stopping through the night. Twenty-five men were acquitted. The rest were executed and buried quickly.
>
> I have no regrets, and we have nothing at all to be ashamed of for our Revolution. I was accused of being a murderer, but this was necessary; it was justice. Much worse executions have taken place elsewhere without such a clamor. There had been a stream of widows, fathers, mothers coming to us demanding justice. Frank País's parents came to see us and were at the trials. You should have seen them. And not a person in Santiago de Cuba ever protested about what I did.

Then it was all over, Raúl claimed. In his eyes, it was obviously a surgical operation, performed once and for all. He defended at length the Havana executions by his brother. For Fidel too, he argued, it was something that had to be done quickly and got over with. Once it was done, the executions stopped until much later, when the death penalty was restored to meet the emergency of a dangerous phase in the Revolution. Underground opposition, guerrillas in the Sierra de Escambray, and raids by exiles with CIA support alarmed the leaders. Even then, Raúl argued, the death sentence was given sparingly; few were executed.

He resents the reputation he realized he had gained in history for being a killer. "I did not like passing sentences of death," he said.

During the first ten days in Havana there were in fact quick, drumhead courts-martial in which perhaps a hundred officers and men were sentenced and executed. After that, the accused received fair trials, conducted by tribunals of Rebel officers and locally known civilians, with a government prosecutor and a defense counsel. Genuine efforts were made to determine guilt or innocence. Many were released as innocent; many were given prison sentences; and many were condemned to death for murder of prisoners or civilians and for torture.

These executions—a few hundred in the first three weeks, perhaps six hundred in all—aroused a storm of protest and expressions of horror in the American press and Congress. Senator Wayne Morse, normally so understanding, led the furious verbal onslaught. Secretary of State John Foster Dulles considered whether something should not be done to ensure "law and order" in Cuba. Ironically, at the height of the American indignation over the executions, according to Hugh Thomas, it was discovered that four members of the U.S. Embassy in Havana had been honorary members of Batista's SIM (the special military police organization so loathed for its tortures and murders). The FBI was also proved to have had links to the SIM.

Fidel and many other Cubans pointed out that the U.S. Congress, the State Department, and the American press had hardly noted the atrocities of the Batista regime. No Cuban who was not a *Batistiano* felt anything but approval for the executions.

North Americans, imbued with traditional Anglo-Saxon ideas of law and justice, were not qualified to pass judgment on the question of the Cuban trials and executions. Nothing seems so trite, as I said before, as to point out that Cubans are not Anglo-Saxon and that Cuban judiciary practices are not in the Anglo-Saxon tradition. Yet this truism was completely ignored and rejected in the United States at the time.

I know of no better qualified Cuban judge of the matter than the economist Rufo López-Fresquet, who became Castro's treasury minister and defected in 1960 because he was an orthodox economist and a liberal democrat. In his book *My 14 Months with Castro* he sees the revolutionary tribunals as the only way to have avoided a massacre.

"The foreigner, especially the North American," he writes, "put his emphasis on the legal aspects of the revolutionary trials. The

Cuban was interested in moral justice . . . Not many calm voices dedicated themselves to explaining the differences. Dr. Agramonte [the *Ortodoxo* foreign minister] expressed the official consensus: 'We reserve the right to act according to our conscience.' The Cuban Catholic hierarchy was more explicit. 'God also punishes sin with terrible and eternal justice,' said Bishop Boza Masdival."

"The treatment that some American newspapers gave Cuba's revolutionary trials," López-Fresquet adds, "was the first victory for extreme right and extreme left in the battle to alienate America and Cuba."

Fidel Castro was so sure that Americans would understand the reasons for what he was doing, and the justice of the procedures, that he naïvely invited a large group of American journalists to Havana to be present at a trial. To give it maximum publicity, it was held in the sports City Stadium before a crowd of eighteen thousand Cubans. Inevitably, it had the atmosphere of a Roman circus, as one of the three Batista officers on trial for murdering and torturing civilians put it. He was Major Jesús Sosa Blanco, whom I wrote about in the previous chapter, one of the worst torturers and killers of the Batista counterterrorism in Oriente Province. The evidence of his guilt was overwhelming, but he gave a spirited defense and died bravely in front of the American television cameras, giving orders himself to the execution squad. It was one of the most famous TV episodes of our times, and Sosa Blanco, a horrible specimen of humanity, became a martyr for the American public.

Castro was astonished and bitterly angry over the American reaction to the executions. He vented his feelings in his first speech to a great mass audience—on January 21, 1959. It began an unending series of anti-American tirades.

By their own standards, both sides were right, but this was Cuba, and Fidel Castro's action was legally justified by Cuban standards and was approved by Cubans. His resentment was justified, but he was naïve in not realizing why Americans were outraged. A lack of understanding between the two countries was from that time on to play a crucial role in their mutual hostility.

I was in Cuba twice while executions were going on and I did not then, or ever, hear or read of an innocent man being condemned. In the early months of the Spanish Civil War I had seen what injustices could be done when "justice" was left to the people.

I felt critical over the summary nature of the Cuban trials, but otherwise agreed with the American sense of shock in one detail only. This was the use of Herman Marks, a native of Milwaukee, reportedly with a criminal record, as the chief executioner at the Cabañas Fortress in Havana. He had joined the rebels toward the end in the Sierra de Escambray and became a captain in Che Guevara's column. I believe that he was used to avoid having a Cuban in charge of killing Cubans. It was a mechanical, cold-blooded, business-like procedure for Marks, like a butcher killing cattle in an abattoir. I was told that the execution squads were rarely lethal and Marks almost always had to deliver the *coup de grâce.* As Mao Tse-tung more or less said, a revolution is not a tea party.

There was a genuinely reprehensible miscarriage of justice by international standards in March 1959, when forty-four Batista airmen were tried and acquitted in Santiago de Cuba. There was a public clamor against the verdict, for it was known, and later proved, that the airmen had bombed open villages, killed civilians, and destroyed homes, but the prosecution had botched the case. Instead of accepting the verdict with a denunciation, Fidel forced a retrial with a specially chosen revolutionary prosecutor and judges. The men were then all condemned to prison sentences of up to thirty years. Even witnesses for the defense and defense lawyers in the first trial were punished.

"Revolutionary justice," said Castro, "is not based on legal precepts but on moral convictions." It was political vengeance for the bitter memories of the way Batista's aviators had acted. There was no demoralization in the air force before the Revolution; they had gone on killing, destroying, and burning with napalm bombs to the very end of the hostilities.

Amateur psychiatrists were already suspicious of Castro's volubility, his restlessness, his inability to be on time, his phenomenal working day of eighteen to twenty hours. There were confident reports that he kept going on amphetamines; some decided that he was paranoiac or even schizophrenic.

He was one of the most extraordinary characters ever to storm his way onto the hemispheric stage, but he was a phenomenon of nature, normally abnormal, larger than life, remarkably gifted, and all too human. It followed that his defects, while not abnormal, had magnified effects leading to colossal errors.

Fidel was communing with and reaching out to the people from the beginning, while his middle-class, reformist President and cabinet ministers tried for moderation. The vast public meetings and long TV speeches by Castro were making the legal government seem useless. Whether Fidel was deliberately building up mass support, or acting instinctively as his character dictated, or whether (as he claimed to me and others) he was overwhelmed by a spontaneous public demand, cannot ever be decided. There may well have been a mixture of all these factors. My guess is that he suddenly realized his strength and, at the same time, saw that the Urrutia administration would not and could not carry out the social revolution on which he had set his heart. One should add that fame, adulation, and power naturally were going to the young man's head. He was still only thirty-two.

It has been difficult for him, his character being what it is, to delegate power. One had to get at him directly if something had to be done. As he rarely settled down anywhere for any length of time, his ministers and heads of departments had trouble getting in touch with him. The result was often frustration and sometimes chaos.

The first government was a façade behind which was an empty lot. Castro told me that he had given President Urrutia "complete freedom to name his own Cabinet." In the first few months Fidel had just about no direct contacts with the ministers, who were older men, high-minded, honest, patriotic, desirous of creating a brave new Cuba—but out of touch with the youths who had fought at Moncada and in the Sierra Maestra, who had other ideas and hopes. It was as if Castro were giving them rope with which to hang themselves. Yet he told me and my wife in January 1959 what he was telling others and had said often in the Sierra—that he had no ambition to run the government or even to be commander in chief. His ambition, he said to us, was to leave Havana and go back to the Sierra Maestra to establish schools, hospitals, and industries. I believe that he was fooling himself and not being deliberately deceitful. As Mirabeau said of the young Robespierre, "He believes everything he says."

In those days Fidel seemed overwhelmed by the incredible popular adulation and the enormity of the task that was being thrust upon him. His diffidence could not last, nor did he in his heart want it to last, but there was that strange moment of hesitation, of doubt, as if he were half paralyzed while his government carried on feverishly in a land of make-believe.

Prime Minister José Miró Cardona resigned on February 13, pointing out that the Fundamental Law just passed granted the Prime Minister "the powers of a true chief of government which, in my judgment, correspond to those assumed by Dr. Fidel Castro who, because of his historic hierarchy, is the chief of the Revolution."

"Fidel was not at all happy about it," Teresa Casuso, who had been with the Cubans in Mexico City and had now joined the government, was to write in her book *Cuba and Castro.* "In my presence he reminded Celia [Sánchez] that it was she who had insisted on his accepting the post. He went through with it, but unwillingly, for it brought more responsibility and restricted even further his cherished sense of personal freedom."

It is true that every instinct in Fidel Castro's body, from childhood, has been to be free, to be himself, to be in his own particular world, alone—always alone. Like the thin man screaming to get out of the fat man's body, there is a captive spirit inside Fidel screaming to fly off. But he was never again to take even a single look backward on the road of power.

Celia Sánchez, incidentally, had remained by Fidel's side in Havana as in the Sierra Maestra. And there she still is in 1975, working near his office in the Presidential Palace, living in the same house in Varadero as Fidel, but on the floor below.

"Castro avoided going to the [old] Presidential Palace," writes López-Fresquet. "Neither Urrutia nor Castro interfered in the affairs of the Treasury. I was free to act at my own discretion. At least on the surface, the other ministers appeared to enjoy similar liberties."

Then, on February 16, 1959, Castro became Prime Minister. As López-Fresquet put it, he "really supplanted Urrutia and not Miró Cardona . . . The only power remaining to President Urrutia . . . was that of signing laws and decrees."

Fidel gradually became disrespectful and even contemptuous of the President. As a result, Urrutia stopped attending cabinet meetings and used the one power remaining to him: he delayed signing laws that required his signature to become legal. By so doing, he created an impossible situation, alienating all the ministers, wrote López-Fresquet.

It will be recalled that Urrutia was chosen because, as a magistrate, he had voted to exonerate the *Granma* and Santiago de Cuba rebels.

"It led to the appointment of a bad President," Che Guevara wrote in 1959, "a man incapable of understanding the revolutionary process, incapable of digesting the profundity of a revolution which was not made for his reactionary mentality."

On the whole, this was a logical judgment, for Urrutia certainly did not believe in radical revolution and he was sabotaging the Castroites with the best of intentions. The problem was more than the simple fact that he was anti-Communist and alarmed by the Communist growth. Had he worked quietly within the cabinet he could, at least, have avoided his humiliating public disgrace. On two occasions in June 1959 he publicly attacked the Communists. On July 13, in a television interview, he not only did so again in the strongest terms ("The Communists are inflicting terrible harm on Cuba") but indicated that Castro felt as he did. Moreover, he made it clear that he would go on attacking Communism.

It was a blatant attempt to pit Castro against the Communists at a time when Fidel was placing great emphasis on unity. However, on past services and as an unquestionably patriotic, well-intentioned man, he did not deserve to be driven out of office so ignominiously.

The anti-Communist interview that Urrutia gave on July 13 was the last straw for Fidel Castro. On the morning of the seventeenth he went on television to announce his resignation as Prime Minister. It was a safe calculation. The public clamor was such that the President took refuge in the Venezuelan Embassy.

Fidel did not make a second mistake on the presidency. He chose Osvaldo Dorticós Torrado, a distinguished and prosperous lawyer and aristocrat, who had led the anti-Batista underground in Cienfuegos, where he was born. Dorticós was then forty, an advanced age for the Castroites. He was drafting the revolutionary laws and was soon to be handling much of the economic planning. As a law student he had been a PSP (Communist Party) organization secretary in Cienfuegos, but had long ceased to be a party member. I never could see—and I talked to him often—that he had any feeling about Communism, but, of course, he easily followed Fidel into Marxism-Leninism. According to the French-Polish journalist K. S. Karol, Dorticós' "intimacy with Socialist writings from Marx to Gramsci is extremely impressive." He proved the most successful appointment that Castro ever made—loyal, brilliant, and steady as a rock.

National fervor was allowed to build up after Fidel's resignation until, at a huge anniversary celebration on July 26, Dorticós announced to a delirious crowd that Fidel Castro had yielded to popular demand and would resume his post as Prime Minister.

For many historians of the Cuban Revolution, what Theodore Draper called "the real point of no return in Cuba" came with the Hubert Matos affair in October 1959. After that, the theory goes, the Revolution became extremist, open to the Communists, populist, anti-democratic, anti-Yankee, et cetera. Matos was depicted as a hero of the Sierra Maestra, martyrized for being anti-Communist.

This is an arbitrary, chronological opinion based on misunderstanding and ignorance of many facts about the case and about the dangerous situation that Matos created at a critical moment in the Revolution.

Like many liberal-minded Cubans, he had become alarmed over the growing penetration and influence of the Cuban Communists. He made his first public anti-Communist speech as early as June 8, 1959, in which he lumped the Moncada–Sierra Maestra group with the PSP, although none of them were Communists.

López-Fresquet, then treasury minister, reveals in his book that when he was in Camagüey (where Hubert Matos was military commander) at the beginning of September 1959, Matos talked to him all one night. He said that there was a Communist conspiracy, but he did not think that Fidel was involved or knew of its extent.

"Raúl, I was informed [by Matos], was the leader of the cabal and, in Matos's opinion, was prepared to kill his brother if need be." (According to López-Fresquet, Matos told the same story to Dr. Andrés Valdespino, undersecretary of the treasury.)

"The [Camagüey] provincial leaders of the 26th of July Movement (who, I had noticed, were very close to Matos) came to see me," the former minister adds. "They talked much as Matos had done."

The next day López-Fresquet heard Matos make an anti-Communist speech at a peasant rally, and "I could see he was trying to gain a following." Matos later told him that "his plan was to inform Castro as soon as possible, in order to save him and the Revolution." During two more days, López-Fresquet writes, Matos talked "with great passion" in the same vein. The minister returned to Havana without being able "to form a clear picture of Matos's political ideas." He said nothing.

On October 15 Raúl Castro joined the cabinet as minister of the armed forces (a post he still holds in 1975). To Hubert Matos, this was sinister and confirmed his worst fears. His mind must have been warped by his emotions. Raúl and Fidel have always been as close and affectionate as two brothers can possibly be. The idea that Raúl could dream of killing Fidel was madness.

Four days later Matos wrote a letter of resignation to Castro as commander in chief. In itself the document seemed unexceptional, saying that he did not want to become an obstacle to the Revolution and ending: "Wishing you every success for yourself and in your revolutionary efforts for the country." It was, however, a clear attack on the Communists, and Matos complained that "great men begin to decline when they cease to be just."

Most of the army leaders in Camagüey, influenced, as Castro saw it, by Matos, likewise sent in their resignations. Camagüey Province was the major cattle region of Cuba. A whole, vital area of the island was, in the eyes of the Castroites, defecting at a delicate and critical juncture of the Revolution. This to them was treachery, containing the threat of a military uprising. Matos had, in fact, written a letter to be circulated secretly after his arrest, which he foresaw, in which he said that he would not have ordered his soldiers to fire "against anyone, not even against the thugs you [Castro] may send."

Fidel did not know of this letter. According to López-Fresquet, his first reaction on receiving the letter of resignation was to say that Matos was "an honest revolutionary" and that he had great affection for him. If he felt that way on October 19, he didn't on the twentieth, for he went down to Camagüey himself to arrest Hubert Matos.

Fidel could not have been concerned one way or another, as so many believed, about the Communist issue. For him, the fate of the Revolution was at stake. He had not yet consolidated his power.

The Matos case had been preceded by the defection of Major José Luis Díaz Lanz, dismissed head of Castro's air force, on June 29. In the United States, Díaz Lanz was to feed the belief in a Communist takeover.

A dangerous guerrilla movement of about a thousand rebels had begun to operate in the Sierra de Escambray, and they were not the only ones. The Cuban exiles and the CIA were active in counterrevolution. Castro, as always, and in this case with good reason, was suspicious of the United States, although presumably wrong in fearing that Hubert Matos was getting encouragement from the Americans.

It was a period when he was working out his policy of "unity," which included the Communists in the power structure. In the best of circumstances, what Hubert Matos was trying to do would have split the Revolution wide open. In fact, there was a serious rift with some of the leaders who were loyal to Fidel Castro but upset by the drift toward Communism.

Matos had hardly been arrested and jailed when tragedy and treachery dealt two hard blows.

On the night of October 25, Camilo Cienfuegos took a light plane to go to Havana, a flight that is partly over water. He was never heard from again. After Fidel Castro he was the most popular hero of the Revolution, brave, gay, and handsome with his long, flowing beard. Che Guevara, in his dedication to Camilo of his book *La Guerra de guerrillas,* calls him "the greatest of the guerrilla leaders who came out of this revolution, the revolutionary without flaw and the brotherly friend. Camilo was the companion of a hundred battles, Fidel's trusted man in the difficult moments of the war, and the fighter who always made out of his self-sacrifice an instrument to temper his character and forge the will of his troops. . . .

"In this war of liberation, there was no soldier comparable to Camilo."

This tribute, taken with Fidel's moving elegy, gives a true measure of what sort of man Camilo Cienfuegos was and what he meant to the Revolution and to his comrades. It is one of the ironies of the historiography of the Cuban Revolution that a man held so dear by Fidel Castro and his other companions should be hinted at darkly, and in so many accounts, as a possible victim of Fidel's sinister machinations.

It was Che, in his *Guerrilla Warfare,* who doubtless explained the cause of Camilo's death as well as anyone could.

"The enemy killed him," he wrote; "they killed him because they wanted him dead; because the pilots could not acquire all the experience necessary; because, weighed down by overwork, he wanted to be back in Havana in a few hours . . . and he was killed by his character. Camilo did not heed danger."

Former ambassador Philip Bonsal writes more matter-of-factly that "he had paid the price for his recklessness in flying in a plane of doubtful airworthiness with a semiskilled pilot late in the evening under unfavorable weather conditions."

Camilo was thought to have been anti-Communist insofar as he had any politics, but he was also fanatically loyal to Fidel. He had supported Castro to the hilt in the Hubert Matos affair. His death, in fact, was the most grievous blow of its kind since the death of Frank País and the greatest personal loss to Fidel until Che Guevara's death in 1967.

There had been added tension over Matos when, on October 21, Major Díaz Lanz flew a B-25 bomber from Florida over Havana where he dropped thousands of leaflets calling Castro a Communist. He does not seem to have dropped any bombs, although some missiles exploded. There was anti-aircraft fire from a Cuban frigate. Three people were killed and forty-five wounded, probably from the ground fire.

Two days later it was flatly asserted that the casualties were caused by bombs. This provided a powerful bit of propaganda against the United States which has gone irretrievably into the mythology of the Revolution. Castro made a virulent speech to an enormous audience on October 26 in Havana.

"It [the speech] was a repulsive spectacle of mass hatred and inspired by the man wholly and knowingly responsible for the lies used to arouse mob passions," writes ex-Ambassador Bonsal.

How Díaz Lanz got the plane is still a mystery. It was one ordered by Batista in the United States but never delivered. The Cubans were all the more suspicious because Díaz Lanz had been given a public hearing by the witch-hunting Senate Internal Security Subcommittee in order to tell the world that the Communists were taking over in Cuba. His testimony, when read in cold print and with knowledge of the facts, was full of inaccuracies, rumors, malicious gossip, and some facts. It was misleading, but the senators and much of the American press loved it.

Hugh Thomas writes that Díaz Lanz was "certainly in contact with" Hubert Matos. Fidel thought so.

Taking all the facts into consideration, the glorification of Hubert Matos and the vilification of Fidel Castro over his case in the United States were unjustified. One can argue that Fidel was unnecessarily harsh. The trial lasted until the end of December 1959. Castro handled the prosecution himself and, as López-Fresquet wrote; "he was implacable." Matos got a twenty-year sentence and the twenty-one officers who resigned with him two to seven years. The evidence given at the trial would not have stood up in a Western court of law, but this was a Cuban court in the midst of a perilous revolution. How could the fears, suspicions, and dangers aroused by Matos be presented in the form of legal evidence?

The psychology behind the judgment was missed by us onlookers at the time. I did not fully grasp the emotional, revolutionary logic behind the Matos affair until it came to me in a flash in 1972 when talking to Juan Almeida about the then recent defection of Carlos Franqui. Almeida's clear, simple, unquestioning judgment was that Franqui could never have been loyal. Once loyal, always loyal—and vice versa. This, I could see, was an inviolable revolutionary law. There is also more than a touch of the Spanish temperament involved where Cubans are concerned.

Matos was at first sent to the same *presidio* on the Isle of Pines where Castro had been imprisoned after Moncada. The prisons of the island have since been closed, but the prisoners were transferred to the mainland. Within a few years Matos was broken in health, his son told me. On the family's behalf I wrote a letter to Fidel arguing that he would gain a propaganda victory if he released Matos. Castro never answers letters, and certainly he never took any advice from me. I must have written a half dozen letters to Fidel about political prisoners, and always in vain. I find the retention still, in 1975, of many thousands of political prisoners to be the ugliest feature of the Revolution.

One immediate result of the Matos affair was that Fidel created a popular militia at the end of October 1959. It was formed of 150,000 volunteers, men and women, and run by army officers. This period also saw the beginning of an excellent military intelligence organization, the G2, under the brilliant and efficient Ramiro Valdés, with Castro since Moncada, Mexico, and the Sierra Maestra. Valdés was a close friend of Che Guevara.

There was an immediate purge of the judicial system in which "counterrevolutionary" judges were dismissed. "Revolutionary tribunals" were set up with wide powers, including the right to pass death sentences. Ordinary courts lost much of their authority. Lawyers who defended those accused of being counterrevolutionary ran the danger of prosecution themselves.

Fidel attacked the old system on December 16, 1959. "There is no reason why all these courts and judges should exist today," he said. Three days later eight supreme court justices resigned. Many lawyers and magistrates fled abroad. A new law was passed giving President Dorticós authority to name new judges and reorganize the whole judicial system. Within a few months the Cuban judiciary was completely "revolutionary." In 1973 another, and hopefully permanent, judicial system was adopted as a part of the forthcoming constitution —but it is still revolutionary and political. It was one of the first elements of Cuban society to respond to an invariable law of politics, i.e., an independent judiciary cannot exist in an authoritarian state —Communist, fascist, militaristic, or revolutionary. There can be no separation of powers.

By an inescapable dialectic, revolution brings counterrevolution. The displaced establishment naturally fights for its former status, property and wealth, privileges and power. In Cuba's case, the Americans tried to hold on to, and then get back, the power and property they were losing. Just to survive, Fidel Castro was going to need a strong military and police establishment and an authoritarian government. This was by no means clear to him or to anybody when the Revolution began. Some enemies guessed rightly, although prematurely and for the wrong reasons, that he would seek the solution to his problems in Communism.

Habeas corpus was suspended in November 1959. By the end of that year there were perhaps as many as ten thousand political prisoners in jail. It was a time of conspiracies, suspicions, and underground activities from sabotage to guerrilla fighting in the Sierra de Escambray and the mountains of Pinar del Río and Las Villas. The CIA was landing groups of exile fighters by sea and air and sending in arms, material for sabotage, and radio transmitters for espionage.

Szulc and Meyer in their book on the Bay of Pigs, *The Cuban Invasion,* claimed that "all these new anti-Castro groups had contact with the American Embassy in Havana."

The prisons were being filled to overcrowding. Latin American prisons are harsh. From whatever I could learn and what I believe, torture was not used. However, Hugh Thomas in his book *Cuba* writes: "Treatment by guards, sanitary arrangements, food were all bad. There were far more prisoners now than Batista ever had . . . The interrogation rooms of the G2 might be more sophisticated than the torture chambers of Batista's SIM, but they were scarcely less vile."

The counterterrorism of the Castro regime did not compare to Batista's, when a great majority of Cubans were sickened by what they saw and learned. There were a number of well-publicized executions under Castro, but in no known case preceded, as before the Revolution, by torture. The counterrevolution against Castro, in fact, never won more than a small minority of Cubans and ceased to be effective anywhere in Cuba after the Bay of Pigs invasion in 1961.

For one thing, Fidel gradually succeeded in winning over the people of Cuba to an understanding and acceptance of the Revolution, despite the hardships, mistakes, deprivations, and disappointments that accompanied its evolution. There was nothing in the way he operated that was more inspired than the realization that he had had from the beginning of his career as a revolutionary, that a revolution would be possible only if the people—that is to say, the great majority of Cubans—could be united. Neither he nor the Cuban Revolution is understandable if this is not kept in mind.

Fidel Castro did not himself realize in 1959 that he and his comrades were embarking on what is surely the most difficult of all exercises in the governance of men and nations—the political, economic, and social transformation of a country by a radical social revolution.

CHAPTER 7

Trial and Error

Of course we have done a host of silly things; no one knows that better than I do.
—Lenin to Alfred Rosmer in *Lenin's Moscow*

Books were written, gallons of ink flowed, and an extraordinary amount of oratory was expended in the first years of the Revolution to say that Fidel Castro had betrayed the Cuban nation and people. Trotsky's phrase "a revolution betrayed" was heard and read everywhere. Washington was to make it the main moral excuse for the Bay of Pigs invasion.

The charge never made a great deal of sense, because it was based on a special choice of promises and a basic misunderstanding (which Castro shared up to a point) about how a social revolution is made, and especially how Cuba's was going to have to be made.

At this late date there is no profit in going over the bewildering, contradictory, and always changing series of *Fidelista* programs from the time of Moncada and Mexico, through the Sierra Maestra, and into the early years of the Revolution. Fidel "promised one kind of revolution and made another," as Theodore Draper put it in an often-quoted epigram.

There is a certain academic interest in following the progress of Castro's proclaimed ideas; a certain fascination in trying to figure out what was deliberately misleading and what was Fidel's sincere belief at a given time that this or that could and should be done; and for opponents, exiles, critics, and Washington, a joyous polemical array of sticks with which to beat Fidel Castro over the head. These articles, books, and white papers had an ephemeral interest during the first five years of the Revolution. Today they are of concern mainly to specializing students.

Most of the later critical emphasis was put on the economic

difficulties, mistakes, and failures of the Castro regime in the 1960s and on its authoritarian and military character. This, too, is a case of using inadequate and unsuitable measures by which to gauge without qualifications a unique state of affairs in which economics and militarism played subordinate roles.

My attitude at all times has been that Fidel Castro was consistent in striving for the goal which was basic to his career and ideals: a radical social revolution, independent of the United States. He did not know how to go about it; his ideas changed; he tried different solutions. And in 1975 he is still trying, still changing, still sure of himself, and perhaps—just perhaps—at last on the right track.

Had he compromised on his social revolution, as Mexico and Bolivia have done; had he come to terms with the United States; had he maintained the corporate-capitalistic-congressional prerevolutionary Cuban system—then, indeed, he would have "betrayed the revolution."

Anyway, do not all politicians and statesmen promise the earth before they take office? Need we compare what Lyndon Johnson promised he would do, or not do, in Vietnam with what he did? What policies Nixon promised in 1968 and 1972, and what he did? No doubt thousands of "betrayals" by thousands of politicians are wrong, but why should a special case be made out of Fidel Castro? It is wrong to judge statesmen by such simplistic standards. The judgment of history on Richard Nixon and Fidel Castro will not be based on broken promises.

Fidel has had some strikingly original ideas, but not in ideology. He has always been impatient with what he called "straitjackets." His Marxism-Leninism is heterodox; he will twist and mold it as *he* pleases, not as the orthodox Cuban, Russian, or Chinese Communists advise. His various programs and manifestos, from *History Will Absolve Me* in 1954 onward, (as Theodore Draper easily demonstrates) are not new or original. The ideas were borrowed and then partly adapted or dropped.

Scholars have traced Marxist ideas to pre-Marxist socialists. What counted was how Marx applied the ideas. What mattered in Cuba was how Fidel Castro applied old ideas. "If reality does not adapt itself to ideas," Hegel wrote, "so much the worse for reality." What made Fidel Castro special was that he moved from ideas into practice. He was not a revolutionary thinker; he was an activist using revolutionary ideas which, in some cases, were innovations.

Many of the ideas in the early manifestos and programs were not revolutionary. A prime example was the repeated promise to hold elections. Once in Havana, Castro saw three things: that he had the power to refuse to hold elections; that there was no popular demand for them; and most important, that he could not hold elections and proceed with his drastic, anti-American social revolution. To accept what would have been a strong Cuban congressional opposition, fighting against his revolutionary policies at every step, threatening his power, backed by a powerful group of newspapers and magazines, with the Yankee colossus on the opposition's side, was impossible, given his aims and ideas.

Salvador Allende's experience in Chile was to provide a good example of the impossibility of making a socialist revolution with congressional opposition and an independent military.

If elections made sense in 1959 to Castro's critics in Cuba and the United States, they will not to history. At least, Castro never perpetrated the hypocrisy of a plebiscite, as in Franco's Spain, Greece, and other totalitarian regimes. He too in those early years could have achieved a 95 percent victory.

Fidel's definitive if demagogic pronouncement on popular elections came in his May Day speech of 1961:

> A revolution expressing the will of the people is an election every day, not every four years; it is a constant meeting with the people, like this meeting . . . What do they want? Elections with pictures on lampposts? The Revolution has exchanged the conception of pseudodemocracy for direct government by the people . . . Do the people now have time for elections? No! What were the political parties? Just an expression of class interests. Here there is just one class, the humble; that class is in power, and so is not interested in the ambition of an exploiting minority to get back in power. Those people would have no chance at all in an election. The Revolution has no time to waste in such foolishness.

The 1940 constitution was buried by Castro in that same May Day speech (which, significantly, came in the aftermath of the Bay of Pigs invasion):

> To those who talk to us about the 1940 Constitution, we say that the 1940 Constitution is already too outdated and old for us. We have advanced too far for that short section of the 1940 Constitution that was good for its time but which was never carried out. That Constitution has been left behind by this revolution which, as we have said, is a socialist revolution. We must talk of a new constitution . . . corresponding to a new social system without the exploitation of man by

> man. That new social system is called socialism, and this constitution will therefore be a socialist constitution.

This was, incidentally, the first official proclamation of the regime's socialist nature. There is still no constitution in 1975, but much work has been done on it by a committee headed by the old guard Communist Blas Roca.

Freedom of the press was completely abolished in the spring of 1960, with virtually no public protest. It has been one of the most puzzling features of the Cuban Revolution to Americans that civic liberties could have been taken away one by one without any but the mildest objections from the Cuban people as a whole. There were, of course, the thousands who went into exile and prison, but there never was any serious internal reaction. Cubans did not place the value on civic liberties that Americans did, or that Americans thought the Cubans did. This was one of the many misunderstandings and miscalculations of American policy toward Castro's Cuba. The great majority of Cubans—peasants, agricultural and industrial workers, artisans, shopkeepers, housewives—would not have known of the Sierra Maestra programs, nor would they have thought of what to expect, except that they hoped for something better than they had.

If the Cubans really wanted the political freedoms that Fidel had promised, would they not have managed a far stronger opposition than they did to the centralizing power? I think that this explains what Ambassador Bonsal calls "the ease with which Castro established a thoroughgoing personal dictatorship over a society which seemed long to have worked and hoped for democracy even though it had not, except fleetingly, enjoyed its substance."

Bonsal gives one reason for what happened when he writes that "Cubans of all classes, especially the wealthy, had climbed on the Castro bandwagon and *were reaching for the steering wheel*" (my italics). None of them knew Fidel personally, which made a great difference, for this was going to be *his* revolution.

In one of his most acute judgments in his massive work on Cuba, Hugh Thomas writes: "A strong democratic and constitutional regime would by the nature of things have received much support from the enlightened section in the government of the U.S.; aid, technical assistance, investment would have poured in; no doubt the Cuban standard of living would have gone up; no doubt most Cubans, above all most middle-class Cubans, but much of the working class too, would have enjoyed a better life; but it would not have been a

Cuban life; it would have been a department of U.S. life, with all its *splendeurs et misères.*"

One of the greatest mistakes that the U.S. government made toward the Castro regime in the beginning is contained in the following sentence from Philip Bonsal's book: "I envisaged my task [on commencing his ambassadorship in February 1959] as one of convincing the new Cuban leaders of the important role the American relationship might continue to play in the improvement of the welfare of the Cuban people as well as of the receptivity I believed that the United States Government and private American interests would wish to show toward reasoned Cuban proposals for alterations in the relationship."

But Castro, as I keep pointing out, was going to make a social revolution! This much he had always made clear. It was also clear that his generation of Cubans was extremely nationalistic and anti-American.

What difference, if any, a true understanding of Castro's revolutionary purposes could have made is beyond knowing, but American policy would at least have been more realistic than the impossible and even naïve task which Ambassador Bonsal says he set for himself. However, it was true that the full extent of Fidel's anti-Americanism could not have been divined at that early stage.

"I did not then realize," Bonsal writes, "to what extent hatred for all things American dominated Castro's spirit, how grossly he was to exaggerate the alleged misdeeds and motivation of the 'imperialists,' and how determined he was to reject any idea of rectification and reform in order to bring about a complete break with the United States."

Within the framework of American policy, aims, and hopes, there is no question that Washington, and, in Havana, Ambassador Bonsal, "endeavored through as many channels as possible to convey goodwill and a readiness to enter into serious negotiations on any matters the Cuban regime might wish to raise." Unfortunately, it was "a dialogue of the deaf." There was no basis for understanding, let alone agreement.

Bonsal did realize that "in the spring of 1959 he [Castro] was far from having fully discovered himself." How could anybody know where the Revolution was going when Fidel Castro himself did not know?

During Castro's April 1959 trip to the United States, his minister of the treasury Rufo López-Fresquet, Felipe Pazos, president of the National Bank, and other Cuban economists, whom Castro had taken along, met a group of two hundred important American businessmen in Washington. López-Fresquet's comment in his book explains as well as anything I have read why there was an unbridgeable gulf between the moderate, liberal, democratic, sincerely patriotic middle-class Cubans and Fidel Castro.

"We talked of Cuba's beautiful future," López-Fresquet wrote, "and beautiful it could have been if we had been permitted to win the confidence of American business. In my opinion, Castro's greatest crime was not merely to have destroyed what existed; he also impeded the creation of the Cuba which was then possible."

Fidel would ask: "Beautiful for whom?" Everything for which he and his followers had fought would have been thrown away. The old Cuba would have been restored, cleaned up, liberalized, with civic freedoms, honest elections, a truly representative Congress and government, and all of it as closely linked to and dependent on the United States as ever. In April 1959 Castro was still far from his socialism and his Marxism-Leninism, but he had fought for a revolution whose benefits, as he saw them, would go to the masses, not the élite, and he had fought for independence from the United States. That a man so intelligent and experienced as Rufo López-Fresquet should still, as late as 1965 when he wrote his book, not have realized this shows how hopelessly Cubans misunderstood each other in the formative years of the Revolution.

The major error we all made—myself certainly and Fidel Castro probably—was not to see that in the historic conjuncture that Castro faced on taking power he would find no solution other than socialism. The turning to Russia was an economic necessity, not an ideological choice. On the Kremlin's part, it was an imperative political response in the existing cold war.

"Revolution is the art of uniting forces; revolution is the art of agglutinating forces in order to engage in the decisive battles against imperialism," Fidel said in a speech in Concepción, Chile, on November 18, 1971. "No revolution, no [revolutionary] process can indulge in the luxury of excluding any force, in undervaluating any force. No revolution can indulge in the luxury of dispensing with the word *sumar* [to total up]. And one of the facts that determined the success of the Cuban Revolution . . . was the policy of unite, unite, unite. Total up incessantly! And it was not easy . . . But we in our movement were the defenders of the thesis of extension [*amplitud*] and fullness, the totality of forces . . . If we, a small group, had followed a policy of closed doors, we would have been isolated; we would never have triumphed."

(It will be noted that many quotations given in this book are from Fidel Castro's speeches, interviews, and discussions on his trip to Chile in November 1971. By then he had thought long and deeply and gone through many years of travail, culminating in the trauma of the 1970 sugar harvest. What he said in Chile—every word of which has been published—contains the fruits of his experiences and the basis on which he has since been constructing a more institutionalized revolution.)

Cuban unity, it can and has been argued, is the other side of the coin of personal power. To get the reins of power in his own hands, Fidel needed unity.

The Communist PSP, in the beginning, offered experienced cadres and the invaluable connection with the Soviet Union. As Castro's thinking gradually went along socialist lines, the obvious way to achieve the unity which obsessed him was through a Communist regime. Of course, many factors—ideological, political, economic, foreign policy—played their roles.

The 26th of July Movement was not a political party and never became one. It was a heterogeneous, unorganized movement, recently swelled by enthusiastic recruits. The role it played from its inception in 1955 to its enforced amalgamation with the Communists in 1961 was a confused one. Fidel was already dissatisfied with its resistance work when I visited him in the Sierra Maestra in February 1957. He had summoned the Havana and Santiago leaders to a meeting at that same time. The Movement was always involved in the conflict between the Sierra and the Plain.

Consequently, when it came to making the sort of revolution that Castro wanted to make, he could not rely on the 26th of July Movement.

Another organization, in which the Movement had taken a dominant role after the triumph of the Revolution, was to succumb to Castro's insistence on unity. The victory went to the Cuban Communists. The CTC, the nationwide workers' confederation, was at first dominated by the 26th of July's Frente Obrero Humanista (Humanist Workers' Front). The Movement also solidly controlled the delegates to the tenth congress of the CTC, held in November 1959. The PSP had been working in vain all year for "unity slates," but they were defeated in twenty-seven out of thirty-three constituent federations. Their chief opponent was David Salvador, who was the underground 26th of July Movement's labor leader during the insurrection. Batista had imprisoned him. After the victory Fidel made him secretary general of the CTC.

The November congress of the Confederation was stormy. The

Communists demanded three members on the executive board, but the "unity slate" was defeated by an overwhelming majority and a second slate with no Communists on it was approved. It was a democratic but unwise move. Fidel went to the congress, mounted the podium, berated the members for their lack of unity, and insisted that a board be chosen containing PSP representation.

This was in the midst of the Hubert Matos trial, and like much that was happening then, made the period a crucial one in the Revolution. A *Comisión Depuradora* was formed which purged the CTC leadership of independents and anti-Communists. The confederation resigned from the Inter-American Regional Organization of trade unions, to which the AFL and the CIO belonged and which Cubans were sure was run by the Americans. Certainly, it was anti-Communist.

In Havana a Communist-oriented CTC board of thirteen members was elected. The Communist newspaper, *Hoy*, began to attack David Salvador. He joined the underground resistance once again, this time against Castro. Industrial sabotage, bombings, and even killings were at their height. Later Salvador tried to flee by boat, but was caught and he has been serving a long prison sentence. Castro, as I have said, never forgives defectors, whatever they have done for him in the past.

As with every facet of the Revolution, Fidel Castro got his way. When the Communists, in their turn, tried to monopolize the CTC, he slapped them down.

The more one studies the dramatic events of the first few years, the greater the personal role of Fidel Castro turns out to be. Not only was he taking measures without consulting the 26th of July Movement, the PSP, or his own cabinet ministers, but he was more radical, more leftist than any of these groups would have wanted. The only approbation came from his faithful, inexperienced Rebel Army commanders and comrades, some of them women, from the Sierra Maestra.

The picture so confidently drawn and believed in the United States of an amateurish, compliant Fidel Castro taking advice and orders from the experienced, disciplined Cuban Communists is almost ludicrous in light of the known facts.

Exactly what part Che Guevara and Raúl Castro played in deciding Fidel to take Marxist-type actions is not clear, but it must have been important. Both were embracing a sort of personal (not organizational, not PSP) form of Marxism. The fact that Raúl Castro was briefly a member of the Communist Youth in 1953 was of no practical meaning in 1959 and 1960. He was disdainful of the old guard Cuban Communists, and I know of one occasion in mid-1959 when he was so angry that he exploded against them in a cabinet meeting and said that if they continued what they were doing he would "cut their throats."

At the same time, Raúl Castro did have young Communists of his own choosing around him in the Rebel Army. He, as Che Guevara did, would have quoted approvingly Danton's slogan, *De l'audace, de l'audace et toujours de l'audace.* But both Raúl and Che were devoted and loyal followers of Fidel, and it was Fidel who made the fateful decisions of those first two revolutionary years.

The slow, intricate, and tortured drift of the Cuban Revolution into Marxism-Leninism was so complex and so important that it must be given extended treatment in a chapter of its own. At this point it is perhaps enough to watch "the specter of Communism" become a reality.

There were many witnesses to the way Fidel Castro thought and spoke in the Sierra Maestra. Not one, not even Che Guevara, who wrote extensively of the period, could claim that Fidel acted like someone who was converted to the ideas of the *Communist Manifesto.* Yet, to some degree, Castro's reading, friendships, and career were a preparation for what happened. Marxism was in the air of the Sierra Maestra. It was read, discussed, argued. Che Guevara, as his first wife, Hilda Gadea, was to write, had steeped himself in the literature of socialism when he was in Guatemala and Mexico. He and Raúl Castro were convinced Marxists in the Sierra, but not Communists. Raúl had never rejoined the party, and Che never had been a member.

Ambassador Bonsal, writing of the early period, said: "There was no serious evidence of effective Communist influence upon the new Cuban Government, either from the local Communist Party or from abroad."

Raúl Roa, who came over from exile in Mexico City immediately and was soon to become foreign minister, wrote of the dawning revolution in the preface to a collection of articles, *En Pie* (1959), as having "its own roots, programs and curriculum. It does not stem from Rousseau, George Washington or Marx." (Roa, a former professor, was twenty years older than Castro and a veteran of the *Machadato,* from which time he has been bitterly anti-Yankee. No speaker at the United Nations for these past sixteen years has matched Raúl Roa in venomous attacks on the United States. He is, incidentally, much the most erudite of the Castro regime's officials.)

Fidel was denying again and again throughout 1959 that he was a Communist or had any intention of becoming one. That he was not a Communist until he said that he was, in December 1961, can be taken as the truth. Affairs reached a point from mid-1960 onward when it could be argued that he might just as well have been—but he was not committed.

The first step, anyway, was a form of socialism. It began, Raúl Castro put it to me, with the Agrarian Reform Law of May 17, 1959. Thousands of cattle ranches, sugar plantations, poultry farms, mills, farming equipment, and the like were expropriated. In theory, payment was to be in bonds, but they never materialized. "It broke the backbone of power of the exploiting classes and imperialism in our country," in the Marxist language of *Granma* in 1973. The drift into socialism was a "process," Castro said to me in 1963, using a favorite word. He agreed that the summer of 1960 (when Guevara first referred to the Revolution as Marxist and socialist) could have been the watershed.

Yet the appearance of Cuba being in the Communist fold in 1961 was deceptive. Not a single member of the cabinet was Communist. Although Communists held many posts in government departments, their alleged control over the army and INRA (the national agrarian institute) was greatly exaggerated. Not for a moment did Fidel Castro lose the power to crush the Cuban Communist Party, the PSP.

One can understand the role of the Communists and Communism in the 1960s by realizing that they were the instruments and methods Castro picked with which to make his revolution. When Fidel and the *barbudos* came down from the Sierra Maestra in January 1959, the PSP's membership was less than twenty thousand. However, in October 1963, Fidel said to me that the party "had men who were truly revolutionary, loyal, honest and trained. I needed them." The PSP did have a unique reputation for honesty.

Andrés Suárez's documentation in his 1967 book *Castroism and Communism* shows that all those drastic socialist and revolutionary measures being taken in the first years were made without even informing the PSP Old Guard, let alone consulting them. Ironically, the Communists profited greatly by the fact that so many Americans —Ambassadors Gardner and Smith, a number of senators, many organs of the mass media—had labeled the Castroites as Communists in the Sierra Maestra, as had Batista.

"The growing role of the Communists was due to the radicalization of the revolution and the fact that they alone possessed a disciplined organization," writes Boris Goldenberg in his book *The Cuban Revolution and Latin America.* Yet Goldenberg, like everybody else, describes how undisciplined, disorganized, and amateurish the Revolution was. The Communists did not bring to it the virtues and qualities they were supposed to, or else they could not exercise them.

The trumpeting from the Cuban rooftop to the world that Communism was openly and doctrinally the political system of the Revolution came in the notorious and perennially misunderstood speech of Fidel's on the night of December 1–2, 1961. It will be discussed more fully in a later chapter. The gist of the sensational event was that in a rambling, confused, five-hour speech, Fidel, with unbelievable humility, regretted that he had not, at Havana University and later, realized the virtues of Communism as he now did. He thumped the table in front of him and, in the sentence that became so famous, shouted: "I am a Marxist-Leninist and I shall be a Marxist-Leninist until the last day of my life." As of 1975, it really looks as though he will be.

In September 1972 Raúl Castro argued with me that, if anything, Fidel should have made the statement sooner. The Revolution had earlier reached a point where this was the reality. Raúl was not interested in my criticisms of the *way* his brother had made the statement, almost boasting that he had been deliberately deceitful, cunning, and scheming all along, and giving his innumerable enemies the chance to pick isolated sentences out of context to have him confess that he had been a Communist back at Havana University. He had not, and he did not say so in his speech, but a legend was created which will never die.

The true importance of the speech was to place the Cuban Revolution irrevocably in the Communist system, domestically and internationally. It did not mean that Cuba had become a satellite of the Soviet Union or that Fidel Castro was now a puppet whose strings would be pulled by the Kremlin. This was not, to their discomfiture, realized by some of the old guard PSP leaders and specifically by Aníbal Escalante, secretary general of the party and a Communist of thirty years' standing.

During 1961 the PSP, the 26th of July Movement, the Directorio Revolucionario, and the youth organizations were gradually merged into the Integrated Revolutionary Organizations, or ORI. Escalante became national organizer and made the mistake of trying to take it over. He put his own men in every position that he could, issued directives on his own, and tried to shoulder Fidel's Sierra Maestra comrades aside. Goldenberg (who had been a teacher in Havana for many years), writing of this period, expressed the common belief that the "Communist apparatus . . . controlled all the positions of power."

What Goldenberg should have said was "all but one." When he had had enough, Castro cracked down hard in a speech on March 26, 1962, ostensibly aimed at sectarianism, but making Escalante the scapegoat for the entire Old Guard of the PSP. He spoke of "privileges, caste spirit, nepotism and even corruption." There has never been any explanation why Fidel Castro put up with this state of affairs as long as he did.

The action was definitive. Fidel was serving notice that he and his loyal followers from the original 26th of July Movement were going to run Cuba. The Old Guard was permanently put down; a new *Fidelista* Communist Party was to arise. Only a handful of the important PSP leaders held on to national posts. The Cuban Communists humbly and sycophantically got into line and, on April 11, 1962, Moscow's *Pravda* applauded Castro's action.

To finish with Aníbal Escalante: he was banished to a diplomatic post in Prague. On his return to Cuba in 1967 he was given an unimportant provincial post, but once again tried to organize his own sort of Moscow clique. This time (January 1968) he and thirty-five others, most of them from the old PSP, were condemned for "microfactional" activity; Escalante is still serving a fifteen-year jail sentence.

Whatever "justice" was involved was revolutionary, as in the Hubert Matos case. A revolution is a law unto itself; it makes its own laws, which is almost like saying that it is lawless. The revolution in effect says: "Necessity knows no law; the revolution is necessary." A lot of traditional legality, morality, and some hard-won fruits of civilization are brushed aside in the process.

But Fidel Castro, neither then nor at any time since, was in a position to be too critical and independent of Moscow. He needed Russian technicians, arms, oil, wheat, credits, and international support. The internal situation had never been worse. The economy was breaking down as the Revolution accelerated. The Castroites convinced themselves that economic orthodoxy—even socialist orthodoxy—was incompatible with their revolution. They were determined to make their own mistakes.

Everything had to be done in the beginning by young, inexperienced men and women, working maddeningly long, hectic hours with little more to contribute than faith, hope, and enthusiasm. Professor Boorstein was an adviser in the newly formed Bancec (Bank for Foreign Commerce) during the 1960s. He tells of the almost fantastically difficult problems that were faced and—to a surprising extent—overcome. But there were many exceptions, many mistakes.

Che Guevara had been made president of the National Bank succeeding Felipe Pazos in November 1959, not only because his loyalty could be trusted but because he knew more about banking—from books he had read—than any of the others. He at least realized the need to conserve U.S. dollars and restrict import licenses. The bank had gold reserves at Fort Knox which, according to Boorstein, Che cannily pulled back to Havana before the embargo.

The impossible hopes and plans of the early years of the Revolution, however, were shared and often formulated publicly by Che Guevara himself. Speeches like a television address on economic planning on April 30, 1961, make for bewildering and incredulous reading today. Che was only relatively more restrained in a much better known speech to the Inter-American Economic and Social Council of the Organization of American States in Punta del Este, Uruguay, on August 8, 1961, where he predicted a Cuban growth rate of 12 percent and "the transformation of Cuba into the most highly industrialized country of Latin America in relation to its population in a period of four years."

The irrepressible instinct of Fidel and his associates, starting in the Sierra Maestra, was to change, transform, reverse—in a word, revolutionize—the Cuban economy. There had been a sugar economy; let us diversify agriculture. There was complete dependence on the United States; let us achieve economic independence of the Americans. The economy was largely agrarian; let us industrialize. The land was heavily committed to large plantations with much idle land; let us make an agrarian reform and put all the land to work. There had been great unemployment and underemployment; let us achieve full employment.

Fidel Castro and his fellow revolutionaries did not grasp the enormity of the tasks facing them until the Cuban economy was just about wrecked in terms of productivity and viability.

The intellectual, the peasant, the worker who today lights the fire of a revolution soon finds that he has burned down the structure that existed. He faces the overwhelming, unsure, uncharted, unguided task of building a new edifice on the ruins. The complexity of modern economic forces, capitalistic or socialistic, makes the task incredibly difficult.

Castro could not find his solution in American-type capitalism, since this was what he had fought against and destroyed, but he could not find it either (as Che Guevara later noted) in the socialism of other countries, such as the Soviet bloc, China, and Scandinavia, for Cuba's problems were unique. Under diverse and powerful pressures, Fidel groped and floundered toward a Cuban variation of socialism, which he ultimately dubbed Marxism-Leninism.

This became inescapable with the nationalization of lands and properties in 1959–1961 and the centralization of power in his person. A sudden revolution creates a completely abnormal state of affairs. Social democracy had to be ruled out because it is reformist, not revolutionary. Fascism had to be ruled out because it is a system allied to big business and banking and, in Cuba's case, to the United States. This left Communism, which Castro had not contemplated and—to begin with, at least—did not want. His critics ridiculed him for not having some special Cuban or Latin American political philosophy and ideas—but what? Certainly his critics had no substitutes, only reform of the existing capitalistic structure.

In modern times a number of basic economic problems are insoluble. What about the economic mess into which the United States, Great Britain, the Continent, and Japan are floundering in 1975? What about the "creeping inflation" which antedated the energy crisis and for which there was no solution? How much better off than Cuba are the other countries of the developing world? The truism that economics is not a science has been too often forgotten in judging the Cuban Revolution.

It is fair enough to point to the economic mistakes that the Castro regime made during the 1960s, but one should here, as in every other respect, guard against applying the mechanistic, orthodox, general theories of economics—even socialist economics—to the Cuba of the Revolution. Fidel Castro had special, *Cuban* economic and financial problems to deal with, and his performance must be judged in Cuban revolutionary terms. Within those terms, there is plenty to criticize, and none have done the job better than Che Guevara in his Algiers speech of February 26, 1965, and Fidel Castro in the July 26, 1970, speech with which I began this book.

"We copied, automatically, from the experiences of brother [socialist] countries, and this was a mistake," Che said in Algiers.

> We have had to learn from practice, by our errors . . . that planning and socialism go together and that one cannot plan everything when the economic conditions present do not allow it . . . The revolutionary leaders consisted only of a group of fighters, with high ideals but insufficient knowledge . . . The superstructure of the capitalist neo-colonial

> state was intact; we had to work to destroy it and to rebuild our society on new bases . . . We had to change the structures, we began to do so without a plan.
>
> The revolutionary group, with Fidel Castro at the head, first issued the Agrarian Reform Law. This indispensable law . . . revealed a terrible instrument: the class struggle—and it pushed the Cuban Revolution to its limits. . . .
>
> We tried to act upon nature subjectively, as if our direct contact with it would accomplish what we were after, ignoring the objective experiences of other countries . . . It was ridiculous to plan for a 15 per cent growth. . . .
>
> Our foreign commerce has totally changed directions, geographically . . . All this international shopping had to be carried out, not in a day by telephone, but with countries which are two months away, and which operate under systems of their own, with internal and external short-range and long-range equipment and raw materials. . . .
>
> In making our plans, we committed errors in our conception of the development of industry and agriculture, and in the balance of our economy. In industry, we evolved a plan based on the hope of becoming self-sufficient in a whole series of consumer products and of medium industry which, however, could easily have been obtained in friendly countries. . . .
>
> In agriculture, we committed the fundamental error of disdaining sugar, our national product . . . this impoverished the cane. An extraordinary drought during the first two years provoked a grave crisis in production.
>
> In the redistribution of wealth we gave too much importance in the beginning to satisfying social needs, to paying more equitable salaries, to increasing employment—all without sufficiently taking account of the general state of our economy.

This talk—of which only some highlights are given here—remains the outstanding *nostra culpa* of the early stage of the Cuban Revolution. Fidel Castro had been frank in admitting mistakes, but he was not to equal Che's extraordinary breast beating until the even more famous speech of July 26, 1970, on the disastrous sugar campaign.

There is no use asking why Fidel Castro and Che Guevara made these mistakes in the face of warnings and advice from their socialist friends and the available written experiences of all economic authorities. The best answer, perhaps, is the most simple one: that they were young, ignorant, and thought they knew better than the experts.

And they were alone. This is often forgotten. The Cuban Communists were last-minute supporters, divided, mediocre (except for Carlos Rafael Rodríguez), and themselves inexperienced. The Soviet Union was of no use during the first year of the regime. By 1960 the Revolution had its own frantic momentum and its headstrong, all-powerful leader. Mistakes are made in such conditions, and Fidel Castro made them. Che Guevara, in his Algiers speech, signed off neatly with a passage of Marxist rhetoric:

"We are building Socialism on our earth, and we are placing our small grain of sand at the service of the great aspiration of mankind —the elimination of the exploitation of man by man. The fiercest enemy of this aspiration is imperialism. We are fighting for the definite realization of Communism—the society without classes."

Which was all very well, but it wasn't making Fidel Castro's problems any easier or bread and butter for the Cuban people more plentiful.

A shortcut to understanding what went wrong is to note what was done in the sugar industry and the attempt to industrialize the economy quickly.

The agrarian reform of May 1959 gave the government the power to do what it pleased with the agricultural sector. Sugar's importance lay in the fact that 75 or 80 percent of all Cuban exports was in sugar. According to the Cuban Economic Research Project of Miami, there were 276 *centrales* (refineries and mills) employing 485,231 people and representing an investment of $1,158,850,000. This was without counting the agricultural sector of the industry.

The Castroites had no sugar policy, but when the United States canceled the Cuban import quota, they had to make one. The industry badly needed reorganization and modernization. It had been static for decades; in fact, the average yield per acre had been declining for twenty years. Instead of reforming and reconstructing the industry, the Castro government tried to break away from sugar dominance of the economy into industrialization.

After the sugar deal that Castro made with Anastas Mikoyan and the Russians, Che Guevara made a remark (March 2, 1960) that became famous. Critics, he said, had "never stopped to analyze what amount of slavery the 3,000,000 tons of our sugar we customarily sell at supposedly preferential prices to the Colossus of the North has meant and means for the Cuban people." He had a point, but it was indiscreet to make it at that time. And he went on rashly to say: "There has been talk of reducing our sugar quota, or suspending it entirely. The sooner the better. For Cuba, it is a symbol of colonialism. We shall be better off without imperialist yokes."

"Sugar has been the eternal affliction of Cuba," Raúl Roa, the foreign minister, said at the OAS meeting in San José, Costa Rica, in August 1960. The phrase in Spanish, *la eterna amargura,* was a play upon meaning, for *amargura* also means "bitterness." "Cuba," Roa said, "has been a country sweet on the outside, and very bitter inside."

Guevara faced and summed up the errors in the Cuban sugar policy as well as any outside critic ever did. In an article for Chatham House's *International Affairs* of London, October 1964, he wrote,

> We believe that we committed two principal errors. Our first error was the way in which we carried out diversification. Instead of embarking on diversification by degrees, we attempted too much at once. The sugar cane areas were reduced and the land thus made available was used for the cultivation of new crops. But this meant a general decline in agricultural production. The entire history of Cuba had demonstrated that no other agricultural activity would give such returns as those yielded by the cultivation of the sugar cane. At the outset of the Revolution many of us were not aware of this basic fact, because a fetishistic idea connected sugar with our dependence on imperialism and with the misery in rural areas, without analyzing the real cause: the relation to the unfavorable trade balance. . . .
>
> The second mistake was, in our opinion, that of dispersing our resources over a great number of agricultural products.

Some of the best sugar-cane areas were ruined for three or four years. The 1963 crop was down to 3,821,000 tons.

The Russians had undertaken to buy a million tons of sugar a year for five years at a good world market price for that period of 2.78 cents a pound. (The United States had been taking about 3,000,000 tons annually, paying 5 cents a pound.) Only 20 percent of the purchase price was to be paid in hard currency; the rest in Russian goods, including some industrial plants and machinery. Cuba was granted a $100 million twelve-year loan at 2.5 percent, and Russia was to provide technical aid for the new factories. In return, Cuba was to send sugar, fruit, fibers, and hide.

Raúl Castro told me years later that the Russians also secretly agreed at the time to supply Cuba with arms. That perhaps was the best part of the rather hard bargain the Russians struck.

The definitive clash with the United States came over oil, not sugar. The Americans and Britons (Standard Oil of New Jersey, Texaco, and Royal Dutch Shell) had built refineries in Cuba to process crude oil from their own Venezuelan producers, paying what the Cubans considered to be inflated prices. Soviet oil, although a bit cruder, could be obtained at lower world market prices. The oil would have to be refined at Texaco's Santiago de Cuba refinery. Havana, incidentally, had run up a debt to the companies in 1959–1960 that, an American oilman told me, totaled about $50 million.

The companies were going to accept the Russian oil under protest, but Washington told them to reject the plan—against Ambassador Bonsal's desire and without his knowledge. United States suggestions to London led to a similar British government request to Shell. The companies refused on June 7, 1960.

It was a futile decision. Cuba cannot exist without importing virtually all her fuel. The idea that supplies could be cut off by a hostile United States, with British connivance, was understandably more than Castro would or could accept. On June 29 the refineries were "intervened," whereupon Cuba found herself 100 percent dependent on the Soviet bloc for oil and gasoline. There were no technical problems.

"The Cuban Revolution," Philip Bonsal concludes, "had won a great victory and had had a powerful ally thrust into its arms."

On July 6 President Eisenhower retaliated by suspending the 700,000-ton balance of Cuba's sugar quota imports for 1960. It meant a loss to the Cubans of about $90 million. Bonsal thought it "most unwise." "With this action," he wrote, "I contend that the United States turned its back on thirty years of statesmanship in the Latin American field."

Certainly the basis for Cuban-American relations was destroyed. The interdependence of the two economies was centered on Cuban sugar exports to the United States in return for tariff concessions on American exports to Cuba.

"I do not believe that a continuation of the policies of nonintervention, nonaggression and restraint which I had advocated would have changed the policies on which Castro and Guevara were bent," Bonsal continues. However, he believed that the Cuban policies would have been made more difficult if Castro could not appear to be defending himself against American actions clearly aimed at his overthrow. The revolutionary process, Bonsal thought, might have taken much longer. "One of those accidents or incidents that would have changed the whole face of affairs" might have occurred. This was a rather coy way on Bonsal's part of saying that Castro might have been assassinated. There were attempts, but, so far as known, not by the CIA, at least not directly.

"A number of plans have been made to assassinate me," Fidel said in a press conference in Concepción, Chile, on December 3, 1971. "I had the opportunity to see, at an exhibit—a sort of small museum—the automatic weapons, the bazookas and the grenades that had been sent from the [U.S.] Guantánamo base to a group of counterrevolutionaries to assassinate me. . . .

"That base is there just to humiliate Cuba; just like a knife stuck in the heart of Cuba's dignity and sovereignty . . . But from a military standpoint, the base is completely useless."

Fidel's intelligence in Washington must have been good, because he knew about a proposal to provoke the Cubans across the border from the U.S. naval base, or even to put in exiles to fake a foray against the base. The Americans, according to the plan, would then send a column in, thus starting a military intervention. Castro spoke about such a plan in one of his speeches.

"As far as we are concerned," he said in Concepción, "we are going to leave that base alone until they get fed up with the whole thing." He added shrewdly that Guantánamo "serves as an added motivation to our revolutionary firmness and our spirit of struggle."

The real calculation behind the American action on the oil was that the Cubans would not be able to run the refineries or get enough Russian oil to keep them going. In both respects, Washington was wrong.

The Kremlin was facing a difficult and costly problem in supplanting the United States in the Cuban economy. Neither the Soviet Union nor the East European bloc could replace broken parts of American equipment or refine the ore from the nickel mines. They did not have any number of products which Cuba had been getting from the United States. Perhaps most important of all, they were not used to dealing with the Cubans, whose character, methods, and language were incomprehensible. The older, sophisticated, worldly wise Russians had to deal with rash young amateurs who had a different sense of values and too much individuality to accept advice, let alone discipline, from foreigners.

The wholesale expropriations of 1960 came as a surprise to the Cuban and Russian Communists. All enterprises and properties owned in whole or part by United States companies or American citizens were seized in August and September. These included all thirty-six American-owned sugar properties. On October 13, Law No. 890 nationalized 376 Cuban enterprises. In all, six million acres of land, half American-owned, half Cuban, were taken over by the Castro government. In theory, 4.5 percent bonds were offered in compensation, but not even paper bonds were forthcoming. Washington's answer to that, on October 19, 1960, was a trade embargo on everything except non-subsidized foodstuffs and medical supplies. Within a few months even those exceptions were banned. The embargo is still in force in 1975.

It was the end—probably forever—of United States control of the Cuban economy, although that could not have been realized at the time. In good years the two-way trade had totaled as much as $500 million. In 1967 the U.S. Foreign Claims Settlement Commission set a claim figure of $2.7 billion, of which $400 million was by individuals. The rest represented claims by 948 American corporations.

Diplomatic relations with the Soviet Union, broken in 1952, had been resumed on May 7, 1960, with Fauré Chomón as the first Cuban ambassador to Moscow.

"I am convinced that Castro's scenario at this time did not contemplate the massive help in the form of economic aid and weapons that he later received from the Soviet Union," Ambassador Bonsal wrote. "His thrust in 1959 was radically and exclusively nationalistic."

Ex-treasury minister López-Fresquet, like Bonsal, believed that "Castro pulled Russia into America almost against its will. Soviet policy was to have a friendly government in Cuba, not a satellite."

There is a subheading to a chapter in the ambassador's book titled "The Soviet Union Driven into Castro's Arms." Many sympathizers with the Revolution put it the other way around—that Castro was driven into the arms of the Soviet Union. I argued that they met each other halfway.

Bonsal's belief, which of course deserves the most serious consideration, is that until the United States' decisions on oil and sugar, the Russians were skeptical of Castro's personality; did not look on him as a Marxist-Leninist; did not contemplate replacing the United States as a trading partner; and did not at the time desire a confrontation with the United States over Cuba.

"I suggest that until July 1960," Bonsal writes, "the Moscow bureaucrats advised Castro to proceed with moderation in his dealings with Washington." Now Moscow was being faced with the choice of helping Cuba or letting the Revolution collapse, and "it was inevitable that a world power engaged in global confrontation with America would decide to come to Castro's rescue."

Bonsal thinks that President Eisenhower's decision to cut the sugar quota caught Castro and Khrushchev by surprise. The Soviet leader's first reaction was his warning on July 9: "Speaking figuratively, in case of necessity Soviet artillerymen can support the Cuban people with rocket fire." The Cubans chose to interpret the threat literally, not figuratively, but Washington knew better and got some useful propaganda out of the threat.

The Kremlin now had to agree to buy the sugar that would have gone to the United States. Bonsal was still counseling some restraint, since he believed that "the Cuban Government was doomed by its own disorganization and incompetence and by the growing disaffection of an increasing proportion of the Cuban people." The validity of this judgment, I believe, has been disproved by the fact that the "disorganization and incompetence" went on and on without weakening the Castro government.

Professor Maurice Halperin, who had worked for years in Havana as a newspaperman and teacher in the 1960s, makes an interesting point in his book *The Rise and Decline of Fidel Castro.* It was Fidel's good luck that his revolution coincided with the first global expansion of Soviet policy. Lenin's Russia had been on the defensive; Stalin's was strictly confined to the solid Communist bloc where Russian military strength could always be exercised. When he died in 1953 and was succeeded in 1957 by the more adventurous Nikita Khrushchev, "socialism in one country" was succeeded by the *sputnik* era. The Soviet Union was both economically able and politically willing to reach out six thousand miles to save a revolution which was fighting against "United States imperialism" and showing clear signs of turning socialist.

It was still the height of the cold war. Castro's field of choice was limited and inescapable: he either gave in to the United States or he turned to the Kremlin for help. The Russians saved the Revolution and have contributed vitally to keep it going ever since. All predictions that they could not indefinitely sustain the cost—usually rated by guesswork at $1 million or more a day—or that they would get fed up with Cuban bungling, or that a *détente* with the United States would make Cuba expendable, have proved wrong. In fact, Fidel Castro was never more cordially or generously received than on his two trips to Russia in 1972. They were followed by exceptionally favorable trade and financial agreements.

Naturally, Fidel could have calculated all along that he had this way out. Russia, in fact, was buying Cuban sugar for three years before 1959. Halperin also points out that between 1950 and 1955 the Soviet Union changed from being a net oil importer to a net exporter.

As time was to show, Cuban trade was not only cut off from the

United States and linked to the Soviet bloc, but also to Western Europe and Japan. In June 1960 Cuba had arranged to sell fifty thousand tons of sugar to Communist China. By July trade agreements had been made with East Germany, Poland, Czechoslovakia, and, more extensively, China.

Since the cold war was still on and the United States' fears of the Communist world were still overpowering, the agreements that Fidel was making constituted a political declaration of independence from the United States. As part of the deal with China, Cuba became the first Latin American country to open diplomatic relations with Peking. By September 1961 there were trade and diplomatic relations with every Communist country including, for good measure, North Vietnam, North Korea, and Outer Mongolia.

No Western country had broken trade and diplomatic relations with Cuba except West Germany, and that was because of Cuba's recognition of East Germany. The Vatican also maintained diplomatic relations. In the Western Hemisphere, Canada and Mexico ignored pressures from Washington. The only limitation was Cuba's inability to produce enough sugar and other products for export to the hard-currency areas. Britain, France, Spain, Italy, Japan, and Canada increased their trade with Cuba over the years, often on credit. In Latin America, Chile (until the overthrow of Allende), Peru, Jamaica, Trinidad and Tobago, and Panama traded with Cuba. In August 1973, Perón's Argentina extended a $200 million credit to Cuba for the purchase of agricultural machinery. A still larger deal was made for automobiles later in 1973. Castro has seen to it that Cuba's credit standing remains good.

After the nationalizations the Castro government had nearly all Cuban industry on its hands, but most of the top administrative, managerial, and technical personnel had been Americans or Cubans trained by, and living like, Americans. By October 1960 most of them had been withdrawn by their American companies, and nearly all of them went back to the United States or into exile.

As Fidel was to say in a speech on December 20, 1969, this led "to anybody at all becoming a manager. There were times when even the village idiot was managing a sugar mill . . . We have been naïve—naïve illiterates and semi-illiterates to the *n*th degree . . . Far from being surprised at the number of mistakes that have been committed, we should be surprised that the number was not even greater."

Fidel and Che did not realize at first how serious the consequences of the U.S. trade embargo were going to be on Cuba's economy. Some of their most extravagant predictions were made after the embargo had started. However, the theme that Cuba has had to struggle against the strangling effects of American policy soon became an oratorical commonplace. For instance, there was hardly a speech or an interview during Castro's sojourn in Chile at the end of 1971 in which he did not stress the difficulties caused by the American trade embargo.

The decline in national income became noticeable and serious in mid-1960, which, by coincidence or not, is the time that Castro seems to have made up his mind that the answers to his problems lay in socialism. By 1961 preexisting inventories had been used up, also spare parts and raw materials. Through good fortune, fine weather helped to bring in a sugar crop in 1961 of 6.7 million tons, the second largest in Cuban history. This was not remotely to be reached again in succeeding years until the abnormal 1970 harvest.

Too many cattle were slaughtered in 1961, bringing severe shortages from 1962 onward. Ambitious orders for new factories contributed to a large balance-of-payments deficit in 1962. Unemployment in June 1960 was still 300,000, Che Guevara said.

These are just some of the specific items, taken at random from a great many. In the summer of 1961 serious shortages of many food items developed. Rationing of food stuffs began on July 4, 1961. The people learned how bad the situation was when a ministerial conference, headed by Castro, was held on August 27–28, 1961. A ridiculously optimistic promise of future improvement was issued which showed that something had gone seriously wrong with the economy. Even in World War II there had been no need for rationing.

And, of course, things got worse. Rationing of most and, in time, all consumer goods began on a systematic basis on March 19, 1962, and it has yet to end. On April 10, 1962, Fidel agreed that "this is a revolution which must be ashamed of itself." It was not only the shortages that were shameful, but the decline in quality of consumer goods that came in shock after shock as 1961 began.

Che Guevara, then minister of industry, reported many errors, and so did everyone else at the National Production Conference in August. To give a few examples: "After a month, toothpaste becomes hard . . . Coca-Cola tastes like cough syrup . . . Matches are one of the worst disgraces we have . . . The glue doesn't dry well"; and so forth. Che's speech, in which he also criticized ministry after ministry, was devastating.

Yet they still did not seem to realize that much of what they were planning was impossible; that much of what they were doing was wrong; that financial discipline was imperative; that land was not a limitless resource; that the economy must in practice, not just in theory, be treated as an organic whole. They saw great possibilities and projected them into great plans. Professor Boorstein quotes Mark Twain's *reductio ad absurdum* on the Lower Mississippi's shortening to a mile and three-quarters if the calculations of the geologists were projected 742 years ahead. "There is something fascinating about science," Twain wrote. "One gets such wholesale returns of conjecture out of such trifling investment of fact."

That was what the Cuban revolutionaries were doing. Even when they came around to the economic planning that their socialist advisers kept telling them was necessary, the plans were ridiculously overoptimistic and, anyway, not much attention was paid to them. Boorstein, whose work in the Cuban Bank for Foreign Commerce makes him one of the best authorities on early revolutionary economics, remarks in his book that, for instance, "the total planned construction exceeded by a large percentage the materials for carrying it out." In general, "the plans were set up without allowing margins for error and unforeseeable contingencies."

The basic and most powerful government agency throughout the 1960s was INRA (National Institute of Agrarian Reform). It was almost a government in itself.

INRA carried out the expropriation and redistribution of the land; it built houses, schools, hospitals, warehouses, and factories, often running them. It granted agricultural credits, constructed roads, imported all kinds of machinery, as well as insecticides, fertilizers, and animal foodstuffs. It imported farm animals—bulls, pigs, chickens. And so forth, interminably. Castro, naturally, was president of INRA, which soon had a long list of subsidiary organizations—the Ministry of Industry, the Petroleum, Mining, and Fishing Institutes, the Agency for Hydraulic Resources, the People's Stores, the Association of Small Farmers (ANAP), et cetera.

"When Major Guevara became President of the National Bank [November 1960]," writes Boorstein, "he was both an officer of the Army and head of the Department of Industrialization of INRA; then he also became Chairman of the Commission in charge of the Bank of Foreign Commerce when it was formed. A number of key revolutionary officials of the National Bank, the Bank of Foreign Commerce, the Central Planning Board, and other agencies, came from INRA."

The prerevolutionary government agencies and the inherited

bureaucracy of civil servants could not be trusted, which was why Fidel used his Rebel commanders for the top posts. They were without administrative experience or technical knowledge, but they were loyal.

"There are many amateurs in the INRA lacking efficiency and with too much zeal," Fidel said to me ruefully in March 1960. But neither he nor the other leaders could adjust themselves then—and for a number of years—to the necessity of establishing a hierarchy where authority was delegated appropriately at each level and everyone played a disciplined role. This was not in the Cuban tradition or character. So a Central Planning Board (JUCEPLAN, or Junta Central de Planificación) was created to control the economy as a whole, but it did little of practical value. Fidel, Che, and a few others had the real authority, which they failed to coordinate or use systematically.

They kept on trying and were still experimenting at the end of 1973, when Russian advisers were given more scope. The planning was never wholly Cuban. Not only Russians, but Czechs, Latin Americans, and United Nations planners were trying their hands in the 1960s. Russian planning has not been notably successful in the Soviet Union. Fidel Castro did not know what to do, but his instinct from the beginning that a Cuban Revolution had to be truly Cuban was probably sound. However, this got affairs back to trial and error.

Blas Roca, one of the few old guard Cuban Communists left in a position of importance, laughed when we talked in 1972 about the early period. "Those were the romantic years," he said.

They were all so young! Youth insists on making its own mistakes. They distrusted the advice of their elders, who, they could see, had made a mess of things. If ever there was a "generational gap" at work in the contemporary world, it was in Cuba in the early years of the Revolution. Add the callousness of youth toward the suffering of others and you get a horde of young enthusiasts and idealists riding roughshod over everything that Cuba's one-time establishment believed necessary and held dear.

Naturally, a huge bureaucracy evolved. Fidel was so annoyed that he appointed a committee to cut down on it, only to end up denouncing the committee for becoming bureaucratic.

Despite all the mistakes and difficulties, the people were fed, clothed, educated, and kept in good health. The Castro regime must have been doing many things right as well as many things wrong. There were unending trials and errors, but the group had any amount of faith, assurance, loyalty, honesty, and energy. They started the Cuban Revolution and put it on the rocky, hilly, zigzagging, and unevenly advancing path it has followed ever since.

As was remarked before, there is so much more to the Cuban Revolution than its economy. We can leave the economists, whether Cubans in exile or foreign, wringing their hands or pouring derision and calamitous predictions upon the often puzzled, but always unbowed, heads of Fidel Castro and his comrades. There were so many other things to do; so much more that was happening. The economy was failing in these years, but the Revolution was succeeding.

CHAPTER 8

The Ties Are Broken

> If the United States did not exist, the Cuban Revolution would perhaps invent it.
>
> —Jean-Paul Sartre

For virtually all Americans, the history of the Cuban republic began on January 1, 1959.

Dean Bayless Manning of Stanford University, in an essay written for the 1967 Brookings Institution book on Cuba, said: "We were ignorant—almost wilfully ignorant—about Cuba . . . If Havana had overnight transformed itself into a hostile power, we would hardly have been more astounded than we were by the sudden snarl and show of teeth in Castro's Cuba." The number of American professors and historians who had specialized on Cuba could probably have been counted on the fingers of one hand.

The dismay in American business and banking circles, and the pressures on the Eisenhower Administration to do something, were understandable. The early notes and statements tried to be conciliatory. One on June 11, 1959, expressed sympathy for the objectives of land reform and referred to the "generally accepted obligation of prompt, adequate and effective compensation." Further negotiations were suggested.

That very night (although there was no connection) Castro abruptly, and without any advance notice, dismissed his ministers of foreign affairs, health, agriculture, the interior, and social welfare.

The next night, June 12, Fidel, who had not seen Ambassador Bonsal for five weeks despite repeated requests, received him cordially and expressed goodwill.

"Years later," writes Bonsal, "Castro remarked to an American newspaperman [it was I] that the American reaction to the agrarian reform of May 1959 'made me realize that there was no chance of an accommodation with the United States.' This is far from a unique example of the manner in which the Maximum Leader's flexible memory permits him statements contrary to the truth of the event he is recalling."

It is also a good example of the problems one faces in interpreting what Fidel Castro says at a particular moment on a particular subject. In his conversation with Bonsal, Castro could have been imposing on the ambassador's credulity, or on mine when he spoke to me, or he may have had second thoughts after speaking to Mr. Bonsal or, quite possibly, he may have been sincere both times.

As likely as not, he was being conventionally courteous to someone who was momentarily his guest. He is never cold, laconic, or reserved in conversation. The courtesy which is bred into every Cuban, as it is into the Spaniards from whom they derive their culture, often fools Anglo-Saxons. Again and again in the book on his mission, Ambassador Bonsal writes indignantly and scathingly of talks with Fidel Castro or Foreign Minister Raúl Roa, or whomever it might be, in which he met cordiality, agreement, and promises which later proved to have been meaningless.

In Bonsal's first conversation with Raúl Roa as the newly appointed foreign minister, for instance, Roa apparently could not have been more friendly or obliging. If he had intended to be anything else, in the circumstances of the time, he would not have recieved the ambassador. By Anglo-Saxon standards Raúl Roa was deceitful, but not by Latin-Cuban standards. He was being polite to his guest, who should have known better than to take him literally, considering the policies that Castro was following. More than language divides Cubans from Americans.

In what proved to be Bonsal's last interview with Fidel, on September 3, 1959, "Castro made no commitments on the special questions I brought to his attention. Both he and Roa exuded goodwill toward me and toward the United States."

"I was aware that Castro's reasonable and friendly attitude at our interview might contain elements of deceit," Bonsal concludes. ". . . Castro had spoken favorably of me in public and he had given the impression that he and I were on a friendly footing based on mutual respect for each other and for each other's country."

The Ambassador was therefore understandably annoyed when, in speaking to the American photographer Lee Lockwood in 1965, Fidel said that Bonsal had come to Cuba "with the demeanor of a proconsul. I [Castro] remember his words, his imposing attitude, and how our reactionary press received him almost as if the Savior had come."

Castro might have been sincere in what he said to Lockwood. His memory is convenient; it suits the way he feels at a particular time. The two men were incapable of understanding each other. Castro would not have considered Bonsal's ideas, suggestions, and requests—however friendly their expression—as evidence of American goodwill. He was convinced that Washington had anything but goodwill for him and his revolution, and by his standards he was right.

Philip Bonsal was in the best and most numerous company in failing to understand the situation in 1959. It was so fluid and chaotic that Castro could not have committed himself categorically. He knew that he was going to make a genuine revolution, and in Ambassador Bonsal he was dealing with someone for whom a radical revolution was anathema.

Philip Bonsal was no Josephus Daniels, the American ambassador who played such an understanding and useful role in the Mexican Revolution. He was a competent, experienced career diplomat, a liberal, a devoted exponent of private enterprise. His strong sense of patriotism included a belief in the righteousness and high moral character of American policy. He was a cultured and charming man, but not one whom Fidel Castro would find warm, friendly, sympathetic, or understanding. It would be hard to choose two men more different from each other in every respect. It was as if they lived in separate worlds. They never really got together or communicated truly with each other. From the beginning to the end of his mission in Havana, Philip Bonsal was a bewildered man. His antipathy toward Castro after his mission ended was so great that he could not bring himself to believe in the possibility of Fidel being idealistic, patriotic, sincerely wanting to do what was best for Cuba and the Cubans, and believing that this was what he was doing. Bonsal denies him any moral qualities—which, to me, represents another of the basic mistakes made by Fidel Castro's enemies. The former ambassador often uses the word "magic" to describe Castro's popular appeal, but the great body of Cuban people who follow him are not so stupid as to succumb to "magic" for sixteen years.

Early in December 1959, Bonsal reported to the State Department that "productive diplomacy was out of the question," but it was agreed "that the channels and the forms of diplomacy should be maintained." He thought that Fidel was disappointed, as "he aimed at an eventual rupture."

There were some men close to the events in 1959 and 1960 who believed that Castro did not expect the United States to permit him to carry out his program. Among them were his Treasury Minister

López-Fresquet and Ambassador Bonsal. In fact, Bonsal was convinced that Fidel desired an American invasion, in which case he would have taken to the mountains and fought a long guerrilla war.

"The bearded leader thought he would not long be in power," wrote López-Fresquet in his book *My 14 Months with Castro.* "He believed that after he began his intended aggressions on American property, the U.S. would surely use its colossal strength to bring about his overthrow."

I saw a good deal of Castro on three visits to Cuba in the first half of 1959, and again in 1960. I agree that he believed an American invasion was possible, but he feared it; he certainly did not court one or expect to be overthrown.

Bonsal expressed a typical American opinion in scathingly and resentfully denouncing much of Fidel's anti-Americanism as "ridiculous . . . fraudulent . . . hate propaganda . . . poisonous nonsense," and the like. Fidel Castro must have known, up to a point, that his anti-Yankeeism was exaggerated and a deliberate political ruse, but anti-Americanism was one of his true and most deeply felt emotions, as well as one of his most effective weapons. It was a key element in uniting a considerable part of the Cuban people behind the regime. It was unrealistic to think that Castro would not use this weapon to the fullest extent possible. There was a large fund of anti-Americanism built into Cuba's social and intellectual structure upon which he could draw.

"It was only months later [after his arrival]," Bonsal writes, "that I was forced to conclude that Castro himself had aimed, through his unscrupulous campaign of historical revision, to create a climate in which diplomacy could not operate."

However, all the evidence points to the fact that when he made his one and only trip to the United States as Prime Minister, Castro was in a conciliatory and undecided state of mind about relations with the United States and about his policy toward the Communists at home. (Fidel had been invited to Washington to address the annual conference of the American Society of Newspaper Editors [ASNE] in April 1959.)

Some of the endless arguments over whether the United States missed a great opportunity to win over or influence Fidel Castro center around that American trip. What if President Eisenhower had stayed in Washington, instead of going off ostentatiously to play golf in California, and had treated Castro royally? What if the U.S. Treasury or Export-Import Bank had publicly offered economic and financial help even though Fidel was not asking for any? And so forth. But this is playing games with history.

President Eisenhower did not have the imagination or desire for such a policy. In fact, as he wrote in his memoirs, he was irritated with the ASNE for inviting Castro to Washington.

Vice-President Richard M. Nixon had a long conversation with Castro which left both men with a low opinion of each other. The Vice-President produced files to show how many Communists there were in the Cuban administration, naïvely believing that this would be news to Castro. He also referred to the bad impression which the executions had made in the United States, which must have infuriated his guest, who was so resentful of the American reaction. Castro, according to what he told Lee Lockwood some years later, responded politely, "explaining the realities of our country, which I believe were similar to those of the rest of Latin America."

The interview had dramatic results, because Nixon convinced himself, as he wrote in his book *Six Crises,* that "Castro was either incredibly naïve about Communism or under Communist discipline." He was neither, but the important sequel was that Nixon acted on his belief, suggesting that a force of Cuban exiles be armed and sent in to overthrow Castro. This was the first move which was to end in the Bay of Pigs fiasco.

There was irony in Nixon's reaction because that period of Fidel Castro's career was undoubtedly the closest he came to turning against the Communists. It was also about the last time that he seemed seriously to be thinking of liberal, democratic policies.

If Nixon had only been understanding and well enough informed to realize that in talking to Castro he was talking to the man who ran the Cuban Revolution—whose revolution it was—there might have been a chance of the United States influencing him and the Cuban situation. It might also have helped if Washington had grasped the strength of the Cuban nationalism that possessed Castro and all his comrades and that had been unleashed by his revolution. The demand for a Cuba independent of United States tutelage or domination had to be faced and met halfway. Instead, there was a head-on confrontation.

I saw Fidel three times on that April trip in Washington and New York, and I would say that nothing irritated him more than the constant and obsessive concern of all the Americans he met, publicly and privately, with the question of Communism. He got the impression that the United States did not care what he did in Cuba or what revolutionary Cuba turned out to be so long as it was not Communist.

The most curious of all the bizarre incidents of his trip was a three-hour private conversation in Washington with the CIA's chief "expert" on Latin American Communism, who, under the name

Frank Bender, was to direct—or misdirect—the whole Bay of Pigs operation. His true name was Frank Droller. López-Fresquet said that Droller told him after the conversation: "Castro is not only not a Communist; he is a strong anti-Communist fighter."

The trip was confusing on the economic side because Castro had said on TV on April 2 that he intended to secure loans in Washington from the World Bank or the Export-Import Bank. The State Department had hinted as early as February 1959 that the United States was prepared to extend economic help. About ten days before the Cuban party left Havana, a note was sent to Washington, presumably with Castro's approval, suggesting a list of economic subjects for negotiation.

Yet on the plane from Havana to Washington, Fidel told López-Fresquet, his Treasury Minister, and Felipe Pazos, head of the National Bank of Cuba, not to ask for aid or even bring up the subject. "I want this to be a good will trip," López-Fresquet quotes Castro as saying. "Besides, the Americans will be surprised. And when we go back to Cuba, they will offer us aid without our asking for it. Consequently, we will be in a better bargaining position."

When I said good-bye to Castro, he told me that he was satisfied with the trip, and he clearly was delighted with the extraordinary public interest he had aroused. On the verge of leaving, he must have had a sudden thought about the Communist issue, which, he realized, was causing such concern in the United States, because he sent two of the women in his entourage to see me and my wife. Along with a thinly veiled courtesy visit was a serious message: Fidel wanted us to know that when he got back to Havana he would take care of the Communists.

On his way from Washington to Buenos Aires to attend a session of the U.N. Economic Commission for Latin America, he made a brief stopover in Dallas, Texas, to talk to his brother Raúl, whom he had summoned. My information was that he raised hell over the way the Cuban Communists were behaving and that Raúl shared his sentiments at the time.

In Buenos Aires on May 2, 1959, Castro made a speech which, if taken literally, was an offer to keep revolutionary Cuba within a more or less democratic, or at least non-Communist, hemispheric community. However, the proposal was that to achieve "a future, humanistic democracy on the basis of liberty with bread for all peoples . . . the economic development of Latin America will require a financing totaling $30 billion over a period of ten years."

He was ridiculed. The American delegation dismissed the idea with amused contempt—and two years later President Kennedy put forward his Alliance for Progress pledging $10 billion for ten years, to which President Johnson was later to add another $10 billion.

There has been no period in the whole Revolution more perplexing than that trip to the United States and Argentina in 1959. It seemed pregnant with possibilities, but nothing whatever came of it, unless one wants to count Richard Nixon's proposals which were to end in the Bay of Pigs. Once Fidel Castro was back in Havana, it was as if he had never left. On May 17 the first Agrarian Reform Law was promulgated. It was interpreted in the United States as pure Communism, although the Cuban Communists had argued as strongly as they dared against such a drastic measure so well designed to antagonize the United States. But the drift toward what was to become Marxism-Leninism continued. So did the expropriations and the quarreling with the United States.

Relations went from bad to worse. The State Department issued a white paper on January 11, 1960, detailing the seizures, confiscations and other undoubted injustices to which Americans and their properties in Cuba had been subjected without even justification in Cuban law. Although factual, the recital infuriated Fidel Castro, who replied, characteristically, with a long television speech so vituperative that Bonsal was called back to Washington for an extended stay of two months.

On January 26, 1960, another statement was issued by President Eisenhower expressing concern at the deterioration of relations, the "unwarranted attacks," and the accusations of aggressive acts by the United States. It told of efforts to restrain illegal raids from Florida, recognized the right of Cuba to make reforms, and pledged continued nonintervention. It ended by stating the U.S. government's "confidence in the ability of the Cuban people to recognize and defeat the intrigues of International Communism."

The ending might better have been left out for diplomatic reasons, but the statement was moderate and kept all doors open. However, there was also a warning that "the United States Government and people will continue to assert and defend, in the exercise of their own sovereignty, their legitimate interests."

Bonsal thought that "the Cuban opposition was sitting back passively because of a predisposition (often inherited) to look to the United States rather than to their own efforts to correct the situation." This was a sad and significant commentary on Cuban-American relations.

It was a combination of the loss of income, property, privileges, and social status, plus the trend toward Communism, that was to set off the massive exodus from Cuba to the United States and, to a lesser degree, to Venezuela, Puerto Rico, and Spain.

In January 1959 Cuba was united as it had never been in its history, but it could not remain so, because different classes and elements had different objectives and ideas for the Revolution. Fidel Castro had at first conceded that the victory had been won "with the help of men of all ideas, of all religions, of all social classes." He changed this judgment later when his conflict with the so-called middle classes became acute.

The most numerous of the disaffected at the beginning, aside from those incriminated in aspects of the Batista repression, were businessmen, bankers, merchants, administrators, directors of enterprises, managers and technicians in the foreign-owned industries. Lawyers, engineers, teachers, artists, writers, and other professionals were at first overwhelmingly pro-Castro, but they soon turned against him also, for they too were losing out materially and they also resented the trend toward Communism and the loss of civic liberties.

Cuban liberal-democratic elements did not make a fight for it, as I have stated. For a great many of the middle-class intellectuals and supporters of Castro and the Revolution, the move toward Communism was the hardest thing to swallow, even for some who trusted Fidel and were loyal to him. Draper rates their opposition as the greatest danger to Castro in 1959–1960, but this element, with some —not many—exceptions, simply ran away and conspired from Florida, or they gave in. I agree in general with Ambassador Bonsal: "Seldom has so much been taken from so many, in terms of both moral and material goods, in so short a time and with so little opposition." But Bonsal's use of the word "moral" is in the Anglo-Saxon liberal-democratic sense of civic liberties, with which the majority of Cubans were not greatly concerned.

One should not think of the Cuban middle classes in the same way as the North American or European. It is true that they were the professional men, businessmen, politicians, high army officers, and government officials, and almost everyone in a certain income bracket. They were, in the Cuban phrase, *las capas medias,* the middle layers; the true upper class—descendants of the white Spanish colonial aristocracy—were so few in number as to be negligible.

Cuba really had only two classes, one that could be called upper-middle and the other the lower class, easily identifiable in the manual laborers, peasants, artisans, petty tradesmen, domestic servants, and the like, who made up the great mass of Cubans. Social mobility was open. A lower-class Cuban could become middle-class simply by earning enough money, getting elected or appointed to a good political post, or (Sergeant Fulgencio Batista was a prime example) rising into the higher ranks of the armed forces.

The middle classes in the European and North American sense are more complicated and less mercenary. They are identified with a way of life, education, culture, attitudes, ideas, philosophy, social values, the acceptance of a certain social status, and—as an important but not necessary feature—a certain income.

The term "middle class," correctly used, is not political, national, or racial. Communist Czechoslovakia has its middle class by standards of Western culture. The social and psychological traits which make an American, a Briton, or a Frenchman middle-class did not apply in Cuba. Moreover, it was inconceivable to a Cuban with a fair income to permit his wife to do any housework or personally take care of their children. The husband would not dream of washing his car, mowing his lawn, gardening, or drying the dishes after supper. Society before 1959 had never lost its feudal traits, inherited from Spain. The upper-moneyed class and the lower classes accepted as natural a relationship in many respects that of masters and servants.

The gap between the few wealthy and the many poor was far greater than in the United States and Western Europe. "Though it is hard to prove statistically," Hugh Thomas writes of the Cuban Republic, "there were probably more Cuban millionaires per head of population than anywhere south of Dallas."

Although his father was a well-to-do landowner and he himself a man of education, Fidel Castro always depended most on people who could not be described as middle class. Little attention was paid by the Cuban rebels—and just about none by the Civic Resistance—to color before the Revolution. Castro had always been "color blind." He accepted, worked with, and fought alongside blacks and mulattos apparently without thinking of them as different in any way. It did not seem to occur to him to mention racial discrimination in Cuba until the Revolution got under way. At first, he appeared little aware of the social and economic inequalities of the races; then he realized how great an asset equality could be, both as a natural part of the Revolution and as a contrast to the United States.

Cuban blacks and mulattos had accepted a degree of economic, political, and social inferiority as normal. Discrimination was not nearly so bad as in the United States, and some blacks managed to rise to higher economic and political, although not necessarily social, levels. There had never been Cuban equivalents of the NAACP, Black Power, or similar organizations, at least not since the first decade of the republic and the Negro uprising of 1912.

Because of the Revolution, racism was being called to the blacks' attention for the moral evil that it was, and they were being given equal opportunities and rights. Only the exceptional black went into opposition and exile.

But what of the Cuban peasants? "Marxists have long argued," Professor Eric R. Wolf writes in *Peasant Wars of the Twentieth Century*, "that peasants without outside leadership cannot make a revolution; our case material would bear them out." This was true of Cuba, as was Wolf's remark that "peasants in rebellion are natural anarchists." That is a good reason why triumphant revolutionaries—the Mexican generals, Lenin, Stalin, Mao Tse-tung, Ho Chi Minh, Boumediene, Castro—all quickly controlled and regimented their peasants by force.

Fidel Castro has never had to face a civic resistance remotely comparable to the great, nationwide, mass build-up that contributed to the overthrow of Batista. And, of course, there was no magnetic, national opposition leader, either among the new guerrillas or in exile.

The main exodus from the island occurred in 1960, starting in the spring and swelling to a flood tide by the end of the year. Many in the business community went in the summer after the large-scale expropriations. Teachers fled with the purge of the schools and universities. Outraged and disappointed professionals and intellectuals, many from the 26th of July Movement, reacted against the trend toward Communism. Skilled and semiskilled workers, losing income and freedom, were in the later waves. At all times, even now in 1975, many more Cubans have wanted to leave than were allowed to go.

The *Fidelistas* soon used the contemptuous term *gusano* (worm) for the exiles. It was not a Castroite invention, for Martí had applied the word to spineless, unpatriotic Cubans.

Professor Lowry Nelson writes in his recent book *Cuba* that "the United States Committee for Refugees (a private organization) has estimated that up to 1970 the Cuban migration to all countries amounted to 570,478." The refugees were a valuable addition to U.S. society; most of them found satisfactory work, and their children have become completely Americanized. There is now a prosperous, self-contained Cuban colony in Miami who have reproduced the prerevolutionary middle-class way of life in Cuba. But it would be callous to forget that exile is a tragedy. As the Florentine exile Dante wrote so many years ago, the bread of others is salt and it is hard to climb someone else's stairs. As was the case after the Russian Revolution and the Spanish Civil War, so many left Cuba expecting to return when, as they felt sure, Castro would either be overthrown or the United States would intervene.

There was quarreling and recrimination, as is always the case with exiles. At one time, it was estimated that there were as many as two hundred squabbling organizations of Cuban exiles in Florida alone. Some of the groups were helped by the CIA; others by donations from wealthy *Batistianos.*

"The imperialists [i.e., the Americans] always count those who leave but never those who stay," Castro said in a speech on May 1, 1966. "They don't say how they close the doors to immigrants from other countries so that they can try to attract the greatest number to come from Cuba and make propaganda. But we don't lose; we win."

Politically, it was a gain in ridding Cuba of a dangerous, powerful, inimical element, but economically it was a great loss. Fidel not only began to concede this in later speeches, but he has blamed the United States innumerable times for crippling the Cuban economy by taking away sorely needed technicians, managers, teachers, doctors, and other professionals. Even before the Revolution, the U.S. government's 1956 study *Investment in Cuba* pointed out, Cuba had "slightly less than half as many professional, managerial, and service workers, proportionately, as the United States."

Castro made up for the loss as best he could by importing Soviet-bloc technicians, but the way out had to be long, patient years of education and training of Cubans in every industrial, service, technical, and professional branch of the economy.

This began sensationally in 1961, the "Year of Education." The prerevolutionary educational system had been very bad, even though it happened to be worse in other Latin American countries. The official illiteracy figure for Cuba before 1959 was 24 percent, or more than a million people, but this was certainly an underestimate. In many rural areas there were no schools. Children from poor families averaged four years' schooling, when they went to school at all. Public education was free, but the classes were overcrowded and the teachers incapable and often absent.

In all of Cuba there were only twenty-one secondary schools. Private schools, many of them run by the clergy, were expensive and generally poor in quality. The Ministry of Education was notoriously corrupt. University education was old-fashioned and concentrated on producing too many lawyers, journalists, and the wrong sort of teachers in a country that desperately needed engineers, agronomists, and all kinds of technicians.

Fidel quickly realized that he had to replace the teachers who were going into exile and, more importantly, that education offered him the opportunity to transform and reconstruct Cuban society. He determined to wipe out illiteracy, offer every child an education, and make the school system suitable to an agrarian but partly industrialized, developing nation. Technology and managerial know-how, he correctly realized, were the key to future independence and viability.

He has succeeded to a remarkable extent and is now—since 1970—embarked on a revitalized educational system which, in its scope and in some features, is unique. Of that, more later.

Fidel's scheme to wipe out illiteracy in Cuba in the year 1961 was imaginative and typically grandiose. All youths from twelve to eighteen were relieved of their own school work, put in uniform, supplied with hammocks and blankets, and sent into the countryside to "alphabetize" the illiterates of all ages. For the teaching, they were given two simple manuals, which did not miss the opportunity to combine anti-imperialism with instruction.

It was revolutionary activity at its best. Thousands of youths who would never have left their cities or towns came into daily contact with peasants. All classes, white and black, experienced a communal life, a sort of social integration such as Cuba had never known. The worldwide publicity gave a sense of pride and enthusiasm to the Revolution in a critical year.

The official figures (which Professor Nelson quotes in his book) were 707,212 adults taught to read and write out of 979,000, leaving an illiteracy rate of 3.9 percent. While the figures were not likely to be quite accurate, no one denied that the results were impressive. It was arguable that a high price was paid in detaching thousands of youths from formal education or training and older people from economically productive work at enormous government expense. But nations do not live by bread alone.

Within a few years there were more new schools and schoolrooms than had been built in the previous quarter of a century. Thousands of students and peasants were sent to Russia for technical training. In Cuba, schools taught new subjects of practical value to agriculture and industry. They also taught Marxism-Leninism. The school-leaving age was raised to fourteen. The budget for education was doubled compared to prerevolutionary years and honestly spent, which was not the case before.

The many houses confiscated from rich *Batistianos* or left by emigrants were turned into homes for boys and girls with scholarships. Women and girls who had been servants, waitresses, even prostitutes, were taught sewing, dressmaking, and nursing. There was special emphasis on female education, a revolutionary development in a Latin country. By 1962 half the students at Havana University were girls.

The University, incidentally, was stripped of what autonomy remained to it in July 1960 and "purged." Two-thirds of the professors went into exile. Juan Marinello, nominal head of the Communist PSP for years, a well-to-do poet with a fine art collection, was made rector. (He is now Cuban representative to UNESCO in Paris.) As with so much that was happening, unscrupulous means had been used to achieve a desirable end. The University naturally became an organ of the Marxist-Leninist government, but it also became a disciplined, serious center of learning which in the 1970s is undergoing an extraordinary rebirth.

For years there was a great shortage of suitable teachers in all schools as a result of the exodus. Standards had to be lowered, with young teachers keeping a step ahead of their pupils, but in time the deficiency was made manageable.

A number of special Escuelas de Instrucción Revolucionaria (Schools of Revolutionary Instruction) were created from 1961 onward. Out of them came a stream of young men and women who today form the cadres for governmental posts, the professions, farms, factories, and the armed forces. They are the new generation on whom the ultimate success or failure of the Revolution will depend. The indoctrination accompanying the instruction is, of course, Marxist-Leninist.

Education potentially represents the greatest and most fruitful economic investment of the Cuban Revolution. Orthodox capitalist economists who point to material failures of the Revolution would do well to keep this in mind. Knowledge, training, skills, higher intellectual levels, professional ability, physical training, and sports—the statisticians cannot put these into their tables, but their economic value to Cuba is enormous. Nor can they put in the fact that all children, however poor the family, are now well fed and clothed; that the new generations of Cubans are growing up healthier than their parents and grandparents.

It has often been noted that the most industrious teacher of all was Fidel Castro. He saw immediately that the Cuban people could be taught and made to understand a great deal if he, President Dorticós, Raúl Castro, Che Guevara, and others would become "teachers" on the highest level. In the process the Cuban masses have listened to more didactic speeches, I imagine, than any people on earth.

If I have seemed to depart here from my narrative, I can only say that there is no understanding of the Cuban Revolution unless there is an appreciation of what Fidel Castro did for education, even in the first desperate, dramatic years when the economy was collapsing, when thousands of Cubans were fleeing, and when the United States was doing its best to overthrow the regime. From the beginning the educational program has been vital to the strength and popular support of the Revolution.

To be sure, the hemisphere's attention was focused on other things in those years. The theme running through Washington's accusations against Castro's policies from the early months was "subversion." Even in 1973, President Nixon brought it up in connection with rumors of negotiations with Cuba.

The year 1959 saw a series of attempted invasions by raiding parties from Cuba. So far as I could find out, only one was organized and sanctioned by Fidel Castro. This was against Trujillo's Dominican Republic on June 14, 1959. I know that Fidel was involved because when I told him that the captive Cuban leader, Major Ochoa, had gone on the Ciudad Trujillo radio to attack him, Castro was upset and incredulous. Ochoa had been a brave and loyal *barbudo* in the Sierra Maestra.

The first of the raids, which was against Panama on April 18, contained about forty Cubans among its eighty men, but Fidel was on his trip to the United States and Argentina at the time. He issued a furious reprimand against the Cubans involved. It was, he said, a case of "inconceivable irresponsibility by adventurers who possibly did nothing in the Revolution."

"The expedition to Panama was organized in Cuba by a group of Panamanians and Cuban adventurers, headed by a certain Cesar Vega, who never had anything to do with the Cuban Revolution," Raúl Roa told the U.N. Security Council on January 5, 1961, "and it was the Revolutionary Government, which was very concerned, acting through the Organization of American States in which I was then Ambassador, which immediately put a stop to this international adventure. To this effect, I sent, in addition, some officers of the [Cuban] Rebel Army to Panama so that they could cooperate with the Panamanian Government in the peaceful liquidation of the invasion . . . The report of the Investigating Commission cleared the Cuban Government of all responsibility."

Roa added that "many Nicaraguans, Dominicans and Haitians who wanted to return to their countries, arms in hand, to free them of the tyrannies were apprehended and imprisoned" by the Cuban Security Corps. All the expeditions failed quickly and ignominiously.

The State Department made effective propaganda out of these invasion attempts, and they have gone into "history" as examples of Castroite attempts at subversion.

At all times the Castro regime has openly and vociferously agitated for Puerto Rican independence. One must remember Puerto Rico's long connection with Cuba as a Spanish colony. For José Martí, the independence of Puerto Rico had an importance second only to that of Cuba. For someone of Fidel's generation, brought up on revisionist Cuban history, Puerto Rico is a colony of the United States whose patriots must, as a matter of course, long for independence from the United States. They don't, as the elections for governor and the legislature proved once again in November 1972. However, for what it may be worth—probably nothing—a resolution was passed by a large majority in the U.N. General Assembly at the end of 1973 calling for Puerto Rican independence.

Any moral judgments on Castro's attempts to overthrow other Latin American countries were weakened for the historic record by the fact that the United States was attempting to overthrow the Castro government. Twelve years later, the CIA was to succeed in overthrowing the Allende government in Chile by using every underhand method of subversion. The Organization of American States Declaration of San José, August 28, 1960, reaffirmed "the principles of nonintervention by any American state in the internal or external affairs of the other American states, and it reiterates that each state has the right to develop its culture, political and economic life freely and naturally, respecting the rights of the individual and the principles of universal morality, and, as a consequence, no American state may intervene for the purpose of imposing upon another American state its ideology, or political, economic or social principles."

Yet by that date the United States was beginning to arm and train the Cuban exiles who were to invade Cuba! Washington was, in fact, intervening in a number of illegal ways. The question of who was trying to subvert whom depended on whether one was North American or Cuban.

The declaration quoted above was made at the Seventh Meeting of Consultation of the Foreign Ministers of the OAS. At the end of his speech as Cuban ambassador to the OAS the following January, Raúl Roa announced that Cuba was leaving the conference. "The Latin American Governments have abandoned Cuba," he said. "I depart with my people, and with my people the peoples of our America also depart from here."

In January 1962, at the Eighth Meeting, which was held in Punta del Este, Uruguay, the United States made its strongest move to isolate Cuba. It called for automatic sanctions against Cuba if she did not break her ties with the Communist countries. The result, as should have been expected, was a failure. However, Secretary of State Dean Rusk did manage to squeeze through a country-by-country vote to expel Cuba from the OAS and the Inter-American Defense Board. There were six abstentions on the vote, and those six countries together contained 70 percent of the population of Latin America.

The process of isolation was concluded at the Ninth Meeting on July 26, 1964, when a resolution was voted to suspend all trade and diplomatic relations between OAS members and Cuba. This resolution is still in force early in 1975, but it is ignored by many of the countries.

Mexico alone retained her diplomatic relations with Cuba during the 1960s, but Allende's Chile breached the wall in 1970 and others have followed. Nevertheless, Fidel Castro goes on stating firmly (as of 1975) that Cuba will not return to the Organization of American States under any circumstances.

The so-called invasions of Latin countries by Cubans had little substance to them, but subversion—or attempted subversion—of Latin American governments was a more solid and serious activity. This started in 1960. The training of foreign guerrillas in Cuba; the arms and money supplied to guerrilla bands in Venezuela, Guatemala, and other countries; the verbal encouragement from Havana for opposition groups; the backing for Maoist, Trotskyist, and other extreme leftist groups—all these went on energetically until after Che Guevara's death in 1967. Since that time the activity has dwindled to unimportant proportions without quite disappearing.

"Of course, and why not?" Fidel said to me and my wife during a conversation in November 1963, when I asked him about it. "The CIA is doing everything to Cuba that you accuse us of. It is training saboteurs and guerrillas; it is supplying counterrevolutionaries with arms and materials; it is supporting raids by sea and air, and landing parties on Cuban shores; it is flooding Latin America with anti-Cuban propaganda; it is using its great influence in every country in Latin America against us.

"If the United States can do all these things, why can't we try to do the same things?"

Raúl Castro once told me that Fidel had started arming his supporters in Cuba the very day he entered Havana in triumph—January 8, 1959. When the British refused to sell Cuba seventeen Hunter jet fighters in September 1959, evidently responding to a request from the United States, hints were dropped that Cuba might get her arms from the Soviet bloc—which is what she did.

The Rebel Army immediately replaced Batista's regular army. The navy and air force were put under loyal officers (at least, so they thought; one was José Luis Díaz Lanz). The key to a revolutionary defense force came with the formation, late in 1959, of a worker-peasant-student militia, which was first a paramilitary organization and then, in September 1960, was turned into an armed militia on military lines.

The Russians first sold and then gave arms to Cuba. They also provided technicians to teach Cubans how to use them and trained hundreds of young Cubans in Russia who became officers in the FAR (Armed Revolutionary Forces). One reason for the timing of the Bay of Pigs invasion seems to have been that the Cubans were soon—probably in May 1961—going to receive a number of Russian MIG fighters, which Cuban pilots had been trained to fly in the Soviet Union.

On March 4, 1960, the Cuban Revolution had had its equivalent of the blowing up of the *Maine* in 1898. A French freighter, *La Coubre,* loaded with seventy-six tons of war materials from Belgium, was blown up at 3:10 in the afternoon in Havana harbor. Seventy-five dockers were killed, about two hundred were wounded, and great damage was done to the port.

Sabotage was naturally suspected. López-Fresquet writes in his book that his assistant at the Treasury, William Burn, told him Castro "immediately asked him [Burn] to request experts from the Belgian factory to determine the cause of the explosion. One of them, a man by the name of Dessard, was at the time in Mexico and arrived the following day. This expert ruled out the possibilities of improper handling, heat, and other accidental causes. He maintained that it was sabotage, but could not determine whether the action took place in port, during the trip, or while loading in Antwerp."

My wife and I reached Havana the day after the disaster. I saw Fidel after he had made a violent speech attacking the United States, and I asked him why he was accusing the Americans. He said that he did not specifically blame the United States and conceded that he had no proof, "but who else would want to sabotage the shipment?" Later he left no doubts in Cuban minds that the explosion was the work of the United States. It became a part of the Revolution's mythology. In 1973, for instance, Havana's *Granma* referred to the event as "a criminal, cowardly imperialist aggression" by the CIA. Actually, as with the *Maine*, the cause of the explosion was never ascertained.

The speech that Fidel made the day after the explosion in Colón Cemetery, Havana, has a special place in the history of the Revolution.

"We will not only resist," he said, "but also defeat any act of aggression, and our only alternative will be those which faced us when we began our revolutionary struggle: the alternative of freedom or death. Except that now freedom means much more; it means fatherland; and thus our alternatives are Fatherland or Death!"

So was born the revolutionary cry *Patria o Muerte!* to which, in another speech, on June 9, 1960, Castro added *Venceremos!* (We shall conquer!) As in so many other cases, there was a parallel with the Wars of Independence. The Montecristi manifesto of March 25, 1895, put out by José Martí and Máximo Gómez, ended with the words *La Victoria o el Sepulcro!* (Victory or the Tomb!)

Ambassador Bonsal thinks that Castro's violent and abusive reaction to the *Coubre* incident "was perhaps what tipped the scales in favor of Washington's abandonment of the policy of nonintervention in Cuba." The government was already frightened by the results of Mikoyan's visit to Havana the month before. The presidential election campaign in the United States was about to begin.

"The new American policy—not announced as such but implicit in the actions of the United States Government," Bonsal writes, "was one of overthrowing Castro by all means available to the United States short of the open employment of American armed forces in Cuba."

The Embassy in Havana was not kept properly informed, he says. Neither, he believes, was the State Department. "As my narrative will reveal, we in the Havana Embassy became aware only gradually and imperfectly, and without real opportunity for comment and discussion, of the new policy of our Government."

A few weeks after the *Coubre* explosion, he continues, "the top-level decision . . . was taken to let the Central Intelligence Agency begin recruiting and training anti-Castro Cuban exiles for military service." This was Eisenhower's decision on a policy which Vice-President Nixon had been advocating for nine months. In addition, according to Bonsal, the Administration, through its advice to the heads of the parent companies in the United States, engineered "the removal of key American and Cuban personnel from leading

American companies in such a manner as to create serious difficulties for the Cuban economy."

Yet at the end of April 1960, less than two months after the *Coubre* incident, Castro named Dr. José Miró Cardona as ambassador to the United States. Miró accepted because, as he said, he believed that there was going to be a favorable change in Fidel's attitude toward the United States.

Perhaps Castro was contemplating one, although it would have been a complete reversal. This was one of those facets of the Cuban Revolution that made no sense—the choice of a nonrevolutionary, professional, middle-class, pro-American ambassador at such a time. But weeks passed and Fidel did not even receive the appointee. In July, Miró Cardona took refuge in the Argentine Embassy, went into exile, and was nominally to lead the provisional exile government at the time of the Bay of Pigs invasion. In October, Castro indignantly complained to me that Miró had professed loyalty to the regime in talking to him on the very eve of seeking asylum. He seemed upset.

Yet on that same trip to Cuba, Fidel questioned me closely about reports that the United States was organizing an invasion of Cuba. I had been on a long Latin American journey and was out of touch, so I was able to answer honestly that I had heard nothing. Fidel Castro knew what I did not know.

CHAPTER 9

Pigs and Missiles

Anti-Communism causes more trouble in the world than ever Communism does or did.

—A. J. P. Taylor
(Introduction to *The Communist Manifesto*)

It would be stupid to underestimate the danger that the Communization and pro-Soviet policy of the Castro regime represented to the United States. After all, it did lead to the missile crisis.

From their beginnings as an independent nation, Americans have feared that a foreign power hostile to the United States could either annex Cuba or use her as a base from which to attack the mainland. The advent of Fidel Castro brought a Cuban regime independent of and hostile to the United States. Moreover, this regime identified itself with the United States' chief antagonist in world affairs—the Soviet Union. Although the Monroe Doctrine had not come to an end, as Nikita Khrushchev boasted in 1960, it had precious little life left in it.

In July 1960, the month Khrushchev spoke of "figurative" rockets, President Eisenhower announced that the United States would not "tolerate the establishment of a regime dominated by international Communism in the Western hemisphere." President Kennedy, in his first State of the Union message on January 30, 1961, declared that "Communist domination in this hemisphere can never be negotiated." Secretary of State Dean Rusk repeated Kennedy's declaration on a number of occasions.

All these words have had to be ignored or forgotten. A Communist regime has had to be tolerated, and there has been negotiation, at least over hijacking.

Put in oversimplified form, in 1960 Fidel Castro's room to maneuver had only two exits. Even granting that he was the one who slammed the normally used door in Uncle Sam's face, it was also true that the Yankee neighbor turned the key and bolted the lock. That left only the other door, which led eastward to the Communist world. Whoever was at fault, by 1960 Fidel Castro had no choice.

It has been difficult or impossible for North Americans to realize the depth and strength of the Cuban revolutionaries' fears of United States intervention. This was not put on, and they have not lost this fear even in the 1970s. It was, of course, much greater in the early years of the Revolution. One of my strongest recollections of many talks with the top Cuban leaders was that their greatest preoccupation was the conviction that the United States was determined to overthrow Fidel Castro and destroy the Revolution. To believe that the Cubans courted such intervention is to fail to realize that their hearts and souls and faith were in the Revolution that they were making. They dreaded a United States intervention, and although they overestimated how far the United States would go, they were right in their fears.

Cuban history had taught only one lesson about antagonizing the United States and damaging American interests. The results had always been military intervention, intolerable diplomatic pressures, economic threats. No Cuban government or leader during the Republic had provoked the United States and gotten away with it.

Times had changed, but Fidel Castro could not know what the American reaction would be. He expected the worst and prepared for it, but he went ahead with his provocations long before he had the Russians to back him up and provide arms. It was daring and reckless, but shrewdly calculated and cleverly timed. The price that Cuba had to pay in economic terms was astronomical, but there was no United States military intervention, and such intervention was the only force that could stop Fidel Castro on his way to a complete social revolution.

Independence from the United States, the dream of Cuban patriots and nationalists since before José Martí, was at last achieved. The special price to be paid was economic dependence on the Soviet Union, but Russia was six thousand miles away and uninterested in acquiring land, utilities, sugar mills, factories, or cultural influence.

Whether or not Cuba got the worst of the bargain depends on the point of view. Nearly all North Americans and a great number of Cubans think so, but the issue cannot be settled in such simplistic terms. History is only tidy for the historians who come long after and draw clear patterns to suit their points of view. Current history is easier to make than to evaluate. In Fernand Braudel's profoundly wise comment, "Events are the ephemera of history." But Fidel

Castro, at least, has always been free of doubts.

"The most likely thing your Government is dreaming of," C. Wright Mills, speaking theoretically in the words of the Cubans, said in his 1960 book *Listen Yankee,* "is some kind of indirect military action, secretly supporting mercenaries and Batista henchmen; something like they did in Guatemala a while back. This intervention would not come from the U.S. soil, but maybe somewhere in Central America."

Mills's book was naïve and full of mistakes, but he had talked at length with all the top revolutionaries, Castro included, and this could well have come from Fidel, who harbored just such a suspicion at the time. It was what happened.

Ambassador Bonsal was recalled to Washington on October 28, 1960, for what turned out to be the end of his mission. The situation was weird—mutual vituperation, blocked trade, seizures of more than $800 million in American properties without compensation, and Fidel Castro knowing quite well that the United States was arming and training an expeditionary force to overthrow him.

Ambassador Bonsal still believed that "Castro's own position seemed shaky." He was doubtless right in saying of the Kennedy-Nixon electoral campaigns then ending: "The notion that the Cuban people were almost to a man anxious to throw off the rule that Castro had violently and mysteriously imposed seemed to be accepted by both candidates." This fallacious belief, based on the way Americans would have felt in similar circumstances and reinforced by faulty CIA reports, was soon to lead to the farcical tragedy of the Bay of Pigs.

In his campaign speeches Kennedy was critical of Eisenhower and Nixon for having been pro-Batista and then "presiding over the Communization of Cuba." Kennedy called for sending an expeditionary force of "democratic" refugees to crush the "Communist enclave," although the exiles of that period were mainly ex-*Batistianos* and the Castroites not yet Communist.

Nixon brazenly condemned Kennedy's "dangerously irresponsible recommendations," although he himself had helped organize the exiles then being trained for the Cuban invasion. He evidently thought that this was still a secret. Nixon came out in one speech for a repetition of the Guatemalan operation of 1954, where, as he incorrectly stated, "a Communist dictator" was overthrown by "the Guatemalan people."

President Jacobo Arbenz of Guatemala, like Castro later, tried in vain to buy arms from normal sources. He too turned to Eastern

Europe. A ship with arms, which sailed from Stettin, Poland, reached Guatemala on May 17, 1954. There was an uproar in Washington. President Eisenhower had been convinced, even before this, that Guatemala was now a Communist country. He knew little about foreign affairs and less about Latin America.

Colonel Castillo Armas, a Guatemalan exile, gathered a band of less than a thousand men just inside the Honduran border. The United States armed them and gave them four planes and money. Starting on June 18, they managed to penetrate about ten miles into Guatemala, but bogged down. The effective job was done in Guatemala City, where the "pistol-packin' " United States ambassador, John Peurifoy, suborned the army leaders—who, anyway, were anti-leftist. They forced Arbenz to resign and depart on June 25.

Castillo Armas peacefully entered the capital in July, where he was duly elected President—and was murdered in 1958, leaving Guatemala as corrupt and with the same mass peasant poverty and tiny wealthy minority as of old—but safe for American strategy and business.

The CIA, the Pentagon, Eisenhower, Nixon, and Dulles had succeeded by wile and force, but had misread the situation. The Arbenz regime collapsed because the army refused to fight for him. Castillo Armas had little to do except to be there. He had no popular support. In Latin America the feeling was widespread that Roosevelt's "Good Neighbor" policy had ended. The successor to Castillo Armas was Miguel Ydígoras Fuentes, who provided the facilities for the Bay of Pigs invasion.

Che Guevara realized that the Cuban Revolution was a warning to the United States and the Latin American governments. "This means that imperialism has learned, fundamentally, the lesson of Cuba," he wrote in the magazine *Verde Olivo* of April 9, 1960, "and that it will not again be taken by surprise in any part of our twenty republics, in any of the colonies that still exist in any part of America."

He showed remarkable prescience. Five years later President Johnson intervened with thirty thousand marines in the Dominican Republic. "The American nations," Johnson said on May 2, 1965, "cannot, must not, and will not permit the establishment of another Communist government in the Western Hemisphere."

President Kennedy had said the same thing in Miami on November 18, 1963, a few days before he was assassinated. But Fidel Castro had nothing to do with the Dominican uprising and was caught by surprise. He could not have helped the Dominican rebels if he had wanted to. Besides, the Soviet Union doubtless would have been dismayed at the idea of having to support "another Cuba" in Latin America. In fact, Russian policy was counterrevolutionary, popular front, and it still is.

The exact role of the CIA in providing arms, bombs, and all kinds of sabotage materials, as well as planes to make drops to the Cuban underground and to parachute men in, and landing others from boats, is naturally not capable of detailed summation. However, it can be taken as certain that from the spring of 1959 onward, the CIA did everything that it could to bring about the overthrow of the Castro government. Beginning in January 1960 at the latest, CIA planes from Florida, some with American pilots, were raiding Cuban fields with napalm-type bombs to burn the sugar cane. The Cubans claimed that four of the planes that crashed had American pilots.

When the John F. Kennedy Memorial Library in Cambridge, Massachusetts, put a great mass of material at the disposal of researchers on August 17, 1970, *The New York Times* printed an article by Henry Raymont, who studied many of the oral-history interviews. One group of talks was with George A. Smathers, former U.S. senator from Florida, who, writes Raymont, discussed and rejected the idea of assassinating Castro on a number of occasions.

"I don't know whether he [President Kennedy] brought it up or I brought it up," Smathers said in an interview dated March 31, 1964, quoted by Raymond:

> We had further conversation on assassination of Fidel, what would be the reaction, how would the people react, would the people be gratified.
>
> As I recollect, he [Kennedy] was just throwing out a great barrage of questions—he was certain it could be accomplished—I remember that—it would be no great problem. But the question was whether or not it would accomplish that which he wanted it to, whether or not the reaction throughout South America would be good or bad. . . .
>
> I did talk to him about a plan of having a false attack made on Guantánamo Bay which would give us the excuse of actually fomenting a fight which would then give us the excuse to go in and do the job. He asked me to write him something about it, and I did.

As I mentioned, Castro knew about this idea and referred to it in a speech. It seems to have been connected with an assassination plot by Rolando Cubela, a former major in the Rebel Army who was arrested in February 1966. Fidel also told me about the Guantánamo plot at the time; either it was common knowledge or there was a leak at the White House.

The former *New York Times* correspondent Tad Szulc wrote in an article for the February 1974 *Esquire* that President Kennedy spoke to him in November 1961 about being under pressure from intelligence advisers to have Castro assassinated.

What Fidel called "revolutionary bandits" were active through the spring and summer of 1960 in the Escambray, Maestra, and Cristal Sierras, especially the first-named. There were also underground groups, one of the most important at that time being the Movimiento de Rescate Revolucionario (Movement of Revolutionary Recovery, or MRR). It included a young Catholic professor, Manuel Artime. Money, supplies, arms, and transportation came from the CIA.

Justo Carillo, a distinguished banker and economist, headed a small underground group in Havana. The outfit that had become the largest and most important of all by 1961 was led by Manuel Ray, former minister of public works under Castro. This was the Movimiento Revolucionario del Pueblo (Revolutionary People's Movement, or MRP). Unfortunately for itself and for the exiles, "Manolo" Ray and the MRP were considered too radical by one of the main CIA organizers of the Bay of Pigs operation (whom I mentioned before), Frank Bender (or Droller), so the MRP got no American help. Their slogan was *Fidelismo sin Fidel* (Fidel's reforms without Fidel).

Castro did not feel able to concentrate on the dangerous Sierra de Escambray guerrilla bands for some time. He knew of the invasion plans, but apparently thought that the attack was coming in December 1960 or January 1961. In a speech on January 2 he told the Cuban people that Eisenhower was planning to attack before he left office on January 20 on the excuse that Cuba was constructing rocket pads on the island. On December 31, Foreign Minister Raúl Roa had called for a Security Council meeting on the subject.

In that same speech (Bonsal thinks that the idea may have come to him on the spur of the moment) Castro demanded that the United States cut the staff in its Havana Embassy down to eleven, the same number as in the moribund Cuban Embassy in Washington. This was the last straw for President Eisenhower, who thereupon broke diplomatic relations between the United States and Cuba.

When the invasion did not materialize, Fidel cleared the Sierra de Escambray of most of the peasants living there. Some of them had been helping the guerrillas. Then he gathered and sent in the rural militia and Rebel Army forces, whom he had organized. They cleaned out the region with a few weeks' leeway to meet the Bay of Pigs invasion in April.

A CIA recommendation to arm and train Cuban exiles for guerrilla warfare had been made to Eisenhower on March 17, 1960. He agreed. From that day on, the United States was caught in an inexorable millrace; something had been started that could not be stopped.

John F. Kennedy, for his part, had committed himself in his electoral campaign to help the exiles and domestic Cuban opposition to overthrow Castro. He was caught in a trap that he himself had laid, and in this respect was as responsible for the fiasco as anybody. It was therefore no more than right that he should have taken the blame on himself.

The President-elect was briefed in mid-November 1960, and learned that the Pentagon and CIA were doing what he had recommended. He gave a keep-going signal, although, according to Theodore Sorensen, one of his White House assistants, he had "grave doubts." In fact, he still had them when the invasion time came around, but since every high official of the CIA and the Pentagon favored the invasion, Kennedy had hardly any support for his doubts. The whole American business community; the expropriated American companies; the overwhelming force of public opinion expressed in an almost unanimously hostile press; and by no means least, the uniquely intense and emotional anti-Communism of the American people and press—all these brought an enormous weight of pressure on Kennedy to do something.

Inexcusably, the President was misinformed and misled by the CIA, the Pentagon, and the Cuban exiles. It was also unfortunate for him that diplomatic relations had been broken, because the American Embassy in Havana had been better informed than the CIA. The only meaningful choice which the President had was whether or not to back the invasion force with American arms, men, and naval and air forces. When he decided against an American intervention, he doomed the invasion to virtually certain failure.

Arthur Schlesinger, Jr., wrote in *A Thousand Days* that President Eisenhower had allocated $13 million for arms, supplies, and training of what, at first, were to be guerrilla bands. Later, it was decided, apparently without consulting the President, to organize an invasion supported by American planes. This was the plan that Kennedy inherited.

The CIA recruited the Cubans, paying them $400 a month, with an additional allotment of $175 for their wives and more for their children. This payment, very generous by Cuban standards, gave Fidel Castro the excuse to call them mercenaries.

The first salvo of the battle of the Bay of Pigs came in the form of a Kennedy Administration white paper on Cuba. It is understood to have been written by Arthur Schlesinger, Jr. As a political and polemical document, it was effective; as a supposedly factual, historical presentation of the Cuban situation, it is best forgotten.

The Cuban revolutionary leaders were told that they had "betrayed their own revolution," turned the country over to the Cuban Communists, and made Cuba a puppet of Moscow.

"It is not clear whether Dr. Castro intended from the start to betray his pledges of a free and democratic Cuba, to deliver his country to the Sino-Soviet bloc, and to mount an attack on the inter-American system," the white paper says in its concluding section, "or whether he made his original pledges in all sincerity but, on assuming his new responsibilities, found himself increasingly dependent on ruthless men around him with clear ideas and the disciplined organization to carry those ideas into action. What is important is not the motive, but the result."

There was no such "either/or." The terms used in the white paper had no valid meaning. Yet American fears were justified. Soviet arms were pouring into Cuba at the time, though it was illogical to condemn the Cubans for arming themselves against the attack they knew was coming. Fidel Castro would have been stupid not to organize what the white paper called "the largest ground forces in the hemisphere." He saved his revolution with the Russian arms.

It was true enough, from Washington's viewpoint, to consider the Castro regime as "a clear and present danger," but it was a danger to the United States, not to a mythical free and democratic Latin America. The missile crisis, only a year and a half away, showed how dangerous Castroite Cuba could be. A devotee of power politics would say, not that the United States had no business intervening in Cuban affairs, but that if it decided to intervene, it should have done so in overwhelming strength. This is what President Johnson did in the Dominican Republic in 1965. In 1961 President Kennedy was wise enough to see that an American military intervention in Cuba would do the United States more harm than good.

The white paper made the interesting concession that "we acknowledge past omissions and errors in our relationship to them [the Cubans]." It also conceded that in 1959 Cuba was ripe for revolution.

"The character of the Batista regime in Cuba," it read, "made a violent popular reaction almost inevitable. The rapacity of the leadership, the corruption of the Government, the brutality of the police, the regime's indifference to the needs of the people for education, medical care, housing, for social justice and economic opportunity—all these in Cuba as elsewhere, constituted an open invitation to revolution."

Yet every one of these "invitations to revolution"—rapacity, corruption, police brutality, indifference to the needs of the people—obtained in any given year back to the founding of the Republic. There was "a violent popular reaction" against Machado in 1933–1934, but no revolution. None of the causes given in the white paper in themselves explain why this time there *was* a revolution. Something new and different had happened, and there was no other possible explanation except—Fidel Castro.

On the verge of the invasion, *The New York Times* emasculated a dispatch from Miami by its correspondent Tad Szulc, leading President Kennedy later to say to Managing Editor Turner Catledge: "If you had printed more about the operation you would have saved us from a colossal mistake."

The arguments about secrecy and preserving American security were nonsense. As early as October 31, 1960, in an interview in the U.N. General Assembly, Cuban Foreign Minister Raúl Roa was able to give full and accurate details about the recruitment and training of the Cuban exiles (he called them "counterrevolutionaries and mercenaries"). He had the names and places where they were being trained in Florida and knew of the connivance of Guatemala and the fact that the preparations were being directed by the CIA. The information he used came from *Life*, the New York *Daily News*, and the Columbia Broadcasting Service. The Cubans, of course, also had their own intelligence information.

"Guatemalan territory has been converted into a refuge and bastion of hardened Cuban war criminals and foreign mercenaries," Roa said, "trained and organized by technicians of the American Army on private plantations and in remote places of the country. A number of secret airports have been established and many military planes and transport-ships have been bought."

Roa added other details, all of them roughly correct, and all ignored or disbelieved.

In the letter dated December 31, 1960, to the then president of the Security Council, which I mentioned, Roa denounced "the imminent military aggression against Cuba by the United States" and called for a meeting of the Council. He claimed that "there exists a Department of State document, which has been sent to all chancelleries and which states, with unheard-of impudence, that the Government of President Eisenhower is preparing to 'prevent the installation of seventeen launching pads for Soviet missiles.' This document purportedly added that for the moment, the construction of these pads had been suspended, but it reaffirmed that [U.S.] intervention 'would take place in case such construction is continued.' "

This was more than a year and a half before such pads began to be constructed. It shows how early the Cuban exiles—or perhaps it was the CIA—began shouting "Wolf! Wolf!" Or else it was a case of inspired foreboding.

When the Security Council met on January 4, 1961, Roa, among other things, told them that "the airport of Retalhuleu was precipitously put into condition by North American engineers." Retalhuleu, on the west coast of Guatemala, was in fact the main training center and air base for the Cuban exiles, and it really was prepared by American army engineers.

The Guatemalan story first broke into print in *La Hora* of Guatemala City in October 1960. About five hundred Cuban exiles were then being trained at the base. Professor Ronald Hilton of Stanford University was in Guatemala, read the item, and published an editorial article about it in his monthly *Hispanic American Report* of Stanford. Hilton, a friend, telephoned me about it, and I passed the information along to *The Times'* News Department.

The Nation picked up Hilton's article for its November 19, 1960, issue. Richard Dudman of the St. Louis *Post-Dispatch* then went to Guatemala and, in a story published on December 1, corroborated Professor Hilton's account. The Washington *Post,* the *Wall Street Journal, Diario de las Américas, U.S. News and World Report,* all wrote about the preparations for the invasion during November and December 1960, and kept on in the new year.

The Nicaraguan and Honduran Cisne Island bases, the five bases in Florida, even the money paid to the Cuban exiles and their families were common knowledge—one would have thought. But "knowledge" and "news" are relative terms in the U.S. press world.

The happenings did not become *news* until *The New York Times,* very belatedly (and, I may add, through my insistence and the cooperation of Emanuel R. Freedman, then foreign editor) published the Retalhuleu story.

In the Security Council, U.S. Ambassador Wadsworth blandly said that the reports were "absurd." *The Times* was soundly berated by some White House and Pentagon officials for lack of patriotism and responsibility in publishing this "secret."

The Bay of Pigs (Baia de Cochinos) is on the south coast of Cuba at the eastern edge of the extensive marsh known as the Ciénaga de Zapata. There is another marshland to the east. Access is limited to two good highways, one coming down from the north, the other going east to the large port of Cienfuegos. Just behind the latter road is a small but serviceable airfield. An established beachhead would have to be enlarged quickly and held firmly, for with the swamps on either side and the sea behind, there is no line of retreat.

The idea was to hold such a beachhead, fly in a "Provisional Government" which the United States would immediately recognize, and then back it strongly with arms, supplies, and advisers. A Cuban Revolutionary Council was formed, comprised of a quarrelsome, mutually suspicious political mixture of anti-Batista but pro-American, pro-establishment moderates headed by Dr. José Miró Cardona. They had no following in Cuba and would not have been welcomed under any circumstances, least of all as representing a Yankee-backed invasion.

The only organization that might have made serious trouble on the island was Manuel Ray's MRP, but, as I have stated, the CIA director, Frank Bender (Droller), would have nothing to do with anyone so liberal. Thus, although Ray was permitted to join the exile Revolutionary Council at the last moment, his underground movement in Cuba had not been kept informed and could not be alerted in time to be used. Before and during the invasion, the members of the Revolutionary Council were held as virtual prisoners in Miami by the CIA without even knowing what was happening.

The Brigade 2506, as it called itself, was taken to Puerto Cabezas, Nicaragua. It sailed in six ships on April 14, 1961. President Luis Somoza, the Nicaraguan dictator, was there to cheer them on, jocularly urging them to bring him back some hairs plucked from Castro's beard.

While Fidel knew that the invasion was coming, he could not tell where it would strike. The Bay of Pigs was an obvious possibility, and he had it constantly patrolled. He had cannily dispersed and camouflaged his small air force. Some obsolete, unusable planes were put out conspicuously to fool the attackers and draw bombs. Early in the morning of April 15, 1961, Castro went to his military headquarters in Havana and ordered a nationwide alert.

Two U.S. B-26 bombers attacked at six in the morning, bombing four Cuban airfields. The planes had been disguised as Cuban by the CIA with Cuban Air Force markings. They did little damage.

Another B-26 bomber, with a pilot who had defected from the Cuban Air Force, flew from Nicaragua to Miami as a diversion, claiming that he had bombed some Cuban airfields. However, one of the two real bombers developed engine trouble and, being unable to return to Nicaragua, also had to land in Miami.

The deception was quickly pierced by American newspapermen, but not before Ambassador Adlai Stevenson at the United Nations and his assistant Harland Cleveland rejected Raúl Roa's complaint to the U.N., saying that the planes were from the Cuban Air Force.

Adlai Stevenson, although he knew of, and had opposed, an invasion, had not been given any details, nor was he advised of the timing. So when Washington told him to tell the emergency meeting of the U.N. Political Committee that the two B-26s "were Castro's own Air Force planes," he complied in good faith. He even produced faked photographs sent to him by Washington. A few hours later he learned the truth. His biographer, Herbert J. Miller, wrote that he was "in a shocked daze," made worse by reports that President Kennedy had referred to him as "my official liar."

For Fidel Castro, it was the occasion next day of a superb and devastating speech against the United States, arousing his people to their successful stand. (It was in this speech of April 16, 1961, that he first said: "This is a socialist and democratic revolution of the humble, by the humble and for the humble.")

Despite President Kennedy's orders—or perhaps interpreting them very loosely—the U.S. Navy as well as the CIA took part in the invasion. U.S. naval landing craft, coming from the Vieques Naval Base in Puerto Rico, met the invasion force thirty miles south of Cienfuegos. A warship with U.S. Marines made a feint off the west coast of Pinar del Río Province, drawing some of Fidel's troops, commanded by Che Guevara.

The invading force comprised about 1,500 men, divided into six battalions. The political chief was the right-winger Manuel Artime, who had made himself unpopular with many exiles but who was the favorite of Frank Bender of the CIA.

(An interesting sequel may be inserted here. Artime, with several other Bay of Pigs participants, was to figure in the Watergate case. The convicted conspirator E. Howard Hunt, Jr., was the CIA operator who supervised the planning and execution of the Bay of Pigs invasion with Frank Bender. Hunt's name did not figure at the time; Bender [Droller] was the man whom the Cubans dealt with in Florida and Guatemala. Hunt remained Artime's friend and was godfather of one of his children.

(Three other Cubans involved at the Bay of Pigs were arrested and convicted in the Watergate case with Hunt—Eugenio R. Martínez, Virgilio González, and Bernard L. Barker, who acted as the exiles' paymaster. In February 1972, Artime, by then the owner of a meat-exporting firm in Miami, organized the Miami Watergate Defense Relief Fund and collected $21,000, which was given to the convicted Watergate burglars.

(A *Time* magazine reporter interviewed Hunt in jail in August 1973. He said that Hunt told him he still felt that the Watergate break-in was motivated by a belief that Cuba was supplying funds to the Democratic presidential campaign. "The main purpose of the Watergate break-in," Hunt is quoted as saying, "was a photographic job to get lists of contributors and check if any were blind fronts for Castro." If this was the case, one can only say that Washington's intelligence about the Castro regime was as bad in 1972 as in 1961.)

The field commander at the Bay of Pigs was José Pérez San Román. There was a strong political "Catholic" conservative tinge to the force, even to taking three priests along. Most of the men were from the upper-middle class—the strongest opponents of the Revolution. About 250 were students, about fifty Negroes or mulattos. In the account later published by Castro, it was estimated that the invaders and their families between them once owned a million acres of land, ten thousand houses, seventy factories, ten sugar mills, five mines, and two banks.

According to Hugh Thomas, a small but deliberately chosen group of thugs in the invasion force were known criminals and killers from the Batista period. They were assigned some special hatchet work on the revolutionary leaders.

The force anchored a half-mile offshore in four vessels. The first men to land were Americans, not Cubans—frogmen to mark the positions. Each ship had an American CIA "adviser." The choice of the landing site was the only unknown factor for the *Fidelistas.* Coral reefs (evidently the maps were faulty) destroyed or delayed several of the landing craft. Other boats had engine trouble. Supplies, reserve ammunition, and one of the battalions were still at sea when dawn came on April 17, but landings were finally made on both beaches of the Bay of Pigs. (The Cubans use the name of one of the two beaches, Playa Girón, for their official designation of the invasion.)

When I was in Havana in 1972, the present minister of education, Major José R. Fernández, showed me one of the battlefield maps used by the invasion force. It had been taken from one of the captured officers. It showed the area in great detail. The spot, Fernández remarked (and Castro once said the same to me), was well chosen.

Fernández, who is one of the very few regular army officers in the Castro government, was then a captain supervising the training of an infantry battalion at the Australia sugar mill on the road going north from the Bay of Pigs. He took over as field commander while Fidel rushed down from Havana to set up an over-all headquarters further back. With few exceptions, the local militia, made up of charcoal burners and other poor peasants who had profited greatly by the Revolution, went into action bravely and held out until Fernández's regulars arrived. They were led by a young Communist, Flavio Bravo, who in 1975 is a deputy prime minister.

Fidel Castro, literally and actively commander in chief, was as preoccupied with events in the rest of the island as in the crucial fight at the Bay of Pigs.

The outcome of the battle itself was never in doubt. The one great question was whether President Kennedy would change his mind and authorize American air and sea support, which would have had to be followed by one more Caribbean intervention with U.S. Marines. The President wisely refused to yield to temptation or advice, including Richard Nixon's counsel, to go in. The United States would have had another Vietnam on its hands, or—who knows?—would have learned such a lesson in Cuba that Vietnam would not have happened. Besides, Kennedy was keeping in mind the possibility that if the United States moved on Cuba, the Russians might move on Berlin.

Fidel had taken care of any possibility of internal trouble by arresting about 100,000 suspects and members of the underground who surfaced, shooting a half dozen leaders and prisoners. It was an emergency police measure; nearly all those arrested were soon released. No effective underground movement would ever be able to organize again. The CIA, incidentally, had not even notified its own agents in Cuba—about 2,500—of the invasion plans.

As with all battles, there are ifs and buts about the Bay of Pigs. Since the decisive element in the quick defeat of the invaders was the devastating work of Castro's tiny air force, there was much controversy over Kennedy's cancellation of a second bombing mission that had been planned. As Roger Hilsman, then director of the Bureau of Intelligence and Research of the State Department, pointed out, it would have been too late.

The official Cuban history, *Playa Girón*, contains an account by the pilots who took part. Their candid stories show what spirit and luck did for the defenders.

> At five o'clock [on the morning of April 17] only three planes were in condition: two Sea Furys and one B26. The latter was used for instructional flights and had only six of its eight machine guns in good

> condition; and it lacked the mechanisms for taking on rockets and guns.
>
> "I had very little practice in aerial shooting and I had no idea what a real war was like," wrote Captain Enrique Carreras Rojas, who piloted one of the two Sea Furys which attacked the *Houston*, a former Liberty ship with troops and supplies. "I assure you that what we tried was a Kamikaze action, like the suicidal Japanese pilots used to do. I set the discharge mechanisms of the rockets and followed the course they took. I confess that I was surprised to see them hit the stern of the *Houston*. I saw smoke coming from the ship and I could observe that its navigator in an urgent maneuver headed it toward the shore, apparently to run it aground."
>
> "I arrived at San Antonio Base at 8 o'clock," writes Captain Álvaro Prendes, who said that he hadn't flown for three months and was out of training. "They were already readying one of the only two jet-propelled T–33's that would fly. Let me explain something: these two planes were not flown often and were used mostly for training, because the injectors through which the fuel passes to the turbines were already worn out. They should have been changed a long time before."

The mechanics somehow patched them up. Prendes shot down one of the B-26s, as well as going on to attack Playa Girón. No B-26 bomber escaped the T–33s, for they were slow, clumsy, and without fighter cover. The *Houston*, about which Captain Carreras wrote, sank with its load of ammunition, oil, and a battalion of volunteers. The defending planes also sank another ship, the *Rio Cándido*, with most of the force's munitions and supplies. The remaining exile ships hastily fled out of the firing zone and could not be coaxed back.

President Kennedy belatedly authorized a flight of six jets from the U.S. aircraft carrier *Essex* to protect the supply ships and several more B-26s coming from Nicaragua, but someone forgot, or did not know, that there was an hour's time difference with Nicaragua. The B-26 bombers, two of them piloted by Americans because the Cuban pilots had refused to fly, were shot down by the T–33s. Four Americans were killed. The fighter planes from the *Essex* learned of the miscalculation in time and did not take off.

President Kennedy also authorized U.S. Navy ships to go to the Bay of Pigs to try to evacuate the now-routed brigade, but by the time they arrived the exiles had scattered and fled into the swamps. The American ships would not come within range of Castro's artillery and turned back.

A North American aviator, Leo Francis Berliss, piloting an

American fighter-bomber, was shot down over Cuba on April 19, the last day of the battle. The Cuban government issued a communiqué giving his name, pilot's license number, Social Security number, and address in Boston—all taken from the body along with other documents. Berliss had "bombed the civilian population and our infantry in the region of the [sugar] refinery Australia," the communiqué stated. "This was one of four military planes shot down this morning, bringing to a total of nine the planes shot down since the mercenary attack on the Peninsula of Zapata began."

Foreign Minister Raúl Roa read the text to the U.N. Security Council. "Naturally—and it is the only commentary that I am going to make about this incident," he concluded, no doubt with Adlai Stevenson's misleading statement in mind, "these planes came from the moon!"

The survivors, 1,180 out of 1,297 who landed, were rounded up and taken as prisoners to Havana. Castro announced casualties of only eighty-seven (which on the tenth anniversary of the battle he raised to 149). Other witnesses gave losses ranging between 1,100 and 1,600. In the early stages of the battle, the Cuban infantry and militia losses must have been heavy.

The prisoners were well treated. The unique flavor of the episode was shown in the astonishing television show in which Fidel questioned, argued, and sometimes good-naturedly took abuse from about a thousand of the prisoners.

"Now be honest," he said to one of the disputing prisoners. "You must surely realize that you are the first prisoner in history who has the privilege of arguing in front of the whole population of Cuba and the entire world with the head of a government which you came to overthrow."

The whole Bay of Pigs episode had elements of good nature, generosity, and chivalry on Fidel Castro's part which were ignored in the United States, where his demand for ransom seemed outrageous. The exchange negotiations, like everything connected with one of the most disastrous adventures in American history, were handled badly and took longer than necessary.

The prisoners were ransomed for medical supplies to the supposed value of $62 million. Fidel released them in time to go back to Florida for Christmas 1962, before the full ransom was paid. Later, he claimed that he had been cheated out of millions of dollars worth of supplies, which seemed true.

In Miami, although it was pure rhetoric, President Kennedy promised the returned prisoners that they would go back some day in triumph. About six months later he grumbled, during a talk I had with him in the White House, "Fidel Castro ought to be grateful to us. He gave us a kick in the ass and it made him stronger than ever."

Many of the Cuban exiles, including those who took part in the invasion, were resentful of Kennedy's refusal to engage American forces. The invaders were given the impression, presumably by their CIA mentors, that the United States would intervene. Major Fernández told me that he knew some of the Brigade prisoners, who had been his pupils. He spoke to several, and their lament was that the promised U.S. military intervention had not materialized.

Maurice Halperin's dispassionate conclusion in his book on Cuba, after reading the four hundred pages of verbatim text of the televised questioning of the prisoners over four nights, was that "the members of the Brigade were not the heroes they were proclaimed to be in the United States or the scum that they were made out to be by their captors . . . The majority were unimpressive and compliant."

By their lights they were well-meaning; most of them fought bravely. But their role in the history of Cuba was ignominious.

Theodore Draper's lapidary judgment on the Bay of Pigs fiasco will always be quoted: "The ill-fated invasion of Cuba in April 1961 was one of those rare politico-military events—a perfect failure."

Ambassador Bonsal approvingly cites the judgment of former Ambassador Ellis O. Briggs: "The Bay of Pigs operation was a tragic experience for the Cubans who took part, but its failure was a fortunate (if mortifying) thing for the United States, which otherwise might have been saddled with indefinite occupation of the island." In other words, the folly was so great that success would have been worse than failure.

The invasion was, as President Kennedy indicated, the best thing that could have happened to Fidel Castro, and it came at the best possible time for him. Cuba was in grave economic difficulties. The Cuban people were going to be asked to accept shortages and hardship for the Revolution. An invasion from abroad, organized and backed by the United States, using "mercenary" soldiers, naturally rallied nearly all Cubans behind the Castro regime.

"The invaders have been annihilated," Castro announced jubilantly over the radio on the evening of April 19, 1961. "The Revolution has emerged victorious. It destroyed in less than seventy-two hours the army organized during many months by the imperialist Government of the United States."

The Bay of Pigs invasion was a Cuban-American affair; the missile crisis of October 1962 was earth-shaking, and while the Cuban role was vital, the effects on the Revolution were of importance only in strengthening the Castro regime and leaving a proud memory of danger shared with monolithic courage.

There was a verbal confrontation between the White House and the Kremlin during the Playa Girón battle which gave a foretaste of the much more serious confrontation that was to come in October 1962. On April 18, 1961, the second day of the battle, Soviet Premier Nikita Khrushchev sent a message to President Kennedy. It was by then obvious that Castro would win unless the United States intervened.

> Mr. President [Khrushchev wrote], I address this message to you at an hour of anxiety fraught with danger to world peace. An armed aggression has begun against Cuba. . . .
>
> I earnestly appeal to you, Mr. President, to call a halt to the aggression against the Republic of Cuba. The military techniques and the world political situation are such that any "small war" can produce a chain reaction in all parts of the world.
>
> As to the Soviet Union, there should be no misunderstanding of our position: We shall render the Cuban people and their Government all necessary assistance in beating back the armed attack on Cuba.

Kennedy hastily replied on the same day:

> You are under a serious misapprehension in regard to events in Cuba. For months there has been evident and growing resistance to the Castro dictatorship. . . .
>
> I have previously stated and I repeat now that the United States intends no military intervention in Cuba. In the event of any military intervention by outside force, we will immediately honor our obligations under the inter-American system to protect this hemisphere against external aggression. . . .
>
> I have taken careful note of your statement that the events in Cuba might affect peace in all parts of the world. I trust that this does not mean that the Soviet Government, using the situation in Cuba as a pretext, is planning to inflame other areas of the world.

In the last-quoted sentence, the President was thinking of Berlin and especially of Laos, where there was what Kennedy called in his letter "a dangerous situation." In the conversation I had with the President about Cuba, he said: "However, that [Bay of Pigs] invasion did some good. If it wasn't for that, we would be in Laos now." But not even the missile crisis saved us from Vietnam!

On Berlin, the Soviet Chairman wrote in *Khrushchev Remembers,* "The Americans knew that if Russian blood were shed in Cuba, American blood would surely be shed in Germany."

"The missile crisis of the fall of 1962," Ambassador Bonsal writes in his book, "does not really belong to the story of Cuban-American relations . . . The issue was entirely one between the United States and the Soviet Union." This is like saying that *Hamlet* can be played without a stage. It also ignores the far from passive role which Fidel Castro played in bringing the missiles to Cuba. At the very least, Khrushchev could not have acted without Castro's consent and support. Besides, the incident naturally affected the course of the Revolution.

Raúl Castro, minister of the armed forces, was in Moscow at the beginning of July 1962. A period of some tension and coolness between Cuba and Russia had just ended. The decision to set up bases and send medium (1,000 miles) and intermediate (up to 2,000 miles) range missiles capable of delivering nuclear warheads on U.S. targets must already have been taken. The Russians started sending new modern military equipment after Raúl's trip, including SAM antiaircraft missiles, and technicians and advisers.

Fidel had what he could have thought were logical reasons to fear an invasion in the spring of 1962. President Kennedy was smarting from his defeat at the Bay of Pigs the year before. The former Cuban-exile Revolutionary Council, headed by Dr. Miró Cardona, continued mistakenly to believe that the United States would intervene; rumors to that effect were going the rounds in Miami. The U.S. Navy and Marine Corps held an unusually large maneuver in the Caribbean in April. Exile groups were making guerrilla and sabotaging raids with CIA support. ("At that time," Fidel said to me ten years later when we talked about the crisis, "the Americans were causing almost daily incidents from Guantánamo, killing our people and sabotaging." I presumed that he meant the CIA sending in Cuban-exile saboteurs, although there were also incidents of firing across the border.)

The economic situation in Cuba was very bad in 1962, and there were demonstrations and some repressive measures.

There was also a still-confusing incident involving Aleksei I. Adzhubei, Khrushchev's son-in-law, the editor of *Izvestia,* which Fidel told me about in 1963. Adzhubei had had an interview with President Kennedy. He made an official report on it to the Kremlin, and a copy was sent to Havana. The Cubans interpreted some of the things that Kennedy said as confirmation of their fears that a U.S. invasion was being planned. The State Department, after I published what Castro told me, denied that the President had been threatening or that the United States was planning an invasion.

Fidel, in the 1972 conversation I had with him, still insisted that "there really was a danger of an invasion from the United States before the crisis. I am sure of it."

Khrushchev wrote in his memoirs:

> We welcomed Castro's [Bay of Pigs] victory, but we were certain that the Americans would not let Cuba alone. Given the continued threat of American interference in the Caribbean, what should our own policy be? . . . The logical answer was missiles.
>
> It was during my visit to Bulgaria [in May 1962] that I had the idea of installing missiles with nuclear warheads in Cuba without letting the United States find out until it was too late to do anything about them. I knew that first we would have to talk to Castro and explain our strategy to get the agreement of the Cuban Government. . . .
>
> The main thing was that the installation of our missiles in Cuba would restrain the United States from precipitous military actions. The Americans had surrounded our own country with military bases and threatened us with nuclear weapons and now they would learn just what it feels like. . . .
>
> Only a fool would think that we wanted to invade the American continent from Cuba. We wanted to keep the Americans from invading Cuba, and we wanted to make them think twice by confronting them with our missiles.

In this account, Khrushchev said that the idea was originally his. On a few other occasions he attributed the action to a request from Fidel Castro. Anatoly A. Gromyko, the son of the Soviet foreign minister, in an article published in 1971 in the monthly *Voprosy Istorii,* quotes his father as saying that "the Soviet Government responded to the appeal of Cuba for help only because this appeal had the purpose of eliminating the threat hanging over Cuba."

Fidel Castro has thoroughly confused the record by a series of contradictory statements about the inception of the missile idea. He gave various questioners different answers—three different ones to me, after which I gave up. However, in September 1972, it being the eve of the tenth anniversary of the crisis and *The Sunday Times* of London having asked me to do an article for the paper, I questioned everybody I met, from Castro down, about *la crisis del Caribe.* I did not ask who had the idea first, but from the way President Dorticós,

Raúl Castro, and Carlos Rafael Rodríguez spoke, I was left with the clear impression that Khrushchev had put forward the idea and Fidel had jumped at it, with enthusiastic support from his brother and Che Guevara. It will be recalled that Che, in his letter of resignation on April 1, 1965, told of his "pride in belonging to our people during those radiant yet sad days of the Caribbean crisis."

Russian arms and men began arriving in July 1962. Khrushchev's plans were very grand, if he had been left alone—SAM and nuclear missiles, MIG fighters, Ilyushin bombers, and Russian ground troops armed with tactical nuclear weapons, plus vehicles and personnel. Professor Thomas writes that one hundred ships were allotted to the task.

By October 22, when Kennedy made his "quarantine" speech, overflights by U-2 planes showed intermediate (IRBM) and medium (MRBM) sites and more than thirty missiles. Actually, there were forty-two in all. Khrushchev boasted in his memoirs, "We had installed enough missiles already to destroy New York, Chicago and the other industrial cities, not to mention a little village like Washington. I don't think America ever faced such a real threat of destruction as at that moment."

On October 22, the day of Kennedy's speech, Fidel Castro ordered a state of alert and the next day, a nationwide mobilization. The government newspaper, *Revolución,* came out with a huge headline: *La Nación en Pie de Guerra* ("The Nation on a War Footing").

On television and radio that night, Fidel in an impassioned speech called on workers, farmers, and students to march to the trenches while the women took their places in the factories and fields.

"We will resist the blockade and repel direct aggression," he cried. ". . . Why has the situation deteriorated? This has happened simply because, up to now, all attempts by the United States to destroy our Revolution have ended in failure . . . They wanted us to be disarmed and at their mercy so they could attack us whenever they felt like it . . . What have we done? We have defended ourselves. That is all!"

As the fateful negotiations went on, the Cuban leaders believed in an American invasion as at least a real probability. "We were aware of the danger," as Raúl Castro put it to me. While the Cuban people may not have realized fully the extent of that danger, they could not have been unaware that the threat of an imminent American invasion and bombing hung over them in the fateful five days of negotiation. Not only had Fidel warned them on radio and television, but the country had been mobilized and hundreds of thousands of soldiers and militiamen and -women had been sent to coastal and urban defense stations. Their families, of course, knew what was happening.

The behavior of the Cuban people—and there is overwhelming evidence—was extraordinary. They were not only not frightened; they joined up by the thousands to aid the militia, even old people. It was a national crisis for them, the defense of their country against a foreign invader, and they showed a willingness to die alongside their own people. This was the way that Spaniards felt in their Civil War; just as they were *muy español* (very Spanish), the Cubans in the missile crisis were *muy cubano.* The regime had not been so united since 1959.

Everyone who was there at the time agrees (and I spoke to foreigners about it, too) that there was a curious mixture of exhilaration and calm. There was none of the acute tension and nervousness that gripped the United States, Europe, or Puerto Rico (where my wife and I happened to be). On Saturday morning, October 27, the very height of the crisis, Foreign Minister Raúl Roa drove to his office along the Malecón, the sea front, quite early in the morning, he told me. It was crowded with people who, he thought, must have heard dramatic and alarming news. They were fishing!

"We had lived through so much danger," Dr. Heliodoro Martínez Junco, minister of public health and a veteran of the Sierra Maestra, said to me, "that we had the strength to face the peril calmly. I said goodbye to my wife and children those few mornings thinking that I might never see them again. Yes, thousands would have been killed, but in the defense of Cuba."

Rolando Chou, now in the Ministry of External Affairs, then a student, was in the militia when it was mobilized. His unit was stationed near Havana. His comment was typical: "Each day we expected to be killed, but we all accepted the danger as necessary for our country."

"Cubans are still resentful of the Russians for letting them down," Edmundo Desnoes, the novelist, said to me. "At the time, they saw the struggle in terms of national survival and of their national identity as having the right to defend themselves in whatever way they considered necessary. It was truly a case of *Patria o Muerte!*"

It was, in fact, a very near thing, and no matter how brave the Cubans were, the result would have been great destruction and death, and the end of the Revolution in the form it had taken. Some congressional, civilian, and military advisers to President Kennedy, including the Chiefs of Staff, had from the beginning urged bombing the sites and invading Cuba. During the fateful days of negotiation, Kennedy had massed a huge invasion force in Florida, ordered the Air Force to prepare to bomb the missile sites, and put all the U.S. nuclear and conventional forces around the world on the alert.

Robert F. Kennedy, in *Thirteen Days*, wrote that on Friday, October 26, "President Kennedy ordered the State Department to proceed with preparation for a crash program on civil government in Cuba to be established after the invasion and occupation of that country." However, as CIA Director John McCone told the President, an invasion would be far more serious than most people realized; the Cubans had "a hell of a lot of equipment and it will be damn tough to shoot them out of those hills, as we learned so clearly in Korea."

Raúl Roa made a shrewd remark to me in 1972 when we were discussing the ten-year-old crisis. If Eisenhower or Nixon had been President in 1962, instead of Kennedy, Cuba would certainly have been invaded. He might have added Johnson, considering that President's reactions in the Dominican Republic and Vietnam.

The crisis was resolved on Sunday, October 28, when Khrushchev capitulated. During the climactic hours of Saturday night, when all hung in the balance, Fidel Castro, President Dorticós, Carlos Rafael Rodríguez, and (I believe) Ramiro Valdés, the intelligence chief, sat in a room of the old Presidential Palace, waiting. Raúl Castro, as minister of the armed forces, was at the headquarters in Havana. Che Guevara was on the west coast of Pinar del Río Province with a force, awaiting the Yankee invasion.

I have the story from one of those present in the Palace. He said that they had no doubts about what would happen if Khrushchev refused to withdraw the missiles. From the moment of decision to accept the missiles, they had realized and faced what they knew to be a terrible danger for Cuba.

The presumption is that they felt it worth doing, first, because they thought the threat of invasion from the United States to be real, and secondly, because with Cuba in possession of the missiles she would be, even though by proxy, a nation powerful enough to threaten the United States and to be a power in the world.

Antonio Núñez Jiménez, head of INRA, the agrarian institute, who was then in Rome for a meeting of the Food and Agricultural Organization of the U.N., telephoned to say that he was coming right back; he wanted to be in Cuba with them. Fidel jokingly told Rodríguez, who answered the phone, to tell Núñez to stay in Rome so that afterward he could write a history of the Cuban Revolution. They really thought that a cataclysm might come. Núñez evidently did not think it was a good joke and was furious—about which, I gather, they have been ribbing him ever since.

Guevara's Argentine friend Ricardo Rojo writes in his biography of Che that Fidel learned the news of Khrushchev's surrender while he and Guevara were talking together. Castro was so furious, Rojo says Che told him, that he kicked at the wall of the room they were in and broke a mirror. To Fidel, of course, it was a betrayal by Khrushchev, and all the worse for his not having consulted the Cubans or even kept them informed. A few days later Fidel told some students at Havana University that Khrushchev lacked *cojones* (balls).

Fidel had been playing for keeps, as he showed when one of his Cuban-manned SAM anti-aircraft guns shot down an American U-2 observation plane.

Kennedy and Khrushchev may have felt as Ambassador Bonsal intimated, that Cuba was no more there than Banquo's ghost at the table, or, as others put it, was a pawn in a chess game that the two statesmen were playing. Whatever figure of speech one wants to use, it was a fact that in October 1962 both the United States and the Soviet Union made Cuba into a vital factor of world politics. Cubans momentarily felt the elation of being of global importance. And then they were let down with a thump, as if Cuba counted for nothing. The disillusionment was correspondingly severe, and so was the resentment against Russia.

"Of course, we had no thought of waging war in 1962—*ni mucho menos* [not in the least]," Castro said to me a decade later in Havana. "It was done for protection. Yes, I was furious. Our relations with Russia started on the downgrade after that for some years."

Ironically, as Fidel had told me in 1963, he was thinking of "the interests of the Soviet bloc." It was "an international proletarian duty." President Dorticós made the same point to me in 1972. Cuba, he claimed, had to place herself in an international frame, as a contribution to the safety of the socialist camp. I made the obvious retort that Cuba may have felt that way but evidently Khrushchev hadn't. The President laughed.

Raúl Roa, the foreign minister, said to me that once the crisis ended, all Castro could do was to try "to save the dignity of Cuba." It was too late. He refused to accept a United Nations inspection team, saying "Cuba is not the Congo." He also tried to make stronger conditions—five points, which were ignored by Washington. They included such impossible demands as ending the trade embargo and withdrawal from Guantánamo Naval Base.

Khrushchev found what he considered to be a face-saving formula. "We sent the Americans a note," he wrote in his memoirs, "saying we agreed to remove our missiles and bombers on condition that the President give his assurance that there would be no invasion of Cuba by the forces of the U.S. or anybody else. Finally Kennedy gave in and agreed to make a statement giving us such an assurance."

The Soviet Premier wrote that "it was a great victory for us . . . but Castro didn't see it that way. He was angry." Indeed he was.

A Cuban cabinet minister who saw Khrushchev in Moscow soon after, and who was the first to talk to him about the missile crisis, told me that Khrushchev was "sincerely repentent." The Russian leader said he had thought he was doing what was best for Cuba and that, after all, he had got Kennedy's promise that the United States would not invade Cuba. For a long time, I was told, Khrushchev kept telling Cubans who went to Moscow how sorry he was.

The most important of the foreign statesmen involved in the missile crisis, British Prime Minister Harold Macmillan, has at last written his account. It is in the final volume of his memoirs, *At the End of the Day,* published in London in 1973, and it proved to be a revelation that has confounded all historians of the missile crisis, myself included. Macmillan, alone among foreign leaders, was in constant touch with President Kennedy, by direct communication over telex and through messages. The two statesmen worked together in one of the most remarkable episodes of Anglo-American cooperation on record. But even more than for Kennedy, Cuba was an object, not a contestant for Macmillan.

"Indeed, in my first draft [of a message to Kennedy on October 22], I had thought of advising him to seize Cuba and have done with it," Macmillan wrote. He thought better of the idea, and, in fact, the British played a restraining role throughout. Their main thought was that Khrushchev was using Cuba as a threat to Berlin.

"He has Cuba in his hands," Kennedy said to Macmillan over the telex on October 24, "but he doesn't have Berlin. If he takes Berlin, then we will take Cuba."

"If Khrushchev comes to a conference," Macmillan wrote in a message to the President on October 22, "he will, of course try to trade his Cuba position against his ambitions in Berlin and elsewhere."

So far as I know or could tell from my many talks with Castro and other Cubans, this seemed never to have occurred to them. The Anglo-Saxon statesmen would have said that if so, Fidel was being naïve. I think he was. I started arguing with Castro, Guevara, Dorticós, and others as early as 1959 that so far as the Russians were concerned, Cuba was expendable. It probably still is, but it would take a far higher price in 1975 than in 1962 to "buy" Cuba from the Communist bloc.

In the exchange on October 22, Kennedy made a surprising remark. "The President finally said that he could not help admiring the Soviet strategy," Macmillan writes. "They offered this deliberate and provocative challenge to the United States in the knowledge that if the Americans reacted violently to it, the Russians would be given an ideal opportunity to move against West Berlin. If, on the other hand, he did nothing, the Latin Americans and the United States' other Allies would feel that the Americans had no real will to resist the encroachments of Communism and would hedge their bets accordingly."

Kennedy's admiration makes one wonder whether, after all, Fidel Castro was as foolishly reckless as he seemed to be at the time. The position and prestige of the United States in Latin America were put at stake. However, even taking it from his own point of view, Fidel's miscalculation was not to realize that Khrushchev was playing a game of chess against Kennedy, with Cuba as a pawn.

"Now that ten years have passed," I said to Fidel on September 12, 1972, "what do you think of *la crisis del Caribe?*" He replied:

> On the whole, I think it did some good, and it worked. We didn't get an absolute guarantee against a United States invasion, but in practice it was enough. We should have got more, and we would have. If, let us suppose, the operation had been a success, Cuba would have insisted on the five points that we later demanded. There was a danger of invasion from the United States before the crisis; I am sure of it. We needed the protection. As it happened, Kennedy was assassinated; Johnson came along, and we were saved by Vietnam. Who can say whether the immense American drive that went into Vietnam in those years would not have turned against Cuba? The missile crisis gave a temporary halt to the American invasions from pirate ships, subversion and other forms of intervention—and then came Vietnam.

Carlos Rafael Rodríguez remembers hearing Fidel say philosophically some years later that perhaps it was all for the best because that confrontation had made the United States and Russia realize the dangers of a nuclear war and they began a period of peace and coexistence which has continued.

The claim that President Nixon made in 1973 that the Middle East crisis was the most difficult for the world since the Cuban missile crisis was exaggerated. Kennedy had to react against a situation so far advanced that it was necessary to risk an open nuclear confrontation with the Russians. In 1973 the American move was a case of anticipating a possible clash before the Russians got under way. There was no real confrontation as in 1962.

I have told the story from the Cuban side. So far as the United States was concerned, President Kennedy's mixture of firmness and wise moderation needs no retelling. Political and strategic factors were equally important. Acceptance of the Russian gambit would have had disastrous effects in Latin America and Europe, while on the military side, the nuclear balance would have been endangered. Weakness might well have invited further bold moves by Khrushchev.

For Cuba the episode was definitive in one sense: President Kennedy gave up any idea of intervening in Cuba, and so did his successors. However, as Theodore Sorensen relates, Kennedy did remain committed to "harass, disrupt and weaken Cuba politically and economically." That has been U.S. policy ever since, but with lessening energy. Kennedy, according to Sorensen, was convinced that Fidel Castro would be out of power within five years, but, as his "few words to the captive people of Cuba" in his "quarantine" speech proved, the President was as badly informed about Cuba in October 1962 as he had been at the time of the Bay of Pigs.

It was common knowledge just before his assassination that the President was considering a new policy toward Cuba. Fidel knew this and, in a talk we had in November 1963, wondered what Kennedy had in mind.

The *crisis del Caribe* was a world crisis of the first order, but it was not a threat to the Cuban Revolution. On the contrary, Fidel Castro could boast with unquestionable truth (in a speech on November 1, 1962) that "the attitude of our people surpassed anything that the most optimistic could ever have imagined by their firmness, bravery and discipline . . . Thousands of men who . . . in these four years of revolution had not joined the militia, did so during the crisis . . . Why, even men and women who were criticizing the Revolution . . . signed up to take part in a struggle which, according to all appearances, was to be a tremendous conflict."

Cuba must have been the only country in the world disgruntled by the outcome. For the one-time rebels of Moncada and the Sierra Maestra who were now the leaders of the Cuban Revolution, those days of the crisis would have been just about the most exciting and happiest of their lives—truly "radiant," as Che Guevara was to write.

In my 1968 biography of Castro, I wrote of the decision to permit Soviet nuclear missiles to be installed in Cuba as "the greatest act of folly in Fidel Castro's hectic career." Neither he nor his comrades think so at all. Their only regret is that Khrushchev backed down and the attempt failed—plus, of course, the humiliating way for Cuba in which the Soviet leader handled the crisis.

I am convinced that the many Cubans I spoke to about *la crisis del Caribe* on the eve of the tenth anniversary of the incident in 1972 were not showing bravado after the event.

If this seems incredible, it must be because none of us abroad understood the Cubans or how they felt at the time. And we underestimated how far and how blindly the ordinary Cuban would go in trusting Fidel Castro and following him wherever he went.

I kept saying to anyone who would listen to me in Cuba in September 1972: "But the risk being run was so far out of proportion to any possible gain even if the move had succeeded!" No one seemed to agree, or at any rate to accept that estimation. Having lived with Spaniards throughout their terrible Civil War, I could at least understand their attitude. They were being *muy cubano.*

The Soviet Premier had been left in no doubt about how Fidel Castro and the Cubans felt about his "betrayal." "We decided to send [Vice-Premier Anastas] Mikoyan to Cuba," Khrushchev wrote in his memoirs. "He will discuss the situation with the Cubans calmly."

As it happened, Fidel was so furious with the Russians that for ten days he would not even see Mikoyan, and then only for a formal talk. The Vice-Premier's wife died while he was in Havana, and he could not go back for the funeral. However, he did reduce the tension enough to open the way for new economic negotiations and, in the spring of 1963, a trip to the Soviet Union by Castro.

"Certainly," Maurice Halperin writes of the visit, "in the 800 years since the founding of the Duchy of Moscow no Russian czar, emperor or ruler of the Soviet Union had received a visiting head of state or any other foreign guest with anything remotely resembling the pomp and ceremony, and out-pouring of attention and honors, that Nikita Khrushchev bestowed on Fidel Castro."

A year and a half later Khrushchev was out of power, and within a few more years—in 1967–1968—relations between Cuba and the Soviet Union reached another low. Castro especially resented the

Russians' remaining on good terms with the Latin American governments for commercial reasons while the Cubans were trying to undermine and overthrow all those regimes. The Moscow-oriented Latin-American Communist parties sabotaged Fidel's support for guerrilla movements. However, the resentment and controversy did not interfere with the development of the Cuban variation of Marxism-Leninism.

CHAPTER 10

Marxism-Leninism

When I use a word, it means just what I choose it to mean—neither more nor less.

—Humpty-Dumpty to Alice

The Cuban Revolution has been a unique experience for the Communist world in general and the Kremlin in particular. It seemed easy at first—a young, favorably disposed novice with a revolution to hand over. Instead, they found a willful leader, prepared to use the Cuban Communists if they adapted themselves to his ideas of Communism, and determined to make and keep a revolution of his own construction. Castro became a Communist, but Cuban Communism became Castroite. His associates and the Cuban people simply followed him, as they would have followed him into fascism, if that had been his choice. Where Fidel Castro conformed—and this was of great importance to the Kremlin—was in the international policies of the Communist bloc, and there he was more orthodox than the Russians.

Boris Goldenberg argues that "Cuba was one of the few Latin American countries where further progress could have been achieved by means of a free struggle within the framework of representative democracy." As an ex-Communist, and one who taught for many years in Cuba, Goldenberg's opinions must be respected, but one wonders when this free, democratic struggle was supposed to take place? And how? And where were the democratic leaders who could bring a poorly prepared people to progress through freedom? Cubans could have had social progress under "representative democracy" anytime they wanted it from 1902 onward. Clearly, they did not want it enough.

Socialism in the twentieth century has to be imposed from above, as it was in Cuba. There is no such thing as a spontaneous, grass-roots Marxist socialism suddenly infusing a complete society. Ideally, it is a highly sophisticated, organized, disciplined system. But considering the Cuban temperament, the inherited capitalism, the unbalanced sugar economy, and the dependence on the United States, socialism was not, like Topsy, just going to grow in Cuba. The only possible method was a form of authoritarianism, and, in the circumstances, that form gravitated—to use Che Guevara's word—into Marxism-Leninism.

This is the framework into which the Cuban Revolution must be set, but it cannot be simplified or left with these generalizations. Cuba has gone through a complex process whose dynamism was—and remains—continuous. We are watching a variation of the Trotskyite "permanent revolution" which cannot end so long as Fidel Castro and his followers are masters of Cuba, if it ends then. In many ways, social revolutions are irreversible.

Neither Fidel, his companions, nor the *barbudos* in general reached any political decisions while they were fighting in the Sierra Maestra. They were determined to make a revolution, but in no ideological or systematic form. In fact, they were all political innocents, even allowing for the strong Marxist bent of Che Guevara and Raúl Castro. None of the leaders was a Communist. Che once said that he knew of only three Cuban Communists who took part in the actual fighting in the Sierra Maestra.

About himself, he told the Cuban journalist José Guerra Alemán, evidently sometime in 1958 when he was in the Sierra: "I am Marxist by conviction. I have never been a militant of any Communist party. Nor of youth leagues, congresses or workers' organizations . . . The indoctrination to which the troops [guerrillas] are subjected, contrary to the accusations of the tyranny [Batista] is pure Martían indoctrination, as Fidel planned. The immense majority of our lads are peasants. We first have to teach them the *abc*'s of political knowledge."

Lisa Howard of the American Broadcasting Company interviewed Che Guevara for a television appearance given on March 22, 1964. She asked Che whether in the Sierra Maestra he had foreseen the radical course that the Revolution would follow.

"Intuitively, I felt it," Che replied. "Naturally, the course and the very violent development of the Revolution could not be foreseen. Nor was the Marxist-Leninist formulation of the Revolution foreseeable. That was the result of a very long process, and you know it very well. We had a more or less vague idea of solving the problems which we clearly saw affected the peasants who fought with us, and the problems we saw in the lives of the workers. But it would be very long to recount the whole process of the transformation of our ideas."

In a letter to the magazine *Bohemia* of June 14, 1959, Guevara said: "If I were a Communist, I would not hesitate to shout it from the rooftops." And he would not have, being Che Guevara. The following year he denied to me that he was then a Communist. However, anti-Communism was already equated with Yankee imperialism in his eyes. And he had been Marxist and revolutionary since his sojourn in Guatemala.

I know of no better statement of Fidel's position in the Sierra Maestra with regard to his later conversion to Marxism-Leninism than what he told Lee Lockwood in 1965:

> Nobody is a born revolutionary. A revolutionary is formed through a process. It is possible that there was some moment when I appeared less radical than I really was. It is possible, too, that I was more radical than even I, myself, knew. Ultimately, a revolutionary struggle is like a military war. You have to set for yourself only those goals that are attainable at a given moment. . . .
>
> If you ask me whether I considered myself a revolutionary at the time I was in the mountains, I would answer yes, I considered myself a revolutionary. If you ask me did I consider myself a Marxist-Leninist, I would say no, I did not consider myself a Marxist-Leninist. If you ask me whether I considered myself a Communist, a classic Communist, I would say no, I did not consider myself a classic Communist. Today yes, I believe I have that right.

Later in the conversation with Lockwood he said that he had had no obligations to any party, "and in no way was I a disguised or infiltrated agent, or anything like that." Neither was Che Guevara, Fidel added. His brother Raúl, he conceded, had joined the Communist Youth when he was a university student but "broke party discipline" to join the Moncada Barracks attack. Raúl almost certainly never rejoined the old Cuban Communist Party (the PSP), and, incidentally, he denied to me that he had done so. In his book *Khrushchev Remembers,* the Soviet Premier says, "Raúl is a good Communist." However, that was written in 1970.

Their political education, like their economic, began on January 1, 1959. When he came down from the Sierra, Fidel's titles were not political. He was commander in chief of the Rebel Army and secretary general of the 26th of July Movement. From 1965 until late 1973 (when military ranks were raised) his titles were always given in documents and the press as: Major Fidel Castro Ruz, First Secretary of the Central Committee of the Communist Party of Cuba and Prime Minister of the Revolutionary Government. He is now formally commander in chief of the Armed Forces of the Revolution (FAR). Much political history was involved in these apparently superficial changes.

During that puzzling and indecisive period in the spring of 1959 when he visited the United States, Castro came up with his one and only ideological—or perhaps one should say, pseudo-ideological—variation. He called it "Humanism," and by Theodore Draper's calculation (in his book *Castroism*) it was not even original. It seems that there was a "humanist movement" in Cuba in the 1950s, founded by the scholar Rubén Darío, "an offshoot of what was known as the Catholic Left." Draper believes that "Castro suddenly appropriated the term."

Fidel defined the concept while in New York on his trip as "government of the people without dictatorship and without oligarchy; liberty with bread and without terror—that is Humanism."

As always with Fidel, he believes what he says when he says it. There is no reason to doubt that his brief (only a few months) excursion into "Humanism" was sincere. In *Revolución* on May 22, 1959, he wrote:

> The tremendous problem faced by the world is that it has been placed in a position where it must choose between capitalism, which starves people, and Communism, which resolves economic problems but suppresses the liberties so greatly cherished by man . . . Capitalism sacrifices man; the Communist state, by its totalitarian concept, sacrifices the rights of man. That is why we do not agree with either of them . . . Ours is an autonomous Cuban Revolution. It is as Cuban as our music . . . Such is the reason for my saying that this revolution is not red, but olive-green, for olive-green is precisely our color, the color of the revolution brought by the Rebel Army from the heart of the Sierra Maestra.

He changed his mind, although he did make a *Cuban* revolution even though the form it took was Marxist-Leninist. It was significant that he said Communism "resolves economic problems" and capitalism "sacrifices man." Communism, he believes, does not sacrifice man, only his rights. Fidel chose to sacrifice what seemed to him, and probably to most Cubans, the lesser of the two desiderata, the rights of man—not that he would concede as much now. Aside from its vagueness, he may have dropped Humanism because it was seized upon by liberals and moderates as a rallying ground against the

Cuban Communists. It was proving a divisive ideology.

When it came to socialism, the Castroites were not honestly going to be able to hold up a mirror to the sacred Wars of Independence, and still less to its "Apostle," José Martí. Writing in *La América* of New York in April 1884, Martí saw socialism as a "slavery" of man serving the state, "a slave of functionaries." This was Castro's position during the brief period of Humanism.

Cuba once had a budding anarcho-syndicalist movement borrowed from Spain, before Martí died. It lingered on stubbornly until, in 1925, President Machado murdered or imprisoned its leaders, broke up its organizations, and destroyed its influence with the working classes. This left a vacuum into which the Communists walked. Cuba was, in fact, the only Latin American country where Communism had been even relatively strong before 1959. Marxism had made little impact on the generally feudal and militaristic regimes south of the Rio Grande.

The Mexican Revolution of 1910 did not move toward a radical socialism because it antedated the Russian Revolution and had no model. Its greatest accomplishment, as the late Professor Frank Tannenbaum of Columbia University wrote, was to forge a unified Mexican nation out of a people divided for centuries by race, religion, culture, class, and languages. It has ended as a capitalist state with some features of its social revolution, not the least its devotion to the revolutionary myth. Only under President Lázaro Cárdenas (1934–1940) did Mexico find a revolutionary leader with socialist, almost Leninist, ideas—but Mexico remained capitalist.

The Cuban Revolution has not taken and cannot ever take the futile, clockwise direction of the Mexican Revolution, which has ended where it began. Both revolutions started with action, but only Cuba's adopted a special ideology. In Russia, the Eastern European countries, and China, the ideology existed before the revolutionary action.

Another difference between Mexico and Cuba was that the Mexicans after seven years (1917) came up with a remarkable constitution. Boris Goldenberg well describes it as "a mixture of radical liberalism, nationalism, democracy, socialism and positivism, and it established the first 'welfare state' of the twentieth century." Cuba is yet to devise a constitution after sixteen years.

I never could find any indication that the Castro brothers, Che Guevara, and other Cuban leaders drew any inspiration from the Mexican Revolution. Perhaps the contrary was true. Their experiences, when preparing for the *Granma* expedition in 1955–1956, were of a pro-Batista Mexican government doing everything it could to prevent the exiles from organizing their invasion. Besides, they could not help seeing, when they lived in Mexico, that capitalism, the wealth of the few and the poverty of the many, the return of the dominant Yankee investors, and the pervasive, ineradicable corruption all made a mockery of the ideals that gave birth to the revolution of 1910.

"In Cuba," Robert J. Alexander writes in his book *Communism in Latin America*, "there is little doubt that the [original] rise of the Communists to influence was due to their deal with Batista, whereby they were given complete freedom of action and positive Government aid in the trade union field in return for political support for Batista's presidential ambitions."

Batista brought the Communists legality, members, a daily newspaper *(Hoy)*, and control of the Confederation of Cuban Workers (CTC).

Lázaro Peña, the mulatto Communist union leader, became a power in the CTC, and although eclipsed for some years by Batista's man, Eusebio Mujal, he returned to leadership under Castro. After several years of semiretirement because of illness, Peña was triumphantly reelected secretary general of the CTC at the Workers' Congress in November 1973. By then he was dying of cancer. He was also a member of the Central Committee of Castro's Communist Party, one of three old-guard Communists (along with Carlos Rafael Rodríguez and Blas Roca) to have performed the remarkable feat of serving both Batista and Castro in important posts.

Hoy, incidentally, was edited by Aníbal Escalante, who was then a member of the Communist National Executive Committee, and who is now in jail. Blas Roca (his real name is Francisco Calderio) said of Batista in 1938: "When Batista found the path to democracy, the Party helped him."

Actually, as Andrés Suárez points out, Cuban Communism was "conclusively Stalinized in 1934," and it stayed that way until Khrushchev's "de-Stalinization" forced it reluctantly to change.

The Cuban Communist Party (founded in 1925) adapted the nominal disguise of the Popular Socialist Party (PSP). In 1942, K. S. Karol writes, it had 87,000 members, with men in the Chamber of Representatives and the Senate, and two cabinet ministers (Rodríguez and Blas Roca) in General Batista's first term as President (1940–1944). This was the Communist Party's reward for helping in the 1940 election, when they joined his Socialist Democratic Coalition. Juan Marinello, one of Cuba's outstanding poets and the nominal leader of the PSP for many years, entered Batista's cabinet as minister without portfolio in 1943. He is still an old-guard survivor, but in minor posts.

Carlos Rafael Rodríguez, the most important figure to emerge from the Cuban Communist movement, was a student rebel against Machado in 1933. He joined the Communist Party soon after, rising to become a member of the Central Committee and Politburo in 1939. He is a true intellectual and just about the only Cuban Communist thoroughly familiar with Marxist literature and theory.

It will be recalled that Carlos Rafael was the first important Communist to realize that Fidel Castro was going to win and that his rebellion had to be supported. In the Sierra Maestra he not only developed a respect and admiration for Castro but a genuine personal affection for him. Rodríguez, besides being a gifted administrator and economist, is a delightful companion with a charming and cultured wife, who is a teacher. His prescience, ability, and attractiveness gave him an open road to favor and power—but always as a follower. He was not, like Blas Roca, a Stalinist, and he was never involved in the machinations of the Aníbal Escalante "sectarianism." He has the unique distinction of being invaluable to Fidel Castro and the Kremlin.

The PSP also supported Batista's candidate in the 1944 presidential election, and although he lost, they gained three Senate and nine Chamber of Representatives seats. Grau San Martín, the *Auténtico* candidate, was elected. The Communists soon quarreled with Grau and were on even worse terms with his successor, Prío Socarrás, who tried to abolish *Hoy* and closed 1010, the Communists' radio station. At the time of General Batista's 1952 *coup d'état,* the party membership was down to about twenty thousand; they had only a handful of members in the CTC and controlled only twenty of the three thousand trade unions.

Although Batista, partly to please Washington, broke diplomatic relations with the Kremlin and officially banned the Cuban Communist Party, he permitted their underground movement to carry on. This was a period when a number of the Communist movements in Latin America adapted the so-called "dual policy" of having two Communist parties or movements in dictatorial countries. One, the official Muscovite party, would openly oppose the dictatorship while the other would support the regime and, in turn, be tolerated.

This is what happened in Cuba. Batista needed working-class supporters. A number of the Communist trade union leaders "resigned" from the party and joined the "Labor Bloc" of Batista's own Partido Acción Progresista. By the end of 1956, when Fidel landed in the *Granma,* the situation was that the Communist Party was illegal but the Communists' political machine flourished. The PSP was in effect made up of legal and illegal Communists. It will be recalled that it criticized and sabotaged Fidel Castro from the time of the Moncada Barracks attack until it realized that the Rebels in the Sierra Maestra were going to win. By then, according to Karol's figures, the party membership was down to seven thousand.

Professor Maurice Zeitlin, in *Revolutionary Politics and the Cuban Working Class,* claims that prerevolutionary Communism and revolutionary socialist ideology "had penetrated to the very fiber of the working-class political culture." However, neither party membership, election results, nor prerevolutionary public manifestations would bear this out.

What the Cuban Communists did have was a political party that had not been broken up; a disciplined membership; a trained core of dedicated organizers; a reputation for honesty; and—most valuable of all—they had the strength and wealth of the Soviet Union behind them. In 1959 they could be trusted to stay in Cuba and do their best to help the Revolution. Their loyalty could be counted upon at a time when loyalty was all-important.

They had to move cautiously at first, because of their dubious record. In the first half of 1959, Fidel was publicly critical of them, but in a speech on July 3 he held out an olive branch. He said that it would be dishonorable to attack the Communists "just to prevent people from accusing us of being Communists ourselves."

Writing of August 1960, Andrés Suárez, who was then in the government, says: "It is certain that at this time there were no active party members in the Council of Ministers, the command posts of the Rebel Army, the top-level administrative positions, or the directing positions of the mass organizations."

An intricate, involved, confusing process was beginning which has yet to end. It carried Cuba into a form of socialism, which is still in a transitory stage.

The situation was confused for Americans by their tendency to label Marxism, socialism, radicalism, the extreme left, and revolution as Communism. When I said in a dispatch from Havana in July 1959 that none of the Cuban revolutionary leaders was Communist, the statement aroused great ridicule. As Suárez wrote, this statement was still true a year later in the only meaningful sense of the word. A Communist is a man or woman who belongs to a Communist party or movement. There is no serious historian who doubts these statements now, or the fact that Fidel Castro did not become a Communist until he proclaimed himself a Marxist-Leninist in the famous speech of December 1–2, 1961.

Huberman and Sweezey were wrong, in their widely read book on Cuba in 1960, to brush aside the Communist potential, but they were right in saying: "This is the first time ever, anywhere, that a genuine socialist revolution has been made by *non-Communists* [their italics]. In the past, no self-styled socialist party has ever made the effort to put through the deeply radical reforms which are essential if capitalism is to be overthrown and replaced by socialism; only Communist parties have had the necessary determination . . . and, it should be added, it is this fact more than anything else that has made Communism the formidable world movement it is today." (Castro was not calling his Revolution socialist in 1960, but one can grant that it was socialistic.)

Several times in the early 1960s I discussed with Fidel Castro the question of when he made up his mind to embrace Marxism-Leninism, but he persuaded me that he truly did not know himself. I quoted him in a paper I wrote for Stanford University as saying to me on October 29, 1963: "I gradually moved into a Marxist-Leninist position. I cannot tell you just when; the process was so gradual and so natural." However, he agreed that it could have been in the summer of 1960, although he said nothing publicly about it in that year.

President Osvaldo Dorticós had been regional organization secretary of the Communist Party in Cienfuegos long before the Revolution. I know, however, that he privately assured an officer of the American Embassy in April 1960 that "having been exposed to Communism, I now understand it and am firmly opposed to it." He assured me as late as August 15, 1960, that "there is no danger of the regime going Communist." Dorticós is a man of such complete honesty that I do not doubt this is what he believed at the time. I presume that he hoped so, too, but that I cannot say.

The situation was confused by the fact (not noted at the time; I confess to being misled by it myself) that a distinction had to be made between being ideologically anti-Communist and being anti-PSP-Old-Guard Communist. Armando Hart, Faustino Pérez, Celia Sánchez, Raúl Roa, Osvaldo Dorticós, and even, on occasion, Raúl Castro, were all "anti-Communist" in the sense of being critical of the individual Communists of the Cuban Old Guard, with their subservience to Moscow and, above all, their maneuvering for power at the expense of the *Fidelistas.* When Fidel made his own, special, Cuban-Castroite Communist party, it was a different matter for all of them.

They did not care much *how* the Revolution was made. The instrument and the methods used were, in a manner of speaking, immaterial. If the best way to do it seemed to be through Marxism-Leninism and an alliance with the Soviet Union, then Communism was the direction to go—not for ideological but for revolutionary reasons. It was like an arranged marriage in which the two parties came to love each other. Once Communism was embraced, a sincere ideological conviction developed. Had fascism, or, for that matter, liberal democracy, offered equally good or better methods, the Revolution might have taken one of those directions.

The Cuban Revolution has many fascinating aspects for political scientists. One of them is the study of how a group of uncommitted, non-Communist young revolutionaries should have found—at least, so they thought—that the only way they could make a radical social revolution in contemporary circumstances with a relatively underdeveloped country was through a form of Marxism.

Fidel Castro's greatest uncertainties from the beginning have been political. In 1960–1961, for instance, there were a number of old-line Communists, crypto-Communists, and fellow travelers in more or less important positions throughout the government, the national institutions, and the armed forces in gradually increasing numbers as the months passed. Why Fidel allowed the "old guard" Communists to get such power and so many important posts is still a mystery. I do not find any of the reasons generally advanced to be entirely satisfactory: that he did not know what was happening; that he was powerless to curb them; that he could not or did not want to antagonize Moscow; that he could see no better alternative; that they were useful; that he needed them. He must have known exactly what was happening and been sure of his ability at any time to put the Cuban Communists in their place.

It was a period of mental travail for Fidel Castro. As I said, he is not a trained, systematic thinker; his mind is not at home in abstractions, philosophical ideas, doctrinaire theories, dogmas, or ideologies. It was as if a realization gradually took hold of him: that the solution to his problems lay in socialism and that the system of socialism best suited to his purpose was a form of Communism, a Cuban form, a Castroite form that he would call Marxism-Leninism.

"It was," he said to me in October 1963, "a gradual process in which the pressure of events forced me to accept Marxism as the answer to what I was seeking . . . With my ideas and my temperament, even in my school and university days, I could not have been a capitalist, a democrat, a liberal. I always had it in me to be a radical, a revolutionary, a reformer, and through that instinctive preparation, it was easy for me to move into Marxism-Leninism."

During a long talk in Santiago de Cuba in September 1972 with Armando Hart, one of Fidel's oldest and closest associates, and who for some years was the organizing secretary of the new Communist Party of Cuba, Hart disputed my opinion that Castro's decision to opt for Marxism-Leninism was a purely pragmatic move. Hart, an anti-Communist in the old 26th of July Movement, argued for the inevitable, inescapable dialectic of history: that in present circumstances in Cuba and in world affairs, Marxism forces itself on a revolutionary situation like Cuba's. However, he agreed with me that Fidel's decision was intellectual, not an act of faith like Saul's on the road to Damascus. But Armando would not go for the thesis that *Marxismo-Leninismo* is *Fidelismo* under another name. (Five years before, I had put the same proposition to Raúl Castro, who laughed and replied: "It was *you* who said that!") Another way of putting it is that Fidel would not join any Communist party until he could make his own special one, and this is what happened. Nevertheless, there is no denying that it really was and is Communism, however Cuban and heterodox it may be.

Dr. Julio Le Riverend, deputy director of the Cuban Academy of Science, a well-known historian and a Marxist, was among those who insisted to me that Castro's Marxism-Leninism is sincere. Fidel, he argues, now believes in it and is not simply using it as a means to exercise his personal power. Dr. Le Riverend concedes that he, like most of us, did not foresee Fidel's evolution into Marxism-Leninism, although Le Riverend now argues, like Hart, that it was an inevitable, almost ingrained process. He agrees that it would be impossible to set a date of conversion, or even for Fidel to do so, since the journey into Communism was so gradual, but "it was genuine."

Fidel Castro's public descriptions of when and how he became a Communist are a mixture of truths, half-truths, and downright misstatements. His open confession of faith was politically motivated. For some reason which has never been clear to me, he felt it necessary to make believe that he had been a Marxist "in embryo" since his university days. Raúl Castro, who knows his brother better than anybody, told me in October 1967 that until Fidel embraced Marxism-Leninism in 1961, he had never accepted any ideology.

One of Fidel's most often quoted early interviews was with a correspondent of *L'Unità*, the Italian Communist newspaper. The interview appeared on February 1, 1961. It was the beginning of a year in which Fidel incredibly and unnaturally seemed to be humbling himself in abject apologetics toward the Cuban Communists. This was completely alien to his nature and, as events proved, to his intentions. It was also factually false.

"You wish to write that this is a socialist revolution, is this not so?" Fidel asked the *Unità* correspondent. "And write it then . . .

> The Americans and the priests say this is Communism. We know very well that it is not. At any rate, the word does not frighten us . . . But if such a great welfare triumph is Communism, then you can even call me a Communist . . . It [the PSP] is the only Cuban party which has consistently called for a radical change of social structures and relations.
>
> It is true that at the beginning the Communists distrusted me and us rebels. They were right . . . because we in the Sierra who were fighting the guerrilla war were still full of petty bourgeois prejudices and defects, in spite of our Marxist readings . . . Then we met with each other; we understood one another and started to work together. The Communists have shed much blood and heroism for the Cuban cause.

This overlooks the many years during which the PSP collaborated with Batista and followed a moderate, bourgeois line. It was false to say that the Communists "shed much blood and heroism for the Cuban cause." As Fidel rightly said on a different occasion, they "hid under their beds." If anything, the Cuban Communists were saboteurs, and no one knew it better than Fidel Castro. Politics had now given him these strange bedfellows, and he was greeting them with open arms.

Perhaps, having decided to take the Marxist road, Castro felt it necessary to rebuild the discredited image of the Cuban Communists. In the process, as I have said, he tried in the December 1, 1961, and a few subsequent speeches to show that he had long been an unborn Communist. Concededly, he was making a very difficult political, economic, and ideological transition from what can be called his 26th of July position into Marxism-Leninism.

Theodore Draper, in *Castro's Revolution,* writes of Fidel in 1961–1962 as "a man who had to reconstruct the past to fit his present in order to make himself retroactively worthy of becoming Secretary General of a 'Marxist-Leninist' party . . . Those who would not believe a word Castro said when he denied having been a Communist were ready to believe every word he said when they thought he was admitting having been a Communist."

Hugh Thomas, like Andrés Suárez, ascribes the declaration of faith to the fact that Castro was hard pressed among his Cuban and Russian Communist allies and "had to survive in order to conquer." It was "a bold bid for admission" to full membership in the Communist bloc.

In other words, Fidel had everybody guessing. The historic speech of December 1, 1961, perhaps purposefully, was confused, rambling, repetitive, and more than five hours long. Since it started at eleven in the evening of December 1, it was December 2 before it ended, but the official date is always given as the first. The speech fooled a United Press International employe, a Cuban exile hired to monitor Fidel's late-night talks in Florida, into believing that Castro had confessed to having been a Communist since his university days. The UPI dispatch, sent all over the world that day and played up sensationally, misled the U.S. government and the American people and, up to a point, distorted the historic record. To this day it is widely believed that Fidel Castro "always was a Communist" and deceived his sympathizers.

The full text of the address became available in a few days, since which time no serious scholar has misread the speech. Fidel was, in fact, apologizing for *not* having properly appreciated the virtues of Communism in his student days.

I agree with Andrés Suárez that the speech "proved to be one of his most unfortunate public appearances," but it served the purpose for which it was made. Castro told lies about himself to establish a truth about his regime. With that speech he placed the Cuban Revolution squarely inside the socialist bloc. He did it in a crude, clumsy, almost humiliating fashion, which was unnecessary, but I have no doubt that it gave him much pleasure to shock a great many people in the process.

Often in the future Fidel was to describe how he became a Marxist-Leninist—but no two versions are quite the same. One that explains what he now wants to be believed was given to a group of students in Concepción, Chile, on November 18, 1971:

> When I entered the University on finishing [preparatory] school, it was as the son of a landowner and—to make matters worse—as a political illiterate. And I studied bourgeois political economy! Luckily, some positive factors were developed at that school. A certain idealistic rationality—something very simple and elementary; a certain concept of what was good and evil, just and unjust; and a certain spirit of rebelliousness against impositions and oppression led me to an analysis

of human society and turned me into what I later realized was a utopian Communist. At that time I still hadn't been fortunate enough to meet a Communist or read a Communist document.

Then one day, he continued, *The Communist Manifesto* fell into his hands. It was "a revelation," as the books of Lenin were to be later. He felt enlightened, but, he asked, "Now, then, was I a Communist? No! I was a man who was lucky enough to have discovered a number of ideas and who was caught up in the whirlpool of Cuba's political crisis long before becoming a full-fledged Communist. I was already in that whirlpool before being recruited. I recruited myself and began to struggle."

The outcome of the struggle, it seems, was announced to the world in the speech of December 1, 1961. Like Monsieur Jourdain in Molière's *Bourgeois Gentilhomme,* who suddenly discovered he had been talking prose all his life, Fidel discovered he had been a Communist since his university days without knowing it.

That Fidel should have been struck by the arguments of *The Communist Manifesto* is natural. As the British historian A. J. P. Taylor writes in his introduction to the Penguin Pelican edition: "Thanks to *The Communist Manifesto,* everyone thinks differently about politics and society, when he thinks at all." Castro, however, was misleading in making believe *ex post facto* that his life was transformed when he read the *Manifesto* as a university student. In Taylor's phrase, it is a "holy book," but only to devotees, and Fidel did not become one until after the Revolution started.

Marx's *Capital* could not have been of much use to Castro even if he had read all of it, which his brother Raúl once told me he hadn't. The main theme of *Capital* is overproduction; the basic assumption is that labor is the source of value. The latter idea has long been discredited, and overproduction has not been a worry to Castro—on the contrary.

In creating a Marxist-Leninist structure, Castro naturally followed some of the precepts of *The Communist Manifesto.* He began "by means of despotic inroads on the rights of property, and on the conditions of bourgeois production; by means of measures, therefore, which appear economically insufficient and untenable, but which, in the course of the movement, outstrip themselves, necessitate further inroads upon the old social order, and are unavoidable as a means of entirely revolutionizing the mode of production . . .

"Confiscation of the property of all emigrants and rebels . . .

"Equal liability of all to labor. Establishment of industrial armies, especially for agriculture."

However, as I have said, the *Manifesto* was not Castro's blueprint; there was none.

Fidel put his knowledge about the technicalities of Marxism moderately, but no doubt fairly, in his May Day speech of 1966: "This . . . is not a class in political economy, nor do I pretend to be an authority on these matters; much more honestly, I should say that I consider myself an apprentice, a student interested in these problems."

The Revolution was then in its eighth year, and it was more than twenty years since he had been at Havana University. Fidel had neither the time nor the inclination to absorb and think about the great amount of Marxist literature which Che Guevara went through. It does not seem that Fidel Castro ever became more than an "apprentice" in Marxist-Leninist studies. Che, however, came close to making himself an authority.

"Marxism," Che said to me in August 1960, "is a vague philosophical concept of a hundred years ago. One might as well talk of Newtonism. Today a nation faced with certain problems follows certain lines which often parallel previous situations."

He liked this idea so much that he used it in an article for *Verde Olivo* in October:

> Cuba's is a unique Revolution, which some people maintain contradicts one of the most orthodox premises of the revolutionary movement expressed by Lenin: "Without a revolutionary theory there is no revolutionary movement." The principal actors of this revolution had no coherent theoretical criteria, but it cannot be said that they were ignorant of the various concepts of history, society, economics, and revolution which are being discussed in the world today . . . When asked whether or not we are Marxists, our position is the same as that of a physicist or a biologist when asked if he is a "Newtonian" or if he is a "Pasteurian." There are truths so evident, so much a part of people's knowledge, that it is now useless to discuss them. . . .
>
> Marx expresses a revolutionary concept: The world must not only be interpreted, it must be transformed . . . We practial revolutionaries, initiating our own struggle, simply fullfil laws foreseen by Marx, the scientist . . . That is to say—it is well to emphasize this again—the laws of Marxism are present in the events of the Cuban Revolution, independently of what its leaders profess or fully know of those laws from a theoretical point of view.

A writer in the *Times Literary Supplement* of London, December 3, 1971, remarked that it "has become increasingly clear that the present fashion for intellectuals . . . to call themselves Marxists because they want to make revolutions has produced some very curious disciples for the master." The reviewer was referring to the French writer Louis Althusser, but he could have had Che Guevara at the back of his mind.

Che argued that Marxism was like an inescapable force of nature or history, but he himself did not think it necessary to go so far as to become a card-carrying Communist. The formality involved did not interest him, not even, as we shall see, when he went along with Fidel's Marxism-Leninism. Che's heart and soul were in his idealized version of socialism. He did not possess Fidel's capacity for self-deception, for being sincerely convinced one day and equally convinced of something quite different another day. Che was not a politician; Fidel was.

Orthodox Muscovite Communism was never attractive to Castro. The old-guard Cuban Communist premises, which were typical of Moscow policy, called for a bourgeois, popular-front drive toward "revolution" based on the industrial workers—the proletariat. But the Cuban workers were not revolutionary. Neither were the peasants. A popular-front government, if one could have been elected, would have had precious little chance of carrying out a social revolution in Cuba.

Fidel was far to the left of, and far more revolutionary than, PSP Communism, which was another reason why the Old Guard had to go. One of the striking features of contemporary politics is that revolutions have to be made in spite of, and against the opposition of, the Muscovite Communists. This was true in Cuba, as it was in Bolivia when Che Guevara was there; in Chile when Salvador Allende was President; in France in May 1968; in the Middle East in recent years.

The organization I wrote about in the downfall of Aníbal Escalante, the Organizaciones Revolucionarias Integradas (ORI, or Integrated Revolutionary Organizations), was announced by Castro in his July 26, 1961, speech. It was to be considered as the forerunner of the Partido Unido de la Revolución Socialista de Cuba (PURSC, or United Party of the Socialist Revolution of Cuba). These were amalgams of the three main political organizations: the 26th of July Movement, the Student Directorate, and the Communist PSP, all of which then melted away.

The function of the ORI, the PURSC, and, finally, the Partido Comunista de Cuba (PCC) was to orient and carry out government directives, not to govern. This was a once-for-all command which is essentially as valid in 1975 as in 1961.

For good measure, Castro reminded the old-guard Communists

in his speech "of certain facts, such as the fact that we waged the war; we led it; we won it." By "we," Fidel as usual meant himself. The July 26, 1961, speech, however, was not a break with Communism or the Cuban Communists; it was a reassertion of Fidel Castro's domination of the Cuban government and the Cuban Revolution.

His method of organizing the successive Communist parties was unique in the world Communist movement. The definitive—and present—organization, the Communist Party of Cuba, was announced by Castro on October 3, 1965. He made it clear that the "path," "ideas," "method," and "system" were going to be Cuban. At the top there was the customary secretary general and his chosen Politburo and Secretariat, but there any similarity to the Soviet-type Communist Party ended. (ORI and PURSC, incidentally, had no Politburos.)

No old-guard Communists were appointed to the eight-man Politburo, but Carlos Rafael Rodríguez and Blas Roca were named to the important Secretariat, joining Fidel and Raúl Castro and Armando Hart. Only President Dorticós and Hart, in the Politburo, were civilians, and only Dorticós had not graduated from the 26th of July Movement or the Rebel Army.

Fidel Castro, the *Jefe Máximo* by courtesy, was head of everything; Raúl was his second in command. The structure then established lasted until December 1972, when an expansion and reshuffling took place.

ORI and PURSC had had a National Directorate of twenty-five; the PCC was given a Central Committee of one hundred. Only twenty-one members of the PCC's Central Committee came from the pre-1959 Communist PSP. The Central Committee is not a policy-making body, but for a person to be a member of it is prestigious and meaningful. All the individual members of the Central Committee have posts in local, provincial, and federal affairs, in industry, government, or the armed forces. Each of the six provinces and the Isle of Pines has a Provincial Committee. Below them are regional and municipal committees and, at the base, factory and farm cells.

Candidates for the Communist Party are taken from the "vanguard," exceptional workers elected by a majority vote of their fellow workers in recognition of their dedication, hard work, discipline, camaraderie, and so forth. These "exemplary" workers and managers would belong to one or more of the mass organizations and to the militia. They would presumably be familiar with Castro's ideas, but no questions are asked. It is not necessary to know the works of Marx, Lenin, Stalin, Mao Tse-tung, or even the theories of socialism or

Communism. However, considering the Marxist indoctrination in the schools, only the older men and women would be ignorant of socialist doctrine. Candidates are warned not to expect higher pay or special privileges for political reasons, but in practice they all get some privileges in the way of transport, housing, and food. The main safeguard is that all candidates for party membership have to be approved by the already-serving PCC members. The Central Committee members, incidentally, are all appointed, not elected, and hence are Castro's men.

About the time that the Communist Party of Cuba was formed, *Hoy* and *Revolución,* which for a while were rivals and critical of each other, were replaced by *Granma,* which has since been the official organ of the PCC. It is supposed to have a circulation of one million. The paper is a little more palatable and attractive than the traditional Soviet or Eastern-bloc journals, as it prints many photographs and uses flamboyant headlines and make-up. It also prints an expensive weekly review in English, French, and Spanish, available in many countries. Its primary value for foreigners is to give the complete texts of all speeches by Castro and many by other government leaders, as well as official documents. But it is, of course, pure government propaganda, with carefully chosen and censored news, presented in typical totalitarian, unctuous, smarmy language. It makes dull and dismal reading for Cubans, and the radio is not any better when it comes to news.

What is presented as news is often shockingly misleading. From what Cubans could learn from their mass media, for instance, it was the Israelis who started the "Yom Kippur" War of 1973 and were the "aggressors." There is a brainwashing process in Cuba as cynical as in any of the totalitarian countries.

Fidel Castro, as I keep saying, is pragmatic and opportunistic, not dogmatic. He thinks something up, or it is proposed to him and he likes it—and there is a new organization. The idea for the CDR (Committees for the Defense of the Revolution), as I wrote, came on the spur of the moment in a speech on September 28, 1960. All the Communist organizations and committees pyramid upward to the person of Fidel Castro. He has reversed the standard Communist procedure whereby the party has the power which the governmental and administrative bodies carry out on the party's behalf. The PCC wields only the power delegated or permitted to it by Castro through the Politburo and Secretariat. Its primary purpose is to activate and consolidate mass support for government policies, which are made *with* but not *by* the Communist Party. The oft-postponed first congress of the PCC is now promised for later in 1975. Neither the ORI nor the PURSC had held a congress.

When I saw Blas Roca in October 1967 he was working at the head of a large and distinguished group of men, drawing up a constitution which, he assured me, would be in operation in a few years. When I saw him next in September 1972, only one section—on the judiciary—had been completed. The bulk of the new constitution was nowhere near ready.

The PCC, as Professor Halperin says, "was not the progeny of the PSP or even an amalgamation of the revolutionary sectors, but a reincarnation of the Movement of July 26th, purged, toughened, polished and streamlined, with Fidel Castro at the head and practically all positions of strategic importance occupied by veterans of the old movement."

Despite its limitations and its unique character, the PCC is of supreme importance to the Cuban Revolution, The whole structure of the Castro regime—political, military, economic, social, cultural—is run by the Communist movement in the sense that an automobile is run by its engine. Like an automobile, the PCC has its driver—Fidel Castro. What importance the party has is relatively new. It is growing in strength (In 1972, Jesús Montané, the party organizer who succeeded Armando Hart, told me that there were more than 140,000 members). A new generation of eager, ambitious, indoctrinated young men and women are active in every sector of the party ranks. More leeway and more authority are being delegated at provincial, regional, and lower levels—and usually to Communist Party members.

It is often said—and I have been saying it of the Cuban Revolution—that the Russian and Chinese Revolutions did not corroborate Marxism; they simply used Marxism. Fidel Castro, like Mao Tse-tung, is an activist, not a theorist. He does all sorts of things and calls them Marxist-Leninist. As Raúl Castro said to me some years ago, "After all, Marxism is a flexible concept; it allows for development and change."

Fidel put it this way in a speech on November 3, 1965, as the new Communist Party of Cuba was being formed: "Marxism is a revolutionary and dialectical doctrine, not a philosophical doctrine. It is a guide for revolutionary action, not a dogma. To try to press Marxism into a type of catechism is anti-Marxist."

Professor Eric Wolf, in *Peasant Wars of the Twentieth Century*, acutely points out that Fidel's strategy from the beginning was what Communists call Blanquist and that Blanquism was always "anathema to most Communists." Wolf cites a passage from Engels, who defined Blanquism as the belief "that a relatively small number of resolute, well-organized men would be able, at a given favorable moment, not only to seize the helm of the State, but also to keep power, by energetic and unrelenting action, until they had succeeded in drawing the mass of the people into the revolution by marshalling them around a small band of leaders."

This is exactly what Castro did. He did not have a party and an ideology, as did Lenin and Mao Tse-tung. Khrushchev, although tolerant of the young Cuban, told President Kennedy in 1962 that so far as he was concerned, Fidel Castro was no Communist.

What future political scientists will have to study and analyze is the *use* to which Fidel Castro has put what he calls Marxist principles, theories, and ideas. The process is continuing and is not susceptible of any definitive judgment, even by historians and sociologists who are thoroughly grounded in the subject of Marxism.

K. S. Karol, the French-Polish journalist who published a sensational book on Cuba in 1971 called in English *Guerrillas in Power*, is an authority on socialism and Communism, but he is anti-Russian and has strongly held views about what a socialist regime should be like. He applies patterns and ideologies on European models to the Cuban scene. They do not fit the heterodox, always changing Cuban picture of Fidel Castro's anarchistic, dictatorial nature. Fidel is still groping for practical and workable solutions to his problems.

He has been often accused of "heresy" to the Communism practiced in Russia, but this is meaningless except when it goes counter to Soviet-bloc policies. It is a feature of Castro's regime that it is closer to the classic definition of Communism than any nation of the Communist bloc: "From each according to his ability, to each according to his needs." However, at the Workers' Congress of the CTC in November 1973, it was strongly emphasized that this was a future goal.

"We do not pretend to be the most perfect interpreters of Marxist-Leninist ideas," Fidel said in his July 26, 1966, address, "but we do have our way of interpreting these ideas; we have our way of interpreting socialism; our way of interpreting Marxism-Leninism; our way of interpreting Communism."

Both Moscow and Peking took their time in conceding that what Cuba was doing could be called socialism. Cecil Johnson, in his book *Communist China and Latin America,* points out that "the Russians did not officially recognize the socialist nature of the Cuban state until April 8, 1963." The Chinese, he adds, were only a little earlier when, on January 1, 1963, the Castro government was referred to as having "courageously led the Cuban people on the socialist path and set up the first socialist country on the American continent."

The Cuban Revolution, as Professor Johnson writes, was nothing like the Chinese (Maoist) description of their own revolution: first, the workers, the peasants, the petty bourgeoisie, and the national bourgeoisie (the so-called "four-class advance") form a united front against the "enemies" of the people; once the first stage, under the leadership of the proletariat, is accomplished, there is a transition to the higher stage of socialism.

Lenin had anticipated Mao in emphasizing the importance of the peasantry in staging a revolution in backward countries, but Mao was the first Communist leader to treat the peasantry as "by nature the most reliable ally of the proletariat" (i.e., the Communist Party), according to Professor Johnson.

Fidel, in 1963, was at odds with the Soviet Union over the missile crisis and Moscow's Latin American policy, but his economy was so bad he needed help which only Russia could give. Unluckily for Fidel, the Sino-Soviet quarrel began in the very year—1959—that he came to power. The Cubans have tried—with considerable success—to keep out of the dispute. It has meant a policy of being pro-Russian but not anti-Chinese, except verbally, now and then.

The official Cuban viewpoint was well expressed by Che Guevara in August 1963: "The Sino-Soviet quarrel is, for us, a sad development. We do not take part in this dispute. We are trying to mediate, but since the dispute is a fact, we tell our people about it and it is discussed by the Party. Our Party's attitude is to avoid analyzing who is in the right and who is not. We have our own position, and as they say in the American films, any resemblance [presumably of Cuba to either contestant] is purely coincidental."

For several years the Chinese Communists were more popular in Cuba than the Soviet bloc. Peking was, at first, generous in its economic aid and financial credits, but the honeymoon ended on January 2, 1966, when Fidel made a verbal attack on the Chinese and repeated the onslaught even more violently on February 6, charging extortion, aggression, piracy, oppression, and filibustering.

The immediate cause for the tirades was Peking's announcement that for 1966 it could supply only 135,000 tons of rice instead of the 250,000 tons that Fidel expected in exchange for 800,000 tons of sugar. As a result, Cuban rice rations had to be reduced by one-half. Castro also objected to the amount and kind of propaganda that the Chinese were exporting to Cuba. The Chinese replied in kind, if with less vehemence. They augmented the rice shipment in 1967, but the old cordial relations became and remained unenthusiastically correct on both sides. It could hardly be otherwise, considering how greatly dependent Cuba is on help from the Soviet Union.

Events, desires, convictions had all pushed Cuba into the Communist fold. Once inside, the commitment was definite and unchangeable. So long as there is a Castroite Cuba there will be a Marxist-Leninist Cuba. In the light of the circumstances he faced, it is arguable that Fidel Castro had no choice.

"Marx conceived of socialism as the direct result of development," he said in a speech on December 20, 1969. "There can be as many political disquisitions as you like, as many doctrinaire discussions as you like, but we know from our own experience how difficult it is, even with every desire to carry it through, with nothing to stop us and with all the revolutionary laws needed to do it—we know that there will be no economic development in any underdeveloped country without socialism, without centralizing all the resources of the economy and channeling them in the needed direction."

This was an easy formulation to make, but Fidel Castro and his colleagues were establishing a socialist system at the same time that they were carrying out one of the most drastic revolutions in history against opposition from the most powerful nation on earth. The process was more than economic; a moral element was involved. Cubans had to feel that "man does not live by bread alone." Without idealism and faith there would be no revolution. That much Fidel had realized from the beginning, before he turned to socialism. It was natural for him to believe that the same qualities of idealism, faith, dedication, sacrifice, and unselfishness were needed to make Marxism-Leninism work.

No one believed more fervently in this than his closest friend and aide, Ernesto Che Guevara. Cuban socialism was the projection of Che's own fanatical, dedicated, self-sacrificing personality. He never seemed to realize that his standards were superhuman. He gave to revolution what a saint and martyr gives to religion. If Che leaves a mark on the history of modern socialism, it will be as an idealist or—who knows?—as a prophet who preached before his time.

In Cuba, the moral element that remains in the economic structure—and it is considerable—is in part a heritage from Che Guevara's idealism, as Fidel Castro concedes. Moral incentives, voluntarism, socialist emulation were and are a part of Castro's philosophy of labor; they became the mainsprings of Che's philosophy of socialism. Authorities on Marxism say that they are not to be found in the writings of Karl Marx, but Cuban Marxism-Leninism is what Fidel Castro and—while he was there—Che Guevara said it is.

CHAPTER 11

Che—Havana

Revolutions are made of passions.
—Ernesto Che Guevara

In Ernesto Che Guevara the Cuban Revolution produced one of the great revolutionaries of all time. But he was much more; he was a human being of extraordinary quality.

His first wife, the late Hilda Gadea, has put history immeasurably in her debt by writing an intimate, loyal, transparently true biography of her husband, *Ernesto: A Memoir of Che Guevara* (1972).

An artless picture was built up by her of a difficult, thorny, hypersensitive, brilliant, fanatically honest and sincere young man, but a warm and compassionate one, capable of deep and loyal friendships. His fortitude under a severe, lifelong asthmatic condition was remarkable, for he never let it interfere with what he was determined to do.

His dedication to his revolutionary beliefs was deeply religious. Che had a missionary's faith in the innate goodness of man, in the ability of workers to dedicate themselves to ideals and to overcome selfishness and prejudices. It was the other side of the coin of his passionate indignation against injustice and exploitation of the humble. He saw the solution in an exalted form of Marxism that would bring freedom and brotherhood. Such men are born to be martyrs.

His testimony as a Marxist was best expressed in a long letter written in 1965 to Carlos Quijano for the Montevideo, Uruguay, weekly *Marcha*, and published in English in 1967 by the Book Institute of Havana as *Man and Socialism in Cuba.* "In our country [Cuba], the individual knows that the glorious period in which it has fallen to him to live is one of sacrifice; he is familiar with sacrifice," he wrote. "The task of the vanguard revolutionary is both magnificent and anguishing." And he added, "Let me say, with the risk of appearing ridiculous, that the true revolutionary is guided by strong feelings of love."

He drew a picture of himself: "The leaders of the revolution have children who do not learn to call their father with their first faltering words; they have wives who must be part of the general sacrifice of their lives to carry the revolution to its destination; their friends are strictly limited to their comrades in revolution. There is no life outside the revolution."

His sternness and stoicism went to bounds that only the fanatic could reach, but Che tried to generalize in his letter about what he called "the danger of weaknesses."

"If a man thinks that in order to devote his entire life to the revolution he must not be distracted by the worry that one of his children lacks a certain article, that the children's shoes are in poor condition, that his family lacks some necessary item—with this reasoning, the seeds of future corruption are allowed to filter through."

In a speech to militiamen on August 19, 1960, Che told how he had traveled in all the Latin American countries except Haiti and the Dominican Republic as a student and later a doctor, seeing the mass poverty, hunger, and disease. "I wanted to help those people," he said. His aim in life could not have been put more simply or truly.

During those travels Che and an Argentine friend, Alberto Granados, both then medical students, went to a leprosarium in Peru where they treated the patients as friends and equals, not wearing masks or gloves. "And the patients loved them," Hilda Gadea writes in her biography. "Whenever he referred to them, it was with respect and affection."

Another Argentine friend of prerevolutionary years, Ricardo Rojo, who was with Che during one of his South American journeys and wrote a biography called *My Friend Che,* says that he asked him why the leprosarium had made such "a remarkable impression" on him. "Because the highest forms of human solidarity and loyalty arise among lonely and desperate men," Che replied. One of his favorite poems was Pablo Neruda's *Canción Desesperada* ("Song of Despair").

"Sometimes we revolutionaries are lonely," he said in a letter written from Havana on May 23, 1963, and printed in *Reminiscences of the Cuban Revolutionary War.* "Even our children look on us as strangers."

To me it is a strange and moving thing that two men so different from each other as Che Guevara and Fidel Castro, and yet bound to each other to the end by the deepest ties of affection, should both have been such lonely men. Che was more articulate about it than Fidel, but Guevara was the artist and Castro the man of action.

The always fascinating differences in character of the two men kept emerging. At the "Battle of Malverde" (a Sierra Maestra skirmish in late 1957) one of the bravest and most valuable of the Rebels, a close friend of Che's, was killed. Javier Milián, a peasant *barbudo* who survived the fight, wrote this note for the magazine *Tricontinental:*

"When Che received the message that Ciro [Redondo] had been killed, it was something tremendous. I thought that Che wasn't a man to cry, but that day he couldn't help himself and grief overtook him. I saw him leaning against a rock, his hand over his face, crying bitterly."

I cannot imagine Fidel doing that, however much he grieved. I know how deeply he felt when Camilo Cienfuegos was lost, and I was in Havana and seeing him when the news of Che's capture and death was gradually confirmed. He was terribly distressed, but if he cried —if he ever cried—it would have been alone.

There is an anecdote in Hilda Gadea's book which helps one to understand the character of Che Guevara and what motivated him. They were living in Mexico City at the time.

> During the first days of our marriage, [she writes] Ernesto was very worried about a patient at the hospital whom he called "Old María." Very moved, he told me about her condition, an acute case of asthma. His interest was so strong that I almost felt jealous of that woman; she was on his mind all the time. Every morning he rushed to see her; when he came home the first thing he talked about was Old María's condition, and sometimes he would even visit her at night. One day he said very sadly that Old María might possibly die that night. He went to the hospital that evening to be at her bedside, helping to do everything possible to save her. The effort was in vain; that night the old woman died of asthmatic suffocation. She was a very old woman, extremely poor; she had only one daughter and three or four grandchildren. She had been a washerwoman all her life, her years sad and hard. For Ernesto she was representative of the most forgotten and most exploited class. His profound emotion was evident as he told me this, but not until later did I realize the mark the tragedy had left on him. When he departed on the *Granma,* I found a notebook of poems in the suitcase that he left with me. One of the poems was dedicated to Old María. It contained his promise to fight for a better world, for a better life for all the poor and exploited.

Once, when he was addressing an assembly of Communist Youth (on October 20, 1963), Che tried to project his own idealism, what he called "a great sensitivity to injustice." Every young Communist, he said, "must develop his sensibility to the maximum, to the point that he feels anguish when a man is assassinated in any corner of the world, and he feels elation when in some place in the world a new banner of liberty is raised."

There is a short, revealing letter from Che in the series published at the end of *Reminiscences.* It is in answer to a Señora María Rosario Guevara, who wrote him from Morocco.

"Truthfully speaking, I don't know what part of Spain my family comes from," he replied. "Of course, my ancestors left there a long time ago, with one hand in front and another behind [a Spanish saying indicating extreme poverty]; and if I don't keep mine in the same place, it is only because of the discomfort of the position!

"I don't think you and I are very closely related, but if you are capable of trembling with indignation each time that an injustice is committed in the world, we are comrades, and that is more important."

"Wherever a man is struck on his cheek," José Martí had written, "every man receives a blow."

The mixture of raillery and seriousness in Che's letter to Señora Guevara was typical. He gave of himself with deadly seriousness, but he experienced a certain malicious pleasure in violating the conventions of society. He was a social misfit, uncomfortable at parties, unable to dance, wanting to talk of nothing but politics.

"Guevara could go without eating for three whole days as easily as he could stay at a table piled with all sorts of food for ten hours at a time," Ricardo Rojo writes of him. "Now that I think back, this way of nourishing himself was one of Guevara's most impressive characteristics."

One of his few indulgences—an Argentine habit that he kept in the Sierra Maestra and the Bolivian jungle—was the drinking of *yerba maté,* the bitter South American tea leaves made into an infusion. He drank it from morning to night. The Cubans taught him to smoke cigars, which he did, with characteristic thrift, down to an alarming nub.

"He was very careful not to use his position in the Government to obtain more than he needed to live on," Ricardo Rojo wrote of a visit to Cuba in 1963. "His house [in Havana], a mansion confiscated from a rich exile, was practically bare, despite the innumerable gifts he was always receiving on his international tours."

His austerity was doubtless a reproach to his more human associates. He lived on such an exalted plane that it made all but his Sierra intimates uncomfortable, as if his behavior was a constant reproach to them.

Although a doctor by training and, in the Sierra Maestra, by practice, Che not only never gave a thought to cleanliness but seemed to glory in dirt, in never washing, in never changing his clothes. Ricardo Rojo, on the trip he made with him up the western side of South America, describes this characteristic.

Enrique Oltuski, who under the *nom de guerre* of "Sierra" was the 26th of July Movement's coordinator in the Las Villas underground, tells in his book *Gente del llano* of an encounter with Che in a hut which was the guerrilla leader's stopping place. A few Rebels had been eating a stew which was so nauseating that Oltuski was revolted. Che arrived about midnight and greeted them.

> While we were talking, [Oltuski writes] Che picked up pieces of the meat with his dirty fingers. Judging from the gusto with which he ate, it tasted glorious to him. He finished eating and we went out. We sat down on a side of the road, Che, Marcelo and I. Che handed out cigars. They were coarse, certainly made in the region by some peasant. I inhaled the strong and bitter smoke. My body felt hot and I felt slightly dizzy. By my side, Che smoked and coughed, with a moist cough as if he were damp up to his teeth. He smelled bad. He smelled of decomposed sweat. It was a penetrating odor, and I combated it with tobacco smoke . . .
>
> When we were going away, Marcelo asked me: "What do you think of him?"
>
> "In spite of everything, one can't help admiring him," I replied. "He knows better than we what is necessary. He lives for that alone. You know? I thought that I was a full-fledged revolutionary . . . until I knew Che. Compared to him, I am an apprentice. How many things hold me down from which he has freed himself!"

His baptismal name was Ernesto Guevara Lynch de la Serna. "Che" is the familiar diminutive for "you" in Argentina, as in "Hey, you!" He began to be called that in Mexico by the Cubans. During his youth in Argentina, Hilda Gadea says, his nickname was "Chancho."

He was born on June 14, 1927, not, as Hugh Thomas writes, on the appropriate day for a future revolutionary, July 14. This made Che ten months younger than Fidel Castro. (But June 14—1845—was the birthday of Antonio Maceo, the "Bronze Titan.")

He came to like the use of "Che" and ended up by making it official: Ernesto Che Guevara, as if it were his middle name. When writing it alone as a signature, he always used a lower-case "c." During his tenure as president of the National Bank of Cuba, all banknotes carried the simple signature "che," which, deliberately or not, showed his contempt for money.

At the time of his birth, his family was living in Rosario, Argentina, a large city on the River Plate. The asthma from which he suffered mercilessly until his death seems to have begun when he was only three. According to Hilda Gadea, it was "a family illness" that he inherited from his mother.

Ricardo Rojo, who remained a close friend of Che's mother until her death in 1965, gives an account of the family's social position which is a little exaggerated.

"The families of his father, Guevara Lynch, and his mother, de la Serna," Rojo writes, "sprang from old aristocratic lines dating back to the days before Argentina's independence . . . The Guevara family was socially broadminded and democratic, intellectually active and progressive in politics, without ever losing sight of its roots in the old aristocracy. In this family atmosphere, certain things were taken for granted: a passion for justice, the rejection of fascism, religious indifference, an interest in literature and love of poetry, a prejudice against money and the ways of making it."

Rojo was right in every respect except perhaps in his snobbish insistence on the family's "aristocracy," which, it will have been noted, Che rather ridiculed. However, the father's connection with the Argentine oligarchy could have been on the Lynch side and a De la Serna was Spanish Viceroy and military commander in Peru in 1824 at the Battle of Ayacucho. Che's parents were not welcomed by Argentina's high society because of their political beliefs. Che's mother, a cultured and charming woman, as my wife and I discovered when we met her in Buenos Aires, adored Che and was inordinately proud of him. She shared his Marxist views.

The father lost his wealth in a variety of businesses because, writes Hilda Gadea, of his "humane refusal to exploit workers." Whenever Che spoke of his parents and brothers and sisters, it was with "warmth and affection; his tie with his mother was very deep." Yet he left them in 1951 intending to be away ten years, as in 1965 he left a wife and five young children in Cuba whom he loved very much to go to his death in Bolivia. He had an older brother, Roberto, a younger brother, Juan Martín, and two sisters, Ana María and Celia. His mother's name was also Celia.

In his lifelong fight against asthma, Che forced himself to participate in sports, especially rugby and long bicycling and walking trips. On December 29, 1951, he began a motorcycle and foot trip up the Pacific coast with his school friend Alberto Granados. They went to Chile, Peru (where the leper colony was), Bolivia, and Venezuela, doing odd jobs to keep alive. Che spent a month in Miami, where he must have done something wrong because he was questioned by the police and shipped back to Argentina. He had an American grandmother who lived in California, he told me once with a mischievous smile—I don't know from which side of his family. On the trip with Granados and on a subsequent journey he learned a great deal about Andean Indians and therefore could have had no illusions about them on his final guerrilla expedition.

On returning to Argentina, he completed his medical studies and graduated as a doctor in April 1953. Both in his studies and his work as a doctor, he specialized in allergies, hoping to help both himself and other sufferers from asthma. Hilda Gadea says that he learned to inject himself with adrenalin at the age of ten. She writes (curiously, considering that she was his wife) that "it must be complicated" to be married to an asthmatic because "children are likely to inherit the disease." The only child by his marriage with Hilda Gadea, Hildita, is not asthmatic. Professor Hugh Thomas makes the odd conjuncture that President Theodore Roosevelt also suffered from asthma and also glorified war.

How much or how competent a doctor Che was is dubious; he was inclined to cast aspersions on his own proficiency. Ricardo Rojo says that he did all his studies for his medical degree "in a period of six months." However, he obviously got a lot of rough-and-ready medical experience in the Sierra Maestra and, at the end, in Bolivia. He joined Fidel's *Granma* expedition as its doctor.

By any standard, Che was an intellectual, an omnivorous reader from childhood until his death.

"Guevara was a man of solid culture," Hilda Gadea writes. "He could speak on Aristotle as he could on Kant or Marx or Gide or Faulkner. He ranged from the poetry of Keats to that of Sara de Ibáñez, his favorite writer of all."

"I discovered that he liked poetry," she says of the time they were living together in Guatemala City in 1953–1954. "He had a wide knowledge of Latin American poetry and could easily recall any poem of Pablo Neruda [the Communist Nobel Prize winner], whom he admired greatly. Among his favorite poets were Federico García Lorca, Miguel Hernández, [Antonio] Machado, Gabriela Mistral, Cesar Vallejo; a few Argentines like José Hernández, whose *Martín Fierro* he could recite completely from memory; Jorge Luis Borges, Leopoldo Marechal, Alfonsina Storni, and the Uruguayans Juana de Ibarborou and Sara de Ibáñez."

Curiously, Kipling's "If" was another poem that, she says, Che knew by heart. So did José Antonio Primo de Rivera, the founder of the Spanish Falangist Party, who was executed by the Republicans.

Hilda tells of their endless reading and interminable conversations on Sartre, Freud, Michurin, Pavlov, the literature of Marxism, and she adds: "I began to see Ernesto transforming his ideas little by little toward the Marxist ideology, which in principle he had already accepted." They evidently read all the writings of Marx, Engels, and Lenin. There is no evidence, however, that Che went beyond the Marxists into the field of sociology. However, when one considers what an active life he led, his knowledge was impressive.

Contrary to general belief, Che apparently had read about the Chinese Revolution and Mao Tse-tung "with great admiration" while in Guatemala, and the two of them "often talked about it." Che also eagerly questioned a Guatemalan who had been in China, Hilda Gadea writes. This means that up in the Sierra Maestra Guevara must have known that the Cuban guerrilla tactics paralleled the Chinese in some respects. Che, she says, even suggested once that they go to China together.

Hilda Gadea, whom Che met in Guatemala City in 1953, was an economist by training and would have helped her lover to grasp some understanding of economics in their reading and talks. In Mexico, she says, Che read and studied about economics, but there must have been something exclusively theoretical about his reading or he would not have made the mistakes he later did in practice as president of the National Bank and minister of industry. However, it is wrong for all of us to believe that Che was ignorant of economics and finance when he assumed the Cuban posts. For instance, according to Hilda, Che was familiar with John Maynard Keynes's *General Theory of Employment, Interest, and Money.*

Marzo Orózco, one of the Rebels who was in the Sierra Maestra with Che, wrote in the magazine *Tricontinental* in October 1967: "I remember that he had a lot of books because he read frequently. He didn't waste a minute. Many times he sacrificed his sleeping hours to sit up and read or write in his diary. If he got up early, he would read if there was light. He would read late into the night, sometimes by firelight. He had very good eyesight."

Music, however, played no part in his life. In a letter to the

Cultural Trade Bureau of the Cuban Ministry of Foreign Trade on June 25, 1964, regarding some disks that had been sent to him for his opinion he wrote: "I cannot speak of the contents. It is not permissible for me to give even a timid opinion about music, for my ignorance reaches down to 273 degrees below zero."

He does seem to have been a superior chess player, and, according to Ricardo Rojo, his principal hobby was archaeology.

No doubt all human beings have a tendency to see what they want to see, but I long ago decided that revolutionaries are especially prone to this failing. Hilda Gadea tells about Che visiting the American-owned Anaconda copper mine at Chuquicamata, Chile, during his odyssey, where he was "able to see the subhuman conditions in which Chilean miners lived." My wife and I visited that mine about the same time and can testify that the miners were exceptionally well treated in terms of pay, housing, medical care, and recreation. Presumably Che would not have been such a good revolutionary if he could see anything good in capitalism—or imperialism, as he preferred to call it.

I learned to my surprise from his wife's book that Che Guevara, like Raúl Castro, had briefly belonged to the Communist Youth organization in Argentina. Even the CIA had not been able to unearth this titbit when they were so feverishly seeking links between the revolutionaries and the Communists in 1959–1961. Che told her, Hilda Gadea writes, that "during his university days, after a short time in the organization, he decided to leave the Communist Youth since he felt the Communists were getting away from the people."

Like Fidel, Che was capable of enormous self-discipline but incapable of anything like party discipline. They were fiercely independent as individuals. Hilda tells how a friend of hers, knowing of Che's poverty, offered him a job through her in Guatemala City on condition that he join the *Partido Guatemalteco del Trabajo*, Guatemala's Communist Party. She told Che about the proposal.

"You tell him," he snapped angrily, "that when I want to join the Party I will do so on my own initiative." However, a few days later he explained: "It's not that I'm not in agreement with the Communist ideology; it's the method I don't like; they shan't get members this way. It's all false."

Hilda Gadea claimed—and she gave ample evidence—that Che's transformation into a militant revolutionary took place in Guatemala. By late 1953, according to her, he was firmly convinced of the need for revolution and that success could be achieved only by violence. The enemy of enemies, even then, was "Yankee imperialism." He was contemptuous of reform movements then being tried in Peru, Bolivia, and Venezuela, although he seems to have had some sympathy for Argentina's Peronism. Reform movements were "betrayals."

Evidently, ideas about a moralistic, idealistic form of socialism were taking root in his mind. "Our points of view about life and our role in society were in complete agreement," Hilda writes of 1954 in Guatemala. "We did not believe that our objectives as professionals were to earn money, to make our personal fortunes. We were aware that we had received from society the benefits of knowledge and culture and that whatever we had learned and would learn in the future had to be put at the service of society."

She said that she had been thinking along these lines for a long time, "but it was during this time that Ernesto began to define his attitude toward these problems. . . . Engel's *Anti-Dühring*, which we had both read, became the subject of many conversations. In accord with this book we shared a materialistic philosophy of life and a socialist conception that takes account of the individual as part of society."

There was a Cuban exile group in Guatemala in 1953 of men who had taken part in the Moncada Barracks attack the previous July. They were youths who had escaped the original round-up and slaughter and taken refuge in the Guatemalan Embassy in Havana. When permitted to leave, they had to go to the Guatemalan capital. Hilda met them and was impressed. In late December 1953 or early January 1954, she introduced them to Che Guevara, thus beginning his Cuban relationship.

Antonio (Ñico) López, who was to be killed at Alegría de Pío after the *Granma* landing, told Che all about Moncada and Fidel Castro in obviously laudatory terms.

Serious historians long ago realized that Che Guevara's role in the Guatemalan crisis and *coup d'état* of 1954 could have been only a slight one. Hilda Gadea confirms this. Che was not allowed to do anything for the pro-Communist government of President Jacobo Arbenz, although he tried. Later he claimed to have "saved lives and transported weapons," although he did not say how. Che was turned down at first for a government medical post and for most of the time scrounged around doing odd jobs until he found work as an intern in a teachers' center.

In the light of the truth, the sensational stories printed for years about Guevara's important role—as a "Communist," of course—in trying to save the Arbenz regime become ridiculous. Che did not even meet Arbenz until the former President turned up as an exile in Cuba, and he was, in fact, contemptuous of the Guatemalan leader's feeble showing during the *coup.*

I earlier mentioned the Guatemalan affair and its role in misleading the CIA and Washington at the time of the Bay of Pigs into believing that the maneuver could be repeated in Cuba. The Arbenz government was not Communist, but it was pro-Communist and radical, and the Reds were influential.

After the excitement was over, Hilda Gadea (a Peruvian citizen) was briefly jailed and then deported to Mexico. Che Guevara took refuge in the Argentine Embassy, also ending up in Mexico City, shortly before Hilda arrived.

He earned a small income in the capital, working in the allergy ward of the General Hospital and supplementing his salary by going around the streets and parks taking photographs. They were developed by a young Guatemalan, Julio Roberto Cáceres, nicknamed El Patojo (Shorty) because of his size. Che was later to bestow a kind of immortality on El Patojo by paying a warm tribute to him at the end of the first Spanish edition of his reminiscences, *Pasajes de la guerra revolucionaria.* Cáceres had been killed shortly before Che finished the book, fighting as a guerrilla in Guatemala.

Che Guevara had a sense of mission by the time he reached Mexico. He inscribed a book that he gave to his fiancée on New Year's Day, 1955: "To Hilda, so that on the day we part there may remain with you the substance of my hopes for the future and my predestined struggle."

Hilda was "very moved." Not every young woman would have appreciated the sentiments, but there was a deep affinity between the two.

Che met Raúl Castro before he did his brother, and, writes Hilda, "a strong friendship developed immediately between them," adding that "Raúl held Communist ideas."

The meeting with Fidel Castro was in the beginning of July 1955 and, typically, they talked for ten straight hours through the night. Fidel had just returned from a money-gathering trip to the United States.

The Argentine saw in the Cuban what he called *un gran conductor* (a great leader), a fellow revolutionary, romantic but foolhardy, ready to die for what he believed in. No doubt, the magnetism of Castro's character played its role with Guevara, as with others. On Castro's part, it must have been the attraction of Che's transparently sincere and ardent character, which, by then, was as revolutionary as the Cuban's. It was the beginning of an undying friendship.

Che also told Hilda that Fidel was "a great political leader." Castro's anti-Yankeeism impressed Guevara, who, in Hilda Gadea's words, "found in Fidel a deep conviction that in fighting against Batista he was fighting the imperialist monster that kept Batista in power." Che was convinced that Castro "will make the revolution. We are in complete accord . . . It's only someone like him I could go all out for."

"As Che expressed it definitely when he joined Fidel Castro's expedition—and I am a witness to this," Hilda adds, "his fight in Cuba was just one stage in his Latin American struggle."

El Patojo, who was a part of the Cuban group through his friendship with Che, also wanted to join the *Granma* expedition, but Castro refused because "he did not want our small army to be a mosaic of nationalities." Such being the case, it is interesting that Fidel nevertheless made an exception for the Argentine Ernesto Guevara.

During the preparations and training in Mexico, Che managed to finish a dissertation and pass tests for a doctor's degree in physiology, still specializing in the field of allergies.

He and Hilda Gadea were married on August 18, 1955, in Mexico City. One of the witnesses was Jesús Montané, veteran of Moncada and still one of Fidel's closest associates. From Hilda's account, it was Che who wanted the marriage. She gives the impression that they were very fond of each other and certainly completely compatible.

A few memoirs and letters are printed at the end of Hilda Gadea's book which are revealing. One is by a Venezuelan friend, Lucila Velásquez, a poet with whom Hilda lived in Mexico City while Che was courting her. Lucila comments shrewdly: "Sister, lover, collaborator, her [Hilda's] pertinacity set up a multiple net of vital opportunities for Ernesto—and he married her. Love? Gratitude? Life is a confusion as subtle as it is inexplicable. Looking beneath the surface, one can only say that Ernesto was necessary to her as she was indispensable to him. Each was one part of a deep and close solidarity."

An expert opinion on Che's character comes in a note printed at the end of Hilda's book, written by a young Guatemalan woman friend, Myrna Torres, who saw much of Che in Guatemala and Mexico. "He was not of an affectionate nature," she writes, but adds later: "Along with his outrage at injustice, Ernesto had his tender side—he was the kind who loves children and dogs." There could be a malicious touch there. One wonders: what about women?

"They were all willing to risk their lives to succeed," Hilda writes of the *Granma* group, "but they all trusted Fidel absolutely, and he guided them like an older brother, with love but with strict discipline. . . . Ernesto had a total trust in Fidel from the beginning. Knowing how profound, disciplined and severe he [Guevara] was in judging himself and others, I could thus appreciate Fidel's stature."

Castro, for his part, appreciated Che. Long after, on November 28, 1971, standing before a statue of Che Guevara in Santiago, Chile, Fidel made a speech which was a beautiful tribute to his dead friend. In it he gave what I would say was an accurate summary of Guevara's politics when they met in Mexico. "Che had a spirit that was always alert," Castro said, "a brilliant mind, a vocation for revolution . . . Although he did not belong to any party, he already had at that time a Marxist turn of mind."

Hilda wanted to join the *Granma* expedition, as did a few other women, but Fidel would have none but men. Anyway, a baby had been born on February 15, 1956, also named Hilda, but known, Spanish fashion, by the diminutive, Hildita. During the whole Sierra Maestra campaign Che wrote Hilda affectionate letters, some of which she quotes.

The day the war ended, January 1, 1959, Hilda flew to Havana with the child and met her husband as soon as he arrived. Then, she writes, "With the candor that always characterized him, Ernesto forthrightly told me that he had another woman, whom he had met in the campaign of Santa Clara. The pain was deep in me, but, following our convictions, we agreed on a divorce."

Che had been in and around Santa Clara during the previous two weeks and could have known the other woman, Aleida March, only for that long. His friends say that it was a case of love at first sight and that Aleida was the only woman he ever truly loved. She was younger, prettier, and sexier than Hilda—and she was there at the perfect moment.

"The divorce was granted on the twenty-second of May 1959," Hilda writes with a stoicism worthy of her part-Indian ancestors. "Ernesto remarried on the second of June."

Che wanted Hildita to be brought up and educated in Cuba, and Hilda agreed. She herself lived mostly in her native Peru and in Mexico until she died suddenly in Havana in February 1974. She was buried on February 12 in Colón Cemetery. Among those at the funeral were Ramiro Valdés, one of Che's closest friends, Jesús Montané, who had been a witness at her marriage to Che, and their now orphaned daughter, Hildita. Neither Raúl nor Fidel Castro attended. The obituary in *Granma* on February 13 did not mention the fact that Hilda was Che Guevara's first wife.

Doctrinally, the Sierra Maestra experience had little effect on the revolutionary leaders or the *barbudos* in general, as I have said. There was no reason why Che Guevara should have been any more or any less Marxist at the end than he was when he left Mexico. The experience strengthened his determination to create social justice, as he saw it.

His first impact on Latin America was in the theoretical field of guerrilla warfare, and this he learned from his Sierra Maestra experience, but as a follower of Fidel Castro and an adherent of Castro's ideas. As was to be the case in other ways, Che Guevara put in writing what Fidel Castro had in his mind. Che's originality in every sphere was in advancing and refining, and carrying to extremes, ideas that he had shared with Fidel. When the two men differed, it was on methods, timing, degree, emphasis, not on basic aims.

For several years Che Guevara's book *La Guerra de guerrillas (Guerrilla Warfare)* was the Bible for Latin American guerrillas. Some variations on the same ideas were widely disseminated in the French writer Régis Debray's *Révolution dans la Révolution?* Guevara's book became required reading in the American Special Forces, who were trained to help Latin American armies suppress guerrillas—as they did in Bolivia against Che and his band with sensational success.

The most authoritative expression of the Castro–Guevara theory of revolution came in the Second Declaration of Havana on February 2, 1962, following Cuba's expulsion from the Organization of American States. It begins by quoting the famous passage from Martí's letter to his friend Manuel Mercado, on the eve of Martí's death which I have already mentioned: "I have lived inside the monster and know its entrails; and my sling is the sling of David." Martí warned of the need to prevent the United States "from extending its control over the Antilles" by "the imperialist annexation of Cuba."

The declaration is inordinately wordy, and in its exposition it is an unoriginal Marxist formulation, but it does contain the basic Fidelista-Guevaraist revolutionary formula:

> The armies, built and equipped for conventional war, which are the force on which the power of the exploiting classes rests, become absolutely impotent when they have to confront the irregular struggle

> of the peasants on their own terrain. . . . But the peasantry is a class which, because of the uncultured state in which it is kept and the isolation in which it lives, needs the revolutionary and political leadership of the working class and the revolutionary intellectuals, for without them it would not by itself be able to plunge into the struggle and achieve victory.

The national bourgeoisie, it continues, "is paralyzed by fear of social revolution and frightened by the cry of the exploited masses."

Then comes the often-to-be-quoted declaration: "The duty of every revolutionary is to make the revolution. One knows that the revolution will triumph in America and throughout the world, but it is not for revolutionaries to sit in the doorways of their houses waiting for the corpse of imperialism to pass by."

Five years later (August 10, 1967), in his speech closing the Organization of Latin American Solidarity (OLAS) in Havana, Fidel was still on the same track. Che Guevara was fighting in Bolivia at the time.

"Whoever stops to wait for ideas to triumph among the majority of the masses before initiating revolutionary action will never be a revolutionary . . . And what distinguishes the true revolutionary from the false revolutionary is precisely this: one acts to move the masses, the other waits for the masses to have a conscience already, before starting to act."

The Cubans gave pretty much the same importance to guerrilla warfare that Mao Tse-tung did in his book on the subject. Cecil Johnson points out that Mao looked on guerrilla operations simply "as one aspect of our total or mass war." For Mao, the guerrillas "are of themselves incapable of providing a solution to the struggle." Both Castro and Guevara concede the need for mass support. "A guerrilla war is a people's war," as Che put it. Régis Debray wrote that it was not until after Batista's 1958 offensive that Fidel and Che first got a copy of Mao's *Problems of Strategy in Guerrilla War Against Japan.* They were surprised when "they found in this book what they had been practicing under pressure of necessity." That may have been true of this book, but, as Hilda Gadea wrote, Che had read about the Chinese Revolution in Guatemala.

In his OLAS speech, Castro had said: "And those who believe that they are going to win against the imperialists in elections are just plain naïve."

Che did not live to see the electoral triumph of Salvador Allende in Chile in 1970. One guesses that he would have been skeptical and said nothing. Castro had to be practical and politic; Allende was an old friend, and his government would be a valuable Latin American ally. When Fidel visited Chile in November 1971, making speeches and answering pointed questions, he felt it necessary to assure his listeners that a revolution had *begun* in Chile through an election.

"If I am asked what is happening in Chile," he said in Concepción on November 18, 1971, "I would sincerely say that a revolutionary process is occurring." But he prudently added: "A process is not yet a revolution."

In Santiago a week later he spoke of "the extraordinary importance of the Chilean process, for this is the first time in the history of revolutionary processes that the way is open for social change through elections, that is, through peaceful means . . . There are some who have tried to present the Chilean process as being in contradiction to the Cuban process, in contradiction to the ideology of the Cuban Revolution." He denied that there was any such contradiction. The key word—a favorite one of his—was "process." He took care not to say that Chile already had a revolution.

When I questioned him about this in September 1972, he denied that he had changed his mind about how to achieve a revolution. This, of course, was well before the overthrow of the Allende regime.

"Chile is just starting to make a revolution," he argued. "The election merely opened up the possibility. We [he and Guevara] never said that revolutions can be made only by violence or by military means. We said that a revolution must have the arms and the people—the masses. Without these two, no revolution is possible anywhere. Allende is in great difficulties. We hope he succeeds and we help as much as we can."

Looking back over my conversations in Cuba with Fidel, Raúl, Dorticós, Raúl Roa, and others, I realize that they held little, if any, hope for the survival of Salvador Allende's attempted revolution. The Cubans were still not convinced that a true revolution could be achieved through elections and parliamentary government. Che had said in his book that a violent armed struggle "to the death" was necessary. Fidel must be more convinced of this than ever, after what happened in Chile.

However, it did not follow that the Cubans could generalize from their experience any more than Mao Tse-tung could from the Chinese Revolution. Moreover, the Cubans were behind the times. Debray quotes Fidel as saying: "The city is a cemetery of revolutionaries and resources." In his 1967 OLAS speech Castro had said: "Guerrilla experiences in this continent have taught us many things —among them the terrible mistake, the absurd concept that the guerrilla movement could be directed from the cities." Che Guevara felt the same way, and acted on his belief in Bolivia.

But in recent years, with the failure of the rural guerrillas almost everywhere in Latin America, it is the urban guerrilla who now holds the stage. Its Bible in Latin America has been the *Handbook of Urban Guerrilla Warfare* by the now-dead Brazilian revolutionary Carlos Marighela. (The pamphlet was published by Penguin in a collection of Marighela's writings.) The tactics of the Irish Republican Army are probably not derivative, but their similarity to Marighela's teaching was noted indignantly in Great Britain.

Carlos Marighela attended the OLAS conference against the wishes of Brazil's Muscovite Communist Party. In 1968 he organized the pro-Castro Action for National Liberation (ALN), which tried to carry on the same sort of guerrilla warfare but in towns, not in the countryside. Like Che Guevara, he made such great demands on his followers that only very exceptional persons could qualify. After some sensational successes—robbing banks, kidnapping the United States ambassador and holding him for ransom—the police caught up with him on November 4, 1969, and shot him dead. Marghela was tough, rough, and brutal, without Che Guevara's compassion and romantic idealism. There are probably few who remember his name now.

Another failure was the Argentine journalist Jorge Ricardo Masetti, who went into the Sierra Maestra in 1958. He and Guevara became friends, and after the success of the Castroites he returned to Cuba, where he was given guerrilla training—not enough, apparently, for he was killed off quickly in Argentina in April 1964. Masetti was credited with convincing Guevara that Peronism approximated his own ideas, but Hilda Gadea wrote that "for Ernesto, the fall of Perón [in September 1955] was a heavy blow." Typically, Che and Masetti blamed it—quite wrongly—on "North American imperialists."

Much the most successful of the urban guerrillas in Latin America have been the Tupamaros in Uruguay, although at this writing (1975) their organization has been shattered. They owed nothing to Castroism and were anti-Communist. Their movement can be expected to surface again.

The international guerrilla or terrorist of recent years was naturally unknown to Fidel, Che, and Régis Debray when they were formulating their ideas, but the terrorists have little or nothing to do with "revolution" as the Cubans see it. There is a Trotskyite "Fourth International" operating out of Brussels which seems to have relations with some Latin American terrorist groups and is given some credit for the switch from rural to urban terrorism in the hemisphere. Carlos Marighela was believed to have had some connection with the Brussels group. The most active of the terrorist movements are nationalistic, like Black September (Palestinian), or racist (Black Power), with little or no revolutionary ideology.

The key word with Fidel Castro, Che Guevara, Carlos Marighela, Camilo Torres, and all the Latin American guerrillas is "anti-imperialism." In general, it is given the Leninist definition of colonial "empires" being created by a bourgeois capitalist class seeking richer markets, cheap raw materials, and labor that can be exploited. In particular, in Latin America it means capitalistic exploitation and hegemony by the United States over the underdeveloped nations of the hemisphere. Authorities on Marxism say that Lenin's theory is far removed from Marx's ideas, but it has proved fruitful in strengthening nationalism in the underdeveloped world and has attracted many revolutionaries from Mao Tse-tung to Fidel Castro and Che Guevara. Aside from its use by the Communists, "anti-imperialism" has had a strong appeal to the intelligentsia of Latin America.

Che Guevara, it seems, made it clear to Hilda Gadea in Mexico that he was going on the Cuban expedition "because it was part of the fight against Yankee imperialism and the first stage of the liberation of our continent."

The story of Guevara's part in the Sierra Maestra has already been told earlier in this book. It was important and heroic, but he did not come prominently into public view until the final stage when he and Camilo Cienfuegos made their epic journeys across the island to Las Villas Province.

I did not—and still do not—give to Ernesto Che Guevara the importance which almost all contemporary writers on the Cuban Revolution gave to him in the period 1959 to 1965, when he was in the government. Professor Robert M. Bernardo of the University of California at Berkeley begins his book *The Theory of Moral Incentives in Cuba* by chiding me for underrating the role that Che played in the political and economic history of the Revolution.

Theodore Draper, in *Castroism, Theory and Practice,* wrote: "The relationship of Fidel Castro and Ernesto Che Guevara is one of the main keys that unlock the innermost secrets of this Cuban revolution. The personal impress of Guevara on the revolution may prove in some respects to be the equal of Castro's, despite the fact that Castro alone can carry the burden of making the final decisions. For

Castro has made different decisions depending on who has influenced him last, whereas Guevara has had the most lasting influence on him."

"Guevara," Draper said in another part of his book, which was published in 1965, "has devoted himself to the deadly game of infighting for the levers of power and to the elaboration of a theoretical mold for the unfolding revolution. For more than five years, [dismissal] was the fate of all who crossed Guevara or whom he marked out for his political destruction in his own good time . . . The surest sign of the direction of the Castro regime has been Guevara's influence in it."

There is nothing left to bear out this judgment except the fact that Che did devote much time to the task of working out "a theoretical mold" for the Revolution. But as Draper's book was being published, Guevara was withdrawing from the Cuban scene, with Fidel's blessing and help. The fact that he could fade away without any effect on the course of the Revolution proved that he was neither dominant nor indispensable. Nor did he ever, even remotely, do any "infighting for the levers of power." He did not want power and never intended to stay in Cuba indefinitely.

The power situation in Cuba was confused by the fact that Che Guevara, Raúl Castro, President Dorticós, and a few others seemed to speak and write for themselves. In reality, they at all times had the tacit or actual concurrence of Fidel Castro, or knew that he would approve. There was no subservience; the Cuban system was not like Italian Fascism or German Nazism, where every official put ideas, admonitions, criticisms, and demands in the name of Mussolini or Hitler. This free-wheeling tone gave Guevara's speeches and writings an apparent personal authority which misled many commentators. When Che Guevara spoke for himself, he knew that Fidel Castro agreed with him.

There was a period when Che seemed to be given the task of saying unpleasant things, but it came natural to him. "You know," he said to some sugar workers in Camagüey on February 7, 1963, "I have a mania for criticism every time I find myself in front of a microphone." Che was also credited with announcing unpopular policies in advance of Fidel in order to break the shock.

It will never be possible to separate Che's ideas from Fidel's, but in all circumstances responsibility for a policy of any importance lay with Castro. Che and Raúl Castro were the only men, so far as I know, who dared to argue with, and even cross, Fidel. No other men were so intimate with the *Jefe.*

Che's earliest speeches were not recorded, which is perhaps just as well. He was never at ease speechifying, but he wasted no words, organized his speeches well, and was clear—in other words, the opposite of Castro. His talks had a theoretical and doctrinal content which Fidel could not match, for Guevara learned to draw on his voracious early readings on socialism and economics. He was sufficiently expert to defend heterodox ideas with respectable authority, as in his widely publicized polemic with the French authority on planning, Charles Bettelheim, and with other Marxists.

Che was caught up in the worldwide socialist controversy over "Libermanism" following the famous article in *Pravda* in September 1962. Professor Y. G. Liberman, chief of the Department of Political Economy of the Technological Institute of Kharkow, was a leading advocate of decentralization and of material incentives and rewards for managers and workers. Libermanism has capitalist features—supply, demand, profit, loss, unequal salaries, bonuses, extra pay for overtime. (Libermanism vanished in Russia under Brezhnev; the central planners are back.)

Guevara was a fanatical believer in moral incentives. Fidel Castro believed in them too, but he found it necessary to hedge and compromise. By 1972, when I was in Cuba, the need for material incentives had been recognized, and in 1973 this became official policy, although retaining as much as possible of the moral-incentive ideals. In this respect, Che was up in the clouds; Fidel had his feet on the ground—the responsibility was his.

An unfortunate official at Havana University once asked Che to deliver a lecture, offering to pay him. He received a dusty answer in a letter dated August 31, 1964. After saying that he had no time, Che added: "It is inconceivable to me that a monetary payment should be offered to an official [*dirigente*] of the Government and the [Communist] Party, for any work of whatever kind it may be. Among the many payments that I have received, the most important is to be considered a part of the Cuban people; I would not know how to gauge that in dollars and cents. I regret having to write you this letter, but I beg of you to give it no other importance than that of a deeply felt complaint for what I consider a grievous insult, none the less painful for not having been intended." (The letter was printed in the Mexican magazine *Sucesos,* January 2, 1967.)

Both Guevara and Castro shared a positive aversion to money and a money economy. Che Guevara's "New Man" would believe in moral incentives, voluntarism, socialist emulation, and exalted ideals. Fidel Castro preceded or accompanied Che with these ideas, but it was Guevara who went all out for them and tried to keep compromises down to a minimum. He went too far, but he achieved partial success, especially in the field of voluntarism.

His illusions did not blind him completely to the difficulties. In a speech to an assembly of Communist Youth in September 1964 he complained: "Youth maintains toward work the old mentality, the mentality of the capitalist world—that is, the attitude that work is, yes, a duty and a necessity but a sad duty, an unfortunate necessity." As Che saw it, "There should be a great sense of duty toward the society we are building, as human beings, with our neighbors, and with all the men of the world."

"And if we are told that we are romantics," he said six months later, "that we are inveterate idealists; that we are thinking about impossibilities; that one cannot find an almost archetypal human being among the masses of a people, we have to answer a thousand times that we can . . . Some fine day, almost without realizing it, we shall have created, together with the other peoples of the world, the Communist society, our ideal." Alas! Che Guevara *was* a romantic.

Che's role as an economist belongs in the story of Cuba's revolutionary economy, where, as I said, he worked with and for Fidel Castro, but one cannot understand Ernesto Guevara the man without recognizing how naturally his character fitted the ideas that he tried to apply in Havana.

Once the Cuban Revolution embraced Marxism-Leninism, Fidel Castro, Che Guevara, and the other leaders felt and expressed a need for the international brotherhood that was supposedly a socialist ideal. No other Communist country, least of all the Soviet Union, shared this missionary zeal. It was to lead to some disillusionments —none greater than in the missile crisis, when the Cubans really thought in terms of international socialist cooperation while the Russians thought of themselves.

Castro is yet to lose this global sense of socialism. Guevara too retained it to the end and never expressed it better than in his last important address, in Algiers, to which I have referred several times. It contained, among other things, a fervent appeal to the strong and more prosperous Communist countries to be less cynically capitalistic and more helpful to the underdeveloped socialist countries.

"There can be no socialism," he said, "unless there is a transformation of consciousness that will bring a greater sense of brotherhood, not only among socialist societies themselves or societies that are becoming socialist, but also internationally, toward all peoples suffering from imperialist oppression."

Che's last major pieces of writing on socialism and revolutionary faith were the letter written early in 1965 to *Marcha* and later published in booklet form as *Man and Socialism* (which I have referred to) and the message to the meeting of the Executive Secretariat of the Solidarity Organization of the Peoples of Africa, Asia and Latin America (OSPAAL) in Havana. It was presumably sent from Bolivia late in 1966 and was published in the magazine *Tricontinental* on April 16, 1967.

Che ended the OSPAAL message with a thought-provoking salutation: "Accept our ritual greetings as a handshake or an *Ave María Purísima. Patria o Muerte!*"

A religious greeting, a comradely clasp of the hands, a Catholic prayer to the Virgin Mary, a revolutionary pledge to fatherland or death—they made a strange mixture, for Che was a very strange, complicated man, as is Fidel Castro, but Che Guevara was profoundly religious, not in the formal church sense of the word, but in its true, human meaning.

Che once referred to himself as *inteligencia fría en espíritu apasionado* ("a cold intelligence in a passionate spirit").

In the message to OSPAAL he made his famous and—at the time—feared threat of "creating a Second or Third Vietnam, or the Second *and* Third Vietnam of the world." Imperialism, as he saw it, "must be defeated in a world confrontation.

> New uprisings shall take place in these and other countries of Our America as has already happened in Bolivia, and they shall continue to grow in the midst of all the hardships inherent to this dangerous profession of being modern revolutionaries. Many shall perish, victims of their errors . . . We cannot harbor any illusions that freedom can be obtained without fighting. . . .
>
> Hatred as an element of the struggle; a relentless hatred of the enemy, impelling us over and beyond the natural limitations that man is heir to and transforming him into an effective, violent, selective and cold killing machine. Our soldiers must be thus; a people without hatred cannot vanquish a brutal enemy.

Yet this was the same man who had said in *Man and Socialism* the year before: "Let me say, with the risk of appearing ridiculous, that the true revolutionary is guided by strong feelings of love."

Love of the humble and exploited; hatred of the oppressors and exploiters—two sides of the same coin to Che Guevara, and not really contradictory.

The two paragraphs ending the OSPAAL message became world famous after Che's death:

> If we, in a small point of the world map, are able to fulfill our duty and place at the disposal of this struggle whatever little of ourselves we are permitted to give: our lives, our sacrifice, and if some day we have to breathe our last on any land, already ours, sprinkled with our blood, let it be known that we have measured the scope of our actions and that we only consider ourselves elements in the great army of the proletariat but that we are proud of having learned from the Cuban Revolution, and from its Maximum Leader, the great lesson emanating from his attitude in this part of the world: "What do the dangers or the sacrifices of a man or of a nation matter, when the destiny of humanity is at stake?"
>
> Our every action is a battle cry against imperialism, and a battle hymn for the people's unity against the great enemy of mankind: the United States of America. Wherever death may surprise us, let it be welcome, provided that this, our battle cry, may have reached some receptive ear and another hand may be extended to wield our weapons and other men be ready to intone the funeral dirge with the staccato singing of the machine guns and new battle cries of war and victory.

Death was coming in less than a year, but surely not as a "surprise."

1. This picture was taken on February 17, 1957, by one of Castro's men during Matthews' interview with the Cuban leader in the Sierra Maestra. It was used (retouched) by *The New York Times* to prove that Matthews actually had been present in the Sierra Maestra.

2. A demonstration at *The Times* in Matthews' favor and against Batista.

3. Matthews with Archbishop Peréz Serantes in June 1957.

4. Castro with Armando Hart en route to Havana, January 1959.

5. Matthews with Armando Hart en route to Havana, January 1959. Behind them is a statue of José Martí.

6. Castro signing the first Agrarian Reform Law on May 17, 1959, at his guerrilla headquarters at La Plata in the Sierra Maestra.

7. Prime Minister Castro and President Dorticos sign the law expropriating all the remaining American properties in Cuba in 1960.

8. Fidel Castro appears before the U.N. General Assembly, September 16, 1960.

9. Harvesting pineapples in the Havana greenbelt.

10. Beginning the great campaign of 1961 to abolish illiteracy. The books say: "Let us alphabetize" and "We Shall Conquer."

11. In Cuba today all children are educated and all education is free. The government furnishes free clothes, lunches, and in many cases, board and lodging.

12. A typical photograph of Castro addressing a crowd.

13. Matthews with Comandante Juan Almeida, Manzanillo, Oriente Province, September 1972.

CHAPTER 12

Che—Bolivia

How dull it is to pause, to
make an end,
To rust unburnish'd, not to
shine in use!
As tho' to breathe were life.
—Tennyson's *Ulysses*

The Bolivian adventure failed, but the elements of heroism, sacrifice, and idealism made it a drama on a grand scale. Out of it could come an epic or a tragedy in the classic Greek style, if a new Aeschylus or Euripides should come along to write it. Che Guevara became a legendary figure, which could only mean that there was a universal quality in his life and death.

One cannot think of Che's departure from Cuba as anything but an abandonment, a flight from the intractable difficulties of creating the "New Man" or building the New Jerusalem of socialism. In Cuba, sitting at a desk, he must have felt desperate and frustrated; he surely saw how little he could accomplish, how long and arduous and dull the journey was going to be. He must have thought of the happy days in the Sierra Maestra, the great days, carefree amidst cherished companions—and fighting days, fighting against men.

But there he was in Havana, facing an invisible, impalpable enemy with prosaic names: productivity, absenteeism, profit, loss, norms, value, material incentives, moral incentives, volunteer work. No romance, no heroism—only drudgery. He heard his own call of the wild and answered it.

I do not say that he abandoned his hopes and ideals. The letter published as *Man and Socialism,* which has been called his ideological testament, is proof that he believed his "New Man" would some day walk the socialist world, but he did not stay in Cuba to fight for him. Che took the easier road, leaving Fidel Castro to struggle with the burdens that Che no longer wanted to shoulder.

As in so many ways, the story of the Wars of Independence was echoing in the present. One of the three national heroes, Máximo Gómez, was a Dominican who went to Cuba, like the Argentine Che Guevara, to help overthrow the existing regime. After the victory Gómez would not take part in politics, feeling a handicap as a foreigner. Che too was never able to rid himself of the feeling that he was not Cuban, although he tried for a while to make himself one. It must be added that for all the respect and admiration he received, Cubans could never look on him as anything but an Argentine. Che, himself, had no particular affection for his native country. He was the universal man at heart, not Cuban or Argentine.

The cruel libel that Che Guevara and Fidel Castro quarreled and the Cuban leader punished his friend, both in Cuba and by sending him off unaided to his death in Bolivia, will, like so many malicious or ignorant lies, live in books and uninformed minds, either as belief or as doubt. Even that most conscientious of scholars, Hugh Thomas, writes: "There seems to have been a quarrel."

I knew, from the time of Che's disappearance in 1965, that there could have been no ill-feeling or quarrel between the two men, but for the record I asked Castro on my last visit to Cuba, in 1972, how the story could have got about and be believed. He became very emotional.

"No one knows how deeply I felt for him," he said. "I kept silent at his request for six months, and it was difficult. People were even saying that I killed him! In Mexico, when he joined the *Granma* expedition, it was agreed that once the revolution succeeded, he would go away and fight other revolutions. I don't know how I was able to keep him in Cuba as long as I did, but I had promised that when he wanted to leave he could go and I would not hold him back.

"Che was a man who had his ideas and he was never afraid to speak up. We had our arguments. But there was no man who was so close to me; who meant so much to me; who was more brave or loyal or honest."

I have mentioned that Hilda Gadea heard Che say in Mexico that his fight in Cuba was to be "just one stage in his Latin American struggle." Faustino Pérez, who was in Mexico training with Che and the others, said to me that Guevara's idea from the beginning was to help Fidel make the revolution and that his task would then be over. At the time of Che's death, Carlos Rafael Rodríguez told me that Che first advised Castro of his desire to leave Cuba in the autumn of 1964.

The last time I saw Che Guevara was in Havana in November

1963. Then, as in previous talks, I had a feeling that he admired Fidel almost to the point of worship. These personal, human feelings that one gets, such as mine about the deep bonds of friendship between Che and Fidel, are not the equivalent of historic documentation, yet they should be weighed in the balance. On my last trip to Cuba, in 1972, I talked about Che to a number of his old Sierra Maestra comrades, partly because *The Sunday Times* of London had asked me to check. The belief in a bitter quarrel had still not died in British journalism. The Cubans all spoke of Che with an affection and sadness that could not have existed if Castro and Guevara had ended their relationship on bad terms. Haydée Santamaría told me that "almost every day" she still has a pang of grief to think that Che is dead.

When Che Guevara went to the U.N. General Assembly meeting in December 1964 as Cuba's spokesman, his decision to go to the Congo along with some Sierra Maestra comrades and young recruits had already been made. The Congo had been on his mind for a long time. In a speech at a workers' rally on August 15, 1964, he had referred indignantly to "Africa,

> where only a few years ago the Prime Minister of the Congo [Patrice Lumumba] was murdered and quartered, where the North American monopolies were established and then the battle for the Congo began. Why? Because there is copper, because there are radioactive minerals, because the Congo contains extraordinary strategic riches. For that reason they assassinated a leader who had the naïveté to believe in right, without realizing that right must be united to force. And thus he was made a martyr of his people. But his people took up that cause. And today North American troops must go to the Congo . . . to get involved in another Vietnam, to suffer inevitably another defeat. . . .
>
> Western civilization disguises under its showy façade a scene of hyenas and jackals. That is the only name that can be applied to those who have gone to carry out "humanitarian" tasks in the Congo. Bloodthirsty butchers who feed on helpless people . . . The free men of the world must be prepared to avenge the crime committed in the Congo.

Fidel then sent Che off on a last diplomatic trip to Africa and Asia. He was in Brazzaville early in January 1965, doubtless planning a guerrilla operation. In Dar es Salaam, Tanzania, he met with the Congolese rebel leader Gaston Soumaliot, whom he knew. His trip took him to Ghana, Guinea, Algiers, and Peking. It was in Algiers on February 26, 1965, that he made his last public speech (which I have quoted), to the Afro-Asian Solidarity Conference.

"We cannot remain indifferent in the face of what occurs in any part of the world," he said. "A victory for any one country against imperialism is our victory, just as a defeat for any one country is a defeat for all."

He was back in Havana on March 15, where Castro met him at the airport. It was the last time that Che Guevara was seen in public.

What he did then was to go off to some secret location in the Cuban provinces to recruit a band and organize the expedition he was planning for the Congo. He was to take along as commanders men who later appeared in the Bolivian campaign. The main purpose of the group seems to have been to train rebel Congolese soldiers, rather than to fight.

Before he left he wrote four letters that became public, one the historic farewell to Fidel and Cuba, and another a letter to his mother, which was to lead to much confusion because it fell into the hands of Ricardo Rojo, who was a friend and confidant of the then dying woman. As he was keeping his movements and intentions secret, Che apparently decided to advise his mother that she should not come to Cuba then, as she wanted, because he would be going into the countryside as a simple worker "to study from the inside, for five years, the functioning of one of the many industries which I directed from above."

Señora de Guevara, according to Rojo, sensed that there was something mysterious and wrote her son *una histórica misiva* ("a historic letter") expressing her misgivings. The letter did not reach Che, as there was no one to take it to Cuba at the time. Meanwhile, the mother's health deteriorated and Rojo telephoned Havana trying to contact Che and tell him that his mother was dying. Aleida, Che's wife, answered the telephone but, being under strict orders not to discuss her husband's whereabouts, simply told Rojo that "Che has gone to the provinces to do some work" and that she would pass the message along.

Haydée Santamaría, Aleida's closest friend, told me the story. It seems that even his wife did not know Che's exact whereabouts, but the message was given to Fidel, who passed it along to Guevara. Castro received a reply from Che, which, I was told, is in the Cuban archives. It was too late to do anything, for the mother died on May 19, 1965.

None of this was explained to Ricardo Rojo, who was not a relative and who anyway could not be let in on the secret of Guevara's whereabouts or plans. As a result Rojo, who had not seen Che since 1963, jumped to the worst conclusions in his book *My Friend Che*

(1968) and constructed a whole edifice of possible quarrel, disgrace, and banishment in a chapter headed "The Burning Mystery." This was picked up in most accounts later, leaving a false impression about Guevara and Castro.

Fidel could have cleared up the whole matter after Rojo's book was printed by publishing the correspondence with Che. However, he felt Che's death too deeply and considered the reports and those who spread them as beneath contempt. Guevara's death was one of the great sorrows of Fidel's life, and, as always, he kept his private life to himself.

He did permit Guevara's farewell letter of April 1, 1965, to be reproduced in facsimile, as it is in the official book *Mil fotos Cuba* ("A Thousand Photos of Cuba"), published in 1966. Enemies and doubters had cast suspicion on the existence and authenticity of the letter because, at Che's request, Fidel held it until October 3, 1965, when he read it at a meeting of the Communist Central Committee. The letter is in Che's characteristic and unmistakable handwriting. It covers five full pages of writing paper and a part of a sixth, ending in the famous cramped signature with its small "c": *che.*

Although it is long, the letter was so important in Che Guevara's life and in the Cuban Revolution that it is worth reproducing in full.

HAVANA
Year of Agriculture [1965]

Fidel:

I remember many things in this hour—how I met you in the house of María Antonia, and how you proposed that I come with you, and all the strain of the preparations.

One day they passed by to ask who should be advised in case of death, and the real possibility of it struck all of us. Later we knew that it was true, that in a revolution one triumphs or dies (if it be a true one). Many comrades were left along the road to victory.

Today everything has a less dramatic tone, for we are more mature, but the event is repeating itself. I feel that I have fulfilled the part of my duty that bound me to the Cuban Revolution on its territory, and I take my farewell of you, my comrades and your people who are now my people.

I formally renounce my posts in the leadership of the Party, my post as Minister, my rank as Major, my status as a Cuban citizen. Nothing legal binds me to Cuba, only ties of another kind that cannot be broken, as can official appointments. Looking back over my past life, I believe that I have worked with sufficient faithfulness and dedication in order to consolidate the revolutionary triumph. My only deficiency of any importance is not to have trusted you more from those first moments in the Sierra Maestra and in not having understood soon enough your qualities of leader and revolutionary.

I have lived through magnificent days and at your side I felt the pride of belonging to our people in the luminous and sad days of the Caribbean Crisis. Rarely has any statesman shone more brilliantly than [you did] in those days. I feel pride, too, in having followed you without hesitation, identifying myself with your way of thinking and seeing and of judging dangers and motives [*principios*].

Other regions of the world claim the support of my modest efforts. I can do what is forbidden to you because of your responsibility to Cuba, and the time has come for us to separate.

Let it be known that I do it with a mixture of joy and sorrow: I am leaving here the purest of my hopes as a builder and the most loved among my beloved creatures, and I leave a people who accepted me as a son; this rends a part of my spirit. On new battlefields I will carry with me the faith that you inculcated in me, the revolutionary spirit of my people, the feeling of having fulfilled the most sacred of duties: to fight against imperialism wherever it be; this comforts and heals any wound to a great extent.

I say once more that I free Cuba of any responsibility save that which stems from its example; that if the final [*definitiva*] hour comes upon me under other skies, my last thought will be for this people and especially for you, that I am thankful to you for your teachings and your example, and that I will try to be faithful up to the final consequences of my acts; that I have at all times been identified with the foreign policy of our Revolution, and I continue to be so; that wherever I may end up I will feel the responsibility of being a Cuban revolutionary, and I will act as one; that I leave nothing material to my children and my wife, and this does not grieve me: I am glad that it be so; that I ask nothing for them, since the State will give them sufficient to live and will educate them.

I would have many things to say to you and to our people, but I feel that they are unnecessary; words cannot express what I would want them to, and it isn't worthwhile wasting more sheets of paper with my scribbling.

To victory forever. *Patria o Muerte!*

I embrace you with all [my] revolutionary fervor!

che

The letter, of course, loses in translation. Since its authenticity is not open to question, Che's warm tributes to Fidel Castro should be enough in themselves to scotch the ignorant and often malicious reports of a quarrel between the two men. The only puzzling feature is the passage in which Che reproaches himself for not having "trusted you more from those first moments in the Sierra Maestra." The explanation, I was told, is political. Guevara was more leftist than Castro in those early days, and there were arguments.

In the spring of 1965, Che Guevara and a number of Cubans who had trained with him went to the Congo. He worked and fought secretly there with the Congolese rebels. If he kept a diary, it must have been captured or lost. President Moise Tshombe, in Brazzaville, was getting United Nations and American help (including some exile Cuban pilots from the Bay of Pigs invasion), and he had about a hundred white mercenaries under the famous Colonel Mike Hoare.

Gaston Soumaliot's rebels were well armed and fought commendably, and at one time controlled half the country. Che is believed to have joined them with his Cuban companions in June 1965 in rough country west of Lake Tanganyika. By that time the rebels were making a last stand, and acted in a fashion which disgusted the Cubans.

Ciro Roberto Bustos, the Argentine journalist captured with Régis Debray in Bolivia, was reported to have told his Bolivian captors that Che said the Congolese rebels would not fight, were corrupt, and acted like butchers.

Clearly, it was a disillusioning experience, and if we know so little about it, the reason doubtless is that the truth would have been harmful to the revolutionary cause in the Congo, besides being a tale of complete failure.

There is no record of how long Che stayed in the Congo; some reports say six months, others nine. He was certainly back in Cuba by April 1966, preparing for the Bolivian venture.

Again he worked in secret and for obvious reasons. Castro was at all times involved. He furnished the arms, money, supplies, and officers from the Cuban Army, and he must have been thoroughly cognizant of the plans. He and Che never lost contact with each other until the last fatal days in Bolivia, keeping in touch by radio and, when possible, written messages.

Che had left two other letters with Fidel Castro on April 1, 1965, one to his parents and the other to his children. They were published in Havana in the spring of 1967, while Guevara was in the midst of his Bolivian adventure.

"My dear Old Ones," he wrote to his father and mother.

> Once more I feel the ribs of Rosinante pressing against my heels. I am back on the road with my shield on my arm. . . .
>
> It may be that this letter will be the last. I do not seek it, but it is within the logical calculations of probabilities. If it be so, I send you a last embrace.
>
> I have loved you very much, only I did not know how to express my affection. I am extremely rigid in my actions and I believe that sometimes you did not understand me. It was not easy to understand me, but believe me—just today.

José Martí—in another curious parallel—wrote a farewell letter to his mother from Montecristi on March 25, 1895. "Today, March 25, on the eve of a long journey, I am thinking of you," it begins. ". . . You mourn, in the anger of your love, at the sacrifice of my life; and why I was born by you to a life that loves sacrifice? Words fail me [*Palabras no puedo*]. A man's duty lies where he can be most useful. But the memory of my mother will go with me always in my increasing and necessary agony."

Tenderness came more easily to Martí. *No padezca* ("Do not mourn") are his last words in a postscript.

Che's third letter was addressed "To my children." The names of these children, all being brought up in Cuba, are interesting: Hildita, for Che's first wife, Hilda Gadea; Aleidita, the first child by Aleida March; Camilo, for Camilo Cienfuegos; Celia, Che's mother's name; and finally his own name, Ernesto. Ernestico was a year old when Che disappeared.

> If ever you must read this letter, [it begins] it will be because I am no longer with you.
>
> You will hardly remember much about me; the youngest ones not at all.
>
> Your father was a man who acted according to his beliefs; he has truly been faithful to his convictions.
>
> Grow up like good revolutionaries . . . Above all, you must always feel deeply any injustice perpetrated against any person in any part of the world. This is a revolutionary's most beautiful quality.
>
> Until forever, my dear children. I still hope I will see you. A great big kiss and a big *abrazo* from
>
> Papa

Che as good as knew that he would never return from Bolivia. Alba Griñán, former Cuban ambassador to London and an intimate friend of Guevara's wife, told me that Aleida wanted desperately to go with Che but that he would not hear of it, as their fourth and last child was only a year old in 1966 and Che wanted Aleida to stay and bring up the children.

Describing the process of forming a guerrilla unit in an article he wrote in September 1963, Che had said: "Their only alternatives will be death or victory, at times when death is a concept present a thousandfold, and victory the myth of which only a revolutionary can dream."

He had survived the Sierra Maestra almost miraculously, suffering a number of wounds. As Fidel said in his elegy: "If, as a guerrilla, he had his Achilles' heel, it was this excessively aggressive quality, his absolute contempt for danger . . .

> When Che took up arms again, he was not thinking of an immediate victory. As an experienced fighter, he was prepared for a prolonged struggle of five, ten, fifteen or twenty years if necessary . . . Bolivia, since it has no outlet to the sea, needs more than any country . . . the revolutionary triumph of her neighbors. Che, because of his enormous prestige, his ability and his experience, was the man who could have accelerated the process . . . Che did not conceive of the struggle in Bolivia as an isolated deed, but as part of a revolutionary movement of liberation which would not be long in extending itself to other countries of Latin America. . . .
>
> Che thought . . . that guerrilla warfare in Bolivia would be a school for revolutionaries who would do their apprenticeship in the fighting. . . .
>
> He had had many encounters with the Bolivian peasants. Their character, supremely suspicious and cautious, did not surprise Che, who knew their mentality perfectly well, having dealt with them on other occasions, and he knew that to win them over to our cause would require a prolonged, arduous and patient labor, but he did not doubt that in the long run he would achieve it.

Che's adventure (which politically was as much Fidel Castro's as his) was timed with Vietnam in mind. The United States was by then heavily committed in Indochina, which absorbed its arms, men, and wealth and which provoked an anti-American reaction everywhere, Latin America included. If successful, the Bolivian expedition would have been like a second front, perhaps easing some of the pressure on the North Vietnamese, to whom the Cubans felt indebted and for whom they had great admiration.

It was an impossible goal. Fidel had to concede that "never in history did so small a number of men undertake so gigantic a task." Not even the Bolivians who joined Che were familiar with the region of Ñacahuasu where they fought. For the Cubans it was a totally different world from the Sierra Maestra, where the terrain and the peasants were adaptable and understandable. The Andean *cordillera* was inhospitable, cold, arid, impenetrable—as were the peasants.

The preparation must have been thorough, because after his return from the Congo, Che seems to have stayed in Cuba from April to October 1966. Castro is believed to have put up something like $20 million for the expedition. They were counting on money and supplies from sympathizers in France, Britain, and Argentina, but none materialized. The bitterest disappointment was the refusal of the Moscow-controlled Bolivian Communist Party to help.

Of the seventeen Cuban officers seconded to Che's unit by Raúl and Fidel Castro, fourteen had fought in the Sierra Maestra and five had been with Guevara in the Congo. (According to Ricardo Rojo, there were sixteen Cubans, most of them veterans of the Ciro Redondo column which Guevara had led across Cuba to Havana. Six of them were *comandantes,* or majors.) Nine of the twenty-nine Bolivians in the band had received guerrilla training in Cuba. Nearly all the Cubans were party members, three of them from the Central Committee. Of those who fought to the end (there were a number of deserters), only three Cubans and two Bolivians came out of the venture alive.

The Bolivian experience showed how difficult, if not impossible, it was for even the hardened Sierra Maestra veterans to live up to Che Guevara's high standards of stoicism and dedication to revolution. It is arguable that Che's greatest mistake was in the locality he chose, which could not have been more inhospitable or—on the results—less suitable for his purpose. It was not even properly mapped. The harsh terrain, the dismal weather, hunger, thirst, sickness, all had played nefarious roles by the spring of 1967 (they had started the previous November) in preparing the way for failure.

"It is always the same story," Che wrote on April 19. "Indiscipline, irresponsibility impel everyone." Only three or four of the men are praised in Che's diary.

The problem with the Bolivian Indians was even worse than Fidel indicated in his speech. Their own Bolivian educated ruling class, whether of Spanish or, more likely, *mestizo* descent, could not fathom their impenetrable minds. Fernando Díaz de Medina, minister of education in La Paz, is quoted by Robert J. Alexander in *The Bolivian National Revolution* as saying: "The Indian is a sphinx. He inhabits a hermetic world, inaccessible to the white and the *mestizo*. We don't understand his forms of life or his mental mechanism."

"The inhabitants have to be chased in order to speak with them, for they are like little animals," wrote Che on June 14, 1967. As potential guerrilla material they were hopeless when friendly and dangerous when, as was usually the case, they were hostile and frightened. The peasants in the Sierra Maestra, backward by Cuban standards, were on a far higher level of political and social consciousness than the Bolivian Indians.

Closing his account of the disastrous month of September, Che bitterly remarks in his diary that the Indians were informers and "also cheated in getting payment for their goods and services . . . They mixed fear with profit."

The band listened to Fidel's speeches on their radio and kept in constant touch with Cuba by messenger, wireless, and letters. Castro was being maligned and even accused of having killed and secretly buried Che Guevara, but he had to keep quiet because the presence of Guevara was not known with certainty to the Bolivians and North Americans until toward the end. Che, for instance, notes in his diary for January 22, 1967: "I am writing a document for Fidel, Number 3, to explain the situation and try out the letter box." In such exchanges they used a code.

At least, no one has ever questioned the authenticity of the *Bolivian Diary;* facsimile pages of it were printed in the official version published by the Instituto del Libro in Havana in 1968, "Year of the Heroic Guerrilla." The title of the original Spanish text is *El Diario del Che en Bolivia, noviembre 7, 1966 a octubre 7, 1967.* Fidel Castro wrote an introduction for it. An English translation was published the same year in New York and London.

The diary was saved for posterity by the mysterious activities of a former minister of the interior of the Bolivian government, Antonio Argüedas. He ended up in Cuba with the diary in his possession. (He also, incidentally, brought with him the gruesome relic of Che's hands, which had been cut off to get fingerprints in order to prove that the dead rebel was, indeed, Ernesto Che Guevara.) The widow, Aleida March, helped in the laborious work of deciphering and transcribing Che's crabbed, minute handwriting.

The government of the Bolivian President, General René Barrientos, seems to have made no effort to prevent the diary's getting out and being published. According to José Guerra Alemán, the CIA was involved. Perhaps it was believed that, being the story of a dismal failure in guerrilla warfare, it would discredit Che Guevara and, indirectly, Fidel Castro, who would be forced to publish it. If so, the opposite result was achieved. The *Bolivian Diary* was translated into many languages and contributed greatly to the apotheosis of Che Guevara.

Argüedas seems to have been a triple agent who served the Barrientos government, the CIA, and the Castro government. Guerra Alemán claims that Argüedas "confessed that he received the photostatic copy of the diary from the hands of Hugh Murray, CIA agent, in November 1967." Whatever Argüedas' connections and motives, the end result was the preservation and dissemination of a document that has great historic and human value.

There was a brave gesture toward fate in the words of the opening sentence of the diary, written on November 7, 1966: *Hoy comienza una nueva etapa* ("Today a new stage of the journey begins").

At the end of November, a satisfied Che writes: "Everything indicates that we can stay here just about as long as we want."

The first months were, in fact, relatively uneventful. The La Paz government had been caught by surprise; the region of Ñacahuasu, down in the southeastern corner of the country where Bolivia borders on Brazil, Paraguay, and Chile, was singularly inaccessible; and there was confusion about how many guerrillas were there and who was leading them.

Régis Debray arrived from Havana with the Argentine Ciro Bustos on March 6, 1967. They were of no particular help to the guerrillas and seem rather to have made Che impatient. They left on April 20 and were arrested in a nearby village. The trial and imprisonment of Debray and Bustos made worldwide news for many weeks. Both men acted with dignity and fortitude.

By April, Che had forty-seven men in his group. It was then that he gave it the ambitious name of National Liberation Army of Bolivia, with an *Estado Mayor* (General Staff), and issued his first war communiqué. It told of a successful encounter near Camiri on March 23 and ended with these hopeful words:

"Hostilities have begun. In future communiqués we will clearly explain our revolutionary position. Today we issue a call to workers, peasants, intellectuals; to all those who feel that the hour has come to answer violence with violence and to ransom a country sold in pieces to the Yankee monopolies and to raise the standard of living of our people, who go more hungry every day."

Communiqué Number 2 told of the victory of April 10, in which ten Bolivian soldiers were killed and thirty taken prisoner. In this communiqué Che, referring to the government's call for North American advisers, wrote: "It was thus that the war in Vietnam began which drained the blood of that heroic people and imperiled the peace of the world."

The result was not only very far from Che's hopes, but the United States sent down a squad of eleven Green Berets, headed by Major Ralph Shelton, who were enough in the circumstances. Ricardo Rojo called them "superspecialists brought into Bolivia from Vietnam to instruct 650 Bolivian Rangers in an accelerated program." The Rangers went into action in the latter part of July 1967. They had learned their lessons well.

There were no more communiqués about engagements. Number 4 was an appeal to the Bolivian people. Number 5 was addressed to the Bolivian miners—an appeal that has its pathos in the light of what was to happen:

"Compañero minero," it ends, "the guerrillas of the E.L.N. [National Liberation Army] await you with open arms and invite you to unite with the workers of the subsoil who are fighting at our side. We will here reconstruct the worker-peasant alliance that was broken by the antipopular demagogy; we will here convert defeat into triumph and the tears of the proletarian widows into a hymn of victory. We await you."

Che Guevara was right to refer to himself as a Don Quixote.

The government in La Paz had been thoroughly stirred up. Sensational accounts were being published in all countries. The American Special Forces Group had begun training the Bolivian Rangers in April, and the CIA had also moved in with other specialists. It will be recalled that it was from Bolivia that Che had sent a "Message to the Peoples of the World," published in Havana on April 16, to the Organization of Solidarity of the Peoples of Africa, Asia and Latin America (OSPAAL). It contained the call to the revolutionaries of the world to rise and "create two, three, many Vietnams."

But already, on March 28, Che had written in his diary: "We are surrounded by 2,000 men in a radius of 120 kilometers and the circle is being tightened, helped by bombardments with napalm; we have had ten or fifteen casualties." In his summary for the month of March he wrote: "The situation is not good."

The first serious setback occurred on April 25 when an attempted ambush failed and "Rolando" (Eliseo Reyes), also known as "San Luis," was killed. At the age of seventeen he had joined Che in Las Villas Province and stuck with him faithfully. In Cuba he had the rank of captain and was a member of the Central Committee of the

Communist Party. "We have lost the best of guerrillas," mourned Che, for whom Rolando's death was also a grievous personal loss.

However, they were fighting and morale improved. They staged three successful ambushes in May, the last two on the 30th and 31st, in each of which three Bolivian soldiers were killed and arms captured without any guerrilla losses.

On April 15 an event had occurred that was to prove a disaster. Guevara divided his force and put a trusted officer, "Joaquín," in charge of a rear guard. He was Major Juan Vitalio Acuña Núñez of the PCC Central Committee, one of the first peasants to join Fidel Castro in the Sierra Maestra. Joaquín and his group went off the next day, and Che was never to see them again. After eight days of silence, he sent two men to seek them and bring them back, but in vain. For some reason which Guevara obviously could not fathom, it was never possible for the two groups to contact each other and join up again.

In Joaquín's group was the young woman known and honored in Cuba now as Tania la Guerrillera. Her full name was Haydée Tamara Bunke Bider. According to Guerra Alemán (in his book *Barro y Cenizas*), she was born in Buenos Aires on November 19, 1937. Her father was a German professor, and her mother was Polish; both were Communists. Tania went to Havana in 1961 with Alicia Alonso's ballet company, Guerra Alemán writes. "Che used her as a courier and on other secret missions," he adds. By marrying a Bolivian in La Paz, she got a citizenship that helped her in preparing for the arrival of Guevara and his band. It seems to have been a *mariage de convenance,* as she divorced the Bolivian after he had served his purpose. It was Tania and the Bolivian Communist Guido ("Inti") Peredo who bought the farm at Ñacahuasu which Che used as his base.

Lionel Martin, an American journalist who has worked in Havana for years, mostly for *Prensa Latina,* told me that he saw a great deal of Tania when she lived in Havana. She was a pretty young woman, very athletic and popular. She used to play the guitar when with a group of friends. In Havana she worked as a translator and was active in the militia, wearing a pistol strapped to her side at all times.

It is clear from the *Bolivian Diary* that Che Guevara felt no affection for her. The report that she was a Soviet KGB agent may have been true, but that she betrayed Che was palpable nonsense. She was tragically unfit for the hardships and almost unbearable demands of guerrilla life. The casual, cold way in which Che records the news of her death shows only too clearly that she meant nothing to him and was probably a burden to the guerrilla group.

Tania la Guerrillera was more to be pitied than glorified. It seems to have been a case of the spirit being willing but the flesh weak. Guerra Alemán, who dug up more about her than any source I know, prints the text of the sad, all-too-human letter to her mother which was found in her knapsack after her death. The original German, translated into Guerra Alemán's Spanish, and now into my English, retains the anguish of a lost soul:

> Dear Mother:
>
> I am frightened. I don't know what will happen to me and all the others. Probably nothing. I am terribly worn out and weep incessantly. My nerves have gone. I try to remember what it is to be brave. Are you, by chance, "Mother Courage"? [the title of Bertolt Brecht's play] Certainly, I am not "Daughter Courage." I am nothing. I am not a woman or a girl. I am only a child, a child who would like to hide herself in some corner where nobody could find her. I wish I could crawl away and hide myself. But where can I hide myself? . . .

Nowhere—she was killed when Joaquín's band was ambushed and wiped out on August 31. She has been glorified for Cuban revolutionary mythology in a book, published in four languages, called *Tania, the Unforgettable Guerrilla,* by Marta Rojas and Mirta Rodríguez Calderón.

On June 14, 1967, Che noted that it was his thirty-ninth birthday, and it set him wondering about his future as a guerrilla *(mi futuro guerrillero).* He had less than four months to live. It was also his daughter Celia's birthday, but he was not sure how old she was, as he wrote: "Celita (4?)"

He mentioned his chronic illness for the first time on June 23: "Asthma is threatening me seriously and there is not much reserve of medicine left." He was to use his last injection of adrenalin on August 2, and had tablets left for only ten days. By then the asthma was very bad. On August 14 he learned that the cave at Ñacahuasu where medicines, documents, photographs, and other supplies were stored had been discovered by Bolivian soldiers. "This is the hardest blow we have been struck," he wrote. "Someone blabbed. Who? Now I am condemned to suffer from the asthma for an indefinite time."

Captain Harry Villegas ("Pombo"), one of the few Cuban survivors, who was a Sierra Maestra veteran and had been in the Congo with Guevara, wrote an article about Che's asthma for *Verde Olivo,* organ of the Armed Forces, printed in October 1971.

> In Bolivia toward the end his asthma attacks were very bad. However, Che's will power and sense of duty and of self-sacrifice were revealed in the fact that he would not allow anyone to go after the medicine he needed, notwithstanding the fact that we had been insisting that it be done for close to two months. He held out until his physical condition was such he couldn't move and it was evident that his handicap would finally have an ill effect on the morale of the guerrillas, because we all had been used to seeing in Che an active man who could make decisions.
>
> Even when suffering an asthma attack, he ordinarily climbed hills and, though he had to stop now and then, kept up with the column. However, toward the last days, he found it too difficult to walk despite his will power and had to ride a horse.

Mercifully, Pombo writes, "in the days preceding the [fatal] La Higuera ambush, he was practically free from his asthma and felt fine."

Another of Che's best men, "Tuma" (Lieutenant Carlos Coello, who had been with him in the Congo), was killed on June 26, which Che puts down as "a black day for me." Tuma was "an inseparable companion for many years, faithful in every trial, whose absence I feel now almost as if he were a son." The guerrillas, who then numbered twenty-four, killed four Bolivians in the skirmish. They were caught in another ambush on July 30, in which two more Cubans were killed and two other guerrillas wounded.

August 7 made nine months since the guerrilla band was set up at Ñacahuasu. The indomitable Che, crippled by asthma, refers to himself on the eighth as *una piltrafa humana.* He was so much of a human wreck that he realized he was temporarily unfit to command. Yet it was typical of his extraordinary will and spirit that he chose to deliver an inspirational lecture on that very day.

"It is one of those moments when great decisions must be taken," he says to his comrades. "This type of struggle gives us the opportunity to turn ourselves into revolutionaries, the highest level of the human species, but it also permits us to take our measure as men: those who cannot attain either of these heights [*estadíos*] should say so and abandon the struggle."

His analysis at the end of August is wholly dark for the first time: "It was, without doubt, the worst month we have had in every aspect of the war . . . We are at a low moment in our morale and in our revolutionary image [*leyenda*]."

On September 4 he learned from the La Paz radio of the tragic fate of Joaquín and the rear guard of seventeen whom he had sent off on April 15. They had been ambushed on August 31. Joaquín and eight others were killed on that day. Che noted the fact without comment. On September 7, Radio la Cruz del Sur announced that the body of "Tania la Guerrillera" had been found on the banks of the Rio Grande. Again no comment from Che, not the least sign of emotion.

His fiercest attack on the Communists, especially in Bolivia and Chile, who would not help him, comes on September 8: "A Budapest newspaper," he writes, "criticizes Che Guevara, a pathetic figure, it seems, irresponsible. It applauds the Marxist position of the Chilean Party which takes practical positions in facing action. How I would love to achieve power, if only to unmask the cowards and lackeys of all breeds and rub the snouts of the swine in their piggishness [*y refregarles en el hocico sus cochinadas*]."

He never seems to have lost his wry sense of humor. "I forgot to list one fact," he notes on September 10. "Today, after something over six months, I bathed. It constitutes a record which others are beginning to reach."

The next day he hears over the radio that Bolivian President René Barrientos has offered $50,000 for his capture, dead or alive. "Barrientos' offer can be considered psychological," he comments, "since the tenacity of the guerrillas is well known, as well as the fact that they are preparing for a long war."

The first mention of Higueras, near where Che Guevara was to meet his end, appears on September 25. The *corregidor* (magistrate or sheriff) is in the region where Che's group has wandered, and Che gives orders to seize the man. The next day they reach Higueras, where the attitude of the Indian peasants is hostile. A patrol that Guevara sends out is ambushed, with three killed, two wounded, and two missing. The two missing men had been taken prisoner, or else, as "Inti" Peredo, the Bolivian with Che, wrote, they deserted. They talked freely to their captors. It was the most costly skirmish to date, for the dead men were *magnificos luchadores* ("splendid fighters"). The Bolivian troops were clumsily but steadily closing in. It was the beginning of the end.

There was a doctor with the band named Morogoro, whom Che had mentioned almost daily for weeks, as the man was ill and getting steadily worse. He had been a constant drag on the guerrillas and was soon to prove a fatal burden to Che, who would not abandon him, although by then he was "very weak." The column was down to seventeen men.

In his résumé for the black month of September—the last full month—Che concedes that "the Army is showing itself more effective in action and the peasant mass does not help us in any way and turn into informers." He is bitter about the Communist apparatus in La Paz, but there is no note of discouragement or weakness. They must "slip away and find a more propitious locality" from which to fight on, he writes.

The army troops on the hunt probably totaled 1,500 at the beginning of October. Che's entry for the sixth shows that he realized the danger of their situation. They rested in a ravine, later identified as the Quebrada del Yuro, "although it was not a tranquil day as we were fully in the sun in a rather populated locality." The next morning they decided to go to a nearby stream "and from there make a more exhaustive exploration in order to determine our future course."

There was to be no "future course." Che and his band were trapped. The next day, October 7, 1967, was exactly eleven months from the time Che Guevara wrote in his diary: "Today a new stage of the journey begins."

It was a "bucolic day," Che says in his last entry. From information that an old peasant woman gives, he notes that "we are approximately a league [about three miles] from Higueras, the same distance from Jagüey, and about two from Pucará."

"We left at seventeen o'clock, with little moonlight," reads his final entry, "and the walk was very tiring and we were leaving a lot of tracks . . . At 2 [A.M., October 8] we stopped to rest since it was useless to keep on walking."

"Inti" Peredo, the faithful Bolivian guerrilla who was to survive, wrote an article about El Yuro for the fourth anniversary of Che's death, published in the Havana newspaper *Granma* on October 8, 1971. It is of considerable historic value, even though he and six others were in another part of the ravine and did not know of the capture of Guevara until too late. Peredo starts by telling about the calamitous ambush they fell into at La Higuera on September 26.

"It was imperative," he continues, "that we establish contact with the city [La Paz] to solve a number of problems in logistics and get reinforcements . . . First, however, we would have to break through two cordons—one spread out practically under our noses and another laid out by the Army."

They "lay in hiding" until October 1, and then made cautious daily treks until the fatal last day.

> It got really cold in the early hours of October 8 . . . At 2 A.M. we stopped for a rest, taking off again at 4 A.M. There were seventeen of

us, walking along a narrow ravine known as El Yuro, not uttering a word and doing our best to blend into our surroundings.

The morning turned out to be bright and clear, which made it possible for us to look over the terrain carefully. We were searching for a crest to make our way toward the San Lorenzo River . . .

At this point, Che decided to send out three pairs of scouts; one, made up of Pacho and Benigno, along the hill on our right; a second made up of Urbano and a second comrade [Pombo]; and the third, made up of Aniceto and Darío, along the path ahead of us. It didn't take Benigno and Pacho long to come back with the news that the soldiers were blocking our way. The question was whether they had seen us or not. . . .

Che took the only decision that could be adopted at that moment: he gave orders to hide in a small canyon to one side, and he deployed the men into various positions. It was approximately 8:30 A.M., and the seventeen of us were sitting in the center and sides of the small canyon, waiting. . . .

About 11 A.M. I went to relieve Benigno, but he remained in his place, lying down. His shoulder wound had begun to suppurate and he was in great pain. So it turned out that Benigno, Darío and I stayed there. Pombo and Urbano were at the other end of the ravine, with Che and the rest in the center.

Sometime around 13:30 o'clock, Che sent Ñato [Darío] and Aniceto to take over from Urbano and Pombo. To get to their position it was necessary to go across a clearing that was controlled by the enemy. Aniceto was the first to make a try, but he was killed on the spot.

The battle was on. We were hemmed in. We could hear the soldiers shouting: "We got one; we got one!"

Up toward a position held by the soldiers, in the narrow part of the ravine, we could hear the steady clatter of machine guns. Apparently, the soldiers were in control of the path we had crossed the night before.

Their little group was pinned down, as it turned out, while Che, in the center, was losing his last battle. In the evening they rejoined their three comrades. Che was nowhere to be found, but they noted traces of his sandals and abandoned food; they pushed on through the night.

The main tragedy had taken place when they heard the clatter of machine guns in the center of the gulley. Che stayed and fought it out. He would not abandon the doctor and a Peruvian guerrilla, both seriously ill. According to the account that Fidel Castro got,

Guevara went on firing until his M–2 rifle was put out of action by a chance shot that hit the barrel, and then Che himself was wounded in the leg. His revolver was empty. This, writes Castro, was why he was captured alive.

Early in the evening he was taken in a litter to a rural schoolhouse at La Higuera (which means Fig Tree), where he was held for twenty-four hours. By an extraordinary chance, "Inti" Peredo and his five comrades were in sight of the building.

> We wound up at La Higuera, [Peredo writes] a place that brought back painful memories. We sat on the ground, practically across from the schoolhouse. The dogs kept barking, but we didn't know whether it was because they were excited by the singing and shouting of the soldiers who were getting drunk, celebrating.
>
> We never dreamed that our beloved Major was there, only a few yards away from us, wounded but still alive.
>
> In retrospect, the idea enters our mind that had we thought Che was there we would have tried a desperate move in an effort to save him, even if it meant dying in the attempt. But on that night of tension and anguish, we hadn't the slightest inkling of what had happened, and told one another, in whispers, of our worry about whether some other comrade besides Aniceto had been killed in the battle. We continued our trek, bypassing La Higuera. . . .
>
> The 9th was a peaceful day. Twice we saw a helicopter fly overhead. It carried the still-warm body of Che, murdered in cowardly fashion by orders of the CIA and the gorillas [President] Barrientos and [General] Ovando, but we didn't know it.

The *New York Times* correspondent Juan de Onis wrote an account of Che's death from La Paz, and returned to investigate the story in March 1968. He learned that an American CIA agent had questioned Che in the schoolhouse for a few hours on the morning of October 9, 1967. The orders to kill Che Guevara had, indeed, come from La Paz. A *suboficial* (NCO) named Mario Terán was told to go in and shoot him.

"At about 11 A.M.," wrote De Onis, "the conversation [with the CIA agent] was interrupted by a burst of gunfire in the adjoining room in the two-room schoolhouse. A wounded Bolivian guerrilla was being slain.

"Mr. Guevara was silent for a moment, and then spoke again.

" 'They are going to kill me, but that will not stop the revolution,' he said. 'The revolution will triumph.' "

Sergeant Mario Terán came in and the CIA agent left.

"When this man, who was quite drunk," Castro writes in his introduction to the *Diary*, "entered the room, Che—who had heard the volleys which had just dispatched a Bolivian and a Peruvian guerrilla [perhaps the ill doctor and the guerrilla whom Che would not leave]—seeing that the executioner hesitated, said to him with fortitude: 'Fire! Don't be afraid.' "

The soldier went out and had to be ordered back. This time "he shot him, firing from the hip with a machine-gun blast."

However, he had been ordered not to disfigure Che by shooting at his head or breast, which prolonged the agony until a sergeant came in to deliver a *coup de grâce* in his left side. The reason for this crude execution, Fidel claimed, was that the authorities had already given out a story that Che had been killed in combat.

Juan de Onis' version is slightly different: "Despite his wound, Mr. Guevara got to his feet and said: 'You are going to see how a man dies.' Four shots killed him instantly."

The body was taken by helicopter (the one Che's comrades had seen) to a hospital in Vallegrande, where two doctors performed an autopsy. Che's hands were cut off for a dactylographic examination by Argentine authorities in Buenos Aires, and then sent back to La Paz.

No exact account of Guevara's death is ever likely to come out. The highest Bolivian authorities lied about almost every aspect of the affair, and they muzzled everyone connected with it. The CIA has naturally divulged nothing. The Bolivian authorities would not say whether Che was cremated or buried, or where the remains were. They even burned down the schoolhouse in La Higuera. Thus, they must have thought, there can be no shrine, because there was no body, no place of death, no known burial spot.

But there remains a name for history, and a memory that can never be erased.

I was in Havana during the agonizing days for Fidel and Che's old comrades as reports started coming in which, they hoped against hope, would prove false. I cannot believe that anything in his life ever upset Fidel Castro so much. Cubans said to me at the time that they had never seen Fidel so moved, but so were his comrades from Sierra Maestra days. I had not realized what a deep personal affection Che had gained from them all.

As Fidel said in his elegiac tribute, delivered to a huge crowd in the Plaza de la Revolución in Havana on October 18, 1967, they mourned

> one of the closest, the most admired, the most beloved and, without doubt, the most extraordinary of our revolutionary comrades . . .
>
> His conduct may have been profoundly influenced by the idea that men have a relative value in history; the idea that causes are not defeated when men fall, that the powerful march of history cannot and will not be halted when leaders fall. And that is true; there is no doubt about it. . . .
>
> But those who are boasting of victory are mistaken. They are mistaken when they think that his death is the end of his ideas, the end of his tactics, the end of his guerrilla concepts, the end of his theses.

In reality, the hopes of the Castro-type guerrilla movements died with Che Guevara and would have died even had he somehow survived his Bolivian adventure. The urban guerrilla was taking his place. But in his eulogy Fidel touched on some of the qualities to which the youth of the world were to respond in an astonishing way:

> When men die it is usual to make speeches, to emphasize their virtues, but rarely can one say of a man, with greater justice, with greater accuracy, what we say of Che: that he was a pure example of revolutionary virtues! But he possessed another quality, not a quality of the intellect nor of the will, not a quality derived from experience, from struggle, but a quality of the heart: he was an extraordinarily human man, a man of extraordinary sensitivity.
>
> That is why we say, when we think of his life, that he constituted the singular case of a most extraordinary man, able to unite in his personality not only the characteristics of the man of action, but also the man of thought, the man of immaculate revolutionary virtues and of extraordinary human sensibility, joined with an iron character, a will of steel, indomitable tenacity. . . .
>
> Che fell defending the interests, defending the cause of the exploited and the oppressed peoples of this continent. Che fell defending the cause of the poor and disenfranchised of this earth. The exemplary manner and the selflessness with which he defended that cause cannot be disputed even by his most bitter enemies. And before history, the men who act as he did, men who do all and give all for the cause of the oppressed, grow in stature with each passing day and find a deeper place in the heart of the people with each passing day.
>
> The imperialistic enemies are beginning to see this, and it will not be long before it will be proved that his death will, in the long run, be like a germ which will give rise to many men determined to imitate him, many men determined to follow his example.

In his July 26, 1970, speech Castro added a comment at the end telling how the hands of Che Guevara, "perfectly preserved," and the death mask had been saved and brought to Cuba by Dr. Argüedas along with the diary. Fidel said then that the hands would be kept intact and placed in a museum to be devoted to Che Guevara and his life. The huge audience cheered. However, when I asked Haydée Santamaría about it two years later, she said that Fidel had had second thoughts, as the idea seemed gruesome. The hands will be saved, but not displayed.

The photograph of the body of Che, taken in the hospital of the remote Bolivian mountain village of Vallegrande, inspired John Berger, the British painter and author of books on art and contemporary life, to write an essay from a painter's point of view. It appears in his book *The Look of Things.*

> There is a resemblance [Berger writes] between the photograph and Rembrandt's painting of *The Anatomy Lesson of Professor Tulp.* The immaculately dressed Bolivian colonel with a handkerchief to his nose has taken the professor's place. The two figures on his left stare at the cadaver with the same intense but impersonal interest as the two nearest doctors on the professor's left. It is true that there are more figures in the Rembrandt—as there were certainly more men, unphotographed, in the stable [hospital] at Vallegrande. But the placing of the corpse in relation to the figures above it, and of the corpse in the sense of global stillness—these are very similar.
>
> Nor should this be surprising, for the function of the two pictures is similar: both are concerned with showing a corpse being formally and objectively examined. More than that, both are concerned with *making an example of the dead* [Berger's italics]: one for the advancement of medicine, the other as a political warning. . . .
>
> I was also reminded of another image: Mantegna's painting of the dead Christ, now in the Brera at Milan . . . Guevara was no Christ. If I see the Mantegna again in Milan, I shall see in it the body of Guevara. But this is only because in certain rare cases the tragedy of a man's death completes and exemplifies the meaning of his whole life.

There is no denying that from a military point of view Che Guevara's tactics were badly conceived and badly carried out. He moved in haphazard fashion, winding in, out, and around an area about two hundred miles long and eighty miles wide. It was a fatal mistake to divide his forces. He should not have left indispensable arms and supplies behind in Ñacahuasu in the midst of a hostile peasantry.

In the Sierra Maestra, Fidel Castro became a skilled military leader; Che Guevara carried out some successful ambushes in Bolivia, but he could not manage to establish a firm base from which to operate. Perhaps it was impossible. Castro had many advantages in Oriente Province that Guevara, isolated in a strange country, amidst a suspicious and hostile peasantry, lacked.

The Bolivian adventure will therefore not take its place in the history of guerrilla wars for any military accomplishment. It belongs on a different plane—human, idealistic, political. It has meaning because of Ernesto Che Guevara; because he lived it and died there. My own reaction, reading and rereading the *Bolivian Diary* and the accounts of Che Guevara's death, has been a literary boyhood memory of the death of Roland in the *Chanson de Roland.*

I admired Che Guevara greatly, and liked him personally. He was a controversial figure. Certain historians of the Cuban Revolution can see no greatness in him. Professor Hugh Thomas, in his huge, scholarly study of Cuba, dismisses Che almost offhandedly. "Guevara was a brave, sincere and determined man who was also obstinate, narrow and dogmatic," Thomas concludes.

Yet Fidel Castro was right when he wrote in his introduction to the *Bolivian Diary:* "Few times in history, or perhaps never, has a face, a name, an example, universalized itself with such swift and passionate force."

This too has been belittled, because the Guevara cult was picked up most sensationally by long-haired, antisocial hippies and had the ultimate indignity of a maudlin film with Omar Sharif playing a sugar-coated caricature of Che. The young who hang Che Guevara's photograph on their walls do not emulate his life, nor do they work for his goal of pure socialism. His appeal to them is as a romanticized rebel.

When I told Fidel in Havana in September 1972 about the huge photographs of Guevara one sees along Oxford Street in London and so many other streets in the world, he shrugged his shoulders in contempt. I said that Che had become a worldwide symbol of youthful rebellion and revolution. "And what do *they* know about revolution?" Fidel asked.

In Cuba that time I saw more photographs and posters of Guevara than of Castro—which was what Fidel wanted. I never heard of or sensed the slightest evidence of jealousy on Fidel's part for the fact that it is Che Guevara, not he, who has won such spectacular, universal fame.

There was a striking parallel in the Mexican Revolution in the figure of Emiliano Zapata, the peasant leader from Morelos. Zapata succeeded initially with his peasant armies, but could not lead a national revolution, which was taken over by Mexico City lawyers and military men. In 1919 Zapata was treacherously ambushed and killed. He had failed. Yet a historian of the Mexican Revolution, Robert E. Quirk, could aptly write that "the inarticulate, militarily ineffectual Zapata accomplished in death what he could not win in life. His spirit lived on, and in a strange, illogical, but totally Mexican twist of fate, he became the greatest hero of the Revolution. In the hagiography of the Revolution, the *caudillo* of Morelos continues to ride his white charger."

And so, we can add, does Che Guevara continue to ride his Rosinante.

The last tribute that Hilda Gadea, his first wife, paid to him was typical in its revolutionary, not its wifely, sentiments. It was written for a January 1968 special issue of the magazine *Casa,* published by Casa de las Americas in Havana. Hilda reprinted the text as the conclusion of her biography.

"And in spite of our pain and the suffering of all revolutionaries," the note says, "we who knew you can say that you have faced all the dangers and that you have gone to the fight with joy as always, happy to offer the best of yourself in the struggle for justice. Happy in suffering, happy in dying for our ideals, with the happiness of knowing surely that other men will follow your example."

The more womanly Aleida was heartbroken, friends told me at the time of Che's death. I know that Celia Sánchez spent the last few days of agonizing uncertainty with Aleida.

She has not remarried. When I asked Haydée Santamaría in 1972 whether she had, Haydée shook her head firmly. *"Ella no puede ser otra que la viuda del Che"* ("She can be only the widow of Che"), she said, as if remarriage would be sacrilegious.

All five children are going to school in Cuba, as Che desired, even Hildita, his daughter by Hilda Gadea. When Hildita was three days old, Fidel Castro was her first visitor. The mother quotes him saying as he fondled the baby: "This girl is going to be educated in Cuba."

Che never failed to note in his *Bolivian Diary* the birthdays of his children and even his parents, brothers, and sisters. Usually it is just the name: *"de Ernestico (2)."* The mothers are not mentioned. On February 15 there had been a simple: *"cumpleaños de Hildita (11)."* He seemed to have had a special affection for his child by his first wife. Hilda told this story of Hildita when she was only eight months old:

"Taking Hildita in his arms one day, he looked at her tenderly and said: 'My dear daughter, my little Mao [Hildita's eyes showed her mother's Indian blood], you don't know what a difficult world you're going to have to live in. When you grow up this whole continent, and maybe the whole world, will be fighting against the great enemy, Yankee imperialism. You too will have to fight. I may not be here any more, but the struggle will enflame the continent.' He spoke very seriously. I was overwhelmed at his words and went to him and embraced him."

Che wrote a letter to Hildita for her tenth birthday in 1966: "Remember that many years of struggle still lie ahead, and though you are a woman, you will have to do your part in the fight. Meanwhile, you must prepare, be a true revolutionary, which at your age means to learn a lot, everything you can, and always be ready to support just causes."

Hildita Guevara is paying heed; she is her father's daughter. When I was in Cuba in 1972, she was sixteen. I was told that she was as passionately revolutionary as her father had been, reading avidly, like both her parents, in the literature of Marxism and revolution. Now both her mother and father are dead.

There are four other Guevara children growing up in Cuba, being educated and indoctrinated. One hopes that "Yankee imperialism" will not be "the great enemy" when they grow to manhood and womanhood. But one thing about them is sure: our world in revolution has not heard the last of the Guevara name.

Ernesto Che Guevara was killed when Americans taught Bolivian Rangers how to track him down. He was an opponent of the United States and, in his way, a threat to American security. He fell victim to the fortunes of war, which should not inhibit Americans from paying respect to the fallen enemy. Che was a human being of great and high qualities. His life burned out with a pure flame.

CHAPTER 13

Economics Cuban Style

Gain understanding though it cost you all you have.
—Proverbs 4: 7

As I remarked before, it is tempting to say that Che Guevara had taken the easy way out, leaving to Fidel Castro the infinitely harder task of struggling with the heartbreaking problems of running the revolutionary economy. Each man obeyed his character and responded to what destiny offered, but I think that Fidel must now and then have envied Che, while Che, had he lived, would never have envied Fidel.

The Cuban leaders, whether consciously or unconsciously, thought of their economy almost from the beginning as something different, unique, specially Cuban, not to be measured or judged in terms of the theories and practices of the world outside. For example, when Professor René Dumont, the French Marxist economist, criticized them in two books for not following accepted or normal socialist practices, they considered him unfair. The Revolution was much more than its economy and, in any event, that economy was going to be worked out by Cubans in a Cuban way. Thus for Che Guevara it was natural, although unsatisfactory, that Cuban work was not "on a level of productivity acceptable by world standards."

He said this in an article he wrote for *Nuestra Industria Económica* of February 1964. In it he listed the "fundamental weaknesses" of the Cuban economic system as ruthlessly as the sharpest critic. The difference was that the Cubans were finding it a slow and painful process to correct their failures, while it took the academic critics only a few minutes to tell them what they should have done.

Economists have had to be—or at least should have been—cautious in describing Cuba's economic system or situation at any given time. By the date an article or a book was published, the situation had changed, and so had economic conditions. But economists, like historians, love to make patterns, build structures, formalize and label. They have found it hard to accept the fact that the reality in Cuba had been so messy, so haphazard, so opportunistic, so hit-and-miss, that any detailed description today would not fit tomorrow. As a sequel to the 1970 sugar disaster, the sensational rise in sugar prices in 1974, and the decisions of the long-delayed thirteenth National Workers' Congress of the Central Organization of Cuban Workers in November 1973, it is now possible to be more confident about the management of the Cuban revolutionary economy.

All writers have noted that Fidel Castro fooled himself again and again, promising great results with complete assurance and sincerity, results that not only did not materialize but had no chance of succeeding. His inexhaustible optimism never flagged. His critics could always say: "We told you so!" or "See how he has deceived the Cuban people!" The climax came in 1970 with the failure of the ten-million-ton sugar target. By then, if not before, it should have been realized that this is how Fidel Castro works; how he keeps going; and how sometimes he progresses.

One tries in vain to analyze why intelligent men, honest, hard-working, well-intentioned, and serious, could have gone on year after year making avoidable errors, failures in planning, management, and production, all culminating in 1970 in a near collapse of the economy. Every measure of austerity and regimentation had to be forced upon them. The bad, foolish, rash acts were partly balanced by the good—but so much of the bad was unnecessary, gratuitous, willful blindness.

Or was it? There was great inexperience, of course, and youthful haste. "A little knowledge" was, as usual, dangerous. Suspicions and distrust were natural. The Cuban temperament was working, as their phrase puts it, *por la libre*—freely, with more than a touch of anarchy.

I remember a talk with Fidel in mid-1959 when he agreed, with a helpless gesture, that many injustices were occurring in the lower bureaucratic ranks where enthusiastic, rough-and-ready young *barbudos* were acting on their own. It was to take him years to get some order and discipline down the line, but they were years when he too was floundering *por la libre* and when loyalty meant more than efficiency.

Business acumen and managerial ability are gifts: you have them or you don't. Fidel and Che Guevara didn't. Raúl Castro had considerable administrative ability, but not in a business way. Sympathetic experts like Felipe Pazos and Rufo López-Fresquet were not trusted. It must be remembered that the best-trained, the most skilled, experienced, and knowledgeable men in Cuba went into exile at the beginning of the Revolution.

It was all unprecedented. Granted the determination to find "Cuban" solutions, was it reasonable or logical to expect anything different? Could Castro have made the kind of revolution he has made, with all its good features in education, health, social welfare, and so forth, if he had been "orthodox" in economics and revolutionary in every other way? The Cuban Revolution is an enormously complex process—to use Fidel's favorite word.

"Fidel is *un intuitif,* who understands quickly, but who is very susceptible to influence," René Dumont wrote in his second book, *Cuba, Est-il Socialiste?* "Instead of basing himself on a scientific observation of facts in order to deduce rules of action, his idea is to mold the facts and to transform the nature of man."

"Economic laws," Dumont says at another point, "which have not all been abolished in a socialist regime, know how to avenge themselves diabolically at times."

Dumont had made such criticisms in articles in 1960 and in a book published in 1964, *Cuba: Socialisme et Développement,* in which he argued against "bureaucratic anarchy," "ultra-centralized leadership of the economy, managed by means of budgetary credits," overoptimism, a lack of realism, unattainable production forecasts, falling quality in tobacco, falling production in many fields, mismanagement, et cetera. Yet, although Castro complained, he invited Dumont back in 1969, whereupon the French professor wrote another and even more devastating book, mentioned above. This time, Fidel was furious and attacked Professor Dumont in a few speeches.

Another friendly French critic, an economist and a Marxist, Professor Charles Bettelheim, who was invited to Cuba four times, likewise angered Castro and—in 1963 and 1964—Che Guevara. Bettelheim, like Dumont, believed in the efficacy of a number of basic economic "laws," whether applied to a socialist or a capitalist economy. He reinforced his arguments by appeals to Marx, Lenin, Stalin, and Mao, as well as to Russian experiences, but Communist orthodoxy was always the least of Castro's concerns.

Che Guevara replied to the critics. His readings made it possible for him to talk and argue with reasonable authority on the technical problems of a socialist economy, such as the conflict in the Communist camp over Russia's Economic Calculus, where government enterprises administer their own financial means under the control of the Central Bank, and Budgetary Calculus, where the capital is entirely handled by the National Bank and Finance Ministry. Cuba had opted for the latter method, and one can suppose that it was on Guevara's advice.

Che, as I noted in a previous chapter, also entered the controversy started by the Soviet economist Y. G. Liberman, who believed in material incentives for workers and decentralization of controls. Guevara (in this regard Fidel came first) was a firm believer in maximum centralization.

Although Guevara and other Cuban revolutionary leaders visited China and presumably studied the economy there, it does not seem that they were in the least impressed by Mao Tse-tung's policy of favoring local initiative and avoiding control by an overcentralized bureaucracy. The Russians retain a higher degree of centralized control than the Chinese, but by all accounts the Chinese peasant is a more contented and more efficient worker than the Russian peasant.

Of course, Cubans argue that their rural population is different from Russia's or China's and that the agrarian problems of a small island are necessarily different from those of two huge countries.

Another of Guevara's pet convictions was that value was a social phenomenon and not, as in orthodox Communist—as well as capitalist—practice, a result of supply and demand. Castro, who had to deal every day with the marketplace and its supply-and-demand values, seems to have been neutral in this controversy.

Che was fascinated in his romantic soul by what he called "this strange and impassioned drama of constructing socialism." Fidel did not interest himself greatly in theoretical controversy, nor did he read the relevant books. His practical, pragmatic mind led him into endless reading of manuals on agriculture and other technical subjects directly affecting a crop or an industry.

The socialist field in which there has been most success—and Castro gives Guevara much of the credit for getting it going—is voluntary labor. Fidel gave great impetus to voluntarism with his *microbrigadas,* especially in the field of construction, in the aftermath of the 1970 crisis. But voluntarism of sorts had started a decade before.

Che was also more responsible than any Cuban leader for creating what he called "a vanguard of the proletariat," which attracted a great many young Cubans. They did useful work for years, but the system has now been reduced and remodeled in the new regulations agreed by the CTC in its 1973 congress, although Fidel gave them a renewed blessing in his speech to the meeting.

A point system was worked out for punctuality, attendance, and quantity and quality of production. Prizes ranged from buttons and diplomas to paid vacations and even trips to a socialist country. Deserving workers were given the right to buy scarce consumer goods like TV sets, refrigerators, and pressure cookers. Those who consistently excelled earned the title "vanguard workers." The most prestigious honor, given annually, was to become a "Hero of Labor." There were a few monetary prizes, but the system was not, like Russian Stakhanovism, based on material awards. The main point of the emulation campaigns was supposed to be the moral satisfaction of being a vanguard worker.

All these honors have to mean something, or they would be derided or resented. Therefore, the Revolution itself must mean something, although one must allow for a certain amount of subtle pressure from managers and party workers and from organizations like the Committees for the Defense of the Revolution. A worker who balked against voluntary work was looked at askance by vanguard members or zealous revolutionary types. He might fear for his future.

Che Guevara realized the impossibility of creating immediately an economy based solely on moral incentives, even though he worked for such a goal and believed that it could be achieved. In the 1966 article I mentioned, he wrote:

"We do not deny the objective need for material incentives, but we certainly are unwilling to use them as a fundamental driving force . . . We maintain that in a relatively short time the development of conscience does more for the development of production than material incentives do."

The furthest he would go was to accept a policy of material incentives as "a necessary evil in a period of transition." He also reluctantly conceded that the Law of Value (prices set by supply and demand) "must be recognized on an international scale as a fact that governs business transactions even within the Socialist bloc."

The hard-headed Communist leader who has played a major role for years in economic affairs, Carlos Rafael Rodríguez, stuck to good Leninist theory, upholding "the necessity for working systematically to reduce the role of material incentives in the construction of socialism, without ceasing to accept the role that they still have to play."

The Revolution never abandoned the law of "historic salary," by which salaries could not be reduced, but only increased.

"The historic salary," Castro explained in his speech to the 1973 CTC Congress, "first arose as a need to establish a certain discipline in wages, taking into consideration the enormous diversity of existing types of salaries, of the need to establish a scale, and the desire and intention of not prejudicing [*afectar*] workers, since many of those historic salaries were the result of great conflicts in the past by the workers themselves, and the Revolution did not want to adopt measures prejudicial to the workers." The basic minimum wage in September 1972 was $75 a month, but salaries of $800 and even $1,000 a month were still being earned. Newly trained engineers, for instance, received $300 to $400 monthly.

"In no way can all salaries be made equal," Castro said in his May Day speech in 1971.

> We cannot simply forget that some work is much harder than another; that there is work which requires much more expertise [*calificación*] and responsibility than other work . . . Sometimes it is difficult getting workers for certain types of activity. Some compensation must be established for them; there is no other mechanism . . . It is true that the salary is not the fundamental factor, not the decisive factor. But all the same it has its weight. . . .
>
> We have reached very high levels of voluntary work . . . But the road to Communism is not only a road of conscience; it is a road of the development of productive forces and of a material basis. . . .
>
> We cannot be misled into the idealism that because we want Communism and because we are struggling for Communism and because conscience is the fundamental factor of development, that therefore we already have a fully-developed conscience, that we already have a material basis, that we are already in a Communist society, and that all men are already behaving exactly the same in their conscience. In reality, this is not the case. All this is a process; but a process that moves upward. . . .
>
> We must understand that we are in a transitional stage; in the socialistic phase of the Revolution, not in the Communist phase.
>
> Some are asking themselves if there has been any change in the line or in the position of the Revolution [on moral values]. There has been no change. There cannot be one! For the day on which we abandon these banners, the Revolution would really be in danger; the Revolution would be disarmed.

The idea in 1974 was "to adopt a policy so that there is not a single new historic salary in the first place, and move progressively and by different paths toward the disappearance of the historic salary

. . . And logically, remuneration must be associated with the amount of work the person is fulfilling."

The Cuban ambassador to France, Baudilio Castellanos (who was one of the defense lawyers in the Moncada trial), told me about a conversation between Fidel and some French visitors in Havana. They expressed doubts about men being inspired by moral incentives, whereupon Fidel asked in a loud voice what inspired a million Frenchmen to die in the battle of Verdun? His appeal, in short, was to the enthusiasm and fervor stirred up by the Revolution. In addition, it still has to be hammered home that it is a moral imperative to work for the good of society and, by extension, the brotherhood of man through international socialism.

All the same, a partial dampener was put on voluntary work in the new CTC rules. While praising unpaid voluntary labor for its "high degree of revolutionary awareness," the theses of the CTC National Congress added:

> However, the wrong use to which voluntary work has sometimes been put and the organizational shortcomings of the mobilizations to carry it out that have developed at times, have distorted the sense of the work and depressed the workers, who are interested in carrying it out and who want their work to be reflected in useful results for society as a whole or for the community or nearby work center. . . .
>
> [Voluntary labor] must be well organized and only be carried out for production, services, projects of interest to society or the community and to compensate for the work of those who go to cut cane or participate in other agricultural tasks and those who join the mini-brigades. . . .
>
> Voluntary work should also be carried out to overcome backlogs in the fulfillment of production plans . . . and for doing things that will improve safety and health conditions on the job, constructing leisure, recreational and sport sites by the workers themselves and cleaning, beautifying and improving the environment.

In other words, voluntarism is to be subsidiary and extracurricular; it will no longer be a vital contribution to the economic system, and it will no longer be spontaneous. In this respect, the Cuban Revolution will be a little less revolutionary and a little better organized, but Fidel did say: "Volunteer work will be continued."

The position of compromise—the moral/material mix—was already evident when Castro made his May Day speech in 1971. This was in part the result of the failure of Cuba's "great leap forward" that preceded the 1970 sugar setback.

It had begun on March 13, 1968, when Fidel launched what was called a "Great Revolutionary Offensive." The aim was to eliminate "bourgeois institutions, ideas, relationships and privileges." The remnants of private trade—556,000 small businesses—were wiped out. Shops, stalls, small factories, and private service establishments (except for fishermen and some farmers) were abolished. Cabarets and bars were closed. Self-employed craftsmen had to go into factories or on farms. Enormous quantities of hoarded consumer goods, much of it black market, were confiscated. Hotel staffs voted against tips. When the "Great Leap" ended, 90 percent of the Cuban economy had been taken over by the state.

"Gentlemen, we did not make a Revolution here to establish the right to trade," Fidel said in the speech announcing the new policy.

> Such a revolution took place in 1789—that was the era of the bourgeois revolution—it was the revolution of the merchants, of the bourgeois. When will they finally understand that this is a revolution of socialists, that this is a revolution of Communists? . . . It must be said very clearly —and it goes without saying—that the Revolution is not out to make enemies for the fun of it, but neither is it afraid of making enemies when necessary—it must be said that private trade, self-employment, private industry or anything like it will not have any future in this country. . . .
>
> We don't feel that the Communist man can be developed by encouraging man's ambition, man's individualism, man's individual desires. If we are going to fail because we believe in man's ability, in his ability to improve, then we will fail, but we will never renounce our faith in mankind.

As Raúl Castro put it in his May Day speech of 1968, "We don't want a small-merchant mentality for our people."

Perhaps in part as a result of the new policy, there was a good deal of sabotage and other crimes in 1968, mostly by the young. Fidel denounced the lawlessness in a speech on September 9. It was a period of much discontent, as production was lagging and consumer goods were in shorter supply than ever. Many thousands of the petit bourgeoisie had been alienated by the nationalization of small businesses.

It was in 1968 that K. S. Karol, the Polish-French journalist, paid his last visit to Cuba and wrote his hypercritical book, *Guerrillas in Power.* Castro was then riding for his hardest fall, as preparations were already under way for the attempt at the ten-million-ton sugar harvest in 1970. The French agronomist René Dumont was to visit

Cuba the following year, 1969, and, as I wrote, come up with an even more devastatingly critical book.

Fidel Castro's career over the last two decades has been assailed by more prophets of doom than the tribe of Israel in the Old Testament—and with no more effect in getting him to change his ways.

"There can be no doubt that worker morale is the basic cause of the faltering Cuban economy," Professor Nelson wrote in his recent book on Cuba.

I do not see how anyone can be so sure of the unprovable. Nelson jumped to the same conclusions as all Western and Cuban capitalist economic experts and, in his case, without any personal, eyewitness knowledge of the Cuban workers, how they feel about the Revolution as a whole and not just their jobs. Because Americans and professional middle-class Cubans would be "weary" of "sloganeering" and "endless meetings," it is concluded that all or most Cubans feel the way Americans would feel. They think that there must be disillusionment "after years of worsening conditions and unfulfilled promises, of being denied the opportunity to work and accumulate goods and property for themselves and their families."

This overlooks so much about the Revolution that is good and is appreciated; it ignores the fact that if in many cases conditions worsened, in many others, at least as many, they were better; it forgets that an abnormal number of Cubans before the Revolution were unemployed and really "denied the opportunity to work."

If Professor Nelson's diatribe were true and all or even most Cuban workers felt so badly, how could one account for the fact that there has been a steady improvement in the Cuban economy, starting just after the prophets of doom began writing their books? The pity and sympathy are being wasted on a majority of Cubans today.

Both Guevara and Castro shared a positive aversion to money and a money economy.

"Money is a vile intermediary between man and the product of his labor," Fidel said in a speech in 1967, the year of Che's death. "We should not collect any interest because that is capitalism . . . Replace money by direct distribution and make it less and less important."

"The great task of the Revolution is to form the new man of whom Che spoke, the man with a truly revolutionary conscience, truly socialist, truly Communist," he said the following year in his July 26 speech. "We aspire to a way of life where man has no need of money to satisfy his essential needs for food, clothing and distractions, as is already the case with his medical needs and with education

. . . The Revolution desires to equalize revenues from top to bottom . . . We must not create conscience with wealth but wealth with conscience."

Castro was talking with his heart and not his head, and in practice he had to change these goals, but they were ideas that he had, at least broadly and vaguely, as early as January 1959. I know because he spoke to me about them. I wrote and said in lectures at the time that Fidel had a medieval objection to interest as the sin of usury. His diatribes against making money could have come out of Deuteronomy. (One of his foibles is to go around without a centavo in his pockets—but this is more regal than socialistic.)

A moneyless world would make moral incentives that much easier to rely upon. Fidel's hopes were at their zenith in the heady days of the "Great Revolutionary Offensive" of 1968. "Are we going to encourage the people by offering them money with which they could buy nothing?" he asked in his March 13, 1968, speech.

> Unfortunately, we cannot eliminate money at this stage of distribution, but we must cut off at least unlimited access to, and any privilege connected with, money. At present, we still cannot eliminate money but someday, if we are to reach Communism, we will do so . . . I know perfectly well what doing some of these things will cost, and how some out-dated academicians devoid of revolutionary sensitivity, some great-grandchildren of revolutionaries, will call us idealists, will say that we propose idealistic, unfeasible things.

(The reference to "out-dated academicians" was undoubtedly to the French critics René Dumont and Charles Bettelheim.)

In another reference he spoke slightingly of "the 'pure' economist, be he capitalist or socialist. In short, just a plain economist. But there is another science, a deeper science which is a truly revolutionary science. It is the science of revolutionary awareness; it is the science of faith in mankind; it is the science of confidence in mankind."

This dream of an ideal non-monetary socialistic world, as the decisions of the 1973 CTC Congress showed, has had to be, if not abandoned, at least considerably modified.

The Castro-Cuban zeal for "international socialism" probably exceeds that of any other member of the Communist bloc. It has not been imposed. Fidel has surely proved over the years that he has a sincere belief in the moral and material value of a unified, worldwide socialist bloc. Perhaps it is his mania for unity—a vital factor in his national policy—expressing itself on a global scale.

He goes beyond his Russian allies in this conviction, as he has done in clinging to as high a degree as possible of moral incentives. The Russians and the whole Eastern bloc abandoned them years before. Under classical Marxism, there had to be material abundance before moral incentives came into play. Morality did not seem to interest Karl Marx very much. Later generations of Marxists did concern themselves with the moral foundations of socialism, and Lenin went in for voluntarism, but by the time the Cuban Revolution came along, the Soviet Union was using material incentives in a big way.

The Russians discovered in 1929–1930 that if the peasants were not given their own private plots, the collective farms *(Kolkhozy)* would fail. Stalin made what he hoped was a temporary retreat, but even now in the 1970s the private plot remains of major importance to Soviet agriculture. Che Guevara never wanted to believe this; Fidel accepts it, but reluctantly and ungenerously. The chances are that he will give ground in agriculture as he is doing in industry with expanded material incentives and wage differentials, as well as private plots for farmers.

Even China has been reintroducing material incentives, surreptitiously but increasingly. It was hardly surprising that Fidel, in his July 26, 1973, speech should have harped on a continuing theme:

"We are in the Socialist stage of the Revolution . . . from each according to his capacity, to each according to his work . . . Together with moral incentive, we must also use material incentive . . . We must act in such a way that economic incentives will not become the exclusive motivation of man, or moral incentives serve to let some live off the work of the rest."

In introducing the new labor organization, the Army of Working Youth, on August 2, 1973, Raúl Castro put it bluntly. The government will "combine moral incentives of all kinds with material incentives, including payment for quantity and quality of work."

This was spelled out unmistakably in the theses adopted by the CTC National Congress in November 1973: "Each one must be remunerated according to the quantity and quality of his work," the declaration reads. "He who does more and better work must receive more. He who contributes more to society on his regular job should receive more from it, in just proportion to his contribution."

However, it was made clear that the reference was to "his regular job, because the great majority of our workers devote part of their free time to voluntary work for the good of society, without expecting or receiving any remuneration other than the moral satisfaction over the job done and the recognition of society for their conduct."

So the Marxist formula for the socialist stage of Communism became the basis for the CTC Congress: "From each according to his ability, to each according to his work." This was displayed in large red letters in the meeting hall and repeated endless times by orators, most emphatically of all by Fidel Castro in his speech at the end.

(This is one of many indications that the Cuban Revolution, like all modern revolutions, is moving inexorably to the "right" and toward institutionalization.)

There had been no special trouble with the labor force. Absenteeism was always a problem—after all, the Russians are still struggling with it after nearly six decades—but I was told in 1972 by Héctor Ramos Latour, then secretary general of the Central of Cuban Workers (CTC), that it was declining. The greatest problem, as always, was the generally low level of productivity. This is where material incentives naturally come in.

The old CTC (Confederation of Cuban Workers; the name was changed to Central of Workers in 1961) was discredited because its leaders, especially Eusebio Mujal, cooperated with the corrupt governments and were themselves corrupt. The new CTC, run until 1968 by the veteran Negro Communist Lázaro Peña, fell into disorganization in the years before the 1970 sugar disaster. From the day that Fidel announced the failure of the ten-million-ton *zafra*, a period of strengthening began, Ramos Latour told me. (He, incidentally, was one of the not very numerous heroes from the labor ranks in the anti-Batista Havana underground.)

Lázaro Peña, who was so honest and conscientious even when he collaborated with Batista that he did not use up his salary, was, as I said, reelected to the post of secretary general at the 1973 congress, but he was a dying man. Castro went out of his way to praise him in the most fulsome terms.

Preparations for holding the thirteenth CTC Congress were under way when I was in Cuba in the autumn of 1972. The twelfth had been held in 1966. It is claimed that some 1.5 million workers were consulted in 70,000 work centers all over the island. They elected 2,230 delegates to the congress. However, their work seemed primarily a case of discussing and modifying details of the "theses" submitted by the government's Organizing Commission for the congress. At least, everyone knew what was being done and why. Moreover, there is the promise now that "trade union representation on the management councils" and "participation by workers in economic management" are going to be improved. At the congress

Fidel attended every session but ostentatiously refrained from intervening.

Another promise is that: "The 13th Congress of the CTC recognizes the deep revolutionary significance of the incorporation of women into work of a social nature with equal rights and opportunities, and it proclaims the determination of the trade union movement to aid in that necessary recruitment."

Just how "democratic" the proceedings were is open to question. The "theses" drawn up by the Organizing Commission in August received a more than 99 percent vote in favor. It is true that the theses had been debated before and during the congress, but there do not seem to have been any significant alterations. Each vote at the plenary was unanimous.

The number of National Syndicates had earlier been raised from fourteen to twenty-two. The cost of belonging to the CTC is minimal —from twenty-five cents to one dollar, depending on the salary, but payment is officially "voluntary." So is membership. However, since 98 percent of Cuban workers belong, it must either be highly desirable or unavoidable.

In a regime like Castro's, which is a variation of totalitarianism, one does not know how to evaluate such statistics or what to believe about labor relations. When I asked Ramos Latour and some other labor leaders about strikes, they were surprised or amused. There are no reasons for them, I was told. "Strikes against whom?" Ramos Latour asked. "If there are complaints or problems there is machinery to handle them. All syndicates, since 1970, elect their leaders by secret ballot and meet every month. Up to now there have been no indications of workers wanting to strike. A meeting can be requested at any time." There is no legislation against striking; it is as if the idea were impossible. Before enactment every labor law is discussed at each work center, I was told.

All workers get one month's vacation with pay, and in some cases they are helped with lodgings on their holiday. When hurt, a worker is paid in full until he recovers. The minimum pension for old age has been $60 a month or higher, depending on the salary at the time of retirement.

"The trade union local," Jorge Risquet, minister of labor, explained, "being an organization of the working class, takes in all the workers in each work center, and the trade union leadership represents the workers who elected it; meanwhile the management represents the organization of the state, that is, it is charged with and held responsible for the correct use of the resources of the entire people and with the fulfillment of the production or service plans established on the basis of such resources."

The Castro regime was the first in Cuba to develop a comprehensive social security system. A Social Security Bank was created as early as 1959. The next year, old age and disability insurance was extended to embrace every wage and salary earner in Cuba. Before the Revolution, the mismanagement and pilfering of social security funds was an open scandal. Anyway, few workers benefited.

Here again, what Professor Dumont unkindly referred to as "economic laws" finally took effect. Social security has become impossibly costly at its present overgenerous rate. The plans as of early 1975 are to honor all retirement and disability pensions still being paid, but to repeal the old laws. New regulations will sustain "our social security in a correct ratio to the resources which our country has at its disposal."

It was frankly admitted that in the past "grave errors" occurred in the trade union system. "These doubts and errors have been criticized by Comrade Fidel, our leader and guide, on various occasions," the CTC Congress stated, "and especially in 1970, when he launched the slogan of strengthening the trade unions and the other mass organizations."

The trade union organization is not a part of the state apparatus or dependent on any ministry or the Communist Party, although the party "orients and directs the trade unions politically." The unions are autonomous in the sense of approving their own regulations or statutes and electing their governing boards.

It was doubtless inevitable that bureaucracy should be inflated in government and industry. As departments, organizations, and institutions increased in number, each one, by a variation of Parkinson's law, expanded to create new tasks, sometimes artificially, to justify its continuance and importance.

Fidel protested on many occasions. In a speech on February 20, 1967, he complained that everybody sought an office job; that far more men were needed to do a job than under capitalist owners; and that there were far too many forms to fill out.

One of the lessons that the 1970 sugar disaster taught Castro was that his government and the Communist Party had overcentralized—a heritage from the era of Che Guevara. He promised a "democratization of the labor movement" and of the revolutionary process generally, and he has taken some steps in this direction, as the 1973 Workers' Congress proved.

Absenteeism and all its kindred ills—malingering, loafing, and dawdling—was an especially acute problem. *"Señores,"* Fidel said in a speech to Cuban workers on August 30, 1966, "there is something that must be quite clear: the Revolution is the abolition of the exploitation of human labor but not the abolition of human work."

Between 1964 and 1967 agricultural labor camps, called Military Units for Aid to Production (UMAP), were established. By all accounts they were pretty harsh. Although abolished in the original form, different types of forced-labor camps continue to be used, mainly for habitual absentees and "loafers." In some cases, would-be emigrants are still being sent to labor camps. There are also a few camps where prisoners are "rehabilitated."

The major effort against absenteeism came in the Anti-Loafing Law, which went into effect on April 1, 1971. It was an example of post-1970 "democratization." As Fidel said in his July 26, 1971, speech, the law was discussed in advance by farmers, students, soldiers, and others in 115,000 meetings in which 3,265,000 people participated. He enlisted the support of the Committees for the Defense of the Revolution (CDR), which discussed the law in 52,707 of their committees with 1,348,666 citizens participating. The radio, television, newspapers, and magazines were used for explanations, suggestions, or arguments.

Article 12 of the law states that when accusations of loafing are made against persons or organizations, the CDR has the task of evaluating and, if warranted, publicly denouncing offenders. Between April and August 1971, 7,453 such cases were published.

"All citizens physically and mentally fit for work have a special obligation to work," the law reads. ". . . Those attached to work centers who absent themselves for more than fifteen days without explanation will be considered predisposed toward laziness [*vagancia*]." Those convicted of loafing will be punished by "a six-month to two-year confinement in a re-education center, where they will engage in productive activities"

Professor Lowry Nelson writes of the pre-1970 situation in his book on Cuba:

> Lamentably, the first dozen years of the revolution saw a steady reduction in agricultural production in absolute amounts. Meanwhile, the population increased from an estimated 6,548,000 in 1958 to 8,-553,395 enumerated in the census of September 1970. The production per capita is therefore much lower than the absolute decline in total amount. . . .
>
> Today more land is cultivated, more fertilizer applied, more trac-

> tors and their attachments and other mechanical aids utilized than ever before. Besides this heavy capital investment in agriculture, there has been since 1962 an extraordinary and ever-increasing infusion of human labor. Nevertheless, the results in production continue to fall short of the goals.

Why did they up to that time (1970)? One reason was the high quality of the emigrants—managerial and professional—who even now have not been entirely replaced. Experienced sugar-cane cutters by the thousands took advantage of the chance to move to easier work in the cities. The cattle, tobacco, and coffee industries all suffered similarly. Every commentator and visitor to the island during the Revolution has noted the shortage of labor in agriculture, although it was a policy of Fidel's to favor the countryside over the city. After 1963 the government controlled everything connected with agricultural production.

On October 4, 1963, the Second Agrarian Reform went into effect. It nationalized all private holdings over five *caballerías* (167 acres). Eleven thousand farms were taken over. The previous upper limit had been 402 hectares (1,000 acres). About 10,000 middle-range farmers were eliminated, leaving 150,000 small private farmers. Fidel promised that this would be the end of expropriations and that so long as they or their heirs farmed the land, their property rights would be respected. They have been, but under more and more controls from their government-run organization, the ANAP (Asociación Nacional de Agricultores Privadas). There are about 40,000 private farmers, who grow 90 percent of the tobacco.

The newly expropriated lands were turned into *granjas del pueblo* (people's farms), the basic form of organization of Cuba's socialized agriculture. The economic cost was enormous, as the middle-sized farms for cattle and dairy products produced far more before the 1963 reform than after. Moreover, great hardships were caused to thousands of families. Presumably, the middle-size farmers were proving a political danger to the Revolution. Farmers are a notoriously conservative element of any society.

As always, the Revolution came first and the economy second. It was a bad period, made worse by the most devastating storm to hit Cuba in her recorded history—Hurricane Flora, which began on October 6, 1963. It was one of those years which proved that the Cuban Revolution did not stand or fall on its economic performance.

Of course, there were better years, and in many respects even agriculture was being permanently improved. Land cultivation had increased by half in 1970 and by more since. The critical Professor Dumont saw "marked progress" in irrigation, artificial insemination, cement, and electricity. He grudgingly admitted, *cahin-caha* (in middling fashion) that despite its mistakes, the Cuban economy managed to progress.

"Fidel," he writes in his 1970 book, "has judiciously put the emphasis on hydraulics and artificial insemination of F1 cows [a cross of the Zebu or India Brahman with the Holstein]; *pangola* [grass] spreads its rich domain; rice has been intensively sown; the planting goes quickly if not under the best conditions."

This great emphasis on F1 cows, artificial insemination, and *pangola* is all Castro's idea. They are important contributions to the permanent structure of Cuban agriculture. When I was in Cuba in 1967 there was one major center for artificial insemination—the Rosafé Signet; in 1972 there were fourteen, with more on the way. Most of the best bulls are bought in Canada, which never broke trade or diplomatic relations with Cuba. It was not unusual for the Cubans to pay $100,000 or more for pedigree bulls. Cuba, I was told, is one of the four or five countries where there has been no hoof-and-mouth disease.

The F1 is a good milk producer. Before 1950 there was relatively little use of milk in Cuba. Only the large cities provided markets for fresh milk. Most of the milk was processed into butter, cheese, condensed and evaporated milk. Fidel has made Cubans into a milk-drinking people, especially the children up to the age of seven, who get a liter of milk a day. Before the Revolution the lower-income classes in Cuba did not use dairy products in their diet; they could not afford to. (Interestingly, one of the first things Salvador Allende did in Chile was to institute the practice of giving every child free milk. "If I were to die tomorrow," he told Cyrus Sulzberger of *The New York Times* in March 1971, "no one in Chile would ever dare to abolish the system.")

As Dumont writes, the Cuban peasants are still the greatest beneficiaries of the Revolution, and the most privileged. Between 25 and 30 percent of the gross national product is invested in agriculture. The nearly always critical Lowry Nelson concludes: "The large investment which the Revolution has made in agriculture could certainly assure Cuba of being one of the most modern and prosperous agricultural countries in the world by 1975–1980, assuming wise decisions are made politically."

Neither Nelson nor Dumont stresses one of the greatest advances being made in the agricultural sector—the intensive cultivation of citrus fruits. It is now Cuba's second largest export, after sugar. To be sure, this has been stepped up greatly only since 1970, but it was started before, especially on the Isle of Pines (which was unofficially renamed the Isle of Youth [Isla de la Juventud] in 1966). It is now a vast center for citrus growing and experimental agriculture for youths of both sexes from the ages of twelve to twenty-seven. The largest citrus fruit development, which Fidel thinks may be the largest in the world—the 200,000-acre Girón Citrus Fruit Plan—is in Matanzas Province.

Despite a natural instinct to suspect government pronouncements, it has generally been safe to accept official figures on *what has been done*—for instance, on the sugar, tobacco, and coffee crops; the production of nickel; housing; the fishing catch; road building; irrigation; and so forth. The Cuban annual reports to the U.N. Economic Commission for Latin America (ECLA) are, I understand, taken as reliable.

The latest published report at this writing, made on March 27, 1973, by Carlos Rafael Rodríguez in Quito, Ecuador, draws a very different picture from those found in any of the books I have mentioned. After my trip to Cuba in August-September 1972, I find the account presented by the Cuban Deputy Prime Minister believable, especially as the economy has since improved.

Nobody is better than Rodríguez at explaining the whys and wherefores of the Cuban political economy. He pointed to the distinction the Cubans make between growth and development. A large growth in industrialization, GNP, national average income, with high gold reserves, can be accompanied by mass poverty, malnutrition, unequal distribution of wealth, high unemployment, increase in nonproductive exports, and so forth. The growth does not lead to *development*. This is the case in Brazil.

Development, Rodríguez argued, "presupposes the economy's capacity to solve—during the process itself and especially upon its crystallization—the basic social problems of the nation: employment, health, education, adequate nutrition for all, housing, creative free time, etcetera.

> We are not going to tire the members of the Commission with a repetition of the figures that we have already presented on more than one occasion. It is well known that in this period of survival and construction we almost doubled the number of roads that existed in 1959; increased reservoirs for irrigation and other uses 150 times, reaching a capacity of 3,000 million cubic meters; doubled the power-generating system before the end of the decade; augmented a fleet which was

> practically invisible, having had less than 50,000 tons of dead weight, until it reached 500,000 tons, and the fishing industry increased its catch six times over. Our work with artificial insemination and cross-breeding of cattle is well known, and, according to experts at the highest world level—not only of the Food and Agriculture Organization—they compare favorably with the achievements of countries that have a more advanced technological level in this field.
>
> All this we have detailed at the meetings of ECLA on other occasions. When asked in the corridors how much our gross national product had increased and how much our per capita income was, we have always replied that we were not interested in an apparent growth that would decline afterward. What we wanted was to create the conditions that would assure us permanent development.

(All the same, figures for growth have been used in speeches by Castro and Dorticós and in articles in *Granma* and other publications.)

"The boom in our building-materials industry more than doubled capacity between 1970 and 1973," Rodríguez asserted. In general, construction made impressive advances all over Cuba after 1970. I watched a one-hour-and-forty-minute documentary film in Havana, made in 1972, of the island-wide construction industry. While it was done for propaganda purposes, the dozens and dozens of new works, built or building, were real: schools, blocks of flats, factories, reservoirs for irrigation, roads, port works, hospitals, dairies, and others. The great new port works in Cienfuegos was nearing completion. The time covered by the film was the two preceding years—after the 1970 sugar setback. Another five or ten years of such construction and Cuba will not only have been transformed, but will be much less dependent on sugar, with a more diversified economy.

I myself, going around the island, saw new housing centers, schools, hospitals, factories, dairies. A great deal of the housing was being done by the *microbrigadas* that I mentioned before—a rather successful invention of Fidel's in 1970. There were 1,058 such minicolumns, composed of 27,619 workers, Castro said on May Day 1973. Each factory, farm or industry assigned a group of men with various skills—carpenters, plumbers, bricklayers, and men or women who could do what they were told or shown. They gave up a year or two of their time, getting their normal wages or, in some cases, working voluntarily after hours or on weekends. Meanwhile, the jobs they left were taken over by the employees remaining, who apportioned the work as overtime without pay.

The *microbrigadas* have been absorbed into the new Army of

Working Youth. There is no doubt that they built a great many blocks of flats which were sorely needed. I had the impression that socially it was salutary, introducing desk workers to manual labor.

President Dorticós, in an interview he gave in Santiago, Chile, on June 4, 1973, claimed that "the construction sector showed a growth of more than 40 per cent in 1972." Overall economic growth in the same year, he said, was 10 per cent, while "the first quarter of 1973 showed a nationwide growth of 16 per cent."

The President was interesting on the fiscal situation, which is rarely mentioned in Cuba. It seems that one of the many shocks that came at the end of the 1970 *zafra* was that there was too much money in circulation.

"This reached truly alarming levels in 1970," Dorticós confessed. It caused "a financial imbalance in the face of which our Government had to, and did, react. This reaction, to be exact, began in the second half of 1971 and developed further in 1972 in the process of the recovery of our internal finances. In 1972 there was a 650 million peso [$650 million] drop in the amount of money in circulation . . . This has already led to conditions of financial health which permit the implementation of a correct wage policy which, in turn, contributes substantially toward raising our working classes' production levels."

"The application of material incentives has no value, no function in a situation of runaway inflation," Castro remarked in his closing speech to the 1973 Workers' Congress. But he added with satisfaction: "Effectively, money is beginning to have some value . . . Since 1971, there has been a process of disinflation, a reduction of money in circulation . . . A little further reduction, and we will be within the limits that are considered by the experts to be the normal limits of money in circulation."

These improvements were made in spite of what Fidel had called "adverse factors" in his July 26, 1971, speech. There was a severe drought in 1970, while 1971 had the sort of drought that occurs once in 140 years. Sugar, tobacco, rice, and pasture suffered. In June 1971, African pig fever was discovered. In Havana Province alone 410,000 pigs had to be sacrificed. From November 1973 to April 1974, there was another severe drought.

Carlos Rafael Rodríguez, in his speech to the ECLA, could say that "for Cuba, 1972 and 1973 are economic periods in which the increase in the production of certain items and the gross national product are not the reflection of accidental circumstances of our economy, but rather the first symptoms of the crystallization we have been talking about all these years and which, from 1975 onwards, will register even more certain and definitive results."

In November 1973, Fidel was able to announce better economic results generally, although, as he pointed out to the CTC Congress, the terms of trade had turned against Cuba as in all developing countries that export raw materials and depend for existence on imports of oil, wheat, and manufactured goods. As he said, while a higher price was being obtained for sugar, the increased cost of imports was "equivalent to selling sugar at 3 cents a pound."

However, in 1974, world sugar prices went on rising sensationally. As Ted Morgan wrote in an article for *The New York Times* of December 1, 1974, "Cuba's hard currency export earnings for 1974 will amount to an unprecedented $2 billion, double the 1973 figure."

For the first time, Fidel can speak with some credibility of the possibility of achieving a balance between payments (salaries, social services, education, health, et cetera) and available consumer goods and services. But this is, of course, at a still low, if improving, level of consumption. It is still an early stage of the worldwide energy and economic crisis, whose dimensions and effects Fidel can no more safely predict than the best financial brains of the greatest countries. However, the Cubans are now bravely working on their first five-year plan (1976–1980) of the Revolution, which, if all goes well, will be ratified at the long-delayed First Congress of the Communist Party in 1975.

"After years of 'socialism,' as Fidel Castro has called his program," writes Professor Nelson in *Cuba, The Measure of a Revolution*, "it is possible to appraise the consequences to Cuba in general and to agriculture especially."

Not at all! Although Nelson's book was published in 1972, his appraisal, as I said, is based on 1970 and preceding years, since which time there has been marked improvement and the very favorable trade agreement with the Soviet Union. There are still plenty of hardships, but Rodríguez's explanation in his ECLA speech in 1973 has some validity.

"In order for a country such as any one of ours [in Latin America] to overcome backwardness," he said, "the people are required to make huge sacrifices. Without them, the necessary rhythm of development will not be obtained."

Whether they had to endure quite so many sacrifices for so long a time is another matter, but one of degree, not substance.

In the first chapter, I gave the dramatic results of Castro's gamble to reach ten million tons of sugar in 1970. The final plans for the campaign were drawn up at a meeting of Fidel and his aides in Santa Clara on November 26–27, 1966. As he said on May 20, 1970, in first announcing the failure, the trade deficit with the Soviet Union and Cuba's debt had grown so steadily and become so large that "a great plan for increasing our sugar exports" offered the only possibility of extricating the country. "Ninety per cent of our articles have to be imported," he pointed out more than once, "for that was the way our economy was developed in the past."

The greatest previous harvest—7.3 million tons in 1952—was achieved in a *zafra* of 110 days. The originally all-American machinery was multinational by 1970, and so was transportation. Two-thirds of the 1,952 mills dated back to the nineteenth century; none was newer than 1927.

"In the old U.S.-built mills," Norman Gall wrote in the November 1971 *Commentary*, "the cane was [now] washed in new French filters, the sugar crystals separated in East German centrifugal machines, loaded by Czech cranes onto Rumanian railroad cars which took them to the ports where new Japanese suction-loading equipment poured them directly into the hulls of Soviet ships."

What was missing—fatally—were the hoped-for Russian cane cutters. The Russians had tried, but their first machine was what Fidel called "a great destroyer." The ground in Cuba is uneven and rolling, unlike Louisiana and Hawaii, where machines have been used successfully for many years. The first crop has to be cut with skill to preserve intact the bulbs on the stubble. This is one reason why the use of volunteers and amateurs was so wasteful. The plan envisaged a gradual build-up between 1967 and 1970, which did not take place.

Even the 1971 harvest was a poor one. Fidel announced afterward that henceforth all cane fields would be burned over to eliminate foliage before cutting the stalks. The cane must be cut immediately after the burning and transported quickly to the mills to grind without delay. Otherwise there is a loss of sugar content. The system requires more fertilizer, more frequent planting, and good maintenance, but Castro had discovered that it works well in Australia; he even bought cane-cutting machines from the Australians.

And, finally, the Russians did come up with what seemed to be a good machine. Fidel visited the Ukhtomski Agricultural Machinery Factory in Liubertsy, near Moscow, when he was in Russia in July 1972. They were finishing fifty self-propelled combines for Cuba, which apparently are satisfactory. (Ironically, the Ukhtomski factory was built in 1902 for the U.S. McCormick interests.) In a speech in

Chile on November 25, 1971, Castro had said that after ten years of experimenting "we have found the technical solution for the problem of the machines. These machines exist at last." Presumably, the machines work on the burned stalks. It will take years before Cuba can get enough of them to help substantially. One hundred fifty of the new improved harvesters arrived from the Soviet Union late in 1973, but Cuba is going to need a few thousand, at least.

After 1970 productivity increased; sugar ports were expanded and modernized; new railway lines and roads to the sugar mills, warehouses, and repair shops were built. Types of cane and planting in rows were improved. More than $500 million was spent in four years on irrigation, fertilizers, and plants. There was also some further rationalization of the *centrales* and plantations.

So it looks as if the Castro regime is at last on the way toward creating an efficient, highly productive sugar industry, a decidedly better one than existed before the Revolution. It has been, to use the Castro word, a long apprenticeship. For two years in a row (1973–1974) Cuba has produced harvests of 5.5 million tons or more, and at a time when sugar quadrupled in price on the world market. In June 1974, for instance, Cuba was selling her sugar at the phenomenal price of 26 cents a pound.

Of the 1974 crop, more than 2,000,000 tons were sold at world market prices for hard currencies. The Soviet Union was paying 20 cents a pound as part of a long-range contract.

However, by an extraordinary stroke of bad luck, 1973 and 1974, as I wrote, were years of such extreme drought that the canefields will be seriously affected through 1975 and 1976. President Dorticós said in October 1974 that the 1975 sugar harvest is going to be "a great challenge."

Sugar prices will most likely remain abnormally high for some years. The Cubans do not expect it to fall below 20 cents a pound in the foreseeable future. At existing prices, the 1975 harvest is expected to bring the equivalent of what 20,000,000 tons would have brought in 1970, the year Castro tried so desperately to reach 10,000,000 tons.

The "revolutionary" years, when every able-bodied citizen was drafted, amateurishly, into the harvesting of sugar, are apparently over. The 1974 *zafra* was done with 100,000 fewer men than the 1973 harvest. Thirty percent of the work was mechanized. The *zafra* was completed in the shortest time of any revolutionary sugar harvest.

For the nationalistic Cubans, it is not entirely strange that they have philosophically endured the vicissitudes, miscalculations, mistakes, and mismanagement of the Cuban sugar industry under the Castro regime. At least, it is now *their* sugar industry, which, by trial and error, they believe they are making efficient.

As with so many aspects of the Cuban Revolution, it is not enough to compile statistics; make comparisons; point out mistakes; and say how much better the American-controlled sugar industry in Cuba worked. This does not mean that the Cubans do not want to reach the level of efficiency and productivity of the American-owned plantations. Fidel did complain at the CTC Congress that "we use a much larger labor force than the capitalists used and we run the mills less efficiently than the capitalists did."

But as I keep saying, the social revolution needs more than economic statistics to be understandable. One has to think of the masses who toiled in the sugar industry before the Revolution—some 500,000 cane cutters and 50,000 mill workers. It was exhausting, intensive work for three or four months, followed by eight or nine months of deprivation in the *tiempo muerto,* the dead time. The Cuban Revolution gave these men and their families a chance to break out of this dismal and degrading cycle. The economic effect on the sugar industry during the 1960s was serious, but what about the human, the social, the health effects on those thousands of workers who either escaped into other fields or found that there would be work for them now during the "dead time" and that they need not go hungry?

One of the most remarkable economic accomplishments of the Cuban Revolution has received surprisingly little attention abroad. Fidel Castro has created a fishing industry with a relatively large and expanding fleet, Cuban-owned and in some cases Cuban-built, where little or nothing existed before 1959. It is bringing in precious hard currency and is growing so fast that the export of ocean fish and shellfish promises to become one of the most important features of the Cuban economy. At the same time, fish is becoming available to the Cuban consumer in ever-growing amounts.

According to official Cuban figures from the National Institute of Fishing, 150,229 tons of fish and shellfish were caught in 1973, which was seven times the 21,900 tons caught in 1958. The Cuban fishing fleet now works the South Atlantic from Brazil to South Africa, the Atlantic Ocean from Florida to Newfoundland, the Pacific off Peru, the Gulf of Mexico, and, of course, the Cuban shelf, where shrimp, lobsters, and crabs abound. Shellfish is the most lucrative export.

The shrimp fleet is completely mechanized. The two deepsea fishing fleets, which go for hake, tuna, and cod, now have forty-five large trawlers and steel long-line ships with the latest equipment. There are four high-speed refrigeration ships.

New ships are being built for Cuba by Spain, Peru, and Japan. Italy, Russia, and East Germany have also sold ships to Cuba. Cuban shipyards are now making boats of over thirty feet; more than one hundred were made in 1973, according to the *Granma* of April 14, 1974.

In mid-February 1974 the first voyage of a new Cuban maritime trade line, Eurocuba, was made. The four cargo ships, each 12,900 metric tons, will ply between Cuba and northern Europe. The vessels were still being paid for in 1975, but they have all-Cuban crews and when the cost is covered they will represent the first shipping line in the history of Cuba run and financed by a Cuban government.

Cuba is the world's second largest exporter of lobster, after Australia. "A plant for processing lobster, equipped by Denmark, Great Britain and Japan, was recently inaugurated in Caibarién," *Granma* reported on June 25, 1973. "It can turn out 5,000 tons of precooked lobster daily and has 150 workers."

I spent an afternoon on my last trip to Cuba visiting the Puerto Pesquera, the now-huge fishing port of Havana, with icehouses and a section to repair ships. The cost of running the port is met by repairing Russian vessels. Originally the shop had sixty Russian technicians, but they were gradually being replaced by Cubans and only seventeen were left in September 1972.

I boarded the *Océano Pacífico*, a large "mother" ship that fishes the Atlantic waters off South Africa. There were then two such ships taking turns at the trip; there are now four. They were bought from Italy for $15 million apiece. The crews, who are trained in Cuban technical schools, are eighteen to twenty-two years old, and the officers twenty-seven or twenty-eight, so it is a youthful fleet, grown up under the Revolution.

An even larger fishing port than Havana's is nearing completion at Cienfuegos on the south coast. Neither port is intended as a naval base for the Soviet Union, or even for Cuba. There was a great flurry in the Pentagon in 1971 when a part of the Russian naval fleet paid a courtesy visit to Havana and two submarines went around for a brief stop at Cienfuegos. The fears were unfounded; the two ports will always be available to Russian naval vessels for harbor or repairs, which is all the Russian navy would ever need, while the Cubans, it should be obvious, are not going to give still another foreign power a naval base on the island, and one that could be destroyed in seconds from the mainland.

Cuba is waiting patiently to see the Americans leave Guantánamo. The parting shot of the captain of the *Océano Pacífico* when I said good-bye was: "One of these days, we look forward to fishing from Guantánamo."

So far as the economy is concerned, I believe that there is enough evidence—some of it presented in this chapter—to bear out the point that I have been making since the beginning of this book: July 26, 1970, was the beginning of a new and better era in Cuba.

It would have been unbelievable even a few years ago, but in 1974 tourists from the non-Communist world began trickling back to Cuba—and on package tours, of all things! The first contingents, mostly from Western Europe, came during the summer. Bookings had already been made by June for Canadian tourists to go to Cuba in the winter of 1974–1975. These would have to be a different kind of tourist from the ones who went before 1959 to gamble or enjoy the luxury of first-class hotels and sunny weather. Cuba can offer an adventure—the fascination of seeing how a full-fledged revolution works—not to mention charm and friendliness, and all can enjoy the beautiful new Lenin Park. New hotels are being built at Varadero and Santa María beaches, partly with Canadian capital.

One cannot discuss the Cuban economy and ignore tobacco. The story makes a sad appendix to this chapter, although the Cubans claimed that the 1973–1974 tobacco harvest was the best in eight years, and exports are expanding steadily. I was told in London that $10 million worth of Cuban cigars were being imported into Great Britain in 1974. The problem is quality, not quantity.

The Cubans themselves—until Castro's 1971 rationing and discouragement of smoking—used to consume about 85 percent of the cigars they produced. They had their cigar chain smokers, as the rest of the world had its cigarette addicts. I had Cuban friends who smoked twenty-five or thirty cigars a day. Fidel, to set an example, gave up cigars early in 1971. There had been a press–radio–TV campaign to assure Cubans that smoking was bad for their health: *Fumar dana la salud* was heard and read everywhere. However, when rationing was dropped late in 1972 and replaced by the capitalist system of "rationing by price," Castro was one of the first to resume his cigar smoking.

The industry never employed many workers. The latest figure I found (1953) gives about 130,000 workers, compared to 485,000 in sugar. It is an intensive, personal-care crop, raised on small farms and requiring experts to grow the tobacco and to make the cigars. Cubans insist that the best cigars are hand rolled, although I suspect that is to protect workers who would lose their jobs if all cigars were machine rolled. In 1950, when Prío Socarrás was President, he managed to introduce some machines, and the Castro regime is bringing in more.

For cigar smokers the Cuban Revolution was a minor tragedy. With nationalization and expropriation, managers, foremen, and many experienced farmers went into exile. The quality of the famous brands dropped strikingly, although in any given year a discriminating buyer could discover that one brand or another—H. Upmann, Punch, Simón Bolívar, Por Larrañaga, Romeo y Julieta, Hoyo de Monterrey—in one size or another (usually No. 1, the largest, or the half-corona, the smallest) would be almost as good as before the Revolution.

For Americans the tragedy has been complete, since the 1962 embargo prevented any Cuban cigars from entering the United States, except by smuggling. Cuban exiles, some from the historic cigar families, produce cigars made from Canary Islands and other relatively smokable tobacco. They are to the real Havanas (the Spaniards call them *puros*) what California wine is to a Château Haut Brion. Before the Revolution the United States took $30 million worth of the $50 million average annual export of cigars and cigar tobacco.

Some famous brand names used to be rolled in Tampa, Florida, which made them cost less but with a considerable loss in quality, like French wine shipped in bulk and bottled in a foreign country. Just as all good wines taste best in the locality in which they are made, Havana cigars taste best when smoked in Cuba. (Curiously, frozen daiquiris also taste better in Cuba than elsewhere.)

Vuelta Abajo cigars are unique, a technician told me in San Juan y Martínez, the very heart of the region near the Hoyo de Monterrey *vega*, because of the deep, sandy soil, the ideal moist, warm climate, and the generations of experience of the farmers and others engaged in overseeing the crop from beginning to end. On my visit to Pinar del Río Province, which has now been developed richly with rice, citrus fruits, and dairies as well as tobacco, I was persuaded that there has been no decline in the quality of the tobacco leaves. The trouble, I decided after some checking, came in the Havana factories where the leaves are made into cigars.

The picturesque old wooden sheds for maturing the tobacco leaves, with their thatched roofs, are being replaced by little prefabricated cement sheds. They are hurricane-resistant, and the temperature can be controlled scientifically.

A great craft is in danger of lasting deterioration. The sons and daughters of the old-time tobacco growers, selectors, and cigar makers now get scholarships and go off to learn easier and better-paying trades and professions.

Cuba has suffered a serious and permanent loss, because already a generation of American cigar smokers does not know what a Havana cigar tastes like. They are satisfied with all kinds of inferior cigars and may remain so. When trade with Cuba is resumed, will they appreciate Havanas and be willing to pay the higher prices?

Cubans are also heavy cigarette smokers. The taste is quite unlike cigarettes smoked elsewhere in the world—excellent, but strong, sharp, and faintly like a cigar. They are not exported. Curiously, Cuban tobacco is quite unsuitable for pipes.

There is still hope for the cigar lover, as the Cubans are proving that when enough care is taken, the finest of cigars can still be produced. A new name has appeared in the last few years in Cuba: *Cohiba,* said to be the word the aboriginal Indians used for tobacco. The cigars are superb but as yet can be bought only in Cuba with foreign currency. Tourists can now enjoy them. Fidel Castro smokes them in a long panatela size *(panatelas largas)*, once made especially for him from the choicest leaves of the Por Larrañaga *vega.* It was one of his rewards for being the Maximum Leader.

CHAPTER 14

The Cultural Revolution

Revolution is the opium of the intellectuals.
—Simone Weil

In an authoritarian regime, the most restive element is the intelligentsia. Intellectuals suffer the most keenly of all citizens from lack of civic liberties, since one cannot write, paint, criticize, or even philosophize in a natural and true way without a free society and a free press. Many intellectuals and artists can and do place the good of a cause—or government—above their art, but then they must hold their creative talent in check.

The problem that a dictatorial regime faces is the extent to which it can permit freedom that includes opposition without too great a danger to the fabric of the government. Fidel Castro decided within a year that a free press was perilous, but he allowed surprising latitude in literature and the arts, off and on, for a number of years.

There were no restrictions on artists and writers for the first few years. Bookshops imported and sold counterrevolutionary books, magazines, and newspapers. There was a temporary setback in 1961 when a congress of writers and artists was held in Havana. Fidel was under strong pressure from the old-guard Communists to introduce "socialist realism." On June 30 he addressed the congress, saying that he did not want to impose any particular line on writers and artists, but added that they should respect revolutionary needs. This means, he said in a Mussolinian paraphrase: "For those within the Revolution, complete freedom; for those against the Revolution, no freedom."

This, of course, did limit freedom, especially since the arbiter of the limits was the Castro government. Out of the cultural congress came a state organization—the Union of Artists and Writers of Cuba (UNEAC). The National Council of Culture was reorganized. The independent, broad-minded literary weekly *Lunes de Revolución* was closed down. Foreign Western publications disappeared. Publishing firms came under government control. The press, television, and radio were, of course, censored.

And yet, in practice, a considerable degree of freedom was tolerated. The openness of the Cuban cultural field for a number of years to "heresies" like abstract painting, black humor, satire, criticism, unorthodox radicalism, and the like was probably a conscious choice on Fidel Castro's part. He told Lee Lockwood in 1965 that he favored the freest intellectual discussion and was opposed to every sort of prohibition or black lists of books and films, even foreseeing the publication in the future of counterrevolutionary works.

No doubt, as usual, he believed what he said when he said it. He would not have had any aesthetic feeling for one kind of art against another. He is not an intellectual and was not educated to a trained appreciation of any art.

The heyday of cultural freedom in Cuba—about 1964 to 1968—coincided with an era of bad feeling or coldness between Havana and Moscow. Soviet-style "socialist realism" was ridiculed. Castro enjoyed and courted support from the radical intelligentsia of Western Europe and Latin America. But once freedom threatened, or seemed to threaten, the stability and ideology of the Revolution, the story was different and so was Castro's attitude. He went back to his stern dictum of June 30, 1961: "For those within the Revolution, complete freedom; for those against the Revolution, no freedom."

The heights of intellectual freedom were reached with the importation in July 1967, at considerable cost, of *avant-garde* painting and sculpture from the Paris Salon de Mai. Scores of well-known artists and writers were invited, all expenses paid. And six months later came the grand climax in Havana when a Cultural Congress with five hundred intellectuals from seventy countries attended a week of performances, lectures, and ceremonies.

Fidel's sensational speech of January 12, 1968, was a barely veiled denunciation of the Soviet Union, as well as a warm expression of thanks to his foreign guests for having come. There was a rare note of bitterness against the Russians that must have been smoldering inside him. Between the OLAS (Organización Latino-Americana de Solidaridad) conference in July 1967 and the Cultural Congress in January, Che Guevara had been killed, abandoned, and, in a sense, betrayed by the official Communist Party of Bolivia. The OLAS meeting had been an attempt by Castro to take over the Latin American revolutionary movements from the Communist parties which were directed from Moscow. It failed.

The death of Che, said Fidel in his January 12 speech, made "the most profound impact" on the intellectuals but not on the Communist organizations and parties, "who are incapable of understanding and will never understand why he died, nor will they ever be capable of dying as he did, or of being revolutionaries, as he was." Marxism, he added bitingly, should act like a revolutionary force and not a pseudo-revolutionary church.

For intellectuals who had come to Havana to attend the Cultural Congress, he had nothing but gratitude. "Our Revolution will not betray the confidence and hopes which you have placed in it," Fidel said in conclusion.

Naturally, the writers and artists went away from Cuba feeling that cultural freedom was safe in Castro's hands. Then came the sensational case of Heberto Padilla, the Cuban poet, which brought worldwide condemnation from intellectuals and signaled a change of the cultural climate of Cuba, no doubt permanently, into the typical policy of all dictatorial regimes.

The change would have come in any event. Padilla could not have done the Revolution serious harm, or perhaps any harm. He was not that important. Through clumsy handling by the Cubans and overreacting by the intelligentsia, what should have been a storm in a teacup turned into a hurricane.

Heberto Padilla was born in Pinar del Río in 1932 and began writing poetry and radio scripts as a youth. He taught in the United States and lived there during the resistance against Batista, returning to Havana only in January 1959, after the Castroites had triumphed. The revolutionaries did not let this be forgotten. Moreover, his parents and a sister went into exile in Miami.

In Havana he worked at first for *Lunes de Revolución*, the weekly literary supplement. After it was suppressed in 1961 he was employed by Prensa Latina, the news agency, and by *Granma*, for which he was a correspondent in Prague and Moscow. The Cuban ambassador to Czechoslovakia, Enrique Finlay, told me in Havana in 1972 that in Prague Padilla professed to be fervently pro-government.

K. S. Karol called him "one of the best poets of his generation." A book of poetry he wrote won a national award from the Cuban writers' union (UNEAC) in October 1968, but they published it with a disapproving introduction.

Here is a poem from it in my own unpoetical translation. It is from a collection called *Fuera del Juego* ("Out of Play," or "Offside";

published in a French translation as *Hors de Jeu*). The poem is entitled "Instructions for Admission into a New Society."

> In the first place: optimism.
> Secondly: be correct, circumspect, submissive.
> (Having undergone all the sport tests)
> and to finish, march
> as do all the other members:
> one step forward,
> two or three backwards:
> but always applauding.

His play, *Seven Against Thebes*, was given a prize at the same time. However, Padilla was forbidden to make the trip abroad which was to have been a part of the prize. Later, he lost his job on the *Granma.*

Padilla was obviously unhappy. The authorities believed that he was using his connections with the Cuban and foreign intellectuals to sow "counterrevolutionary" ideas and information. Haydée Santamaría, whose institute had published his books, said that Padilla had ideas of becoming a spokesman for the intellectuals and thought that because he was a poet he should have privileges ordinary mortals would not have. The authorities felt that there was an incipient danger, as with the Hubert Matos case. *Verde Olivo,* organ of the Armed Forces, attacked Padilla and other "counterrevolutionary" writers.

On March 20, 1971, without any specific reason being given or charges made, Heberto Padilla was arrested and kept in jail. The news got around, of course. One of his close friends was Carlos Franqui, former editor of *Revolución,* who was then living in Paris. The Castroites believed that Franqui mobilized the formidable group of intellectuals who signed a letter to Castro which was published in *Le Monde* on April 9:

> The undersigned, supporters of the principles and objectives of the Cuban Revolution, address you in order to express their disquiet as a result of the imprisonment of the poet and writer, Heberto Padilla, and to ask you to reexamine the situation which this arrest has created. . . .
>
> At this moment . . . the use of repressive measures against intellectuals and writers who have exercised the right of criticism within the revolution can only have deeply negative repercussions among the anti-imperialist forces of the entire world and most especially of Latin America, for which the Cuban Revolution is a symbol and a banner.

Among the distinguished signers were Simone de Beauvoir, Carlos Franqui, Carlos Fuentes, Juan Goytisolo, Alberto Moravia, Octavio Paz, Jean-Paul Sartre, Jorge Semprún, Mario Vargas Losa, and Julio Cortázar. These had been some of the most important sympathizers among the intelligentsia of the Cuban Revolution. They saw the arrest of Padilla—I believe wrongly—as due solely to his literary criticisms of the regime. After the firm promise Castro had made at the OLAS conference in 1968 that the Revolution "will not betray the confidence and hopes" that the intellectuals had placed in it, the arrest of Padilla came as a shock. The intellectuals felt deceived.

Yet anyone who knew Castro could be sure that at the OLAS meeting and Cultural Congress he had spoken in complete sincerity. He must have been carried away, as so often, by enthusiasm, excitement, and adulation. Evidently, he had not at the time made the connection, which was later to strike him so forcibly, between cultural freedom and political freedom. To be sure, when UNEAC was formed in 1961, its declaration of principles contained this sentence: "We consider it to be absolutely necessary that all writers and artists, regardless of individual aesthetic differences, should take part in the great work of defending and consolidating the revolution."

Padilla was doing the opposite. He was held in jail, incommunicado, for thirty-nine days and was released only after writing a long, abject letter confessing wrongdoing and wrong thinking. This was the real shocker, because its resemblance to the form of confession of Communist prisoners in the Stalin era was so striking that there was an inevitable worldwide reaction of protest. The Cubans were surprised, dismayed, and outraged. Cuban naïveté, displayed at the time of the 1959 executions, had repeated itself. The Padilla letter was ingenuously distributed in New York by the Cuban Mission to the United Nations with complacent self-righteousness.

The confession was four thousand words long. These excerpts are from the Cuban Mission's text:

> I have meditated profoundly before deciding to write this letter. I am not doing so through fear of the inevitable and just consequences of my contemptible, well-known and demonstrated attitudes—demonstrated far beyond what I myself could ever have imagined possible. I am moved by a sincere desire to make amends, to compensate the Revolution for the harm I may have occasioned and to compensate myself spiritually. I may prevent others from losing themselves stupidly.
>
> But, above all, I desperately want to be believed and my action not

to be taken for cowardice, although I myself am overcome with shame at my own actions. . . .

Under the guise of the writer in revolt within a socialist society, I hid the opposition to the Revolution; behind the ostentations of the critical poet who paraded his sickly irony, the only thing I really sought was to leave conscience [*sic*] of my counterrevolutionary hostility. Among both Cubans and foreigners I accused the Revolution unjustly of the worst things. I discredited every one of the initiatives of the Revolution, striving to look like an intellectual who was an expert in problems on which I neither had information nor knew anything about. . . .

I, who had not achieved anything either before or after the Revolution, wanted fame and looked for it along a road that could only lead to counterrevolution. . . .

My egoism was growing by leaps and bounds . . . Because my vanity then had no limits, I carried my disaffected political position to heights I never should have scaled: in my poetry I was convinced that a poem which would represent a supposed criticism of the Revolution would awaken the interest of certain international circles: the circles of skepticism and hatred toward revolutions. That is how I came to write insidious and provocative poems which . . . expressed nothing more than the temperament of the unbeliever, the cynic, a versemaker trapped by his own moral and intellectual limitations. . . .

Since one of my aims was to attract the attention of our leaders and show them that I was a writer respected abroad who had to be consulted and listened to, I began to feel great despair when the months went by and nobody paid any attention to me. So after a year of sterile waiting to be called and to be given a position that would correspond to what I imagined my intellectual rank to be, I decided to write a short letter to the Prime Minister, Major Fidel Castro, telling him that I had no work and that I needed work. Almost immediately I received a reply from the Prime Minister through the Rector of the University of Havana, granting my request for work which after an analysis of my aptitudes and desires would consist of translation for the University, because of my knowledge of foreign languages. . . .

I have been tremendously ungrateful, unjust to Fidel, and the deep repentance I feel for having acted that way motivates me to make amends for my cowardly and counterrevolutionary virulence. . . .

I can speak of these gross faults of mine with clarity, without any subterfuge, because I have been able to measure the degree of decadence I had reached and the force and vehemence with which I want to rectify everything.

This experience is and will always be unforgettable in that it has

> divided my life in two: that of the past and that which I want it to be today.
>
> I beg the Revolutionary Government to give me the chance of carrying this out. If I desperately ask to be granted this opportunity, it is because of the deep conviction I have that this experience of mine can have value not only for myself but can go far beyond my own person: that this experience of mine can be of extraordinary use to other Cuban writers, for the reason that a great part of the despicable activities I have described and the style of living and the social conduct I have maintained until now have been, and I should say still are, those of a large number of our writers. . . .
>
> I ask to be allowed to expose these facts publicly, to discuss and to argue with those who are falling or are going to fall into the same errors as my own. I am convinced that my personal experience and my words will be irrefutable and some good talents will be able to free themselves from the crude traps laid by the enemy, and perhaps they may be of use to the revolutionary cause.

Enrique Finlay of the Foreign Ministry, who, as I said, knew Padilla well in Prague and Havana, has a theory that the letter was deliberately couched by Padilla in the terms of a Stalin-type confession, knowing what the worldwide reaction would be. He sees it as the poet's sardonic revenge on his Cuban enemies.

Padilla's self-abasement seems exaggerated, and his newly professed dedication to the cause of the Revolution is a factor that would have to be accepted with caution. He was never a revolutionary. His behavior and his letter show weakness of character, not coercion. What manner of man calls himself "contemptible, deceitful, unworthy, false, vain, a defamer, a hypocrite," and similar epithets? One cannot say that since the torment of "brainwashing" works in Russia it could have worked in Cuba, because Padilla was a unique case. The groveling note arouses either distaste or, in the case of the critics abroad, pity for him and condemnation for the regime.

He told James Higgins, a freelance newspaperman, who quoted him in *The Boston Globe* of August 5, 1971: "Perhaps the best way to put it is to say that I was accused of damaging the Revolution on the cultural front by shooting off my mouth incessantly to enemies of the Revolution." He said to Higgins that he believed he had influenced K. S. Karol and René Dumont by "my personal, bitter view of things, which reinforced their own cynicism."

When Higgins asked him what methods had been used to change his outlook, he said: "Discussions."

"Many Western observers assumed that the confession had been extracted from him [Padilla] by psychological pressure and 'brainwashing,'" it is stated in the *Amnesty International Report on Torture* published in London in November 1973. It refers to the charge as "an allegation." There is no evidence that Padilla was questioned or "brainwashed" in a cruel or unusual way.

Padilla agreed with security officials to destroy the manuscript of a new novel which, among other things, contained a caricature of Fidel.

The reaction to the letter abroad made Heberto Padilla a worldwide sensation for weeks. Sixty European, United States, and Latin American intellectuals wrote a letter to Castro which was given to the press on May 20, 1971, expressing their disillusionment with him. They were, on the whole, writers of high distinction who had favored the Revolution. The second letter, like the first, was published in *Le Monde* of Paris.

One of the signers, the Cuban novelist Juan Arcocha, seems to have been the source of the accusation, also in the same issue of *Le Monde*, that the Padilla letter could have been obtained only by torture. He wrote an article, "Le Poète et le Commissaire," in which he said: "I tremble when I think of the future of the Cuban Revolution. We have already seen in other countries where such practices can lead."

A prominent French authority on Latin America, Marcel Niedergang, also in *Le Monde* on the same day, said that the letter marked the effective break of Western intellectuals with the Cuban regime which they had so enthusiastically supported in the 1960s.

It did nothing of the sort. The intellectuals struck out blindly, in haste, with the best motives but with insufficient knowledge of the case and of Fidel Castro and his revolution. The letter they wrote was unfair, simplistic, and politically unsophisticated. What was worse, the signers had missed the forest for one insignificant tree. Between the dates of their two letters, the Castro regime had come out with a declaration of intent that was truly disheartening to all believers in cultural liberty.

The text of the intellectuals' letter, in translation, was printed in *The New York Times* of May 22, 1971:

> We hold that it is our duty to inform you of our shame and anger.
>
> The deplorable text of the confession signed by Heberto Padilla can only have been obtained by means that amount to the negation of revolutionary legality and justice.
>
> The contents of this confession, with its absurd accusations and

> delirious assertions, as well as the pitiable parody of self-criticism to which Heberto Padilla and Comrades Belkis Cuza, Díaz Martínez, César López and Pablo Armando Fernández submitted to at the seat of the National Union of Cuban Writers and Artists, recall the most sordid moments of the era of Stalinism, with its prefabricated verdicts and its witch-hunts.
>
> [It is] with the same vehemence that from the very first day was ours in defending the Cuban revolution, which seemed to us exemplary in its respect for the human being and in its struggle for liberation, that we exhort you to spare Cuba dogmatic obscurantism, cultural xenophobia and the repressive system imposed by Stalinism on the socialist countries and of which events similar to those now occurring in Cuba were flagrant manifestations.
>
> The contempt for human dignity implied in the act of forcing a man into ludicrously accusing himself of the worst treasons and indignities does not alert us because it concerns a writer but because any Cuban comrade—peasant, worker, technician or intellectual—can also become the victim of similar violence and humiliations.
>
> We would want the Cuban revolution to return to what made us consider it as a model in the realm of socialism.

The names put to it were the same as those who signed the first letter in *Le Monde*, with some equally distinguished additions: Susan Sontag, Marguérite Duras, Giulio Einaudi, Pier-Paolo Pasolini, Alain Resnais, Nathalie Sarraute, and others.

The New York Times, on the same day, gave Padilla the honor of its daily profile, written by someone who knew little of the true situation.

José Iglésias, who knows Cuba so well and has written so well about the Revolution, came out with an emotionally hostile article in *The New York Review of Books*. Even I. F. Stone, in his *Weekly*, called the Padilla confession "as phoney as the worst in the Stalin era and in Czechoslovakia's Slansky affair." It is a pity that anyone so honest and sincere as "Izzy" Stone should know so little of Fidel Castro as to put him in a category with Stalin.

This was where the letter was so unfair. To criticize the Cuban regime and Fidel Castro for disappointing the hopes of the intellectuals everywhere that the Revolution could carry on in an atmosphere of cultural freedom is one thing. To jump to the conclusion that Padilla's letter *must* have been forced out of him by violence was unjustified. Suspicion may have been warranted, but not certainty. To imply that Fidel Castro would allow or condone torture and to compare his regime to Stalin's was outrageous.

The charges still rankled when I talked to the Cuban leaders about the Padilla case more than a year later. Armando Hart, in Santiago de Cuba, pointed out that no Cuban intellectual or author of any prominence (he was dismissing Juan Arcocha) backed Padilla except Carlos Franqui. It was the one Cuban name that had struck me among the signatories.

Franqui was the son of a poor peasant from Las Villas. He joined the Communist PSP and worked for its newspaper, *Hoy,* but he was fractious and was expelled from the party in 1947. ("Carlos Franqui never was a revolutionary," Castro said to me. "He couldn't even stay in the Communist Party.")

Although Fidel denied him the right to call himself a revolutionary, he had run an underground anti-Batista newspaper in the Havana resistance, and he joined Fidel in the Sierra Maestra at the end of 1957. There he edited material for Radio Rebelde and the mimeographed *Revolución,* the organ of the 26th of July Movement. (Even at that, Castro was sarcastic to me. "He had ambitions to be a world-famous writer," said Fidel. "Why, many times up in the Sierra I had to write the bulletins for Radio Rebelde. He couldn't even write them properly!")

Franqui fell from favor in June 1963 when, on returning from a visit to Russia, Castro sharply attacked *Revolución* in a speech because of the way it had covered the story of his trip. Franqui was dismissed from his editorship and spent the next four years on odd jobs, including helping Castro compile an autobiography for the Italian publisher Feltrinelli. Nothing came of the venture. I asked Fidel about it in 1972 and he gave me much the same answer he had given me five years before: "I decided that first I would make history, and then write it." In 1967, he had said: "I want to make history, not write it."

Franqui's former colleagues and the government leaders believe that he was resentful because he had been pushed aside. His health was poor and, Fidel told me, they agreed to send him to Paris to help him.

When I remarked to Juan Almeida that I was surprised to see Franqui, of all people, turning against the Revolution, he exclaimed: "*No, señor!* he never was with the Revolution; he was always disloyal." It was an old story—by their standards a truly loyal revolutionary never would or could change; past appearances, therefore, were deceptive.

The two letters by the Western intellectuals in *Le Monde* were answered by a letter from a group of nearly fifty Cuban artists and writers. Most of the major figures in the Cuban cultural world had remained loyal. Among the signers of the reply were Alicia Alonso, Alejandro Carpentier, Nicolás Guillén, Lisandro Otero, and Julio Le Riverend.

Their letter was likewise intemperate and uncomprehending. It accused the critics of serving Yankee imperialism, of falsely claiming to have defended the Revolution out of "snobbism and vanity." It was especially vehement against "the infamy of saying that physical or moral violence is used against prisoners held for counterrevolutionary activities."

Extraordinarily, no one was hitting the mark. Between those two letters of the intellectuals, the first and presumably permanent guidelines for Cuba's world of news, literature, and art had been published. It was the final blow to any official freedom of culture.

A National Congress on Education and Culture had been held in Havana from April 23 to 30, 1971. It ended with a long "Declaration" that was dismally similar to the policies of all totalitarian regimes, Communist and Fascist, of modern times. It expressed the conviction that culture must serve the state, or, in Cuba's case, the Revolution, as its *raison d'être,* thus putting limits to purely artistic expression as well as to free opinion.

Every form of "bourgeois ideology" was condemned in the Declaration. No half measures were to be permitted "in the field of the ideological struggle" (i.e., Marxism-Leninism). "All trends are condemnable and inadmissible that are based on apparent ideas of freedom as a disguise for the counterrevolutionary poison of works that conspire against the revolutionary ideology on which the construction of socialism and Communism is based." Measures were to be taken to change the rules for national and international literary contests, and more care would be exercised in inviting foreign writers and intellectuals.

Here are some excerpts from the long Declaration which adequately explain the new policies:

> Art is a weapon of the Revolution . . . Our art and literature will be a valuable tool for the formation of our young people in the spirit of revolutionary morals, excluding selfishness and other aberrations typical of bourgeois culture . . . True genius is to be found among the masses and not among a few isolated individuals. . . .
>
> The radio, television, cinema and press are precious instruments for ideological formation and for the creation of a collective con-

science. The mass media cannot be left to chance or be used without directives. . . .

We want ideological coexistence only with revolutionary peoples, socialist culture and the forms of expression of the Marxist-Leninist ideology. . . .

Culture, like education, is not and cannot be apolitical or impartial, for it is a social and historic phenomenon motivated by the demands of social classes, by their struggles and their interests during all of history. . . .

We condemn the false Latin American writers who, after their first success due to works which express the drama of their peoples, have broken the links with their countries of origin to install themselves in the capitals of the decayed and decadent societies of Western Europe and the United States and become the agents of metropolitan imperialist culture.

Paris, London, Rome, West Berlin, New York offer these Pharisees a terrain propitious for their ambiguities, their hesitations and their contradictions, motivated by the cultural colonialism which they accept and profess. Revolutionary peoples will accord them only the scorn which traitors and deserters merit. . . .

We reject the pretensions of the mafia of bourgeois intellectuals, calling themselves leftists, to become the critical conscience of society.

Fidel made an exceptionally bitter and violent speech to close the Congress on April 30, full of vituperation against his critics, many of whom had been invited to the previous cultural meeting in January 1968, where they were praised and thanked by Castro. They were "pseudo-leftists who hope to win their laurels living in Paris, London and Rome." They will never again "be able to use Cuba . . . Our contests will never again give them the chance to come here as jury members . . . Only revolutionaries will find the doors open to them.

"Now you know it, bourgeois intellectuals and bourgeois libelers, agents of the CIA and intelligence services of imperialism," he raved on.

You will not be allowed to come to Cuba just as the UPI and AP are not allowed to come. Our doors will remain closed indefinitely. . . .

Our standards are political. There cannot be aesthetic value without human content or in opposition to man, justice, welfare, liberation and the happiness of men. For a bourgeois, anything can have aesthetic value, anything which entertains, amuses or helps him to overcome his boredom as a lazy, unproductive parasite. But these cannot be the standards of a worker, of a revolutionary and a Communist. . . .

For our revolutionary people, the value of cultural and artistic creations is in direct function to their utility; we recognize a value to the degree that they contribute to the liberation of man, to the happiness of man.

The crux of the unending dispute over cultural freedom was in his repeated assertion that "our evaluation is political." He did not mean, literally, that such entertainments as whodunits should be banned. In fact, Cuba's first detectiver—a very good one—came out in 1971 and was a best seller. The speech must be taken as polemics and as evidence that Fidel was in a state of fury.

"Why, they even compared me to Stalin! *Yo!*" he said indignantly to me a year and a half later.

"There have been many calumnious accusations against the Revolution by the imperialist enemy," Castro said for *Verde Olivo* of June 6, 1971, "but some truths are so clear, so universally recognized that we consider the statement that even a single citizen of this country could have been the victim of physical torture to be an act of the utmost baseness, a most infamous calumny against the Revolution. This Revolution will *never* pardon those who even insinuated that our Revolution could have recourse to physical tortures to obtain any objective."

Haydée Santamaría, who as director of the Casa de las Americas was deeply involved in the whole affair, had her own instinctive reaction. She is, as she has amply proved, a very brave human being. After denying to me, in typically voluble and passionate terms, that any pressure or torture was brought to bear on Padilla, she scathingly made the point that if he did not want to write his letter of confession, he was a coward to have done so, and therefore beneath contempt.

"Thousands of Cubans, thousands of women, who are the weaker sex," she said, "stood torture for the Revolution under Batista without speaking or yielding."

The criticism I made to her and others in Havana was that even granting that Padilla had volunteered his letter, it was most unwise (I was thinking, even stupid) to publish it. Reading the letter in London before going to Cuba, I had a natural shock of disbelief in its genuineness, for it was, indeed, exactly the type of confession extracted in Russia during the Stalinist purge. I ascribed the whole incident to the inveterate Cuban ignorance and innocence about the "free world's" reactions to what Cubans do and say in all self-righteousness. The inability of Fidel Castro and his associates to understand the system of Western democracy or the character and temperament of North Americans and Western Europeans has been a source of unending dismay to friends and sympathizers. Criticism of their mistakes or policies that they consider honest or fair is not resented when it comes from friends, well-wishers, or detached observers. It is when criticism is hostile, and especially when it impugns their patriotism, dignity, or honor (the Spanish *pundonor*), that the reaction is fierce.

The lack of understanding is, of course, mutual. The two letters by the intellectuals were another proof of that. They thought the Cuban Revolution was something that it wasn't. One of the irritations to the Cubans was that their accusers acted as if intellectuals were a special, privileged class who must rush to the defense of other intellectuals simply because they are members of the same cult.

In talking to me on the subject in 1972, Fidel said that one trouble with the intellectuals of Europe and Latin America who turned against him was that they were romantics; they constructed an ideal revolution in their heads and had no idea of the tremendous difficulties that have to be faced or of the dangers from counterrevolution.

He might have been quoting De Tocqueville on Lamartine and the *Carbonari* who became revolutionaries *pour se desennuyer*—a relief from boredom.

So far as Heberto Padilla was concerned, as Haydée Santamaría said, he was not arrested because he was a writer, but because of his activities against the Revolution. After all, his poems and play had been printed and even given an award.

Padilla stated a truth in his confession when he said: "I knew that every skillful blow that I aimed at any aspect of the Revolution would increase my popularity with the so-called liberals and democratic journalists and writers." It has been highly unpopular in the United States to be pro-Cuba. Hence, there is a temptation for a discontented, unsympathetic writer like Padilla to play to the liberal gallery and thus become important. He clearly did not aim for martyrdom, or he would not have signed the letter. (In 1975, incidentally, he is living quietly and without molestation in Havana, working in a government bureau.)

He was no Alexander Solzhenitzyn or Andrei Sakharov or Andrei Almarik fighting for intellectual freedom and deliberately seeking martyrdom. There are no Cuban equivalents. Nor can one say for either Cuba or the Soviet Union that the *people* are concerned about cultural freedom. Their wages, working conditions, and social services are not touched by the intellectuals.

Besides, the Cuban Cultural Congress had been preceded by six months of discussions by ten thousand teachers and intellectuals. There had been a week of plenary sessions and committee meetings before the Congress. In its way, the Declaration was the result of a national debate on cultural problems. No doubt there were many dissidents at heart, but they did not speak up.

When I was in Cuba I did not feel that the rigid precepts of the 1971 cultural declaration were being followed very strictly. The concern is political, not aesthetic.

There was a socio-cultural feature in the declaration and in the conflict with the intelligentsia: homosexuality. This had nothing to do with the twice-married father Heberto Padilla.

A fierce campaign against homosexuals began in mid-1965. They were drafted into the UMAP (Military Units to Aid Production). Intellectuals were especially persecuted, and there was a severe purge at Havana University. It brought a protest from UNEAC (Union of Cuban Writers and Artists) which led to the dissolution of the UMAP in 1967, but it did not end the ill-treatment of homosexuals.

There seems to be an unusually strong emotional aversion to homosexuals in Cuba—which Castro shares. The repression evidently upset many foreign intellectuals.

> As for homosexual deviations, [the 1971 Declaration reads] they bring up the question of social pathology. It is our principle not to admit its manifestations in any way. Its propagation must be avoided but this complex problem should be resolved on the basis of a profound study which will indicate the measures to be taken. . . .
>
> On the subject of homosexuality, the Commission arrived at the conclusion that it was inadmissible that under the pretext of "artistic talent," notorious homosexuals should gain influence over our youth. . . .
>
> It must be avoided that persons whose morality damages the prestige of our revolution can be members of artistic delegations sent abroad.
>
> Finally, severe penalties will be applied in the case of the corruption of minors, of systematic depravity and of incorrigible antisocial attitudes.

The battle over cultural freedom must not be allowed to hide the fact that the Revolution has done a great deal for the arts and has taken culture to the people for the first time in Cuban history.

Before the Revolution there was only one orchestra—the Philharmonic Orchestra of Havana, which never left the capital. There are now three important orchestras—the best of them the National Symphony, created in 1960 "to offer concerts for all people and work assiduously to educate our people in the love of music." It regularly tours the island. Some of the smaller provincial towns now have their own local orchestras, aided by the government.

"The regime spent a great deal on artistic promotion," Hugh Thomas wrote in his book, "and it can fairly claim to have brought poetry, ballet, music, travelling libraries and theatre to the countryside of Cuba."

Castro invited the world-famous prima ballerina Alicia Alonso, who is a *Habanera,* to form a national ballet. Her husband, Fernando Alonso, was named director. The Ballet de Cuba has been recognized as one of the best *corps de ballet* in the world. It has toured extensively abroad, but it likewise performs all over the island. An international ballet festival, including dancers from the United States, was held in Havana late in 1974.

The theater has consistently been weak in Cuba. In 1959 Fidel began supporting a National Theater of Cuba. It awarded prizes and scholarships to playwrights, but it has not been successful.

There has been much greater success with films. The short documentaries produced in Cuba are often of the highest class. An attempt was made in 1972 to put on a New York Festival of Cuban Films, but the U.S. Treasury Department closed it down. However, one film, made in 1968, was allowed back—*Memories of Underdevelopment,* which was taken from Edmundo Desnoes' novel, published in the United States as *Inconsolable Memories.* The picture was directed by Tomás Gutiérrez Alea. Peter Schjeldahl, in a long article in *The New York Times,* wrote: "It is a miracle . . . a beautifully understated film, sophisticated and cosmopolitan in style, fascinating in its subtlety and complexity."

I have not seen the film, but I have read the book and know the author, who is now teaching and writing in Havana. The book has passages quite as critical as some of Padilla's poems, but this did not make Desnoes a "counterrevolutionary" or prevent the filming of his novel.

This was not the only Cuban film to receive international acclaim in recent years. The atmosphere in New York became calm enough to make it possible for sympathizers to establish a Center for Cuban Studies.

When I was in Havana in September 1972 there were at least fifty cinemas showing films of many nationalities—Italian, French, Japanese, and North American. On a particular day, the *Granma* listed eleven American films, all made after the trade embargo went into effect. There is either a black market, or they are bought through foreign sources.

The National Printing Works, which did so little before 1959, has been producing huge quantities of books, by no means all revolutionary or technical in nature. Cubans claim that book production has increased tenfold during the Revolution. The Book Institute of Cuba, which was founded in 1967, celebrated the production of book number 100,000,000 on June 8, 1973. Before the end of November it had passed a total of 25 million books printed in 1973 alone, without counting millions of pamphlets and magazines. Most of the books were school texts, but more than a third were in the general cultural field.

In Havana in 1972, I was at first distressed to find that there were no books I could buy. Haydée Santamaría explained the reason: they simply cannot keep up with the demand. Eighty thousand copies of *Don Quijote* had been published earlier in the year, and they disappeared in days. Cubans do not have the habit of using public libraries. They buy books and keep them in their homes. At Havana University, which has a lending library, books can be taken out for a month, but large numbers of them are never returned. Imported books are snapped up in a day or two. There is also a problem of priorities. They have to print 20 million textbooks each year now. Imported books in Spanish have to be paid for in hard currency, and there is not much money to spare.

Fidel solved one problem in dictatorial fashion: copyright. In a speech on April 19, 1967, he said:

> Because of the existing copyright concepts we found that in order to satisfy the demand for books, we had to spend tens of millions of pesos on their purchases, often paying for them most dearly . . . We had to arrive at a decision, a defiant one, indeed, but a fair one. Our country, in fact, decided to disallow copyrights . . . We state that we consider all technical knowledge the heritage of mankind, and especially of those peoples who have been exploited . . . Cuba can, and is willing to, compensate all its intellectual creators but, at the same time, she renounces, internationally, all the copyrights that she is entitled to . . . That is, our books may be reprinted freely in any part of the world, while we, on the other hand, assume the right to do the same. If all countries did the same, humanity would be the beneficiary.

It was hardly a bargain for the outside world, but at least it permitted a number of technical manuals and textbooks to be picked up free and printed in Cuba. While humanity might benefit from the abolition of copyrights, it would be tough on us authors, who would lose the proceeds of foreign publication. Even the Russian system—a royalty credit in rubles to be spent in the Soviet Union—is fairer.

Some of the best writing that has been done in Cuba has come from the revolutionaries themselves. Che Guevara's account of the guerrilla war in the Sierra Maestra and his epic foray with Camilo Cienfuegos across the length of the island, as well as his *Bolivian Diary,* are classics of their kind. Faustino Pérez's story of the crossing on the *Granma;* Fauré Chomón's and Luis Goicoechea's accounts of the March 13, 1957, attack on the Presidential Palace; the vivid, moving story of their experiences during the July 26, 1953, assault on the Moncada Barracks by Haydée Santamaría and Melba Hernández, as related in Carlos Franqui's *Il Libro de los Doce*—these and other writings will live as literature whatever happens to politics in Cuba. Rarely has such dramatic history been written so graphically by those who made it.

The exception is the chief character, the protagonist of the drama, Fidel Castro—who, as I remarked before, is no writer. He is a great orator, but his speeches have no literary flavor. His writing has been confined to long, often florid, political manifestos and newspaper articles. As he had said to me, he is interested in making history; others can write it. (When Clemenceau was asked to write his memoirs, he is supposed to have said: "Never! Life is made to be lived, not written.")

The decline of Havana as a beautiful capital, as well as a notorious center of gambling, prostitution, and high living, has been noted by every visitor to Cuba since the Revolution settled down. The city gets worse with the years because, although kept clean, no painting, repairs, or refurbishing of buildings have taken place, nor has there been any new building in the center of town.

Since no private automobiles could be imported or bought, the streets looked strangely empty when I was there in 1972, except for the crowded British Leyland and Japanese buses and the official Alfa Romeo and Russian Volga cars, plus some Fiat and Alfa Romeo taxis. The situation is now changing.

The shops that were open were almost bereft of consumer goods. The famous streets and squares—the Prado, the Malecón, the Parque Central—were dismally bare during working hours and in the evening. The once wealthy, fashionable districts of Miramar and Country Club were, however, beautifully kept and made a startling contrast to the rest of the city. Diplomats and *becarios* (students on scholarships) live there now.

But Havana has one new glory. It is the Parque Lenin, ten miles south of the capital, covering about a hundred acres. It was about three years old when I saw it and still being built up, although nearly completed. Without doubt, it is one of the finest public parks in the world—Fidel's greatest and most permanent gift to Havana.

It has a big artificial lake on which floating cabaret shows are given, with boating for the people. There are facilities for horseback riding, a sports stadium that is also used for rodeos, and a superb restaurant built like Roman ruins in an original architecture. There is a room for protocol meals and a public restaurant with a dance floor; all very elegant and expensive, with meals that cost $15 to $20 a person. Even at five in the afternoon when I visited it, it was fairly crowded with Cubans. It is open to everyone, as is every park, beach, club, and facility in Cuba. The view stretches over miles of the Havana green belt.

The aquarium (I have seen many in my travels) ranks with the best in the world, charming in its conception, architecturally like the convolutions of a shell, with fish of many kinds and huge crocodiles. It was amazing to me that no word of this beautiful adornment to Havana and Cuba has reached the outside world, at least so far as I know, and I read everything I can get hold of about Cuba.

Access to the park is by frequent bus, although those with ancient cars and the diplomats and official visitors can drive there on specially built roads. The restaurant is set in a grove of trees, every one of which, even a few very large ones, was transplanted there.

That Fidel Castro, who almost seems to hate Havana and gets away from it whenever he can, should have created the Parque Lenin is ironic. The Revolution brought a reaction against Havana, as if the city were being punished for its past sins. Aside from its unsavory reputation, it had lived unfairly off the rest of Cuba. More than three-quarters of all Cuban imports went to Havana alone; more than half of the nation's hospital beds were located there; in public works, entertainment, the arts, education, publicity, it hogged the most and the best. Yet it had only a fifth of Cuba's population.

The Revolution swung the pendulum back, and more or less let Havana take care of itself. One result is that its population—about 1,750,000—has hardly grown at all. The Castro regime deliberately favored other provinces, putting much more emphasis on smaller communities and rural areas. Fidel could point out that José Martí also disliked Havana; perhaps it is a poor milieu for revolutionaries.

The people of Havana—meaning the once poorer people, the once lower classes, the ones who could not enjoy its *douceur de vivre* —have little to complain about, or at least, nothing special. The paucity of life would seem immensely depressing, but perhaps only to the middle-aged and old. At the big hotels like the Nacional, where I usually stay, and the Habana Libre (the old Hilton) and the Riviera, hordes of young people pour in to dance in the evenings. They not only seem, but obviously are, gay and pleased with themselves, and surprisingly well and attractively dressed. The parties are generally multiracial, but at the Nacional I did see some all-black and all-white gatherings.

Tipping is firmly abolished by law. A hotel chambermaid, waiter, porter, or clerk who accepts tips will be discharged if caught. The food in all the hotels and restaurants except three in Havana—La Torre, 1830, and the Parque Lenin—is appalling and very expensive. Restaurant meals are a deliberately permitted outlet for spare cash that cannot be spent on consumer goods. There will have to be new restaurants for future tourists.

Driving around Havana's streets, I did not see a single policeman. There are roving police patrols in autos, I was told, although I never noticed any, and they must be few. The Committees for the Defense of the Revolution help the police and call them if they see trouble or suspect it. A foreign diplomat told me that on his street someone from the CDR telephoned the police that they had seen suspicious characters loitering near his house late at night and the police came around to check.

Cuban cities, all through the Revolution, have been relatively free of violence or crime, from what I could learn. Havana, it hardly needs saying, is infinitely safer than New York, or even London.

There is obviously an intellectual life, but I imagined that it was confined to cliques at the university, the Instituto del Libro, the Casa de las Americas, the Academy of Sciences, and the ballet, concert, film, and theater worlds.

Hoi polloi have the movies and theaters, the very poor radio, and, on public occasions, television. They come into their own on weekends and holidays, when beaches, clubs, and resort hotels are open to all. On a Sunday morning I went out with a Cuban friend to the beach at Santa María, about fifteen miles east of Havana. It is a long, beautiful beach with fine, gently sloping sand. Families go there for vacations, living in tents. It is crude, ill-tended, and noisy, but before the Revolution all such beaches were reserved for the well-to-do. A new hotel is being built there. We passed many trucks coming and going. On Sundays offices and factories turn over their trucks to employees so that they can go to the beaches with their families for the day.

CHAPTER 15

School and Church

> A man whose work is purely intellectual is just as unhappy as a man whose work is purely manual.
> —Fidel Castro

The field of education is one of the few aspects of the Cuban Revolution where even its worst enemies concede that great and praiseworthy accomplishments have been made. Since 1970 a work-study educational system, unique in its scope, has got off to a good start. It is Fidel Castro's brainchild, and he will have to stay in power a long time to nurture it to maturity.

But from the beginning, education was an important reason for the strength of his Revolution. Castro's work in that field has nothing to do with doctrinal ideology, even though Marxism-Leninism came to be taught in the schools. He has developed basic ideas which will not be changed, whatever happens to the Revolution.

The 1970 sugar disaster, as I keep saying, was a turning point in the history of the Revolution in many ways, education included. The new program had its germination in earlier years, but its fruition came out of the sudden pressures of the sugar crisis.

The working of the system is best told in the words of Fidel Castro on the occasion of the graduation of 2,095 students at Havana University on December 8, 1972. This was the first graduation after the principle of study and work was put into effect the year before. (These excerpts are from the *Granma Weekly* of December 17, 1972.)

> Tonight we would like to refer chiefly to what we consider the most novel, the most difficult and the most revolutionary of the changes that have taken place in the University in these last years—to a degree that we could not even have imagined in the early days of the Revolution. . . .

This group of graduates has had ample participation in productive activities and, to a certain extent, they combined work and study. But the combination of study and work did not yet have, at that time, the character and the meaning that it now has. Needless to say, the procedure of separating a large number of students from their studies completely, from their universities when the harvest got under way, and sending them to the sugar mills to take part in it for two, three and even four months, was not exactly what we call the ideal method. . . .

And finally it was decided . . . to take a decisive step in university education by combining study and work, a combination which took on the character it has today.

It is quite possible that the very people who played a role in those events—which began in this university—have not yet fully realized the enormous significance that this step will have on our country's life and also the impact it is already making outside our country and the impact it will have in the future changes that are going to take place in the universities in other countries.

We believe that it was a historical event and constituted a real revolution in education . . . We are not yet going to judge the efforts by the results. The results are highly satisfactory. But what is really admirable is that such encouraging and really positive results were obtained in the first year that the system was put into effect. . . .

The old concept of study went hand in hand with the old society —the class society, the capitalist society, full of contradictions of every kind, among them the contradiction between the interests of a minority of intellectual workers and those of the entire society. . . .

Castro explained how and why the new system was first tried in the field of medicine, as the government had been forced "to pay special attention to the school of medicine" because "the imperialists took away 3,000 of the 6,000 doctors who were in our country prior to the Revolution . . .

There was quite an exodus of teachers at the very time when the struggle against illiteracy, the struggle for the education of the masses, was getting under way. What kind of sensitivity, of social conscience could theirs be? What could possibly be their idea of what a human being is, of the needs of a human being? What did they really care about the struggle against ignorance?

At that time [1959] there was a surplus of teachers. Today we don't have enough teachers to meet our needs. When more than a million and a half children are attending elementary school; when an effort is being made to improve the quality of education—not only quantitatively but also qualitatively; when the number of intermediary level students has doubled or even tripled; when the number of university students is on the increase; when a real struggle was waged to eradicate illiteracy and to give our workers and farmers an education; when an effort is being made to have all the people studying, it is logical that the number of teachers we have is insufficient to meet our needs . . . We will have to continue training teachers on a mass scale for many years to come. We have had to resort to what is known as people's teachers in order to solve the problem in many schools. These are people who have not yet graduated as teachers and are now working and studying to win their title. . . .

In our country, the need to combine study and work was more than obvious. No poor country, no underdeveloped country can proclaim the principle of universal education. No poor country can set itself the goal of giving all its children and young people the opportunity to study, because such a possibility is out of reach of that country's economy in the old concept of education. A poor country with the old concept of education would have to settle for the principle that only part of the population could study, thus the majority of the population would be deprived of an education. By following the old concept, a country would be forced to do exactly the same thing the capitalist society did, thus giving only a few the opportunity to study while condemning the immense majority to ignorance. That would be unfair, immoral and in no way revolutionary. That would never make it possible for any country to solve its problems in the long run.

If we analyze the cost of education, for example, we will find that the cost of education in Cuba will run to more than 700 million pesos [$700 million] by 1973. That is more than the entire budget of the Republic prior to the Revolution . . . Therefore, in reality, the application of the principle of universal study is possible only to the extent that work is also made universal.

Fidel went on to point out that the economic cost of providing universal education for "an ever-growing mass of students" would be impossible if they merely studied and did no work.

If we go a little further, in keeping with these ideas, there will come a day when those who graduate from the university will realize that all they have done is to get past a stage, that they have been awarded a diploma, but that they will have to keep on applying the principle of study and work for the rest of their lives. . . .

Therefore, whether he likes it or not, life makes it more and more

> imperative for a man to work with his mind. And the gap between intellectual workers and manual workers must gradually disappear as a result of the development of human society.

He gave some figures for advanced education. In 1972 nearly 16,000 students at Havana University started to work as well as study. From the other side, 14,000 workers were registered for courses at the University while retaining their jobs.

There had been a sensational increase in the building of junior high schools between the opening of the school year in September 1971 and September 1972—from six to fifty-one. I saw a number of the new schools. The figure for the year ending September 1973 was 102 new schools for 60,000 students; in 1974, 108 new schools were opened. A great many new elementary schools for work and study have been built in rural areas where the children can spend some hours in the fields, but Castro confessed that no solution had yet been found for urban elementary schools.

He argued that "class society," by which he meant capitalist society, had always "underestimated children and young people."

In the long talk I had with Fidel on September 12, 1972, this was the idea and the achievement of which he was most proud. He told me that UNESCO has become interested in his system. It is, indeed, one of the most remarkable experiments in education taking place anywhere in the world, and it has attracted a good deal of attention from educators abroad—although not from the United States, of course, due to the "Cuban Wall" between us.

I spent a morning at Havana University with the then rector, José M. Millar Barrueco (now with INRA), who was only forty and had been the university head for seven years. His devotion to and admiration of Fidel Castro were boundless, obviously genuine, and typical of the way almost everyone who works with the *Jefe* feels. At the University the ideas had come from Fidel, and so have drive and constant watchfulness. He is a frequent visitor, letting nothing escape his persistent questioning.

Back in the early 1960s Fidel had the idea of applying a system of work and study, and he made some attempts and some progress at it. However, a promising new drive, which was started in 1965, was set back, like everything else, for the 1970 *zafra*.

The idea, as Dr. Millar explained it, is the total socialization of education through the *integration* of work and study. There is no separation of the individual student as a member of society, a worker, a peasant, or a professional. All citizens are "students." "Social participation of the student is the basis of revolutionary education," as Millar put it.

The student—an engineering student, for instance—does not go to the factory for a brief period to learn superficially how others do the work; he goes there and works himself and stays there, studying at the same time. A worker is brought to the university not to study books while he leaves his work, but to study as he continues working, contributing his practical knowledge to the university; he teaches as he learns, and in the factory he teaches the university student who comes to work there.

There are plans to keep on developing the idea, and by 1980, according to the rector, the "university" will in reality be a vast complex of schools, factories, farms, mines, hospitals, et cetera, where students are workers and workers are students. The concept is a revolution in education, Dr. Millar said (as did Castro to me, later), not just a reform of the university system. The program encompasses the whole of society, since even the primary-school pupil is being taught the importance of work. The process carries through to the adult, forming a new man as it forms a revolutionary society.

"What is the Revolution but ideas?" the enthusiastic rector exclaimed. It was a reminder of Max Weber's dictum that "the interests of society are the great rails on which humanity moves, but the ideas throw the switches." Revolutions are also driven along the rails by ideas.

"A new factory is the same anywhere," Millar said, "but in Cuba a factory is, in addition, a branch of the university, a part of the educational system. Before the Revolution, Havana University was a place apart from society, where those who could afford it studied books and learned their professions out of books. Today, Havana University is an integral part of the revolutionary economy and social system.

"There are many work centers all over the country that are already factory schools and, as such, have the characteristic of university units," Castro said in a speech to the Second Congress of the Young Communist League (UJC) on April 4, 1972. "The Moa Bay and Nicaro nickel plants are provincial and local extensions of the Universities of Havana, Las Villas and Oriente, and the Camagüey University Center. There are also a number of 'educational hospitals' where teaching and study are combined with practice."

The Russians had nothing to do either with the question of culture or the educational system. The policies were examples of Fidel Castro going ahead on his own with *his* revolution. Any resemblance to the Soviet bloc's cultural system came naturally out of the demands faced by every sort of totalitarian or authoritarian regime.

The Cuban work-study system of education that Fidel has introduced does resemble China's in some respects, but it is much more comprehensive. China's "May Seventh" cadre schools, where bureaucrats, teachers, medical professionals, and the like do farm work for several months, are like the civilians going out to cut sugar cane in the Cuban harvest. But in China the basic reason for government functionaries and others to work in agriculture is ideological—to prevent revisionism, dogmatism, ultra-leftism, élitism, and other doctrinal deviations. In Cuba the cane-cutting and coffee-picking practice was primarily economic; there was a shortage of labor.

For Cuba the basic reason behind the work-study program is educational. Of course, it is all done in the name of Marxism-Leninism—everything is given that label in Cuba now—but in reality it is a form of *Fidelismo.* Castro picked up a socialistic idea and gave it a special, Cuban form.

"We run a risk because our Revolution is a socialist revolution," he conceded to a group of Chilean students at the University of Chile on November 12, 1971. "We might form a youthful bourgeoisie . . . We run the risk of replacing the father by the State . . . Much revolutionary formation, much political instruction, much indoctrination—but in the end these are nothing but abstract ideas which cannot transform man. It is life, habits, daily work which forms a man . . . A university cannot form a man better than a factory can."

In that same conference, he came back to one of his most strongly held ideas: "We want to avoid university diplomas making an intellectual élite removed from the realities of life, foreign to the mentality of the workers . . . Man cannot be solely an intellectual, just as he cannot be merely a machine."

At the same time, it is true of Cuba, as elsewhere, that persons having had higher education at the universities or technical schools are forming the new élite of the nation's government and army, civil service and industry, as well as the professions. This makes for social and economic inequalities which Castro hopes will be ironed out, or at least reduced, by his worker-student system. There will always be some "socialist inequality."

"What is to some extent discouraging," Fidel had said to the UJC Congress, "is that in 1971 and 1972 fewer and fewer students want to study agricultural and industrial subjects. With all due respect to philosophy, we cannot say that we can make this a nation of philosophers . . . I ask myself why there are only 7,757 studying agriculture and 16,203 in our industrial institutes? And I ask you: who is going to produce the material goods in the future, and how?"

Castro was touching a sore spot. For Latins, manual labor is demeaning, almost degrading. No Cuban of the middle-upper class did manual work before the Revolution. Fidel is aiming to change that.

"Today," he said in a speech on February 5, 1967, "our children will learn the meaning of work from the youngest age. Even if they are only six and in the first grade of school, they will learn how to grow lettuce. In addition, they will learn how to water a plant or tend a flower bed so as to make their surroundings more pleasant. They will do what they can, but the important thing is that as soon as they are old enough to reason, material goods are produced . . . In this way, they will acquire a noble concept of work."

After successful experiments in different parts of the island, the Ministry of Education ordered the establishment of vegetable gardens in all elementary schools in December 1972. "The school vegetable garden will be educational in nature," it was stated.

The principle had been put into practice in junior high or secondary schools, but on a commercial basis to produce vegetables for markets. This too had started in a rudimentary way in 1967 in what was called *escuelas en el campo* (schools in the field). Children participated for six weeks after following special television courses. (TV education, incidentally, is well developed in Cuba.)

Now, as one of the many sequels to the 1970 economic setback, Castro ordered the system to be extended to full-time study and farm work for secondary schools which were to be built in the countryside. This was one goal that was more than fulfilled. He had called for forty junior high schools to be built in the year following September 20, 1971. While I was in Cuba in September 1972, forty-four such schools were inaugurated for the opening of the school year, with a half dozen more virtually completed. A year later, with the start of the 1973 school year on September 3, eighty-eight new secondary schools had been inaugurated, according to *Granma.*

I visited a half dozen of them. One was the Plan Ceiba Secondary School for boys and girls of eleven to fifteen years old, 1,500 in all. It was in the fertile green belt of Havana Province where there is now an extensive dairy community with many new cow sheds and new roads.

The students live in the school dormitories on weekdays, working four hours in their classes in the morning and three hours in the fields in the afternoon, cultivating citrus fruits, coffee, pineapples, and sugar cane on forty *caballerías* (about 1,325 acres). The children return to their homes every Saturday and Sunday and for their holidays. The director was twenty-one years old, a recent graduate in pedagogy at Havana University.

At the other end of the island on the rich plain from Santiago de Cuba to Manzanillo, I visited two just-opened secondary schools in a big new agricultural development (started in 1970 after the sugar *zafra*) called the Plan Viandero de Vaguitas. The director of one of the schools, this time a prerevolutionary educator, assured me that the children's work in the field was not amateurishness and not play, but a serious contribution to agriculture. Being so young, he remarked, they are quicker and more supple and do not mind bending over so much. They do not, of course, have the strength or stamina of adults, but their contribution is real, especially considering the shortage of farm labor.

I was struck at all these schools by the happy, animated, and obviously healthy life the children were leading. The bright graduates go on to technical or pre-university schools. The teachers not only supervise but also work in the fields. Apparently, so do some of the parents when they come to visit.

The zeal and enthusiasm of the youth of Cuba are something that nearly every visitor notes. Because so many of the young are out and about doing things, one gets an impression of a youthful country, although the demographic proportions are unchanged.

A contented Fidel Castro, inaugurating a new secondary school on September 25, 1972, told his audience: "I believe that any country that succeeds in carrying out this [educational plan] will have thereby created endless possibilities in the field of social, technological and educational development."

The progress is by leaps and bounds, even among industrial workers. "Whereas 166,021 workers were studying in 1972, we now have 517,803 registered for courses in the various branches of adult education, technical and professional training, higher education and technological studies," said Castro in a speech on May Day 1973. "This means that 27.3 per cent of all Cuban workers are studying . . . Last year, throughout the country, we had 963 cultural groups, composed of 8,357 workers who were interested in the arts. Now there are 3,105 such groups, composed of 21,604 workers."

There was no adult education in Cuba before the Revolution. In 1970, according to Castro, there were 1,365,344 adults getting some form of education. When the school year began on June 1, 1974, 445,695 adults registered for courses.

In a speech on April 4, 1972, he conceded that Cuba too has its dropout problem. From the ages of eight to ten, 99.8 percent go to school. By age twelve, it is down to 94.5, and then it drops sharply to 55.7 at fifteen years and 39.8 at sixteen. This means that well over 200,000 children between twelve and sixteen neither go to school nor work.

Other, more gratifying figures that he gave were that in 1958–1959 there were 717,417 pupils in primary schools and in 1970–1971, 1,664,634. In 1958–1959, 811,345 went to universities; in 1970–1971, 2,345,188.

Cuba, Fidel said in 1972, spends $400 million, or 10 percent of its budget, annually on education, which is about twice what Costa Rica, one of the most advanced countries in Latin America, spends. It was planned to spend $700 million on education in 1973.

Theoretically, the dropouts should cause a substantial delinquency rate, but Major José R. Fernández, the minister of education, assured me that the rate is very low. This was a problem that the Committees for the Defense of the Revolution (CDR) were beginning to tackle. One drawback is that education is compulsory only through the age of twelve but no one under sixteen is allowed to do gainful work. At sixteen, boys are conscripted into the armed forces for three years.

Fernández said that a new law was in preparation making education compulsory up to the age of conscription. Fidel spoke of compulsory education up to the age of nineteen, when we talked about it. When I asked how this would go with obligatory military service, he said: "We will arrange for part study, part training." (I suspected that the idea had just entered his head.)

One does not see any hippie types at the universities and higher schools. When I asked, I was told that long hair is not forbidden or frowned upon, but I had the impression that a long-haired youth would feel conspicuous. The girls are advised not to wear miniskirts. All the lower-grade pupils wear uniforms and parade like soldiers.

The Revolution has always had a puritanical flavor, but not to the extent of separating the sexes.

A Cuban report to a conference of Ministers of Education in Caracas, Venezuela, in December 1971, said:

"Coeducation is a factor of great importance in the development and formation of mankind. It is applied on all levels and in all types of education in our country and it is based on the criterion that the separation of boys and girls in school creates an artificial climate since boys and girls are together in their homes, working centers, entertainment places, the street and daily life, and if school prepares one for life it should reflect this situation."

The Cultural Declaration of April 1971 had mentioned sex education. "As a rule," it said, "coeducational schooling should be generalized, except in cases where the characteristics of the teaching branch do not permit it. Sufficient information should be given on sexual relations, telling children and youths the truth when they ask questions in school or at home. In order to dissipate any existing ignorance and prejudice, sexual questions should be approached in the framework of teaching, without it being necessary, however, to create special courses on this subject."

One of the great changes brought by the Revolution is that any boy or girl, however poor their parents or wherever they live on the island, can get to a university or technical school and become a doctor, engineer, agronomist, or any other professional.

Most infants are kept in the *círculos infantiles* while their mothers work. Older children whose parents live in isolated rural areas are boarded, clothed, and fed in central schools. In the cities they go to elementary schools where they are given lunch and a liter of milk a day. The brighter ones get scholarships and become *becarios*, living in Havana and other cities in the homes of the formerly wealthy exiles.

"In the school years of 1970–1971," the report to the Education Ministers in Caracas said, "there were 201,300 scholarship students, and 251,500 semi-boarding school students. The scholarship includes educational services, sports, recreation, culture, room and board, clothing, transport, medical attention and, according to the level and type of education, a small sum for personal expenses."

Then come the universities and technical schools. It is no longer enough, as in all Latin countries, to get the *bachillerato* (our Bachelor of Arts degree) to be a "Doctor." The title, I was assured, is now the equivalent of the United States Ph.D, to be earned, first, by up to five years' study for *licenciado* (Master of Arts), and then a few years' work on a thesis and another examination.

Naturally, every type of education is free. And understandably, every pupil is now indoctrinated with Marxism-Leninism and taught to revere the revolutionary heroes, with special emphasis on José Martí in the past and Ernesto Che Guevara in the present. There is no cult or worship of Fidel Castro in the sense that there is of Mao Tse-tung or was of Hitler and Mussolini.

There are some specialized schools now for the blind, deaf, and handicapped. There were none before the Revolution.

The teacher problem is still serious, as Castro said, although lessening each year. Numerically, the exiles have been replaced, but experienced teachers for the lower grades are still too few. In the universities, Dr. Millar, the rector of Havana University told me, there are now 2,500 professors, which is enough. Some of them are foreigners, from Latin America, Eastern Europe, Italy, and France. Many of them visit Cuba just to give summer courses.

Dr. Millar drove me out to the Country Club section of Havana, once the most fashionable part of the capital with its finest mansions. Aside from the diplomatic corps, who still live there, the houses are now full of *becarios* and teachers. There were many new school and technical buildings and other impressive ones being built. It is now one of the largest educational centers in Latin America.

Our trip was made in part so that Millar could prove to me that Cubans are making computers on their own. He said that some years earlier Fidel called a meeting of the educational heads and ministerial officials in Havana and told them that he wanted to see a computer industry created in Cuba, since computers were so important nowadays. They said that it was impossible. Fidel said "No"—and ordered them to go ahead. I saw computers in operation, built by Cuban engineers and students, one model of which was being sold to Chile, "in competition with the IBM," as one engineer said jokingly.

The only criticism of the new educational system that I heard in Havana (it came from a foreign diplomat) was that it leaves little or no scope for the scientific brains, the men in secluded offices and laboratories who work out the crucial problems of pure science, the discoveries, the inventions, that provide the impetus for economic advances. However, even he conceded that Castro's system would create the broad basis of technicians, managers, and skilled workers that Cuba desperately needs for its development, and will need for twenty years or more. Castro knows that it is a long haul.

"For the near future we will have only moral satisfactions," he said to the Havana Congress on Education and Culture in April 1971. "For the next five or ten years this enormous mass of more than a million children in primary school; these 100,000 pupils who enter secondary schools each year, will bring us only moral satisfaction."

The Declaration of the Congress summed it all up in more ideological terms: "Education must reflect and stimulate the changes flowing from the revolutionary transformations. It must above all tend to create a new man, a new people who, at the same time that they untie the strings of the past, are capable of creating conditions for higher individual and social existence."

This is like an echo of Che Guevara's voice, calling for the "New Man," but one should not miss the fact that Fidel Castro's ideas on education are rooted in the solid earth. He wants more farmers, more engineers, more builders, more doctors, dentists, teachers. He wants boys and girls, men and women, who will learn and work at the same time. He will tell them that this is Marxism-Leninism.

There is, of course, no religious education in any of the schools. But in the field of religion, as in nearly everything else, Cuba is special.

On my first Sunday in Havana during my last trip, in September 1972, I spent the morning visiting four churches. No new churches have been built since the Revolution began, of course. There is no encouragement to go to church; in fact, play and work are arranged instead for children on Sunday mornings. Cuba is perhaps unique in its indifference to religion; for most Cubans, except middle-class urbanites before the Revolution, neither church nor religion occupied their minds or emotions.

The first church I visited, Santa Rita, in the once fashionable Miramar district, was shockingly empty—no more than sixty worshipers in a big edifice, a few young men, a half dozen children brought by their parents. Most worshipers were middle-aged. The priest was finishing his sermon. He was alone, and when he needed help a woman or a man went up to the altar. There was a fine organ, no choir, but a young man with a superb tenor voice sang the hymns. There was something sad in the church as the lovely voice soared almost plaintively over the nearly empty pews. During the offering I noticed that no one gave less than a peso (dollar). The women were moderately well dressed. There was not a Negro in the congregation, but this was a prosperous, white, upper-middle-class neighborhood before the Revolution.

I went up to the priest when the service had ended, and he invited me into the sacristy, where we talked. He was an old Spaniard, a diehard, critical of new Church trends, conducting his service in Latin. When I said something about Fidel being Marxist-Leninist, he said: "No, he is not a Marxist here," tapping his heart. Evidently, he wanted to believe well of Castro.

In all of Cuba there are only two seminaries, one at El Cobre in Oriente, but only for the young and first years, after which the seminarians must go to Havana to finish their studies and be ordained; so, effectively, Havana has the only seminary in Cuba. No more than forty or fifty priests had been ordained in the previous eleven years, he said, but another priest later told me he thought that about forty novices would be starting courses the next day.

There are few church marriages, the Spanish priest said. Rather more baptisms, but still not many. Foreign priests, monks, and nuns are not allowed to come to Cuba to live. The Church of Santa Rita is Augustine. The priest was afraid to give me his name. He was so reactionary that he felt that Franco Spain is being "lost" by modernizing its economy; it is "losing its *espíritu moral.*" Martí, he insisted, was an atheist (in reality, he was a deist and a Freemason). For the priest, even Rome has been going backward since Pope John XXIII.

I went on to the larger, much more imposing Church of San Antonio de Padua on the same beautiful avenue. Here three priests were officiating, and the church was a good third full. There was a full choir of male and female voices.

Heriberto, my Negro chauffeur, about forty, said that he went to church when he was young and was taken there, but not after. He does not go now, nor does his wife, and their five children have not been baptized. He has nothing against religion, but nothing for it, and he sees no value in it for his children. This was typical.

The Cathedral of Havana, a lovely old colonial church in the old center of town, was closing. I was told that it opens only early in the morning for a low mass and is closed the rest of the day. Yet it is the only cathedral in the capital, and it is administered by the Archbishop of Havana, Monseñor Francisco Oves.

The largest of Havana's churches, the Church of the Sacred Heart *(Sagrado Corazón)* on the Avenida de Bolívar—Gothic in style with a high spire dominating much of the city—was almost half filled, this time with poorly dressed people, as it is in a poor section of the city. For the first time, I saw a fair number of blacks and mulattos. As in the other churches, they gave peso bills when the basket was passed around. Again, the worshipers were mostly middle-aged, with few children, but in this church there were some young men.

There had been virtually no adolescents in any of the churches. It made me realize that a generation is being lost to the Catholic Church in Cuba. I noticed in all the churches that few in the congregations took communion.

After the service at the Church of the Sacred Heart, I spoke briefly to one of the priests. He said, "there are no difficulties of any sort with the regime [*No hay dificultades*]. There is "complete respect" [*respeto completo*] from the government.

Coming out of one of the churches, a busload of chattering, singing children passed, no doubt en route to a picnic or a beach. This is what the regime prefers the children to do, and it sees to it that the opportunities are there, but parents can take their children to church if they want.

That basic document to which I keep returning—the "Declaration" of the 1971 Cultural Congress—has a passage on the church:

> The policy of the Revolution concerning religion is based on the following principles: not to make the religious problem the center of our preoccupations; absolute separation in all domains of Church and State and of Church and school; not to encourage, support or help religious groups and to expect nothing of them; we have no religious belief and practice no cult; the Revolution respects religious beliefs and worship as an individual right: no one is persecuted for his convictions; obscurantists and counterrevolutionaries must be fought.

The objectionable sects were listed separately as Jehovah's Witnesses, Seventh-Day Adventists, and Gideon's Evangelists. However, I was told about groups of Jehovah's Witnesses and Seventh-Day Adventists carrying on without molestation. Members of these sects, by their beliefs, cannot be good revolutionaries, and they were in trouble early in the Revolution. After some American pastors were expelled, it was realized that the sects were politically harmless and socially commendable. So far as I could find out, they are ignored.

In theory, practicing Catholics cannot become members of the Communist Party, but as Haydée Santamaría said to me: "We only worry if someone is very devout." And then what they worry about is politics, not religion. They do not trust the clergy. Priests and pastors, incidentally, have to do military service.

There is no interference with parents who want to teach their children religion at home, since they get none at school. "The churches can remain open," as Castro put it. "That is where religion can be taught." Nor is there any official objection or impediment to baptism, communion, church marriages, or the last sacraments. Cubans have been deprived of many freedoms by the Revolution, but not freedom of worship—with one proviso: that the Roman Catholic Church, the Protestant sects, the Jewish community, the Afro-Cuban cults, and the Freemasons keep their beliefs out of politics.

In modern times the Roman Catholic Church was not an important force, politically, economically, or even socially in Cuba. What trouble occurred during the Revolution was not due to Marxism-Leninism but to the fact that the chronic shortage of clergymen had led to the introduction of many Spanish priests who could not accommodate themselves to the radical revolution.

The hierarchy, which was 100 percent Spanish before independence, was linked to the ruling classes throughout colonial and prerevolutionary republican times. The Church wanted stability, not change, and still less, revolution. In the popular mind the Church was identified with the Spanish colonial masters and, later, with pro-American political, business, and landowning interests. Few Cuban youths chose the priesthood as a vocation.

There was little anticlericalism in Cuba at any time. Liberalism, secularism, and a strong Freemasonry played important roles in the struggle for independence and for the successful separation of church and state, but there was no anti-Catholicism to speak of, and the anticlericalism never remotely reached the degree of mad fury which again and again led to church-burning and priest-killing in Spain.

Opposition was centered in the Freemasonry movement. José Martí and many other leading nineteenth-century intellectuals and revolutionaries were Masons. Martí, in fact, was excommunicated by the Church. It is ironic that he is known to all Cubans as *El Apóstol.* The European type of Freemasonry, which Cubans copied, held that human reason, freely exercised, would lead to universal moral truths without the aid of the church. For Martí, Christianity "died at the hands of Catholicism." In twentieth-century Cuba, Freemasonry became much less political and more social, aping the United States. It was always middle-class and had close connections with North American lodges.

But Cuba must, of course, be considered a Roman Catholic country. Perhaps as many as 85 percent of Cubans are Catholics by birth. MacGaffey and Barnett, in their book *Cuba* (1962), estimate that only 10 percent were practicing Catholics before the Revolution. There were few churches in rural areas, and priestly visitations were generally rare. Perhaps half—mostly the lower half—of Cuban society never had anything to do with the Church.

There were 200 parishes in 1959 for a population of more than 6.5 million, served by only 700 priests, mostly Spanish. The religious orders also were composed mostly of Spaniards. In 1960 and 1961, Castro expelled about 140 Spanish priests, but for political reasons. He was glad to see 400 Cuban priests go into exile for the same reason. Some Canadian priests were expelled and then brought back, at Cuban expense, as a recognition of the Canadian government's uninterrupted friendliness.

Protestantism hardly existed in Cuba before the United States occupation in 1898, after which many denominations established missions, schools, and hospitals, virtually all in urban districts. The peasants were too poor, too illiterate, and too indifferent to be attracted. Insofar as there was conflict with some Protestant sects during the Castro revolution, it was because they were run by Americans and, in some cases, politically motivated against the Revolution as well as against Communism. All told, there are between 90,000 and 100,000 Protestants in Cuba.

When the Revolution began, there were between 8,000 and 10,000 Jews in Cuba, of whom 5,000 were in Havana. Many of them came from Eastern Europe between the World Wars. Since as many as three-quarters of them had shops or were merchants in retail trade, the proportion leaving Cuba was the highest of any religious sect. By 1969, according to Professor Lowry Nelson, only about 1,000 remained. The reasons were undoubtedly economic, not religious, for there is no anti-Semitism in Cuba. What Jews have remained practice their religion, but they must now be deeply worried by Castro's pro-Arab, anti-Israel policy.

"A rabbi [Everett Gendler] who visited the island in 1969," Nelson writes, "reported that all five Jewish congregations were still active and not subjected to any harassment."

MacGaffey and Barnett devote some interesting pages to the persistence of African religious beliefs among black Cubans. The worship of African deities is known as *santería.* The cults are derived mostly from the Nigerian Yorubas of western Africa, who furnished many of the slaves in early days. Another group, the Arará, descend from the Dahomeyans. Haitian immigrants imported their *vodún,* or voodoo rites.

William R. Bascom, in the *Southwestern Journal of Anthropology,* found *santería* in 1950 to be "a vital, growing institution." "The members of *santería* cults," he wrote, "regard themselves as Catholics" but he concluded that "while Catholicism is outwardly embraced, it is inwardly rejected." According to MacGaffey and Barnett, "Catholicism is viewed as the Spanish tribal version of *santería.*"

Christ is identified with Obatala, the most important of the *orishas,* or spirits of great men. Oshun, the Yoruba Aphrodite, has a shrine in El Cobre, the old copper-mining town of Oriente Province, which houses Cuba's miracle-working statue of the *mestizo Virgen del Cobre,* to whom childless women burn candles.

The most intriguing of the Afro-Cuban secret religions is *Ñañiguismo,* which was so secret that it had to be rediscovered by a Cuban sociologist only a few decades ago. *Ñañigos* are members of the Abakuá secret society, which flourished in nineteenth-century Cuba but seems to have greatly declined (no one is sure) in this century. The oath of secrecy is formidable. The spirits of the dead are worshiped and must be placated.

While white Cubans dismiss *santería* and *Ñañiguismo* as *brujería* (witchcraft), few know anything precise about them. Fidel has referred to the *ñañigos* in derogatory terms, but the government is tolerant of Afro-Cuban worship, as it is of all the others.

Marriage became a civil ceremony, although couples can be married again in church if they desire. There is a puritanical streak running through the Cuban Revolution, as I said, and one evidence is that Fidel wanted to encourage marriage. In prerevolutionary days rural couples often could not afford to pay for a church marriage. In 1967 a law was passed providing that an engaged couple need only present themselves, with two witnesses, at a local Collective Law Office and sign an affidavit. Low-price honeymoons were made available. After that, the number of marriages, already much higher than before the Revolution, took a 60 percent spurt. But divorces are also much higher. (Although Latin America is nearly 100 percent Roman Catholic, divorce has been acceptable for many years. The Revolution did not bring divorce to Cuba; General Batista was a divorcé.) The old-style Cuban family life has been weakened in many ways by the Revolution.

Birth control, like religion, is a take-it-or-leave-it practice. Contraceptives are provided freely as a matter of the sexual rights of the individual. Abortion is permitted only for medical reasons, especially where the mother's health is at stake. The island's population is not considered excessive, and the government does not want to slow down the birth rate, which ranges around a rather high 2.2 to 2.5 percent.

Castro "suppressed" Christmas during the great sugar *zafra* in 1969, and it has never been resumed. December 25 comes at the height of the beginning of the harvest. Every man who can cut cane is needed in the fields. Fidel, instead, incongruously offered July 26 as "Christmas," with August 6 as the children's "Epiphany." It was a politico-economic, not a religious, measure. This is to continue until better days and more mechanization come, when the traditional Christmas celebrations will be resumed. They will be expected, anyway, by the tourists.

The Vatican recognized the new regime early in 1959, but there was a period when the Holy See was critical. So was the Cuban hierarchy for a while. There were pastoral letters criticizing the growth of Communism, met by angry retorts of counterrevolution from the Prime Minister and the President. Some priests were expelled, as I said. All church property, schools included—Catholic and Protestant—was expropriated in 1961.

When, on December 4, 1960, the hierarchy issued a pastoral letter urging Castro to reject Communism, his answer was typical of an unchanging attitude toward religion. After remarking that "to be anti-Communist is to be counterrevolutionary," he added that it was also counterrevolutionary "to be anti-Catholic, anti-Protestant or anti-anything which divides Cubans."

The excitement gradually died down. Pope John XXIII's great encyclical of April 1963, *Mater et Magistra,* undoubtedly helped. It made the now historic distinction between Communism and the Communist.

"One must never confuse error and the person who errs," it says, "not even when there is a question of error or inadequate knowledge of truth in the moral or religious field. The person who errs is always and above all a human being." To be sure, citing his predecessor, Pope John added: "Salvation and justice are not to be found in revolution, but in evolution through concord."

The Holy See never broke diplomatic relations with Cuba, nor did Fidel Castro ever contemplate a break. He had the same ambassador in Rome throughout—Luis Amado Blanco, who, ironically, was the Dean of the Vatican diplomatic corps and who while we were in Rome on January 1, 1974, conveyed the good wishes for the New Year to His Holiness on behalf of the assembled envoys. Ambassador Amado Blanco was the only Communist diplomat present throughout the recent Ecumenical Council sessions. The papal representive in Havana for nearly a decade has been Monseñor Cesare Zacchi, who is on friendly terms with Fidel and some of the other revolutionary leaders. He was consecrated a bishop during his term in Havana and in December 1974 was elevated to the rank of Nuncio.

At the end of March 1974, Archbishop Agostino Casaroli, secretary of the Council of Public Affairs of the Holy See (the pope's "Foreign Minister"), arrived in Havana on the first visit of a high Vatican official since the Revolution began. While he was officially welcomed at the airport only by Deputy Foreign Minister René Anillo, Foreign Minister Raúl Roa and other high Cuban officials saw him off at the airport on April 5.

The *Granma* of April 6 printed a news item which ended: "On the night of April 4, Monsignor Casaroli held a long and cordial interview with Commander in Chief Fidel Castro, Prime Minister of the Revolutionary Government."

The talk lasted for ninety minutes and, typically with Fidel, went on until long after midnight. Raúl Roa returned the visit when he was in Rome a few months later.

An incident noted in a number of books about the Revolution gave evidence of Castro's insistence that religion be respected. On March 13, 1963, the sixth anniversary of the attack on the Presidential Palace was celebrated, as it is every year. José Antonio Echevarría, the student leader killed in the attack, had left a political testament which contained this sentence: "We are confident that the purity of our intentions will bring us the favor of God, to achieve a reign of justice in our land." The chairman of the meeting omitted the sentence in reading the text, which brought Castro to his feet with a long, sharp harangue. "Can we be so cowardly, so mentally crippled, that we have the moral poverty to suppress three lines?" he asked. ". . . We know that a revolutionary can have a religious belief."

"In our country," Fidel said to the students of the University of Concepción in Chile, on November 18, 1971, "Christianity does not exist in the sense that it does in many Latin American countries, because the Catholic religion is not a popular religion . . . It was fundamentally the religion of the rich in our country. . . .

"Our Revolution could never be characterized by anti-Catholicism, by anti-Christianity or by any form of anti-religiosity . . . We have always taken great care in our country to avoid any form of persecution or anti-religious struggle."

He told his listeners about Padre Sardiñas staying in the Sierra Maestra with the rebels. "Peasants would present themselves, asking that their children be baptized," he said, "and Father Sardiñas baptized them, and I was the godfather. So, I have many godchildren in the Sierra Maestra."

While he was in Chile, Fidel had an audience with Raúl, Cardinal Silva Enríquez, who was criticized for it by right-wing Chileans. Castro invited a group of Chilean priests to visit Cuba. They accepted. When told about it, Monseñor Francisco Oves, Archbishop of Havana, said, "They will be welcomed fraternally by the Cuban Church."

One day Fidel had a meeting with a group called the *Ochenta Sacerdotes* ("Eighty Priests"). The discussions were taped and published in a pamphlet called *Fidel y los Cristianos.*

"Religion," Fidel said at one point, "is for man and has man as its object. I say 10,000 times that the needs of men are satisfied more through socialism and Communism, and therefore there is more coincidence of Communism with Christianity than Christianity can have with capitalism."

"When did you have your religious crisis?" Fidel was asked.

"The problem is that I had no religious crisis and that I had no religious education; it was superficial; I did not understand it."

The best statement I know of by Fidel Castro of his beliefs as a Christian, a Marxist, and a revolutionary was made in Santiago, Chile, on the eve of his departure for home, December 2, 1971. It was his last speech in Chile.

> We [i.e., I] have often spoken of the history of Christianity—that Christianity which gave rise to so many martyrs, to so many men who sacrificed themselves defending their faith. Men who can lay down their lives for the sake of their faith will always have our deepest respect. . . .
>
> We examined the many points of coincidence that may exist between the purest precepts of Christianity and the objectives of Marxism. There are many who have tried to use religion to defend exploitation, poverty and privilege; to transform people's life in this world into a hell, forgetting that Christianity was the religion of the humble, of the slaves of Rome, of the tens of thousands who were devoured by the lions at the circus and who had very definite ideas about human solidarity or human love and condemned greed, gluttony and selfishness.
>
> That was a religion which, 2,000 years ago, called the merchants and the Pharisees by their name, which condemned the rich and said virtually that they would not enter the kingdom of heaven. That was the religion which multiplied the loaves and the fishes—precisely what the revolutionary man of today intends to do with technology, with his hands, with the rational, planned development of the economy.
>
> When you search for the similarities between the objectives of Marxism and the most beautiful precepts of Christianity, you will find many points of coincidence. You will see why a humble priest who knows what hunger means—who knows what sickness and death and human pain mean . . . Or why some of those priests who practice their religion among the miners or among humble peasant families become identified with them and fight shoulder to shoulder with them. You will see why there are unselfish people who devote their whole life to the care of people afflicted with the worst diseases.
>
> When you find all those points of coincidence you will see how a thing like a strategic alliance between Marxist revolutionaries and Christian revolutionaries is possible.

Monseñor Oves, the Archbishop of Havana, gave an interview to the *Cuba Internacional* of March 1972. He is Cuban, born in Camagüey in 1928, and was named to his post by Pope Paul VI in the fateful year, for Cuba, of 1970. The pontiff had invited the then

Bishop Oves to Rome and sent him to several important synods, including the one at Medellín, Colombia, in 1969.

The Archbishop was quoted in the interview as saying that he considered the United States trade blockade against Cuba "unjust." He praised "the role played by the Cuban Revolution in the evolution of the Latin American combination of events [*coyuntura*] in confronting a continental situation of injustice."

However, there is no doubt that formal religion is weakening in Cuba. I could see a difference between 1972 and my previous visit in 1967. On the earlier trip I could write that the Cubans went on taking the sacraments, having their children baptized, getting married in church, and seeking priests to administer the last rites. This was no longer true five years later, although there were no objections or impediments so far as the government was concerned.

The inevitable is happening: children and youths who have grown up under the Revolution have not gone to church or had any religious teaching in school and, in most cases, they have heard little or nothing of religion at home.

Yet one cannot forget in Cuba that Christianity means far more than church practices. Cuba is a Roman Catholic country; calling it Marxist-Leninist cannot change that.

CHAPTER 16

The Egalitarian State

That there may be equality: As it is written, "He that had gathered much had nothing over; and he that had gathered little had no lack."

—2 Corinthians 8:14,15

Cubans are a healthier people today than they were in 1958. In the field of public health, as in education, the achievements of the Revolution are remarkable, but little is known outside of specialized international organizations like the World Health Organization (WHO) about the advances in Cuban public health. There is no country in Latin America that can show anything comparable.

The Revolution began reorganizing and improving health services in its first year, but it was not until 1965 that the present system was established, starting with provincial health and hospital centers down to polyclinics at the local level.

The general practicioners who stayed in Cuba, and who are now the oldest and most experienced doctors, work in the health centers. As they retire, they are replaced by primary-care specialists, such as internists, pediatricians, and gynecologists. All physicians must serve two years in the rural health centers after their medical training, a revolutionary move of the first order considering the abysmal neglect of rural health care before 1959. Most physicians are required to divide their time between the hospitals and the health centers.

The most authoritative recent unofficial survey, "Health Services in Cuba," appeared in the *New England Journal of Medicine*, November 9, 1972. It was written by an American, Dr. Vicente Navarro, editor of the *International Journal of Health Services* of Johns Hopkins University. Dr. Navarro made two extensive trips to Cuba, the second for a United Nations agency. His article is based on his first stay in Cuba. He wrote me that the second trip bore out the findings of the first, with steady improvement being shown.

"Today Cuba is providing care to the majority of the population and minimizing the striking inequalities that existed between urban and rural areas in the distribution of health services before 1958," Dr. Navarro writes. A great deal has been done, he asserts, to equalize the historic inequalities between Havana and the other regions, especially Oriente Province. Most of the new hospitals and services have gone to rural and regional areas.

Among the statistics Dr. Navarro provides are these: two-thirds of the hospital beds existing in 1969 were added after 1958; the number of nurses almost doubled between 1958 and 1968; the patient bed-days per 100 inhabitants in 1969 was 92.6, "the highest in Latin America."

Equalization of health care around the country had the natural effect of reducing some services in Havana while they increased elsewhere. Dr. Navarro gives figures to show that the ratio of hospital beds per 1,000 population declined in Havana from fourteen in 1958 to twelve in 1969, while the ratio rose everywhere else. "The rate of increase of hospital construction during this decade," he writes, "was only 8 per cent in Havana compared with 184 per cent in Camagüey and 147 per cent in Oriente . . . Of the 236 new health centers which were built, over 50 per cent of them were allocated to the rural areas where they were totally nonexistent before 1958." In 1958, 65 percent of Cuba's physicians practiced in Havana; in 1971 the figure was 42 percent.

According to the Cuban Ministry of Health, there were 6,300 physicians in Cuba in 1959, of whom about 3,000 emigrated in the first five years of the Revolution.

"In response," writes Dr. Navarro, "the new government launched a massive campaign to attract university students to the medical profession. As part of the campaign, physicians were and are paid the highest salaries of all professionals in Cuba and are given special privileges . . . In 1970, applicants to medical schools represented 30 per cent of all applicants to university programs.

"The result of this intensive effort was that 5,293 new physicians were trained between 1959 and 1970, bringing the total number of practicing physicians today [1972] to over 7,000. Of these physicians, 600 are in part-time private practice and eighty in full-time private practice." (In December 1974, Fidel said there were 9,000 doctors with 6,000 in medical schools.)

To replace the émigrés, the new doctors had to be trained in a very short period in the early years. This naturally affected quality —a problem now fairly well taken care of by time and experience.

A new feature is that medicine, like other professions, is now equally available to young women as well as young men. As a result, half the medical students in 1971 were women, many of whom would have studied nursing before. Numerically, Cuba was getting more doctors and fewer other professionals than she needed. Starting in 1971 only 20 percent of all university applicants were allowed to choose medicine.

The education and training take a normal length of time—five years in medical school after the baccalaureate, followed by a year of internship and two years in compulsory rural medical service. Another three to five years as a clinical resident are required to qualify as a specialist. It was 1965 before young Cubans could even begin to practice. None of them, even in 1975, can be considered very experienced. However, since more than one-half the prerevolutionary physicians remained in Cuba, there is a solid basis for the medical professions. One is inclined to forget that the majority of the Cuban middle class in all professions did not emigrate.

Medical students, incidentally, like all students, must do their stints on the sugar plantations, although not cutting cane. This is part of Castro's determination that every Cuban will now be in contact with—and usually do—some physical work in field and factory. After 1970 the worker-student formula was applied to medicine first of all.

Dr. Navarro is critical of the fact that while the organizational and administrative structure of the health services changed substantially after 1959, medical education and curricula did not begin to change until 1963 and were not suitable to the demands of the Revolution until about 1968. The effort was to make up for the number who had emigrated rather than to create new types of physicians. But a more suitable curriculum was applied in 1968, oriented toward community care with special emphasis on social motivation. This placed the study of medicine where it belonged—in the revolutionary educational system.

The health services work up from localities to health centers for towns, regional hospitals, and provincial hospitals, all under the control of the Executive Committee of the Ministry of Health. Cooperating with them are four national institutions: the Committees for the Defense of the Revolution, the Federation of Cuban Women, the Association of Small Farmers, and the trade unions of the CTC.

> Health campaigns for the public [writes Dr. Navarro] in developing countries cannot succeed unless there is massive public participation in their implementation. The impressive progress witnessed in

> Cuba, for instance, in the reduction of most infectious diseases, would not have been feasible within the rather limited time period were it not for the massive participation of the Cuban population in the public health programs. . . .
>
> The Cuban experience puts a question mark on the well accepted argument used by some health planners that a lack of resources prevents the provision of health services to entire populations in most developing countries. Contradicting this argument, Cuba, a small country . . . is, in fact, providing comprehensive health services (not without great sacrifice) to the whole population without direct payment involved, as the result of its philosophy of equalization and comprehensiveness in health care . . . Because of its social and economic commitment to equalization, the Cuban Government is redistributing its health resources, both old and new, thus minimizing the striking inequalities so apparent before the Cuban Revolution . . . and thereby providing health services to the whole population . . . The redefinition of social groups and their decision-making power (which is taking place in Cuba) with all the economic, political and social ramifications that this change implies, seems to have been a requirement and consequence of that country's commitment to health as a human right.

Dr. Navarro referred in his article to the underreporting of and unreliability of prerevolutionary Cuban mortality and morbidity statistics. "However," he asserts, "it is to the credit of the new Cuban Government that, especially since 1965, high priority has been placed on establishing a reliable system of data gathering within the health sector in order to cover the whole population."

In 1974, according to government figures, there were 235 hospitals and 314 clinics in areas where there was little or no medical care before the Revolution. In 1958 there were 54 hospitals and only a handful of rural clinics in all of Cuba.

The Pan-American Health Organization of WHO, in its annual reports, noted that with mass mobilization 20 percent, or more than 2 million, of Cuban children under fifteen received polio vaccinations in eleven days in 1962; again in 1969 in just seventy-two hours, and in 1970 in only one day. The work was done mainly with the help of the Committees for the Defense of the Revolution. There has been no polio in Cuba since 1963. The same organization stated in 1971 that only the United States, Canada, and Cuba have eliminated polio, which makes Cuba the only Latin American country to have done so.

Malaria was eradicated by 1968; diphtheria by 1971. The incidences of typhoid fever were very low by 1967 and have undoubtedly been reduced since. Tetanus has been cut down to a very small figure and eradicated in childbirths. There have been significant decreases in mortality from such waterborne diseases as gastroenteritis and dysentery.

One of the most impressive figures of the public health program has been the reduction in infant mortality. There was a puzzling increase from 37 per 1,000 live births in 1965 to 40 in 1969. This may have been due to improved statistics gathering, as the nutritional level was relatively high and the incidence of infant diseases low. However, a sharp improvement began, and, according to World Health Organization figures, Cuba now has the lowest infant mortality rate in Latin America, with a figure of 27.7 per 1,000 births a year.

The maternal death rate (during pregnancy or while giving birth) was reduced from 11.5 to slightly less than 6 deaths out of every 10,000 women between 1959 and 1963, Dr. Armando Peralta of the Cuban Ministry of Health stated in an interview printed in *Granma* on August 11, 1973.

"Moreover," he added, "we should take into account that the former figure . . . does not include all the deaths it should, as deaths as a result of abortions were not reported as such at the time. The maternal mortality rate in our country now is the lowest in Latin America and similar to those in developed countries."

Dr. Peralta said that "a substantial reduction in deaths through abortions" was achieved by making intrauterine loops and other contraceptives "easily accessible to the population."

"In our country," Castro said in a speech on November 17, 1971, "the majority of women used to bear their children in their homes, without any medical attention . . . Today almost 100 per cent of the Cuban women bear their children in hospitals, in conditions of maximum security for themselves and their infants."

Babies and young children, in fact, are the most favored of Cuban citizens—helped into the world, fed, clothed, cared for, and, when old enough, educated.

Dr. Navarro, in one of his reports, writes that due to "the public's demand, translated through the mass organizations," there is a now-accepted and successful practice of allowing mothers to live at the hospitals with their hospitalized children.

All Cubans, of course, receive medical treatment, including dentistry, free, and all get the same treatments. Medicines, with some minor exceptions, are also free. However, as I stated, there are a certain number of doctors and dentists in private practice, mostly in the large cities. It is one way of using up otherwise unspendable pesos.

My own experience with dentistry, forced on me by a painfully broken tooth in Havana in September 1972, was impressive. It was a complicated job, done with as much skill as the best dentist in New York or London could have shown. And I could not pay, since I was, perforce, sent to one of the public health dentists. All dentists and doctors who joined the Public Health Service or who began to practice in 1964 have to take an oath that they will accept no pay for their work. The idea is that their education and their salaries having been paid for by the state, they have no right to charge.

My dentist, a thirty-nine-year-old mulatto, Dr. Llanes, had begun his studies in 1955 but started his practice under the Revolution, which sent him to Paris for a year of study. Being colored, he could not have hoped to practice with well-off white patients in Havana in prerevolutionary times. And what makes it revolutionary is that if I had been a poor old worker from a Havana slum I would, presumably, have had much the same care, except that I would have had to wait my turn after the initial emergency treatment, and it could well have been a long wait. However, even in London and Adelaide, Australia, I discovered, it was necessary to wait two or three months for an appointment with a reputable dentist except for emergency treatment.

Social services, such as free public health, education, old age and retirement pensions, are an especially heavy drain on the economy of a more or less underdeveloped nation, whether socialist or not. One has only to think of the intolerable burden of Uruguay's social services during its democratic period. This has been doubly so in the case of Cuba, which faced the supremely difficult task of changing over from a capitalist to a socialist economy. As I have already written, the cost and extent of the social services will be brought down to an economically bearable amount, but it is still planned to keep them at a generous level for all Cubans equally.

It is not possible for a work on a current and highly dynamic situation like Cuba's Revolution to be up to the minute when one's book is published. Important changes in the political, economic, and social structure of Cuba are taking place all the time. Nevertheless, the economic situation as I saw it in September 1972, and as it has been developing since, contains enough stable factors to write about safely. Some important changes took place in 1973 and 1974. The present trends—upward trends—were set in motion after the fiasco of the ten-million-ton sugar harvest in 1970, and they continued through 1974.

Deputy Prime Minister Carlos Rafael Rodríguez gave a summarizing speech to the U.N. Economic Commission for Latin America (ECLA) on March 27, 1973 (about which I wrote in a previous chapter), which contained a passage that for all its obvious partisan and nationalistic bias was, in my opinion, a fair statement of the facts and is still valid:

> There are not as many new cars in our cities as in certain Latin American capitals. There are not any luxury resorts in Cuba, because our vacation spots cater to a hard-working people. But neither are there any barefooted children begging, or any unemployed pleading for work. . . .
>
> But, even if we aren't satisfied with [our] rate of development, we are very happy over its form. While Latin America as a whole is plagued by internal and external difficulties that threaten to postpone this objective for more than a century, Cuba is marching confidently ahead. There are two basic reasons for this: we have made a revolution, and we have formed external connections that are helping us in the transition from backwardness to progress. . . .
>
> With these physical sacrifices and temporary lacks of consumer goods—which are enabling us to carry accumulation to unprecedented levels—we have taken the first step, and we know that our people don't complain about this added sacrifice, because they know what goals and objectives lie behind them. That is why those who had lost hope in the success of a military invasion or acts of sabotage, but trusted in the effects of a lack of economic efficiency, lost their last bit of hope on that unforgettable 26th of July in 1970 when, from the distance of their reason-inspired exile, they heard the response of the people to the words of Fidel Castro as he assumed responsibility, on behalf of the entire leadership, for our failure to reach our ambitious goal of the 10 million tons.

Cubans have been on short rations since 1962, but no Cuban has gone hungry or been undernourished. "According to a 1969 report by the Food and Agricultural Organization," Professor Thomas writes in his book on Cuba, "there was an estimated average intake of 2,650 calories per person per day in Cuba. (This was higher than both the Latin American average and the daily requirement of 2,500 calories.)"

Professor Nelson points out that the annual meat ration in 1962 was 36 pounds per capita; in 1972 it was 38 pounds. In 1958, he writes, 70 pounds per capita "was available." However, at that time meat was rationed by price, with large numbers of Cubans eating no meat at all. As of early 1975, *every* Cuban gets three-quarters of a pound of meat every nine days.

Joe Nicholson, Jr., who spent six weeks in Cuba in late 1972 and published his findings in a well-observed article, "Inside Cuba," for the April 1973 *Harper's*, listed the rations the Cubans were getting:

> Luxury items are rarely available and food is strictly rationed, except for such things as fish, beer and soft drinks. Even sugar, Cuba's principal product, would be limited to three and a half pounds monthly per person, assuming Fidel's proposal [to donate a half pound a month to the people of Chile] is accepted. [After the fall of Allende in September 1973, this sacrifice became unnecessary.]
>
> Other monthly rations per person include: six pounds of rice, three pounds of meat, three pounds of beans, two pounds of macaroni, two pounds of spaghetti, one and a half pounds of noodles, one pound of salt, twelve ounces of flour, six ounces of coffee, fifteen eggs, three containers of canned milk (fresh milk is for children and the old), fifteen servings of jello, four containers of yoghurt, two servings of cream of wheat, etc. . . .
>
> Workers usually eat an inexpensive and well-balanced lunch on the job: some eat all three meals there, leaving their rations to their families. Rural families and even some city dwellers keep poultry and small vegetable gardens. Finally, the absence of most consumer products generally leaves families with plenty of money to dine out. Most Cubans say they eat better now than they did before the Revolution. Clothing rations are a bigger problem than the food, especially for men, who every year receive two pairs of trousers, two shirts, and several pairs of shoes.

The black market, Nicholson writes (I was told the same), "has been virtually eliminated," for food, but clothing can still be bought, although "it has become increasingly scarce." Since Nicholson's visit, there has been a great increase in the production of textiles.

The bread ration is one pound a day, which is more than a great many people want—at least to my knowledge, in Havana. As a result, bakers often find themselves with extra bread, which they are allowed to put on general sale in the last hour of the day.

Fish is rationed, but it was so plentiful when Nicholson (and I) were in Cuba that one could buy more than the ration.

"Booths selling soft drinks and sandwiches have appeared on the streets of Havana and other large cities for the first time in five years," according to a Reuters dispatch printed in *The New York Times* on January 20, 1974. "The new stands are obviously state owned, as are the ice cream vans that made their appearance last summer." By mid-1974, the supply of consumer goods had improved so much that more than eighty products were taken off the ration list.

Rationing is simply a mechanism used in all countries to provide an equitable distribution in times of scarcity—such as the gasoline rationings of 1974. It has nothing *per se* to do with socialism or revolution, but on a day I spent in the green belt of Havana I had a lesson in what revolution means. I was in a pineapple-growing district and was told that two months previously, when the harvest was in and the export allotment had gone, pineapples were sold on ration, one pineapple for three persons, two for five, and so on. It was possible to do this twice for the 2,300,000 inhabitants of Havana Province, of whom 1,750,000 lived in the capital. Before the Revolution those who could afford the price bought all the pineapples they wanted, or ate them in the Floridita, Zaragozana, and other restaurants. Most *Habaneros* could not then afford to buy any pineapples at all.

In this harvest 20,000 *quintales* (hundredweights) were rationed —but for everybody. So each one had his taste of ambrosia, but no one had his fill. It was what Winston Churchill called "the equality of misery"—but it *was* equality. To be sure, it exposed an insoluble problem of socialism. To grow enough pineapples so that *every* inhabitant of Havana could have all he wanted whenever he wanted it, the whole fertile province would have to be given over to pineapples and then what about other fruits, vegetables, coffee, dairy products? But to leave the available supply of pineapples to the operations supply, demand, and price would not only be capitalist; it would be counterrevolutionary.

The problem of who could or could not acquire new automobiles was solved in simple fashion—no private person could import or buy an automobile. The new ones are all official cars or taxicabs. Small Alfa Romeos were the most favored. I was told that the government had had the opportunity to buy a large lot at $2,000 each from Italy. Many of the taxis are Italian Fiats. The rest of the new, or newish, cars were Russian Volgas, no doubt acquired on credit. They are not as good as the Italian cars. Since then the French have moved in with Citroëns and the Germans with Mercedes Benz's. Under the new Argentine trade agreement, Fords, Chryslers, and General Motors cars and trucks are going in. There are still plenty of prerevolutionary cars, looking very dilapidated. Fidel boasted in 1969 that "we only imported about 1,000 automobiles in ten years, but we imported 50,000 tractors." Those days are gone, doubtless forever.

There is no income tax in revolutionary Cuba. In fact, virtually all taxes had been eliminated by 1970. This not only suited Castro's revolutionary soul, but the government was able to sweep away a huge bureaucratic structure, while managers or other equivalents of private employers were saved that many accountants and much paperwork.

Rents were scheduled to disappear by 1970, but did not. However, they are enviably low—8 to 10 percent of wages, whatever is earned and however big or small a house or apartment may be. Electricity, water, and local telephone services were free until the end of 1973, when small charges were introduced. Sports events and funerals are still free. Bus fares within city limits are five centavos.

"The regime has dedicated upward of 25 per cent of its gross national product to development works," writes Lowry Nelson in his book *Cuba*, "most of them directly or indirectly affecting agriculture."

The investments are showing signs of paying dividends at last. How much time has been needed to hit a promising rate of progress, and how much more time is still needed to achieve a modest prosperity! Those early years of euphoria and dazzling dreams are gone. Publicly, at least, Fidel is not letting the boom in sugar prices go to his head.

In Havana, on my last trip, I had a talk with the men who run JUCEPLAN (the Central Junta for Planning), which manages the whole Cuban economy. They were modest in their claims, even though the recovery from the 1970 crisis was clearly under way. They talked realistically of needing seven to eight years before the sugar industry was fully mechanized and capable of averaging six to seven million tons a year. In order to mechanize properly, some land has to be leveled. They too claimed that the proper cane-cutting machine has been developed in Russia, but 2,500 of them will be needed and only fifty were in production when Castro visited the Russian factory in July 1972. There will have to be an investment of $300 million for the machines. For the next fifteen years the economy must concentrate on sugar, they told me.

The cattle industry, they said, was only then recovering from the 1970 *zafra*. It will be five to ten years from 1975 before cattle or meat exports become important. Deputy Prime Minister Rodríguez frankly said to me that "cattle is of no great importance; it has not yet been a big success despite what you have been told and read.

Sugar, citrus fruits, nickel and tobacco are all ahead of cattle in exports."

The JUCEPLAN directors told me that it takes five to fifteen years before trees bearing citrus fruits are fully matured. At a big farm outside Havana, which was a new development, they said that it takes five years for avocados to reach full growth, three for strawberries, and two for pineapples. In Pinar del Río and Oriente provinces, where rice is now being grown extensively (and in Las Villas, which I did not visit), it was explained to me that while production has increased and although rice can be produced in one year, the preparation of the ground and the necessary irrigation works take a long time.

The third-largest export today, and potentially the most important, is nickel. (The export of citrus fruit is at present in second place.) Cuba ranks after the United States in her supply of nickeliferous ore. Both the formerly American-owned mines—Nicaro and Moa Bay—have been fully restored to working order, with some Russian help. The 1958 production was 18 million tons; in 1967 it totaled 35 million, and the figure has gone up since. A new program of expansion, with a Russian credit said to total $100 million, is supposed to get under way now. The nickel ore is sold to France, Spain, and Germany as well as to the Soviet Union. Fidel has complained that the United States has made exports of nickel difficult to some countries by the American ban on importing any goods made with Cuban nickel.

Despite all the errors, floundering, and time lost, almost everything about the Cuban economy today (early 1975) points toward a slow but steady strengthening of the infrastructure (the industrial and agricultural base), to which the advances in the professions must be added. Above all, there has been the fantastic rise in sugar prices on the world market.

In addition to what I have mentioned here, there were 60 percent more new roads built in the eight years before 1973 than in the whole previous history of the Republic. Reforestation only began with the Revolution, which planted more than 550 million trees between 1960 and 1971, of which 330 million were usable for timber. (The figures were given to the Food and Agricultural Organization at the conference in Cali, Colombia, in August 1972.) This constituted thirty-three times the number of trees planted between 1898 and 1958.

Housing—one of the most stubborn of all problems in underdeveloped (and for that matter, developed) countries—has made fair progress, but there is a long way to go. I visited new *viviendas* (blocks of flats) in and around Havana, Pinar del Río, and Santiago de Cuba. One big development, Alamar, was being built by the volunteer *minibrigadas.* The accommodations seemed comfortable and adequate, a great improvement for those who lived in slums before or in the miserable, poorest kind of huts I saw in Santiago next to the new *viviendas.*

There have been vast and much-praised irrigation works around the island; a steady growth in electric plants for water power, with some new Russian technical and financial aid coming along; new factories for fertilizers; and so forth.

In the old, expropriated factories, the newcomers are very conscious of the fact that their enemies, domestic and foreign, scrutinize every product to be able to criticize it. There was much scope for criticism in the early years, with Che Guevara as the most caustic critic of all. Results are generally better now.

If the famous ex-Bacardi rum factory of Santiago de Cuba is a fair example, the lesson has been learned. The factory now turns out Bacardi rum, but calls it El Caney for domestic consumption and Havana Club for export. As a rum drinker, I would say the quality is as good as it was. Two of the foremen had been with the firm, they said, for fifty years. One of them remembered a visit my wife and I made in 1958 with the famous proprietor, José M. Bosch, who helped Fidel at first, then went into exile, and has Bacardi factories in Puerto Rico, Florida, Mexico, and Brazil.

The Cuban factory is being enlarged, and the welcoming committee, headed by a young Negro, claimed that they now produce much more of the high-quality rum than before. The workmen, I was told, had almost all stayed on; only the owners and managers fled.

In his July 26, 1970, speech Fidel had said that "there remain 75,000, neither housewives, students nor disabled, who simply do not work." While this was a complaint, the unemployed figure in the 1958 "dead season" was given as 686,000. However, I was assured in 1972 by government leaders and by the heads of the labor CTC and JUCEPLAN that "there is no unemployment." By technical economic standards this is true.

"Cuba," Dr. Vicente Navarro wrote for the U.N. Food and Agricultural Organization's review, *Ceres,* in 1969, "displays one fundamental characteristic which distinguishes it from most other underdeveloped countries: it has no unemployment problem; on the contrary, it has a painful labor shortage." Among the reasons he gave were the abolition of child labor through compulsory education; "the considerable expansion of the agricultural area"; and "the building of roads and dams, reafforestation, house construction, etc."

Of course, it must never be forgotten that Cuba has no oil, coal, or iron, no steel industry, and is only now getting some water power and lumber. These are unavoidable handicaps. When it comes to commodities, nature is not to be revolutionized.

Claude Begin, Reuters correspondent in Havana, wrote in an article for *The New York Times* in January 1974: "Economic growth was 5 per cent in 1972 and 13 per cent last year."

In 1972, 1973, and 1974, there were important moves toward the long-awaited and inevitable institutionalization of the Revolution. In August 1974, a start was made at changing and partially democratizing the grass-roots structure of Cuba. It is potentially the most important political development since the start of the Revolution in 1959. The process is beginning as an experiment, but one that was carefully worked out, and it has gotten off to a good start.

The province of Matanzas has been placed, administratively under "organs of People's Power" *(organos de Poder Popular)*, secretly and democratically elected and free of any interference by the Cuban Communist Party. The functions of these "organs" will cover much of the responsibility for the National Councils and Institutes of culture, broadcasting, sports, cinema, tourism, transportation, communication, public health, and some fields of industry and agriculture. Certain functions of the Committees for the Defense of the Revolution will also be taken over by the new bodies.

"A total of 5,597 production and service units throughout the province will be handed over to the organs of People's Power," Fidel Castro said in his July 26, 1974, speech. "This is the basic criterion: all production and service units that serve the community—that is the grass roots—must be controlled at the grass roots level."

It is a move toward decentralization of adminstration and institutionalization—a word that Fidel himself now uses. As he explained in his speech:

"The Revolutionary Government is provisional in nature. . . . We seized state power, installed a revolutionary government and began to carry out the Revolution. . . . Now we must think of the definitive form that the socialist state of Cuba will take. . . . To put it another way, we must replace our destruction of the old laws with discipline and respect for the new laws. . . .

"The [Communist] Party does not adminster the state. The state must be administered by the masses through their organs of People's Power. The Party has other functions."

The process of extending the system to every province in the country is to be completed in 1976, Castro said, at which time "the socialist state of Cuba" will have assumed its definitive form.

The delegates elected to the Matanzas organs of People's Power were given a seventeen-day seminar on their functions, at the end of which Raúl Castro delivered a long exposition of the meaning and ideas behind the new institution. Raúl called the new system "democratic centralism." It is to put an end to "bureaucratic centralism" and "make the participation of the masses in state power something real."

Fidel Castro still remains very much the *Jefe Máximo*, but Cuba is becoming less of a one-man operation than it used to be. This is more or less what Fidel promised in his speech of July 26, 1970.

There already is such a bewildering array of governmental, party, economic, social, professional, and other national institutions that one wonders whether the Revolution is not too well organized. Every year has brought new organizations to fit new needs and new ideas. This has been true especially in the last three years. These manifold organs are now being streamlined and decentralized. As Fidel Castro keeps saying, a revolution is a process.

An experience of Dr. Vicente Navarro in the field of public health was typical.

"I was invited to sessions of the Executive Committee of the Ministry of Public Health," he wrote me, "as well as to the Executive Committees of the provinces, regions, even health centers. All these sessions were completely unrehearsed and my speaking Spanish gave me a great opportunity to see how decisions were made in the health sector . . . It seems that decision-making is highly centralized while the implementation of these decisions is highly decentralized."

The political power structure was haphazard until November 24, 1972, when an Executive Committee of the Council of Ministers (i.e., a Cabinet) was created, "pursuant to orientations from the Political Bureau of the Communist Party of Cuba." The Committee is composed of Fidel Castro as Prime Minister, several deputy prime ministers, and President Dorticós.

The Council of Ministers was enlarged by the addition of the heads of those state agencies that have ministerial rank. These included seventeen ministries, agencies like JUCEPLAN, the National Bank of Cuba, the National Institute of Fishing, the Secretariat of the Presidency (i.e., Celia Sánchez), et cetera.

A subordinate group of state agencies are to be considered as "annexes" of the Council of Ministers. Seventeen more organizations are involved, such as the Academy of Sciences, the Book Institute, and the Institute of Civil Aeronautics.

"With the aim of establishing conditions under which the Prime Minister [Castro] can give his best and most steady attention to such agencies," they are grouped under seven deputy prime ministers, all close associates of Fidel.

At the intermediate levels, and as a temporary measure, Provincial Councils are set up of delegates appointed by the deputy prime ministers "in coordination with the delegates of the [Communist Party's] Political Bureau." These Provincial Councils will merely have "a coordinating character," carrying out "orientations and directives" from above "which in no case are to be altered without the previous knowledge and approval of the corresponding central authority."

And Fidel Castro? Here is where the new governmental set-up places him: "The Prime Minister, Major Fidel Castro Ruz, who presides over the Executive Committee of the Council of Ministers, will also be directly in charge of the following agencies: Ministry of the Revolutionary Armed Forces, Ministry of the Interior, Secretariat of the Presidency and Council of Ministers, National Institute of Agrarian Reform and Ministry of Public Health, as well as the Children's Institute as an annex to the Council of Ministers."

This makes Fidel Castro—or keeps him—all powerful. It is still *his* Revolution. All the primary organs of power—the Armed Forces; the Ministry of the Interior, which includes the police and intelligence units; the INRA, the all-embracing agricultural institute—are among the institutions under his direct charge. This is without counting the fact that he is first secretary of the Central Committee of the Communist Party, through which the orders came to establish the new Executive Council of the cabinet ministers. Moreover, every minister and agency head would belong to the PCC, which now—it can be said with finality—runs Cuba under Fidel Castro. One can say of the PCC what is said of the British monarch: it reigns but it does not rule.

An interesting feature of the new set-up is that the Ministry of Foreign Affairs is made subordinate to a "Foreign Agencies Sector" headed by Deputy Prime Minister Carlos Rafael Rodríguez. This means that Foreign Minister Raúl Roa is responsible to Rodríguez and is not a member of the Executive Committee although he remains in the Council of Ministers. In the same way, Raúl Castro, minister of the armed forces, is responsible to his brother and is not a member of the Executive Committee.

Although the organizations and institutes named in the Council of Ministers' resolution are bewildering in number and type, there are other important ones not listed. One is the most important non-governmental mass organization in Cuba—the CDR (Committees for the Defense of the Revolution), which is under the control of the Communist Party. Another is the ANAP (National Association of Small Farmers).

A third is a new and very important paramilitary national labor organization under the Ministry of the Armed Forces (FAR). Since it was created only on August 2, 1973, there has not been time at this writing to see how well it will work. It is linked to a new social service law and to regulations for obligatory military service. These steps seem to take Cuba further toward regimentation and militarization of the regime, although one can also say that the recent changes do not represent much more than a tidying up, streamlining, and institutionalization of loose and disorganized practices.

The new organization is called the Army of Working Youth (Ejercito Juvenil del Trabajo). It absorbs the five-year-old Centennial Youth Column (CJC) of the Young Communist League—about 110,000 youths in the construction, sugar, fishing, and other industries. Its main purpose, Raúl Castro, Minister of the Armed Forces, said in a speech on August 3, is to relieve the army of "devoting many thousands of its forces to production work for long periods of time." This had been "leading to a gradual decline in the defensive capability of the country and increasing the cost of defense." The units will be "part of the frontline reserves in case of war." In peacetime they will concentrate on agricultural work, especially the sugar harvest.

The texts of these laws are reprinted from the official gazette of August 2, 1973, in the magazine *Verde Olivo* of August 19.

"The Army of Working Youth," says Article 2, "will incorporate all youths under obligation to fulfill active military service." Students whose conscription has been postponed because they are in universities also become part of the organization. The soldier-work units of the armed forces, who played such a great role in the sugar harvests, are dissolved.

The new Social Service Law is based on the idea that "a man's education is a permanent process of carrying out social services" after graduation, on the theory that the knowledge he acquired—"technical, scientific, and cultural"—was a free gift of the state.

"All Cuban citizens of both sexes," Article 2 continues, "are obligated to fulfill Social Service on graduation from university, technical school, or teaching courses [*Educación Superior*]." Article 3 states: "The Social Service will last three years and can be combined with Active Military Service" (which also lasts three years).

The new conscription law *(Ley del Servicio Militar General)* holds that "it is the inescapable duty and the right of all citizens to serve the *Patria* in arms, and to defend with them the conquests of the Socialist Revolution against the attacks of the imperialist enemy."

(The enemy is the United States. It is interesting to note that the Castro government is officially called the Revolución Socialista, which, as with the Union of Socialist Soviet Republics, does not make it any the less Communist.)

Article 5 denominates as "militiamen" the workers and peasants who belong as reservists to the FAR's Wartime Units *(Unidades de Tiempo de Guerra)*. They are to continue preparing "victoriously to repel the imperialist enemy." All members of the Civil Defense are also considered to be *milicianos.*

Women over the age of seventeen can volunteer to enlist in the armed forces and can take courses in the Military Instruction Centers. After proper training, women from seventeen to forty years old can become reservists.

A chapter of Cuban revolutionary history was ended on that same August 2, 1973. Celia Sánchez, in her capacity of secretary of the Presidency, issued a decree that must have saddened the hearts of many veterans of the Sierra Maestra and the Rebel Army. They now become reservists and are forbidden to wear olive-green uniforms or any insignia unless they are actively serving in the Armed Forces.

At Raúl Castro's suggestion, the size of the Armed Forces was reduced from 300,000 to about 150,000, and Raúl told me in September 1972 that they would be further reduced in the near future. The August 1973 decrees have made that possible. Even at the reduced figures, the army is a great economic and labor drain. Batista had only about 30,000 regulars in his army.

The clear trend has been toward professionalism—fewer "citizens in arms" and more regulars. Also, fewer women defending the regime with rifles and more working in factories, fields, and the professions. The Revolution has changed their family lives and their role in society. They play a major part in the all-important Committees for the Defense of the Revolution. There are more girls in the universities. Young peasant women, who never before in Cuban history could get a proper education or leave the drudgery of their rural hovels in villages and on farms, now go to sewing schools, take handicraft courses, learn nursing. Rationing and food shortages give them all a hard scramble, since working women in Cuba, as in all countries, generally have to do the housework as well as their jobs. One truly revolutionary advance for a great many of them is that their babies and young children are taken care of in the Círculos Infantiles while the mothers work or study.

They have a remarkable national organization—the Federation of Cuban Women (FMC)—headed by a remarkable woman, Vilma Espín, wife of Raúl Castro and mother of his four children. At a plenary meeting of the FMC in December 1972, it was announced that there were 1,615,478 members, two-thirds of them between the ages of fourteen and sixty-five, with 400,700 working.

So far as it is possible in any society, prostitution has been eliminated. Havana alone was said to have had 270 brothels before the Revolution. They were a source of abundant graft for government and police officials. As Castro said to Lee Lockwood, prostitution is "a vicious, corrupt, cruel thing, that generally affects women of humble origin who, for a number of economic and social reasons, wind up in that life." However, Fidel let the traditional *posadas* stay open and even financed them, because, as he put it, "they satisfy a social need." *Posadas* are literally "inns" where couples can go and stay for some hours.

Nevertheless, as Professor Thomas points out, of the one hundred Communist Party Central Committee members, only five are women. Of these, three—Celia Sánchez, Vilma Espín, and Haydée Santamaría—are revolutionaries. One, Elena Gil, is President Dorticós' secretary. The fifth is an old-guard Communist, Clementina Serra. "Feminine membership in our Party is only 12.79 percent," Fidel lamented in a speech on November 29, 1974. He conceded that women do not get their share of "leadership posts."

Of course, traditional Cuban (really Spanish) attitudes of men toward women and vice versa could not change suddenly, or even in the course of sixteen years, revolution or no revolution. Yet the life that Cuban men and women lead has changed, and with it the relationship of the sexes surely must be changing. No doubt, as with the advent of the "permissive society" everywhere, the changes affect young Cubans more than their parents.

There are more men than women in Cuba, according to the 1970 census (the most thorough and accurate ever taken). The total population was 8,553,395, of whom 4,374,624, or 51.1 percent, were male and 4,178,771, or 48.9 percent, women. It is a young country —40.3 percent below the age of seventeen, compared to 27 or 28 percent in the United States.

The island is more urbanized than before the Revolution—60.5 percent in 1970, compared to 57 percent in 1958.

A revolutionary dictator is piloting his ship of state through a violent storm which, like a Sorcerer's Apprentice, he himself has conjured up. He can never be free of the forces that he cannot control; up to a point, the ship is driven, not steered.

Fidel does not want—perhaps he does not dare—to create a self-governing central administration, a managerial apparatus, an autonomous political party, a powerful military élite. Any one of these could not only threaten his power but, more importantly in his eyes, weaken, distort, or divert the social revolutionary process for which he has fought and lived.

The recent government, army, and labor laws prove that the dynamism which infuses every revolution is forcing Fidel into a gradual widening and decentralization of his authority. One of the lessons of the 1970 sugar-crop failure, as he conceded, was the need to disperse power and to make room for the new generation of trained, zealous, and ambitious young men and women.

Cuba in 1975 is superficially a highly militarized state, but without losing its revolutionary character and without turning Fidel Castro into a military dictator. The top Cuban "militarists" are ex-Rebel civilians in uniform.

The Cuban process was unique, for it was not a case of a political (Communist) party creating its military organization and controlling it, as in Russia, China, and Vietnam, or of a military clique organizing a political party, as in Mexico. In Cuba there was a political and military vacuum to begin with. In the early months of the Revolution, it was the Rebel Army which performed most of the tasks of government, since the remaining members of the Batista administration could not be trusted. Military courts superceded civil. The Rebel Army took over the property of the *Batistianos,* repaired bridges, turned barracks and the homes of the rich into schools, set up rural hospitals, worked on the farms, provided personnel for government agencies, including the INRA (the agrarian institute). Fidel never abandoned his olive-gray uniform of *comandante* even in his new rank as commander in chief.

Now—in 1975—the army seems to be returning to its original position, but with a difference. It is politicized, and it is Communist. *Granma,* in an editorial on December 2, 1972 (the sixteenth anniversary of the landing from Mexico), was frank about it:

> The FAR is a class army, a socialist army, one that is educated in the principles of Marxism-Leninism, solidarity with all peoples who are struggling for their national and social liberation, fraternal unity with the Soviet Armed Forces and other armies of the sister socialist states and staunch unity around the Party and our Commander-in-Chief.
>
> A large percentage of the officers of our FAR, at all levels of authority, are members of the Party or the Young Communist League. This is an indicator of the political and ideological force concentrated in them.
>
> With the help of the Soviet Union and its military specialists, our Revolutionary Armed Forces have been forged as a mighty regular army equipped with modern and effective combat material, high combat readiness and discipline and organization. They are ready to deal with and crush any enemy attack.

On January 2, 1974, the fifteenth anniversary of the triumph of the Revolution, the armed forces put on by far the most impressive military display ever held in a Latin American nation. From infantry, militia, and cadets to artillery, tanks, anti-aircraft missiles, and MIG jets flying overhead in formation, it was a show that Israel could not have bettered. On December 29, at the Isle of Pines, the Revolutionary Navy displayed how formidably it is armed for a sophisticated missile defense against ships and planes.

"It was not a case of piling up weapons for the sake of having them," Castro said in his speech at Camagüey. "It has been a vital need of our people."

And the "need"? In the military exercises held in Camagüey on December 30, the "enemy" invaders were pointedly labeled as the "northern" forces who had landed in the zone of Nuevitas on the coast and who, of course, were routed and driven back to their transport ships, which, in turn, were "sunk" by units of the Revolutionary Navy and Air Force. So much for the Colossus of the North!

The proliferation of army titles and olive-drab uniforms at every stage of government and industry has led a number of historians of the Revolution to conclude that Cuba has succumbed to what Professor Dumont called "*cette néo-stalino-militarisation.*" He sees careerists *(arrivistes)* developing "as in all Communist countries."

"The New Class—the new power élite," Lowry Nelson calls it. He puts it in typical fashion: "Privileges of many kinds are enjoyed by members of the new inner circle and dispensed by favorites as they wish." The latter half of the sentence is not true. The "privileges" are in all cases modest—extraordinarily so when one considers what comparable officials would have got in prerevolutionary governments. Moreover, many of these so-called privileges are necessary or suitable for the work being performed.

It is hard to see what argumentative point is gained by remarking that a cabinet minister or some equivalent official or a commanding officer in the FAR has a car and chauffeur, a better house to live in so that he can invite guests, a servant or two, a better and bigger supply of food, rum and cigars on hand, and so forth. The important fact—and all Cubans know it—is that such a cabinet minister, or whatever he is, is not enriching himself, not sending money abroad, not buying real estate in Florida, not living in arrogant luxury, and is working very hard. Human nature being what it is, he may be envied and criticized, but he will not be despised, nor will patriotic Cubans be ashamed of him as they used to be with so many officials in prerevolutionary times.

Still, one must face the fact that the all-pervading Communist apparatus of government and industry is clothed in uniforms and carries military titles. Fidel Castro, as I said, commands the most powerful armed forces in Latin America. It is arguable that, historically, he comes out of the *caudillo* tradition of Latin America, out of the father figures of the great *haciendas,* out of *personalismo.* He can change the Revolution, as he has several times; he cannot change himself or his character.

There was no *caudillismo* in the Cuban Republic until Sergeant Fulgencio Batista came along in 1933. The Americans had disbanded the Rebel Army in 1900, leaving a sort of vacuum which they themselves felt constrained to fill with Marines on several occasions. There was no Cuban army as such until 1909. Generals did not become presidents in typical Latin American fashion. Instead, they became partners of the politicians, for whom they tried, unsuccessfully, to maintain law and order and with whom they collaborated heartily in graft. The biggest peculators during Batista's last stretch of power were his generals and colonels.

When Fidel Castro came along, he in his turn disbanded the army and dismissed or arrested those officers who had served Batista too well and who were unable to flee to hospitable Florida. Then he had to create his own Rebel Army, which became the FAR. This army was originally formed of Rebels, all volunteers. Fidel had promised that there would be no conscription, but this was one of those promises that he could not or did not want to keep. As the years passed and younger men were trained as officers, the generally apolitical character of the amateurish officer corps turned into its present Communist cadre. More and more posts are being entrusted to those young men who were boys or children when the Revolution began. The decrees of August 2, 1973, which I have written about here, are signs of the old giving way to the new.

Without agreeing with Dumont, Nelson, Karol, Thomas, and some others about the significance of the militarism, one is entitled to wonder what this forebodes. The young ones, who did not fight in the Sierra or in the underground, will become true career officers. So long as the Castro brothers (Raúl has always been minister of the armed forces) are there, supported by the ever-loyal Sierra Maestra group, there can be no significant change in the course of the Revolution, nor is the nominal "militarization" very significant. However, Latin American history has provided a great many examples of what can happen when generals and colonels are given their chance to seize power.

Cuba is not a police state; there is no police terror. The Castro government is not remotely like the sinister military regimes of Brazil, Paraguay, Chile, and Uruguay (to name only South American examples), where widespread, systematic use of torture has become a normal instrument of "law and order."

The worst that can be said of the revolutionary regime—at least, as I see it—is that the practice of holding political offenders in prison and rehabilitation labor camps goes on, year after year. Even Generalissimo Franco in Spain and—when he was in power—General Papadopoulos in Greece (whose countries I am not comparing to Cuba) gave amnesties to political prisoners. Fidel Castro has not given one in sixteen years.

In July 1964 he told Richard Eder of *The New York Times* that the political prisoners totaled "something under 15,000," conceding that "this is a great many." A year later, talking to Lee Lockwood, he said: "I think that there must be 20,000 . . . Unfortunately, we are going to have prisoners for counterrevolutionary reasons for many years to come . . . In a revolutionary process, there are no neutrals; there are only partisans of the revolution or enemies of it. In every great revolutionary process it happens like this: in the French Revolution, in the Russian Revolution and in our Revolution."

There has been little direct news about the political prisoners in the last ten years. No international body has been allowed to visit the prisoners, and no foreign journalists. Trials are not open to observers.

According to Hugh Thomas, "Accounts by ex-prisoners of appalling conditions during interrogation or in Cuban political prisons . . . are too numerous to be discounted. It is true that most accounts of inhumanity date back to 1960–1961 . . . On the other hand, conditions in ordinary prisons for common criminals have certainly improved since 1959, with serious efforts being made at re-education."

A much graver charge was made by Amnesty International, the respected organization with United Nations and Council of Europe connections that seeks to hold a watching brief and alarm system over what they called in an October 1973 pamphlet "Epidemic Torture."

"In over thirty countries," writes Victor Jokel, director of British Amnesty, "torture is systematically applied to extract confessions, elicit information, penalise dissent and deter opposition to repressive governmental policy."

In the list of more than thirty countries was Cuba. At the bottom of the page is a line in fine print stating: "Substantial allegations of the use of torture in these countries have been reported by Amnesty International in 1973."

I wrote Victor Jokel, expressing incredulity and pointing out that "aside from the fact that 'substantial' is a vague word, my Concise Oxford Dictionary gives 'allegation' as 'an assertion (especially one not proved).' "

He telephoned me, saying that in the book *Report on Torture* (which was published by Amnesty in London the following month) no claim was made that torture was used "systematically" in Cuba, and he conceded that they had no information to that effect. He also admitted that they were exercising "caution" with regard to Cuba because no international organization has been allowed to enter the country and investigate the allegations.

The passage on Cuba in Amnesty's book is based on reports made by the Inter-American Commission on Human Rights of the Organization of American States and by the International Commission of Jurists. Here is the key passage referring to Cuba, headed "Political Prisoners and Their Families in Cuba":

> The information has been gathered from allegations made by Cuban prisoners and their families. In these reports there is a wealth of allegations of physical and psychological torture, executions and simulated executions of prisoners, and inhuman prison conditions. Most of the allegations are gathered from the early 1960's, although the most recent report (of April 1970) includes allegations made up to 1969. Prisoners have alleged that, when they refused to accept the ideological Rehabilitation courses imposed by the Cuban Government, they were subjected to manifold tortures. The report concluded that the

> situation of political prisoners in Cuba displayed serious characteristics incompatible with the UN Declaration of Human Rights.
>
> As the Cuban Government has consistently refused to accept an international commission of inquiry, it has been impossible to check these allegations.

The book gives "two recent allegations of torture." One I have already mentioned: Heberto Padilla, the poet. The other is Pedro Luis Boitel, "who died in Castillo del Principe Prison after a long hunger strike, allegedly after torture by prison guards."

The section on Cuba concludes: "Amnesty International has received no allegations of torture in Cuba during 1973." If, as Professor Thomas wrote, prisons for common criminals have improved, it is reasonable to suppose that they would have improved for political prisoners.

Since Cubans have not permitted foreign observers to investigate, one has to remain either in the realm of "allegations" or, in my case for instance, on the plane of personal knowledge. I am as certain as I can be of anything that Fidel Castro and his close associates would not authorize or knowingly stand for the use of physical torture. I do not know where they—or any other ruling group in any country, including the United States—would draw the line at so-called psychological torture. Police everywhere have to use more or less forceful measures and long and perhaps maddening questioning of suspects. Even the British employed measures in Northern Ireland in 1973 that Amnesty International branded as torture. When torture is used as a regular practice—"systematically," to use Amnesty's word—as it is in Brazil, Chile, Turkey, Spain, Vietnam, and the Soviet Union, it becomes common knowledge. There is certainly no such knowledge about Cuba. If there was torture in the first few years of the Revolution, it would have been the unauthorized work of petty sadists.

The haphazard, arbitrary methods of the judicial system in Cuba did make injustices, one must suppose, inevitable at times. There was no habeas corpus until June 1973. A judicial code has, at long last, gone into effect, regularizing and codifying Cuban law, which had been working without rules or standard procedures. It is, as no doubt has to be expected under a form of totalitarianism, political justice.

A "Law for the Organization of the Judicial System" was concluded on September 1, 1972. It will form part of the new *Codigo Legal,* which, Blas Roca told me at that time, was almost completed. Blas, as president of the Secretariat of the Commissions of Juridical

Studies, has been working on the new constitution since 1966.

Article 6 of the judicial law says:

> It is the duty of the tribunals [courts] to elevate the juridical social conscience as a means of contributing to the development and realization of *political* [my italics], economic, cultural and social tasks which the construction of socialism requires, making opportune pronouncements in their decisions to educate citizens in the conscientious and voluntary observance of their duties of loyalty to the country and the cause of socialism; in the fulfillment of working discipline; in their duties to the State and society; and in respect for social propriety, the rights of others and in the norms of socialist living-together in general.

"We will be respectful of the Law," Castro said at a meeting to celebrate the event, "but of the Revolutionary Law; respectful of Right [*Derecho*], but of revolutionary Right, not of the old Right but of the new Right which we are going to make. Nothing for the old Right; no respect, but all respect for the new Right; no respect for the old Law, but all respect for the new Law."

As part of the new system, a "Council of Government of the People's Supreme Court" was launched in Havana on July 2, 1973. *Granma* called it "the first practical step in the inauguration of the new judicial system." The chairman is Dr. Enrique Hart, a jurist from prerevolutionary days and father of Armando.

"Lay judges" will participate in the courts, who are "elected by the political and mass organizations . . . and in the case of courts at the grass-roots level, by the people in the neighborhoods." *Granma* calls this "a firm step on the road to the democratization of the administration of justice."

"The new Criminal Law has already gone into effect, and the Civil Law is being worked on," President Dorticós said in inaugurating the Supreme Court Council. "One day, there will have to be a new Civil Code. I think it won't be long before we should work, too, on the elaboration of a new Constitution."

On October 23, 1974, Blas Roca announced the formation of a commission to draw up a "Draft Constitution" to be submitted to a referendum. The plans are to make it much shorter and clearer than the 1940 constitution. It will contain only articles that can and will go into effect and not remain on paper, as with the 1940 constitution, Blas Roca told me.

The time and care taken on the constitution are typical of the assurance that Castro and his associates feel about the durability of the Revolution. Fidel sees the Revolution as a continuing process, and he has always been reluctant to do anything that would hamper its dynamism.

However, a new constitution will be completed before 1975 ends. As with governments from Moscow to Madrid, it will have an elected national assembly. After a predictably favorable referendum in 1976, the Cuban Revolution will be fully institutionalized but it will still be Fidel Castro's Revolution.

CHAPTER 17

The Russian Connection

De omnibus dubitandem (You must have doubts about everything).

—Karl Marx's favorite motto

The failure of the Castro government in its efforts to achieve the ten-million-ton sugar harvest in 1970 made Cuba more dependent than ever on the Soviet Union and the Communist bloc. She got more help, but it stands to reason that she has had to pay some price to the Russians. This seemed evident when the terms of the agreement that Fidel signed in Moscow on December 23, 1972, were revealed by him in a nationwide television and radio address on January 3, 1973.

The differences from before 1970 are technical, material, and practical, not ideological or political, nor do they affect the conduct of the Revolution as such in Cuba. The Soviet Union is still six thousand miles away; still uninterested in acquiring any property or business control; still aiming to make Cuba as economically viable as possible and not, as was the case with the United States before the Revolution, as economically dependent.

The present situation, so far as one can tell, is a temporary accommodation by which—hopefully—Cuba will benefit to the point where she either ceases to be a burden on the Soviet Union or becomes a greatly lessened one. In the meantime—five, ten, twenty years?—Cuba will be a part of the international socialist trading bloc through COMECON (Council for Mutual Economic Assistance), which she joined in 1972. The greatly increased returns from the high sugar prices could shorten the term of dependence.

It is impossible to know what part the Russians and Eastern Europeans may have played in bringing the many improvements that have occurred since 1970. The role could not have been a great one, because there has not yet been much time for the new trade agreement to take practical effect. There may well be more Soviet-bloc technicians, advisers, planners, and managers about, but if so, they are not visible. A few diplomats told me in September 1972 that they noticed more Eastern Europeans in Havana, but I could see no difference from the picture five years before. It could be that Fidel Castro now takes more advice or lets foreign advisers do more managing and planning.

The 1972 agreement may be one of the most important developments in the history of the Revolution. We have seen the earlier phases of Cuban-Russian relations. They started glowingly with the Mikoyan trade pact early in 1962; were relatively unfriendly after the missile crisis in October 1962; improved somewhat for a few years; and then hit an all-time low around 1967–1968, partly as a reflection of the Soviet Union's friendly relations with Latin American dictators whom Castro was trying to overthrow. As recently as 1969, K. S. Karol wrote in his book *Guerrillas in Power* of Cuba's "possible or rather probable expulsion from the Communist family."

Fidel Castro was not exactly sitting on the fence, but he was not wholeheartedly on the Russian side. Yet Cuba could not do without the Soviet Union, and when the Russians invaded Czechoslovakia in August 1968, Fidel had to face that reality. As I wrote, he shocked his liberal European and North American sympathizers by approving the Russian action, although he plainly labeled it for what it was —a violation of Czech sovereignty. (The incident, it will be recalled, coincided with that other and greater shock to the Western intelligentsia—the affair of the Cuban poet Heberto Padilla.)

Castro explained his reasons to the Central Committee of the Communist Party of Cuba at a meeting on August 23, 1968:

> Of course [speaking of the Dubcek regime] in our opinion everything that receives the praise, support and enthusiastic applause of the imperialist press, naturally begins to arouse suspicions in us . . . The Czechoslovak regime was marching toward capitalism and was marching inexorably toward imperialism. We don't have the slightest doubt of that. . . .
>
> And our point of view is that it is not permissible, and that the socialist camp has the right to stop it in one way or another.
>
> What we cannot say is that the sovereignty of the Czech State was not violated. That would be a fiction and a lie. And, besides, that the violation has been flagrant . . . In our opinion, the action in Czechoslovakia can be explained only from the political point of view, not from

> the legal point of view. It had no aspect of legality, frankly and absolutely none. . . .
>
> We all know that the administration which Czechoslovakia on the whole had for twenty years was saturated with many vices, with dogmatism, bureaucratism and, in short, with many things that cannot be considered models of a truly revolutionary administration . . . We must remember, that so far as we are concerned, that administration, with which we had relations from the beginning, sold to this country at good prices many weapons which were war booty from the Nazi occupation, and that we have been paying, and are still paying, for arms that belonged to the Hitlerian troops who occupied Czechoslovakia. . . .
>
> Sovereign right, in this case, has to give way before the much more important interest of the demands of the world revolutionary movement which, in our opinion, is the fundamental question, and to which, without the slightest doubt, the breakaway [*desgajamiento*] of Czechoslovakia and her fall into the arms of imperialism would have constituted a very hard blow . . . We must analyze these realities, and when one interest has to give way to another interest, we must not take up romantic and idealistic positions which do not fit these realities.

Castro took advantage of his opportunity in 1968 to scold the Soviet bloc for not putting some of the blame on "Yankee imperialism" and for not doing enough, or demanding enough, for Vietnam. These were *his* main preoccupations. The press—Western and Communist—ignored his criticisms of the Soviet Union and noted with blame or praise his support for the invasion.

Times changed and Fidel Castro, the politician and statesman, changed with them. In April 1973, Gustav Husak, general secretary of the Communist Party of Czechoslovakia, visited Cuba. Castro's opinion of the Czechs was expressed very differently from that of 1968.

"We remember the tremendous amount of machinery from Czechoslovakia that has been used in our country and the valuable factories that have been built with the cooperation of the sister Republic of Czechoslovakia," he said, with much more of the same. ". . . We recall the firm determination with which our Party and people supported the correct line in that [1968] situation."

Visiting Prague on September 19, 1973, Castro blandly ignored what he had said about Cuba being cheated on arms deliveries by the Czechs and gratefully said that "it must not be forgotten that our first arms came from Czechoslovakia."

Such is life in the world of politics, but history will note that what

Fidel said about Czech arms sales in 1968 was correct, and what he said in 1973 was ceremonial gush.

As a general proposition, Fidel Castro and the Cuban Revolution have been stigmatized again and again for policies which are no different from those followed by the United States or other Western democracies and yet which are considered uniquely reprehensible in Cuba's case. No number of wrongs can make a right, but a holier-than-thou attitude and a lack of sophistication could be dispensed with.

How many Americans realize that the Soviet government's justification for invading Czechoslovakia was, *mutatis mutandis,* the same as the American government's justification for intervening in Guatemala in 1954? Or that the 1968 "Brezhnev Doctrine" limiting the sovereignty of small nations within a sphere of influence was as good as copied word for word from President Johnson's statements justifying his invasion of the Dominican Republic in 1965?

Fidel Castro was running Cuba in 1968 under incredibly difficult conditions. He could not allow himself the luxury of joining the United States in condemning the Soviet invasion of Czechoslovakia. It was easy for foreign intellectuals and journalists with no responsibility to sit at their desks and condemn Castro. He had no choice, but within the range of his possibilities, he was critical.

His policies set him again—this time it would seem definitively—on a course of unstinted friendship and cooperation with the Soviet Union. The difference in tone between 1968 and 1972 can be noted in the joint Cuban–Czechoslovak communiqué issued on June 26, 1972, after Castro's visit to Prague.

"The existence of the Soviet Union is objectively to all free nations and to those nations struggling for independence, their principal support and bulwark," the communiqué states. It also expressed appreciation for "the Soviet Union's efforts to impose the principles of a peaceful coexistence that strengthens the cause of world peace."

When Che Guevara was in Bolivia in 1967, being sabotaged by the Kremlin-oriented Communist parties in Latin America while Moscow sought greater trade deals in the hemisphere, Fidel was openly critical of "peaceful coexistence." By 1973 he was brazenly asserting that even the attack on the Moncada Barracks in Santiago de Cuba twenty years before was an example of Marxism-Leninism.

"Without the extraordinary scientific discoveries of Marx and Engels, and without the inspired interpretation of Lenin and his prodigious historic feat, a 26th of July could not have been conceived of," he said on the twentieth anniversary of Moncada.

This, factually, was pure nonsense. As I wrote, there was at most only one Communist in the 1953 attack and he a political accident. None of the participants could have given a thought to Marx, Engels, or Lenin, least of all Fidel. Afterward, the Cuban Communist PSP condemned the attack. As in 1961, Castro was rewriting history to suit present political needs. What is alone meaningful is that in 1973 Fidel Castro placed maximum importance in the Communist Party of Cuba and in Cuban Marxism-Leninism, and he is giving practical significance to what he says. The PCC is playing an ever-expanding role, under Fidel, in the running of the country.

One of the parlor guessing games about the relations between Cuba and Russia is to estimate how much the connection costs the Soviet Union. For many years the figure of $1 million a day was generally accepted abroad, although there were no statistics to bear it out. It was a nice round figure and a good debating point. If the amount was too high for the early years, it would be too low from the late 1960s onward. Lowry Nelson quotes Robert A. Hurwich of the State Department as saying on July 8, 1970, that "we estimate" the daily cost of Cuba to the USSR as $1.4 million a day, or $511 million a year.

Nelson calculates the Cuban debt to Russia for the years 1960–1969 at $1,380 million, without counting the arms supplied free of charge by Moscow at a value that Castro, in April 1970, estimated to be $1.5 billion. René Dumont cites a statement by Carlos Rafael Rodríguez, made in an interview in Lima, Peru, at the end of 1969, that Cuba had cost the Soviet Union the equivalent of $4 billion, without counting the military aid.

These figures on Russian aid were always treated by Americans as something sensationally burdening to the Soviet Union. Yet for the first half of 1972, *Al Ahram*, Cairo's semiofficial newspaper, gave Egypt's debt to Russia as about $2.5 billion and said it was piling up at some $2.5 million a day. The State Department's estimate in 1972 was an Egyptian debt to Moscow of more than $3 billion. *The Economist* of London in its November 10, 1973, issue estimated the Egyptian debt at that time as $3.6 billion. These figures do not include the cost to the Soviet Union of the 1973 Middle East war.

So—is Cuba really so intolerably expensive to the Russians?

Economically, the Soviet Union has little interest in trade with Cuba. She needs sugar, despite being one of the world's largest sugar producers. The Russians sometimes resold Cuban sugar on the world market, but usually at a loss. Cuban nickel is useful. But on the whole, Russian aid is politically and strategically motivated. In those fields, "value" is subjective, intangible, and unmeasurable.

One of the most serious efforts to analyze Cuban-Russian trade was made in an article entitled "Cuba's New Dependency" by Leon Gouré and Julian Weinkle for the March-April 1972 issue of *Problems in Communism,* a U.S. government publication.

Using Moscow's *Statistical Handbook of Foreign Trade,* they give Russia's share of Cuban exports in 1960 as 16.7 percent and imports as 13.8 percent, compared to 52.1 and 58.3 percent respectively for 1967. (This apparently has not changed much, for on January 7, 1974, *Granma* wrote: "The Soviet Union's share in Cuba's foreign trade ranges from 50 to 52 per cent.")

The writers estimated the cumulative trade deficit with Russia for 1960–1970 as approximately 900 million rubles, or $1 billion. This is without counting military aid, interest charges, the cost of maintaining Soviet technical and military advisers in Cuba, and other items. The authors guess at a total debt for 1972 of about $3 billion. An added cost factor is the four hundred or so Soviet ships that carry five or six times more cargo to Cuba than they take back.

Gouré and Weinkle refer to a sentence from a Russian book by V. V. Volskii on the first ten years of the Cuban Revolution. "The Soviet Union," they say, "claims to 'fully or almost fully' fill Cuba's needs for oil and petroleum products, mineral fertilizer, sulphur, asbestos, cotton, saw-timber, trucks and special automobiles, and metal-cutting lathes."

All of Cuba's wheat imports come from the Soviet Union via Canada, which must be creating a difficult problem, considering Russia's need to import great quantities of wheat for herself. Many thousands of tractors and harvesters came from the Soviet bloc, although a great many were bought in France.

"Russia has re-equipped sugar mills, built electricity plants, hospitals, factories, irrigation plants and roads," writes Hugh Thomas in his book on Cuba.

There has been a string of trade agreements between Cuba and Russia, none of them lasting their time because of Cuban mismanagement, mistakes, and growing demands. They started with the historic 1962 agreement with Mikoyan. There was a pact in 1964 that provided for sugar shipments at 6.11 cents a pound, which was well above the world market price. But the Cubans never could meet their quotas to the Soviet Union because of one poor crop after another.

A 1969 trade pact called for an exchange totaling nearly 1 billion rubles annually (the ruble is worth $1.11), but the total, according to Moscow's figures, reached only 770 million rubles in 1969. The target figure was met in 1970, but the near-collapse in Cuba brought on by the sugar-harvest fiasco meant that it all had to be done afresh. This was when the new agreement began to be worked out, with the evidence pointing to Russian demands that serious reforms had to be made and a greater role given to Soviet-bloc planning and management.

The cost to the Soviet Union all along does not appear to have been a basic consideration, despite belief abroad. A million or 1.4 million dollars a day is not a very large expenditure for Moscow, any more than it would be for the United States. During the late 1960s the Americans were probably spending more in a week on Vietnam than the Russians spent in a year on Cuba. In both cases, the money appeared to be going down a bottomless pit.

It seems a safe bet that both the Russians and the Cubans (i.e., Fidel Castro) would have realized in 1970 that it was the end of an era. Drastic reforms were needed in Cuba, and massive aid had to come from the Soviet bloc.

Fidel Castro did his part at home, coming up with some striking new ideas and a program of inspiration plus discipline to get more and better cooperation from the Cuban people. Presumably, the Russians were impressed by Castro's attitude, policies, and the popular support he was getting during the year and a half or so after his July 26, 1970, confessional speech.

An ambitious journey was worked out for Castro while the negotiations inside the Communist bloc were coming to fruition. In April 1972 he left Cuba on a trip of more than two months to Africa (the first time for him) and to every country of the Communist bloc in Europe.

Although the journey received hardly any notice from the Western media (except for a false Associated Press report that Fidel had had a heart attack), the people's, as well as the official, reactions in the Eastern European countries could not have been more impressive. They left no doubt that Fidel Castro was still a popular romantic revolutionary figure in Communist Europe, even allowing for the extent to which demonstrations were arranged and audiences were captive. What was more important was the evidence of official governmental support in every country.

Fidel went on perpetuating the Sorelian-type myth of his early Marxism, which he had first developed in the sensational December 1–2, 1961, speech proclaiming his lifelong Marxism-Leninism. Although he was tying himself still closer to Russia and must, by the same token, have weakened his relations with China, there was no hint in any speech he made of criticism of Peking or sign of an alignment with Moscow against China. This is a price that Cuba has not paid, at least to date, to the Russians. (The nearest he has come was a sideswipe at the Chinese, without mentioning them, in a speech in Havana during Leonid Brezhnev's visit in January 1974.)

Cuba's relations with China, in fact, got back to a mutually cautious normal friendliness after Mao Tse-tung's "Great Cultural Revolution" had run out of steam. However, by that time Castro's anger or resentment or rebellion—whatever one wants to call it—against Russia had ended. Peking has accepted the fact of Cuba's close relations with Russia, and Castro has had to accept the new Chinese policy of trade expansion and diplomatic friendliness with Latin American countries, even Brazil, which has a harshly anti-Communist military dictatorship but is a source of sugar for China. Among the many messages from all over the world congratulating Cuba on the fifteenth anniversary of the triumph of the Castroites, January 1, 1974, was an exceptionally cordial one from Chou En-lai which ended: "May the friendship between the Chinese and Cuban peoples grow."

In Europe in 1972, Fidel did speak in every country about Vietnam, with implicit criticism toward both Moscow and Peking. It was his most consistent theme, perhaps with the idea that Russia and China, new friends of the United States, were letting Hanoi down. Every joint communiqué mentioned Vietnam. In Warsaw, on June 6, Fidel spoke of "our willingness to send combatants to Vietnam, should it become necessary . . . Vietnam is today the supreme test of proletarian internationalism; Vietnam is today the supreme test of Marxist-Leninist principles."

But, of course, Russia and China at that period abandoned North Vietnam to Nixon and Kissinger and to the realities of their new politics, and made no move to help Hanoi during the "stone age" bombings of December 1972 and January 1973.

Fidel was in the Soviet Union from June 26 to July 5, 1972, going around the country and getting extraordinarily warm receptions. Leonid Brezhnev, general secretary of the CPSU Central Committee, welcomed Castro to Moscow on June 27 in a speech that embraced Cuba, once and for all, as a member of the Communist club. "Socialist Cuba is not alone," he said. "She is an integral part of the world socialist system."

Alexei Kosygin, chairman of the Council of Ministers, in his farewell toast to the Cuban delegation on July 3, put his emphasis on Cuba's satisfying Russia and integrating her economy with the Communist bloc:

> We are satisfied with the results of the analysis of important aspects of our bilateral cooperation and with the solution of a number of problems to the benefit of the peoples of both our countries and of our common cause. We understand the statements made by Comrade Fidel Castro with regard to the further development of Cuba's economy, and we are of the opinion that the coordination of the economic plans of our two countries will make it possible for us to take a new and great stride forward in improving our collaboration and tackling the tasks involved in the building of the economy. . . .
>
> The Soviet-Cuban talks are a brilliant manifestation of proletarian internationalism.

This sounded very much as if Kosygin were saying: "We are pleased that you have agreed to follow our advice, accept our ideas, and make Cuba's economy an integral part of the economy of the Communist bloc."

Castro has never put this interpretation on his policies, nor does he concede that Cuban independence has been sacrificed in any respect.

However, on July 11, 1972, the premiers of the eight nations in COMECON, the international Communist trading bloc, unanimously endorsed Cuba's application for full membership in the community. Previously, Cuba had the status of observer.

Entry, it was stated, means that Cuba joins the "Comprehensive Program of Socialist Economic Integration" of 1971, which will take the special features of the Cuban economy into account for the 1976–1980 period. This indicates that it will take some time to work out the details and that Cuba is committing herself for a long time, since the program is to stretch over fifteen or twenty years.

"Today," Carlos Rafael Rodríguez said in his speech of thanks to the COMECON council in Moscow, "it is impossible to conceive of the development of the Cuban economy without that systematic economic collaboration provided by the socialist community or without Cuba's incorporation into the process of socialist integration, which geographical distance may limit but not utterly prevent."

I asked Carlos Rafael about all this when I spoke to him in Havana a few months later. The entry into COMECON is not a case of surrendering to Russia, which would thereupon dominate Cuba as Stalin did the European satellites, he claimed. There had been long arguments in 1971 among the members of the group, with Rumania holding out because she did not want to accept the concept of, or even use the word, "integration," so it was agreed that each member would retain its independence within the integrated economic structure—and this will go for Cuba.

Blas Roca, the other old-guard Communist in the government, also insisted to me that there will be no need, ever, for Cuba to get approval from the Russians for any of its plans or decisions that do not require Russian aid. The complete integration of COMECON under the "Comprehensive Program," Blas pointed out, is a future goal. He and others remarked on the fact that Cuba is joining COMECON at a time when the individual members of the Soviet bloc have become more independent of the USSR economically and politically.

Rodríguez told a correspondent of the Chilean magazine *Hoy* in August 1972:

> The fundamental idea is that without integration there is no development. This is an era of great communities, both capitalist and socialist. We believe that there cannot be development if there is not integration within the framework of socialism . . . At present, integration with Latin America is not possible. For historic reasons, our economy has been united to the socialist economy by the process that has taken place in the last fifteen years . . . Comecon is achieving more and more forms of collective participation through an investment bank and through the international socialist division of work in which each country assumes a concrete activity in accordance with its possibilities.

The flowery, esoteric language that is conventional in the Communist world, so dull and repetitive to read and hear, must not be allowed to bury the significance of Fidel Castro's trips to the Soviet Union in 1972 and the agreements that were reached there. His own realization that he might be putting on a Shirt of Nessus that could hold him in an unbreakable embrace was shown by his careful insistence at every point during his first journey that Cuba's natural future lay in and with Latin America, not Europe.

The supreme importance to the Cuban Revolution of the agreements that Castro reached during that trip was conveyed to the Cuban people in three stages. The first came immediately after his return to Cuba when Fidel, in three long sessions on July 15, 16, and 17, 1972, made his report to the Central Committee of the Communist Party. Afterward, on July 20, the CC passed a long resolution, in customary terms but with two special angles. The first went to extremes in praise of the Soviet Union and in commitment to its policies.

"The Central Committee," says one passage, "shares Comrade Fidel Castro's recognition of the fact that the Soviet people, educated by the Communist Party of the USSR in the principles of Marxism-Leninism and internationalism, constitute, without a doubt, the highest expression ever attained of social, political and human progress. Soviet society, characterized by a highly-developed political awareness and culture, has a revolutionary soundness that makes it invulnerable to ideological penetration by imperialism and capitalism."

The other unusual angle was a passage ending the resolution expressing confidence in the future of "the anti-imperialist struggle in Latin America,

> in which regard Comrade Fidel Castro had the opportunity to inform the leaders of the countries he visited about the understanding of the Communist Party of Cuba . . . The Cuban people are in solidarity with all the revolutionary forces in Latin America . . . They also consider that it is impossible to better the relations that exist between Cuba and the United States as long as U.S. policy is directed by the ideas of domination, by its position as a reactionary gendarme, and by the arrogant attitude toward Cuba and her sister nations of Latin America that has characterized its policy.
>
> As a result of historic circumstances, the Cuban people have been accorded the privilege of heading the transforming process in Latin America that will lead it toward socialism.

Few Cubans would read such a long resolution printed in their official newspaper, *Granma*. However, millions would have heard the next statement, which came in Fidel Castro's annual July 26 speech, less than a week later.

It was a complete, effusive, enthusiastic hymn of thanks to the Soviet Union and a pledge of adherence to the socialist bloc. However, he once again hedged it as much as he could with his insistence that Cuba is a Latin American country, that her future lies with Latin America, and that her economic aims are someday to become part of an integrated, revolutionary union of Latin America. All the same, the commitment to the Soviet Union was present and real; the hopes of detaching Cuba from the Soviet Union and joining a Latin American confederation are for the distant future, as Fidel conceded:

> We say here, and we will always say it: our people are proud of the friendship of the Soviet people. Our people are united to the Soviet people by the bonds of internationalism and by the bonds of elemental gratitude. And they are proud of this. For we know other friendships, and when we recall those friendships, we appreciate in all its immense

> worth the friendship of the Soviet Union; altruistic, disintegrated, revolutionary. . . .
>
> We are Latin Americans. We know that no small country will have the slightest possibility of getting ahead in tomorrow's world, a world of great powers, human and economic, in the midst of a gigantic scientific and technical revolution, in the midst of a struggle against an imperialism which exists and will exist for an indefinite period of time, and that in the future we should integrate ourselves economically with Latin America. We will not, of course, integrate with the United States for, in reality, the differences of language, customs, mentality, everything, are very great, despite the fact that we are internationalists . . . But for there to be economic integration and political integration there must be a social and antiimperialist revolution in Latin America . . . However, this will take time. We cannot make plans looking to an integration that may take ten, fifteen, twenty, twenty-five, thirty years —that, at the most pessimistic. In the meantime, what are we to do? a small country, surrounded by capitalists, blockaded by the Yankee imperialists? We will integrate ourselves economically with the socialist camp.

If Fidel, understandably, was worried about his new commitments to the Soviet bloc, he also had the best of reasons to be grateful to the Kremlin. He went back to Russia on the occasion of the fiftieth anniversary of the USSR and signed a remarkably favorable trade and financial settlement on December 23, 1972. After his return to Havana he made a telecast on January 3, 1973, happily announcing the provisions.

There were five separate economic agreements. The first arranged for a prorogation to a twenty-five year period, beginning in 1986, without interest, of payments on the huge Cuban debt to Russia from the beginning of the Revolution in 1959.

The second pact promised additional Russian credits to cover the expected unfavorable balance of trade between Havana and Moscow in 1973, 1974, and 1975. These too are not to be repaid until 1986 and after.

The third agreement merely lists articles to be exported and imported between the two countries.

The fourth calls for the "collaboration" during 1973, 1974, and 1975 of the two countries in development of the textile industry, nickel mining, oil refining, transport, communications, et cetera. This seems to mean that the Cubans committed themselves to accepting Russian advice and planning in their key industries for three years.

Under the same fourth agreement, Cuba will get a credit of 300 million rubles ($333 million) to pay for Soviet machinery, equipment, and materials. Repayment is to be in twenty-five years, starting in 1976 at "a very low interest." The Russians will "collaborate" in the construction of two new textile plants, the repair and reconstruction of the nickel plants of Moa Bay and Nicaro, and the construction of a new nickel-cobalt combine with a capacity of 30,000 tons a year, thermoelectric plants, a railroad line from Havana to Santiago de Cuba, a factory to make reinforced concrete, the "reconstruction" of Cuba's ports, a factory to build radio and television sets, et cetera, et cetera.

In the fifth and final agreement, the Soviet Union agreed to pay the equivalent of 11 cents a pound for Cuban sugar (a very high price at that time) and $5,000 a ton for nickel-cobalt (against a world market price then of $2,000 to $3,000). As I wrote, the sugar price was raised to 20 cents a pound in 1974.

On paper, this is the most favorable trade agreement the Castro regime has made since the beginning of the Revolution, and the most important. If it is carried out as planned, it will transform the Cuban economy, making it sounder, more diversified, and even prosperous. Everything depends on that "if." The Russians failed to fulfill some earlier promises, and their own economy has been going through a difficult period. Moreover, since then the great economic and energy crisis of the Western countries following the Middle East war of 1973 has been in full spate. The Communist bloc, although not directly affected, is bound to feel the consequences.

Much will also depend on the Cuban workers and managers rising to the challenge. "Our people have an inescapable moral duty," Fidel said in his report, "to make the maximum use of the foreign aid that we are going to receive."

At best, such ambitious plans will take many more than three years to materialize. The Russians are obviously counting on a long duration for the Cuban Revolution, during which its economy will be integrated as much as possible with COMECON and the Soviet Union's economy. However, Cuba will have more trade with the rest of the world, including most of Latin America, and conceivably may resume trade with the United States.

The Soviet-Cuban accord looked too good to be true, but it was, and perhaps is, within the realm of possibility. The Russians are not fools or philanthropists.

"We should point out something important," said Fidel in his TV address, "which is that the initiative for the solution of these problems came fundamentally from the Soviet Union itself, which considered our objective problems, our difficulties, the characteristics of the Cuban economy, our dependence on the production of sugar and a few other products, as well as the inconveniences imposed on our country by the [U.S.] economic blockade."

According to Fidel, "There is no precedent in the history of humanity for such generous treatment." He even argued that it was "truly disinterested."

His speech ended on a sober note, expressing satisfaction with the progress made within Cuba, especially since his *mea culpa* speech of July 26, 1970, but pointing out that Cuba has few resources and a long, hard road to climb "of effort, sacrifice and struggle."

Why has the Soviet Union "decided to become receiver in bankruptcy for the Cuban economy," as a *New York Times* editorial of January 13, 1973, unkindly put it? Russian aid, of course, is not "truly disinterested," as Castro said. There has to be a *quid pro quo* which Moscow considers to be satisfactory. One can grant that the Cuban debt was irrecoverable, and might just as well have been put off to the Greek kalends, but not that Russia has to go on pouring additional millions of rubles into a highly risky economic venture. The answer, obviously, is political and strategic, not economic. The Kremlin has a sort of beachhead in the Western Hemisphere so long as Cuba remains Marxist-Leninist and economically dependent on Moscow. There might come a time when the United States would pay a high price to get the Russians out of the Caribbean, but just lifting the trade embargo and finding a *modus vivendi* with Cuba is not going to do that.

Meanwhile, Moscow has to think of Russia's position as a leader of the world Communist movement in rivalry with China. The Kremlin cannot afford to be blamed for the collapse of the Cuban Revolution. Cuba has to be fit into the long-range, never-to-be-abandoned Russian-led campaign of spreading Communism to every possible region of the globe. The Kremlin did not give up Egypt after the disaster of the Six Day War in 1967—on the contrary, the Egyptians got even more aid to try again. The Russians did not give up Cuba after the 1970 sugar disaster. Again one can say, on the contrary—and the Russians may get their reward there too.

Fidel Castro, for his part, has not forgotten the lesson of the missile crisis. Several high government officials made it clear to me on my last trip that while Fidel's praise and gratitude toward the Russians in his public pronouncements were genuine, I should keep in mind his insistence that Cuba's future lies with Latin America, not

Europe. He needs the Russians now and for the foreseeable future, but it is not possible for him, by temperament or character, to become Moscow's puppet. Whatever the cost could be, he would not sacrifice Cuba's sovereignty. He is 100 percent nationalistic. The men in the Kremlin have had enough experience with him to know that he can be wooed and persuaded, but he cannot be commanded. He lives for Cuba and his Revolution; nothing else counts for anything.

This probably does not worry Moscow any more than Egyptian President Anwar Sadat's rebelliousness toward the Russians in 1972 and 1974, or the anti-Communism of King Feisal of Saudi Arabia and some of the other Arab leaders: the enemy of my enemy is always a friend.

The new agreement with Russia should not interfere with Cuba's Revolution or Castro's leadership of it in those fields which have made what has happened in Cuba a true social revolution: national independence and sovereignty, a socialist system, a welfare state, egalitarianism, the abolition of dire poverty, advances in education, public health, housing, and so forth.

If the agreement with the Russians works, and if sugar prices remain above 20 cents a pound, Castro will get a strong economic base on which to go ahead with the revolution for which he has lived and fought. His economic errors and deficiencies were wrecking the Revolution. The Russians are looking out for their own interests, but in the process they have a good chance of providing what is needed to make the Cuban Revolution an economic as well as a social success. They have nothing to lose but their rubles—and much to gain in other respects.

Fidel Castro is in possession. The Cubans own Cuba—all of it; the Russians none and the Americans none.

In arguing with Carlos Rafael Rodríguez about Cuba's dependence on the Russians, he told me how, when he first teamed up with Batista, it was decided that Cuba should build a wheat mill, saving that much money in imports of flour from the United States. Senator Ellender, when he learned of it, sent word that if the Cubans went ahead and in the process hurt some American exporters, he, as senator from sugar-producing Louisiana, would see to it that the Cuban sugar quota was reduced. They dropped the plan. In 1944, during the war, when Carlos Rafael was a cabinet minister, a plan was drawn up to build a small fleet of coastal vessels to carry freight between Cuban ports and the East Coast. Washington sent the Cuban government a note saying that if one ton of American shipping was going to be lost through this fleet, the United States would not permit it.

All the Cuban leaders I spoke to, including Fidel Castro, made the same points. The dependence on the United States was "a typical neocolonial process," preventing diversification and development and involving a vast foreign ownership of resources. The Russians are helping the Cubans to diversify and become self-sufficient. They supply complete plants and materials for development, which remain in Cuban hands.

When the two nickel mines were American-owned, the ore was taken to the United States for refining, and the profits of the companies went to the United States. Russia has helped to get the nickel mines in order, buys most of the product, and is providing machinery and credits for a considerable expansion and modernization of the properties.

Before the Revolution greater industrial growth meant greater dependence on the United States; a similar expansion now would have a different effect with regard to the Soviet Union, perhaps a contrary one.

The dependence in present circumstances is on the aid that Cuba must have and Russia could withhold or reduce. Moreover, the Soviet Union is Cuba's main market for exports and sole supplier of wheat and oil. In the case of oil, the dependence is especially chancy. The Soviet Union is short of oil in 1975. Russian tankers have to sail six thousand miles through the Black Sea, the Mediterranean, and the Atlantic to take oil every two or three days to Cuba. When one or two are delayed as much as forty-eight hours, it is upsetting to some sector of Cuban industry. Venezuelan oil traveled only 750 miles. (With the new Venezuelan government planning to nationalize the oil industry and diplomatic and trade relations with Cuba being resumed, the time may not be far off when Cuba gets crude oil from Venezuela again.)

The idea of Russia taking over much, or perhaps most, of the planning and direction of the Cuban economy has aroused some sarcastic comment. It has been pointed out that the Soviet Union has not fulfilled any of her own agricultural plans for forty or more years.

"Why have repeated changes in Russia's planned economy failed to yield the objectives of effective management, an abundance of high-quality goods and rapid technological progress?" *The New York Times* asks. "For fifteen years of organizational and administrative turmoil, Soviet planners have searched in vain for a satisfactory system of economic management."

If they cannot find one at home, can they do so in Cuba? The Soviet Union is a nation endowed with human and natural resources the equal of the United States, yet Russians still have the lowest living standards of any developed, industrial country. Productivity is about half that of the United States, and in the last few years the rate of growth seems to be declining.

Castro sees the picture differently. The Russian Revolution started in 1917 from a far lower base than the United States. When I spoke to Fidel in Havana a few months after his return from Russia, he went into a glowing account of how greatly he was impressed by what he saw.

"The United States was not touched physically by World War II," he said. "Most of Western Europe remained, but Russia was destroyed and lost 20 million men, and from that basis she has constructed a strong economy and a good life for her people." He was especially impressed by how hard the Russian people worked—no doubt thinking of his problems with his own Cubans.

Fidel's reasons for being impressed are significant. The fact that over the years the Russian people are slowly but steadily getting more to eat, more to wear, better housing, and so on, would mean more to the Cuban leader than any statistical or real comparisons with Western capitalist countries.

Whether he realizes that the Russian five-year plans are never more than partially fulfilled, I do not know. I suspect that he would be sympathetic. He might even think that if the Soviet Union, after trying for fifty years to achieve an economic system comparable to capitalism, has so far failed, one need not wonder at the Cuban failures, which, aside from inexperience, also displayed overoptimism, self-deception, and administrative chaos. Everything is relative, and whatever the deficiencies of the Soviet economic planners, the Russian economists would certainly be better than the Cuban.

Cubans are now, for instance, copying the Russians in placing a new emphasis on value and costs. In his May 1, 1971, speech Castro had said that "under socialism some things are sold below price . . . Prices in themselves have nothing to do with [market] value, but much more with their utilitarian value." A "System of Economic Registry" has gone into effect linked to the problem of costs, and now market values and material incentives are involved in the planning.

The reliance on the Soviet bloc should not be exaggerated. As I mentioned earlier, for thirteen years Cuba has been acquiring products, credits, markets, even to a certain extent technicians and know-how, from Canada, Western Europe, Japan, and China. Automobiles, trucks, tractors, fishing vessels come from Britain, France, Spain, Italy, and Japan.

Commerce with Japan has grown steadily, and she is now the

biggest trader with Cuba outside the Communist bloc. Cuba sends Japan more than a million tons of sugar yearly and actually has had a favorable trade balance since 1972. Australia is selling agricultural machinery, meat, and milk and is planning to reestablish diplomatic relations when it will not annoy Washington too much. Sweden extended a credit of $30 million to Cuba in 1974 to cover the construction and complete equipment of two technological institutes. A group of European and Canadian banks loaned Cuba 150 million German marks in May 1974.

The U.S. blockade was, therefore, never successful outside Latin America, and then only for a while. Mexico never broke relations with Cuba. Chile (under Allende) became an ally; Peru, Argentina, Venezuela, Jamaica, and Trinidad-Tobago began trading with Cuba. Panama restored diplomatic relations in August 1974. Other nations were preparing to follow suit; they saw no reason to fight an American battle. They needed export markets; credit risks were normal thanks to Soviet backing or, as in Britain, government guarantees; the United States had little or no power to retaliate. Some nations, like Spain and Japan, are big sugar importers. The only limitation on Cuba was the scarcity of hard currency, and in some years the Russians helped by releasing some of the Cuban sugar due to them to be exported to hard-currency countries. And now Cuba is earning great sums in hard currencies thanks to the boom in sugar prices.

The old established trade pattern between Cuba and the United States has been destroyed, not just interrupted. Cuba has crossed a historic watershed in transferring her economic and trade relations to Europe and Asia. From the time of the discovery and colonization of the New World until 1959, the island's economic relations were with Spain and, later, the United States. The Cubans no longer need —and cannot use—the once-necessary spare parts for American machinery and other products. The United States will have no distribution lines, no contacts, no agents, and perhaps not much, if any, goodwill. In many ways, Americans will have to start all over again.

The old pattern could not have lasted much longer. Whether Cuba had a revolution or not, the United States cannot behave toward her in 1975 the way it did in 1945 or 1958. International investment and trade have taken new forms; great powers can no longer as easily bend small ones to their will; nationalism is stronger than ever. A friendly Cuba could, tomorrow, have the same degree of independence toward the United States that Mexico has today. Mexico is an independent, sovereign country, holding 51 percent control of her vital subsoil industries. Yet the United States buys two-thirds of her exports, provides three-fifths of her imports, and has made 80 percent of Mexico's foreign investments.

As Fidel has said, Cuban exports depend overwhelmingly on five products: sugar, citrus fruits, nickel, tobacco, and seafood, in that order. But thousands of different products have to be imported, many of them inescapably from the capitalist—i.e., hard money—countries.

In the case of Spain, Cuba's position was strong enough to drive a hard bargain in 1971. A four-year agreement provides for an exchange of about $900 million and, interestingly, the gradual repayment of Cuba's debt to Spain resulting from the nationalization of Spanish property, as well as the trade deficit. A new three-year trade agreement with Spain began on January 1, 1975.

The 1971 pact presumably indicates that when or if Cuba and the United States reach a trade agreement, the Cubans will make a settlement on the American property that was expropriated. However, the claims of U.S. investors for losses in Cuba total between $1.5 and $2 billion. What future Cuban government could afford to pay such a sum? The United States is still bargaining with the Soviet Union over the World War I debts and the lend-lease accounts of World War II.

The super-generous agreement that the Russians made with Cuba in December 1972 indicated that the friendly arrangement Nixon made with Brezhnev in June 1973 would not dispose the Kremlin to help Washington on the Cuban question. The same was true of Brezhnev's trip to Cuba in January 1974, which aroused so many unfounded hopes among American journalists. "What the world will be watching for from Mr. Brezhnev's visit," *The New York Times* wrote editorially on January 30, "is an indication that he is urging Premier Castro to seek better relations with the United States." The American media were still working on ideas and beliefs that had no relation to Cuban realities. The United States helped Yugoslavia when she broke away from the Soviet bloc in 1948; the Soviet Union helped Cuba when she broke away from the "imperialist yoke" of the United States. This is normal international politics.

At the same time, it has to be recognized that the strategic factors involved in the two cases were quite different. The use of Cuba by the Russians as a possible base for all kinds of military purposes is a constant and natural worry for the United States. Space tracking, electronic monitoring, ports for "fishing trawlers" with sophisticated intelligence devices, repair bases where any kind of ship, even submarines, can be fixed, and what has anxiously (but very probably wrongly) been described as a "Russian naval base" in Cienfuegos—all stir up anxious thoughts in the Pentagon.

When I was in Cuba in September 1972 the Cubans ridiculed the idea that Cienfuegos and the new port at Havana were anything but repair bases and fishing ports. The Havana port, which I visited, certainly does not look like a naval base. The vulnerability of Havana and Cienfuegos to American power would make Russian bases immediately useless in a military crisis, but that Russian vessels can visit and be repaired in Cuban ports is an asset for the Kremlin and a worry for the Pentagon. In a minor way the Caribbean, like the Mediterranean and the Indian Ocean, has become a zone of operations for the Russian navy. This is surely worth some millions of rubles in aid to Cuba.

American indignation over the Russian presence in the Caribbean is a typical case of applying double standards. During the years of the containment policy the United States kept formidable nuclear forces close to Russia's frontiers. So far as the complaints over Cienfuegos are concerned, here is a pertinent item from *The Observer* of London, July 1, 1973:

"The port of Athens—Piraeus—is the Sixth Fleet's home port, with 10,000 U.S. servicemen and their dependents. There are thirteen other installations, including nuclear bases in Crete . . . More than 12,000 Greek officers have had training in the United States."

It is worth remembering, as the 1973 Middle East war proved, that Israel's dependence on the United States for military support is just as great as Cuba's on the Soviet Union.

"Cuba as a Russian-equipped base," wrote Hanson Baldwin, former military editor of *The New York Times*, in the Brookings Institution's book (*Cuba and the United States*, 1967), "costs us many millions annually, and it demands a diversion of a sizeable fraction of our most specialized and skilled forces to what is essentially a static, defensive task on our doorstep . . . We cannot—and must not—forget that in the fall of 1962 some forty odd missiles and perhaps (at a maximum) 40,000 Russians forced the mobilization and concentration by the United States of more than half a million soldiers, sailors, marines and airmen."

The United States keeps warships, marines, radar stations, and fighter interceptors in Florida, Puerto Rico, and the Caribbean at all times, more with an eye to the Russians than the Cubans, according to Baldwin. SR71 reconnaissance planes and satellites keep constant vigil. Baldwin calls "Gitmo" (Guantánamo) "perhaps the most important naval facility outside of our shores in the Western Hemisphere." The treaty with Cuba (reaffirmed in 1934 when the Platt Amendment was abrogated) gives the United States "complete jurisdiction and control" indefinitely, unless abandoned by *mutual* consent. Cuba, for what it is worth, has "ultimate sovereignty." Naturally, the Americans have it in mind that if they gave up Guantánamo, the Russians could replace them there even without sovereign or treaty rights.

As early as 1963 Baldwin considered the Cuban Air Force to be "the most modern and potentially the most powerful in Latin America." It has been greatly strengthened since then with MIGS and other Russian equipment. On April 17, 1972, Raúl Castro, as minister of the armed forces, accepted some of the then newest type MIGS. "Your handing over these planes to us," he said, "is another example of the confidence the Soviet Union has in us." It was the eleventh anniversary of the day Cuba's few old fighter planes shot down the B-25s with their American pilots over the Bay of Pigs.

Cuba also has a formidable array of anti-aircraft missiles and coastal artillery, radar stations and ground-control intercept centers. These were on display in the celebrations of the fifteenth anniversary of the triumph of the Revolution. All the equipment is Russian and Czech, but all the pilots, gunners, and technicians, so far as known, are Cubans who were trained in the Soviet Union. Every item of war material from the Soviet Union was given to Cuba free of charge.

The professionalism of the Cuban armed forces made it necessary to establish "an adequate order of hierarchy," as the Council of Ministers' law establishing a new system of ranks put it. Relations with other countries which had the customary military hierarchy had become awkward. The Revolution in this, as in other ways, was becoming institutionalized.

Law 1257, as it is called, leaves Fidel Castro as commander in chief. Raúl Castro, Minister of the Armed Forces, becomes the only "division commander," whose equivalent rank in other countries is lieutenant general (in fact, he is now called "Lieutenant General Castro" in Cuba). Four "brigade commanders" were named, who are the equivalents of major generals. A number of "first commanders," or colonels, were also appointed. Below the rank of "commander" (lieutenant colonel), the titles of major, captain, first lieutenant, and sub-lieutenant are used as in other armies.

Similar changes were made for the Revolutionary Navy ("ship commander" for admiral down to "Corvette captain" for the equivalent of commander in other navies.)

"As the Revolution becomes more mature," Castro said at the presentation ceremony, "so do we." He expressed pride in the way the old *comandantes* (majors) had carried on and warned: "We must never abandon this modesty, no matter what symbols, uniform or rank we may adopt, because there is a symbol, a rank that is higher than all the rest: the respect of the people."

All the same, the free-and-easy, happy-go-lucky, personalized guerrilla revolution had taken one more step backward into history.

On July 22, 1973, on the eve of the twentieth anniversary celebration of the Moncada Barracks attack, Havana saw its first military parade in years. The soldiers now march ceremoniously with the goose-step. Well before the 1973 year-end maneuvers, it was disclosed that Cuba, in addition to previous material, now had Russian-built multiple rocket launchers, long-range cannons, light amphibious tanks, and T–55 tanks equipped with 100mm cannons.

However, the number of Russian military advisers and technicians had been reduced. A report by the U.S. Defense Intelligence Agency (DIA) in 1972 estimated that for the three years there had been no more than three thousand in Cuba. "The Soviet weapons systems which are in Cuba have a good defense capability," Major General Richard Stewart of the DIA told a House of Representatives committee in September 1972, "but they do not give the Soviets or the Cubans an offensive capability,"

Not only is another Bay of Pigs exile invasion unthinkable, but even an American invasion would face a high cost in men and material.

"Our country can now mobilize half a million men," Castro boasted on May Day 1972, "and as many as 600,000 men in a matter of hours, ready to go into action."

He was counting in the militia and paramilitary forces. The regular army, which was 300,000 when he spoke, was halved at Raúl Castro's suggestion, as I wrote.

Where Israel looks to defend herself from a host of Arab enemies, Cuba has only one enemy: the United States. Like Switzerland in World War II, Cuba's objective is to make an attack by her immensely stronger neighbor too expensive to be worth trying. The calculation, of course, is on a defense against conventional weapons. In a nuclear attack, Cuba would be destroyed in a matter of minutes.

The Russians, it stands to reason, are not being charitable, nor is Cuba their first consideration. They are compelling the United States to keep a great force on the *qui vive.* Because the arms are Russian and there is an unlimited supply of them in case of need, the

United States must think of Cuba as a Russian ally—ninety miles from Florida. The Kremlin has a potential beachhead in the Western Hemisphere that in geopolitical terms can be accounted as priceless.

The Middle East war of 1973 came close to bringing on a military confrontation between the Soviet Union and the United States. At the time that President Nixon called an Alert Grade 3 mobilization, the Israelis were on the point of breaking through to Cairo and the Russians were mobilizing airborne divisions in Eastern Europe to stop them. The Israelis were forced to halt in time by the two great powers, but it is not hard to envisage a spillover into hostilities if there is another time around. In such a case, a heavily armed and hostile Cuba, allied to the the Soviet Union, would be a threat of considerable proportions. Cuba, Castro said on December 5, 1974, is going to start building a nuclear power plant in 1977–1978, with Russian help. And more will follow, Fidel asserted.

All things considered, it looks as if the Soviet Union is getting value for the $1.4 million a day, or whatever Cuba costs. Once upon a time, Cuba was worth a great deal to the United States. She is still worth a great deal—but the Soviet Union, in a manner of speaking, has bought an interest in her.

Fidel Castro, the proprietor, is more than satisfied; he keeps his island and uses the payments to make a bigger and better revolution. But I wonder sometimes how he feels in his heart of hearts. He is not a forgiving man. Has he forgiven the Moscow-oriented Communists of Bolivia who abandoned Che Guevara? Has he forgotten the years and events—Moncada, the Sierra Maestra, the Escalante affair, times when the Cuban Communists attacked and sabotaged him, and the missile crisis, when the Kremlin brushed him aside? How he must long for that day, which now seems so very far away, when Latin America unites as he dreams of it, and he no longer needs the Soviet Union! Meanwhile, he makes a virtue of a necessity; he has always managed to do that.

In spite of all that he says in praise of the Soviet Union, is it possible that he does not realize that for the men in the Kremlin Cuba was, is, and always will be expendable? This was very much under discussion abroad when General Secretary Leonid Brezhnev visited Cuba early in 1974 and Soviet Foreign Minister Andrei Gromyko went afterward to Washington. Yet both the Russians and the Americans denied that Cuba was even discussed, nor could any knowledgeable authority on Cuba have expected any kind of a decision. At that time neither Castro, Brezhnev, nor Nixon had the desire or possibility to take action. The communiqué issued after Brezhnev's visit left the situation exactly as it was.

So far as the United States was concerned, the situation changed dramatically with the resignation of President Nixon. What this may mean is for the future to tell. All one can say is that it does not seem to be in the interest of Cuba, the Soviet Union, or the United States to change the *status quo.* At the same time, one knows that a break in the complete separation of Cuba and the United States must come soon. One may get a better idea of the possibilities by taking a closer look at Cuban-American relations.

CHAPTER 18

The Yankee Colossus

It is a narrow policy to suppose that this country or that is to be marked out as the eternal ally or the perpetual enemy of England . . . Our interests are eternal, and those interests it is our duty to follow.
—Lord Palmerston

A judgment on U.S.–Cuban relations which seemed plausible in the early years of the Revolution needs rethinking today. Dr. Milton Eisenhower, the President's brother, in a book that was published in 1963, *The Wine Is Bitter,* put it this way:

"If, during the heyday of its interventionism in Cuba the United States had initiated even a reasonable degree of social justice, universal education, and true democracy—which it seems to me it was in a position to do . . . there would surely never have been a Batista or a Castro."

The United States could not have played God; it could not have changed the Cuban character, way of life, and complex but profound inheritance from Spain. Dr. Eisenhower was quarreling with the eternal, structural basis of Cuban history. Batista and Castro were as much products of Cuba as her sugar cane. Nothing that the United States did could have made Cuba into another Long Island. What Dr. Eisenhower considered to be social justice would not have suited Cuba; his "universal education" would not, in Cuba, have resembled American schools and universities; his "true democracy" would have been a foreign implantation quite unworkable by the Cubans of this century.

Most Americans are convinced that their system of government, inherited from English common law and parliamentary practice, is universally applicable; that it has absolute value. After a long newspaper career in foreign countries, I can only marvel at what Denis Brogan, the British scholar, once called in a famous article in *Harper's*

"The Illusion of American Omnipotence." Global humanity is infinitely complex; its values are varied. In all cases there is naturally a mixture or balance of good and bad. These truisms need saying, for they are too generally disregarded.

Communism *per se,* it should be obvious, is not simply bad or wrong, and liberal democracy good or right. Cubans are getting a regime in which the good and bad are mixed.

We in the United States have learned through Watergate that our democratic system does not protect us from evil practices. A nation can pay a high price for the virtues—and they are, of course, virtues—of the civil liberties we cherish. If a Cuban says: "It means more to me to have equality, the freedom to eat enough, to clothe myself and my family properly, to get free medical care, to be well educated, to have no racial discrimination, than to have civic freedoms," we North Americans have no right to disapprove. We can say that *we* cannot and will not live without popular elections, freedom of the press, speech, assembly and similar liberties; we cannot then conclude that Cubans also must want to live the same way, and pity them because they don't.

More than 150 years have passed since the Latin American colonies (except for Cuba and Puerto Rico) won their independence. Only a few of them achieved forms of government that could safely be called democratic in the liberal, Western sense of the word, and two of these—Uruguay and Chile—have lost their democratic standing in the past few years.

It does seem about time that North Americans asked themselves whether this is due to the backwardness of the people and the difficulties inherent in a liberal, democratic system, or whether it simply means that Latin Americans do not—at least at this stage of their history—want the American-European type of democracy. It does not fit or satisfy the traditions, the mores, the ethos, the logic, the categorical aims and principles of the vast majority of Latin Americans—and I include the Cubans.

When the Cubans had freedom of the press they abused it through venality and corruption; when they had elections they were, with few exceptions, fraudulent; when they had strong trade unions their venal leaders betrayed the workers; when they had capitalism it benefited a few Cubans and brought social injustices and misery to most.

Latin America is yet to achieve one of the dreams of José Martí—to find a suitable, indigenous way of government that was different from United States democracy and (in his day) Spanish autocracy. It would be ridiculous at this early stage to say that Castro's Cuba has found the way, but it would be obtuse to ignore such innovations as the new organs of People's Power, the Committees for the Defense of the Revolution, or the worker-student form of education as it is developing, or the method of acting through national institutions like the Federation of Cuban Women and the Central of Cuban Workers, or the system of choosing a Communist élite and other types of vanguards.

Cuba under Fidel Castro is so much more than just a new Communist state which happens to be in the Western Hemisphere. There is no country in or out of the Communist bloc with which to compare the Cuba of 1975. In the word that Fidel Castro has used every year since 1959—and which I too keep using—we are watching a "process," dynamic, developing, changing.

The anti-Americanism in Cuba is not new except in its intensity and in the word used by Castroites to describe it: anti-imperialism. Anti-Yankeeism is a deep-seated disease of the Cuban body politic, and it will take years or generations to work itself out.

However, nothing can change the realities of geography which placed Cuba ninety miles from the shores of Florida. Nevertheless, John Quincy Adams' prediction that "Cuba, forcibly disjoined from its own unnatural connection with Spain, and incapable of self-support, can gravitate only toward the North American nation," is no longer valid. Both in lines of trade and in sovereignty, Cuba has become a member of the global community. This would continue to be the case even if her primary economic dependence shifted back from the Soviet Union to the United States. In these sixteen years of Revolution the world, as well as Cuba, has changed.

Once Fidel had consolidated his rule in Havana, there was only one force capable of overthrowing his regime—the United States. Vice-President Nixon, the CIA, the Pentagon, and President Kennedy foolishly believed that it could be done by helping the Cuban exiles in the Bay of Pigs landing. An American bombing attack and invasion, at an appalling cost, could have done the job in the missile crisis of 1962, but President Kennedy had too much sense for that. The conditional pledge which the President gave Khrushchev at the time—that the United States would not invade Cuba—has been kept. Unless that policy is changed, the Castro regime is safe against any but internal forces of revolt—which are not visible in present circumstances—or assassination.

The CIA, however, made it its business from the early months of the Revolution to do everything it could to overthrow, or failing that, to harass and sabotage, the Castro regime. The Bay of Pigs invasion, it will be recalled, was run by the CIA. The harassment has diminished, but never stopped. In recent years nothing more could be done than to help, along with other U.S. government agencies, to land small sabotage groups and, on some occasions, killer bands. Weapons are provided for underground groups. Spies are frequently sent in and brought out. SR71 planes take photographs to make sure that no offensive arms are being installed.

For years after the missile crisis, according to the Cubans, whose evidence is convincing, the CIA transported invaders on launch carriers, known as "mother ships," whose crews were armed and specially trained. The vessels would remain sixty or seventy miles from shore and send in launches or speedboats to land armed Cuban exiles. At times the boats stayed offshore to fire mortars or bazookas against warehouses, port installations, and oil refineries. Almost always, the operations would be carried out at night.

In May 1964 the existence of a training camp for Cuban exiles at Punta Presidente in the Dominican Republic was revealed when a band of twenty-five Cubans landed in Cuba and were captured. The leader was Eloy Gutiérrez Menoyo, who had headed one of the guerrilla groups in the Sierra de Escambray during the insurrection against Batista, and who later defected. He is now in a Cuban prison.

The CIA "mother ship" system seems to have been abandoned after 1966 for another method—cooperating with Cuban exiles using commercial freighters under Liberian and Panamanian registry. A wealthy and numerous Lebanese-Cuban family named Babún (Cubans also spell it Babúm), who sent several of their young sons on the Bay of Pigs invasion, used two ships flying the Panamanian flag which made a number of trips, sending in saboteurs and infiltrators. The ships were the *Layla Express* and *Johnny Express.* The Castroites quickly identified them and knew what they were doing, but since they stayed far out in international waters they did not do anything about them until 1971, although some Cuban militiamen were killed and wounded and property damaged.

The organization—RECE—through which the Babúns worked was based in Miami, and the vessels usually sailed from there. The Cubans believed that RECE was financed by the CIA.

A serious incident, which occurred on October 12, 1971, made Castro decide to act. In this case, it was the use of a "mother ship," the *Aquarius II* of Panamanian registry, to send in a speedboat which machine-gunned the village of Boca de Samá, near Banes on the north shore of Oriente Province. Two militiamen were killed and among the wounded were two young girls, one of whom had to have a foot amputated. An exile in New York, José Elías de la Torriente of the Cuban Liberation Front, which the Cubans had long considered to be financed by the U.S. government, publicly claimed credit for the attack. The vessel was seized by the authorities in Miami on its return.

As Castro explained later in a TV appearance and interview on December 22, 1971: "We decided to proceed against the ships which had carried out actions against Cuba. From the information we had, we knew that the *Layla Express* and the *Johnny Express* were among them. So instructions were given to intercept and capture these ships."

This was done one hundred miles out, leading to the sharpest Cuban-American conflict since the missile crisis. The captain of the *Johnny Express,* which was captured on December 15, was a naturalized American citizen born in Cuba, José Villa Díaz, who was wounded by gunfire when he refused to heave to. The *Layla Express* crew had offered no resistance when she was captured on December 5.

Strong and threatening statements came from the White House and State Department. The Latin American members of both crews were sent unharmed to Panama, but Cuba kept the others, including the captain of the *Johnny Express.* Washington ordered its naval vessels and fighter planes to aid all merchant vessels which the Cubans might attack in the Caribbean. A statement was issued saying that "attacks on United States citizens on the high seas would not be tolerated." It demanded the release of Captain Villa Díaz. Castro had made his point.

"The actions which are effected from U.S. territory are the responsibility of the U.S. Government" was his conclusion. "Let the United States declare clearly that there will be no pirate ships and there will be no problems of any kind."

The United States, in fact, took public measures on December 22, 1971, to stop further incursions of the type by exiles. Villa Díaz was not released.

There has been only one period in the more than sixteen years of the Revolution when Cuba and the United States carried out anything resembling negotiations of a general nature for some sort of reconciliation. This was done secretly in the autumn of 1963. William Attwood, then a member of the U.S. delegation to the United Nations, wrote about it in his book *The Reds and the Blacks* (1967). There were talks at the U.N. with Cuban Ambassador Carlos

Lechuga and with Castro's aide Major René Vallejo. The White House was brought in through McGeorge Bundy. Robert Kennedy was also involved. In the midst of the exchange, President Kennedy left for "a brief visit" to Dallas, Texas. Castro's instructions to Ambassador Lechuga reached him on November 23, the day after Kennedy's assassination. Bundy then told Attwood that the discussions would have "to be put on ice for a while."

In July 1964, during a long interview with Richard Eder of *The New York Times,* Fidel "suggested that the discussion of issues between the two countries would be useful," Eder wrote, and he quoted Castro as saying: "If there is a desire for talks, a form of holding them will suggest itself." But he felt that the initiative had to come from the United States.

I do not believe that anything could have resulted from negotiations in 1963 or 1964, even if Kennedy had lived, but the President was open-minded and probably willing to attempt negotiations. When I saw Fidel at the end of November 1963 he expressed regret over Kennedy's death and asked, almost wistfully, what I thought the President had had in mind about Cuba, and could he have changed his policies? I did not know.

On several future occasions Fidel expressed a willingness to talk, bargain, explore the issues, but always vaguely and in situations where it was inconceivable that either side could offer terms that the other might accept.

In recent years Castro has made it clear many times that he will have nothing to do with the United States unless its policies changed. Here is a typical statement, made during a speech at Havana University on August 27, 1971:

> Now, then, our position with respect to the imperialist U.S. Government is quite clear: we have nothing to negotiate with the imperialist Government of the United States. Debts to the imperialist Government? Mines, Cuban lands, natural resources, banks, factories and trade rights which were recovered by the Cuban people? Such property cannot be paid for, should not be paid for and will never be paid for! No question about it! We will never pay one single penny to the imperialists who exploited us, who made millions at the expense of our sweat and blood. That is clearly understood.

Richard Nixon, understandably, was the blackest of *bêtes noires* to Castro and the Cubans. For years his name was printed in the newspaper *Granma* with a swastika in place of the letter "x." It was Vice-President Nixon who first proposed the arming and training of

Cuban exiles for what was to end in the Bay of Pigs invasion. It was President Nixon who commanded the merciless bombings of North Vietnam, to which Cuba felt indebted and whose people the Cubans admired with sincere emotion. "Therefore," to quote Castro again, this time in a press conference in 1972, "we have nothing to talk about with Nixon." This was still Castro's attitude when Nixon resigned.

On other occasions Fidel made the point that "we won't discuss anything with the United States as long as the [trade] blockade lasts," and he has said many times that the United States must stop "trying to play the role of gendarme" in Latin America.

There has been a movement within the Organization of American States (OAS) to invite Cuba back into the fold. Cuba was expelled at an OAS conference on January 31, 1962, in Punta del Este, Uruguay, which unanimously passed the following resolution:

> 1. The adherence of any member of the Organization of American States to Marxism-Leninism is incompatible with the Inter-American System and the alignment of such a Government with the Communist bloc breaks the unity and solidarity of the Hemisphere.
>
> 2. The present Government of Cuba, which has identified itself as a Marxist-Leninist Government, is incompatible with the purposes and principles of the Inter-American System.

Incompatible or not, Cuba went on being Marxist-Leninist, and it was President Osvaldo Dorticós' parting shot which proved most prophetic: "You may expel us [from the OAS] but you cannot remove us from the Americas . . . The United States will continue to have a revolutionary and socialist Cuba 90 miles from its shores."

In July 1974 as I mentioned, the OAS voted to break diplomatic relations and ban trade with Cuba.

"How can they admit us into the OAS," Fidel ranted in a speech on the tenth anniversary of the Bay of Pigs invasion, April 19, 1971, "if we say that the OAS is a filthy dunghill [*una sentina inmunda*], foul and despised; if, besides, we say that in this country the OAS makes us vomit—the very name of the OAS? . . . Historically, the OAS must disappear, for it is the historic expression of the degree of balkanization and division that imperialism has introduced into Latin America."

"There aren't any words in the dictionary with which we can state more clearly that Cuba will never return to that filth, that trash, that rotting corpse," Castro said once more at Havana University on August 27, 1971.

Nevertheless, either on the theory that if invited, he might change his mind, or recognizing Castro's well-known pragmatism, the movement to lure Cuba back continued.

At an annual meeting of the Inter-American Economic and Social Council three weeks after Fidel's August 27 speech, Galo Plaza, secretary general of the OAS, called for an end to the economic and diplomatic sanctions that the OAS had imposed against Cuba. "My opinion is that the politics of isolation have been neither constructive nor effective," Galo Plaza said.

On May 25, 1972, Peru introduced a resolution at an OAS meeting to the effect that "the member states who deem it desirable might normalize their relations with the Republic of Cuba, being free to do so at whatever level they deem convenient." Seven were in favor, three abstained, and thirteen were against, including the United States. In Mexico in February 1974, during a meeting of hemispheric foreign ministers attended by Secretary of State Henry Kissinger, Peru and other friendly nations brought the subject up again, but as Kissinger said it was not the time or place to do anything about Cuba.

The General Assembly of the OAS met in Washington in April 1973 and agreed to a simple declaration that the OAS accepts "a plurality of ideologies" among its members. This, presumably, included the ideology of Marxism-Leninism.

Castro's answer was made in his May Day speech of 1973: "We are grateful to those countries that, in a positive spirit, have proclaimed the right of Cuba to belong to the regional organization. But we cannot and shall not ever return to the OAS as it now stands."

"It is still not possible to set up a regional organization of our own because the United States still controls many governments," Fidel said in his July 26, 1973, speech. "But it is also impossible to revive the OAS and there is no sense in doing so. Cuba will wait patiently. Our Revolution is now stronger than ever, and it will still be young when the OAS has died—and together with it all the humiliation and shame it represents for our people."

So far as is publicly known, this remains Fidel Castro's attitude in early 1975. He can change his mind, but there are no obvious reasons why he has to. The last time I spoke to him (September 1972) he was firm in rejecting the OAS, but stressed at length how the situation was changing in Cuba's favor in Latin America. "We will be friendly with those countries who want to be friendly with us, whatever their form of government," he said to me.

A significant move was made at an informal meeting of hemispheric foreign ministers in Washington in mid-April 1974. The Argentine foreign minister, Alberto J. Vignes, proposed that Cuba be invited to another ministerial meeting in Buénos Aires scheduled for March 1975. Mexico, Venezuela, and Peru supported the proposal. The United States did not object, but was not in favor. No decision was taken, but Fidel Castro indicated in May that if Cuba were invited to such a meeting she would be willing to attend, providing that it was held apart from the OAS. Another attempt to end the diplomatic and trade sanctions against Cuba was made at Quito, Ecuador, in November 1974. It won a simple majority but not the two-thirds vote required.

The collapse of the Allende regime on September 11, 1973, and the death of the President were heavy blows to Castro, but there was no surprise. When I spoke to the Cuban leaders about Chile on my last trip, it was clear that they had little hope for President Salvador Allende.

Castro and the others were skeptical because Allende was trying to make a socialist revolution without the power to do so. He did not control the armed forces and had a hostile majority against him in the legislature. Moreover, he did not have a mass following. In addition to all that, as President Ford publicly confessed in September 1974, Allende was being fought clandestinely by the CIA, which spent millions of dollars in every kind of underhand trickery. Even so, the situation was not comparable to Fidel's in 1959–1961 because Castro destroyed Batista's army, replaced it with his own, abolished the Congress and civil freedoms, and sustained an uninterrupted mass support.

Fidel did all this before leading Cuba into Marxism-Leninism or even having any conviction that to make his social revolution he would have to make it Marxist. He had demonstrated how to go about making a radical social revolution before he found it necessary to carry it on by socialistic, Communistic, or, as he labeled it, Marxist-Leninist means. Thanks to his own charisma and to the power structure that he created and controlled, Fidel Castro was able to carry Cuba and his Revolution through an economic collapse as great as Chile's.

Salvador Allende was a human being of high moral stature and great courage, idealism, humanity, and faith. He tried to make a socialist revolution by peaceful, parliamentary means. Cuba was ripe for revolution, as the U.S. white paper said before the Bay of Pigs invasion; Chile badly needed drastic reforms, perhaps even revolution, but the people and the country were not ready. Moreover,

Allende and his followers hopelessly bungled their task and opportunities.

As the Allende experience proved, the problem is not so much how to get to the top as how to stay there. Allende could not convert his legality into authority. He could not impose his policies on the armed forces, the political opposition, or even on many workers or a number of his own supporters. In any event, many of his policies were wrong and bad.

Castro was away on an eighteen-day trip to the nonaligned countries' conference in Algiers and from there to Hanoi and New Delhi when the Chilean revolt occurred. He automatically blamed the United States for the "fascist coup," as did the Cubans at home.

Soon after his return, on the anniversary of the formation of the CDR, September 28, he addressed a hugh crowd in Havana. The speech contained a remarkably graphic, almost minute by minute, account of Allende's last day from "the testimony of those who were with the President that morning and the reports of some survivors." It was a picture of a man who fought heroically to the end, wounded in the stomach but "keeping on shooting at the fascists, who are only a few yards away, until a second bullet hits him in the chest. The impact throws him to the floor and, already dying, he is riddled with bullets."

Allende's personal guard, Fidel continued, took the body of the President to his office, sat it in the presidential chair, put the President's sash on it, and wrapped it in the Chilean flag.

This would be the explanation, according to Castro, for the story that Allende killed himself in his office. Fidel did not entirely rule this out.

"But even if Allende, seriously wounded, had shot himself so as not to fall prisoner to the enemy," he said, "it would not have been a blot on his record. Rather, it would have been an act of extraordinary courage."

Castro's final speculation about what may have happened is the most likely explanation. Fidel, by all accounts, made a thorough and careful investigation, and his conclusions were never denied by the Chilean junta. The cultural attaché of the Cuban Embassy, Lisandro Otero, who was in Santiago at the time, told me that he spoke to Chileans in the palace who saw Allende just before he died, and there seems to be no question that he had been seriously wounded.

On the other hand, the evidence that he ended by killing himself is hard to dismiss.

On March 22, 1974, the *Corriere della Sera* of Milan printed an interview by its correspondent in Santiago with Dr. Patricio Guijón, the personal physician of the President, who says that he saw, through the door of an adjoining room, Allende seat himself on the sofa of his office, place his submachine gun between his legs, and almost blow his head off with the shot. There is no reason to doubt Dr. Guijón's account, for he was a friend and follower of Allende—but revolutions live by myths as well as realities.

Fidel Castro's speech was intended to create another "heroic revolutionary" for Latin American history along with Che Guevara "and all the other giants who dedicated their lives to liberty in this continent."

He drew the obvious lesson for the future, as he saw it: "Chilean revolutionaries know that now there is no alternative other than revolutionary armed struggle." But he conceded that the struggle "will be a long one."

Eleven days before, in a press conference, Fidel had drawn another lesson that seemed obvious to him.

"The hand of imperialism is behind the events in Chile," he said. ". . . Naturally, given the state of affairs in Latin America, imperialism was able to pull a coup; to do so is a part of its policy. There was the coup in Bolivia, the coup in Uruguay. And now the coup in Chile. All these movements were directed by Yankee imperialism, in complicity with the Government of Brazil, which is playing the role of subimperialism, the role of gendarme in Latin America." After President Ford's confession, it must be conceded that Castro was right about the United States and Cuba.

A favorable trend had been interrupted only temporarily. On December 8, 1972, Barbados, Guyana, Jamaica, and Trinidad and Tobago had all recognized the Castro government, "moved by the common desire of promoting friendly relations and developing an effective cooperation between the Caribbean nations," as a joint communiqué stated.

The tide was so strong that at a Senate hearing where a top State Department official sought to justify continuing the U.S. policy of isolating Cuba, Senator Gale McGee asked: "Who is being isolated in the hemisphere—Cuba or the United States?"

At the end of May 1973, Cuba resumed relations with the now-Peronist Argentina. But Argentina, which seemed so safe and compatible when Héctor Cámpora, the interim President, embraced Osvaldo Dorticós in Buenos Aires, became dubious when Juan Perón took over. After all, he was a fascist type and set about crushing his left-wing extremists, but after his death in 1974, his widow, who became President, left relations with Cuba unchanged.

Argentina and Cuba had signed a five-year, $1.2 billion trade pact in the autumn of 1973. It is as part of this deal that the Argentine subsidiaries of Ford, Chrysler, and General Motors are to sell $145 million worth of cars and trucks to Cuba.

Until 1974 Mexico was not as friendly as she seemed, although her refusal to break relations with Cuba was priceless for the Castro government. Mexico's was not a pro-Cuban policy. It was a gesture of independence against the United States; it was pro-Mexico. Least of all was it pro-revolutionary. Mexico has long left the heart of her great Revolution of 1910 behind her, although some of the soul remains in the mythology and in a number of reforms.

Mexico, in fact, provides an example of the way a revolution can become a mockery of half-truths, rhetoric, the invocation of the noble ideals of its origins but not the practice of them. The country had a violent and sweeping agrarian reform, only to have more landless laborers today than ever. Capitalist exploitation is as bad as in the days of the dictator Porfirio Díaz. Corruption in high and low places is unchecked. Censorship, violence, work regimentation, negate the original revolutionary promises. Mass povery has hardly declined.

I made many trips to Mexico for *The New York Times* and on vacations, but the last one—a three-day stopover in Mexico City on the way to New York from Havana in September 1972—was a revelation. I thought I could see a basic reason why the Mexican Revolution has failed to bring honest administration and the end of corruption, as the Revolution did for Cuba. Both countries had long, uninterrupted generations of corrupt rule, but in Mexico it was an accepted part of life; it was taken for granted that there would always be the *mordida* (the bribe, literally "the bite") and other forms of corruption. In Cuba this was not the case; there was incessant opposition; an influential sector of the Cuban people wanted honesty, and they fought for it. They appreciated it when it came with the Castro Revolution.

A great weakness in the relationship of Mexico and Cuba until recently was that Mexico is almost as dependent economically on the United States as Cuba is on the Soviet Union. The interests of Mexico's ruling class are pro-Yankee, and capitalistic, and, by the same token, anti-Communist and antirevolutionary. The remarkable stability of the Mexican political system is another asset appreciated in Washington. All the same, President Echeverría of Mexico sent an important trade delegation, headed by Foreign Minister Emilio O.

Rabasa, to Cuba in April 1974, which was warmly welcomed. A new commercial agreement was negotiated. The Cubans had good cause to be grateful to Mexico. Whatever the reasons for Mexico's policy toward Cuba, there is no doubt that it provided an invaluable link to Latin America during the long years when all the other hemispheric nations had joined the United States in isolating Cuba.

Relations with Brazil's right-wing military dictatorship come at the other extreme. Before the coup of 1964 the government of President João Goulart was sympathetic toward the Castro regime. I know because I had a long conversation with "Jango" Goulart in Brasília a few months before he was overthrown.

Brazil's trade relations with the United States are bound to grow. American government, business, banking, and military sectors pragmatically care nothing about the Brazilian government's odious domestic policies. Brazil became the world's greatest producer of sugar in 1973 and in the next five or ten years will be a greater exporter of sugar than Cuba ever was. Presumably, this will mean that the United States will import more Brazilian sugar, leaving less room for Cuban sugar if or when the time comes that trade is restored.

The use to which Brazil's extraordinary economic boom is being put is instructive when one considers what is happening in Cuba. *The Times* of London had a special supplement on Brazil on October 15, 1973. Tucked away on a back page amid a large number of favorable articles was one by John Mulholland about the economy being run by a partnership of the military and some civilian technocrats. In the middle of it was this paragraph:

"The whole concept of the more equitable distribution of wealth has, at least temporarily, been dismissed. The chief economic slogan in Brazil today is 'grow rich.' There is no doubt that it has worked out only in favor of a tiny percentage of the population. Some 80 percent of Brazilians live barely above the subsistence level and their plight in the last few years, as the Government admits, has become worse rather than better."

If those 80 percent of Brazil's 100 million population could be asked whether they preferred their present system to Cuba's, could there be any doubt what they would say?

"We are of the opinion that this hemisphere carries a child in its womb that is known as Revolution," Fidel said in a news conference in Concepción, Chile, on December 3, 1971, "that is on its way and that, inexorably—due to a biological law, a social law, a law of history —it will be born."

The goal that he dreams and works for, as I have said, is a new pan-American union—but without the United States.

"There is no need to wait for an advanced or super-advanced or Marxist consciousness," he had said in the same city on November 18. "Oh! if only we were all agreed on one thing: to free ourselves from imperialism!"

Castro's emphasis on Latin American confederation is one of the oldest aspirations of hemispheric history. It is not just the "subversion" that Washington complains about; it is a response to a long and emotive tradition that began with Simón Bolívar early in the nineteenth century. José Martí was a champion of the idea of a unified political and cultural Latin America, free of United States as well as Spanish intervention. There has been an affinity at work through the generations, a sort of hemispheric nationalism that has seemed gradually to be reasserting itself in recent years. Setbacks may well be temporary, like the Spanish dance where the participants go three steps forward, two steps back, three steps forward, two back . . .

In his farewell address at the end of his Chilean trip on December 2, 1971, Fidel said:

> The day will come when we will all have the same citizenship, without losing one iota of our love for our homeland, for that corner of our hemisphere where we were born; for our flags, which will be sister flags; for our anthems, which will be sister anthems; for our traditions, which will be sister traditions; and for our cultures, which will be sister cultures. The day will come when our peoples will have the power to take an honored place in the world, when the powerful will no longer be able to insult us, when the empire, proud and arrogant, will no longer be able to threaten us with tragedy and defeat or make any other kind of threat . . . Because it is not the same thing to threaten a small country as it is to threaten a union of sister nations that may become a large and powerful community in the world of tomorrow.

"How hollow the rhetoric that ushered in the Alliance for Progress in 1961 sounds in the wake of Chile's tragedy," wrote Graham Hovey of the Editorial Board of *The New York Times.* "Why have things gone so terribly wrong? Why have there been more coups since the beginning of the Alliance than in any comparable period in the modern history of the hemisphere? . . . Even in disillusionment with the Alliance for Progress and recognizing that American influence will be only marginal, can Washington be comfortable with a nothing policy for a continent largely out of control but clearly lurching toward revolution?"

"Cuba has come closer to some of the Alliance objectives than most Alliance members," wrote Juan de Onis and Jerome Levinson in their book *The Alliance That Lost Its Way* (1970). "In education and public health, no country in Latin America has carried out such ambitious and nationally comprehensive programs. Cuba's centrally planned economy has done more to integrate the rural and urban sectors (through a national income distribution policy) than the market economies of other Latin American countries."

The irony of this judgment lies in the fact that President Kennedy's Alliance for Progress was created as a democratic answer to the Cuban Revolution.

Until Pat Holt, staff director of the Senate Foreign Relations Committee, visited Cuba in July 1974 and returned with a favorable report, there was no public evidence that government or political leaders in Washington—and still less the press—understood what had been happening in Cuba or what the situation was there, but there are signs that many Americans want to change U.S. policies toward Cuba. A possibly historic breakthrough came with an article by Senator Edward M. Kennedy in *The New York Times Magazine* of January 14, 1973.

"After a quarter of a century of hostility," he began, "the United States cast off its cold war veil last year and acknowledged the existence of the People's Republic of China. Now it is time to lift the veil once more and begin the process of normalizing relations with Cuba."

Referring to a recent statement by Nixon that "there will be no change, no change whatever, in our policy toward Cuba unless and until—and I do not anticipate this will happen—Castro changes his policy toward Latin America and the United States," Kennedy continued:

> I think President Nixon's judgment on this matter is wrong. The original rationale for the policy has lost all validity. . . .
>
> Another pillar of the policy of isolation has also crumbled with the passage of time. Cuban intervention in the hemisphere has diminished almost to the point of insignificance. . . .
>
> We cannot know beforehand whether the enterprise of normalizing relations with Cuba will meet with success or failure. But we can be sure that our current policy is out of touch with reality. We can be sure that a growing number of our Latin American allies are rejecting that policy. And we can be sure that there will be no opporutnity to know whether Castro is ready to respond to our initiatives unless we try them.

Senator Kennedy was writing without any apparent knowledge of what was happening in Cuba or how strongly Fidel was rejecting any idea of a reconciliation with the United States. However, he was right in saying that one could not be sure of Castro's response before an effort was made from the American side.

When Henry A. Kissinger, then Secretary of State–designate, was first asked on September 10, 1973, about a possible relaxation of the Cuban trade embargo, he said that the United States would consult with Latin American countries about it but would make no unilateral move. The next day the Allende regime was overthrown in Chile, an event Castro blamed on the United States.

In Mexico City in February 1974, Kissinger had his chance to consult with Latin American countries about Cuba and rejected it. However, while he was there, Argentine businessmen were on their way to Cuba to arrange for the deal whereby the Argentine subsidiaries of Ford, General Motors, and Chrysler could sell 44,000 vehicles to Cuba over three years. At the same time, two hundred other Argentine businessmen and government officials were going in and out of Havana consolidating sales contracts under the $1.2 billion credit that Argentina gave to Cuba in 1973. The American cars were competing with France's Citroën and Germany's Mercedes Benz, which had already muscled in on the Cuban market. The U.S. trade embargo was being breached by proxy.

No doubt there will be many foreign trade agreements in 1975 and thereafter. If the Americans are left out in the cold, it will be politics, not business, that fails to surmount the "Cuban Wall."

What with Chile, Watergate, and the Middle East war, the Cuban question faded for a while into the background, but there is a groundswell that may take effect in time. *Newsweek* of April 16, 1973, referred to an opinion poll taken early in the month indicating that 51 percent of the American public favored reestablishing diplomatic ties with Cuba, compared with only 21 percent two years before.

The Ford administration finally responded to the combined Latin American and domestic pressure when, in a speech in Houston, Texas, on March 1, 1975, Kissinger said that "the United States will consider changes in its relations with Cuba. We are prepared to move in a new direction if Cuba is."

Senator Kennedy, who had broken the ice with his article in *The New York Times* more than a year before, picked up the challenge and introduced legislation in the Senate the following week to end the trade embargo and the sanctions against countries which trade with Cuba and the ban on Americans traveling to Cuba. Kennedy by then was sure he could count on passage of the legislation by Congress and approval by the Ford administration, but he was starting what would have to be a long and difficult process of negotiations with a Fidel Castro and a Cuba in no mood to make a quick settlement on easy terms.

This book must go to press before the final results are known, but the drive toward closing the thirteen-year-old rift between Havana and Washington is obviously too strong to stop.

How greatly American opinions have changed is evident when one re-reads the much-applauded book by Theodore Draper, *Castroism, Theory and Practice,* published in 1965. He ends his book with a criticism of a tolerant speech on Cuba by Senator J. William Fulbright on March 25, 1964. Draper's attack shows the fear and alarm that still permeated American opinion in 1965.

"Those who may be willing at this stage to give up all hope and effort to bring down the Castro regime should take into account the total magnitude, the full enormity, on a world scale, of this decision," Draper wrote.

Little of that feeling is left in 1975, although, ludicrously, the supposed threat from Cuba had its place in the Watergate scandal. Bernard L. Barker, one of the three naturalized Cuban-Americans convicted of burglary in the case, told the Senate investigative committee that the Watergate raids were prompted in part by fears that Castro's government was providing funds for Democratic candidates in the 1972 presidential election. Barker said he had been enlisted by E. Howard Hunt, Jr., one of the top CIA officials in the Bay of Pigs invasion.

It has often been noted with great satisfaction in the United States that Castro's Cuba was not an example that other Latin American countries have wanted to follow. This is a doubtful proposition now, and as I said about Brazil, should not one ask whether conditions in Latin America have been such that Cubans would have wanted to live as the other Latin Americans do? There have been economic, political, and social crises uninterruptedly since the mid-1950s throughout the hemisphere. In many ways—education, public health, social services, equality—Cubans are surely envied by knowledgeable Latins. And how many Latin American leaders must wish that they could defy the United States as Fidel Castro has done?

"American power over Cuban destinies has gone," ex-Ambassador Bonsal concedes in his book on Cuba. "The fact of confiscation is a political fact, whatever one may think of its morality or its equity."

Some payment will doubtless be made someday, but return of

most properties will be impossible or, at least, unmanageable, and indemnity will be financially unbearable. Nationalism will prevent renewed foreign control of major utilities and vital industries like mining, oil refining, and perhaps even sugar.

"We are disposed to go five, ten, fifteen, twenty, thirty years without relations with the United States," Castro said on July 26, 1972. ". . . Tourists here to play roulette? Tourists here for prostitutes? Tourists to corrupt us? No! No profit, no economic benefit can compensate for the morals that Yankee tourism signifies in our country." (However, as I wrote, tourists by the thousands were welcomed in the summer and winter of 1974. One sees advertisements for package tours in Canadian, Mexican, and even European newspapers.)

The one successful Cuban-American negotiation since the diplomatic break was the hijacking agreement reached on February 5, 1973. The worldwide era of hijacking began in August 1961 when Charles Cadon, an Algerian-born Frenchman, commandeered a U.S. airliner over Mexican territory and forced the pilot at gunpoint to fly to Havana.

The Cubans proposed very early in the game that the two countries negotiate an accord, but it had to be reciprocal. If the Cubans returned planes and hijackers, the United States must return Cuban planes, boats, and their hijackers to Cuba. Washington left the various suggestions unanswered.

Cuba always returned hijacked aircraft, crews, and passengers immediately, after hospitable treatment, but held the hijackers. Most of them ended in jail. Cuba was the first country to enact a law against hijacking. The text was presented to an assembly of the International Civil Aviation Organization in Montreal, Canada, in June 1970. It had been enacted on September 16, 1969.

"The provisions of the present Law will be applied solely on the basis of equality and strict reciprocity," reads Article 3. This was the stumbling block for the United States until the hijacking became intolerable.

"It can be seen," Major Claudio Rey Moriña, head of Cuba's delegation to Montreal, said, "that under this law the Cuban authorities, far from encouraging the hijacking of planes and ships, make instead the perpetrators of such crimes subject to abide by applicable laws in force in Cuba and render them liable for any criminal acts that might be deriving therefrom, without prejudice to the principle of political asylum that is granted under the law in Cuba to whoever is being politically persecuted."

A government statement of November 14, 1972, made it clear that Cuba did not want to be a refuge for American criminals or for planes or ships leaving the United States illegally. "However," it added, "the Government of Cuba cannot settle this question in a unilateral, isolated manner without a reciprocal and broad commitment on the part of the United States."

Such a commitment was agreed to by Washington on February 5, 1973, in a joint "memorandum of understanding on hijacking of aircraft and vessels and other offenses." It begins: "The Government of the United States of America and the Government of the Republic of Cuba, on the basis of equality and strict reciprocity, agree . . ."

There is a passage which states that either country will punish those who promote expeditions, violence, or depredation "in the territory of the other party." This was a guarantee that Cuba long sought, although there still are breaches in the observance.

Article 4 allows both sides to "take into consideration any extenuating or mitigating circumstances" where political prisoners are concerned.

The eight-year-old refugee airlift from Havana to Miami was ended by Castro in April 1973, at which time it was estimated that more than 50,000 Cubans still wanted to leave.

According to a study financed by the U.S. government, published on December 13, 1973, there were 612,648 Cuban refugees in the United States. Of these, 268,200 were living in Dade County, Florida, 98,479 in New York, and the rest spread around the country.

Life was made harsh for Cubans who applied over the years to leave the island. They lost their jobs, professions, and property, working meanwhile on farms for the minimum pay. Some had to wait two years or more for their turn. The procedure was not much better than the fate of Jews applying to leave Russia for Israel during the same period.

At one time there were an estimated two hundred organizations of exiles in Florida, quarreling among themselves. By April 17, 1971, when the tenth anniversary of the ill-fated Bay of Pigs invasion was commemorated, George Volsky, *New York Times* correspondent in Miami, wrote that "only a handful of exile organizations are barely active."

The Cuban refugees have made Miami equal to the second-largest Cuban City; Santiago de Cuba, the island's second, has a population of only 276,000. A lavish social life in restaurants and clubs by one-time Havana socialites is going on, Volsky wrote. The median annual income of a Cuban family is about $8,000. Miami has an all-Spanish television channel and three full-time radio stations, the *Diario las Américas* newspaper, and a dozen weekly publications in Spanish.

"On the whole," Volsky concludes, "concern among exiles over what is going on in Cuba is on the wane."

In a dispatch sent on July 28, 1973, about Cuban exiles becoming active in political life, Volsky wrote that it took until 1965 for "the refugees to realize that, with the Government of Fidel Castro firmly in power, they were here in Florida to stay."

It was natural for the emotion-driven refugees to take so long to reconcile themselves to what had been obvious for years. There was no excuse for Washington's failing to understand the facts of Cuban life from the early years. Today the continued existence of the Castro regime is taken for granted.

"We will be friendly with those countries who want to be friendly with us, whatever their form of government," Castro had said to me in September 1972. But a détente was never possible while Richard Nixon was President. As Fidel put it in a press conference in 1972, "We have nothing to talk about with Nixon." On a number of occasions, Castro said—as he still says—"We won't discuss anything with the United States so long as the trade embargo lasts."

Then, in August 1974, with the resignation of Nixon, the succession of Gerald Ford, and the naming of Nelson Rockefeller as Vice-President, the picture changed. One major obstacle had been removed, but perhaps another had been introduced. Ford had played no known role in Cuban-American affairs, but in Nelson Rockefeller history ironically has given to the situation another Vice-President who, like Nixon, has wanted to destroy the Cuban revolutionary regime. At the times of the Bay of Pigs, the missile crisis, and even in later years, Rockefeller's advice on Cuba, as on Vietnam, was hawkish in the extreme. Castro can look only to tolerance from Nelson Rockefeller, not amity or trust. For Fidel, Rockefeller represents all that he has fought against as a revolutionary.

So far as the Organization of American States is concerned, it is still likely that Cuba will be invited to rejoin the fold, but right into 1975, Fidel was talking with contempt of the OAS.

He is in no hurry, as he showed when he blasted President Ford and the United States for the CIA intervention in Chile against President Allende. This was in a speech on September 28, 1974, the anniversary of the founding of the CDR. Unluckily for them, Senators Jacob Javits, Republican of New York, and Claiborne Pell, Democrat of Rhode Island, had chosen that very weekend to visit Havana in a presumably friendly and hopeful mood.

This did not mean that Castro would not, at some future date, negotiate with the United States. What Americans can never discount is the inborn, inbred, ineradicable anti-Yankeeism of Fidel Castro. In that September 28 speech, he still referred to the OAS as "shameful . . . discredited . . . prostituted . . . this ridiculous institution." As I said, he wants a Latin American organization without the United States—and he may get it.

The stature of Fidel Castro as an international statesman of considerable importance was first shown by his appearance at the conference of the so-called nonaligned nations in Algiers in early September 1973. Seventy-six nations were represented. Castro was a dominant figure with his spirited championship of the Soviet Union, his public controversies with Colonel Gaddafi of Libya and Norodom Sihanouk of Cambodia, and what the correspondent of *The Observer* of London felt was his appeal to "the twenty-five poorer countries against their richer rivals."

"These countries now find that Castro and Cuba as one of the 'have-nots' represent their interests more effectively than Libya and the oil and copper millionaires of the Middle East and Africa," the newspaper stated.

The countries at the conference represented more than half the population of the globe. To play a major role among the leaders of such a meeting was a triumph for Fidel Castro.

At the close of the conference on September 9, Castro announced that Cuba was breaking diplomatic relations with Israel. He was alone in this action at the time, which was a gesture toward the Arabs, an alignment with the Soviet bloc—and a contravention of what had been Cuban policy to date. There had always been normal and friendly relations between Havana and Tel Aviv. Israel had never done anything to harm Cuba. It was a callous move of *realpolitik.* Unlike the Czechoslovak incident in 1968 where Castro had no choice, this was a deliberate political decision. After his announcement Colonel Gaddafi, who had attacked Fidel during the conference, went over and shook his hand. As was learned at the time of the October 1973 Middle East war, Fidel sent a Cuban military contingent of fifty to a hundred men to the Syrian front to fight against the Israelis.

In the Middle East conflict in October 1973, Fidel was not only completely pro-Arab, but set a foreign news policy in Cuba that was blatantly false. The Cuban people were told by *Granma* and their radio that the Israelis were the aggressors. This was only too typical of the way foreign news is handled in Cuba. In the case of the "Yom

Kippur" War, it was an insult to the Cuban intelligence, but few would have had the means to learn the truth.

In November 1974, Castro invited Yasser Arafat of the Palestine Liberation Organization to Havana after the Arab's United Nations appearance and gave him a hero's welcome. There is now a PLO representative in Havana.

The clearest proof that the Castro government has become an established part of the global community of nations was the flood of congratulatory messages that poured in from all over the world on the fifteenth anniversary of the Revolution on January 1, 1974. One addressed to President Dorticós from London read:

"I have much pleasure in sending to Your Excellency on the Cuban Day of Liberation My cordial congratulations and warm good wishes for the prosperity of your country and its people." It was signed: "Elizabeth R."

Among the dozens of other messages were those of Pope Paul VI, President Pompidou, and Generalissimo Franco.

Castro has had to face one of the great facts of the 1970s—that the world powers are coming to terms with each other, coexisting and putting their emphasis on economic factors. China and Russia, while quarreling with each other, are forgetting about "wars of liberation." Small powers like Cuba are losing some of the importance they may have had. Fidel had to sit back, in bitterness, and watch Moscow and Peking let Hanoi down during the "stone age" bombing by President Nixon of North Vietnam. Castro played the game as it is, and not as he wished it could be.

In that famous speech of July 26, 1970, he had said wistfully:

> Someday we will form part of the community of the peoples of Latin America, of the revolutionary peoples of Latin America. Someday our nations will not be fragments of a balkanized continent subjugated by imperialism. We are the pioneers along this revolutionary road; the first, but not the only ones. And one day, sooner or later, we will be the peoples of Latin America, with the resources and strength of hundreds of millions. And it will not be just so that we can confront a powerful imperialism, but in order that a great people can live united; the day when the imperialist yoke will have been lifted and the day when a revolution will have been made in its [imperialism's] own country: the people of the United States. We are not the enemy of those people, but of its criminal governors, its imperialistic rulers.

In 1975 this is a dream that he has not relinquished, nor is he ever likely to, although he must know that it could not become real for many a long year.

For Fidel Castro, the United States has been a nightmare, not a dream. He does not understand the United States or North Americans, and they do not understand him and the Cubans. The American historiography on Cuba—what little there is—provides some wise, shrewd, and enlightened interpretations, but these are the exceptions. The journalism has been worse than the history. The coverage of the Castro Revolution in the American news media has been one of the greatest failures in the history of American journalism. Yet the Cuban Revolution is undoubtedly one of the most fascinating subjects in the world for newspapermen, students, teachers, sociologists, political scientists, and, most of all, historians of revolution. A social revolution in process is a rare and enthralling phenomenon to watch. And how few Americans have been watching it these last sixteen years!

One of our most perceptive and knowledgeable Latin Americanists, Professor Kalman H. Silvert of New York University (who revisited Cuba in July 1974), has realized the meaning as well as the importance of the Cuban Revolution from the beginning.

In a paper published in the American Assembly's 1971 book *The United States and the Caribbean,* he wrote:

> To a social scientist or anyone interested in the sociology of knowledge, Cuba is one of the most interesting cases of guided social change to be found anywhere in the world . . . Castro and his associates are attempting to create an absolutely equalitarian, national community based on a theory of value that has nothing to do with economic criteria and everything to do directly with the affective meaning of man's activities in the community. Only Maoist China approaches the degree of radical innovation being pursued by Cuba's leadership, who unabashedly speak of the creation of a new man—new in his sense of good and bad, in his world view, in his approach to work and labor, and in his identification with community.

For Silvert, "the price in cultural change seems impossibly high." I do not believe that the great majority of the Cuban people feel that it is in 1975.

CHAPTER 19

Revolution

When one makes a revolution one cannot mark time; one must always go forward or go back.
—Lenin, as quoted by John Reed

"Purity of heart is to will one thing," Kierkegaard wrote. Mao Tse-tung, Lenin, Robespierre, had that pure certainty of revolutionary purpose, which is an attribute of will, not of good or evil. Those who have missed this all-absorbing simplicity of Fidel Castro's revolutionary aims have misunderstood both Castro and the Cuban Revolution.

His drive, from the time he set himself on a revolutionary course after General Batista's coup in March 1952, has been unwavering. It has moved like the relentless progress of a bulldozer, now and then stopped by obstacles but always gathering power to forge ahead. The end is not in sight. "I am more revolutionary than ever," as he said to me in September 1972.

Addressing a Santiago, Chile, audience on November 11, 1971, he said:

> To our understanding, a revolution is a way, a process. There is no such thing as a ready-made revolution. No revolution is made in one day, either. There are not even preconceived revolutions, because revolutions, which are the result of reality, the result of life itself, the result of the laws of history, cannot be preconceived. Even though they are the result of history, revolutions do not make themselves. They are made by men. And men play an important role in the interpretation and application of those laws. . . .
>
> If we said that we had a revolution already made, we should be sent to an asylum. We Cubans are trying to make a revolution, and the more we advance the more we realize how great and how complex the task is—but, at the same time, we realize how stimulating it is.

> So, we are still making revolution. And I believe that we will have to go on making revolution for another fifty or one hundred years.

Fidel never ceases to brood over his problems and the meaning of revolution. In this sense, at least, he is an intellectual. He seeks—perhaps "gropes" is a better word—for reasons, explanations, interpretations. The years when he seemed to act with little or no thought—impulsively, intuitively—are gone.

"Revolution alone does not provide the solution for problems," he now concedes. (This was in a speech to the students of University City in Cracow, Poland, on June 8, 1972.)

> Revolution is only a beginning! Problems are solved through technological development, through the development of productive forces, through the development of the masses' capacity to produce. However, in order to accomplish this, revolution is necessary.
>
> We can say to the young people from the various countries in Asia, Africa and Latin America that we are convinced of the fact that revolution is necessary for development. As long as there are landowners and latifundists, oligarchs, capitalists and foreign monopolies in control of the economy, there will be no solution to social problems. What the world of the future needs is revolution, the revolution that remains to be made in many parts of the world.

This is how his faithful group of followers also see it. None of them has lost his or her zest for carrying on the revolution that they helped Fidel Castro to make.

Looking back over the years, I think that none of them has given me a keener sense of the all-absorbing revolutionary fervor which has sustained and driven Cuba than Haydée Santamaría. She is the *Marianne* of the Cuban Revolution. Haydée and I talked for hours on my last visit in her office at the Casa de las Américas, which she directs, and I marveled, as always, at her ardent faith. She still glows with the purest flame of any of the revolutionaries, perhaps because she is so articulate, so emotional, so dedicated.

"I thank God every morning when I wake up that I still live to devote myself to the Revolution," she exclaimed.

Haydée said something during our talk that had struck me before, but without my being able to give expression to it. There is a compulsive quality about the Cuban Revolution for those taking part in it. They have a fatalistic impulse to devote themselves to it, to work for it, to keep it alive, to give it a propulsion that must never stop. What Haydée was describing was the equivalent of a profound religious emotion expressed in secular, revolutionary terms.

Except for the Chinese Communist leaders, no individuals in the chain of social revolutions that began in France in 1789 were submitted to such a test of character, stamina, morale, and loyalty as the group who fought with Fidel Castro for two years in the Sierra Maestra. Those same qualities are there in 1975, and they earn Fidel the same degree of loyalty and devotion.

There has been no break-up of the Cuban leaders, as in China, no defections among the Moncada–Sierra group. The Revolution did not "devour its children" as so many critics and historians were saying in 1959–1961. Those who defected were not legitimate members of the revolutionary family.

In none of the modern revolutions has a leader attracted such a united, dedicated, and enthusiastic band of followers, men and women who went through extreme dangers and hardships in the field, followed by long years of exhausting and often heartbreakingly unfruitful sedentary work in government.

A true social revolution, such as Cuba now has, transforms the quality of life at least as much as it does the economics and politics. The Cubans of 1975 are a different people from the Cubans of 1959.

The Jamaican playwright Barry Reckord, who has written one of the most perceptive personal studies of the Cuban Revolution under the ridiculous title *Does Fidel Eat More Than Your Father?* (1971), was struck by this fact. Writing of a Cuban girl who had been trained as a mechanic ("her Jamaican equivalent would be an ignorant servant"), Reckord says:

"I think her articulateness comes from being brought up on Fidel's speeches which, rhetoric aside, often state problems succinctly—very direct, very clear, no jargon, full of definitions, facts and figures. Dull Cubans merely repeat the ideas. Bright Cubans pick up the method and the confidence. There are thousands of Cubans like this girl, light-years away from their parents. This is more than social mobility; it is mass migration of a whole generation from one level of civilization to another."

Kalman H. Silvert has stressed the modernity and uniqueness of the Revolution. "It is taken for granted in Latin America that Cuba has broken out of traditional Latin American molds and into the early stages of modern nationhood," he wrote in a contribution to the Brookings Institution book, *Cuba and the United States* (1967), edited by John Plank.

Professor Silvert calls Cuba "socially and politically the Iberian cultural world's first almost-modern state . . . The Cuban Government seems to have been the first to evoke as well as impose forcefully a kind of national coherence throughout its society."

For Silvert, "modern social organization refers to a social system sufficiently open to permit broad interclass mobility—a system possessing communications and attitudes that transcend class lines." Cuba fits this definition.

The survival of the regime, he wrote eight years ago, "implies a strength that can only be based on a high degree of consensus from certain groups and a special kind of opposition from others."

Discussing why the Cubans, who are so individualistic, so Spanish, so easily violent, should be so quiescent for years, a European ambassador in Havana suggested to me that it was because they had no alternative. This is no doubt true for some. There must be the disaffected, the discontented, the antagonistic, the disillusioned. But they are disorganized and have no popular support and no leader. They have no alternative because they are weak and a small minority. In the Batista era the alternative was revolution; the alternative to Fidel is counterrevolution, but there is no strength for this, in or out of Cuba, and little evident desire.

The Cuban character is positive and assertive; in that respect it is very Spanish—*muy español.* It does not permit neutrality, nor does it favor compromise. When faced with a man like Fidel Castro or a revolution of this type, a Cuban is not objective, philosophical, or apathetic; he is passionately for or against. The objective foreigner is damned by both sides—and rightly, because it means that he does not understand or does not care.

One factor in Fidel's continuing popular support is that it is impossible to be cynical about him, as Cubans have been throughout their history with their rulers and politicians. Cubans do not shrug their shoulders and say resignedly, as they have done so many times: "Well, what can you expect?" The mass of people, the so-called lower classes, would think in clichés: "He means well; he tries hard; he works like a dog; he is honest and runs an honest government; he is for us peasants [or workers, or Negroes], not for the rich people, not for Americans." Simple men and women think in simple terms and appreciate common, basic qualities, which they can understand. They would not feel that Fidel Castro has betrayed them.

A saying of Martí's was given new force in Cuba after 1959 and has been cited many times. "When a people enter into a revolution," Martí wrote, "they do not come out until they have achieved it." (The Spanish is more vivid: *hasta que la corona*—"until they have set a crown upon it.")

I did not feel in the early years, when Cuba "entered" the Revolution, that one could truly use the word "people." The people were not ready; they did not understand what the Revolution represented, what it specifically meant to them, and they were a divided people. As the years passed, I could see that more and more of the Cuban people understood and supported Fidel Castro. In September 1972, on my last visit, I felt sure that now, finally, perhaps irrevocably, the Revolution had taken hold of the people.

The fact that the Revolution today has grass roots is one of the most important judgments that can be made about it. This is all the more true now with the elections for "organs of People's Power." There is an enormous mass following for it and a commitment that embraces the old and the middle-aged as well as the young. The grumbling one hears is about the discomforts of life, the shortages, the lack of things to buy, a certain drabness, and, with the older generations, a sense of nostalgia for what was for many an easier, freer life. Many must feel a vague sense of oppression conveyed, especially, through the Committees for the Defense of the Revolution, but also through the regimentation of their lives in so many ways, the restrictions and limitations, a certain monotony. The older, prerevolutionary educated Cubans must feel, more or less keenly, the loss of civic liberties. The measure of the Revolution's acceptance is not in the lack of opposition and disaffection, but in the degree and quality of the support that it receives, and these are impressive.

In his very first speech in Camp Columbia, Havana, on January 8, 1959, Castro had said: "When I speak of columns [of Rebel troops], when I hear speak of fronts of battle, of more or less numerous troops, I always think: here is our steadiest column, our strongest troop, the only troop capable by itself of winning the war—this troop is the people."

Fidel realized and argued from the beginning—even before 1959—that revolutions succeed to the extent that their leaders are able to mobilize mass, nationwide support. He had that backing overwhelmingly in the beginning, but it broke down under confused and wrong expectations among a large part of the community.

Today the Revolution has passed its most difficult and dangerous hurdles. The first decade saw the economy collapse and then flounder through a morass of errors and handicaps. Politically, there was the Bay of Pigs invasion, the missile crisis, with a dangerous five years of internal strife, complicated by constant incursions, underground resistance, and guerrilla bands, most of them armed, supplied, and financed by the U.S. Central Intelligence Agency. One of the most severe tribulations was the American trade embargo. On the favorable side, the abandonment of any idea of American intervention and the uninterrupted military, economic, and political support of the Communist bloc gave Cuba a solid, secure place in the game of power politics.

The Cuban people—more than enough of them—have educated themselves at the same time that their leaders were learning. As I wrote before, there could be no better evidence of this than the way the Cuban people rallied more strongly than ever behind Fidel Castro after the great fiasco of the 1970 sugar *zafra.*

"Of course the Revolution was unable to give the people all that they needed," Fidel said in a speech on September 28, 1966.

> The people could not be given what the Revolution did not have to give. But the Revolution did give the people all that it could. . . .
>
> And there is something that cannot be calculated mathematically, simply by multiplying and dividing, by adding and subtracting —and that is the moral benefits that the Revolution has meant for the people; what it has meant for every man and woman in this country to feel for the first time like human beings, like men and women in in the fullest sense of the word; what it has meant for millions of men and women in this country to cease being nothing, in order to become something. . . .
>
> There is not one family, one farmer, one single worker, one common man in our country who does not feel security in the face of death, accidents, illness, in the face of anything. And all this has been creating in our citizens a sense of their own worth, a sense of their own dignity.

Fidel in that speech quoted the biblical saying: "For man does not live by bread alone." Thus the "Humanism" of 1959, which as an official philosophy was used only for about three months, was, one can see now, a permanent form of idealism.

Talking to some fishermen in Iquique, Chile, on November 16, 1971, Fidel told them:

> One of the nicest [*mas bellas*] things that some of the visitors to our country find is the enormous human change that has taken place in our people. The accomplishments of a revolution are not to be measured only in stones; they are not to be measured only in factories. They *are* to be measured in these, but essentially they ought to be measured in moral and human terms [*factores*].
>
> Already it gives us [me] much satisfaction when visitors are able to see this sense of fraternity, of disinterestedness, that characterizes

our people as a result of their revolutionary education. We are struggling to construct upright [*justas*] human societies, societies that really merit the name of human. The exploitation of man by man converted human society into a jungle where the law of the strongest held sway, the weightiest, the most astute, the richest. It converted human society into a zoo.

Talking, as I did in August-September 1972, to President Dorticós, Raúl Castro, Celia Sánchez, Juan Almeida, Armando Hart, Haydée Santamaría, Melba Hernández, Jesús Montané, Vilma Espín, and others of the close-knit group who have always been with Fidel, it was striking how strong their feeling for him was. I had never sensed the depth of their affection, loyalty, and faith in Fidel and the Revolution so vividly as I did during that sojourn. Admiration too was to be found everywhere, but it was only since 1970 that Castro could be said to have merited respect for his economic policies.

A ruler with his power is always accompanied by sycophants, flatterers, the overawed, the blind worshipers, but this would not apply to the Sierra Maestra group. In any event, Fidel does not command by fear, although he has a formidable temper that no one wants to arouse. As a type he is not remotely like Stalin, Hitler, Mussolini, Franco, or even the *caudillo* generals of Latin America. He radiates a warmth that permits the humblest peasant not only to talk to him freely but to scold him because he did not get the tools or the fertilizer he needed. I have seen that often, and Fidel's response would always be a patient, fatherly explanation of how difficult things were and how hard they were all trying. There always has been this direct contact between Castro and the people. He seems to be everywhere, tending personally to everything, talking to everyone.

I thought in the early years of the Revolution that power had corrupted Fidel. I now incline toward the opposite; it has matured him, deepened a sense of responsibility to the masses, the people; made him realize that he had sometimes abused his power—as in 1970—and must now use it with more discretion. We in the United States, who have seen one of the most striking cases in history of power corrupting, in the case of Richard Nixon, should be able to understand why Cubans appreciate the character of the man who heads their government.

The top group of men and women—the generation of Moncada—have also matured in more than age and experience. They have a sense of the responsibilities of power that I did not note before. The dash, the exuberance, the rashness, the euphoria—all the youthful excesses of the early years—have turned into a sober exercise of what is still seen as a great mission and a glorious ideal. They are working better, doing a better job, cooperating more smoothly, and they have a quiet confidence that, to my knowledge, is new.

Of course, one must realistically keep in mind that Fidel Castro and all his group have no alternative to the present method of rule. They stand or fall together—not that they consciously act from a sense of self-preservation. The idealism is genuine.

There cannot be another Fidel Castro. There is certainly no man and no group of exiles abroad with any following in Cuba. Even the names of the refugees who set themselves up with Washington's help in the Bay of Pigs invasion of 1961 would be unknown to the new generation of Cubans. No one wants them back—or wanted them then, for that matter—except for the few older folk longing for and living in the past.

Cuban exiles cannot ever be used again. Some were corrupt politicians; some sincere and honest patriots; some true democrats; a few were gangsters, adventurers, gamblers, or criminals. Virtually all are disillusioned, without hope, or satisfied with their lot in the United States, Puerto Rico, Venezuela, or Spain. There is no unity among them, and never was; no leader; no agreed program. Across the Florida Strait is a different island from the one they left. Those who do not realize that under no circumstance, least of all through a Cuban-American reconciliation, would they be welcomed back in Cuba are living in a dream world. It seems, however, that very few would now want to go back.

When Fidel is out of the country, Raúl Castro is Acting Prime Minister. After Fidel and the others have died or become incapacitated, a whole generation of "revolutionary" children will be there to take over should the Revolution create its line of legitimacy. There are Fidel's son, Fidelito; the four children of Raúl Castro and Vilma Espín; Juan Almeida's four; and the two of the Haydée Santamaría–Armando Hart marriage. And there is Hildita Guevara, the daughter of Che and Hilda Gadea, not to mention Che's four children by Aleida March. The list could go on. There is no nepotism as yet in Cuba, and most of these children are anyway too young, but they are being brought up as revolutionaries and they will be heard from. One should, perhaps, make an exception for Fidelito, who in 1975 is doing postgraduate work in physics in a Moscow university. He will be twenty-six years old when this book appears. While his loyalty is unquestioned, he has shown no desire to follow in his father's footsteps.

When the Revolution was beginning in 1959, there was much

talk of the possible assassination of Fidel. He took note of it one day in a speech in which he said that the destiny of Cuba would not depend on one man. "Behind me come others more radical than I," he warned, naming his brother Raúl as the man to succeed him if he were killed.

The statement was received with disbelief or skepticism. It would be foolish to brush it aside now that the Revolution is so far advanced. The qualities that Raúl displayed in organizing and administering the large and elaborate guerrilla structure in the Sierra de Cristal, with its minigovernment; the able way in which he has commanded the Cuban armed forces since 1959; his shrewd and keen intelligence; his dedication to the socialist revolution—these and other achievements and qualities show that Raúl is *capable* of running the government if anything happened to Fidel. Like the others, he has grown in stature with maturity and years of experience. He is also more popular, being a family man with a distinguished wife who is also constantly in the news as head of the Federation of Cuban Women. Raúl lacks his brother's charisma, oratorical gifts, and expansively warm personality, but he would have with him a strong administration, a powerful military and police force, and the Politburo of the Communist Party.

Assassination is the ever-present danger. In one of his press conferences in Chile in 1971, Fidel said that "a number of plans had been made to assassinate me. I had the opportunity to see at an exhibit—a sort of small museum—the automatic weapons, the bazookas and the grenades that had been sent from the Guantánamo base to a group of counterrevolutionaries to assassinate me."

If the party, the PCC, continues to grow in power and influence, it could take over, post-Castro, in much the same form as the Communist Party of the Soviet Union. The Politburo would then hold the power, and it is now composed of the Castro group. The Cuban military leaders are all Communist Party members. The Central Committee has an impressive membership which includes young Communists who have made their mark. Cuba would then have one-party in place of one-man rule. The Revolution would lose much of the *cachet* that has made it unique and peculiarly Cuban.

It is the fate of all revolutions to move to the right, which is toward conservatism. This comes with institutionalization and the growth of measures that have to be "conserved." For ex-Ambassador Bonsal, the Revolution signalizes "the end of the Republic" that was created in 1902. The *Fidelistas* do not think of their country in those terms. Officially, it is still simply the Republic of Cuba.

My own approach to the Cuban leaders and their Revolution has always been influenced by my respect for their character and ideals. I never believed that the Revolution had to be measured primarily in economic, materialistic terms. Ideally, the rule of a man over men is to be justified by reconciling power to ethics.

The impulse behind true revolutionary action must be spiritual, which is to say moral and/or patriotic, not material and not simply an exercise of power. If a revolution loses this quality, if its leaders enrich themselves or cling to power without popular support by harsh and repressive police force, the revolution will have lost its justification. The transformation that all revolutions, by definition, achieve would not then represent social progress.

It has been argued in this book that Fidel Castro and the men and women who during the past two decades fought and worked with him to make the Cuban Revolution have responded to and acted upon idealistic motives. They have sought to make a better Cuba for the Cuban people and to achieve for Cuba a stronger, more dignified position in world affairs.

No one can say yet whether Marxism is going to provide the right answers for Cuba's problems. As long ago as 1926 John Maynard Keynes, in an essay, saw how Communism could make its appeal:

> I feel confident of one conclusion, that if Communism achieves a certain success, it will achieve it not as an improved economic technique, but as a religion . . . Modern capitalism is absolutely irreligious, without internal union, without much public spirit, often, though not always, a mere congeries of possessors and pursuers. Such a system has to be immensely, not merely moderately successful to survive. . . .
>
> Our problem is to work out a social organization which shall be as efficient as possible without offending our notions of a satisfactory way of life.

The Cuban Revolution is beginning to offer "a satisfactory way of life." It has achieved "a certain success" and done so by means which could, in Keynes's broad use of the word, be called religious. As with religion, there is a powerful element of irrationality and emotion, a heavy reliance on faith, an element of worship. These are not measurable by statistics, nor can they be gauged in economic terms. No one has a right to condemn—or for that matter, to praise—the Cuban Revolution except in what Fidel called "human" terms.

At the television panel discussion on June 26, 1973, to which I referred in the chapter on Moncada, Haydée Santamaría, one of the survivors who answered questions about the attack, was asked how she and Melba Hernández felt when they realized that the attack had failed. Haydée answered:

> Today, being the same person who was at Moncada—and yet I tell you this without really being the same person who was at Moncada—and I tell you this without boasting—today I would be the happiest woman on earth if I should be sent to some place where I was needed to fight, because the terrible thing is to see the years passing and one's life ending not as one wished. . . .
>
> Now I have a son named Abel [after her dead brother]. And if that son of mine should take a step backward I would be the unhappiest woman on earth. Yet at that moment [1953] I would have been the happiest woman on earth if I had learned that Abel was alive. And now I would be the unhappiest woman on earth if my son, when he gets old enough, doesn't have the same readiness to undertake anything that comes along, even though it might mean that I would never see him again. Just look how times have changed! For the better. . . .
>
> I can tell you that now the only thing I need in order to fight is for the sun to keep on shining. Today this is the so-different situation. Today, all I need is for the sun not to fall out of the sky. If the sun should fall out of the sky, I could not fight. But as long as there is a sun, and as long as the sun doesn't fall out of the sky, I can fight for another twenty years.

The nostalgia for the Sierra Maestra, the heroic, comradely days, remains in the hearts of all the participants. Lee Lockwood, in his book *Castro's Cuba,* heard Celia Sánchez say of the Sierra: "Ah, but those were the best times, weren't they? We will never be so happy again, will we? Never."

George Kennan, in an article for *Foreign Affairs* of October 1972, entitled "After the Cold War," saw Russia as trapped by its system of politics. "The Soviet regime," he wrote, "continues to be inspired by an ideology hostile in principles to the Western nations, from which it dares not depart."

Cuba is in a similar position, but in both cases one must question whether the Russians and the Cubans *"dare* not depart" from their ideology. It does not look as if either of them want to. Certainly neither would choose to depart from socialism to embrace the "principles of the Western nations, least of all in this period of crisis for world capitalism."

President John F. Kennedy had a more rational idea in launching his Alliance for Progress. "Our unfulfilled task," he said, "is to demonstrate that our democratic, capitalistic, free enterprise system is better for underdeveloped countries than the totalitarian systems; that it will provide the social justice which the masses demand."

The United States has not proved its case; nor has Marxism-Leninism yet done so. This is Castro's "unfulfilled task," but the Alliance for Progress faded ignominiously into history as the Cuban Revolution grew stronger.

There are at last clear signs of an economic takeoff, thanks both to the Russians and to the Cubans' own efforts, and no doubt one should add the dizzy rise in the price of sugar. As President Dorticós said to me in 1972, all the planning now is for a slow, steady climb toward viability. A solid base has been constructed. All the years of "apprenticeship," of struggle, of investment in the infrastructure, of rationalization, as in the sugar industry, and, most of all, of national, popular education, are beginning to pay off. The hundreds of thousands who have gone through technical schools and universities, training and practicing in fields and factories, are unquestionably an enormous asset for Cuba and the Revolution. The trees that the Revolution planted are bearing fruit, literally and metaphorically.

"It [the Sierra Maestra] was the first heroic period in which men strove to earn posts of greater responsibility, of greater danger, with the fulfillment of their duty as the only satisfaction," Che Guevara had written in the message published as *Man and Socialism.* "In our revolutionary educational work, we often return to this instructive topic. The man of the future could be glimpsed in the attitude of our fighters."

This was the sort of dream on which Che built his life—and lost it. In the Spanish Civil War, many of us thought of the International Brigade and its volunteers as "men of the future," but we can see now that the Brigade, its inspired appeal, and the way men died for an ideal that to them represented good against evil, can never be resurrected.

The adventure of the Sierra Maestra can never be repeated either. It required a unique and complex conjuncture of history, with an extraordinary leader. The men and women of the Sierra, now in middle age, were of a different world than today's. Che's hope that "such heroic attitudes" could be perpetuated in everyday life was asking too much of human nature. The exaltation of a people cannot be sustained in the humdrum affairs of daily life, although Fidel and his group have retained their revolutionary fervor to a remarkable degree. The enthusiasm and dedication of a new generation have a different quality.

As Castro said in a speech on April 4, 1972, "We still don't have the new man, and we no longer have the old one."

For those who created the Revolution and for those, like myself, who have lived with it from the beginning, there is a consistency. The changes one saw with each visit as the years passed were a process of growth. It was always the same Revolution, the same leader, the same followers.

Fidel Castro, like Mao Tse-tung, has worked steadfastly to a grand design within which he has shown flexibility of thought and ideas. His design has been a radical social revolution. He has never ceased to keep it in mind and to work at it through defeats and mistakes that would have discouraged a less sanguine and rocklike character. It has been an impressive accomplishment, and clearly an inspiring one to a majority of the Cuban people, especially the young.

Those of us—I suppose that we were not many—who retained all through the Revolution a belief in its survival and a continuing hope in its struggle toward economic viability, had to rely, as I said, on high opinions of the character, abilities, and ideals of Fidel Castro and the young men and women who fought and worked with him.

They and their revolution need more time—ten years? twenty years?—before the question of economic viability can fairly be answered. Politically, one cannot speak of success or failure; this is for Cubans, not foreigners, to decide. But socially—and it is a *social* revolution—there is no doubt that in many ways the Revolution has been a great and enduring success.

Throughout, the patience, understanding, and intelligence of the Cuban people have been extraordinary. They have borne hardships, frustrations, disappointments, hopes deferred, year after year. Some rebelled; hundreds of thousands fled; and heaven knows how many of those who remain are in varying degrees unhappy, but most are clearly convinced that the Revolution is worth living and working for and, as the Bay of Pigs and missile crisis showed, worth fighting for.

Having seen in Italy, Spain, and Argentina how quickly popular moods can change, I would hazard no guess about the future. I am a journalist and live for today. It is enough for me that in 1975 the Cuban people understand the revolutionary process through which they are going and that a great majority of them approve of it. Their leader, Fidel Castro, retains their trust and admiration.

The fate of Allende's Chile is the best possible argument for the thesis upon which Fidel Castro made his Revolution: that there are no halfway revolutions any more than a woman can be slightly pregnant. It is all or nothing. Castro made a workable and genuine social revolution because he did not compromise, because he went for total change, not half-measures. He gave a lesson in revolution for all time.

His task has not been divorced from the world revolution of our time. Cuba is an island, but the bell of John Donne's aphorism was tolling at all times for Fidel Castro. There is no guessing, at this writing, what effect the worldwide inflation, unemployment, and energy crisis, with its shattering economic and financial developments, will have on Cuba. Much will depend on how the Soviet Union weathers the storm. The Revolution itself, as I have said, is irreversible, but Cuba, like every country in the world, will have to adjust itself to a new era.

History may give Fidel Castro a leading place as a forerunner. He was the first—perhaps the most important—of the rebel youth of our time. He anticipated 1968—a year of revolution whose place in history is not yet clear. Nineteen sixty-eight was not 1789, although it was descended from that revolutionary ancestor. It was not 1848, which seemed so fruitless at the time and to decades of historians until it was realized that in 1848 a document had formulated a new ideology—Communism—which was to transform much of the contemporary world.

We do know that a worldwide movement of protest by the young and by a vaguely labeled "New Left" such as occurred in 1968 must leave a mark on history. Political contagion, like an epidemic, is caught from a germ or virus that can appear everywhere or anywhere, but is the same agent. The Cuban Revolution is a symptom of our profoundly disturbed times; it is not a freak or an aberration.

One hopeful guess is that we are seeing a new flowering of the Protestant ethic—the revolution which transformed not just a religion, but the whole Western world in the sixteenth century. The meaning of life and the political instruments to express this meaning turned from a monarch, an élite, a central authority, to the individual, upon whom devolved the responsibility for his government, his economy, and his way of life. At least, this was the idea which, however imperfectly, has dominated thought and action in the Marxist "people's democracies" as well as in the liberal democracies.

The Max Weber thesis, of course, is not the Marxist one of Western individualism arising through the development of commodity production and accompanying the rise of a new middle class. I am not arguing that Cuban sociologists are concerning themselves with philosophical considerations of this sort. It just seems to me that Castro's actions and thoughts fit better into a thesis like that of the Protestant ethic than into an orthodox Marxist ideology.

The greatest weakness of the method of rule that Lenin applied to Marxism is its concentration of power in a handful of men in the Politburo, with one man standing out—Lenin, Stalin, Khrushchev, and now Brezhnev. This, basically, has been the method used in Cuba. In 1970 Fidel grasped the fact that this was a threat to the continuity of his revolution, and he is changing the system, slowly but steadily.

But individual responsibility demands that individuals work together as a community, delegating authority and voluntarily accepting that authority. This presupposes a high degree of equality, not natural equality, but legal equality, equality of opportunity regardless of race or religion, equality in those necessities that permit a decent and dignified life: food, shelter, clothing, education, medical care, leisure, and the like.

To claim that the Cuban Revolution has yet achieved this ideal would be an exaggeration. However, it is possible to say that Fidel Castro has in some instinctive, intuitive way been driving toward such a goal. He seems to be groping for a new social ethic. His experiment in equality resulted in a genuine social revolution; his experiment in moral incentives for work has surpassed any such attempts in the Western world, even though it is in process of modification now. Only in Maoist China, and perhaps North Korea, has the concept of moral incentives been used for any length of time, but in both those cases with peoples who never in modern history knew any lot that was not a form of wage slavery or subsistence living in ignorance of the world outside. The new "organs of People's Power" are an experiment in genuine democracy.

Cubans are a sophisticated, knowledgeable, Western-minded people, imbued with their Spanish-European culture, and subjected to the liberal ideas and way of life of the United States. It would not have seemed possible, even in theory or a pipedream, that so many contemporary Cubans would accept the voluntary, moral-incentive work system for a day, let alone for years.

We in the Anglo-Saxon world would say that the system goes against human nature. Fidel and his followers say that we have a debased, materialistic, faithless idea of human nature.

I mentioned Castro's using the phrase "For man does not live by bread alone." In 1958, during the insurrection against Batista, a pastoral letter was issued by the bishop in Pinar del Río. It contained that biblical phrase, and there was a sensation. It was taken in a revolutionary sense, not a religious sense. In the Castro regime it was given the meaning that man does not work, or should not work just to make money, more and more money and worldly goods for himself and his family.

"History is an argument without an end," Pieter Geyl wrote as the last sentence of his book *Napoleon, For and Against.* The arguments about the Cuban Revolution will never end, any more than they have about the French Revolution. But all revolutions must end. There is no such thing as a permanent revolution, even though Fidel sometimes talks as if there is. However, there are permanent effects. We still live under the effects of the French Revolution. True social revolutions like Cuba's are irreversible. The eggs are scrambled and can never be put back in their shells.

All previous revolutions moved from left to right, which is to say they became conservative. At this writing—early in 1975—the Cuban Revolution is in flood tide, but the signs of a conservatism, institutionalism, economic orthodoxy, a settling-down, a conformity to convention (as with the new military ranks) are evident. But "the process," to use Fidel's favorite word, of making the Revolution continues.

We—or at least a great majority of us in the United States—have lost our belief in what in my childhood was called "America the Golden." Vietnam and the Nixon era have made a mockery of the phrase. In Cuba I know men and women who hope for and dream of a "Cuba the Golden." I cannot find it in me to mock them.

I treasure the inscriptions that Che Guevara wrote in two of his books. In the *Guerra de guerrillas* he said:

> To the journalist Matthews, always a friend despite ideological differences that go on increasing.
>
> Revolutionarily [*revolucionariamente*],
> che

In the first edition of his *Pasages de la guerra revolucionaria* (Sketches of the Revolutionary War) he put:

> For H. Matthews, ideological enemy at all times and our friend since the luminous days of the Sierra Maestra, as a cordial witness to the understanding between men who speak different tongues.
>
> che
>
> Havana, November 3, 1963

He did not mean by the word *lenguas* ("tongues") that his language was Spanish and mine English; he meant that we saw things differently, had different ideas, were "ideological enemies"—but we remained friends.

Americans are entitled to look upon the Cubans of today as opponents of their government and its policies, but not as enemies of the American people. Cubans do not feel themselves to be such and are constantly told by Castro not to be.

A liberal like myself, who finds more than enough in Fidel Castro and the Marxist-Leninist Cuban Revolution to consider it praiseworthy and beneficial for Cuba and the Cubans, faces problems in reconciling the two positions. I have not found them insuperable. I believe that Castro is himself groping for a form of government and society that respects human dignity and self-development.

Equality is at the heart of his revolution, not just economic and social equality, but the development of the individual's capacity to think by means of education and the inculcated ability to choose, compare, create. He has sought a means by which the individual can express opinion, and perhaps he is finding it in the Committees for the Defense of the Revolution, in the "organs of People's Power," and in his version of Marxism-Leninism.

The "process" continues. So does Fidel Castro's search for new ideas. He keeps going, and the island goes with him. It is too soon to pass final judgments. A sun has risen in Cuba, but this is still the early morning of the Revolution.

In his most famous prediction, made at the end of the court trial in 1953 after the attack on the Moncada Barracks, Fidel Castro said: "History will absolve me."

I believe that it will.

BIBLIOGRAPHY

INDEX

BIBLIOGRAPHY

A brief bibliography of some basic works in English, Spanish, and French for the general reader. Students will find the most comprehensive bibliography—up to 1970—in Professor Hugh Thomas' book.

GENERAL

Background to Revolution, edited by Robert Freeman Smith. New York: 1966.

What Happened in Cuba?, by Robert Freeman Smith. New York: Twayne Publishers, 1963.

Cuba, by Wyatt MacGaffey and Clifford A. Barnett, for the American University. New Haven: HRAF Press, 1962.

(These three books contain much valuable documentation and comment on the Cuban people and the causes of the Revolution.)

FIDEL CASTRO

History Will Absolve Me, by Fidel Castro. New York: Lyle Stuart, 1961. (Castro's self-defense in court after Moncada.)

Fidel Castro, by Herbert L. Matthews. New York: Simon & Schuster, 1969. Also in Penguin Pelican Book paperback, 1970.

Fidel Castro Speaks, edited by Martin Kenner and James Petras. New York: Grove Press, 1969. (A selection of important speeches with commentaries.)

Cuba Chile: Encuentro Simbólico Entre dos Procesos Históricos. Havana: Instituto del Libro, 1972. (The complete texts of Castro's speeches, interviews, and statements during his trip to Chile, Peru, and Ecuador in November-December 1971. Important for Castro's mature thoughts after thirteen years in power and the 1970 watershed.)

SIERRA MAESTRA

El Libro de los Doce, by Carlos Franqui. Havana, 1963. (This valuable transcript of tape-recorded accounts by a number of the revolutionary leaders is now available only in its French edition, *Le Livre des douze.* Paris: Gallimard, 1965.)

La Sierra y el Llano. Casa de las Américas, Havana: 1969. (First edition, 1960. An important collection of accounts of the rebellion against Batista by such participants as Fidel and Raúl Castro, Ernesto Che Guevara, and Camilo Cienfuegos.)

M-26, Biography of a Revolution, by Robert Taber. New York: Lyle Stuart, 1961. (The best all-around history of the fighting in the Sierra Maestra.)

Reminiscences of the Cuban Revolutionary War, by Ernesto Che Guevara. Translated by Victoria Ortiz. New York: Grove Press, 1968. (The most complete collection in any language of Guevara's articles in Cuban periodicals on the Sierra Maestra, written between 1959 and 1963.)

CHE GUEVARA

Ernesto: A Memoir of Che Guevara, by Hilda Gadea. New York: Doubleday & Co., 1972. (An indispensable and uniquely important biography of Che Guevara by his now deceased first wife.)

My Friend Che, by Ricardo Rojo. New York: Dial Press, 1968. (Useful for many personal details of the prerevolutionary life and career of Che by an Argentine family friend.)

Venceremos! The Speeches and Writings of Ernesto Che Guevara, edited by John Gerassi. New York: Macmillan, 1968. (A selection with commentaries. For readers of Spanish, much the largest selection yet published is to be found in *Ernesto Che Guevara, Escritos y Discursos,* three volumes. Havana: Instituto del Libro, 1972.)

Man and Socialism in Cuba, by Ernesto Che Guevara. Havana: Instituto del Libro, 1967. (The English version of Che's letter to Carlos Quijano for the Montevideo, Uruguay, weekly *Marcha.* The most important expression of his socialist faith.)

THE REVOLUTION

Castro's Revolution, Myths and Realities, by Theodore Draper. New York, Praeger: 1962.

Castroism, Theory and Practice, by Theodore Draper. New York: Praeger, 1965. (The two best-known works on the early years of the Revolution; hostile, polemical, with much valuable but selective documentation.)

Cuba: The Pursuit of Freedom, by Hugh Thomas. New York: Harper & Row, 1971.

(A unique and massive work of scholarship on Cuba from 1762 to 1970. The most valuable reference book on the historical data of the Revolution; politically hostile.)

Guerrillas in Power, by K. S. Karol. Translated from the French by Arnold Pomerans. New York: Hill & Wang, 1970. (The hostile and sensational concluding chapters were widely serialized in the United States. A mixture of useful scholarship and misleading opinions.)

Cuba, Castro and the United States, by Philip W. Bonsal. Pittsburgh: University of Pittsburgh Press, 1971. (By the U. S. Ambassador to Cuba at the beginning of the Revolution. Lacking in understanding, but important for its official viewpoint.)

THE ECONOMY

Cuba: The Economic and Social Revolution. Edited by Dudley Seers, who wrote the economic sections. (A valuable early study of the economic situation and the beginnings of the educational revolution.)

The Economic Transformation of Cuba, by Edward Boorstein. New York: Monthly Review Press, 1968. (A sympathetic study by an American left-wing economist who worked for years in a Cuban government bank during the early part of the Revolution. Valuable because of its understanding and authority.)

Cuba, Est-il Socialiste?, by René Dumont. Paris: Editions du Seuil, 1970. An English edition, *Is Cuba Socialist?,* was published in London by Dent in 1974. (The second of two highly critical studies by a French Marxist economist whose advice Castro sought.)

Cuba: The Measure of a Revolution, by Lowry Nelson. Minneapolis: University of Minnesota Press, 1972. (The author of the classic study *Rural Cuba* [1950], Nelson provides much useful economic information up to 1970, but entirely on second-hand documentation with often misleading deductions.)

INDEX